Handbook of Victims and Victimology

Handbook of Victims and Victimology

Edited by

Sandra Walklate

WILLAN
PUBLISHING

Published by

Willan Publishing
Culmcott House
Mill Street, Uffculme
Cullompton, Devon
EX15 3AT, UK
Tel: +44(0)1884 840337
Fax: +44(0)1884 840251
e-mail: info@willanpublishing.co.uk
website: www.willanpublishing.co.uk

Published simultaneously in the USA and Canada by

Willan Publishing
c/o ISBS, 920 NE 58th Ave, Suite 300
Portland, Oregon 97213-3644, USA
Tel: +001(0)503 287 3093
Fax: +001(0)503 280 8832
e-mail: info@isbs.com
website: www.isbs.com

First published 2007

Reprinted 2008

Hardback
ISBN 978-1-84392-258-2

Paperback
ISBN 978-1-84392-257-5

British Library Cataloguing-in-Publication Data

A catalogue record for this book is available from the British Library

Project management by Deer Park Productions, Tavistock, Devon
Typeset by GCS, Leighton Buzzard, Beds
Printed and bound by T.J. International, Padstow, Cornwall

Contents

About the contributors

Tracey Booth is a Senior Lecturer in Law at the University of Western Sydney in Australia and the Director of Pro Bono Students Australia. She has written extensively in the area of victims of crime with a particular focus on victim impact statements from family victims in homicide matters. Tracey is currently completing her PhD thesis, entitled 'The involvement of family victims in the process of sentencing homicide offenders in NSW: progressive or retrogressive?' Much of the research for Tracey's work on her contribution to this book was undertaken while she was a Visiting Fellow at the Centre for Sentencing Research at the University of Strathclyde in 2006.

Kerry Carrington is a Professor in Sociology and Director of the Centre for Applied Research in Social Sciences at the University of New England. She has published widely in the fields of criminology, gender studies and sociology. Her publications include six books, 13 book chapters, 15 refereed journal articles, and five social policy research briefs for the Australian Parliament. Her latest a co-authored book (with Russell Hogg) *Policing the Rural Crisis* (Federation Press, 2006) contrasts the visibility of Indigenous crimes against the invisibility of the victims of violence in rural communities governed by dense networks of informal social control.

Kate Cook, after undertaking the Open University module 'The Changing Experience of Women' in 1990, joined Manchester Rape Crisis and became an enthusiastic member of the collective. During her years there she worked the line, gave talks and training to outside agencies, worked on fund-raising and on training new volunteers. This was the beginning of a period of change in her life which has led to teaching about the law on rape, domestic violence, child sexual abuse and pornography, while working within the Truth About Rape Campaign and Campaign to End Rape, to try to change the world.

Pamela Davies is Senior Lecturer in Criminology in the Division of Sociology and Criminology at Northumbria University. Pamela is programme leader for BSc (Hons) Criminology and Sociology and teaches on a range of core and option modules on criminology-related programmes. Pamela has also worked as a civilian researcher with Northumbria Police engaging in community consultation exercises and performance indicator projects. She spent a year on secondment to the Scarman Centre for the Study of Public Order at Leicester University on a project funded by the European Commission. While at Northumbria she has been a key member of a team exploring domestic violence in rural Northumberland and she has conducted a city-centre customer theft survey. In recent years her research interests have been focused primarily on female offenders and in particular on women who commit crimes for economic gain. Her most notable publications reflect this particular research interest and have included articles on women who shoplift casually and women who shoplift as a profession. Additionally she has written and co-edited books on the subjects of doing criminological research, crimes and victimisations of the powerful, criminal victimisation generally and on gender, crime and victimisation.

James Dignan is currently Professor of International Criminal Justice at the University of Leeds, having been previously Professor of Criminology and Restorative Justice at the Centre for Criminological Research, University of Sheffield. He has conducted research in the fields of restorative justice and community mediation and has written on a variety of theoretical, practical and policy issues relating to the development and implementation of restorative justice.

Peter Dunn qualified as a probation officer in 1984 with an MSc and Certificate of Qualification in Social Work from the London School of Economics. He worked as a probation officer in London, then Bristol, before moving to Berkshire where in 1993 he was appointed senior probation officer and manager of a probation and bail hostel. At this time Peter was a member of the management committee of Victim Support Reading. In 1999 Peter went to work for the Youth Justice Board as a policy adviser, where he was responsible for devising the first National Standards for Youth Justice. Joining Victim Support's national office in 2001, Peter became their head of research and development in 2002. As well as working for Victim Support, he is now at LSE again as a part-time student, doing research for a PhD into the impact of hate crime. He is also a trustee of Galop, the London lesbian and gay anti-violence charity. Peter was made a Fellow of the Royal Society of Arts in 2005.

Barry Godfrey is Director of the Research Institute of Law, Politics and Justice at Keele University. He researches the history of crime and policing and has recently published or co-authored *Criminal Lives: Family, Employment and Offending* (Clarendon Series in Criminology, Oxford University Press, 2007); *Crime and Justice, 1750–1950* (Willan, 2005); *Crime and History* (Sage, 2007). He has also edited or co-edited *Markets, Risk and 'White-collar' Crimes: Moral Economies from Victorian Times to Enron*, Special Edition of the *British Journal of*

Criminology (2006); *Crime and Empire: Criminal Justice in Global and Local Context 1840–1940* (Willan, 2005); and *Comparative Histories of Crime* (Willan, 2003).

Jo Goodey (PhD) is Programme Manager for Research at the Vienna-based European Fundamental Rights Agency. She previously worked as a research fellow at the UN's Office on Drugs and Crime, and as a lecturer in criminology at the University of Leeds and the University of Sheffield. She is the author of *Victims and Victimology: Research, Policy and Practice* (Harlow, 2005), co-editor of the book *Integrating a Victim Perspective within Criminal Justice* (2000), and European editor of *Critical Criminology*.

Hannah Goodman is a Research Fellow with the Community and Criminal Justice Research Centre at De Montfort University in Leicester. Her main research interests are victims of crime and restorative justice. Her previous relevant experience includes working for the probation service, the Victims and Witnesses Action Group, Leicester Witness Cocoon and also volunteering for Victim Support and the Probation Service in London. She is working on a *Reader on Victims and Victimology* to be published by the Open University Press.

Simon Green is Lecturer in Community Justice and Criminology at the University of Hull. He is currently co-editing a text called *Addressing Offending Behaviour* for Willan Publishing and co-authoring a new edition of *Understanding Crime Data* for the Open University Press. His current research interests are in the fields of social and criminological theory, victimology, probation and community studies. He is Hull University's programme director for undergraduate criminology and for the Diploma in Probation Studies. Current projects include developing an online MA in restorative justice, investigating people's stories of offending and reoffending and, as part of the Restorative Justice Group at the University of Hull, an early stage project to explore how people resolve their own conflicts.

Marc Groenhuijsen has been Professor in criminal law, criminal procedure and victimology at Tilburg University, the Netherlands, since 1987. In 2005, he became the founding director of INTERVICT, the International Victimology Institute Tilburg (see www.intervict.nl). He has published extensively on topics relating to victims' rights in the criminal justice system. As a practitioner he was involved in service provision. For many years he served as chairman of the Dutch National Victim Support Organisation and of the European Forum for Victim Services. In 2006 he was elected vice-president of the World Society of Victimology.

Tim Hope is Professor of Criminology at Keele University. His research interests lie in the fields of victimology, communities, crime prevention and community safety, and the relationship between science and government in criminal justice (including the role of evidence in policy-making, and evaluation research methodology). He has published both widely and internationally on these topics, including the USA, Canada, Germany, Italy, France and Poland.

He has extensive experience of analysing crime victimisation surveys and statistics, particularly using the British Crime Survey. He has directed evaluation studies for the Home Office, including that of the Priority Estates Project and the Reducing Burglary Initiative, and was Director of the Economic and Social Research Council Crime and Social Order Research Programme. Recently, he has completed research for the UK Statistics Commission on users' perspectives on crime statistics.

Carolyn Hoyle is Reader in Criminology, and Fellow of Green College, University of Oxford. After almost a decade of research on domestic violence, culminating in the publication of her book, *Negotiating Domestic Violence* (Oxford University Press, 1998), she has spent much of her time over the last decade conducting research into restorative justice. Recently she has moved back into the field of domestic violence, focusing in particular on the use of risk assessment and management tools. In addition to publishing widely in these areas, she teaches courses on restorative justice, victims, and the death penalty to masters and undergraduate students studying law and criminology in Oxford.

Helen Jones' background includes working with a number of rape crisis groups and campaign groups on legislative and media-based issues. She was a member of the Sexual Offences Review (Home Office) which culminated in the Sexual Offences Act 2003 and currently holds two national consultancies. The first is on the Victims of Violence and Abuse Prevention Programme headed by Professor Catherine Itzen (joint initiative between the Department of Health and the NIMHE) and the second is on the Sexual Violence and Abuse Stakeholder Advisory Group at the Home Office. Her day job is lecturing in criminology (Manchester Metropolitan University).

Imogen Jones completed her LLB at the University of Manchester in 2005 and went on to do an MA in International Criminology at the University of Sheffield the following year. She is currently an associate lecturer and PhD candidate in the School of Law, University of Manchester. Her current research interests focus on recent changes to evidential procedures and rules in criminal trials contained within the Criminal Justice Act 2003, and on how the rhetoric of 'rebalancing the criminal justice system in favour of victims' is used by the government for political purposes.

Tony Kearon is a Lecturer in Criminology at Keele University. His interests include relationships between media representations of crime and public attitudes to punishment; processes of criminalisation and the relationships between crime, cultural practices and identity in high and late modernity, and the construction of offender identities in British sociology and related social enquiry in the late nineteenth and early twentieth centuries. He is currently writing a book on popular culture and crime.

Rob Mawby is Professor of Criminology and Criminal Justice at the University of Plymouth. His PhD and first book, *Policing the City* (Saxon House, 1979) assessed the role of the police and crime victims in the creation of crime statistics, and his subsequent research interests have centred on policing and victims issues. In the latter case, books include *Crime Victims: Needs, Services and the Voluntary Sector* (Tavistock, 1987, with Mark Gill), and *Critical Victimology* (Sage, 1994, with Sandra Walklate). His subsequent research in the victimology field includes a cross-national interest, a local interest as co-ordinator of the 2001/2004 Cornwall Crime Surveys and Cornwall Business Crime Surveys, and a focus on the experiences of specific groups of victims (older people; tourists; burglary victims). His most recent text is *Burglary* (Willan Publishing, 2001).

David Miers is Professor of Law at Cardiff Law School. He has a long-standing research interest in particular in the law governing the compensation of victims of crime and, more generally, in the position of the victim in the criminal justice system. He is the author of *State Compensation for Criminal Injuries* (Oxford University Press, 1997), a leading account of the application of the Scheme, and of many other contributions on crime victim compensation to journals and edited works. He is regularly consulted by government and other official bodies, both within Great Britain and abroad.

Gabe Mythen is Senior Lecturer in Sociology at Liverpool University. He has published work in the areas of risk perception, representations of danger and the discursive construction of new terrorism in journals such as the *Sociological Review*, *Current Sociology*, *British Journal of Criminology*, *Security Journal* and *Environmental Politics*. He is author of *Ulrich Beck: A Critical Introduction to the Risk Society* (Pluto Press, 2004) and, with Sandra Walklate, co-editor of *Beyond the Risk Society: Critical Reflections on Risk and Human Security* (Open University Press, 2006). He is presently writing a third book to be published by Palgrave Macmillan entitled *Understanding the Risk Society: Crime, Security and Welfare*.

Paul Rock is Professor of Social Institutions at the LSE. He took his first degree at the LSE and then a DPhil at Nuffield College, University of Oxford. He has been a Visiting Scholar at the Ministry of the Solicitor General of Canada; a Visiting Professor at a number of Canadian, Australian and American universities; a Fellow of the Centre for the Advanced Study of the Behavioral Sciences in Stanford, California; Fellow of the British Academy and of the Royal Society of Arts; and a resident at the Rockefeller Foundation Centre at the Villa Serbelloni, Bellagio. He is currently a Visiting Professor at the University of Pennsylvania.

Andrew Sanders has lectured at Manchester Metropolitan, Birmingham, Oxford and Bristol universities. He is now Professor of Criminal Law and Criminology at the University of Manchester and is, until August 2007, head of the Law School. He is the author of several books including (with Richard Young) *Criminal Justice* (3rd edn, Oxford University Press, 2006). He has carried out many empirical projects on victims and other aspects of criminal justice, including Home Office evaluations of a pilot scheme for victim impact statements and of special measures for vulnerable witnesses and victims. He is currently writing *Victims, Criminal Justice and Social Exclusion* for OUP, which should be published in 2009.

Jan Van Dijk was a Professor in Criminology and policy adviser at the Ministry of Justice in the Netherlands, then joined the United Nations Office of Drugs and Crime in 1998 and served in several senior positions, including as Officer in Charge of the Centre of International Crime Prevention. He currently holds the Pieter Van Vollenhoven Chair in Victimology and Human Security at the International Victimology Institute, Tilburg University, the Netherlands. He served as President of The World Society of Victimology from 1997 till 2000 and received the Stephen Schafer Award of the National Organisation of Victim Assistance in the USA for his contributions to the international victims' rights movement. He has published extensively about comparative crime statistics, crime prevention and victim assistance. His forthcoming book on these topics, titled *World Atlas of Crime*, will be produced by Sage USA in the summer of 2007.

Sandra Walklate is currently Eleanor Rathbone Chair of Sociology in the School of Sociology and Social Policy at the University of Liverpool. She has worked extensively throughout her career with victim support organisations and police training programmes designed to better understand the impact of crime on the victim and how to respond. Her latest book is *Imagining the Victim of Crime* (Open University Press, 2007) and she is currently working on the third edition of *Gender, Crime and Criminal Justice* for Willan Publishing.

Dave Whyte is Reader in Sociology at Liverpool University. His main research interests are in crimes of the powerful and various aspects of the regulation of corporate crime. Main publications include *Unmasking the Crimes of the Powerful* (Peter Lung, 2003, with Steve Tombs), *Expanding the Criminological Imagination* (Willan, 2006, with Alana Barton, Karen Corteen and David Scott) and *Safety Crimes* (Willan, 2007, with Steve Tombs). His articles have appeared in numerous edited collections and journals, including *British Journal of Criminology, Journal of Law and Society, Urban Studies, Crime, Law and Social Change, Studies in Political Economy, Policy and Politics* and *International Comparative Law Quarterly*.

Brian Williams was Professor of Community Justice and Victimology at De Montfort University in Leicester. His main research interests were services for victims of crime, restorative justice, community justice and criminological research ethics. He previously worked at Keele, Sheffield and Teesside universities and as a probation officer. He was an Executive Committee member of the British Society of Criminology and chair of its Professional and Ethics committees. His most recent book was *Victims of Crime and Community Justice* (Jessica Kingsley, 2005).

[Brian Williams died as a result of a tragic motor accident in March 2007. He will be greatly missed by his wife Suzanne, his young family, and all those who knew and worked with him.]

Figures and tables

Figures

Tables

Introduction and overview

Sandra Walklate

Despite the current political preoccupation, and perceived consensus with, rebalancing the criminal justice system to take better account of the victim of crime, it is easy to forget that the concept of victim, understanding the nature of criminal victimisation, and even measuring victimisation, are hotly contested issues. As Garland and Sparks (2000) have commented, a concern with and for the victim of crime has become not just a symbolic reference point but also a dominant one. This reference point has been made all the more poignant and impactive in recent years with the graphic media coverage given to (crime) victims and victimisation. That coverage ranging as it does from victims of natural disasters to victims of terrorist attacks, to more mundane and routine, though nonetheless harmful events, such as burglary, rape and murder, has arguably contributed to the drive to rebalance the criminal justice system in the victim's favour. Yet, in the midst of such media coverage and political preoccupations, real and harmful things do happen to people. What is of interest to those (and others) who claim the label of victimologist, is the changing nature of how such 'things' have been articulated, responded to, and by whom. While on the one hand the publication of a volume of this kind stands as testimony to the extent to which victims and victimisation have become an increasing source of political, policy, and academic concern, on the other hand it also evidences that the way in which that concern has unfolded, especially in recent decades, is neither simple nor straightforward. The chapters in this volume evidence some of this complexity. Before going on to consider that complexity, it is of value to consider some of the key moments of change in this rising concern with (criminal) victimisation.

Key moments of change?

It is probably a moot point as to whether or not the Home Office consultation document, *Rebuilding Lives*, published in December 2005, constituted a key moment of change in the rising concern with the victim of crime, but what it does do is list the achievements that have been made in delivering improved services to victims of crime in England and Wales in recent years and at the same time explores where further work needs to be done. One of the main concerns of this consultation document was with improving the operation and delivery of the work of the Criminal Injuries Compensation Authority (CICA) especially in respect of the speed with which it operates. This particular focus emerged in the aftermath of the bombings that took place in London on 7 July 2005, and questioned not only the efficiency with which the CICA operated but also what it understood, and was permitted to understand, were appropriate levels of compensation, for what kind of injury and for whom (see Miers in this volume). The fact that this concern about the operating practices of the CICA emerged in 2005 says much about how understandings of, and responses to, criminal victimisation have changed since the first establishment in 1964 of what was then called the Criminal Injuries Compensation Board, which was considered at the time a trail-blazing initiative (Waller 1988) and an example of good practice to follow. The changes that have occurred since the 1960s that have focused on criminal victimisation are worthy of further comment.

These changes have been marked at every level but especially at the political, legal and cultural levels, with much of the latter (referred to above) epitomised by what Valier (2004) would call a fascination with gothic horror. One only needs to reflect upon the media coverage of the various (international) terrorist events since 9/11 to appreciate the value of her description. Indeed, some of these media and political processes have resulted in what Cole (2007) calls 'anti-victimism', especially in the United States where processes to overcome a victim mentality appear to have produced an ever more deeply entrenched vision of what she calls 'True Victimhood'. It is worth exploring in a little more detail how Cole (2007: 5) delineates this and it is worth quoting her at length on it since it resonates with some of the concerns within this book.

> True Victimhood is defined in opposition to victimism: a victim is 'true' because the victimist is evidently a bogus victim ... The True Victim is a noble victim. He endures his suffering with dignity, refraining from complaining or other public displays of weakness. The True Victim commands his fate; he does not exploit his injury to excuse his failures ... A True Victim is not a victim by affiliation or by engaging in 'victim politics'; victimization must be immediate and concrete. Innocence: the most important virtue of True Victimhood ... This totalizing conception of innocence encompasses every facet of the True Victim's character.

And then she goes on to say: 'The truest of True Victims are victims who refuse to be victims' (2007: 6). Of course, her analysis of True Victimhood purposely echoes the Victorian construction of True Womanhood and neatly captures some of essence of the early conceptual work of victimology especially around the idea of victim precipitation. Indeed, as many feminists would argue this notion of True Victimhood has never disappeared when it comes to responding to the female (or latterly the male) victim of rape (see Cook and Jones in this volume). However, Cole's analysis is not from the late

1940s, but is reflective of the United States in the twenty-first century, in the aftermath of an event that some would argue was envisioned as an attack on the whole American body in which the nation is victim (Cole 2007). Moreover it is apposite to observe the coalescence of this notion of True Victimhood and the political expression of an 'axis of evil' in which 'you are either with us or against us'. This is a political rhetoric that has fuelled policies in the UK and elsewhere as well as the United States: a reflection of refusing to be victims? Yet simultaneously the current criminal justice policy context is endeavouring to embrace a more effective rebalancing of the criminal justice system in favour of the (crime) victim. Much of this book is about what that embrace looks like, and in its later sections, what might be considered as the continued presences and absences in that embrace.

As a result of the changes that have impacted upon our understanding of victimhood, it is difficult to offer a full appreciation of the changes that have occurred in the local context of England and Wales, in which the Home Office might produce a document like *Rebuilding Lives*, without situating an understanding of those changes within the wider changing global context. Some attempt will be made at contextualising these changes here, though it is important to note that many of the contributions in this handbook have set their concerns with the UK within a wider appreciation and understanding of developments in other countries.

Victim-oriented developments

In England and Wales the early 1960s were marked, in policy terms, by a consolidation of the achievements of the welfare states in the post Second World War era (see Mawby and Walklate 1994). Victims of crime, *per se*, were not part of political or policy rhetoric, neither was there any substantive available or influential research conducted on victims of crime. Much of the early victimological research was conducted by emigré lawyers cum criminologists in the United States. These commentators took the Holocaust as their problematic and the World Society of Victimology, in its early life, shared in the intellectual origins of understanding and giving voice to the impact of the events that led up to the Second World War. Indeed the overlap between the academic and the humanist, as Fattah (1991) would say, has remained within the world of victimology and one that continues to give it a particular character and vibrancy (see Cook and Jones, and Dunn in this volume). However, central to the rise in interest within intellectual and policy arenas about the victim of crime was the development of the criminal victimisation survey.

The first criminal victimisation survey was conducted in the United States in 1967. The development of this research instrument, designed in the first instance so that policy-makers could say something about the nature and extent of what was then called the 'dark figure' of crime, marked the beginning of a turning point both for victimology and for policy responses to the victim of crime. This research instrument provided researchers and policy-makers with a wealth of information about what concerned people, not only about crime, but also about the criminal justice system, and provided one route through which concern about the victim of crime rose on the political agenda. It was during the 1970s and early 1980s, as crime rates rose, that concern for the victim of crime emerged in a rather informal and patchy way within the voluntary sector. In conjunction with this rising concern there was a pilot criminal victimisation survey done by Sparks, Genn and Dodd in 1977. This was to be the forerunner to the development of the British Crime Survey, first conducted in 1982 then conducted biannually and latterly annually, which now constitutes an essential component of academic, policy and political debate about the nature, extent and impact of crime. Indeed the conduct of such a survey became a required activity for local authorities when devising their Crime and Disorder Reduction Strategies under the 1998 Crime and Disorder Act. In the interim the use and deployment of the International Criminal Victimisation Survey has grown apace. First conducted in 1989, this survey has grown in influence both in Europe and elsewhere, and stands as a good exemplar of both a 'travelling method' and the inherent problems of occidentalism embedded within victimology (see Walklate 2007, Chapter 3, for a fuller discussion of these problems).

Faced with rising crime rates, and a criminal justice system in which, it would appear, nothing worked, the data from the first British Crime Survey was deliberately used politically to underplay the nature and extent of crime (see Mayhew and Hough 1988). This was seen to be a way of not only allaying public concerns about crime but also justifying the demand for economy and efficiency that was increasingly expected of the different branches of the criminal justice system in England and Wales at that time. The links between this further politicisation (a process that Miers (1978) argued began in the 1960s), and reconstruction of the crime victim from being a complainant in the criminal justice system to being a consumer of criminal justice services evidences the impact of the global recession of the mid-1970s, repeated in the early 1990s, that took its toll on the local service delivery context (see also Mawby and Walklate 1994; Williams 1999). The management strategies that have been embraced as a response to these (global) economic demands have been referred to as a form of 'actuarial justice' (Feeley and Simon 1994) in which the victim became constituted as a central feature of achieving justice, and are processes that have been keenly felt not only in the UK but also elsewhere (see Booth and Carrington in this volume). Evidence of the impact of these kinds of changes in the UK can be traced from the reorientation of services to women as victims (consumers) of services through to the more explicitly audit culture driven modernising agenda of contemporary government policies in, for example, embracing restorative justice. Indeed there is a sense in which some of these policies now carry a global passport as governments in different contexts grapple not only with the problem of delivering justice and securing all the necessary participants to the process in order to deliver justice, but also with ensuring that this happens as cost effectively as possible. Two policies, in particular, that claim the victim voice and seem to have such a passport are the use of victim impact statements in court and the development of restorative justice initiatives (both discussed in detail in this volume by Sanders and Jones, Booth and Carrington, and

Dignan). So along with the increasing influence of the ICVS it is possible to argue that there has been an increasing presence of the Anglo-speaking world on policy development worldwide, thus widening the influence of a particular kind of victimological agenda and simultaneously narrowing its remit: what kind of victim it is concerned with.

During this time research on the impact of crime has continued apace, in some respects led by the Home Office sponsored criminal victimisation survey and the response that it generated. In other respects such research was also responsive to the emergent work of the voluntary sector, both feminist in dealing with woman abuse and non-feminist in responding to other kinds of crime. In addition increasing academic space was given to criminology and victimology in the UK as the popularity of undergraduate degree programmes in this general area mushroomed. So by the mid-1990s the academic, political and policy concern for the victim of crime was well established.

However, arguably these concerns took a sharper edge in the aftermath of a number of high-profile crimes that were taken (by the media, at least) to signify the state of decay in some aspects of society in England and Wales. The murder of James Bulger in 1993 in particular provoked some considerable debate (in a shape and form that the murders committed by Mary Bell in the late 1960s did not), not only politically but also socially. The screaming mob chasing the prison van that contained Jon Venables and Robert Thompson is an image that arguably belongs to a different era. Yet nevertheless these images marked an (acceptable) expression of emotion in the face of victimisation. This too has changed since the late 1940s in which Cole's (2007) observation on the 'propriety' of being a victim, of suffering with dignity, is clearly redolent. Furedi (2002) would argue that these changes are part of wider cultural changes that encourage victimhood in all of us, a process that Cole's (2007) analysis clearly suggests is under siege in the United States. Whatever the underlying cause of these changes, the management of emotion constitutes an increasingly important feature of criminal justice policy responses to the victim of crime that have changed in their tenor contemporarily. In some respects, of course, these concerns have become elided and hidden by the political rhetoric and continued politicisation of the crime victim, but the perpetual invocation of the image of the victim – not just any victim but the suffering innocent victim – as a justification for policy needs to be related to these wider concerns about how to manage emotion that has a different shape to it now than it once did.

It is, of course, also important to take account of the questions raised by a world in which, post-9/11, things will never be the same again (Worcester 2001) or, as Jenks (2003) suggests, some fundamental line has been transgressed. This event, alongside those in Madrid in 2003 and London in 2005, and others given a lower profile in the West (for example, the train bombings in India in 2004), raise all kinds of questions about what can be considered as legal/illegal, criminal/not criminal, and who as a consequence is considered to be a victim or otherwise of crime, the cultural concerns of Furedi (2002) and Cole (2007) notwithstanding. Victimology, as a discipline, demands a theoretical framework that can work with the questions that the events listed above pose, as well as those raised by events and issues more conventionally understood as criminal or problematic for the victim of crime in their relationship with the criminal justice system. In the social sciences over the last 40 years increasing space has been given to the risk society thesis, most famously explicated by Beck (1992) as a way of making sense of the precariousness of contemporary social life. It is necessary to add to this the concerns posed by a 'post terroristic world society' (Beck 2002) and point to areas where policies and debates could be differently shaped if such events had a more central place on the victimological agenda.

Elsewhere (Walklate 1990) I have argued for the adoption within victimology of a theoretical position that recognises that human beings actively construct and reconstruct their daily lives; that these constructions reflect practices of both resistance and acceptance of their social reality; that these constructions are made in a context of observable and unobservable generative mechanisms that have a real impact on people's lives, whether or not they are aware of them; and that these processes have both intended and unintended consequences that further feed the knowledgeability of human beings and set the scene for future action. However, Flynn (2006), in discussing the relevance of the risk thesis to his own area of work on health, adds to this by suggesting the adoption of a critical realist perspective. He says:

> What is critical about this approach is that it assumes the possibility of alternative conditions, it asks what must and what might happen, and it is critical of existing structures and processes – critical realism aspires to offer a potentially emancipatory analysis associated with normative structures.

This is the critical edge to a critical victimology implied in my own work. Put rather simply, this posits a meaningful, if not straightforward, relationship between individual action and the social conditions of and for action. In the context of understanding some important features of the contemporary social condition it means recognising that there are real risks of victimisation, independent of people's knowledge of them; there are actual risks (what happens when people encounter victimising situations); and there are the risks/victimisations that people experience for themselves. For example, those in positions of power long knew about the real risks of terrorist attack in London, which is distinct from the actual risks for those people who encountered those attacks, and how those who survived dealt with them. Then, in addition, there is the empirical reality of what people may choose or choose not to do in the aftermath of such an event: do they embrace victimhood or resist it? The latter two types of choice bear very little if any relationship with the real chance of further victimisation. However, a critical realist approach, with its intrinsic commitment to the possibility of change, offers up the opportunity not only of being critical of the structures and processes that engender or prevent victimisation, but sets that critical approach within the realm of the normative: what should and should not be the case. In other words, in the case of the crime victim, it meets head on the political, structural and moral processes that lie embedded within the delivery of criminal justice policy and the drive to use criminal justice policy as a vehicle for change. It leads us to ask who gets what and why. The extent to which the contributions to this volume aid in the development of such a victimological agenda is a moot point, but as this brief introduction has intimated, the problems and possibilities for those concerned with the victim (of crime) take their toll contemporarily in quite a different shape and form from when Miers (1978) first addressed the politicisation of the crime victim. It is hoped that the reader gains some sense of that current shape and form from the chapters that follow.

Structure and organisation of this handbook

While each of the chapters in this handbook can be read as stand-alone contributions to understanding the contemporary theoretical and policy problems facing victimology and those concerned with victims, the book has been organised in five parts. Part One contains what might be considered to be the staple diet of the victimological agenda, addressing as it does the perspectives on the victim and victimology. In Chapter 1, Barry Godfrey and Tony Kearon explore the changing status of the victim in her/his historical context and illustrate the value of appreciating what can be learned from history for the contemporary criminal justice context. Paul Rock (Chapter 2) explores the problems and possibilities of theory for the study of criminal victimisation. In so doing he eschews the more usual categorisations of victimology in terms of positive, radical or critical victimology, and opts instead to ask the reader what the role of theory might be in an area of study that, like criminology, constitutes a meeting place for people from many different disciplinary backgrounds. In similar fashion, Tim Hope in Chapter 3 also eschews the more conventional approaches usually taken to the problems of measuring victimisation. He again asks the reader to think critically about not just the problems of measurement *per se* but also the problem of relating what it is that is being measured to explaining what has been measured. Taken together, Chapters 2 and 3 offer a significant challenge to what has become a rather stultified theoretical and empirical victimological debate. In Chapter 4 Simon Green takes an in-depth and critical look at the impact of crime and usefully offers a detailed map of vulnerability. He offers a critical exploration of Christie's (1986) concept of the 'ideal victim' (as do other contributors to this volume, in particular Davies in Chapter 7 and Whyte in Chapter 17) and considers the way in which victimhood has become a commodity, in which vulnerability has become the currency, in contemporary society.

Part Two of the book deals with what has been historically one of the most conflict-ridden arenas of concern in relation to victimisation. It addresses the relationship between feminism and victimology. This part of the book brings to the fore the relationship between the academic and the activist, admirably reflected in Chapter 5 by Kate Cook and Helen Jones, which deals with responding to rape. Chapter 6 takes up this academic/activist understanding of responding to criminal victimisation in a different way as Carolyn Hoyle discusses the policy and practical issues of responding to domestic violence. Finally, in Chapter 7 Pamela Davies shifts this agenda further by offering a detailed consideration of the 'gender agenda' for both the theory and practice of victimology.

In Part Three we move our attention from questions of theory, measurement and gender-specific issues to questions of policy and service delivery in general. As was intimated above, the shift in focus of the criminal justice agencies over the last 25 years to becoming more victim-oriented has been considerable and aspects of this change in orientation are differently addressed by each of the chapters in this section. Rob Mawby, in Chapter 8, deals with the changing focus within public sector service delivery. Using the new Victims' Code of Practice as his benchmark, he considers the changing role of the police, probation and the Crown Prosecution Service. In Chapter 9 Brian Williams and Hannah Goodman examine the changing face of the voluntary sector in terms of the nature and support that is offered to victims of crime, and review these developments in their European context sensitive to the increasingly diverse services that seem to be available contemporarily. In Chapter 10 Peter Dunn explores what might be considered the question that underpins all the policy delivery discussed in the previous chapter: whether or not it is possible to match service delivery to victims' needs. Here he examines this issue in relation to the organisation for which he works, Victim Support, but as already suggested the questions raised here are pertinent for the criminal justice system as a whole, and by implication, of course, whether or not this is the purpose of the criminal justice system. Andrew Sanders and Imogen Jones take a close look at the role of the victim in court in Chapter 11. Here efforts to introduce a greater voice for the crime victim are situated within an understanding of the adversarial system considered alongside what may or may not be on offer in the inquisitorial system. In this chapter we get our first taste of one of the policies with a global passport: victim impact statements. As was suggested above, restorative justice is another policy with a global reach, and in Chapter 12 Jim Dignan considers the problems and possibilities of what may or may not be delivered to the victim with this kind of disposition from the court.

In Part Four the contributions reach out from the UK context and encourage us to consider those local developments within a wider comparative perspective, beginning with a contribution by David Miers on the development of criminal injuries compensation schemes. In the 1960s the UK was considered to be the 'trail blazer' (Waller 1988) in introducing the (then) Criminal Injuries Compensation Board, and such schemes have emerged in Europe and elsewhere since. In Chapter 13 Miers explores what can be learned from comparing and contrasting the differing initiatives in this area. Following the European connection, Jan Van Dijk and Marc Groenhuijsen (Chapter 14) explore the extent to which European benchmarking has a role to play in understanding service delivery to victims of crime. Finally in this section we move to the world stage. Tracey Booth and Kerry Carrington in Chapter 15 take us on an all-encompassing tour of the way in which responses to victims of crime have developed within the Anglo-speaking world, and document quite a complex picture of those developments.

The last part of this collection, Part Five, encourages us to think about both the continued absences and the newer presences on the victimological stage. In Chapter 17 Dave Whyte examines the nature and extent of our victimisation from corporate crime and considers why it is that this form of victimisation still occupies a relatively marginal space within victimology. In contrast, Jo Goodey (Chapter 16) explores the increasing presence of racial and religious victimisation on contemporary European policy agendas. This is not totally unconnected from the issues raised by Gabe Mythen in Chapter 18, who considers the possibility of a cultural victimology returning us to the issues with which this Introduction began. How do we make sense of the symbolic use of the victim in a culture preoccupied with control without losing sight of the fact that, while culturally we are all encouraged to think 'victimhood', structurally, the impact of crime, whether it be committed by the state, the corporation or the next door neighbour, takes its toll on some of us more than others. In the Conclusion, I endeavour to explore the remaining tensions for victim-oriented policy and how victimology might move to make sense of these tensions, in a western world preoccupied with safety and the problem of 'the other'. It is hoped that the reader is as challenged by these contributions as I have been as editor of them.

References

Beck, U. (1992) *The Risk Society*. London: Sage.

Beck, U. (2002) 'The terroristic threat: world risk society revisited', *Theory, Culture and Society*, 19(4): 39–55.

Christie, N. (1986) 'The Ideal Victim', in E. Fattah (ed.) *From Crime Policy to Victim Policy*. London: Macmillan.

Cole, A. (2007) *The Cult of True Victimhood*. Stanford, CA: Stanford University Press.

Fattah, E. (1991) *Understanding Criminal Victimisation*. Scarborough, Ontario: Prentice Hall.

Feeley, M. and Simon, J. (1994) 'Actuarial Justice: The Emerging New Criminal Law', in D. Nelken (ed.) *The Futures of Criminology*. London: Sage.

Flynn, R. (2006) 'Health and Risk', in G. Mythen and S. Walklate (eds) *Beyond the Risk Society: Critical Reflections on Risk and Human Security*. Maidenhead: Open University Press.

Furedi, F. (2002) *Culture of Fear: Risk Taking and the Morality of Low Expectation*, revised edn. London: Continuum.

Garland, D. and Sparks, R. (2000) 'Criminology, social theory and the challenge of our times', *British Journal of Criminology*, 40(2): 189–204.

Jenks, C. (2003) *Transgression*. London: Routledge.

Mawby, R. and Walklate, S. (1994) *Critical Victimology*. London: Sage.

Mayhew, P. and Hough, M. (1988) 'The British Crime Survey: Origins and Impact', in M. Maguire and J. Pointing (eds) *Victims of Crime: A New Deal?* Milton Keynes: Open University Press.

Miers, D. (1978) *The Politicisation of the Victim*. Abingdon: Professional Books.

Sparks, R.F., Genn, H. and Dodd, D. (1977) *Surveying Victims*. London: Wiley.

Valier, C. (2004) *Crime and Punishment in Contemporary Culture*. London: Routledge.

Walklate, S. (1990) 'Researching victims of crime: Critical victimology', *Social Justice*, 17(3): 25–42.

Walklate, S. (2007) *Imagining the Victim of Crime*. Maidenhead: Open University Press.

Waller, I. (1988) 'International Standards, National Trail Blazing, and the Next Steps', in M. Maguire and J. Pointing (eds) *Victims of Crime: A New Deal?* Milton Keynes: Open University Press.

Williams, B. (1999) *Working with Victims of Crime: Policies, Politics and Practice*. London: Jessica Kingsley.

Worcester, R. (2001) 'The world will never be the same again: British hopes and fears after September 11th 2001', *International Journal of Public Opinion Research* (http://www.mori.com).

Part One

Perspectives on the Victim and Victimisation

Sandra Walklate

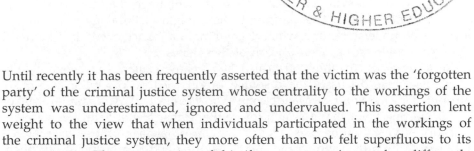
Until recently it has been frequently asserted that the victim was the 'forgotten party' of the criminal justice system whose centrality to the workings of the system was underestimated, ignored and undervalued. This assertion lent weight to the view that when individuals participated in the workings of the criminal justice system, they more often than not felt superfluous to its requirements. The presumption of this 'forgotten party' status has differently fuelled political and policy responses to the victim, many of which are documented in the chapters that follow. However, one of the first questions to consider is whether or not this 'forgotten party' status has any real historical currency.

Barry Godfrey and Tony Kearon trace the changing place of the victim in the criminal justice process from Anglo-Saxon times until the present day. Their analysis highlights the important role the victim played in bringing private prosecutions prior to the nineteenth century. Indeed they assert that without the victim, from the Norman Conquest to Queen Victoria's Silver Jubilee there would have been very few criminal prosecutions at all! However, this analysis is also careful to point not only to the historical disjunction that occurred as modern police forces took up the role of prosecutor on behalf of the state but also to the historical continuities in respect of who actually had access to justice. Thus the demise of the role of the victim took its toll on those who had had such access, but for women and children, whose access to justice had always been minimal, little changed. Indeed, as the role of the state extended in its various regulatory forms, through, for example, the developments in education, insurance, and the tax system, and most significantly through the workplace and the nineteenth-century Factory Acts, a new kind of victim was created: who Godfrey and Kearon call the 'pure victim'. At this historical moment, understandings of who was a victim shifted from a simplistic notion of a victim of crime to more generic constructions tied into increasingly public debates about morality and crime. For Godfrey and Kearon, at precisely this point in time the role of the victim of crime was becoming increasingly marginal to the operation of the criminal justice process, while there was a rise in importance of the symbolic or mythical victim rooted in Victorian melodrama – use of the gothic that is not too far removed from the current media coverage of the victim commented on in the Introduction and overview. So for these authors the victim has moved from being an essential actor, key to the prosecution process, to a symbolic actor, a construction that has much contemporary resonance, to a fragmented actor: for example, the fear of terrorism on the one hand or rising concerns about domestic violence on the other, has effectively both widened and diffused constructions of victimhood. Indeed, much evidence of this fragmentation is to be found in the chapters that follow. What Godfrey and Kearon also point to in their historical analysis is the emergence of victimology in the mid-twentieth century; they argue that this might be best understood as a response to the processes of symbolic construction of victimhood that emerged during the nineteenth century. The question is, how might victimology as an area of analysis be understood and what, if anything, has it achieved? In Chapter 2 Paul Rock addresses aspects of each of these questions.

Rock asks us to think critically about any claims to theory within victimology. He discusses the disputed origins of this 'discipline' variously attributed to the work of Mendelsohn, Von Hentig and Wertham, and takes as his starting point that a search for anything that could claim the status of a theory of victimisation presents very similar problems to those encountered in a search for a theory of crime. Yet as Godfrey and Kearon point out, there have been various claims made for the label of victimological theory. These claims, largely emerging in the post Second World War era, became especially focused in the 1980s as both in the UK and elsewhere the struggle over what might be done about crime, and hence the struggle for the victim of crime, became particularly acute, with those of a more radical persuasion resisting political and policy efforts to downplay the impact of crime favoured by those of a conservative viewpoint. Such political wrangles notwithstanding, it is clear that those working within victimology recognised and lent some weight to the labels of positive, radical, and critical victimology. (For a more detailed discussion of these theoretical positions see Walklate 2007; Dignan 2005; Goodey 2005.)

Despite this, Rock reflects the view that theory within victimology is in a poor state. His approach takes us on a tour that, while refracted through the discipline of criminology, nevertheless clearly outlines the neglect of that discipline of the victim of crime. He suggests that there have been four main developments within the study of criminal victimisation: the differential development of the concept of victim precipitation, the feminist contribution to understanding the nature and extent of criminal victimisation (a theme taken up in Part Two of this book), and the popularisation of criminal victim surveys (also discussed in Chapters 3 and 4), and the later influence of routine activity theory on understanding who is likely to be victimised and when. He also points to the different but important influence of particular empirical studies of criminal victimisation in extending our understanding of the impact of crime. In particular he points to the work of Shapland *et al.*

(1985) on victims of violent crime, Maguire and Bennett (1982) on burglary victims, Morgan and Zedner on child victims (1992) and interestingly adds to this list the ideas of Braithwaite (1989) in contributing to the foregrounding of restorative justice (addressed in detail in Chapter 11). Nowhere does Rock discuss those efforts that have been made to make greater claims of a coherent theory for victimology, for example, Miers (1989, 1990) on positive victimology; Fattah (1992) on critical victimology; Mawby and Walklate (1994) and Walklate (2007) on critical victimology; Kauslarich et al. (2001) on radical victimology. These efforts, he would argue, comprise what he calls 'opportunistic theorising', borrowing as they variously do from criminology and/or sociology. From this point of view, victimology is no more than another *rendezvous* sub-discipline, a meeting place for all those who share a common interest in the victim of crime.

Acceptance of Rock's analysis, of course, rather depends upon whether or not the reader considers that victimology (or criminology for that matter) carries with it the status of a discipline with a clearly defined unit of analysis, as opposed to a meeting place for people interested in a particular substantive problem. It is perhaps fair to suggest that those who have been keen to develop a theoretical framework for victimology have also been keen to establish a clearer line of demarcation between what Fattah (1991) referred to as the activist victimologist and the academic victimologist. Given the increasing symbolic use to which constructions of victimhood have been put, highlighted by Godfrey and Kearon and developed in Chapter 18 by Gabe Mythen, alongside the contemporary preoccupation in the policy arena with the crime victim not only in the UK but elsewhere (see especially Chapter 15), then concerns to separate these two strands seem eminently defensible whether or not this implies a resulting claim to the status of a discipline. However, Rock is right to encourage a deeply critical stance towards theoretical thinking about the victim (of crime). This is an issue we shall return to in the Conclusion. In a similar vein, Tim Hope takes up the problem of the measurement of criminal victimisation in Chapter 3.

Rather than taking us through a rather conventional discussion of the advantages and disadvantages of the criminal victimisation survey, which has formed the bedrock of data on criminal victimisation in the Anglo-speaking world and which is increasingly forming the basis of victim-related policy on an international level given the investment in the International Criminal Victimisation Survey (see Walklate 2007, Chapter 3 for a discussion of this), Hope takes a much more critical stance towards the problems of studying victimisation. So his chapter is not concerned with the problems and possibilities of the criminal victimisation survey, whether done as a national survey, a local survey or an international one. Nor is it concerned with the findings from these enterprises *per se*. (For this kind of coverage see Maguire 2002.) Indeed, if one were to add to this list of data sources the now almost compulsion to engage in a criminal victimisation survey subsequent to the requirements of the Crime and Disorder Act (1998), there is indeed a wealth of information on victims contemporarily that was very much absent in the 1960s. Moreover it should be noted that this search for more and more data on criminal victimisation is variable from country to country, as Jo Goodey alludes to in Chapter 16. So while there have been some significant technical developments in the criminal victimisation survey methodology and much more widespread use and acceptance of this research technique especially in England and Wales, some of the issues that relate to how to make sense of the data gathered remain the same. It is this problem that Tim Hope draws our attention to, and by implication, also addresses the problem of theory foregrounded by Rock in Chapter 2.

Hope cogently argues that understanding the data generating process is crucial in understanding the problems and possibilities of policy intervention. He asks us to think about the problem of the 'counterfactual condition'. Put simply, what is it that we know about not being a victim as opposed to being a victim? What are the conditions that result in our non-victimisation? If we think about this problem, two scenarios suggest themselves. The first is what he calls a 'discrete outcome model': you are either a victim or you are not. In computing terms this would amount to being either counted as zero or counted as 1. In the second model, victimisation is the outcome of a continuous process (think, for example, about some of the issues associated with domestic violence, discussed by Carolyn Hoyle in Chapter 6). This latter model is more about exposure to risk and connects with the routine activity approach that has informed some of the thinking behind the criminal victimisation survey methodology. So, it is important to consider whether victimisation is a discrete or continuous experience, and the implications of each of these different positions for understanding the cause of criminal victimisation. Hope's argument is that only by understanding the counterfactual position that each of these views implies is it possible to appreciate how, for example, in certain high-crime areas some people are immune from criminal victimisation and others are highly vulnerable to it. The idea that these conditions coexist is central in the search for the causes of victimisation, as it is in positing the possibility of policy intervention, neither of which flow readily from the current use of criminal victimisation survey data. As a result, in different, though clearly connected ways, Hope, like Rock, points to the paucity of what has currently been achieved by those involved in the criminal victimisation survey industry. In Chapter 4, Simon Green draws our attention to not so much the data generating process that concerns Hope, but the findings of that data generating process.

Green presents these findings in a critical and thought-provoking manner. Taking what he calls the 'axis of vulnerability' as his central organising theme, this is used to offer a critical exploration of Christie's (1986) concept of the ideal victim. This exploration resonates well with the gendered critique developed of it in Chapter 7 by Pamela Davies and the extent to which it falls short in helping us understand victims of corporate crime considered by Dave Whyte in Chapter 17. Green uses his 'axis of vulnerability' to consider the class, age, gender and ethnic basis to vulnerability from crime, but this also becomes his tool for considering the extent to which the status of victim itself has become a commodity in the Marxist sense in contemporary society. This process of commodification, he argues, utilises fear as its marketing strategy to which we have all become victim. This emphasis on the economic and its relationship with fear and victimhood usefully reminds, and encourages us to consider the relationship between the criminal victimisation industry, the rise of the culture of victimhood discussed in the Introduction and Overview, and the nature of the neo-liberal capitalist state in which these developments have occurred (see also Walklate 2007).

Of course, in reality it has become increasingly difficult to separate the theoretical and empirical findings with respect to criminal victimisation from the way in which the victim has been used more and more as a political and symbolic reference point, part of the riding tide of penal populism that has been witnessed in the UK and the USA since the early 1980s. Garland (2001) refers to this as the 'culture of control'. Many of the policy initiatives discussed within this book need to be understood and referenced within this wider socio-economic and cultural context: the express political use to which criminal victimisation survey findings were put in the early 1980s (see Mayhew and Hough 1988) have become implicit to the agenda-setting of criminal justice policy. So, victimological developments and debates, as with criminology, need to be understood within their socio-economic and cultural context. The chapters here are suggestive of an emergent resistance to the presumptions that have become embedded within those developments and are indicative of the potential for the debate to come.

References

Braithwaite, J. (1989) *Crime, Shame and Reintegration*. Cambridge: Cambridge University Press.

Christie, N. (1986) 'The Ideal Victim', in E. Fattah (ed.) *From Crime Policy to Victim Policy*. London: Macmillan.

Dignan, J. (2005) *Understanding Victims and Restorative Justice*. Maidenhead: Open University Press.

Fattah, E. (1991) *Understanding Criminal Victimisation*. Scarborough, Ontario: Prentice Hall.

Fattah, E. (1992) *Critical Victimology*. London: Macmillan.

Garland, D. (2001) *The Culture of Control*. Oxford: Polity.

Goodey, J. (2005) *Victims and Victimology*. Harlow: Longman.

Kauslarich, D., Matthews, R.A., and Miller, W.J. (2001) 'Towards a victimology of state crime', *Critical Criminology*, 10: 173–94.

Maguire, M. (2002) 'Crime Statistics: The "Data Explosion" and its Implications', in M. Maguire, R. Morgan and R. Reiner (eds) *The Oxford Handbook of Criminology*, (3rd edn.). Oxford: Oxford University Press.

Maguire, M. with Bennett, T. (1982) *Burglary in a Dwelling*. London: Heinemann.

Mawby R. and Walklate, S. (1994) *Critical Victimology*. London: Sage.

Mayhew, P. and Hough, M. (1988) 'The British Crime Survey: Origins and Impact'. in M. Maguire and J. Pointing (eds) *Victims of Crime: A New Deal?* Milton Keynes: Open University Press.

Miers, D. (1989) 'Positivist victimology: A critique, part 1', *International Review of Victimology*, 1(1): 1–29.

Miers, D. (1990) 'Positivist victimology: A critique, part 2', *International Review of Victimology*, 1(3): 219–30.

Morgan, J. and Zedner, L. (1992) *Child Victims: Crime, Impact and Criminal Justice.* Oxford: Oxford University Press.

Shapland, J., Willmore, J. and Duff, P. (1985) *Victims and the Criminal Justice System.* Aldershot: Gower.

Walklate, S. (2007) *Imagining the Victim of Crime.* Maidenhead: Open University Press.

Chapter 1

Setting the scene: a question of history[1]

Tony Kearon and Barry S. Godfrey

Introduction

For much of the twentieth century, the victim of crime was either ignored in criminological debates or portrayed as a marginal and passive figure in the criminal justice system (Hoyle and Young 2002: 526). As Miers (1978: 15) noted, the very term 'victim' inevitably promotes an image of passivity, where the victim has 'traditionally been viewed as the "sufferer" in a simple "doer-sufferer" model of criminal interaction'. This perception has (notwithstanding growing debates about the role of the victim in restorative justice), become something of a 'given' in modern criminology, although essays in this collection will go a long way towards reassessing that view. Historical research has provided a measure of empirical evidence to challenge the 'marginality' of victims in past centuries. However, debates about the historical position and importance of victims in the criminal justice process have had to be pieced together from disparate sources. Victims make an appearance in essays on the development of policing services, descriptions of change in the prosecution process, but only as bit-part actors. If Rude's opinion in 1985 that historical research had pretty much bypassed victims is now looking a little dated, it is certainly true that victims, and the part they have played in the operation of the criminal justice system, are not well served by historians (see Rude 1985: 76). However, let us start with something positive. There are some recent publications that have significantly increased our knowledge, and described concepts that help to make sense of the role of the victim. Rock's (2004) exploration of the development of the state's prosecution apparatus has been added to King's work on victims' use of the law in the eighteenth and nineteenth centuries (King 1984, 2000; and see Storch 1975, 1976); Kirchengast (2006) has attempted recently to produce a Foucauldian account of the history and development of the crime victim, and some crime history textbooks now contain chapters on victims as prosecutors (Emsley 2005; Godfrey and Lawrence 2005).[2] This chapter presents further knowledge and contextualises the place of victim in society in previous centuries; and attempts to describe the beginnings of interest in victims by academics and policy-makers – interest that later came to be termed 'victimology'. In doing this, we illustrate the confused and contradictory position that victims have occupied as both symbolic and real actors in the detection and prosecution of crime and in the public conception of the crime 'problem'.[3]

The centrality of the victim?

Despite the view presented in modern criminological studies, victims have been both central to and indispensable for the processes of justice. Indeed, if it was not for the activity of victims there would hardly be any recorded crime at all before the late Victorian period. The role of the victim in the prevention, prosecution and detection of crime has been altered by the increasing centrality of the national authorities and their vacillating desire to take control of the prosecution of offences. However, private action by aggrieved individuals was for centuries the mechanism and impetus for legal proceedings.

Perhaps some of the earliest examples of this (in an English context at least) can be found in the role of victims in late Anglo-Saxon justice. Anglo-Saxon society was organised around small agricultural communities in which social cohesion was maintained by ties of family and kinship but also by the mutual interdependence of members of the community through the need to pool resources and labour at key points in the agricultural calendar. An essential issue for these communities was how intra-communal conflicts could be managed and resolved. The 'blood feud' as a means of resolving conflicts through violence was a long-established and accepted tradition in Anglo-Saxon society, but such feuds could undermine the fragile patterns of interdependence in small communities (Jolliffe 1937). Thus, by the eighth century, many conflicts at the local level were managed by the 'Moot' (a semi-formal court made up of members of the local community). These courts dealt with complaints brought directly by victims or their families against an alleged perpetrator, with a complex system of financial compensation paid directly to the victim or victim's family by the 'convicted' offender. These fines covered offences ranging from theft or damage to property through personal injury of varying degrees of severity up to the 'Wergeld', the fine paid by a convicted murderer directly to the family of the victim. In the absence of a strong state, compliance with the decisions of the Moot was enforced through local sanctions – the threat of ostracism, expulsion from the community or being formally declared as outside of the law. Ultimately, non-compliance could result in the victim resorting to blood feud with the support of the community (Wormald 1999). In the reign of King Alfred (871–99) the emerging state began to be more explicitly involved in the enforcement of laws and punishment. In cases where a relatively powerless victim brought a charge against a powerful perpetrator, the local nobility (or ultimately the king) could be enlisted by the victim to support their claim. In such cases the perpetrator would be required to pay both compensation to the victim and also a separate fine, the 'Wite', to the king. Alfred and subsequent Anglo-

Saxon Kings attempted to produce and enforce codified national laws and to introduce the concept of offences being a breach of the King's peace (and hence subject to a Wite). Although the punishment of offenders remained a largely victim-centred process throughout this period, involving direct financial restitution and the local/informal resolution of conflict, these developments marked the beginning of the process by which the state selectively replaced the victim as the instigator of charges against perpetrators and also the first challenges to the hitherto taken for granted assumption that the victim would automatically be the recipient of any fines paid by the offender (Kirby 1992).

The Norman invasion of 1066 resulted in a number of modifications, additions to and revisions of the Anglo-Saxon legal framework. While still ostensibly a victim-centred process, a number of shifts in the relationship between victim, offender and state began to emerge. Henry I (1100–35) continued the trend of the late Anglo-Saxon kings by attempting to shift the emphasis away from crime being an offence against the victim towards an offence against God and the King's peace. Henry II (1154–89) attempted to codify legal practice and produce a 'common' law for the kingdom, which in part involved attempts to increase the role of the state in the prosecution of offenders. In theory prosecution was still a victim-instigated process but the state increasingly adopted powers to allow it to take up and pursue cases instigated but subsequently dropped by a victim. The state also employed 'Kings Approvers' – individuals who were paid to press charges on behalf of the state, and allowed accused felons to instigate charges against their fellow criminals in return for reduced sentences (Rawlings 2002). Thus, in a small but growing number of cases during this period the state began to intervene to press charges and bypass the victim as instigator of proceedings. This period also saw the introduction of the concept of the 'Deodand' (literally 'given to God'). A Deodand was any object, artefact or possession that had inflicted death or injury, which would subsequently be forfeited to the Crown. Income raised by the confiscation and sale of a Deodand was held by the Kings' High Almoner for the benefit of the local community (or, in reality, often simply kept by the state). In many respects the introduction of this concept can be seen as a significant shift in the distribution of compensation for victims – severing the direct link between the victim and the repayment of a 'debt' by the offender, with the 'debt' owed by the offender increasingly shifted towards society and the state. Fines became an increasingly lucrative source of revenue for the state (during this period tax collectors also served as itinerant magistrates, underlining the increasing blurring of the two functions). The range of offences punishable by a fine paid directly to the state increased significantly, including fines for accusers who made false charges or withdrew their complaint before the completion of a trial, and harsh penalties introduced to compel victims to bear witness in cases brought by agents of the state. But it would be crude and slightly misleading to suggest that these developments in the power of the emerging state to bypass victims of crime in the prosecution process was purely driven by the imperative of financial gain. Growing national trading networks and increased levels of geographical mobility and labour migrations in the late medieval period increasingly problematised semi-formal prosecution systems based on small, close-knit and static communities and created a growing role for a regulatory state that transcended local feudal structures. As Zedner (2004: 8) argues, this is a period in which 'the notion of the crime as an interpersonal dispute was overlaid by the notion of crime as a threat to social order'.

So the period between the eighth to the seventeenth centuries was marked by a number of interlinked transitions in the role, rights and status of the victim of crime. By the end of this period, the state had firmly established its right to selectively bypass victims and to intervene directly in the prosecution of offenders for particular offences, and many of the attributes of the marginalised and disempowered victim of crime, who has figured so heavily in contemporary debates, were becoming embedded within legal processes. This period sees a shift from the commission of an offence being regarded as a direct act against the victim, towards an act against the peace or person of the monarch and ultimately to an act against 'society' in general. It sees a shift from the victim as direct recipient of compensation towards a more general and abstract notion of the offender owing a debt to 'society'. It is marked by a transition from the victim as essential instigator of proceedings to the victim reduced increasingly to the status of potential witness in cases instigated by the state. This period also saw the beginnings of a shift away from informal and semi-formal strategies for dealing with victimisation to an increasingly state-centred and bureaucratised response in which the victim's desire for restitution was increasingly policed, restricted and marginalised. This is not to suggest a steady and unproblematic shift away from a victim-centred approach to criminal justice. The movement towards the state's monopoly control of retribution and the punishment of offenders was slow and uneven (and by the end of the nineteenth century the process was still incomplete, as is discussed later in this chapter).

However, the state became an important if infrequent prosecutor during the eighteenth century, reserving action only for major offences which threatened the economic or political well-being of the ruling elites. In practice, this meant that many offences such as coining (the production of counterfeit coins) were prosecuted by the Treasury Solicitor. Forgery of paper money was also taken very seriously by government officials, although the Bank of England was the main prosecuting agency, having established its own private police force for this task (McGowen 2005). The attorney-general would from time to time undertake the prosecution of cases of sedition and treason, and the publicity surrounding these high-profile cases served to reinforce the authority of the state.[4]

In the case of ordinary offences against persons or property that did not threaten the security or well-being of the state the chances of government funded or conducted prosecutions were still minimal. In fact, until the Prosecution of Offences Act of 1879 there was no public prosecutor who could take criminal cases to court, and even then only significant or important cases were taken forward (Rock 2004).[5] State prosecutions in the higher courts, attended by a mass of government-paid lawyers and a good deal of media attention, lay like a layer of cream over the mass of privately initiated prosecutions for everyday offences. However, although the vast majority of prosecutions were privately funded, it is certainly not the case that the prosecution of offenders lay within the means of everyone. Although direct state intervention in the prosecution process remained relatively minimal during this period up to the latter half of the nineteenth century, and victims remained largely responsible for the pursuit of prosecutions, the period from the mid-seventeenth to the early nineteenth century in particular can be characterised as one in which a number of the mechanisms of support for victims of crime become increasingly eroded, particularly in terms of the formal and informal obligations placed on fellow members of the community to provide support to the victim (ranging from active participation in the pursuit and apprehension of suspects through to the provision of evidence in prosecutions: Rawlings 2002; Beattie 2001). This left poorer and less influential victims of crime increasingly marginalised and excluded from formal processes of prosecution and restitution. Increasingly the prosecution of crime could be a costly business, and often relied on people with social or financial capital being able to draw upon private prosecution agencies of one kind or another – thief-takers (Hay and Snyder 1989: 301–40); the Bow Street Runners, or additional constables, for example, who were available to anyone who could afford the appropriate fee (Steedman 1984).[6] The main redress for wealthier victims of crime were the numerous 'associations for the prosecution of felons' which had been established in most parts of the country from the 1760s (Beattie 1986; Philips 1989; Gatrell *et al.* 1980). For an annual subscription, prosecution associations would advertise the loss of people's property and offer a reward for its return. When an offender could be tracked down (sometimes by detecting inspectors belonging to an association) they arranged for a prosecution and paid for its costs. By the early nineteenth century these associations were firmly established, and they could be extremely active although only in very local contexts (Hay and Snyder 1989). For example, a group of textile employers in Yorkshire formed an organisation that prosecuted over 3,000 workers for taking home workplace materials from their factories (Godfrey 1997, 2002). The impact of the associations on national prosecution rates was probably slight, and they served only a small number of victims from a particular section of society (Beattie 1986: 50). Nevertheless they added to the large number of private prosecutions brought in this period. As Hay and Snyder (1989: 24) have noted, private prosecution was the dominant mode in the eighteenth and nineteenth centuries. More than 80 per cent of all criminal cases were prosecuted by private individuals mainly through the use of agents of one kind or another (Hay and Snyder 1989: 167). National and local government bodies were infrequent prosecutors by comparison.

Those cases which complainants pressed through the courts[7] through the activities of private agencies, or by action themselves, for example by the taking out of summons and securing warrants from the courts, were but one option in the range of reactions to criminal victimisation. For those who may have lacked the financial means to bring a formal prosecution,[8] or those who simply preferred to retain control in their own affairs (see Storch 1975, 1976), there were informal routes to 'successful' dispute resolution. As Godfrey and Lawrence (2005: 30–1) note:

Minor offences would in all likelihood be ignored or even tolerated. These will not show up in criminal statistics and there is, therefore, no way of knowing the real extent to which crime was tolerated. However, some anecdotal evidence does exist that can give us a flavour of public opinion. There are a number of documented instances, for example, where prosecutors were attacked or pressurised in some way for their bringing cases to court. Sometimes this was a reaction to severe sentencing by the court – especially if the death penalty had been inflicted – but was also motivated, so it seems, by a general community feeling that the case should not have been presented because the circumstances did not warrant it. Often this reflected the status of the offender. Much which would currently come within the purview of criminal justice system was in earlier times simply ignored or settled privately between the individuals concerned.

Alongside individual retribution, personal retaliation and vigilantism, community-wide forces came into play (Wood 2003: 111, 114; Beattie 1986: 135; Emsley 2005: 182). For example, during episodes of 'rough music', local people, mostly in rural areas, were treated to displays of public shaming (villagers banging pots and pans outside the houses of abusive husbands or local 'gossips').

The most common form of extra-judicial action was the simple agreement of two disputing parties not to take the matter to court. A vast number of 'crimes' disappeared with a handshake between the parties or the payment of some compensation (a process known as 'compounding', which was illegal but which was also widely practised).

We should remember, of course, that some victims have never enjoyed the same access to the criminal justice system as others. Victims (usually women) of domestic violence have faced structural, familial, economic and religious barriers to prosecuting their abusive partners (see Clark 1987; D'Cruze 1998; Ross 1982; Tomes 1978).[9] Those victims rarely had the opportunity to use methods outside the criminal justice system either. Only in the late twentieth century did the state put resources into supporting domestic violence victims, and this has led to a rise in prosecutions, but before then the numbers of prosecutions was but a shadow of the number of offences committed within the family home.

From the Norman Conquest to the silver jubilee of Queen Victoria the victim was central to the whole business of detecting and prosecuting crime. They were as yet not involved in the punishment of offenders (and would not be, in theory at least, until the late twentieth century) but until the late nineteenth century this was the only area of the criminal justice system where the victims did not appear to play a major part.

So far this chapter has presented a picture of gradual, piecemeal and apparently marginal changes in the role of victims *vis-à-vis* the state in criminal prosecutions. But by the end of the First World War this picture had changed significantly, with the police taking over from victims as the instigators of the vast majority of criminal prosecutions, and with private prosecutions becoming increasingly rare occurrences.

The disappearance of the victim?

In many respects, the 'disappearance' of the victim of crime from the process of prosecution during a quite short period of the latter stages of the nineteenth century can be equated with the growing regulatory role of the local and national state within the context of local police services.

The development of the 'policemen-state' has been charted in local and national context (Johnson and Monkonnen 1996; Jones 1992; Taylor 2002). Early examples of this regulatory state and the increasing role it accorded to the discretionary power of the police to intervene in hitherto largely unregulated areas of social life for the 'public good' include the Contagious Diseases Acts of 1864, 1866 and 1869, which gave the police power to detain women suspected of engaging in prostitution, subject them to medical examinations and (if found to be infected with venereal diseases) confine the women to 'lock hospitals' until they were cured. Another aspect of the extension of police jurisdiction was their increasing willingness to act as prosecutors in court. In the early and mid-nineteenth century, the police were mainly interested in taking only major crimes to court (murders, serious sexual violence, woundings, burglaries, larcenies and other serious property offences). The majority of complainants were present in court to press their cases as witnesses to the offence committed against them; individual victims accusing individual defendants was the norm. However, by the 1870s and 1880s, the police preferred to prosecute a range of offences (now including cases of drunkenness, disorderliness, fighting, violent offences and sexual offences) either for themselves, the state, or on behalf of victims who otherwise could or would not prosecute cases themselves. By the First World War, this practice had become so established that individuals carrying out private prosecutions were very rare. The professionalisation of the court, with police prosecutors and advocates representing victims, and lawyers defending the accused, 'pacified' the court and eventually reduced the 'carnivalesque' atmosphere that had pervaded magistrate's and high courts in the eighteenth and early nineteenth centuries.

Concomitant with these changes in prosecution practices came the rise of what might be termed the 'regulatory state' – which ushered in a huge range of very active prosecutors (including market inspectors, nuisance inspectors, NSPCC and animal inspectors, rates and truancy inspectors, and appointees of the town clerk), all purporting to be working on behalf of the community (or sections of it), but without the aid of the 'victims' appearing in court. As Emsley (1993: 360) states, 'In the second half of the century penal punishments were imposed to back up legislation on education, registration and vaccination; legislators saw failure to comply with the requirements of the state as the products of a defective conscience'. Contemporaries estimated that half a million parents were prosecuted in the 20 years following the passage of the 1870 Education Act for failure to send their children to school. If one adds together the people prosecuted for not sending children to school or to be vaccinated; having a chimney fire or unsanitary drains; riding a bicycle without lights or a bell; selling unsound meat or margarine disguised as butter; or buying scrap metal without proper documents; leaving curtains open during an air-raid; or not paying local authority rates, the numbers are considerable (there were, for example, over 18,000 prosecutions just in the small northwest town of Crewe between 1880 and 1940, see Godfrey, *et al.* 2007). Indeed, nationally, regulatory offences comprised the main business of the courts in the late nineteenth and early twentieth centuries and processes of civilisation, social control and governmentality were carried forward by the routine enforcement of health, safety, family and traffic regulations. Offenders who breached bylaws or health and safety legislation, and so on, might not be considered to be '"criminals" in the accepted sense' (Emsley 1993: 360) but they did find themselves in court through the action of locally or nationally appointed officials, and answering for offending against the 'community' rather than against individuals. One way or another, by various means, individual victims had been largely squeezed out of the courts. At almost every stage, professional bodies were intervening in the prosecution process to represent individual victims and reduce their role to an abstract representation. This was, of course, even more complete when the Crown Prosecution Service was formed in 1985 to conduct prosecutions (with professional solicitors and barristers replacing legally trained police sergeants).

However, discussion of the 'disappearance' of the crime victim during this period needs to be qualified. Undoubtedly, the victim of crime as a living, breathing actor playing a crucial (if mundane) role in the prosecution process was relegated to a very minor walk-on role in the performance of criminal justice during this period. But this does not entirely equate with the disappearance of the victim in every sense. Rather, during this period the role of the victim in criminal justice processes was re-imagined and reconfigured, with the socially located victim of crime as a real actor in the day-to-day practice of criminal justice becoming usurped by the 'victim of crime' as a symbolic and generic construct in popular/public discourse. This period was also, as we have already demonstrated, characterised by the rapid expansion of an interventionist state. The liberal sensibilities that emerged during this period were fundamentally wedded to the identification and amelioration of diverse social problems (Evans 1982); they were implicitly paternalistic and explicitly interventionist (Gunn 2000). The interventionist state engaged in an implicitly and explicitly evangelical fashion with a range of social causes, from universal education and suffrage, cruelty to animals and public drunkenness to the provision of sewers and the moral and spiritual welfare of the urban poor (Crossick 1977, 1983; Morris 1983; Kidd and Nicholls 1999). The state (often pushed and cajoled by moral entrepreneurs and activists) was particularly active with regard to women and children.

For example, the Factory Acts passed between 1819 and 1864 increasingly curtailed child and female labour in 'dangerous' occupations, and the 1885 Criminal Law Amendment Act included a number of measures, such as raising the age of female consent from 13 to 16, aimed at curbing unacceptable sexual behaviour towards girls. All of these measures, particularly the Factory Acts, faced opposition when they were mooted. The proponents of reform were keen to evoke images of vulnerable and innocent girls and boys, images that fitted well with Victorian mentalities and sentimentalities. Paintings, literary descriptions and documentary news reports depicting the 'victims' of an uncaring social environment essentialised and universalised the purity and vulnerability of women and children. Not all women and children, of course, for there were always the 'undeserving' poor to focus on.

In the context of criminal justice during this period, the state (in both local and national contexts) engaged in processes of differentiation and delineation between those to be surveilled, policed and punished and those to be protected – those to be watched and those to be watched over. This in part reflected attempts at a general level to reassert moral and normative frameworks within a rapidly urbanising and industrialising British society. Brooks (1995) captures these processes in the context of his exploration of the emergence of a 'melodramatic imagination' in late Victorian culture. Informal strategies for the maintenance of social order and the production and informal policing of norms and values, which worked effectively in small, static and close-knit communities, became increasingly problematised by this social revolution of urbanisation and industrialisation. In this context, the sketching out of moral and normative boundaries and frameworks became an increasingly mediated process (through the growing cultural representation of moral transgression and moral resolution and the campaigning zeal and moral enterprise of the growing print media and the 'new journalism' of the late Victorian era). Fundamentally this moral enterprise involved the creation of symbolic (and quite literally melodramatic), ideal types of offender and victim whose publicly rehearsed travails reaffirmed normative frameworks in Victorian society (Brooks 1995; Kearon 2005). Examples of this include Josephine Butler's high-profile campaign against 'white slavery' in the late nineteenth century and W.T. Stead's series of articles in the *Pall Mall Gazette* in 1885 on the sexual exploitation of young girls in London, contributing to the public furore which resulted in the 1885 Criminal Law Amendment Act (Walkowitz 1992).

Thus, in the context of victims of crime, this shifted the focus away from mundane individual crime victims to the creation/identification of social 'types' as pure victims – the vulnerable widow, the 'plucky' orphan, the innocent maiden seduced into a life of vice and so on (Hendler 2001). This was a significant transition in the nature/role of the victim of crime, from active individual to a series of generic symbolic archetypes, to be mobilised in public debates about crime and moral transgression. This symbolic role for the victim of crime relied on the construction of 'pure' and unambiguous victim identities designed to engender unqualified public sympathy and support. The messy, complex and fragmented identities of real victims did not sit well with these ideal types and in many respects these symbolic and melodramatic constructions of the victims of crime, which became firmly entrenched in law and order discourses during the late Victorian period, shaped the role of the victim of crime in these debates for much of the twentieth century. By the end of the First World War this symbolic/mythic centrality of the victim in criminal justice narratives (underscored by the *de facto* marginalisation of *real* victims of crime from criminal justice processes) was firmly embedded and remained so for most of the twentieth century. Indeed it could be argued that the victimology that emerges in the last quarter of the twentieth century sets out to critique and problematise precisely the image of the victim that is symbolically constructed during this period.

25

The re-emergence of the victim?

Hoyle and Young (2002: 526) have recently stated that 'The modern Anglo-American professional and bureaucratic criminal justice system, with decisions on whether to prosecute concentrated in the hands of the state, did not emerge until the latter part of the nineteenth century'. A century later, victims had re-emerged as important components in the criminal justice system, or at least the 'idea' of the victim had claimed an importance in politicised debates on crime and punishment carried out in the public and academic realm.

During and in the immediate aftermath of the Second World War campaigning reformers and academics began to focus on victims and Mendelsohn was the first to coin the term 'victimology' in 1940. In 1948, Von Hentig published *The Criminal and His Victim* in which he outlined 13 psychological and sociological classes of victim. However, victims were hardly at the forefront of academic debate. Mawby and Walklate commented that 'by 1945 there was no sense in which victims of crime had a voice in the political or the policy arenas' (1994: 69), and Margery Fry argued in *Arms of the Law* published in 1951 (see Rock 1990) that 'the injured individual [has] rather slipped out of the mind of the criminal court'. Nevertheless, the post-war welfarist social agenda did key in with the willingness of the criminal justice system to protect the vulnerable. In the 1950s and 1960s the state increasingly put into place structures to protect people who were 'at risk' as well as those who were suffering deprivations of one kind or another (as we have argued, this was a trend that in many respects originated in the nineteenth century, see Wiener 2004). Fry's campaigns eventually led to the system of Criminal Injuries Compensation for the victims of violent crime in the 1960s, for example.

The academic studies relating to victims of crime that were published in the 1960s and 1970s were fairly conventional and conservative, with a continued emphasis on the offender and offence – the lens through which the role and experience of the crime victim continued to be visualised and interpreted. Von Hentig's work, for example, examined the role of victims in criminal incidents; Wolfgang (1958) and Mendelsohn (1963) similarly examined the contribution victims made to their own victimisation. Academic research was primarily focused upon the risks faced by various social groups, concepts such as victim proneness, victim precipitation, victim vulnerability/lifestyle and attractiveness and with the situations in which victimisation might occur – see Hindelang *et al.* (1978), for example. Not surprisingly, this approach to victims (most notably in the context of gender, class, ethnicity and victimisation) became increasingly problematised in an emerging body of more critical work. It is perhaps no surprise that in one of the earliest exemplars of this more overtly victim-focused approach, Schafer (1968) chose to highlight the symbolism of this shift in thinking about crime victims by calling his book *The Victim and His Criminal.* Subsequently, a range of interventions in these debates (see *inter alia* Stanko 1988; Walklate 1992; Newburn and Stanko 1994) criticised studies which restricted the debate to the measurement and identification of 'victimisable' individuals, the needs of 'pure' victims and the exploration of public rather than private victimisation (Walklate 1992: 105–6).

This emerging literature on victims of crime needs to be placed against the backdrop of wider concerns about crime, justice and 'law and order' across the Anglophonic world during this period. Debates about victims of crime came to a head during a period of apparent increases in recorded crime and a significant emergence of 'law and order' as an electoral issue (Hall *et al.* 1978). This in turn sparked a range of crime prevention and victimisation reduction initiatives across the developed world. However, while these initiatives potentially had a significant impact on *average risk* of criminal victimisation (Hough and Mayhew 1983), policy-makers and criminal justice researchers continued to express concerns about what they saw as the mismatch between *actual* and *perceived* risk of criminal victimisation by the public. General and situational crime prevention initiatives to attempt to reduce recorded crime were recognised as only one aspect of policy. Increasingly it was felt that the management and ultimate reduction of *real* crime needed to develop in tandem with initiatives to address public *perceptions* of levels of crime. The growing electoral significance of the 'law and order' agenda in the 1960s and 1970s placed a growing emphasis on the management of public concerns about and perceptions of crime, which appeared to increasingly have a life of their own, independent of changes to 'objective' official crime statistics.

In this context, during the 1960s and 1970s the crime victim became linked to emerging debates about 'fear of crime'. Fear of crime was regarded increasingly as a means by which the negative social consequences of victimisation could be reproduced on a wide scale, regardless of actual levels of victimisation. In part, this fear was regarded as rooted in uncertainties about levels of crime, which stem from the 'dark figure' of crime – the amorphous, unknown mass of unreported and unrecorded victimisation which by its very existence casts doubts on the veracity of official statistics. The policy response to this problem of the unknowable aspects of victimisation was the implementation of national crime and victimisation surveys (initially in the US, but subsequently across most of the developed world). In many respects, these surveys key aim was to make knowable the unknown of unreported victimisation, to question the public's perceptions of the stereotypical crime victim and to emphasise the relatively low risk of criminal victimisation. As Hough and Mayhew (1988: 157) stated in the context of the British Crime Survey (first carried out in 1982):

> It was thought within the Home Office that distorted and exaggerated ideas of crime levels, trends and risks were widespread among the public; information on crime risks would demonstrate the comparatively low risks of serious crime and puncture inaccurate stereotypes of crime victims. In other words, the survey was envisaged in part at least as a way of achieving what might be called the 'normalisation' of crime – to help create a less alarmist and more balanced climate of opinion about law and order.

So ironically, at a time when apparently the victim of crime was beginning to be taken more seriously in criminal justice policy, national crime/victimisation surveys implicitly set out to defuse the long-established symbolic power of 'the victim'. They demonstrated the 'irrationality' of the fear of becoming a victim of crime for most of the population, indicated that the 'purest' and (symbolically) most powerful victims featured in contemporary debates about crime (such as the elderly, women, children and middle-class suburbanites) were actually the groups *least* likely to become victims and compartmentalised the crime problem by reasserting that the 'typical' victim (like the typical offender) was young, working class and male.

The radical victimology that arose during the 1970s and 1980s set out to challenge these classifications of victimisation by examining domestic violence; the victimisation of ethnic minorities; victims of corporate and state criminality and other crimes of the powerful; and by turning away from the analysis of criminal statistics towards more qualitative sources for an epistemologically and methodologically informed position. All approaches up until this point had emphasised the importance of criminal statistics and highlighted the need for better and more quantitative data. However, in the 1980s, experiential data such as local crime surveys were designed to lessen reliance on criminal statistics produced by the government and produce a more 'accurate victimology' (Young 1986: 23).

This laudable aspiration was never really possible unless it is taken as simply an attempt to 'get nearer' to the experiences of neglected victims and criticism came from Newburn and Stanko (1994) for the continuing false distinction between 'victims' and 'offenders' and refusing to acknowledge the overlap between those two groups. As Farrall (2002) noted:

> Ultimately, realist victimology may be remembered not for its accurate victimology [sic], but for its inability to: perceive men as victims; uncover in greater detail the experiences associated with victimisation; or, accurately record the extent to which victims and offenders were the same individuals.

The critical victimology that emerged in the 1990s attempted to address these debates: Miers (1990) and Holstein and Miller (1990) focusing upon the ways in which labels such as 'victim' are applied, how such concepts are defined and who has the power to apply such labels. Nevertheless, whatever the disputes between the theorists, it is clear that victimology had been established in the criminological canon by the start of the twenty-first century.[10] But while victimology may have become firmly established, what has happened to the victim? To what extent can these more recent changes be characterised as the re-emergence of the victim of crime as a newly re-empowered and increasingly central actor in criminal justice?

The symbolism of victimhood and the rise in punitive attitudes and policies

The brief discussion above of the rise of various forms of 'victimology' in the second half of the twentieth century cannot really do justice to the complexities of this area of theoretical, political and cultural re-engagement with the victim of crime during this period, but one of the things that this discussion does highlight is the continuing symbolic power of the crime victim. It could be argued that the rise of 'victimology' as a topic for academic debate has not altered substantially the perception of victims as passive actors (Rock 1990: 84). In fact, some argue that victimology has bolstered punitive attitudes in society by again reinforcing the passivity and vulnerability of victims (and by extension, all respectable citizens). It has also preserved the distinction between those who offend and those who are victimised. As Godfrey, Cox and Farrall (2007) note (and see Walklate 1992: 104; Fattah 1993: 230–3):

> Despite realist and critical critiques of 'conventional' victimology; despite the introduction of concepts like repeat victimisation into the debate; and despite the obvious policy-related interest; one is still left with the feeling that victimology has not yet fully got to grips with one of the most consistent findings in its own field: the overlap between 'offenders' and 'victims'.

This situation has led Newburn and Stanko to conclude that 'in much recent victimological literature, victims are characterised as helpless and vulnerable' (1994: 154). Recent research on the emotional responses to criminal victimisation has suggested that victims may actually be significantly less passive and 'victim-like' than they are routinely constructed (see Ditton *et al.* 1999).

This growing realisation that victims of crime are complex actors, linked to the growing political salience of 'victims' rights', within criminal justice debates, would suggest that they are becoming re-empowered due to policy initiatives to deal with crime victims, most notably in the context for restorative justice. Indeed, Zedner (2004: 15) argues that it is perfectly feasible to view recent trends in restorative justice as 'indicative of a larger reversion to the historic responsibility of lay actors for preventing and prosecuting crimes'. Restorative justice has its roots in a range of 'victim–offender' reconciliation/ mediation programmes that were initially developed in North America in the mid-1970s and have been followed by a plethora of similar programmes across the Anglophonic world. Such initiatives, which appear to relocate real crime victims at the heart of the restorative process, could indeed be interpreted as an indication of the inclusion of crime victims. But questions remain about this renewed inclusion and the benefits to the victim. Indeed, Ashworth (2000) has characterised restorative justice as an exercise in 'victim prostitution', with the victim playing a new role in a process that is still implicitly concerned with the rehabilitation of the offender rather than addressing the wrongs suffered by the victim. The rhetoric of justice may have shifted, but it would appear that the new role of the crime victim in criminal justice processes is a much more fragmented, diffuse role which maintains many of its largely symbolic functions.

Conclusion

Clearly, then, the part that victims and the idea of victims have played in the conception and prosecution of crime is a complex one. We have attempted to capture this complexity, but, while it is easy to inappropriately force social phenomena into false chronologies, the history of victims does seem to fall into three distinct periods.

Period 1 – the victim as essential actor

As we have has already clearly demonstrated, before the late nineteenth century one could be forgiven for suggesting that without the victim there would be no prosecution process to speak of, beyond that small number of offences that directly threatened the state itself. In the vast majority of cases (those deemed too mundane or insignificant for the attentions of the state), the victim provided the evidence, the impetus and the financial means to the detection and prosecution of crime. Victims of crime sought redress for wrongs they had suffered and although there was some collective action (such as in raising the hue and cry or less formal community-based strategies for seeking redress), individualistic response to offending predominated in the formal pursuit and prosecution of offenders (obtaining warrants, securing arrest and so on). The rise of various private prosecution associations and related non-state agencies to aid those victims of crime with the financial means to secure their services is merely a veneer on the mundane daily reality of the prosecution process as a genuinely victim-centred process in which the crime victim was an essential (if often lonely) actor.

Period 2 – the victim as symbolic actor

The victim-centred approach to prosecutions that characterised this first period does not survive the emergence of the increasingly proactive interventionist and investigatory state, which was developing in the latter half of the nineteenth century. The growth of modern public police agencies from the 1840s onwards (who increasingly took over the role of detecting, apprehending and later prosecuting offenders) was simply one aspect of this process. The majority of victims in this period had their grievances filtered through a range of public agencies who kept in mind the needs (and finances) of the state and a slightly vague, amorphous and implicitly paternalistic conception of the 'public good'. Thus, from the 1880s, the public servants of the local and national state were the routine prosecutors of crime. But paradoxically, if victims were now less able to initiate prosecutions, or control the court process – now appearing in court as witnesses to a case brought in the *public* interest – the concept of 'the victim' was becoming much stronger. From the Victorian period onwards the powerful symbolism of vulnerable victims was developed and has significantly shaped public, media and governmental attitudes towards crime and offenders. After the Second World War, the power of symbolic constructions of crime victims has grown stronger and could be said to drive governmental policy to an unprecedented degree. The image of innocent victims plagued by rapacious and rampaging criminals is at least contested now by academics (victimologists) and to an extent by actual victims of crime themselves. The directions that academic victimology took in the late twentieth century are charted in Karmen (1990) and Miers (1989).[11] The sub-discipline had matured sufficiently for it to have fairly discrete theoretical perspectives by the late 1980s. The key texts, beliefs and perspectives of victimology (positivistic, radical and critical) have all contributed to a vibrant debate about victims, how they should be studied and how their concerns could be foregrounded in public policy debates (Mawby and Walklate 1994).

Yet somewhat paradoxically, while the symbolic power of the victim of crime continues unabated, we would argue that the history of the victim of crime has recently entered a third, much more fragmented period.

Period 3 – the victim as fragmented actor

The last quarter of the twentieth century can be characterised as a period in which 'the victim' begins to be mobilised in a range of diverse (and often) contradictory or mutually exclusive narratives, public debates and policy initiatives, leading to an increasingly fragmented conception of the term 'victim of crime'. This fragmentation is rooted in a tension between two competing and contradictory conceptions of the crime victim which had begun to coexist in the late twentieth century. As we have already suggested, in many respects this period continues to be characterised by the political salience of the 'pure' symbolic victim (alongside 'pure' and unproblematic offender identities) in the rise of punitive populism (Garland 2002; Young 1999). The crime victim also continues to maintain a socio-political salience through the actions of a diverse range of political parties, media commentators and pressure groups claiming to speak on behalf of 'the victim' in a generic (and largely symbolic) sense (Mawby and Walklate 1994). The concept of the 'victim' of crime as a symbolic construct in the latter stages of the twentieth century even begins to transcend the *actual* experience of criminal victimisation itself, with the emergence of the 'vicarious' victim in debates around the fear of crime and the rise of endemic/ambient anxiety in the context of the 'culture of fear' (Furedi 2002).

But alongside these continuities in the symbolic power of 'the victim' we have also seen the re-emergence of real, complex, contradictory and often politically inconvenient victims of crime as real actors in critical debates about crime in contemporary society and (increasingly) in the operation of criminal justice and the punishment/rehabilitation of offenders. This is reflected in the increasing awareness and salience of a diverse range of 'new' forms of victims highlighted by academic studies and political struggles in the post-war period. These developments (which we outlined in the second half of this chapter) led to the identification of hitherto ignored forms of criminal victimisation (sexual assaults, domestic abuse, intra-familial victimisation, racially motivated crimes, victims of corporate and state crimes and so on) and these developments are mirrored in the rise of pressure groups and victims' rights groups trying to address the needs of these specific groups of victims, often linked to explicit critiques of the state, legal structures and criminal justice agencies rather than just perpetrators *per se* (see *inter alia* Tombs and Whyte 2003; Mawby and Walklate 1994). Many of these 'new' victims, most notably victims of the crimes of the powerful, have engendered an awareness of forms of victimisation that are less interpersonal and direct and much more diffuse. Others, like domestic violence, have challenged comfortable assumptions about domestic and familial relationships. What these emerging forms of victimisation shared was their refusal to map neatly onto established typologies of 'the victim' or to be unproblematically mobilised in public/ political debates about law and order in the same fashion as the symbolic 'crime victim' that had begun to emerge in the late nineteenth century.

Thus, by the end of the twentieth century the 'victim' had begun to assume an increasingly complex, fragmented and contradictory role in debates about the operation of criminal justice and in the delivery of legal and social justice. That complexity will be explored elsewhere in this collection.

Further reading

Emsley, C. (2005) *Crime and Society in England, 1750–1900*, 3rd edition. Harlow: Longman.

Godfrey, B., Cox, D. and Farrall, S. (2007) *Criminal Lives: Family Life, Employment and Offending*, Clarendon Series in Criminology. Oxford: Oxford University Press.

Godfrey, B. and Lawrence, P. (2005) *Crime and Justice, 1750–1950*. Cullompton: Willan Publishing.

Kirchengast, T. (2006) *The Victim in Criminal Law and Justice*. London: Macmillan.

Rawlings, P. (2002) *Policing – A Short History*. Cullompton: Willan Publishing.

Rock, P. (1990) *Helping Victims of Crime: The Home Office and the Rise of Victim Support in England and Wales*. Oxford: Clarendon Press.

Rock, P. (2004) 'Victims, prosecutors and the state in nineteenth-century England and Wales', *Criminal Justice*, 4(4): 331–54.

Notes

1 Passages in this section of the chapter draw upon Godfrey and Lawrence 2005, and Farrall and Maltby 2003.

2 There are some areas of historical research on victims which this chapter does not describe in detail, mainly because they are emerging areas of interest where a density of research does not yet exist. The first is the right of victims to defend themselves from offenders. It has been argued that the 'right' of self-defence was implicit in the earliest laws of England and was in fact essential in a time before police officers could rush to the aid of victims (there is a detailed historical discussion of the use of self-defence in Godfrey and Lawrence 2005). The right was guaranteed in the Bill of Rights of 1689 (Malcolm 2002: 4; 1996, but see Williams 2004) but its use remains contentious as a reading of guidelines issued on the use of force against intruders by the Crown Prosecution Service and ACPO

(Association of Chief Police Officers) will demonstrate. The second area deals, obliquely perhaps, with the victim/offender overlap – treating some offenders as victims of the criminal justice system – juvenile delinquents suffering cruelty and humiliation as part of the reformative process, for example (see Godfrey and Lawrence 2005), or women alcoholics in inebriates' homes forced to conform to a concept of femininity they could never adhere to upon release (Morrison 2005).

3 Perhaps renewed interest in 'victims' stems in part from the desire to identify 'where' power resides in the criminal justice system, who operationalises it, and to what effect.

4 Paradoxically, due to the cost of prosecuting these types of cases, the state often urged late-eighteenth century magistrates to seek other means to fund the prosecution of sedition cases rather than relying on the Crown Law Officers to finance them (see Emsley 2005: 183).

5 Scotland together with many European states instigated the office of Public Prosecutor much earlier.

6 The use of thief-takers encouraged informal agreements between offenders and victims, usually compensating the thief for the return of stolen property.

7 Or any of the quasi-judicial bodies that could be accessed by private individuals, at least until these routes were limited by the Judicature Act (1873) and the Appellate Jurisdiction Act (1876) (see Arthur 1985).

8 Sweeping statements should be avoided. King (1984, 2002) found that complainants in assault cases in the eighteenth century were drawn from a fairly wide cross-section of society, including the working population. Davis (1984; Hay and Snyder 1989: 413) found this also to be the case in the late nineteenth century. 'Working-class' prosecutors accounted for between a fifth and a quarter of all prosecutions for theft during the 1860s and 1870s. It seems that only the lowest strata of society failed to be able to press their cases through legitimate means.

9 Abusive husbands could also be targets for 'rough music', however (Hammerton 1991, 1992: 15–33).

10 For example, there are chapters on 'victims' and 'victimology' in editions of M. Maguire, R. Morgan, and R. Reiner (eds) *The Oxford Handbook of Criminology* (Oxford: Oxford University Press) and also in many of the best-selling textbooks for the undergraduate market.

11 Subsequent chapters in this volume describe more recent writings on victims, and describe significant studies published in the late twentieth and early twenty-first centuries.

References

Arthur, H. (1985) *Without the Law: Administrative Justice and Legal Pluralism in Nineteenth-Century England.* Toronto: University of Toronto Press.

Ashworth, A. (2000) 'Victims' Rights, Defendants' Rights and Criminal Procedure', in A. Crawford and J. Goodey (eds) *Integrating a Victim Perspective within Criminal Justice.* Aldershot: Ashgate, pp. 185–204.

Beattie, J. (1986) *Crime and the Courts in England 1660–1800.* Oxford: Clarendon Press.

Beattie, J. M. (2001) *Policing and Punishment in London, 1660–1750: Urban Crime and the Limits of Terror.* Oxford: Oxford University Press.

Brooks, P. (1995) *The Melodramatic Imagination.* New Haven, CN: Yale University Press.

Clark, A. (1987) *Women's Silence, Men's Violence: Sexual assault in England, 1770–1845.* London: Pandora.

Crossick, G.J. (1983) 'Urban Society and the Petit Bourgeoisie in Nineteenth Century Britain', in D. Fraser and A. Sutcliffe (eds) *The Pursuit of Urban History*. London: Arnold.

Crossick, G.J. (ed.) (1977) *The Lower Middle Class in Britain 1870–1914*. London: Croom Helm.

Davis J. (1984) 'A poor man's system of justice? The London Police Courts in the second half of the nineteenth century', *Historical Journal*, 27(2): 309–35.

D'Cruze, S. (1998) *Crimes of Outrage: Sex, Violence and Victorian Working Women*. London: University College of London Press.

Ditton, J., Farrall, S., Bannister, J., Gilchrist, E. and Pease, K. (1999) 'Reactions to Victimisation: Why has anger been ignored?', *Crime Prevention And Community Safety*, 11(3): 37–54.

Emsley, C. (1993) '"Mother, what did policemen do before there weren't any motorists". The law, the police and the regulation of motor traffic in England, 1990–1939', *Historical Journal*, 37: 357–81.

Emsley, C. (2005) *Crime and Society in England, 1750–1900*, 3rd ed. Harlow: Longman.

Evans, N. (1982) 'Urbanisation, elite attitudes and philanthropy: Cardiff, 1850–1914', *International Review of Social History*, 27: 290–323.

Farrall, S. (2002) *Rethinking What Works With Offenders*. Cullompton: Willan Publishing.

Farrall, S. and Maltby, S. (2003) 'The Victimisation of Probationers', *Howard Journal of Criminal Justice*, 42(1): 32–54.

Fattah, E. (1993) 'The Rational Choice/Opportunity Perspectives as a Vehicle for Integrating Criminological and Victimological Theories', in R.V. Clarke and M. Felson (eds) *Routine Activity and Rational Choice*. New Brunswick, NJ: Transaction Publishers.

Fry, M. (1951) *Arms of the Law*. London: Gollancz.

Furedi, F. (2002) *Culture of Fear*. London: Continuum.

Garland, D. (2002) *The Culture of Control: Crime and Social Order in Contemporary Society*. Oxford: Oxford University Press.

Gatrell, V.A.C., Lenman, B. and Parker, G. (eds) (1980) *Crime and the Law: A Social History of Western Europe since 1500*. London: Europa Publcations.

Godfrey, B. (1997) 'Workplace Appropriation and the Gendering of Factory "Law": West Yorkshire, 1840–1880', in M. Arnot and C. Usborne (eds) *Crime and Gender in Modern Europe*. London: University College of London Press.

Godfrey, B. (2002) 'Private Policing and the Workplace: The Worsted Committee and the Policing of Labour in Northern England, 1840–1880', in L.A. Knafla (ed.) *Policing and War in Europe: Criminal Justice History*. London: Greenwood Press.

Godfrey, B. and Lawrence, P. (2005) *Crime and Justice 1750–1950*. Cullompton: Willan Publishing.

Godfrey, B., Cox, D. and Farrall, S. (2007) *Criminal Lives: Family Life, Employment and Offending*, Clarendon Series in Criminology. Oxford: Oxford University Press.

Gunn, S. (2000) *The Public Culture of the Victorian Middle Class: Ritual and Authority in the English Industrial City, 1840–1914*. Manchester: Manchester University Press.

Hall, S., Critcher, C., Jefferson, T., Clarke, J. and Roberts, B. (1978) *Policing the Crisis: Mugging, the State and Law and Order*. London: Palgrave/Macmillan.

Hammerton, J. (1991) 'The targets of "rough music": respectability and domestic violence in Victorian England', *Gender and History*, 3(1): 23–44.

Hammerton, J. (1992) *Cruelty and Companionship: Conflict in Nineteenth Century Married Life*. London: Routledge.

Hay, D. and Snyder, F. (eds) (1989) *Policing and Prosecution in Britain, 1750–1850*. Oxford: Oxford University Press.

Hendler, G. (2001) *Public Sentiments: Structures of Feeling in 19th Century American Literature*. University of North Carolina Press.

Hindelang, M.J., Gottfredson, M.R. and Garofalo, J. (1978) *Victims of Personal Crime*. Cambridge, MA: Ballinger.

Holstein, J.A. and Miller, G. (1990) 'Rethinking Victimisation: An Interactionist Approach to Victimology', *Symbolic Interaction*, 13.

Hough, M. and Mayhew, P. (1983) *The British Crime Survey: First Report*. London: HMSO.

Hoyle, C. and Young, R. (2002) 'Restorative Justice: Assessing the Prospects and Pitfalls', in M. McConville and G. Wilson (eds) *The Handbook of The Criminal Justice Process*. Oxford: Oxford University Press.

Johnson, E.A. and Monkonnen, E. (eds) (1996) *The Civilisation of Crime: Violence in Town and Country since the Middle Age*. Chicago: University of Illinois Press.

Jolliffe, J.E.A (1937) *The Constitutional History of Medieval England – From the English Settlement to 1485*. London: A. & C. Black.

Jones, G.S. (1992) *Outcast London*. Harmondsworth: Penguin.

Karmen, A. (1990) *Crime Victims: An Introduction to Victimology*. Belmont, CA: Wadsworth.

Kearon, T. (2005) 'We have never been Liberal – bourgeois identity and the criminal(ized) other', *Social Justice*, 32(1).

Kidd, A. and Nicholls, D. (1999) *Gender, Civic Culture and Consumerism: Middle-Class Identity in Britain, 1800–1940*. Manchester: Manchester University Press.

King, P. (1984) 'Decision makers and decision-making in the English criminal law 1750–1800', *Historical Journal*, 27: 25–58.

King, P. (2000) *Crime, Justice, and Discretion in England, 1740–1820*. Oxford: Oxford University Press.

Kirby, D. (1992) *The Earliest English Kings*. London: Routledge.

Kirchengast, T. (2006) *The Victim in Criminal Law and Justice*. London: Macmillan.

Malcolm, J. (2002) *Guns and Violence: The English Experience*. Cambridge, MA: Harvard University Press.

Mawby, R.I. and Walklate, S. (1994) *Critical Victimology*. London: Sage.

McGowen, R. (2005) 'The Bank of England and the policing of forgery 1797–1821', *Past and Present*, 186: 81–116.

Mendelsohn, B. (1963) 'The origin of the doctrine of victimology', *Excerpta Criminologica*, 3: 30.

Miers, D. (1978) *Responses to Victimisation*. Abingdon: Professional.

Miers, D. (1989) 'Positivist victimology: A critique', *International Review of Victimology*, 1: 3–22.

Miers, D. (1990) *Compensation for Criminal Injuries*. London: Butterworth.

Morris, R.J. (1983) 'The Middle Class and British Towns and Cities of the Industrial Revolution, 1780–1870', in D. Fraser and A. Sutcliffe (eds) *The Pursuit of Urban History*. London: Arnold.

Morrison, B. (2005) 'Ordering Disorderly Women: Female Drunkenness in England *c*. 1870–1920', unpublished PhD thesis, Keele University.

Newburn, T. and Stanko, B. (1994) 'When Men are Victims: The Failure of Victimology' in T. Newburn and B. Stanko (eds) *Just Boys Doing Business?* London: Routledge.

Philips, D. (1989) 'Good Men to Associate and Bad Men to Conspire: Associations for the Prosecution of Felons in England 1750–1860', in D. Hay and F. Snyder (eds) *Policing and Prosecution in Britain 1750–1850*. Oxford: Oxford University Press, pp. 113–70.

Rawlings, P. (2002) *Policing – A Short History*. Cullompton: Willan Publishing.

Rock, P. (1990) *Helping Victims of Crime: The Home Office and the Rise of Victim Support in England and Wales*. Oxford: Clarendon Press.

Rock, P. (2004) 'Victims, prosecutors and the state in nineteenth-century England and Wales', *Criminal Justice*, 4(4): 331–54.

Ross, E. (1982) '"Fierce questions and taunts": Married life in working-class London', *Feminist Studies*, 8(3): 575–602.

Rude, G. (1985) *Criminal and Victim: Crime and Society in Early Nineteenth-Century England*. Oxford: Clarendon Press.

Schafer, S. (1968) *The Victim and His Criminal: A Study of Functional Responsibility*. New York: Random House.

Stanko, E. (1988) 'Hidden Violence Against Women', in J. Pointing and M. Maguire (eds) *Victims of Crime: A New Deal?* Milton Keynes: Open University Press.

Steedman, C. (1984) *Policing the Victorian Community: The Formation of English Provincial Police Forces, 1856–80*. London: Routledge and Kegan Paul.

Storch, R. (1975) 'The Plague of Blue Locusts: Police reform and popular resistance in northern England 1840–57', *International Review of Social History*, 20: 61–90.

Storch, R. (1976) 'The policeman as domestic missionary: Urban discipline and popular culture in Northern England, 1850–1880, *Journal of Social History*, 9: 481–511.

Taylor, D. (2002) *Policing the Victorian Town: The Development of the Police in Middlesbrough, c. 1840–1914*. London: Palgrave Macmillan.

Tomes, N. (1978) 'A "Torrent of Abuse": Crimes of violence between working-class men and women in London', *Journal of Social History*, 11(3): 328–45.

Tombs, S. and Whyte, D. (eds) (2003) *Unmasking the Crimes of the Powerful: Scrutinising States and Corporations*. New York: Peter Lang.

Von Hentig, H. (1948) *The Criminal and His Victim*. New Haven, CT: Yale University Press.

Walklate, S. (1992) 'Appreciating the Victim: Conventional, Realist or Critical Victimology?', in R. Matthews and J. Young (eds) *Issues in Realist Criminology*. London: Sage.

Walkowitz, J. (1992) *City of Dreadful Delights: Narrative of Sexual Danger in Late Victorian London*. Chicago: University of Chicago Press.

Wiener, M. (2004) *Men of Blood: Violence, Manliness, and Criminal Justice in Victorian England*. Cambridge: Cambridge University Press.

Williams, C. (2004) 'Review of *Guns and Violence: The English Experience* by Joyce Lee Malcolm', *Journal of Modern History*, March: 168–9.

Wolfgang, M.E. (1958) *Patterns in Criminal Homicide*. Philadelphia: University of Pennsylvania Press.

Wood, J.C. (2003) 'Self-policing and the policing of the self: violence, protection and the civilising bargain in Britain', *Crime, Histoire et Societies/Crime, History and Societies*, 7(1): 109–23.

Wormald, P. (1999) *The Making of English Law: King Alfred to the Twelfth Century*. Oxford: Blackwell.

Young, J. (1986) 'The Failure of Criminology: The Need for a Radical Realism', in R. Matthews and J. Young (eds) *Confronting Crime*. London: Sage.

Young, J. (1999) *The Exclusive Society: Social Exclusion, Crime and Difference in Late Modernity*. London: Sage.

Zedner, L. (2004) *Criminal Justice*. Oxford: Oxford Univerfsity Press.

Chapter 2

Theoretical perspectives on victimisation

Paul Rock

Introduction

Almost any discussion of theoretical perspectives on victimisation (which I shall clump together and call victimology) tends to begin with the pronouncement that they are intellectually thin and underdeveloped,[1] and there is a temptation, to which I shall also succumb, to devote space to speculating on why that should be so. Theory, according to the *Oxford English Dictionary*, is 'A scheme or system of ideas or statements held as an explanation or account of a group of facts or phenomena; ... a statement of what are held to be the general laws, principles, or causes of something known or observed'. Social theory, adds Marshall (1994), 'embraces a set of interrelated definitions and relationships that organizes our concepts of and understanding of the empirical world in a systematic way'. It would be difficult to argue that there is a fully coherent victimological theory in that sense, and, at the very outset, it should perhaps be observed that there is no good reason why so diverse and complex an entity as victims and victimisation should or could be covered by one consolidated set of arguments. Helen Reeves, first the director and then the chief executive officer of Victim Support, the largest voluntary organisation for victims in England and Wales, and as knowledgeable as anyone about the field, once remarked that to search for a single theory or description of victims and victimisation would be quite as quixotic as a search for a single theory or description of criminals and crime. But there is more that can be said about the theoretically emaciated state of victimology, and, in saying it, one may begin to learn something interesting about the intellectual world centred on the victim.

The neglect of the victim

It is commonplace to remark that, until very recently, victims were neglected in Anglo-American criminal law and procedure (Christie 1977). Victims' activists used to talk about the 'forgotten person' who appeared only as a witness, an applicant for compensation or as a complainant or *alleged* victim until the conclusion of a trial. The prime conflict at law did not touch significantly on the victim: it was deemed to be between two parties only, the prosecution and the defendant, and the individual victim merely provided evidence of an offence that, for all practical purposes, was committed not so much against him or her but against the collectivity in the form of the Crown, the State or the community. Private wrongs were a matter for tort and civil procedure, not the criminal trial (Elias 1983: 2). Garland observed that 'individuals and victims featured hardly at all, other than as members of the public, whose complaints triggered state action. Their interests were subsumed under the general public interest' (Garland 2000: 357).

Almost without exception, the foundational writings of criminology followed suit and made (and, in some cases, continue to make) no reference to victims (see, for instance, the following more or less randomly selected works: Barnes and Teeters 1943; Becker 1963; Matza 1969; Sutherland and Cressey 1970; Taylor *et al.* 1973). The crimes they described were curiously intransitive, as if they lacked an object and impact. Kenneth Burke once said that a way of seeing is always a way of not seeing, and, focusing on crimes and criminals, many criminologists most emphatically did not see the victim. Even where victims did come into view, they were observed only through a highly focused lens. For instance, one of the premier sociologists of crime of the 1960s, Matza, summarily invoked an unresearched and abstract conception of the victim simply to flesh out what he conjectured to be the delinquent's reasoning in neutralising guilt. The victim could figure as one whose 'qualities may be so debased as to disqualify him from [the assumed] right' to press charges (1964: 174). That was all. No more was said. It was a most fleeting and unsatisfactory appearance.

The explanation of that neglect is not mysterious. Criminology is a minor discipline with few practitioners and many gaps, and it is not remarkable that the victim should also have been overlooked for a while. After all, we know very little about crime and justice in Asia, Latin America and Saharan Africa; very little about rural crime and policing in Europe and North America; the crimes of the elderly (see Stephens 1976) or of *Roma*; and trafficking in people, weapons, art and archaeological artifacts. In such an ill-mapped world, victims could be taken as little more than just another tract of *terra incognita*. But other epistemological and methodological issues were in play. Each of the major theoretical approaches seemed to have had good reasons to ignore victims and victimisation.

The more positivist criminologists looked for the origins and development of crime in the body and mind of the criminal, the principal causal factors being constitutional, genetic, psychiatric or psychological, and the victim appeared not at all because he or she lay outside the central field of inquiry. Functionalist writers were interested less in the surface appearances of crime and control – appearances, they held, that could be misconstrued by naïve common-sense reasoning. If that reasoning *did* pay attention to them, if what is sometimes disparaged as saloon-bar criminology pointed at them, victims became all the more invalid. The theorist's eye was turned elsewhere, towards what were represented as the deep structures of society where crime and control were instruments of the unseen hands that performed unrecognised services for the collectivity: prostitution buttressing marriage and the family; the stigma of illegitimacy buttressing primogeniture; organised crime introducing order into otherwise chaotic markets and ineffectual political regimes; deviance resolving problems of anomaly and ambiguity in classification schemes (Douglas 1966); crime reinforcing social cohesion (Erikson 1966); and, in a later, radical twist, offenders and prisoners deflecting popular discontents from structured inequalities on to mass-produced scapegoats (Foucault 1979; Reiman 2003). There was no place there for the pathos and pains of individual victimisation or the personal and communal costs of everyday crime.

Symbolic interactionism or 'labelling theory', the approach ostensibly wedded to an empathetic description of how people jointly construct lines of action, *should* have accommodated the victim in its analyses of rule-breaking, but it failed to do so because it chose chiefly to hearken to what were called crimes *without* victims: the crimes that are 'created when we attempt to ban through criminal legislation the exchange between willing partners of strongly desired goods or services' (Schur 1974: 6), and their repression was used to illustrate the folly and oppressiveness of many rules and much formal control (Schur 1965). (Stan Cohen once remarked that, while lawyers tend to see laws and control as benign, sociologists almost invariably regard them as malign.) The interactionist's was a largely self-regarding focus that, for purposes of appreciation and easy access to research populations, allowed them to examine themselves and others in their own *milieu*, the sexual deviants, political radicals, nudists and drug-users who may have had no discernible individual victims. Indeed, Cohen and Taylor confessed they had been merely reporting themselves: they 'took notes about our own "normal" deviance; smoking dope with our students, organising anti-Vietnam war demonstrations, watching porno movies' (1976: 2). They had no notion of rule-breaking as harmful. Rather it was fun, romantic and sometimes heroic. Lacking a clear vision of the victim, formal control became little more than an aggravating factor that amplified and confirmed deviance (see Schur 1973), generating so-called 'secondary deviation' (Lemert 1951), and exerted, in many cases, to no good purpose other than to express the inflated moral indignation of the community and provide work for agencies of social control (Becker 1963; Erikson 1966; Sutherland and Cressey 1970). In that formulation, in a relativised, negotiated and confused world, there was a 'vacillation between the image of the deviant as mismanaged victim and the deviant as cultural hero' (Cohen 1979: 19). It 'is not easy', said Sagarin on one occasion, 'to divide the world into victims and offenders. The hunted fugitive is a victim, but so are people upon whom he preys; and, potentially, the hunters – the decision-making, overdog, and putatively oppressive police – may be victims as well' (1975: 133).

Radical criminologists preferred to talk of crime as the ephemera of a capitalist society in transition – the fruit of possessive individualism, class resentment or primitive rebellion (Hobsbawm 1971) – that would not survive the coming of socialism. And, while capitalism lasted, it was argued, there were other, more pressing issues to consider: the problems of class conflict, racism, structured oppression and exploitation (Hillyard *et al.* 2004). In the language of the time, criminology should 'constitute its own object' and occupy itself with a core critical agenda, not with the petty distractions of volume crime that capitalism and its legislators placed in its path. Not untypical was Herman and Julia Schwendinger's introduction to what was then a new journal, *Crime and Social Justice* (1974: 1): radical criminology, they recalled, had emerged in the United States of the 1960s where

> political movements were scourging American institutions: when the endemic causes of gender, racial and class inequality were being laid bare; when crimes against humanity and violations of constitutional law were being exposed at the highest levels of government; and when popular rage over the carnage produced by the U.S. government in Southeast Asia, Latin America, and Africa had ruptured the political fabric of our country.

Those were held to be the drivers and topics appropriate to a critical criminology, not, say, routine household theft, burglary and malicious damage (and see Schwendinger and Schwendinger 1970). A terminology of moral crusade (Becker 1963), moral panic (Cohen 2002) and moral censure (Sumner 1990) could in its turn be deployed, sometimes carelessly, to dismiss popular fears about crime as ideologically manipulated, misdirected and irrational. Anxieties about everyday crime became tantamount to figments of false consciousness. If there *were* authentic victims to be acknowledged, they were the immiserated proletariat, the racial underclass, the poor and unheeded victims of corporate crime (Pearce 1976), and the prisoners and criminals, who were the real casualties of class-based, racist societies and their repressive criminal justice systems (Crime and Justice Associates 1982; Mathiesen 1974). Dignan complained of Quinney, one early radical, that he

> drew attention to structural factors relating to the way society is organized, and also the role of the state itself and the legal system in the social construction of both victims and offenders ... such insights tend to see offenders as the principal victims of state oppression and to downplay or ignore altogether those who were in turn victimized by them. (2005: 33)

The personal victim of mundane crime could readily be represented as an instance of obfuscation,[2] demagoguery, penal populism, authoritarian populism, or some other term for the political malaise that was thought to distract the so-called subaltern classes. Some even took it that Marxism should not deign to busy itself with crime at all (Hirst 1975).

There was, by extension, something of a distaste in criminology at large, and in radical criminology in particular, about any involvement with the victim and problems of victimisation conventionally defined. To study victims was in effect to collude with the politics of the mob and the machinations of the powerful, heeding a group whose world-view contradicted the authority and competences of the criminological expert. Take an observation made by

Garland, an astute, disinterested and far from polemical writer, a man who currently wields great influence in criminological theory: 'The dominant voice of crime policy is no longer the expert or even the practitioner but that of the long-suffering, ill-served people – especially of "the victim" and the fearful, anxious members of the public' (Garland 2001: 13).[3] One wonders why the word 'victim' should have been conveyed in such a deprecating fashion and such a context, as if it were intended to suggest that the victim's status was merely alleged or *soi-disant*, and not really achieved in good faith at all.

And there was something else permeating that unease. Victims do have something of the uncomfortable 'other' about them. They have been described informally by David Downes as a hybrid of pariah and saint. They are necessarily somewhat disreputable, stigmatised figures, blighted by misfortune, often portrayed as angry and vindictive, perhaps best avoided by lay person and criminologist alike. Their very existence is disturbing because it can challenge the belief in a just world where people simply cannot incur harm unless they have somehow earned their suffering through their own misdeed or foolishness (see Lerner 1980). To think otherwise would turn the moral order quite upside down.

The New Shorter Oxford English Dictionary defines victim as a sacrifice, 'A person killed or tortured by another; a person subjected to cruelty, oppression, or other harsh or unfair treatment or suffering death, injury, ruin, etc., as a result of impersonal agency ... A person who is taken advantage of; a dupe.' It is a word that evokes strong images of submissiveness, pain, loss of control and defeat. Those bereaved by murder and manslaughter have certainly told me of the primitive fear and embarrassment they believed they could excite, how people would not know what to say to them, sometimes crossing the road in an attempt to avoid them lest their bad luck become contagious (Rock 1998a). Victims are riddled with taboos.

The origins of victimology

There is a conventional account of the genesis and evolution of victimology (see Maguire 1991: 374) and, although there may be room for dispute about some of its particulars, its very acceptance has become a shaping academic and ideological influence that must be taken seriously. Victimology, we have been repeatedly told, was founded more or less independently in the 1940s by – and the histories vary somewhat – three or four men (see Sebba 1982: 225), a Romanian lawyer, Beniamin Mendelsohn;[4] a professor of law at the State University of Colorado, Boulder, Hans Von Hentig;[5] a Hungarian criminologist resident first in England and then the United States, Stephen Schafer (see Doerner and Lab 1995); and a German-American psychiatrist and campaigner against the corrupting influence of comic magazines, Fredric Wertham.[6] Criminology proper being barren, and victims being tainted, victimology could not but appear with an odd genealogy, late and from the side-lines, and it exhibited some peculiar traits. The website of the World Society of Victimology (www.victimology.nl), one of its parent bodies, candidly admitted:

> Not only has the 'science' of victimology suffered because of its inauspicious origins as the wayward sub-discipline of criminology, but its very subjects, 'victims' have been weighed down by negative imagery that connotes their status with that of the 'weak' underdog. Victimology ... does not carry the academic weight of theory and critique that is the domain of criminology.

It was inevitable that the first victimologists were unconventional scholars, lying on the outer reaches of the academic study of crime, psychology and the law, wedded to doctrines that may now appear somewhat eccentric or *passé*, later to be described by one unfriendly critic as 'the lunatic fringe of criminology' (Becker 1981: 4). A man claimed by some as the father of victimology, Hans Von Hentig, declared, for instance, that he was attached to the Italian school of criminal anthropology (a school associated with the largely reviled figure of Cesare Lombroso[7]) and to ideas of moral imbecility and constitutional immorality. And it was Beniamin Mendelsohn, also claimed as the father of victimology, who first awarded the sub-discipline a name and declared it his ambition to analyse the victim from the 'the bio-psycho-social point of view' (1963: 239), a project that betrayed a certain grandiosity of purpose.

Victim-precipitation

The principal foundational idea of those first scholars was *victim-precipitation* (Meier and Miethe 1993: 464) and, for good or bad reasons, it came to dog the political and analytic standing of the sub-discipline thereafter. Victim-precipitation was propounded first by Mendelsohn, and it alludes to the criminally provocative, collusive or causal impact of the victim in a dyadic relation variously called the 'penal couple' (Mendelsohn 1963: 241); the 'reciprocal action between perpetrator and victim' (Von Hentig 1940: 303); the 'duet theory of crime' (Von Hentig 1948: 397); a 'situated transaction' (Luckenbill 1977); 'the functional responsibility for crime' (Schafer 1968: 55), or, simply, 'the victim–offender relationship' (Wolfgang 1957: 1).

At one pole, victim-precipitation portrays crime somewhat neutrally as an interactive process or evolving relation between victim and offender, in which each influences not only the conduct of the other but also the form and content of any crime that may ensue. Douglas and Waksler (1982: 249) argued perfectly sensibly that 'perpetrator and victim commonly appear to be involved in a social encounter where the acts of each affect those of the other'. And Reiss said much the same when he stressed 'the importance of theories about victimisation focusing upon the behavior of all parties to crime events rather than resorting to separate theories about victimisation and offending or about victims and offenders' (1981: 710). Little exception could be taken to those formulations. Of course, not all crime is significantly interactive – some burglaries are only tangentially so – but the attention of the early victimologists was fixed on the graver instances of law-breaking, on rape, assault and murder, and it is important to note that it was framed from the start in a very special way that has perhaps been too little appreciated.

Aspects of victims and victimisation become visible through the assumptions, ambitions, methods and questions that scholars apply to observe them. In this, victimology's first big idea, victimisation was seen through the eyes of Mendelsohn, a practising defence attorney, and his epiphany occurred during the course of a murder trial. Thoughts of victim-precipitation (and victimology) welled up in the construction of a defence case. As he recalled:

> It was while preparing for the trial of Stephan Codreanu arraigned in 1945 for a *crime passionel*, he recalled, that I began to elaborate the doctrine of Victimology … There can be no doubt that, had it not been for the perversity of his former wife, he would never have been guilty of two crimes. (1963: 241) Responsibility for Codreanu's offence should, in effect, be assigned to his wife. The implications are startling.

There are perhaps three principal defences in any murder trial: the defendant was not there at the time of the alleged offence; someone else did it; or the victim provoked the offence or struck the first blow, thereby lessening the charge to one of manslaughter, on the one hand, or self-defence, on the other. Defence lawyers are not obliged to be disinterested and impartial. They must be fearless in the discharge of their obligations to promote their clients' interests. They must accept instructions. If, as one counsel said to me, 'my client instructs me that Martians landed on the lawn and forced him to act, that is the case I will put'. In murder cases fought in the adversarial system, not only is the victim silent but there is no one briefed formally to speak on his or her behalf. A defence, in other words, is a lop-sided and motivated construction, one of a pair of competing narratives, that is almost invariably balanced by an equal and opposite account. What Mendelsohn introduced into victimology from the beginning was but one side of that pair, and it is not remarkable that victim-precipitation could occasionally take a peculiar and distorted form. Victims were to be represented just as their perpetrators would have wished, as people who were causally and, indeed, often culpably complicit in their own downfall. They provoked, conspired or were gulled into becoming a target. They deserved their fate.

So it was that Porterfield and Talbert could remark: 'It is amazing to note the large number of would-be murderers who become the victim' (1954: 48). So it was that Von Hentig, having also taken up the baton of victim-precipitation, produced a curious taxonomy of murder victims which included the *depressive*, 'who lacks ordinary prudence and discretion'; the *greedy of gain*, 'who lack all normal inhibitions and well-founded suspicions'; the *wanton type*, where 'female foibles play a role'; and the *tormentor-type*, 'the most primitive way of solving a personal conflict [being] to annihilate physically the cause of the trouble' (1940: 304–6). 'Are we permitted', he continued, 'to say that in some cases criminality is a self-consuming process of anti-social elements in which criminals prey on criminaloids, killers on suicides or other killers, oversexed on oversexed, dishonest individuals on dishonest?' (1940: 309).

Despite its lack of balance, victim-precipitation played an influential part for a while in the development of theories of criminal victimisation. It certainly inspired a pioneering study, *Patterns in Criminal Homicide*. Marvin Wolfgang, its author, acknowledged that 'Von Hentig ... provided the most useful theoretical basis for analysis of the victim–offender relationship' (Wolfgang 1957: 1), and then proceeded to employ police and other official records to examine patterns of victim involvement in killings in Philadelphia (Wolfgang 1958). He was followed by Luckenbill (1977), Polk (1994) and others, all of whom leaned heavily on Von Hentig, Wolfgang and the 'duet theory of crime'. Quite typical was Avison (1973: 58), who argued that

> the role of the victim is not restricted to precipitation of the crime ... The victim can contribute in many different ways to the interaction preceding the aggressive behavior, and it may be more meaningful to consider such involvement on a continuum ... culminating in active participation by the victim.

Feminism and victimology

The second, double-edged strand of ideas injected into victimology was both internally contradictory and quite at odds with the theorising I have just described, and it only uncertainly belongs to the body of victimology proper at all. What was called second-wave feminism arose in the 1960s and 1970s to protest the injustices inflicted on women and girls; to locate those injustices in the structure and functioning of a patriarchal order; to disclose the everyday experiences of women as politically-freighted; and, in the conduct of research, to restore dignity and humanity to those who were studied by eschewing imbalances in power between the scholar and subject, levelling hierarchy, and letting women themselves speak as authorities about their own lives (Oakley 1981).

Feminist criminology had a radical tinge, and it arose in large measure as a protest against the domain assumptions of radical criminology. Women, it was said, were raped, abused and assaulted, and their neglect by male criminologists constituted not only a political and sexist affront but an analytic and empirical gap. It was not good enough to dismiss crimes against women as epiphenomenal, an ideological mystification, or as a canker which would disappear when a 'fully socialist society' (see Taylor *et al.* 1973) at last came into being. Wrongs were real and immediate, and they required exposure, analysis and redress. Smart, a *protégée* of Ian Taylor, the author of the polemical *The New Criminology*, wrote her own countering feminist manifesto, *Women, Crime and Criminology* (1977), in which she lambasted the way in which women as offenders and victims had been anathematised, and she proposed their reinstatement within an analytic framework emphasising the workings of patriarchal power and male myopia. Women, her successors came to argue, are kept firmly in their social, spatial, economic and sexual place by the exercise of male coercion (Brownmiller 1977; Madriz 1997: 352; Pagelow 1981: 1476). They are encouraged through fear of male violence and male censure (Hollander 2001: 85) to remain submissive and unambitious (Bourgois 1996; Kurz 1989: 490) within the private, domestic sphere. Daly (1994: 779) observed that, although 'feminist analyses of the causes of men's violence toward women were (and are) varied, the structural sources of men's power and entitlement over individual women was prominently featured'.

Women were, in short, constituted as victims generically and individually in the workings of patriarchy (Wright 1995: 111). And looming large, the first stirrings of victimology supplied an appropriate foil not only for contesting the meanings of victimisation, gender and power but also for establishing a countervailing feminist criminology. Like *The New Criminology* (Taylor *et al.* 1973) before it, early feminist criminology was elaborated through 'immanent critique', a series of running criticisms which amounted to the provision of an alternative theory, and one of its prime objects was the failing of criminology and victimology to comprehend female victimisation.

Matters came to a head when a student of Marvin Wolfgang, Menachem Amir, applied without significant modification his supervisor's formulae, methodology and even the style of his book title, not to cases of homicide, but to rape (Amir 1971). Murder victims tend not to be available for observation and interview[8] but rape victims might well be so. Yet Amir followed Wolfgang and faithfully relied on official records, talking neither to rape complainants nor to any other participant, and hearing no insider's account of what might have happened (see Lotz 1975: 381). Quoting Von Hentig once more, he said: 'We are accustomed to believe that forcible rape is an act which falls upon the victim without her aid or cooperation, but there is often "some reciprocal action between perpetrator and victim" in such cases' (1967: 493). He then advanced to produce an inventory of victim characteristics that could trigger a rape, and they included meeting an offender in a bar, picnic or party, possessing a 'bad' reputation and consuming alcohol. That was a cluster of allegations too far and it was timely. It became an iconic target for a number of feminists who renamed victim-precipitation 'victim-blaming' (Clark and Lewis 1977). Lamb (1996: 78, 79) protested:

At the root of all victim-blaming are the perpetrator's own attempts to present the victim as the cause of his violence or abuse ... Perpetrators will ... claim that their victims are almost directly responsible for their fates, that the little girl wanted to be fondled, that the raped woman was asking for it, and that the abused wife provoked her beating ...

The political and intellectual standing of victim-precipitation plummeted in some quarters and, with it, that of victimology itself. Said Meier and Miethe (1993: 463)

The implication of blame in victim-precipitation analyses has inhibited full development of the concept. When Wolfgang's student Menachim Amir ... adopted the concept in a study of forcible rape that parallels Wolfgang's research on homicide, it caused a major political controversy.

Fattah may have protested about what had been said, describing it as 'unwarranted attacks and unfounded ideological criticism' (Fattah 2000: 2) that revealed no flaws in the integrity of the idea of victim-precipitation itself, only in its execution (Fattah 1979: 200), but damage had been done.

Once feminism had been established as a solid enterprise in the 1980s and 1990s, it became possible for women criminologists to move on, distance themselves critically from its early writings and embark on a flurry of revisions. They remonstrated that, in concentrating on the woman as victim, there was an all too frequent collusion in the manufacture of an imagery that stressed defeat, passivity, submission and resignation. There had been an exclusive but indefensible preoccupation with the victimisation of women that obscured criminal acts committed against men, as if men were never victims and always perpetrators (Walklate 2000: 189). There were abundant male victims of domestic violence (Mirrlees-Black 1999; Grady 2002: 77).[9] There were male victims of rape and violence (Stanko 1990). There were female *offenders* (Carlen 1985, 1988), including, exceptionally, violent (Shaw 1995) and sexual offenders (Matravers 2000). There were *varieties* of women differentiated by class and race, not just a solidary mass (hooks 1982). Gender became interpreted as a dialectical concept, taking its meaning from the paired contrasts of male and female, and portions of academic feminism began to progress towards a more balanced consideration of *masculinity* as a counterpoint to their work on femininity (see Newburn and Stanko 1994). Criminology itself was recognised as intellectually *diverse*, subject to no one orthodoxy but fissured by the debates which ran through its parent disciplines of sociology, psychology, law, statistics and social anthropology. And it then became possible to speak not of a unitary feminist criminology (or victimology) but of *feminisms* (Adamson *et al.* 1988) and *criminologies* (see Gelsthorpe and Morris 1990). One of the mothers of feminist criminology, Carol Smart, even came to question whether it was any longer politically or analytically defensible to consider women in a context of crime, victimisation and criminal justice at all (1989). Placing them in such a restricted setting dwarfed analysis and invited uncongenial associations.

Feminist criminology had been galvanised in part by a practical and political preoccupation with the victims of rape, incest and domestic violence, and by a methodology and epistemology that restored a voice to those whom it studied. There was to be a concomitant strain: those who had founded the early rape crisis centres and women's refuges in the 1970s extolled the authenticity of victims' experiences and of practical action, and, on occasion, they challenged the right of academic writers and clinicians to pronounce on what they were doing and who they were. They subordinated the cold analysis of the monograph and textbook to hot testimony, and their evidence lay in narratives of pain and transcendence relayed by the victims themselves (Eastel 1994; Plummer 1994). Muir, the president of an Australian victims' organisation, the National Association for Loss and Grief, said quite characteristically: 'The telling of individual stories about the human experience of being a victim of crime is an attempt to give voice to an experience which cannot adequately be described through the interpretation of crime statistics' (1998: 179). In common with other primary and secondary victims of traumatic crime (Caffell 1994; Dardenne 2005; Ivison 1997; Spungen 1983), theirs were stories of suffering and fortitude, and there was a discernible shift over time away from the quietism and defeat of the language of victimisation. They were *survivors*, not victims, and they were casualties of patriarchy, not of crime commonly conceived. In their methods of accounting, they drew away from the world of crime, criminal justice, criminology and victimology.

But they (and other activists)[10] were also frequently to be found in the same spaces – the conferences, workshops and seminars – as the academic writers with whom they were in uneasy relation and whose legitimacy they questioned. At the beginning, too, they were mistrustful of men (the Women's Aid Federation of England would not allow men into their buildings, although the 'independent' refuges did otherwise). To be sure, alignments were not always uniform (members of the Canadian women's movement were always more pragmatic than many of their English counterparts, for example). Neither were they unchanging over time. But a series of political and ontological tensions about definition, authority, hierarchy and ownership were planted in and around victimology and there they remain. Consider the following excerpt from an activist text which perfectly condenses the family of core themes, and hints at the contradictions, I have described:

SISTERHOOD IS POWERFUL! INTERNATIONAL SISTERHOOD IS EVEN MORE POWERFUL! This slogan captures well one of the assumptions of those who organized the International Tribunal. Our struggle must not only be conducted within nations, but across national boundaries. Nations are man-made. 'I belong to No-man's land' proclaimed one of the buttons sold at the Tribunal. Unlike a traditional Tribunal there was no panel of judges at the International Tribunal on Crimes Against Women. We were all our own judges. Moreover, the women present completely rejected patriarchal definitions of crime; all man-made forms of women's oppression were seen as crimes. Most of the crimes testified about are not recognized as such by patriarchal nations ... Personal testimony was emphasized because of the belief that it is through sharing our personal experiences of oppression that we become politicized and motivated to struggle against that oppression and the societal conditions producing it, rather than by engaging in abstract theoretical debates divorced from our personal experiences. (Russell and Van de Ven 1976: xv)

Coming from within the radical fold, the feminist challenge had legitimacy and it made its mark on radical criminology. In tandem with the new instrument of crime surveys, which I shall touch on next, it obliged some radical criminologists to trim and admit that not all mundane crime could be lightly dismissed, and that the victimisation of women should certainly be taken seriously as a political and social problem. Jones, MacLean and Young remarked how there had been 'a general tendency in radical thought to idealize [its] historical subject (in this case the working class) and to play down intra-group conflict, blemishes and social disorganisation. But the power of the feminist case resulted in a sort of cognitive schizophrenia amongst radicals' (1986: 2–3). To be sure, shibboleths remained: it proved awkward politically for those three recanting authors to probe too extensively into the background of the high numbers of black women victims they had unearthed in a local crime survey, because that would have dangerously exposed black *offenders*, but a dent had been made, and it prepared the way for what was to be called 'left realism', the new socialist criminology which more readily accommodated the brute facts of crime and victimisation, and inserted victims into a new conceptual contrivance, a quadrilateral of forces, that was built on the offender, the victim, informal social control and the state (Lea and Young 1984).

Crime surveys

The third principal source of victimology was empirical – but no empirical inquiry is ever free of theorising. Large household surveys of victims were conducted first in the United States, in 1973,[11] in the wake of the urban riots of the 1960s (Lipsky and Olson 1977), and they were designed principally to assist the curtailing of violence by ascertaining the extent and character of criminal victimisation (President's Crime Commission 1967). They were followed by similar surveys in Canada in 1981 (where they were at first opportunistically presented as an exploration of trends in violence succeeding the imminent abolition of capital punishment (Rock 1986)), the United Kingdom in 1982 (where they were at first opportunistically presented within government as a purposive way of responding to the 1981 Brixton riots, and later as a mechanism to improve what was called 'the criminal justice data base' (Rock 1990)), and elsewhere. There were eventually to be international crime surveys in 1989, 1992 and 1996–97 which compared victimisation rates across nations and over time (Van Dijk *et al.* 1990) and local surveys which looked intensively at crime in small areas (Anderson *et al.* 1991; Bottoms *et al.* 1987; Jones *et al.* 1986; Smith 1982).

Crime surveys chart a population's experience of crime over a given period, usually of a year. They are plastic instruments, adaptable to different purposes and changing in significance. In the beginning, they were a means of securing a better measure of offending, and they concentrated on the victim chiefly as a source of data closest to the crime that could act as 'an important alternative to police records' (www.homeoffice.gov.uk/rds/bcs). The authors of the first British Crime Survey reported in 1983: 'It is one thing to identify the shortcomings of statistics or recorded offences as a measure of crime, quite another to provide an alternative. Only recently has a research technique been developed with this aim in mind – the sample survey of victimisation, or "crime survey"' (Hough and Mayhew 1983: 1). The international crime surveys were similarly prompted by 'two main reasons ... The first was the inadequacy of offences recorded by the police for comparing crime in different countries. The second was the absence of any alternative standardised measures' (http://ruljis.leidenuniv.nl/group/jfcr/www/icvs/introduction).

But it was inevitable that crime surveys also began to yield copious information about the impact, distribution (Clarke *et al.* 1985; Home Office

2004a, 2004b), incidence, trends and severity of crime; victims' experiences and perceptions of crime and the criminal justice system (Home Office 2002); their fear of crime and incivilities (Block 1993; Garofalo 1979); and much else. They mapped crime in ways hitherto conceived impossible, and victimology was flooded with new data. An analytic industry was established on their back, showing, for example, how crime was massively concentrated spatially (in what became known as 'hot spots' (Pease *et al.* 2004), socially and temporally (Tseloni and Pease 2003)). Victimisation was not distributed broadly and evenly across society, but in relatively dense pockets where groups and individuals (Pease and Farrell 1993) could expect repeatedly to be subject to burglary, theft, robbery and assault (over two-fifths of reported crime was experienced by 4 per cent of victims in a report published in 1994 (National Board for Crime Prevention). The best predictor of *who* might be a victim of property crime is recent victimisation (Polvi *et al.* 1991). The best predictor of *where* a property crime might take place is a home recently burgled and the homes adjacent to it (Bowers *et al.* 2004). Crime is so concentrated that offenders, victims and witnesses could not but be recruited from very much the same populations (so that, for instance, the young men who assault young men in city centres at night are most likely to have been observed by other young men, because it was they who are abroad at that time and in those places). Crime predominantly took place *within*, not across, social strata, the proletariat attacking the proletariat, the young the young, males males, minority ethnic groups minority ethnic groups. At the very epicentre, where offending was most rife in the eye of the victimological storm, such social areas could be chaotic and confused indeed. Consider the graphic observations of one 'hot spot', life in an apartment reported by Hazel Genn 'where fights, verbal abuse, sexual assault and property theft were commonplace, and where the use of violence in the resolution of conflict was virtually automatic' (1988: 99):

> Endless streams of neighbours coming in and out. Aggression is very noticeable. There are many mock fights both between women and between men and women. There is some pride displayed in the extent to which the women are knocked about by men. During the afternoon when Kath mentioned the new bruises on her arm, a neighbour took down her trousers to reveal a sizeable bruise on her thigh ... [The next day] the women become more and more agitated and restless. They kept joking about 'feeling like a good fight', and it is easy to see how fights occur. The women are bored and become angry with the children, so that by mid-afternoon everyone is dying for something to happen. (Genn 1988: 96–7)

Those new maps of crime were to supply the second dent to radical criminology: crime was evidently not centred on the equitable redistribution of property. It did not serve, as the radicals used to say, to expropriate the expropriators or to exercise class justice, but, in David Downes' words, as a 'regressive tax on the poor'. Lea and Young confessed somewhat ruefully that they had believed that 'property offences are directed solely against the bourgeoisie and that violence against the person is carried out by amateur

Robin Hoods in the course of their righteous attempts to redistribute wealth. All of this is, alas, untrue' (1984: 262).

Smith and Gray (1985: 124) reported of a survey in London that 'to a considerable extent the police deal with a limited clientele of people who tend to be in trouble both as victims and as offenders ... people who tend to be repeatedly victims also have a much higher chance of being arrested'. It became increasingly difficult to conceive of victims and offenders as groups apart, the one innocent and the other guilty, but as members of substantially overlapping groups, no longer a confrontation between black and white, but of 'grey versus grey' (Antilla 1964: 8). Elias (1983: 253) remarked that in certain volatile areas, 'it becomes almost a matter of chance as to who will be the victim and who will be the offender for any particular crime, almost a matter of who strikes first. Consequently, it is difficult to clearly attribute guilt.' The contours of the moral economy of victims became a little more insecure in the academy, even though broader political, lay and activist accounts remained substantially unaffected.

Routine activities

If victim-precipitation is recognised conventionally as the first victimological theory, a second is routine activities theory (or what some call life-style theory; Walklate 1989: 6) victimologically construed, and it flowed in part out of the crime survey. There is an obvious and strong affinity between hazard-based theories and crime surveys which 'reveal that some persons may be prone to victimisation' (Gottfredson and Hindelang 1981: 123) and which present the 'tabulation of crime data in ways that would be indicative of risk' (Gottfredson 1981: 714).

The theory is economy itself: it predicts that crime will occur where there is a convergence in space and time of what are named 'likely offenders, suitable targets and an absence of capable guardians', and that 'the spatio-temporal organisation of society affects patterns of crime ... Strong variations in specific predatory crime rates from hour to hour, day to day [affect reporting] ... and these variations appear to correspond to the various tempos of the related legitimate activities upon which they feed' (Cohen and Felson 1979: 588, 592).

Convergence is likely to be enabled by the increased mobility and capacity to remove goods offered by motor vehicles; by the building of roads that encourage movement and the dispersal of populations (particularly in the United States, Canada and Australia); by shifting patterns of employment that may leave homes unattended; by the demographics of divorce, late marriage, physical longevity and small families that lead to a proliferation of single-person households with their weak guardianship; by new forms of technology which may reduce the size and increase the portability of electrical and electronic goods, and much else. Ken Pease was wont to begin public lectures by reflecting on the lack of highwaymen on freeways and motorways: technology had moved on, he would say, and with it there were companion changes in patterns of criminality and exposure to victimisation.

Miscellaneous victimological ideas

Victim-precipitation, feminist criminology and routine activities theory are the main home-grown constituents of a full-blown victimology. But victims have also been studied by several sociologists, psychologists and criminologists who might never elect to call themselves victimologists, knowingly contribute to the body of victimological theory, or regularly subscribe to the journals or attend the conferences of victimology.

Those writings are necessarily piecemeal. There is, first, what might be identified as standard scholarly work which alighted on victims, discovering new facts and new patterns of association, but not fully warranting or claiming the title of victimology, unless victimology includes *any* piece of academic writing that refers at some point to the victim. Take Braithwaite's work. It alludes to the role that can be played by victims and their supporters in mobilising sentiments of shame and animating rituals of reintegration in confrontations with offenders and their supporters, and it has reawakened an interest in the potential role of the victim in areas of criminology, criminal justice policy and dispute resolution. But Braithwaite's victim is a minor figure who hardly occupies centre stage and it would be difficult to claim that *Crime, Shame and Reintegration* (1989) is a piece of *victimology*. Perhaps a better candidate would be the evaluation of RISE, a restorative justice experiment conducted in Canberra by his colleague, Strang (2002), which looked squarely at victims' responses, although it was instigated somewhat as an afterthought and late in the planning of the larger project.

Another instance would be the influential study of Shapland and her colleagues of the passage of victims of violence through the criminal justice system (1985), in which they reported a decaying of satisfaction with police responses, a hunger for information and control, an interest in monetary compensation that was far outweighed by a yearning for symbolic recognition, and an experience of their vicissitudes in the criminal justice as, in effect, a form of 'secondary victimisation'. The reiterated complaint made by victims after cross-examination in court was that they were made to feel on trial, as if *they* were the wrongdoer. After all, lawyers in the adversarial system do indeed subject witnesses to identical techniques of questioning, irrespective of whether they testify on behalf of the prosecution or the defence, in the hope that they will expose (or be seen *trying* to expose) flaws of memory, inconsistencies of testimony, and defects of character (Rock 1993).

A further instance would be Maguire and Bennett's study of burglary (1982), which was conceived initially as a study of crime and criminals, but whose chapters on victims and the impact of crime were to create a stir because it had hitherto been supposed that trauma and trauma-like reactions stemmed only from the graver forms of violent crime (Waller and Okihiro 1978). Burglary, it appeared, can (but does not inevitably) generate many of the same experiences of invasion and defilement as crimes against the person. Significant numbers of victims were distressed, and distressed for long periods. Some, indeed, were so upset by the knowledge that an outsider had entered their home and rifled through their possessions that they never returned (Maguire 1980). Crimes against property, it appeared, can have a profound and often unappreciated impact on what William James once called the 'material self', the self constituted through its possessions, and quite visceral responses suggestive of pollution may ensue.

A final example would be Morgan and Zedner's work (1992) uncovering the extent of anguish suffered by child victims at first and second hand, victims who, as witnesses and household members, had often previously been overlooked unless it was as the direct and obvious target of abuse or violence. Children tend to be mute bystanders, all too readily overshadowed, but they could be as discomfited as any by mundane crime such as burglary. Morgan and Zedner's research was one of the first of a number of empirical studies that began to map formerly unexplored victim populations (for a more recent summary of work on child victimisation see Finkelhor *et al.* 2005). Running in tandem to their book, there was, for instance, research on racist (Bowling 1998; Sampson and Phillips 1992) and 'homophobic' crime, and crimes against the elderly and the disabled, and the population of known victims began to grow ever more crowded, possibly, indeed, overcrowded (see Sykes 1992), as they became swollen with groups newly identified or clamouring for recognition. It became evident that fresh groups of victims were continually emerging or being invented (Pendergast 1997); that generalisation was becoming more fraught; and that definitions and boundaries were unstable and more eagerly disputed (Jacobs and Potter 1998). And clearly at stake are questions of recognition, compensation, exculpation and much else. It seemed that there were not only 'primary' victims, the immediate casualities of crime, but 'secondary' victims, who had a family connection with those casualities; and others more distant still.[12] Debates about eligibility could become quite heated. Were the police officers, court staff, medical and paramedical staff who responded to traumatic incidents to be called 'tertiary victims'? Were the families of those killed in homicides or, more contentiously still, in traffic 'accidents'? Who was to count as family? And what of the families of serious offenders, some of whom laid claim to the title of 'the other victims of crime'? (Rock 1998b). Holstein and Miller reflected that

> 'victim' is a categorisation device ... an interpretive framework ... that provides a set of instructions for understanding social relations ... As an act of interpretive reality construction, victimisation unobtrusively advises others in how they should understand persons, circumstances, and behaviors under consideration. (1990: 105, 107)

And those social relations and that framework are not fixed but emergent and contested, and they may well be anything but unobtrusive.

Opportunistic theorising

There was to be another tier of incidental theorising that was the outcome of even more minor encounters between victimology, criminology and sociology. Sprey (1979: 255) said of one collection of papers that it 'fails to suggest even a semblance of order or generality ... the overall picture ...

remains confused ... the reader is confronted with a large number of rather loosely related papers in which, with very few exceptions, the focus simply has been shifted from the criminal to the victim'. And it is to that mode of theorising which I shall now turn.

Criminology has made occasional use of victims and victimology to develop points about questions lying squarely in its heartland. It was in that sense that victims have been described instrumentally as failures of crime prevention (Block remarked, for example, that 'the study of victims of crime is most importantly the study of the failure of crime prevention by citizenry and by the police and secondarily the study of the active participation and precipitation of criminal events by their victims' (1981: 761)). They have been construed as checks on the adequacy of official, recorded crime statistics ('"Citizens", it has been said, decide whether or not to invoke the law in the first instance ... The best available data for the systematic study of this most important juncture in the application of criminal law (and of the forces driving its application) are victimisation surveys' (Gottfredson and Hindelang 1981: 118, 119)). They offer, by extension, opportunities to promote the better measurement of vulnerability to crime, propensities to report crime, and trends in crime data over time. Those are all interesting enough areas, but it is not clear that they should be classified as victimology.

A final variation on that theme has been the transposition of criminals and victims in the analysis of familiar criminological questions. There has, for instance, been a modest interest in the growth of victims' movements and campaigns but it has sometimes been lodged in a stock criminological frame (see Davies *et al.* 2003: 4). Take Boutellier (2000), who represents the new focus simply as part of a demagogic politics of reaction in which victims are no more than a pretext for class oppression. Take Elias' *The Politics of Victimisation* (1986), which elaborated established radical arguments about the need to supplant ruling class-generated, state-based categories of crime and insert in their place a list of broad structural and human rights abuses, including inequality, alienation, competition, bureaucracy and violence, that victimise the powerless. The book is of interest, but it tends merely to offer the standard arguments of radical criminology in a new key.

Conclusion

Theoretical perspectives on victimisation have succeeded in introducing the victim into criminological analysis, filling a central void; they have promoted the idea that crime is processual, emergent and interactive, although that is an idea besmirched by the murky origins of victim-precipitation; they have illuminated the negotiated and contested character of claims to victim status, showing, obliquely, that those claims are sometimes resisted; they make it clear that there is no straightforward or transparent connection between victimisation and the fear of crime, or between types of crime and their impact on different groups; they show how crime is concentrated in time, space and society; they have underscored how sharp moral, political and ontological separations between victim and offender may not always be empirically defensible; they have exposed the hazards of generalising and imputing traits to victims; and they have pointed to the manner in which exposure to the criminal justice system may exacerbate victimisation and encourage what some call 'secondary victimisation'. We have moved far away from simple stereotypes of vulnerability and victimisation, away from the little old lady who represented Christie's 'ideal victim' (1986), and towards a more nuanced appreciation of crime and its effects. We have, in effect, come to appreciate more intelligently what theoretical perspectives on victimisation cannot and do not reveal, and that is helpful indeed. But beyond that it would be difficult to conclude that victimology amounts to a coherent whole. So diverse and discordant are its origins that victimology should probably best be represented as yet another *rendez-vous* sub-discipline where different approaches meet around an empirical content and share as a common denominator the word 'victim' (Levine 1978). Consider two self-critical observations made in the formative days of the sub-discipline. The first was framed as the conclusions of a conference, the International Study Institute on Victimology held in Bellagio in 1976 (604):

> so far it can only be stated that the universe of events that have some probability of being defined as victimizing, conceptually define the parameters of victimology. Beyond this admittedly circular definition, little consensus has emerged.

The other was culled from the prospectus for the World Society of Victimology, also drafted in the 1970s:

> From its beginning, victimology has been an international and an interdisciplinary subject. The need for information about the victim's contribution to the commission of crime, the offender–victim relationship, the victim's vulnerability and recidivism, the victim's role in the criminal justice system, the potential victim's fear of crime and attitudes towards legislation and law enforcement stimulated victimological research throughout the world.

It would be difficult to pretend that much has changed in the last few decades.

Acknowledgement

I am grateful to Heather Strang for reading an earlier draft of this chapter.

Further reading

Fattah, E. (1991) *Understanding Criminal Victimisation*. Scarborough, Ontario: Prentice Hall.

Hoyle, C. and Young, R. (eds) (2002) *New Visions of Crime Victims*. Oxford: Hart Publishing.

Zedner, L. (2002) 'Victims' in M. Maguire, R. Morgan and R. Reiner (eds) *Oxford Handbook of Criminology*. Oxford: Oxford University Press.

Notes

1 There are exceptions. Robert Elias, for instance, claimed that victimology 'has sought to build a scientific discipline substantially defining and framing the aspect of society it wishes to study, by devising a set of specific question, and some general theories, and by developing scientific methodologies' (1986: 21). But the poverty of victimological theory is a reiterated complaint. Adler (1979: 266), reviewing a special issue of the journal *Victimology*, remarks: 'The lack of attention to theory building is a weakness both of this collection of articles and of the literature in this area as a whole.' Very similarly, Silverman (1988: 214) asserts: 'I find it difficult to take victimology seriously as a sub-discipline, since it offers no unique theory or methodology.' And Meisenhelder (1980: 586) says in yet another review of a victimological compendium, 'There is ... one serious defect – the essay fails to address the glaring need for serious theoretical work in the area of victimology ... papers are almost totally devoid of theoretical content.'

2 Consider the tone and burden of the following statement by Stuart Hall and his associates: mugging 'has – when accompanied by violence – sometimes resulted in serious physical and emotional consequences for its victims, many of whom are old or unable to cope with the shock of the encounter, and few of whom have very much of the world's wealth at their command. This is not a pretty social development to contemplate ... [But] [o]ur argument is simply not conducted within [an] individual frame of reference, or within the given, common-sense calculus of individual praise or blame. To blame the actions of individuals within a given historical structure, *without taking that structure itself into account*, is an easy and familiar way of exercising the moral conscience without bearing any of its costs. It is the last refuge of liberalism' (Hall *et al.* 1978: 181–2, emphasis in original).

3 Elsewhere he states 'The interests and feelings of victims – actual victims, victims' families, potential victims, the projected figure of "the victim" are now routinely invoked in support of measures of punitive segregation' (Garland 1996: 445).

4 Robert Elias (1986: 17) names Mendelsohn as the founder of victimology.

5 Sandra Walklate (1989) locates the beginnings of victimology in H. Von Hentig's *The Victim and His Criminal* (1948). For an early reference of Von Hentig to the importance of the victim, see Von Hentig (1940).

6 Lucia Zedner (2002: 420) claims that the progenitor of victimology was Wertham, who, she says, invented the word in 1949 in *The Show of Violence*.

7 Charles Goring (1919: 16), the man appointed eventually by the Prison Commissioners to assess Lombroso's anthropometric claims, concluded that Lombroso worked 'not by methods of disinterested investigation, but, rather, by a leap of the imagination, the notion thus reached then forming the basis upon which he conducted his researches, and constructed his theory – the whole fabric of the Lombrosian doctrine, judged by the standards of science, is fundamentally unsound.' Mannheim (1965: 215) said that Lombroso's 'style and his basic approach ... were often highly intuitive, not to say fanciful. While imagination and inspiration are truly indispensable elements of scientific research, the flashes of insight have to be rigidly controlled to guard against the dangers that unconscious

bias may lead to imaginary discoveries not borne out by the facts.'

8 Those who may eventually be identified as victims of homicide do not necessarily die immediately. Under the so-called 'year and a day rule' rule, for instance, it was sufficient In England and Wales that a person died within a specified time to become eligible as a murder victim. Presumably, a number of such people could be amenable to interview.

9 Although it should be noted that the frequency and severity of their injuries seemed less than that of women.

10 For instance, the Australasian Society of Victimology was founded in 1988 by victims' organisations that were themselves largely the creation of people who had been traumatised by serious crimes such as murder (see Robinson 2004: 64).

11 Although the British General Household Survey of 1972 (OPCS 1972) did contain a question about experience of burglary.

12 For example, the Victims of Crime Review Report 3 disseminated by the Government of South Australia (Justice Strategy Unit 2000) recommended that the definition of a victim contained in the Criminal Injuries Compensation Act 1978 should be repealed and replaced by three categories: *primary*, *secondary* and *related*.

References

Adamson, M., Briskin, L. and McPhail, M. (1988) *Feminist Organizing for Change*. Toronto: Oxford University Press.

Adler, E. (1979) 'Review of *Victimology: Special Issue on Spouse Abuse and Domestic Violence*', *Contemporary Sociology*, 8(2): pp. 266–7.

Amir, M. (1967) 'Victim precipitated forcible rape', *Journal of Criminal Law, Criminology, and Police Science*, 58(4): 493–502.

Amir, M. (1971) *Patterns in Forcible Rape*. Chicago: University of Chicago Press.

Anderson, S., Kinsey, R., Loader, I. and Smith, C. (1991) *'Cautionary Tales': A Study of Young People in Edinburgh*. Edinburgh: Centre for Criminology.

Antilla, I. (1964) 'Victimology – A New Territory in Criminology', *Scandinavian Studies in Criminology*, 5.

Avison, N. (1973) 'Victims of Homicide', in I. Drapkin and E. Viano (eds) *Victimology: A New Focus*. Lexington, MA: Lexington Books.

Barnes, H. and Teeters, N. (1943) *New Horizons in Criminology*. New Jersey: Prentice Hall.

Becker, C. (1981) 'Criminal Theories of Causation and Victims' Contributions to the Etiology of Crime', PhD thesis, University of Cambridge.

Becker, H. (1963) *Outsiders*. New York: Free Press.

Block, R. (1981) 'Victim–offender dynamics in violent crime', *Journal of Criminal Law and Criminology*, 72(2): 743–61.

Block, R. (1993) 'A cross-national comparison of victims of crime: victim surveys of twelve countries', *International Review of Victimology*, 2: 183–207.

Bottoms, A., Mawby, R. and Walker, M. (1987) 'A localised crime survey in contrasting areas of a city', *British Journal of Criminology*, 27(2): 125–54.

Bourgois, P. (1996) 'In search of masculinity: Violence, respect and sexuality among Puerto Rican crack dealers in East Harlem', *British Journal of Criminology*, 36: 412–27.

Boutellier, H. (2000) *Crime and Morality: The Significance of Criminal Justice in Post-Modern Culture*. Dordrecht: Kluwer Academic.

Bowers, K., Johnson, S. and Pease, K. (2004) 'Prospective hot-spotting: The future of crime mapping?', *British Journal of Criminology*, 44: 641–58.

Bowling, B. (1998) *Violent Racism: Victimisation, Policing, and Social Control.* Oxford: Clarendon Press.

Braithwaite, J. (1989) *Crime, Shame and Reintegration.* Cambridge: Cambridge University Press.

Brownmiller, S. (1977) *Against Our Will: Men, Women and Rape.* Harmondsworth: Penguin.

Caffell, C. (1994) *In Search of the Rainbow's End: A Father's Story.* London: Hodder and Stoughton.

Carlen, P. (ed.) (1985) *Criminal Women: Some Autobiographical Accounts.* Cambridge: Polity Press.

Carlen, P. (1988) *Women, Crime and Poverty.* Milton Keynes: Open University Press.

Christie, N. (1977) 'Conflicts as property', *British Journal of Criminology*, 17: 1–15.

Christie, N. (1986) 'The Ideal Victim', in E. Fattah (ed.) *From Crime Policy to Victim Policy*, Basingstoke: Macmillan, pp. 17–30.

Clark, L. and Lewis, D. (1977) *Rape: The Price of Coercive Sexuality.* Toronto: Women's Press.

Clarke, R., Ekblom, P., Hough, M. and Mayhew, P. (1985) 'Elderly victims of crime and exposure to risk', *British Journal of Criminology*, 24(1): 1–9.

Cohen, L. and Felson, M. (1979) 'Social change and crime rates trends: A routine activity approach', *American Sociological Review*, 44: 588–608.

Cohen, S. (1979) 'Guilt, Justice and Tolerance', in D. Downes and P. Rock (eds) *Deviant Interpretations.* Oxford: Martin Robertson.

Cohen, S. (2002) *Folk Devils and Moral Panics*, 3rd edn. New York: Routledge.

Cohen, S. and Taylor, L. (1976) *Escape Attempts: The Theory and Practice of Resistance to Everyday Life.* London: Allen Lane.

Crime and Justice Associates (1982) *The Iron Fist and the Velvet Glove: An Analysis of the U.S. Police.* San Francisco: Synthesis Publications.

Daly, K. (1994) 'Men's violence, victim advocacy, and feminist redress: Comment', *Law and Society Review*, 28(4): 777–86.

Dardenne, S. (2005) *I Choose to Live*, London: Virago.

Davies, P., Francis, P. and Jupp, V. (2003) 'Understanding Victimisation: Theory, Research and Policy', in P. Davies, P. Francis and V. Jupp (eds) *Victimisation: Theory, Research and Policy.* Basingstoke: Palgrave Macmillan.

Dignan, J. (2005) *Understanding Victims and Restorative Justice.* Maidenhead: Open University Press.

Doerner, W. and Lab, S. (1995) *Victimology.* Cincinnati, OH: Anderson Publishing.

Douglas, J. and Waksler, F. (1982) *The Sociology of Deviance: An Introduction.* Boston: Little, Brown and Co.

Douglas, M. (1966) *Purity and Danger.* London: Routledge and Kegan Paul.

Eastel, P. (1994) *Voices of the Survivors.* Melbourne: Spinifex.

Elias, R. (1983) *Victims of the System.* New Brunswick, NJ: Transaction.

Elias, R. (1986) *The Politics of Victimization*, New York: Oxford University Press.

Erikson, K. (1966) *Wayward Puritans.* New York: John Wiley.

Fattah, E. (1979) 'Some recent theoretical developments in victimology', *Victimology*, 4(2): 198–213.

Fattah, E. (2000) 'Victimology past, present and future', *Criminologie*, 33(1).

Finkelhor, D., Ormrod, R., Turner, H. and Hamby, A. (2005) 'The victimisation of children and youth: A comprehensive national survey', *Child Maltreatment*, 10(1): 5–25.

Foucault, M. (1979) *Discipline and Punish.* Harmondsworth: Penguin.

Garofalo, J. (1979) 'Victimization and the fear of crime', *Journal of Research in Crime and Delinquency*: 80–104.

Garland, D. (1996) 'The limits of the sovereign state: strategies of crime control in contemporary society, *British Journal of Criminology*, 36(4).

Garland, D. (2000) 'The culture of high crime societies', *British Journal of Criminology*, 40(3).

Garland, D. (2001) *The Culture of Control*. Oxford: Oxford University Press.

Gelsthorpe, L. and Morris, A. (eds) (1990) *Feminist Perspectives in Criminology*. Milton Keynes: Open University Press.

Genn, H. (1988) 'Multiple Victimisation', in M. Maguire and J. Pointing (eds) *Victims of Crime*. Milton Keynes: Open University Press.

Goring, C. (1919) *The English Convict*. London: HMSO.

Gottfredson, M. (1981) 'On the etiology of criminal victimisation', *Journal of Criminal Law and Criminology*, 72(2): 714–26.

Gottfredson, M. and Hindelang, M. (1981) 'Sociological aspects of criminal victimisation', *Annual Review of Sociology*, 7: 107–28.

Grady, A. (2002) 'Female-on-Male Domestic Abuse: Uncommon or Ignored?,' in C. Hoyle and R. Young (eds) *New Visions of Crime Victims*. Oxford: Hart Publishing.

Hall, S. Critcher, C., Jefferson, T. and Clarke, J. (1978) *Policing the Crisis*. London: Macmillan.

Hillyard, P., Sim, J. and Tombs, S. (2004) 'Leaving a "stain upon the silence": Contemporary criminology and the politics of dissent', *British Journal of Criminology*, 44: 369–90.

Hirst, P. (1975) 'Marx and Engels on Law, Crime and Morality', in I. Taylor, P. Walton and J. Young (eds) *The New Criminology*. London: Routledge and Kegan Paul.

Hobsbawm, E. (1971) *Primitive Rebels*. Manchester: Manchester University Press.

Hollander, J. (2001) 'Vulnerability and dangerousness: The construction of gender through conversation about violence', *Gender and Society*, 15(1): 83–109.

Holstein, J. and Miller, G. (1990) 'Rethinking victimisation: An interactional approach to victimology', *Symbolic Interaction*, 13(1): 103–22.

Home Office (2002) *Crime, Policing and Justice: The Experience of Older People: Findings from the British Crime Survey*, Statistical Bulletin 8/02. London: Home Office.

Home Office (2004a) *Violence at Work: Findings from the 2002/2003 British Crime Survey*, Home Office Online Report 4/04. London: Home Office.

Home Office (2004b) *Ethnicity, Victimisation and Worry about Crime: Findings from the 2001/02 and 2002/03 British Crime Surveys*, Home Office Research Findings 237. London: Home Office.

hooks, b. (1982) *Ain't I a Woman: Black Women and Feminism*. London: Pluto Press.

Hough, M. and Mayhew, P. (1983) *The British Crime Survey: First Report*. London: HMSO.

International Study Institute on Victimology (1976) 'Conclusions and Recommendations', in E. Viano (ed.) *Victims and Society*. Washington: Visage Press.

Ivison, I. (1997) *Fiona's Story*. London: Virago.

Jacobs, J. and Potter, K. (1998) *Hate Crimes: Criminal Law and Identity Politics*. New York: Oxford University Press.

Jones, T., MacLean, B. and Young, J. (1986) *The Islington Crime Survey: Victimisation and Policing in Inner-City London*. Aldershot: Gower.

Justice Strategy Unit (2000) *Review on Victims of Crime: Report 3*. Adelaide: Government of South Australia.

Kurz, D. (1989) 'Social science perspectives on wife abuse', *Gender and Society*, 3(4): 489–505.

Lamb, L. (1996) *The Trouble with Blaming*. Cambridge, MA: Harvard University Press.

Lea, J. and Young, J. (1984) *What is to be Done about Law and Order?* London: Penguin.

Lemert, E. (1951) *Social Pathology*. New York; McGraw-Hill.

Lerner, M. (1980) *The Belief in a Just World: A Fundamental Delusion*. London: Plenum Press.

Levine, K. (1978) 'Empiricism in victimological research', *Victimology*, 3: 1–2.

Lipsky, M. and Olson, D. (1977) *Commission Politics: The Processing of Racial Crisis in America*. New Brunswick, NJ: Transaction.

Lotz, (1975) 'Review of Menachem Amir. *Patterns in Forcible Rape*', in *Contemporary Sociology*, 4(4): 381–2.

Luckenbill, D. (1977) 'Criminal homicide as a situated transaction', *Social Problems*, 75(2).

Madriz, E. (1997) 'Images of criminals and victims: A study on women's fear and social control', *Gender and Society*, 11(3): 342–56.

Maguire, M. (1980) 'The impact of burglary upon victims', *British Journal of Criminology*, 20: 261–75.

Maguire, M. (1991) 'The needs and rights of victims of crime', *Crime and Justice*, 14: 363–433.

Maguire, M. and Bennett, T. (1982) *Burglary in a Dwelling*. London: Heinemann.

Marshall, G. (1994) *Oxford Concise Dictionary of Sociology*. Oxford: Oxford University Press.

Mathiesen, T. (1974) *The Politics of Abolition*. London: Martin Robertson.

Matravers, A. (2000) 'Justifying the Unjustifiable: Stories of Women Sex Offenders', PhD thesis, University of Cambridge.

Matza, D. (1964) *Delinquency and Drift*. New York: John Wiley.

Matza, D. (1969) *Becoming Deviant*. Englewood Cliffs, NJ: Prentice Hall.

Meier, R. and Miethe, T. (1993) 'Understanding theories of criminal victimisation', *Crime and Justice*, 17: 459–99.

Meisenhelder, T. (1980) 'Review of W. Parsonage (ed.) *Perspectives on Victimology*', *Social Forces*, 59(2) 586–7.

Mendelsohn, B. (1963) 'The origin of the doctrine of victimology', *Excerpta Criminologica*, 3: 239–45.

Mirrlees-Black, C. (1999) *Domestic Violence: Findings from a New British Crime Survey Self-Completion Questionnaire*. London: Home Office.

Morgan, J. and Zedner, L. (1992) *Child Victims: Crime, Impact, and Criminal Justice*. Oxford: Clarendon Press.

Muir, H. (1998) 'Voices of Victims of Crime – The Wounded Storytellers', in B. Giuliano (ed.) *Survival and Beyond*. Curtin, ACT: National Association for Loss and Grief.

National Board for Crime Prevention (1994) *Wise After the Event: Tackling Repeat Victimisation*. London: Home Office.

Newburn, T. and Stanko, E. (eds) (1994) *Just Boys Doing Business? Men, Masculinities and Crime*. London: Routledge.

Oakley, A. (1981) 'Interviewing Women: A Contradiction in Terms', in H. Roberts (ed.) *Doing Feminist Research*. London: Routledge and Kegan Paul.

OPCS (1972) *General Household Survey*. London: Office of Population Censuses and Surveys.

Pagelow, M. (1981) 'Review of R. Dobash and R. Dobash, *Violence Against Wives: A Case against the Patriarchy*', *American Journal of Sociology*, 86(6): 1475–6.

Pearce, F. (1976) *Crimes of the Powerful: Marxism, Crime and Deviance*. London: Pluto Press.

Pease, K. and Farrell, G. (1993) *Once Bitten, Twice Shy: Repeat Victimisation and its Implications for Crime Prevention*, Home Office Crime Prevention Unit 46. London: Home Office.

Pease, K., Bowers, K. and Johnson, S. (2004) 'Prospective hot-spotting: The future of crime mapping?', *British Journal of Criminology*, 44(5): 641–58.

Pendergast, M. (1997) *Victims of Memory: Incest Accusations and Shattered Lives*. London: HarperCollins.

Plummer, K. (1994) *Telling Sexual Stories: Power, Change and Social Worlds*. London: Routledge.

Polk, K. (1994) *When Men Kill*. Cambridge: Cambridge University Press.

Polvi, N., Looman, T., Humphries, C. and Pease, K. (1991) 'The time course of repeat burglary victimisation', *British Journal of Criminology*, 31: 411–4.

Porterfield, A. and Talbert, R. (1954) *Mid-Century Crime in Our Culture*. Fort Worth, TX: Leo Potishman Foundation.

President's Crime Commission (1967) *The Challenge of Crime in a Free Society*. Washington, DC: US Government Printing Office.

Reiman, J. (2003) *The Rich get Richer and the Poor get Prison*. Boston, MA: Allyn and Bacon.

Reiss, A. (1981) 'Foreword: Towards a revitalisation of theory and research on victimisation by crime', *Journal of Criminal Law and Criminology*, 72(2): 704–13.

Robinson, J. (2004) *Crime: It Can Happen to You*. Kent Town, SA: Wakefield Press.

Rock, P. (1986) *A View from the Shadows: The Ministry of the Solicitor General of Canada and the Justice for Victims of Crime Initiative*. Oxford: Clarendon Press.

Rock, P. (1990) *Helping Victims of Crime: The Home Office and the Rise of Victim Support in England and Wales*. Oxford: Clarendon Press.

Rock, P. (1993) *The Social World of an English Crown Court*. Oxford: Clarendon Press.

Rock, P. (1998a) *After Homicide*. Oxford: Clarendon Press.

Rock, P. (1998b) 'Murderers, victims and "survivors": The social construction of deviance', *British Journal of Criminology*, 38: 185–200.

Russell, D. and Van de Ven, N. (eds) (1976) *Crimes Against Women: Proceedings of the International Tribunal*. Millbrae, CA: Les Femmes.

Sagarin, E. (1975) *Deviants and Deviance*. New York: Praeger.

Sampson, A. and Phillips, C. (1992) *Multiple Victimisation: Racial Attacks on an East London Estate*. London: Home Office Police Department.

Schafer, S. (1968) *The Victim and His Criminal: A Study in Functional Responsibility*. New York: Random House.

Schur, E. (1965) *Crimes without Victims*. Englewood Cliffs, NJ: PrenticeHall.

Schur, E. (1973) *Radical Nonintervention: Rethinking the Delinquency Problem*. Englewood Cliffs, NJ: PrenticeHall.

Schur, E. (1974) 'The Case for Abolition', in E. Schur and H. Bedau (eds) *Victimless Crimes*. Englewood Cliffs, NJ: Prentice Hall.

Schwendinger, H. and Schwendinger, J. (1970) 'Defenders of order or guardians of human rights?', *Issues in Criminology*, 5: 123–57.

Sebba, L. (1982) 'The victim's role in the penal process', *American Journal of Comparative Law*, 30(2): 217–40.

Shapland, J., Willmore, J. and Duff, P. (1985) *Victims in the Criminal Justice System*. Aldershot: Gower.

Shaw, M. (1995) 'Conceptualising Violence by Women', in R. Dobash, R. Dobash and L. Noaks (eds) *Gender and Crime*. Cardiff: University of Wales Press.

Silverman, R. (1988) 'Review of R. Elias, *The Politics of Victimisation: Victims, Victimology, and Human Rights*', *Contemporary Sociology*, 17: 2.

Smart, C. (1977) *Women, Crime and Criminology: A Feminist Critique*. London: Routledge and Kegan Paul.

Smart, C. (1989) *Feminism and the Power of Law*. London: Routledge.

Smith, D. and Gray, J. (1985) *Police and People in London: The PSI Report*, Vol. 1. Aldershot: Gower.

Smith, S. (1982) 'Victimisation in the inner city', *British Journal of Criminology*, 22(2): 386–402.

Sprey, J. (1979) 'Review of E. Viano (ed.) *Victims and Society'*, *Contemporary Sociology*, 8(2): 255.

Spungen, D. (1993) *And I Don't Want to Live this Life*. New York: Villard Books.

Stephens, J. (1976) *Loners, Losers, and Lovers: Elderly Tenants in a Slum Hotel*. Seattle, WA: University of Washington Press.

Stanko, E. (1990) *Everyday Violence: How Women and Men Experience Sexual and Physical Danger*. London: Pandora.

Strang, H. (2002) *Repair or Revenge: Victims and Restorative Justice*. Oxford: Clarendon Press.

Sumner, C. (ed.) (1990) *Censure, Politics and Criminal Justice*. Milton Keynes: Open University Press.

Sutherland, E. and Cressey, D. (1970) *Principles of Criminology*. Philadelphia, PA: J.B. Lippincott.

Sykes, C. (1992) *A Nation of Victims: The Decay of the American Character*. New York: St Martin's Press.

Taylor, I., Walton, P. and Young, J. (1973) *The New Criminology*. London: Routledge and Kegan Paul.

Tseloni, A. and Pease, K. (2003) 'Repeat personal victimisation', *British Journal of Criminology*, 43: 1996–212.

Van Dijk, J., Mayhew, P. and Killias, M. (1990) *Experiences of Crime Across the World*. Deventer: Kluwer Law and Taxation Publishers.

Von Hentig, H. (1940) 'Remarks on the interaction of perpetrator and victim', *Journal of Criminal Law and Criminology*, 31: 303–9.

Von Hentig, H. (1948) *The Criminal and His Victim*. Hamden, CT: Archon Books.

Walklate, S. (1989) *Victimology: The Victim and the Criminal Justice Process*. London: Unwin Hyman.

Walklate, S. (2000) 'Researching Victims', in R. King and E. Wincup (eds) *Doing Research on Crime and Justice*. Oxford: Oxford University Press.

Waller, I. and Okihiro, N. (1978) *Burglary: The Victim and the Public*. Toronto: University of Toronto Press.

Wertham, F. (1949) *The Show of Violence*. New York: Vintage.

Wolfgang, M. (1957) 'Victim-Precipitated Criminal Homicide', *Journal of Criminal Law, Criminology and Police Science*, 48(1).

Wolfgang, M. (1958) *Patterns in Criminal Homicide*. Philadelphia: University of Pennsylvania Press.

Wright, R. (1995) 'Women as "victims" and as "resisters": Depictions of the oppression of women in criminology textbooks', *Teaching Sociology*, 23(2) 111–21.

Zedner, L. (2002) 'Victims', in M. Maguire, R. Morgan and R. Reiner (eds) *The Oxford Handbook of Criminology*, 3rd edn. Oxford: Oxford University Press.

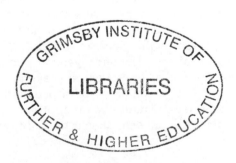

Chapter 3

Theory and method: the social epidemiology of crime victims

Tim Hope

Introduction

Empirical victimology is concerned both with the study of people's experiences of crime victimisation and of the people who experience crime victimisation (i.e. victims). As such, it is fraught with conceptual problems, though many of these often tend to be overlooked or remain unexamined in empirical research. Most forms of social activity involve people interacting with their environment, and crime victimisation is no exception. Each crime victimisation event is embedded within, and sets in train, complex webs of social action and meaning, stretching backwards and forwards in time for the people involved, and intersecting with the lives of others. Crime events also occur in specific instances of space-time – including 'cyberspace'. Yet we cannot readily observe the complexities and ramifications of these events and their settings – not just in the sense of being unable to observe people's motives towards them or their interpretations of them, but even being able to capture the full complexity of the systems of social interaction that converge upon and are brought about by the act itself. So, the data that we have to work with are typically only partial selections from these complexities, focusing on limited slices of time-space in which such events occur and, at any one time, usually upon only one of the many parties to the event – in this case, the crime's immediate victim. Inevitably, then, there are considerable difficulties of interpretation and inference, including problems of partiality, bias and distortion, raised by the essential *selectivity* of the available data.

This chapter sets out to review what we might know about the distribution of the general population's experiences of crime victimisation from the data we have available. The term 'general population' is used here not necessarily in any normative or 'statistical average' sense but as a catch-all term to mean any population or group of people from which it is possible in principle to select a representative sample for study. Again, though, empirical research encounters the problem of selectivity. Studies of victims and victimisation (of both a quantitative and a qualitative nature) invariably have been *opportunistic*, in the sense that they have sought to understand people's crime victimisation experiences from data usually assembled for other primary purposes: for example, from the respondents of social surveys designed to count crime, or among the users of social and clinical programmes and interventions. In this sense, much that we know empirically about victims is the result of secondary analysis of these data sources. It is rare indeed to encounter studies that set out specifically to investigate the phenomenology of crime victimisation, or test explanatory hypotheses derived *a priori* from theory. Yet the selectivity and partiality engendered by the usual circumstances in which data is acquired (see Hope 2005) also continues to limit the capacity of empirical research to support explanations of crime victimisation. Consequently, this chapter is as much concerned to describe some of the problems for explanation that arise from the various processes of selection which underpin the generation of data, as it is to advance explanation of the phenomenon of crime victimisation risk itself. Its emphasis is upon exploring what is, or should be, entailed in specifying hypothetical models that might be useful for exploring and describing the *data generating processes* (*dgp*) that presumably might underlie the observable data on crime victims and their experiences that are available.

Some problems of studying aetiology

Since there is no objective, impartial nor universally applicable way of defining who is or who is not a 'victim' (as discussed in many contributions to this volume), and thus no agreed system for counting or measuring victims, it might be thought futile or disingenuous to proceed any further (as many do), especially to explore the distribution of victims within particular populations. Be that as it may, even where we might be reasonably confident on measurement issues – for instance, that persons who are prompted in the context of questionnaire surveys to report their experiences broadly understand the questions put, and give truthful answers, and that our interpretations of these answers conform to commonly agreed notions as to what a victimisation event might look like – even so, substantial issues of selection bias remain to confront attempts at explanation. These reflect the fundamental conceptual and operational difficulty of framing and estimating the *counterfactual condition* for crime victimisation events, compounded by the consensus that such events are experienced as part of the victim's everyday or normal life (regardless of whether or not this might seem 'abnormal' to anyone else). The source of this difficulty stems from the problem posed for causal attribution by the nature of observation itself: namely, in this case, that an individual cannot be observed (or rather self-reported to have been) in both a victimised and a non-victimised condition simultaneously. We only have available the 'fact' (i.e. victimisation) but we cannot observe its precise 'counterfactual'. That is, since we cannot observe what would have happened if crime victimisation had not happened (i.e. the counterfactual condition), we have no empirically certain means of knowing what factors 'caused' the specific occurrence of the crime victimisation event. Because the counterfactual remains unobservable for 'singular events' of victimisation, we cannot evaluate the actual probability of the event in question occurring against the unactualised probability of it not occurring.[1]

The empirical social sciences, including the empirical study of victims, have sought generally to overcome this kind of problem by inference, particularly through observing regularities from variation in supposedly temporal antecedents of events or statuses, in order to deduce causal antecedents. In this, they are following Hume in the empirical tradition of causality (Russell 1946/2005: 603–12). With regard to victims, the method seeks to infer the causal antecedents of the likelihood of a person becoming a crime victim by tracing the biographical pathways leading towards crime events, or through comparison with 'non-victims', and preferably both. Nevertheless, for all its operationalisability, for a number of reasons the approach does not fully overcome the counterfactual problem with regard to the causes of crime victimisation:

1 Since it is generally felt that there is no *a priori* condition that leads axiomatically to crime victimisation,[2] the acquisition of the status of 'crime victim' comes from people's *actual* experiences of crime victimisation, over variably defined segments of their life-courses. Crime-victimhood is thus a status that is attached to people retrospectively, occasioned by the occurrence of a crime victimisation event; people *become* victims, attaining a status and label that they did not have before. Yet if we simply looked back over the circumstances of people's lives that lead up to the event, we would be likely to risk teleological fallacy. This is because we would risk selecting only those past events that actually occurred (assuming they were recalled) and would have no means of evaluating whether they were the real reasons that led up to the event, since we could not compare the observed routines and pathways with all the possible counterfactual alternatives that the victim could have taken but did not, for whatever reasons (including those that we would want to uncover).

2 A conventional scientific way of overcoming this problem is through some kind of prospective longitudinal 'experiment'. In this case, such an experiment would set up conditions whereby people were randomly exposed (or not) to conditions that are presumed likely to give rise to a victimisation event. In the pure experimental design, those persons assigned to non-exposed conditions represent the counterfactual condition because the process of random assignment to the 'exposed' and 'non-exposed' conditions means that members of either group are 'exchangeable' and that the subsequently observed differences between the two represents the difference between the factual and the counterfactual, and hence indicates causation (Hernán and Robins 2006). Of course, such a research strategy risks rejection on ethical grounds in the case of crime victimisation, entailing as it would do the contrived exposure of human subjects to potential harm. Paradoxically, any experiment that contrived to minimise the risk of harm – say by somehow simulating victimisation in laboratory settings or other similarly

constrained environments – would risk losing generalisability since such a set-up would be an artificial *abstraction* from the conditions in which the phenomenon of crime victimisation is embedded, that is, within everyday life.

3 Paradoxically, experiments that seek to expose people to benefits – in this case exposing people to conditions that would protect them against crime victimisation, likewise cannot be used to infer antecedent causes, if these are unknown, since they risk confounding the causes of the 'dependent variable' (i.e. crime victimisation) with the 'causes' of the intervention. For instance, an hypothetical experiment that offered intruder alarms for purchase to randomly selected households would not be able to assess the protective effect of alarms since it is known both that more affluent households are likely to purchase alarms and that they are less likely to be victimised from household property crime (Hope 2001). Thus, in this case, it would be the condition of 'affluence' rather than the condition of 'alarm' that was the causal antecedent of victimisation. And 'affluence' would then *confound* observation of the effect of 'alarm', even though the experimental set-up was predicated on testing the latter effect. Again, the difficulty of abstracting victimisation from the realm of everyday life in which it is embedded makes it hard to identify its causal antecedents.

4 Given these problems, empirical research into the antecedents of crime victimisation has had to be content with inferential (statistical) methods of association – typically between victims and non-victims (as defined by self-reported admissions) – in order to estimate effects, usually by setting non-victimisation as the counterfactual condition. Yet as discussed below, this seemingly commonsensical model may well be a misleading depiction of the *dgp* of crime victimisation leading to mis-specification and mis-identification of explanatory models.

5 Some compensation might be had by building 'controls' into the design and analysis of studies of observed data: for example, to establish temporal order (from which to infer causation) by implementing longitudinal 'panel' designs (i.e. repeated measurement on the same people at different points in time) and/or to control for extraneous or confounding effects by utilising appropriate, multivariate statistical models. Regrettably, longitudinal panel data are rarely available on victimisation;[3] ironically, an absence that severely hampers investigation of processes that have been seen of much policy-relevance, such as *repeat* (sic) victimisation – a concept that clearly implies a temporal causal ordering (but see Hope and Trickett 2004).

Thus, much of the available empirical data for studying the aetiological circumstances of crime victims are to be found in cross-sectional sample surveys. Since, as discussed below, the average prevalence of crime victims in populations (at least over periods of 12 months or less), is relatively low, large-scale samples are necessary, perforce leading to a reliance upon government-supported surveys, often with national coverage such as the US National Crime Victimisation Survey, or the British Crime Survey for England and Wales. Notwithstanding the fact that these surveys may lack adequate sets of measures of covariates of theoretical (aetiological) interest, due to possible conflicts with their public service functions,[4] all cross-sectional survey data remain vulnerable, nevertheless, to three kinds of selection bias:

1 *Sample selection bias,* arising from failure of eligibility for inclusion in the sampling process.

2 *Response bias,* arising from the failure of those selected to participate in answering some or any of the questions either accurately, truthfully or at all (for summaries of commonly observed sample and response biases see Hope 2005; Mayhew 2000).

3 *Conditional selection bias.* This latter form of selection bias (sometimes called conditional censoring) again reflects the concerns of the counterfactual approach. As discussed below, in the case of testing theories of crime victimisation which rest upon the notion that people might be differentially exposed to the chance of becoming a victim, it is necessary to distinguish between those who are never likely to be exposed to the risk of crime, for example, because they never go out on foot, or to places where they might encounter street-robbers, from those that are so exposed to crime-risk but nevertheless do not become victimised (see Clarke *et al.* 1985).

Generally, counterfactual reasoning suggests that explanatory models are likely to be incomplete, mis-specified or biased to the extent that they fail substantively to take each of these sources of selection bias into account (Heckman 2001).

In sum, the nature of the available data, combined with the *ex post facto*, event-referenced nature of the definition of 'crime victim', present formidable problems for researching the aetiology of the condition of crime-victimhood. Such research has had to proceed empirically by the method of statistical association, from which inferences about underlying data generation and aetiological processes might be deduced. Counterfactual reasoning suggests that such methods of empirical analysis are likely not only to be causally weak (because of the difficulty of identifying satisfactory conditional counterfactuals) but may also lead to erroneous or biased results – which might only be overcome, partially at least, by careful attention to *ex ante* theoretical development, model specification (including an incorporation of selection bias) and data collection. Nevertheless, empirical analysis of this kind has continued over the past 30 years or so, though the difficulties and inconsistencies encountered in interpreting its results have been disappointing, on the whole, arguably through inattention to the issues of causal analysis identified here.

Specifying the data generating process

Sample surveys of general populations generate *counts* of crime-victimisation events experienced by their respondents. Typically they ask their respondents to report the numbers of incidents of a set of offences that they or their households have experienced over a particular recall period (usually no more than the previous 12 months). Naturally, tabulations of responses to such questions yield frequency distributions for the number of crime victimisations experienced by the sampled respondents. Typically also, those experiencing one or more incidents over the recall period are usually considered to be 'victims', and thus distinguished from non-victims (i.e. people not reporting any incidents), while persons reporting more than one incident have come to be termed 'multiple victims' or, following Farrell and Pease (1993), 'repeat victims'. Because the surveys are representative samples, so also have these categories come to be thought of as representative of the crime victimisation experiences of the general population.[5] Since the surveys also ask a range of other questions about respondents' background, experiences and so on, these questions have been correlated with crime victimisation frequencies and, in turn, have been considered as covariate proxies of causal antecedents, used to support, substantiate or test various explanatory theories of crime victimisation.

When the sampled count data of self-recalled crime victimisation are arranged as a frequency distribution, they invariably display two characteristics: first, that crime victimisation seems to be a probabilistically *rare event* – that is, the majority of the sampled population do not report victimisation over the recall period; and second, the population distribution is *over-dispersed* – that is, the sample variance exceeds the sample mean, for example, that there are more higher-frequency crime victims than would be expected, or conversely, that the zero response observation is over-inflated (see below). Table 3.1 and 3.2 show that these characteristics appear across a variety of types of crime and types of victim. The similarity suggests that there might be a similar data generating process (*dpg*) underlying these different frequency distributions. The difficulty, however, lies in finding out what such a *dgp* might look like.

The data generating process

While measurement issues are concerned with how we count crime victimisation, the form of the *dgp* is a particular stochastic process that best describes how the observed frequency distribution is produced. Any particular *dgp* cannot be observed itself but its presence and form can be identified by the degree to which a sample frequency distribution conforms to, or 'fits', a particular theoretical statistical distribution. If there is found to be a good fit, we can then infer that the unobserved *dgp* for the observed frequency distribution has the same general properties as the theoretical distribution which, in turn, provides us with basic building blocks for developing and testing theories about the processes that produce the frequencies observed.

In general, the *dgp* for crime victimisation distributions possesses three basic characteristics (Hope *et al.* 2001). First, *repetition* – that is, whether an observed frequency distribution implies a time-ordered sequence of crime victimisation events suffered by the same individual victim (which is the case in self-report, recall-based crime victimisation surveys). Second, *specificity*, that is, whether such an ordered sequence occurs within a specific crime type or

Table 3.1 Recalled-frequency crime distributions for the previous 12 months according to the British Crime Survey (2002/03): general adult population (percentages)

	Proportion of non-victims in population	Proportion of victims experiencing two or more incidents
Property		
Burglary – households	96.6	18
Vehicle-related theft – vehicle-owning households	89.2	19
Violence		
Mugging	99.9	10
Stranger	98.4	21
Acquaintance	98.6	28
Domestic	99.4	45

Note: Adults in the BCS are persons over 15 years of age.
Source: Simmons and Dodd (2003)

Table 3.2 Recalled-frequency domestic violence distributions for the previous 12 months according to the British Crime Survey (2001): adult women (percentages)

	Proportion of non-victims among adult women	Proportion of victims experiencing two or more incidents
Domestic violence – threat or force	95.8	72
Domestic force	96.6	68
– minor	97.4	63
– severe	98.4	73

Source: Walby and Allen (2004)

across crime types or both. Most research has focused on victimisation within specific crime types. Exceptionally, Hope *et al.* (2001) model the conditional probabilities for cross-crime type victimisation between household property crime and personal crime victimisation, also taking into account (self-reported) prior victimisation experiences of offences in both crime types. While the study is restricted to cross-sectional BCS data and cannot determine causal order between immediate victimisation experiences, it suggests a degree of *generality* present in crime victimisation experience: first, having taken into account covariate risk factors specific to each offence type (though there is also a degree of commonality in these too), there still remained a significant, positive association between the chance of becoming a property crime victim and that of becoming a victim of personal crime; and second, that prior victimisation experiences seem to affect immediate victimisation risk, both within (see also Ellingworth *et al.* 1997) and also across crime types.

This leads on to the third, and most elusive element, the existence and form of the *mechanism of risk-transmission* – that is, whether there is a non-random link between incidents suffered by the same individual over time and, if so, what might be the characteristics of the process linking incidents together? The Poisson model is regarded as the benchmark model for count data that consist of a number of discrete events occurring over a fixed time interval (Cameron and Trivedi 1998). The simple Poisson model assumes that successive events for any individual occur independently of each other over time at a constant rate. However, in the case of crime victimisation data this would mean that the probability of victimisation would be the same for all persons in the population and that the probability of being victimised would not depend upon the number of previous victimisations (Nelson 1980: 871). Yet not only has much recent research on the aetiology of crime victimisation proceeded as though neither of these conditions were true (see below) but the observable properties of the frequency distribution, particularly its over-dispersion, violate the assumptions of the simple Poisson distribution, leading to an extremely poor fit. Thus, early research on both American and British crime victimisation surveys suggested there was a need for an alternative to the simple Poisson process that might be producing the underlying distribution of the observed condition of crime victimisation (Nelson 1980; Sparks *et al.* 1977). Yet, it has not been established precisely what form the *dgp* for the distribution actually takes. Empirically, there have been various strategies taken to overcome this problem when seeking to estimate covariates to stand as proxies for causal influences or risk factors.

The discrete outcome model

By far the most common approach taken to date has been to conceptualise the distribution as a 'discrete outcome' model[6] where the observed frequency distribution is truncated into two outcomes: typically, zero to indicate non-victimisation, and a positive value (usually 1) to indicate victimisation frequencies of one or more incidents over the recall period – commonly designated as 'victim'. This approach has a number of advantages: it conforms to 'common-sense' and policy priorities – that is, interest in the process of acquiring the status of victim; it reflects legal distinctions that operate on an individual case basis, which assigns status to the different parties to a criminal event (i.e. 'victim' and 'offender'); and it obviates the problem of the uncertain nature of the underlying *dgp* by converting it into a simple discrete binary outcome. It also capitalises on empirical observation – that the majority of sampled populations are not victimised over the typical recall period (Tables 3.1 and 3.2). Thus, by truncating the positive values of the count of victimisation incidents, the discrete outcome approach brings the average risk rate, called *incidence* (defined as the number of victimisation incidents divided by the number in the sampled population), closer to an assumed true mean of the distribution (*prevalence*), approximating to zero. The approach removes the explanatory problems posed by over-dispersion by ignoring the contribution to explanation of the statistically rare sub-population of higher-frequency 'multiple victims', thereby 'normalising' the distribution, 'fixing' the *dgp*, and thus making the distribution easier to analyse, without apparently much loss to explanation (Nelson 1980).

The theoretical assumption of the discrete outcome approach is thus to focus on the 'normal' condition – that is, close to a zero likelihood of victimisation for the majority of the population. Victimisation is thus conceptualised as a *deviation* from normality – a relatively rare risk that individuals encounter in their daily lives and routine activities. The empirical task is thus to look for those risk factors present in the environments in which people normally find themselves (Miethe and Meier 1994). The primary reason for asking the question in this way is to identify the factors that might contribute to, and thus predict on the basis of *a priori* risk, the general population's likelihood of *exposure* to crime victimisation – an approach first developed by Hindelang, Gottfredson and Garofalo in their book *Victims of Violent Crime* (1978). To the extent to which patterns are found, this indicates the risk of exposure to the likelihood of crime victimisation that is part of the structure of the social environment. The null hypothesis (the conterfactual) is thus that crime victimisation – in the rare chance that it should occur – is a random event, at least from the point of view of the victim. This approach has been termed *positivist victimology* reflecting an empirical strategy of analysing population distributions in terms of deviations from norms, with the theoretical intention of identifying and explaining what those norms might be (Mawby and Walklate 1994).

Exposure to risk

Central to the discrete outcome empirical approach is the concept of *exposure to risk*. Bearing in mind the conventional *ex post facto* definition of victim status, it is not surprising that when first encountering these distributions, researchers gravitated towards the concept of exposure – that persons who became victims did so because they were likely to be exposed to criminogenic risks, typically through social and/or physical propinquity to the carriers of the 'disease of crime', that is, those who offend (Hindelang *et al.* 1978). In part, this may have arisen because criminology came first, reflecting a primary preoccupation with explaining crime and offending (Lauritsen and Laub 2006). Thus, it was assumed that the observed distribution of crime victimisation mirrored the data generating process of differential exposure to criminogenic sources and conditions in the population. Further support for this assumption came from Cohen and Felson's (1979) specification of the necessary conditions for the occurrence of criminal incidents.[7] The probability of these convergences occurring could be explained primarily by reference to common, socially structured *routine activity patterns*, such as travelling to work, leaving dwellings unoccupied, frequenting public spaces or places of entertainment. And these patterns could be extended to residential proximity to neighbourhoods also plentiful in the supply of 'offenders' (Cohen *et al.* 1981).

Correspondingly, at the individual-level of analysis, a *lifestyle explanation* of exposure to criminal victimisation was originally proposed by Hindelang *et al.* (1978) as a way of accounting for apparently non-random differences in victimisation risk observed between different demographic groups (i.e. groups distinguished by age, gender, race, income, etc.) in survey data. In an effort to explain these observations, individuals' status characteristics – which are presumed to be measured by their demographic characteristics – were held to imply role expectations and structural constraints which result in differing routine activities and patterns of social relations. These activities and associations may also entail differing levels of 'exposure' to others who might victimise them (Miethe and Meier 1994). The analysis has been essentially inductive – with researchers seeking to provide *ex post facto* explanations for observations obtained from survey data.[8]

Within this tradition of research, four central concepts have been used to explain the risk of individual victimisation (Miethe and Meier 1994):

1 *Proximity to crime.* This might be thought of as the degree of permanent, physical proximity to places where offences might be committed. Risks of victimisation may be heightened in many kinds of place where people who are likely to commit crimes might congregate, and where circumstances are conducive to their being encouraged to commit crimes (Cohen and Felson, 1979); in the residential context, proximity is generally taken to mean a victim's residence in an area which is also likely to have a high rate of resident offenders whom it is presumed may be likely to victimise their fellow residents.

2 *Exposure to crime.* Aside from physical propinquity, certain individuals and households may also have a heightened risk of victimisation by virtue of their lifestyles and routine activities which provide them with additional exposure to the likelihood of risk. Their routine activities and lifestyle choices may take them to risky places, or among dangerous people (as in the proximity hypothesis), and may take them away from the location of their residential and mobile property, which then becomes more exposed to the risk of appropriation or damage. Alternatively, their routines might allow them to avoid such risks.

3 *Attractiveness.* In addition to proximity and exposure, some targets (property or persons) may be seen by offenders as more attractive or worthwhile to attack or steal than other targets. Possibly, it may be the different values or subjective utilities attached to particular targets within a range of suitably 'exposed' targets in any residential community which shapes the decisions of offenders to select particular targets (Miethe and Meie 1994).

4 *Capable guardianship.* Finally, targets may or may not be selected depending upon the degree of effective protection – what Cohen and Felson (1979) call capable guardianship – which is available to them. Such protection might take the form of physical security measures, and activities by residents or owners carried out either individually (i.e. locking-up, keeping a dog) or collectively (i.e. participating in watching actions with neighbours).

Individuals may also benefit from guardianship 'services' available collectively in the locales in which they find themselves, including physical-environmental opportunities facilitating surveillance (i.e. street layout, building design, street lighting), informal surveillance by other residents, organised citizen surveillance (block watches, citizen patrols), and public or private police patrolling.

Is crime victimisation risk a discrete or continuous process?

Much of the research effort which has sought to apportion individual likelihood of risk between these elements has been hampered by inadequacies both in the selection and measurement of indicators, the specification of appropriate analytical models, and underlying difficulties in conceptualising the way in which these effects might operate and the relationships between them (see Miethe and Meier 1994). Research has tended to produce discrepancies and difficulties of interpretation, and it is difficult to work out whether these are substantive or merely artefactual. At least part of the difficulty may reside in conceptualising crime victimisation as a discrete, binary choice. If the underlying *dgp* for crime victimisation is actually a continuous process (or if there is actually a non-random link between events), then this cut-off point is essentially arbitrary. Other or more salient thresholds may exist than the distinction between no incidents and one incident, or that there might be an underlying continuous distribution with no empirically meaningful thresholds at all. Theoretically, the discrete outcome approach reifies the *status* of 'victim' as a stable quality at the expense of conceptualising the *process* of victimisation – which may be one reason for the apparent confusion of empirical research, or the lack of covariate consistency between samples.

Osborn *et al.* (1996) specifically test the possibility that crime victimisation is a discrete or a continuous distribution by testing a 'double-hurdle' model of household property crime victimisation: first, the transition from non-victim to victim household; and second, whether the victimised household progressed to become a multiple (two or more) victim. It was assumed that the probability of a second or subsequent victimisation would not be independent of the probability of an initial victimisation. This allows both for the possibility of a contagious link between victimisation incidents (see below) and that the process of victimisation risk may be similar for each of the hurdles, that is, a continuous process of *heightened exposure to risk*. Having taken into account the (individual and area) risk factors associated with the first hurdle, no further or additionally significant risk factors could be identified for the second hurdle (of repeat household crime victimisation). The inference was that there were no measured *a priori* predictors that would distinguish multiple victims from victims generally, other than those that are common to all victims and distinguish them from non-victims (Osborn *et al.* 1996). Two interpretations were invited by this result: first, that there might be *unmeasured* risk factors that would distinguish higher from lower frequency victims (Tseloni *et al.* 2002)[9] – that is, that would substantiate a discrete outcome model with a further cut-off between 'single' and 'multiple' victims;

but second, that there remained the probability that a victim experiencing higher frequency victimisation was dependent to some extent upon the initial (or rather *a priori*) risk of victimisation – that is, that victimisation was a continuous process.

It is also theoretically possible that truncating the distribution at the zero (positive) value masks important qualitative distinctions among those classified as members of the 'non-victims' sub-population. For example, there may be persons who, for various reasons, are not 'at risk' of victimisation and those who are theoretically 'at risk' but who have not been victimised over the recall period. If the frequency distribution of crime victimisation is held to measure the risk of victimisation, then the zero category may also be masking both discrete differences – for example, those never likely to be at risk – and continuous differences – that is, those who depart with increasing degrees from the likelihood of being victimised; in this latter case, not only would the victimisation risk process be continuous but that there should also be *negative* exposure values on such a victimisation risk continuum. Yet these cannot be observed empirically, especially if the risk continuum is measured by actual events of victimisation. Again, this points up the limitations to explanation of an inadequate or incomplete conceptualisation of the counter factual (or antonym) to the experience of crime victimisation. So, while the measurement of victimisation can only be positive, the underlying *dgp* may be capable, theoretically, of producing unobservable negative risk values. As we shall return to below, the possibility not only of continuing, incremental risk but also of possible negative values, poses difficulties both for the discrete outcome model, and the concept of exposure that underpins it.

Conceptualising risk

The concept of exposure also presupposes that there is something that victims are exposed to – that risk is a property of their environment (rather than something intrinsic to them). Nevertheless, there are problems in conceptualising the role of environmental effects and how they might be distinguished from individual risk factors. For example, numerous empirical studies in both the UK and the USA, have found a correlation between lone (female-headed) household status and the risk of property crime victimisation (Hope 2001). A variable 'lone-parent household' is an individual-level characteristic, while a variable 'proportion of lone-parent households in the resident population of a neighbourhood' is a characteristic of an environment, in this case the residential neighbourhood in which the household is located. Correlations between *rates* of lone-parent households and *rates* of victimisation have been found across neighbourhoods; and lone-parent households have also been found to be at greater risk of victimisation compared to other household types.

But what does this mean? Are these correlations indicators of:

1 *Individual vulnerability* – for example, lone parents may have to leave their property unguarded more often because they go out to work (Cohen and

Felson 1979), or are victimised more often by intimates, including past and estranged partners (Maxfield 1987; Genn 1988), or their children's friends (Sampson and Lauritsen 1990). In other words, are these correlations evidence of an essentially *micro-level effect*? Or:

2 *Neighbourhood-level vulnerability* – for example, high proportions of lone-parent households in a neighbourhood might mean that there are fewer adults to carry out day-to-day surveillance of property (guardianship), or to supervise local youth activities (social control) (Sampson and Groves 1989). In other words, providing evidence of a *macro-level effect*: or even

3 *Context-specific vulnerability* – for example, lone parents who live in areas of predominantly lone parents are not only more vulnerable than other types of household (in 1 above) but are also more vulnerable than single parents who live in other kinds of area (in 2 above). Here, individual vulnerability is enhanced by the particular neighbourhood-level context of risk (Miethe and McDowall 1993). In other words, providing evidence of a *macro-micro interaction effect*.

Why these different interpretations matter is that, if one or another is true, and the others false, it would then help to support different theories of crime victimisation, particularly those that give different explanatory weight to one or the other levels of analysis. For example, if the true interpretation operated at the micro-level rather than the macro-level, it would be evidence of so-called *life-style/routine activity theories* of certain households' and individuals' (lone parents') differential likelihood of exposure to criminal victimisation risk (Smith and Jarjoura 1989; Maxfield 1987). In contrast, the macro-level correlate could indicate diminished levels in the community of informal social control over children and teenagers, and would be supportive of theories of *social disorganisation* (Sampson and Groves 1989; Sampson 1985).

Cross-level mis-specification

Yet the problem remains, in the example given above, that lone-parent household status appears related empirically to the risk of victimisation at *both* levels of analysis (Hope 2001). So, how could we set about sorting out which one is right? In the context of differentiating whether an effect operates at the macro-level or the micro-level, we encounter the general theoretical problem of *cross-level mis-specification* – that is, of misinterpreting effects measured at one level as representing explanations operating at another level, and *vice versa* (Sampson and Lauritsen 1994), and thus committing errors of inference. Each source of variation – whether attributed to micro-level or macro-level sources – constitutes a threat to the validity of explanation couched at the other level.

There are different kinds of potential cross-level mis-specification error, depending on whether one is seeking to explain micro-level phenomena from macro-level observations, or *vice versa*. Mouzelis (1991) sees both of these as problems of reductionism (of reducing explanation to one or the other of the two levels), and are the pitfalls of methodological individualism. One type of reductionism – *downward reductionism* – lies in erroneously explaining micro-level phenomena from macro-level observation. Here one might encounter two kinds of mis-specification error:

1 *The ecological fallacy* – that is, inferring that unobserved individual actions can be deduced from aggregate-level observations. Following Robinson's classic exposition (1950), it is possible to demonstrate logically that, say, an observed correlation between rates of lone-parent households and criminal victimisation at the macro-level does not *necessarily* mean that, within any given community, it is the lone-parent households who are being victimised more than other types of household.

2 *The contextual fallacy* – that is, what might be asserted to be contextual effects, requiring macro-level explanations, may turn out to be merely unmeasured, residual variance at the micro-level which might have disappeared had the micro-level variables been better or more comprehensively measured. For example, the capacities and abilities of families to supervise their teenaged children have not been properly measured. If they had, then the seemingly contextual effect produced by the lone-parent proportion indicator could be explained by the distribution of families with variable supervision capabilities.

Similarly, when seeking to move from micro-level evidence to macro-level explanation there is the risk of *upward reductionism* (Mouzelis 1991), again in various forms:

1 *The aggregation fallacy*. This is the opposite side of the coin from the contextual fallacy – that what might purport to be genuine contextual (macro-level) effects are merely biased aggregations of individual-level measurement. For example, in a frequently cited study, Sampson and Groves (1989) aggregate data collected from individual respondents in the British Crime Survey and, taking advantage of its sampling design, aggregate these responses together to form macro-level data on 'pseudo-communities'. Thus, they derive contextual variables – such as the presence of teenagers on the streets – from respondents' individual perceptions of neighbourhood teenagers as a problem. The risk in this approach is that the macro-level variables so constructed may compound the sampling error of the survey, leading to biased estimates of the macro-level parameters used in analysis at the macro-level; in preference, it may be better to use genuinely contextual variables about the area in which the respondents lived, derived from an independent source, such as the national Census (Osborn *et al.* 1992). Unfortunately, in this case, the Census does not contain information on the kinds of concepts of substantive significance for Sampson and Groves' (1989) analysis.

2 *The individualistic fallacy*. It follows from the aggregation fallacy that analysts may refuse to countenance that the effect of a variable observed at the individual level, or based on an individual's response, is anything

other than an attribute of the individual, in this sense, it assumes that what is important is the way that individuals interpret or respond to their environment, which can be gauged by asking or observing them, without needing to look at what it is in the environment that may be prompting, shaping or structuring their responses, nor at the role that the environment might play in mediating these influences to shape individual propensities to victimisation. In simple form, this may amount to saying that a neighbourhood crime rate is merely due to features of its population's composition, such as the number of families that fail to supervise their teenage children.

3 *The selection-compositional fallacy.* The chief threat of individual-level variance for macro-level explanation is that observed community-level variation may simply be the product of *selective population composition*, in other words, it may be that the *differential selection* of particular vulnerable individuals to certain communities may be the source of any observed community effects. Thus, systematic (macro-level) social selection processes could be the main way in which individuals with similar characteristics (such as propensity to crime victimisation) are brought together in specific spatial areas. If so, macro-level explanations would become substantively trivial or spurious, for what we might observe in the aggregate in neighbourhoods may be merely individual characteristics writ large – simply the *compositional effect* of bringing individuals together (Sampson and Lauritsen 1994). Thus, neighbourhoods with high crime rates also have high rates of lone parent households, and many other problems besides, merely because they are unpopular or undesirable so that only 'problem populations' find themselves living there, and thus express their problems, including youth crime and consequently victimisation.

While we might suspect cross-level effects in cross-sectional data, we may be able to do little to sort out the appropriate levels of analysis. This problem is compounded by the inherent, socially structured heterogeneity of the social world that renders it impossible in natural settings to 'abstract' individuals from their environments.[10] For example, Trickett, Osborn and Ellingworth (1995) estimate a multivariate statistical model of household property crime victimisation that includes both variables representing household characteristics (micro-level) and characteristics of households' area of residence, taken from the Census (macro-level). Again, pursuing our illustration of the lone-parent household, when the significant influence of area-level variables on households' likelihood of property crime victimisation is taken into account – including the separate influences of the proportions of adult residents who may be living as lone parents, single-person households, and who are adult women, alongside other socio-economic and demographic indicators – we find that lone-parent households do *not* have any greater risk of victimisation than any other type of household.

While this example could be taken as evidence that households' risk of property crime victimisation is a consequence of the social environment or context of different kinds of neighbourhood – and hence would seem to explain the apparently greater vulnerability of lone-parent households – it does not rule out a relationship between lone-parent household composition and crime rates, via social selection processes at the macro-level. Thus, using the same data, although this time aggregated to represent 'pseudo-neighbourhoods', Osborn, Trickett and Elder (1992) find not only that the proportion of lone-parent households is significantly related to area-level property crime rates but also that lone-parent households are likely to be found disproportionately in areas with other social characteristics related to crime rates, including a larger teenage/young adult population, single-adult households, and households in non-self-contained accommodation; taken together the effect of these neighbourhood characteristics is substantial. Yet, in neither analysis does the data itself explain the folowing:

1 The macro-level social-selection processes that allocate lone-parent households to particular kinds of neighbourhood.

2 Why it is that such neighbourhoods with particular social compositions have an influence on the crime rates experienced there, i.e. a contextual (structural) influence that is not reducible simply to the fact that they may contain household types or individuals prone to be involved in crime in one way or another.

Both these processes are relevant to shaping the crime victimisation rate at an observed macro-level but nevertheless involve different *movements in explanation* going from the macro-level to micro-level and back again. Thus, point (1) above, needs to explain a macro-level observation by a process that links micro-level actors (lone-parent households) to macro-level locations (neighbourhoods); while point (2) is a process that seeks to interpret a macro-level observation by collective, micro-level processes – i.e. the effect of the compositional structure of the neighbourhood upon individual actions or events (offending or victimisation). Not only do both require a theory but the resulting explanations depend upon moving between the levels of analysis. Thus, a more complete explanation requires not only explanation at each level of analysis but also *cross-level explanation* that links each level with the other in a causal sequence (Coleman 1990). Otherwise, it becomes very difficult to disentangle individual victimisation risks *produced* by environments from the *contribution* to risk that individuals make to their environments.

Understanding the data generating process

An obstacle that has stood in the way of developing aetiological understanding of crime victims on the basis of the discrete outcome approach has been the perhaps unwarranted readiness of empirical researchers to make assumptions as to the nature of the *dgp* that might underpin observed frequency distributions, and thence to interpret covariate associations as indicators of aetiology in the light of their assumptions. The discrete outcome approach naturally leads to normalising the distribution around non-victimisation and focusing explanation on deviations from that condition. While, on the one hand, research suggests that there is nothing to distinguish a subsequent hurdle (of multiple victimsation) from the primary hurdle (Osborn *et al*. 1996), there nevertheless remained an unmeasured dependency between the probability of becoming a multiple victim and that of becoming a victim at all. Additionally, this study estimated that, irrespective of initial differences in risk, once victimised, the probabilities of subsequent victimisation converged. So while there may be only one hurdle (between non-victim and victim), victimisation itself may be more of a continuous process – as indicated by the entire frequency distribution – than the discrete outcome approach allows.

As illustrated in Tables 3.1 and 3.2, the discrete outcome approach recognises one part of the distribution – the preponderance of non-victimisation – that would seem common to all observed victimisation distributions, including interpersonal violence (Table 3.1) and domestic violence (Table 3.2). Yet it ignores the second consistent element of the distribution – the high frequency of victimisation of the apparent minority of 'multiple victims'. Although these frequency rates differ between crime types – with property crime at one end of the spectrum and domestic violence at the other – the survey data nevertheless suggest a common pattern of multiple victimisation, ranging from a fifth of victims of burglary to around three-quarters of victims of domestic violence. Yet while the assumption of deviation from normality inherent in the concept of exposure might fit common-sense explanations of household property crime – committed apparently by predatory strangers – they hardly fit common-sense understandings of acquaintance and domestic violence – committed by familiars who are party to a routine relationship, with *persistent frequency* of risk over time.

Not surprisingly, from the outset, victimology has seen a polarisation between explanations of property crime, on the one hand, and domestic violence, on the other; interpersonal violence has had an uneasy position between them, splitting primarily on the fact of the prior relationship between the two parties, resting on a distinction between 'stranger' and 'acquaintance'. While the discrete outcome empirical model has suited quantitative survey-based methods, the study of domestic violence has proceeded primarily on the basis of qualitative methods. Similarly, the discrete outcome model focuses exclusively on issues of *onset* – why people become victims, and completely ignores issues of *process*, including the duration of victimisation experience and its cessation (see Miethe and Meier 1994). In contrast, the latter are of paramount interest in the victimology of domestic violence. Issues of onset are at best irrelevant and at worst inappropriate, since domestic violence is a condition that develops *after* the 'onset' of a relationship. Ostensibly, different normative counterfactuals apply: in the case of domestic burglary, it is the expectation of privacy and protection from trespass that underpin property norms (Hope, 1999); in the case of domestic violence, it is the social and cultural norms of intimate human relationships.

Yet the empirical similarity of all observed crime victimisation distributions (Tables 3.1 and 3.2) suggests that there might be a common data generating process uniting all forms of crime victimisation. Conceptually, what would be required for a general theory to express the commonality of the crime victimisation data generating process would be to bring the respective counterfactual conditions into common alignment. Yet, since it is both archaic and unacceptable to apply the norms of property relations to the conduct of interpersonal relationships,[11] the only possible strategy to unite the two empirical traditions of victimology is to apply the norms of personal relationships to the explanation of property crime and 'stranger' victimisation, especially to consider issues of victimisation duration and cessation, which have been central the study of domestic violence.

The conceptual strategy that would need to be applied to property crime would be to mimic more precisely the 'relational' or processual characteristics found in the phenomenology of domestic violence. Two broad strategies are possible: first, to focus on the duration of victimisation. Central to this line of enquiry is whether there could exist a property of *contagion* between victimisation events – that is, that the probability of one event influences the probability of subsequent events. This is the case in domestic violence where violence becomes established in a relationship and may escalate in severity as a result of repetition. A second strategy is to focus particularly on the conditions that lead to *immunity* – both those things that lead to the cessation of victimisation once it has started, for instance by removing victims to a place of refuge, as well as those things that inhibit it from starting in the first place – which in the case of violence means addressing factors leading men to perpetrate violence in relationships.

However, the specialism of victimology (as distinct from criminology) suggests that the focus remains upon *individual victims and their specific time-space locations and trajectories*. Part of the confusion that has grown up recently has been a result of shifting the focus away from the specific perspective of victims. For example, an interest in repeat victimisation can include an interest in working out relationships between victimisation *incidents*, particularly from a crime prevention perspective. Such studies may be concerned with whether there is any contagion between incidents occurring among neighbouring properties (e.g. Townsley *et al*. 2003), or within residential areas (Morgan 2001). Similarly, some (perhaps most) studies of repeat victimisation are concerned primarily to study the target-selection activities of *offenders*, again with a concern to intervene in these activities to reduce crime, again defined as consisting of the quantity of incidents (Pease 1998; 1993; Farrell and Pease 1993). Yet these interests tend to divert attention away from exploring the *position and agency of the victim*, who remains a passive 'host' to these phenomena which are, strictly speaking, occurrences emanating from their external environment. But notwithstanding the conceptual and moral difficulties of introducing the concept of victims' agency in their victimisation (see elsewhere in this volume), the aetiological analysis of victims necessarily requires some notion of victims' agency, particularly how victims *interact* with their environments. In so doing, it may be possible to move beyond the normative and explanatory inadequacies of the discrete outcome model of exposure to risk (Walklate 1997).

True contagion

Many instances of count data, like those of crime victimisation (Table 3.1 and 3.2), are characterised by over-dispersion. The standard parametric model used to account for over-dispersion is the *negative binomial model* (Cameron and Trivedi 1998), which Nelson found to have an 'astoundingly good fit' to the observed sample distribution of crime victimisation (1980: 872). Yet, despite its empirical robustness, the negative binomial model is theoretically ambiguous since its assumptions can support a variety of probability mechanisms that might be producing the data generating process (*dgp*).[12] Because of this, although multivariate regression models based on the negative binomial distribution can be used to estimate the predictors of the distribution of crime victimisation by allowing for over-dispersion (Osborn and Tseloni 1998; Tseloni 2006), there is not a unique specification of the *dgp* for the negative binomial model and hence the problem of identifying a general specification of the distribution of crime victimisation remains unresolved.

There are two archetypical processes producing over-dispersion in count data (Cameron and Trivedi 1998): first, a dynamic dependence between the occurrence of successive events which are reported by each respondent – what is termed here as *event-dependency*. Event-dependency can be regarded as an instance of *true contagion* between victimisation experiences. The hypothetical illustration often used is where crime victimisation events occur over time in a *series* against a target (or victim) because they are committed by the same person, who returns to the scene on a number of occasions because he or she is attracted to the target in some way (Farrell *et al.* 1995). A second source of over-dispersion in the observed sample distribution is where there is unmeasured variability in *a priori* risk between respondents that affects the observed distribution in a systematic way – what is termed here as *risk-heterogeneity*. For example, two households reporting different frequencies of victimisation may possess different characteristics, signifying differential risk or vulnerability, that render them *differentially prone* to being victimised. This interpretation conforms more to the assumptions of the risk-exposure model. Thus, any repetition of victimisation over time for any individual may merely indicate separate occurrences (even if these consist of separate series or spells of victimisation occurrences) of a stable and persistent risk. Crucially, in the risk-heterogeneity interpretation, incidents occur randomly over time with no direct link between one incident and the next.

As Pease (1998) helpfully puts it, the repeat victimisation of a person or household over time may serve either as a *flag* for a stable probability of victimisation risk or indicate that victimisation events can serve to *boost* the likelihood of subsequent events over and above chance. Yet merely aggregating risk occurrences across heterogeneous individuals can yield an *apparent* contagion effect which is indistinguishable in cross-sectional data from the effect produced as if true contagion (event dependency) existed. So, despite the fit yielded by the negative binomial distribution, the underlying *dgp* cannot be identified, nor can true contagion (event-dependency), using only cross-sectional data (Cameron and Trivedi 1998). Both Nelson (1980) and (Sparks 1981) rejected as implausible the idea that true contagion characterised the *dgp* since this would mean, contrary to the risk-exposure model, that everyone faced the same *a priori* risk. Nelson (1980) substantiated this recommendation by showing that the correlates of victimisation differed very little whether one used individual probabilities (i.e. whether a person will experience one or more victimisations over the recall period) or rates (the individual frequency-rate of victimisation over the period).

Nevertheless, theoretically, the negative binomial distribution is capable of accommodating different *mixtures* of flag and boost processes (Cameron and Trivedi 1998). In particular, the hypothesis that victimisation is repeated by virtue of event-dependency has been justified more recently by arguments in terms of 'routine situational risk-transmission' (Hope *et al.* 2001), primarily by hypothesising that revictimisation is a consequence of revisits by the same offender or his/her direct associates over the short term (Farrell *et al.* 1995). In this, there is an attempt to incorporate elements of true contagion into the risk-exposure model. As Pease (see also Farrell *et al.* 1995) puts it:

> the key reasons for repeats are ... the presence of good, and lack of bad, consequences of the first crime for the offender, and the stability of the situation which presents itself to an offender on the first and subsequent visits to the scene of his or her crime. (Pease 1998: 6)

Two pieces of evidence are often cited as suggestive of the existence of true contagion: first, analysis of aggregate recorded crime data appears to suggest a short time-period between offences, if they repeat (Polvi *et al.* 1990);[13] and second, *series offences* comprise a very large proportion of offences reported by victims to the British Crime Survey (Chenery *et al.* 1996).[14] The emphasis on short-term, event-dependent repetition lends itself congenially to the application of immediate situational control methods of crime prevention (Laycock 2001; Pease 1998).

Osborn and Tseloni (1998) were able to estimate a multivariate negative binomial model for the whole frequency distribution of household property crimes using British Crime Survey (BCS) data with the assumption that over-dispersion arises through unexplained risk-heterogeneity. Using *a priori* risk factors identified from their model, they were able to predict the probabilities for the various frequency levels of victimisation observed in the data. Comparisons of predictions from the negative binomial model were made with predictions derived from a simple Poisson model: for low levels of predicted *a priori* victimisation risk, the two distributions gave very similar results. However, for higher risk levels, the negative binomial model diverged from the Poisson model, more closely resembling the observed distribution of crime victimisation, with fewer victims than under a Poisson assumption but correspondingly more multiple-victim households (Osborn and Tseloni 1998: 325), and suggesting a much better fit. They conclude that 'our models indicate that crime is more concentrated [on multiple victims] than random events would predict ... the effect of this concentration is most marked for those whose household and area characteristics make them most vulnerable' (1998: 328).

Nevertheless, despite further model refinement (Tseloni 2006), the use of negative binomial regression methods cannot *prove* the presence of true contagion. That is to say, it does not imply that multiple victims are 'repeat' victims, in the sense that each event is dependent upon prior events. If anything, the reverse is more likely, since the model specification utilised in applications to date tests specifically for risk-heterogeneity and relegates any possible contagion effects to residual error.[15] Even so, the limitations of cross-sectional data also limit efforts to test properly for the existence of event-dependency, in practice. While modelling refinements, such as those introduced by Tseloni (2006), can help further to identify the extent of risk-heterogeneity – for instance, by estimating the degree of unmeasured heterogeneity – by the same token they reduce further the possibility of event-dependency. Thus, while considerable confidence can be had that the distribution of crime victimisation fits the negative binomial model, less can be said as to which generalisation of the model is the most appropriate description of the underlying process generating the distribution, even though the success of the risk-heterogeneity version to date reduces support for true event-dependent (i.e. repeat victimisation) contagion (Tseloni and Pease 2003).

Vulnerability

Nevertheless, even if there may be no event-dependent link between incidents, that does not mean that the occurrence of events are not related, though the mechanism linking them may reside in the biography or life-course of the victim – including relationships with others – rather than intrinsically in the victimisation events themselves (Hope *et al.* 2001). Risk-transmission via the life-course becomes more persuasive when incidents are contextualised as part of people's lives – for example, when they reoccur over the longer term, or reoccur in variant or generic situations, or are clearly part of a long-term life-course attribute, such as a cohabiting relationship. In a 'life-course' explanation, the 'carrier' of risk is the victim. People might become vulnerable to crime victimisation by virtue of some predisposing risk factors acquired early on, which renders them abnormally and persistently vulnerable to being victimised during their subsequent life-course.[16] This view of vulnerability, however, lends itself too readily to the reification of unwarranted and immeasurable traits such as victim-proneness, which logically must precede any instance of victimisation, must constitute a prior cause of subsequent victimisation but which must not be defined by reference to them. Here, again, problems are raised by the difficulty in deciding upon what would be an appropriate counterfactual condition for life-course victim vulnerability.

Immunity

In preference, the continuing occurrence of incidents that persistently instantiate the victims' vulnerability may eventually become part of victims' biographies. Regular experiences of victimisation may shape their life-course to such a degree that crime victimisation itself becomes part of the 'normal' pattern of their everyday lives (Genn 1988). These patterns may then continue into the future, unless and until something happens to *rupture* the expected life-course – for example, the abused woman leaves the abusive relationship, or the victimised household moves to a safer neighbourhood. Yet while they remain in such victimising circumstances, victims will simply continue to experience victimisation, the frequency of which is largely in the hands of offenders. So, while the concept of risk-exposure has been deployed to account for the onset of crime victimisation, the possibility of life-course persistence (duration) calls, in turn, for an explanation also of the *cessation* of victimisation.

Hope and Trickett (2004) propose an *immunity model* to explain the *dgp* driving the observed micro-level frequency distribution. Rather than see 'repeat victimisation' as a consequence of excessive selective exposure to crime risk – primarily selection by prolific offenders (Pease 1998) – frequent (multiple) victimisation could also reflect certain victims' *inability to remove themselves from risk*, by virtue of their relative powerlessness to change their life circumstances. In support of the concept of *powerlessness*, Hope *et al.* (2001) found that multiple crime type victims experienced also other forms of social vulnerability – such as suffering a domestic fire in the past two years (also a rare occurrence) – and were also more likely to be younger adults, living with children, renting from the local (social) housing authority and living in poorer, urban areas. Thus multiple victims shared many of the social characteristics of economically marginal social groups – sectors of society that are also likely to suffer other misfortunes, including ill health.

Yet, unlike many forms of ill health, the source of crime victimisation risk (i.e. motivated offenders) comes primarily from victims' environments. Thus very vulnerable residents in high-risk environments continue to be victimised because they are unable to attain immunity – that is, to remove or protect themselves from risk within those environments. Rather than being selected specifically for repeat victimisation on the basis of prior victimisation (Pease 1998), victims in these environments may only *appear* to have a non-random probability of repeat crime victimisation over time because they are more likely to remain unprotected in an environment where the probability of victimisation itself remains high and constant. Their contagiousness is apparent rather than true. In contrast, those who have attained 'immunity' by virtue of their removal from risk have a censored (negative) exposure to crime risk – that is, they are no longer eligible for selection as victims and thus unavailable to register at higher frequency levels. Thus, while repeat victims do not possess any additional risk factors that mark out their excessive risk (Osborn *et al.* 1996), their continued vulnerability may indicate an (as yet unmeasured) incapacity to remove themselves from risk; while the category of non-victims may mask a variety of types of immunity, again unmeasured.[17] As such, powerlessness to avoid the probability of exposure may allow the conceptualisation of negative values of risk that are missing from the more positive conception of exposure discussed above.

As described in most of its technical reports, the Primary Sampling Unit (PSU) of the BCS (however it has been defined) is a *nested cluster sample* of respondents living in close, spatial proximity to each other. From these it is

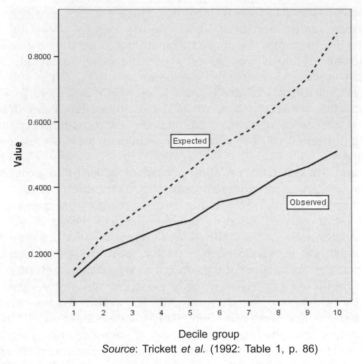

Decile group
Source: Trickett *et al.* (1992: Table 1, p. 86)

Figure 3.1 Observed and expected prevalence – household property crime victimisation.

possible to aggregate individual responses according to the strata and clusters present within the BCS sampling structure – for instance, to form 'pseudo-neighbourhoods' based on such clusters. Trickett *et al.* (1992) estimated expected prevalence from observed prevalence rates, over the deciles of the distribution of pseudo-neighbourhood crime victimisation rates for both personal and household property crime victimisation. As illustrated in Figure 3.1, observed prevalence rates differed significantly from that expected, over all decile groups, though dramatically so in higher rate areas.[18]

Their analysis implied that significantly *fewer* people are victimised than would be anticipated if the chance of crime victimisation was distributed randomly amongst the population. Yet neither is this likely to be random selection: while the disparity described in Figure 3.1 has been interpreted as evidence of excessive exposure of a minority of people (repeat victims), it can also be seen just as easily as indicating a non-random prevalence of immunity (i.e. non-victimisation) among other residents. Thus 'what is different about high crime areas' is not only non-random repeat victimisation but also non-random immunity. The possible non-random co-presence of *both* immune and chronic groups within the same risk-producing environment has not hitherto greatly influenced either theory or policy. Even so, it is possible that the social environment of any high crime community may be composed at any one time of a *segmented order* comprising *both* the extremely vulnerable and the highly immune. The resulting neighbourhood risk environment may reflect the outcome of 'conflicting forces' of exposure and immunity – a process documented during a crime reduction 'experiment' in Hope and Foster (1992)

– resulting in a particular macro-level pattern of crime-flux (Hope 1995) and a distinctive micro-level frequency distribution.

Very little is known about either the varieties of immunity or the forms of relationship between immune and victimised groups or, needless to say, how these relationships shape the data generating process of observed crime victimisation distributions. Some people, e.g. the elderly, may be immune because they are never exposed to risk, or because of moral inhibition (see Clarke *et al.* 1985). Some may be immune to victimisation because they are themselves offenders, or members of family networks, capable of retribution should they be attacked. And some people may be victimised excessively because they do not conform to the prevailing culture, or because they 'stand out' in some way (Walklate and Evans 1999). In any event, detailed ethnography reveals a variegated, micro-social pattern of group relations, social networks and contrasting cultures that warns against reliance upon a 'black box' conceptualisation of the environment of crime victimisation.[19] Whatever the conceptualisation, it seems likely that all victims have *relationships* of one kind or another with the sources of their victimisation risk, even if these are not intimate or identifiable.

Conclusion

Crime victimisation is conceptualised as a phenomenon that is embedded in everyday life. 'Victims' are members of populations in society and experience victimisation while being 'normal'. Nevertheless, the empirical study of crime victims, especially derived from population sample surveys, has suffered from the illusion of actuality fostered by the 'real' and 'normal' appearance of these data. It is not as though such data were not real themselves nor that they do not represent real phenomena but that the embeddedness of victimisation in everyday life makes it hard, if not impossible, to *abstract* crime victimisation so that its true causes and processes might be observed. Victimisation is defined by its observed actual occurrence which makes it impossible to observe the data generating processes that underlie the production of these observations, including continuous processes of risk that might be inherent in victimisation. And it is also impossible to observe the counterfactual conditions that give meaning to the factual condition of crime victimisation. In sum, we are hindered in explanation because we cannot observe non-victimisation in the same way that we observe victimisation and we cannot therefore observe the complete manifestation of the phenomenon.

Nevertheless, the positive perspective has dominated empirical work, leading analysts too readily to interpret observations as positive evidence of crime victimisation – especially, that crime victimisation is a product of exposure to abnormal risk, and that victims deviate from the normal condition. Yet efforts to apply statistical models to the data reveal problems and difficulties with the approach, in part because positive data are being used to prove the normal condition – non-victimisation – which, paradoxically, is defined by its absence, or as an unobservable negative. It may be impossible to overcome the limits to observing the data generating process of crime victimisation.

Operational research efforts to abstract victimisation from everyday life risk both selection bias and artificiality. But equally so does unreflexive 'realism' based on direct observation. The only viable research strategy, then, is to work with the observations of crime victimisation that we are able to gather but to approach these in a fundamentally reflexive and hypothetical manner. And this requires careful attention to how we frame and test our hypotheses, not just about the facts of victimisation that we can observe but also about the necessary counterfactuals, which we must infer.

Further reading

Many of the sources for this chapter are contained in the References, though these tend to be in the form of rather technical academic journal articles. Somewhat dated books concerning analyses of victimisation survey data include: R.F. Sparks, H. Genn, and D. Dodd (1997) *Surveying Victims*. London: John Wiley; M.S. Hindelang, M. Gottfredson and J. Garofalo (1978) *Victims of Violent Crime*. Cambridge, MA: Ballinger; and T.D. Miethe and R.F. Meier (1994) *Crime and its Social Context*. Albany, NY: SUNY Press. A useful textbook, again somewhat dated, is C. Coleman and J. Moynihan (1996) *Understanding Crime Data*. Buckingham: Open University Press.

More recent overview chapters on crime surveys are: P. Mayhew (2000) 'Researching the State of Crime: Local, National and International Victim Surveys' in R.D. King and E. Wincup (eds) *Doing Research on Crime and Justice*. Oxford: Oxford University Press; and T. Hope (2005) 'What Do Crime Statistics Tell Us?', in C. Hale, K. Hayward, A. Wahidin and E. Wincup (eds) *Criminology*. Oxford: Oxford University Press.

Details about the British Crime Survey can be found in annual reports published in the Home Office Statistical Bulletin series (http://www.homeoffice.gov.uk/rds/pubsstatistical.html). Information on the social and political context of crime victimisation surveys in Britain can be found in *Crime Statistics: User Perspectives*, Statistics Commission Report No. 30, London: Statistics Commission, 2006 (www.statscom.org.uk).

Recent reviews of research, focusing particularly on issues concerning repeat victimisation include: K. Pease (1998) *Repeat Victimisation: Taking Stock*, Crime Detection and Prevention Series Paper 90. London: Home Office; and A. Tseloni, D.R. Osborn, A. Trickett and K. Pease (2002) 'Modelling property crime using the British Crime Survey: What have we learnt?', *British Journal of Criminology*, 42: 109–28.

Finally, a primer on some of the statistical analysis issues touched on in this chapter can be found in A.C. Cameron and P.K. Trivedi. (1998) *Regression Analysis of Count Data* 1998 (Cambridge: Cambridge University Press).

Notes

1 Counterfactual theories of causation have emerged as (arguably) a more useful way of conceptualising causation than the traditional Humean empirical regularity approach, particularly for observable phenomena. As Menzies (2001) puts it, the basic idea of counterfactual theories is that 'the meaning of a singular causal claim of the form "Event c caused event e" can be explained in terms of counterfactual conditionals of the form "If c had not occurred, e would not have occurred"' (Menzies 2001). Increasing interest in, and use of, counterfactual reasoning is occurring, for example, in the cognate fields of epidemiology (e.g. Maldano and

Greenland 2002), micro-econometrics (Heckman 2001), quantitative sociology (e.g. Harding 2003) and, recently, criminology (Sampson *et al.* 2006).

2 For example, no hereditable proneness to crime victimisation has yet been identified.

3 Presumably due to the point made above, that much data is collected for other primary purposes, for example, in the case of national victimisation surveys such as the British Crime Survey, to estimate annual (cross-sectional) prevalence and incidence rates for its jurisdiction (England and Wales).

4 For example, competition for questionnaire space with apparently more 'policy-relevant' variables.

5 Specifically, national victimisation surveys such as the British Crime Survey (BCS) sample representative adult populations of permanent residence, in the case of the BCS, respondents are aged 16 years or over and answer questions about themselves and their households. Respondents are selected using a complex multi-stage sample design and are interviewed in person using Computer Assisted Personal Interviewing (CAPI) techniques.

6 Referred to in the econometrics literature as 'discrete choice' models.

7 '… the probability that a violation will occur at any specific time and place might be taken as a function of the convergence of likely offenders and suitable targets in the absence of capable guardians' (Cohen and Felson 1979: 59).

8 Marsh (1982) disparages such an approach as 'face-sheet sociology'.

9 These could either be similar to or different from hypothetical unmeasured differences distinguishing generally victims from non-victims. These possibilities have been explored recently using US National Crime Victimisation Survey data by Tseloni and Pease (2003).

10 Which are further compounded by the problems of 'experimentation' noted above.

11 Indeed, this has been the paramount project of feminist victimology.

12 Cameron and Trivedi (1998: 102) cite 13 distinct stochastic mechanisms.

13 Although this assumption has been questioned by employment of alternative stochastic models (Spellman 1995).

14 A 'series offence' is defined in the British Crime Survey by respondents answering the question 'Were any of these very similar incidents, when the same thing was done under the same circumstances and probably by the same people?'

15 i.e. implementation as a risk-heterogeneity model – a characterisation of the Negative Binomial as a Poisson-gamma mixture (Cameron and Trivedi 1998; Tseloni 2006; Osborn and Tseloni 1998).

16 Of course, this approach has been adopted by developmental perspectives on offending.

17 This interpretation is consistent with a compound-Poisson specification of the negative binomial distribution (Cameron and Trivedi 1998) which has been found via multivariate modelling to have both a good fit to the micro-level distribution (Osborn and Tseloni 1998), and to indicate substantial unmeasured risk-heterogeneity in the population (Tseloni 2006).

18 This finding was replicated using data from the 1988 BCS (Trickett *et al.* 1995).

19 See Merry (1981); Foster and Hope (1993); Walklate and Evans (1999).

References

Cameron, A.C. and Trivedi, P.K. (1998) *Regression Analysis of Count Data*. Cambridge: Cambridge University Press.

Chenery, S., Ellingworth, D., Tseloni, A. and Pease, K. (1996) 'Crimes which repeat: Undigested evidence from the British Crime Survey 1992', *International Journal of Risk, Security and Crime Prevention*, 1: 207–16.

Clarke, R.V.G., Eckblom, P., Hough M. and Mayhew, P. (1985) 'Elderly victims of crime and exposure to risk', *Howard Journal*, 24: 1–9.

Cohen, L.E. and Felson, M. (1979) 'Social change and crime rate trends: A routine activities approach', *American Sociological Review*, 44: 588–608.

Cohen, L.E., Kluegel, J.R. and Land, K.C. (1981) 'Social inequality and predatory criminal victimization: An exposition and test of a formal theory', *American Sociological Review* 46: 505–24.

Coleman, J.S. (1990) *Foundations of Social Theory*. Cambridge, MA: Belknap Press.

Ellingworth, D., Farrell, G. and Pease, K. (1995) 'A victim is a victim is a victim? Chronic victimisation in four sweeps of the British Crime Survey', *British Journal of Criminology*, 35: 360–5.

Farrell, G. and Pease, K. (1993) *Once Bitten, Twice Bitten: Repeat Victimisation and its Implications for Crime Prevention*, Crime Prevention Unit Paper 46. London: Home Office.

Farrell, G., Phillips, C. and Pease, K. (1995) 'Like taking candy: Why does repeat victimisation occur?' *British Journal of Criminology*, 35: 384–99.

Foster, J. and Hope, T. (1993) *Housing, Community and Crime: The Impact of the Priority Estates Project*, Home Office Research Study 131. London: HMSO.

Genn, H. (1988) 'Multiple Victimisation', in M. Maguire and J. Ponting (eds) *Victims of Crime: A New Deal*. Milton Keynes: Open University Press.

Harding, D.J. (2003) 'Counterfactual models of neighbourhood effects: The effect of neighbourhood poverty on dropping out and teenage pregnancy', *American Journal of Sociology*, 109: 676–719.

Heckman, J. (2001) 'Microdata, heterogeneity, and the evaluation of public policy: Nobel Lecture'. *Journal of Political Economy*, 109: 673–748.

Hernán, M.A. and Robins, J.M. (2006) 'Estimating causal effects from epidemiological data', *J. Epidemiol. Community Health*, 60, 578–86.

Hindelang, M.S., Gottfredson, M. and J. Garofalo (1978) *Victims of Violent Crime*. Cambridge, MA: Ballinger.

Hope, T. (1995) 'The flux of victimisation', *British Journal of Criminology*, 35(3): 327–42.

Hope, T. (1999). 'Privatopia on Trial? Property Guardianship in the Suburbs', in K. Painter and N. Tiley (eds) *Surveillance of Public Space: CCTV, Street Lighting and Crime Prevention*. New York: Criminal Justice Press.

Hope, T. (2000) 'Inequality and the Clubbing of Private Security', in T. Hope and R. Sparks (eds) *Crime, Risk and Insecurity*. London: Routledge.

Hope, T. (2001) 'Crime Victimisation and Inequality in Risk Society', in R. Matthews and J. Pitts (eds) *Crime Prevention, Disorder and Community Safety*. London: Routledge.

Hope, T. (2005) 'What do crime statistics tell us?', in C. Hale, K. Hayward, A. Wahidin and E. Wincup (eds) *Criminology*. Oxford: Oxford University Press.

Hope, T. and Foster J. (1992) 'Conflicting forces: Changing the dynamics of crime and community on a "problem" estate', *British Journal of Criminology*, 32(4): 488–504.

Hope, T. and Trickett, A. (2004) 'La distribution de la victimation dans la population', *Déviance et Société*, 28(3): 385–404.

Hope, T. Bryan, J. Osborn, D. and Trickett, A. (2001) 'The phenomena of multiple victimisation: The relationship between personal and property crime risk', *British Journal of Criminology*, 41: 595–617.

Lauritsen, J.L. and Laub, J.H. (2006) 'Understanding the Link between Victimisation and Offending: New Reflections on an Old Idea', paper presented at the colloquium

'The British Crime Survey: Past and Present', Cumberland Lodge, Windsor Great Park, October.

Laycock, G. (2001) 'Hypothesis-based research: The repeat victimization story', *Criminology and Criminal Justice*, 1: 59–82.

Maldano, G. and Greenland, S. (2002) 'Estimating causal effects', *International Journal of Epidemiology*, 31: 422–9.

Marsh, C. (1982) *The Survey Method*. London: Allen and Unwin.

Mawby, R.I. and Walklate, S. (1994) *Critical Victimology: International Perspectives*. London: Sage.

Maxfield, M.G. (1987) 'Household composition, routine activity and victimization: A comparative analysis', *Journal of Quantitative Criminology*, 3: 301–20.

Mayhew, P. (2000) 'Researching the State of Crime: Local, National and International Victim Surveys', in R.D. King and E. Wincup (eds) *Doing Research on Crime and Justice*. Oxford: Oxford University Press.

Merry, S.E. (1981) *Urban Danger: Life in a Neighborhood of Strangers*. Philadelphia, PA: Temple University Press.

Menzies, P. (2001) 'Counterfactual Theories of Causation', *Stanford Encyclopedia of Philosophy*, http://plato.stanford.edu/entries/causation-counterfactual/ (accessed 10 August 2006).

Miethe, T.D. and McDowall, D. (1993) 'Contextual effects in models of criminal victimisation', *Social Forces*, 71: 741–59.

Miethe, T.D and Meier, R.F. (1994) *Crime and its Social Context*. Albany, NY: SUNY Press.

Morgan, F. (2001) 'Repeat Burglary in a Perth Suburb: Indicator of Short-term or Long-term Risk'? in G. Farrell and K. Pease (eds) *Repeat Victimization*. Monsey, NY: Criminal Justice Press, (Crime Prevention Studies, 12, 83–118).

Mouzelis, N. (1991) *Back to Sociological Theory: The Construction of Social Orders*. Basingstoke: Macmillan.

Nelson, J.F. (1980) 'Multiple victimization in American cities: A statistical analysis of rare events', *American Journal of Sociology*, 85: 870–91.

Osborn, D.R. and Tseloni, A. (1998) 'The distribution of household property crimes', *Journal of Quantitative Criminology*, 14: 307–30.

Osborn, D.R., Ellingworth, D. Hope, T. and Trickett, A. (1996) 'Are multiply victimized households different?', *Journal of Quantitative Criminology*, 12(2): 223–45.

Osborn, D.R., Trickett, A. and Elder, R. (1992) 'Area characteristics and regional variates as determinants of area property crime levels', *Journal of Quantitative Criminology*, 8: 265–85.

Pease, K. (1993) 'Individual and Community Influences on Victimisation and Their Implications for Crime Prevention', in D.P. Farrington, R.J. Sampson and P-O.H. Wikstrom (eds) *Integrating Individual and Ecological Aspects of Crime*, BRÅ-Report 1. Stockholm: National Council for Crime Prevention.

Pease, K. (1998) *Repeat Victimisation: Taking Stock*, Crime Detection and Prevention Series Paper 90. London: Home Office.

Polvi, N., Looman, T., Humphries, C. and Pease, K. (1990) 'Repeat break and enter victimisation: Time course and crime prevention opportunity', *Journal of Police Science and Administration*, 17: 8–11.

Robinson, W.S. (1950) 'Ecological correlations and the behavior of individuals', *American Sociological Review*, 15: 351–7.

Russell, B. (1946/2005) *History of Western Philosophy*. London and New York: Routledge Classics.

Sampson, R.J. (1985) 'Neighborhood and crime: The structural determinants of personal victimisation', *Journal of Research in Crime and Delinquency*, 22: 7–40.

Sampson, R.J. and Groves, B.W. (1989) 'Community structure and crime: Testing social disorganisation theory', *American Journal of Sociology*, 94: 774–802.

Sampson, R.J. and Lauritsen, J.L. (1990) 'Deviant lifestyles, proximity to crime, and the offender–victim link in personal violence', *Journal of Research in Crime and Delinquency*, 27: 110–39.

Sampson, R.J and Lauritsen, J.L. (1994) 'Violent Victimisation and Offending: Individual-, Situational-, and Community-level Risk Factors', in A.J. Reiss and J.A. Roth (eds) *Understanding and Preventing Violence: Volume 3 Social Influences:* Washington DC: National Academy Press.

Sampson, R.J., Laub, J.H. and Wimer, C. (2006) 'Does marriage reduce crime? A counterfactual approach to within-individual causal effects', *Criminology*, 44: 465–508.

Simmons, J. and Dodd, T. (2003) *Crime in England and Wales 2002/03*, Home Office Statistical Bulletin, HOSB 07/03. London: Home Office.

Smith, D.A. and Jarjoura, R. (1989) 'Household characteristics, neighborhood composition and victimization risk', *Social Forces*, 68: 621–40.

Sparks, R.F. (1981) 'Multiple victimization: evidence, theory and future research', *Journal of Criminal Law and Criminology*, 72: 762–88.

Sparks, R.F., Genn, H. and Dodd, D. (1977) *Surveying Victims*. London: John Wiley.

Spellman, W. (1995) 'Once bitten, then what? Cross-sectional and time-course explanations of repeat victimisation', *British Journal of Criminology*, 35: 366–83.

Townsley, M., Homel, R. and Chaseling, J. (2003) 'Infectious burglaries: A test of the near repeat hypothesis', *British Journal of Criminology*, 43: 615–33.

Trickett, A., Osborn, D.R. and Ellingworth, D. (1995) 'Property crime victimisation: The roles of individual and area influences', *International Review of Victimology*, 3: 273–295.

Trickett, A., Osborn, D.R., Seymour, J. and Pease, K. (1992) 'What is different about high crime areas?', *British Journal of Criminology*, 32: 81–9.

Tseloni, A. (1995) 'The Modelling of Threat Incidence: Evidence from the British Crime Survey', in R.E. Dobash, R.P. Dobash and L. Noaks (eds) *Gender and Crime*. Cardiff: University of Wales Press.

Tseloni, A. (2006) 'Multi-level modelling of the number of property crimes: Household and area effects', *Journal of the Royal Statistical Society, Series A*, 169: 205–33.

Tseloni, A. and Pease, K. (2003) 'Repeat personal victimization: 'boosts' or 'flags?', *British Journal of Criminology*, 43: 196–212.

Tseloni, A., Osborn, D.R., Trickett, A. and Pease, K. (2002) 'Modelling property crime using the British Crime Survey: What have we learnt?', *British Journal of Criminology*, 42: 109–28.

Walby, S. and Allen, J. (2004) *Domestic Violence, Sexual Assault and Stalking: Findings from the 2001 British Crime Survey*, Home Office Research Study 276. London: Home Office.

Walklate, S. (1997) 'Risk and criminal victimisation – a modernist dilemma?', *British Journal of Criminology*, 37: 15–34.

Walklate, S. and Evans, K. (1999) *Zero Tolerance or Community Tolerance?* Aldershot: Ashgate.

Chapter 4

Crime, victimisation and vulnerability

Simon Green

Introduction

The aim of this chapter is to strike a balance between a descriptive overview of what is known about victims and vulnerability and an analysis of how social conditions can be used to explain the way in which we have come to think about these two concepts. The objective is to construct an argument that demonstrates how victimisation and vulnerability have been socially constructed to serve political and economic interests. The purpose of doing this is to explain why it is that despite the research evidence very little time is spent addressing victimisation among the group most at risk: the heavily offending, young, male, economically disadvantaged. It will be argued that this is because debates and policies around victims and vulnerability are neither neutral nor independent from wider ideological and economic interests. An analysis of these interests is used to reconsider what is meant by both the 'ideal' victim (Christie 1986) and the concept of vulnerability.

The ideal victim has been typically understood as the 'deserving' victim and is encapsulated by notions of the sort of victim that evokes our sympathies and in whose name victim services are justified (Spalek 2006). Christie (1986) argues that this idealisation provides an image of the victim, and correspondingly the offender, which is out of kilter with messy social realities. Victims are not always entirely good, and offenders not always entirely bad. The ideal victim represents an abstraction of what it is to be a victim. For Christie (1986) the ideal victim is a person who is weak, respectable, blameless, unconnected to the offender and able to command just enough power to establish their identity as an ideal victim. (The importance of this concept is reiterated in the chapters by Davies and Whyte in this volume.) Yet Christie's (1986) construction of the ideal victim is one firmly located in the attributes of the victim themselves. Idealness is therefore a presentation of the personal qualities and circumstances individuals, or possibly social groupings, find themselves in. This construction is clearly still both valid and instructive when thinking about victimisation. Yet 20 years after Christie's

(1986) original work, there is a need to consider the social and economic conditions that both shape and provide meaning to what is understood by an ideal victim. Hence, this chapter attempts to develop Christie's (1986) ideal victim by looking at the social conditions and processes that define certain characteristics as ideal.

The many meanings of vulnerability

Vulnerability appears to have a somewhat varied history when considered in relation to criminal victimisation. The concept has rarely been explored in its own right, its meaning and application generally considered in relation to the fear of crime (for example, Hale 1996; Killeas 1990; Killeas and Clerici 2000). Killeas (1990) provides a useful taxonomy of vulnerability which explores physical, social and situational components; which, while still located within a wider discussion of the fear of crime, at least manages to begin a discussion about what might constitute the different aspects of vulnerability. His inclusion of physical, social and situational factors clearly demonstrates an appreciation that vulnerability is both internal and external to the individual. A sense of vulnerability is shaped by the conditions of existence, whether they are biographical, environmental or cultural.

Vulnerability is often used to express the level of risk posed to certain groups or individuals. The more vulnerable a person is the more at risk they are of victimisation. It can also be used to refer to the level of harm we are likely to suffer when we are victimised. The greater the impact and consequences of victimisation the more vulnerable a person is. Hence vulnerability can be measured on two axis, risk and harm. This would mean that those individuals least likely to be victimised and most capable to cope with victimisation are the least vulnerable, whereas those most at risk and least capable to cope with harm caused would be the most vulnerable. If these two variables of vulnerability were plotted on an axis they would look like Figure 4.1.

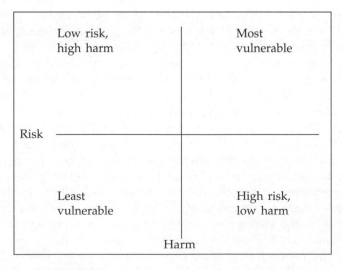

Figure 4.1 Axis of vulnerability

Figure 4.1 demonstrates that using risk and harm as the two prime measures of vulnerability every person can conceivably be plotted on this axis. Given the established wisdom gleaned from over two decades of the British Crime Survey some social groups could be plotted on these axes. Young men would find themselves in the low harm, high risk corner, whereas the elderly might find themselves in the low risk, high harm space. The least vulnerable might most easily be stereotyped as affluent, middle-aged men. Interestingly, the hardest corner of this axis to attach a group to is the most vulnerable. Who is most at risk and most likely to be seriously harmed by criminal victimisation? This might be low-income, single-adult households who can do little to prevent their victimisation and are often more susceptible to harm (Maguire and Bennett 1982) but there is comparatively little evidence that regularly suggests an appropriate group. This may be because many people at high risk of victimisation take preventative action to reduce their chances of being harmed.

While this diagram is conceptually useful when thinking about how vulnerability might be understood it does little to help explain what leads some people to be more vulnerable than others. Measuring the risk of victimisation is the one of the main features of the British Crime Survey and of a variety of local crime surveys (e.g. Jones *et al.* 1990; Crawford *et al.* 1996; Kinsey 1985). While like any survey they suffer from methodological flaws, and while there is a recognised 'dark figure' of crime (Maguire 2002; Coleman and Moynihan 1996), these surveys do tell us something about the distribution of victimisation among some parts of the population. Of course, these surveys have been criticised on a number of grounds relating to their methodological and ideological assumptions (e.g. Lea and Young 1984; Skogan 1986; Young 1988; Walklate 1989). Hence, what the surveys show about levels of risk is contestable both in terms of how categories of victims are constructed (Miers 1990) and how meaning is attributed to survey findings (Lea and Young 1984). Even if these concerns are ignored, risk is not a constant, most people being more at risk of some forms of victimisation than others. Young males, for example, may be more likely to be the victims of street crimes because of the amount of time they spend socialising in public spaces but are far less likely to become the victims of domestic violence in the home (Home Office 2006).

Measuring the level of harm is an even harder task. There can be no easy and objective measure of the amount of harm caused to an individual by a particular crime. The circumstances, personality, and physical, economic and cultural resources of a person will affect how much harm a person suffers from any given crime. As Young (1988) reminds us, the impact of a punch

> can mean totally different things in different circumstances: it can be the punch between two adolescent boys – of absolutely no significance on the level of victimisation. It can be the punch of a policeman on a picket line or the punch of the picket against the police. It can be the drawn-out aggression of a violent man towards his wife. It can be the sickening violence of a parent against a small child. (Young 1988: 174)

Spalek (2006: 91) goes on to suggest that not enough attention has been given to the diversity of different victims and that research into harm is 'theoretically and empirically rather limited'. Spalek argues that this area of research has tended to ignore important differences between victims that might affect how they experience harm. She goes further, suggesting that non-traditional forms of victimisation such as corporate or institutional victimisation have also received limited attention. Despite these limitations, there is a growing body of research that attempts to explore harm in reference to a fairly wide range of variables that include different types of harm (for example, physical and emotional), different levels of harm (degree of offence and type of offence) and how harm is experienced by different social groups (for example, men and women). Spalek (2006) herself provides a good review of the different types of harm, while Newburn (1993) rounds up the research on the long-term effects of victimisation. Stanko (1985) and Stanko and Hobdell (1993) provide some of the best research into the relationship between gender and the experience of harm.

Measuring vulnerability is therefore a complicated business. Even using risk and harm provides nothing more than a conceptual framework for thinking about what vulnerability is. Even if vulnerability could be ordered and measured, such research would probably still fall into the positivist trap of ignoring the social processes that both label people as victims and define their appropriate responses to the harm caused. For example:

> victims may be expected to express gratitude for sympathy or other compensating behaviour, and should not be perceived as exaggerating the extent of the harm suffered, or of the excusing opportunities presented for suspending the expectation others normally have of them. A victim should not, conversely, appear to enjoy his suffering, and should try to avoid for the future the circumstances that occasioned it. A victim may be expected to express anger, and possibly vindictiveness against those who caused the harm; but here again, such sentiments have traditionally been expected to be constrained within tolerated limits. (Miers 1990: 226–7)

Both the label of victim and the response to the harm caused are socially constructed. Measurement of this can only be epistemologically sound when approached as an ethnographic or phenomenological enquiry into the social processes and power relations that structure how behaviour is invested with meaning. For example, a woman who is raped is expected to behave in a certain way. She is traumatised, depressed, possibly angry and suffering from feelings of helplessness and so forth (Newburn 1993). Women are not supposed to exhibit great resilience to this crime, they are not supposed to get over it easily and move on. Yet, research by Burgess and Holmstrom (1979) suggests that women who make the most positive self-assessments and have the highest levels of self-esteem recover the most quickly. Despite this, women are not allowed to shrug it off and get on with life as normal. When women do respond in such atypical ways aspersions are cast about the truthfulness of their accusation, whether it was really rape at all and so on. The courtroom has often been the arena where these kinds of perspectives have been both formalised and reinforced (Holmstrom and Burgess 1978). A set response is therefore culturally prescribed:

> Victims of crime occupy a social role, and where they are seen not to conform to the expectations associated with it, they diminish their chances of being sympathetically treated, and may even forfeit their occupancy of the role. (Miers 1990: 227)

This is not to trivialise the seriousness of rape, or the potential consequences for the victim, but to understand the harm caused and how victims respond requires an investigation of gender roles, personal resources, legal categories and social conditions. Therefore victim responses to the harm caused to them are constrained by role expectations culturally embedded in society. In this sense, vulnerability is part of Christie's (1986) conception of the ideal victim. To be an ideal victim you must not have deliberately put yourself at risk and you must evoke sympathy for your plight. Hence, any consideration of vulnerability cannot simply be a measure or count of particular variables, but must also engage with the wider social conditions that shape which people are afforded the vulnerability label.

The contention will be that social conditions simultaneously reinforce Christie's (1986) notions of the ideal victim while extending it to include new elements of idealness that go some way in helping to understand how notions of vulnerability are deployed in relation to different social groups. The purpose of this is to build an argument where vulnerability will be considered in terms of a 'currency' by which the value of the victim can be measured.

Vulnerability and the social construction of age

The most recent data (Home Office 2006) confirms what has long been the trend: young people between the ages of 16 and 24 are the most victimised group, regardless of whether it is crimes of violence or crimes of property. Inevitably there are one or two exceptions to this trend, but in general over two decades of British Crime Surveys consistently reproduce this finding. Of course, this is a measure of the level of risk, the frequency by which young people are victimised. Explanations for this trend are usually located in lifestyle and routine activity theories (Hindelang *et al.* 1978; Cohen and Felson 1979). Young men are the group most likely to spend leisure time in public spaces, frequenting pubs and nightclubs, staying out late at night and generally not being very afraid of these environments. Hence, they are more heavily victimised than other age groups. Young women between 16 and 24 are also the most heavily victimised age group among the female population, reproducing the findings from the male population. As the age groups get older the risk of victimisation reduces, meaning that the older you are the less likely you are to be victimised. This can also be explained using lifestyle or routine activity explanations. Elderly people do not generally socialise in pubs and clubs late at night.

This general trend masks differential rates of victimisation according to other types of cross-cutting variables such as economic status or ethnicity and is drawn from crime survey data that does not include children or people living in institutional settings. Hence, there are patterns of victimisation that disproportionately affect both children and the elderly that are not reflected in the data. Muncie (2003) cites the extent to which independent research (Mawby 1979; Anderson *et al.* 1990) demonstrates the high rates at which children are victimised in cases of theft and assault. Harassment, violence and sexual abuse of children within the family and within children's homes is further discussed by Muncie (2003: 46) who suggests that 'youth victimology is virtually non-existent'. Muncie attributes this to a predominant focus on youth as offenders and a reluctance by the state to address directly issues of child abuse in the home for fear of threatening the stability of the family unit. Instead of addressing youth victimisation the focus is on youth offending and the control of young people.

At the other end of the scale is the elderly. Much like young people, they often suffer a significant power disadvantage when compared to other adults (Aitkin and Griffin 1996) and crimes committed in either the home or an institutional setting (McCreadie 1996) are unlikely to be recognised or reported through any normal process. Yet there is also evidence that suggests that older people are increasingly becoming the victims of harassment in their communities. Pain (2003: 65) argues that 'stone-throwing, name-calling, nuisance and vandalism' are increasingly common against elderly people.

So the risk of victimisation is generally higher for young people, though this masks important variations in the level of risk posed to different age groups by specific types of criminality, in specific types of environments, namely within the family and within residential care. Using the second measure of vulnerability, harm caused, the general trend would appear to be in direct contrast with the first. The highest risk group, young people, are probably the most quick to recover from harm while the seemingly lowest risk group, the elderly, are likely to suffer more enduring consequences (Newburn 1993). Yet even this is a contestable conclusion. Pain (2003: 73) rightly argues that using age as the sole determinant of impact is both simplistic and reductionist:

> The structures of class, gender, race and ability are the key determinants of how old people experience old age. It is these which underpin where they live, their socio-economic status and their risks of victimisation, whether from property crime, harassment in the community or abuse by carers within domestic spaces.

If this is the case it would seem as applicable to the young as it would to the old. Childhood and old age are bound by some physical conditions that are, by and large, inescapable, but social constructions of different age groups are at least partly responsible for how victimisation by different groups is understood and responded to. As Fattah (1986: 7) astutely observes:

> The labelling of certain crime victims as a weak, vulnerable group in dire need of assistance, care and compassion carries with it the danger of

attaching to those who are victimized a social stigma similar to the one attached to welfare recipients, beneficiaries of unemployment insurance and other unprivileged groups.

Fattah (1986) goes on to explore some of the consequences of this victim stereotyping, including how it can shape state responses to victimisation. This concern can clearly be identified when thinking about age. Young adults tend to be stereotyped as an anti-social and dangerous group and thus seem to receive fairly little attention as victims (Muncie 2003). On the other hand, children and the elderly appear to have the harms committed against them routinely ignored or redefined as a welfare issue. The reasons for this are varied, including the difficulty some people have accessing the authorities to report the harms they are suffering, through to a wider cultural distaste about being confronted with the details of harms committed within families or residential care settings (Brogden and Nijhar 2000). Pain (2003) and Muncie (2003) make a similar point for both the elderly and children by arguing that harm is often constructed in terms of welfare or medical needs rather than criminal victimisation.

Therefore, although there are clear trends in the distribution of victimisation by age, it is doubtful that age alone can provide adequate explanation for this trend. Further, there is a danger of age essentialism (for a good discussion of essentialism see Young 1999) and applying fixed and concrete characteristics to different age groups. The old are weak, children are innocent and so on. What becomes apparent in this brief review of age and vulnerability is that although physical age can clearly affect physical health it is not a gauge by which we can measure any other characteristic. To do otherwise would be to make the same mistake as early positivist criminologists such as Lombroso (1876) or Sheldon (1949) and attribute personality traits to physical attributes. This is nonsense by any contemporary empirical benchmark. Age may be a physical characteristic, but how societies understand and respond to different age groups is socially constructed.

Vulnerability and the gendered victim

Men are victimised more than women. Or so the vast majority of victim survey evidence consistently tells us (Fattah 1989; Dignan 2006). This is for most categories of violent crime, though women are significantly more victimised by domestic violence or violence by someone they know. This illustrates the gendered nature of certain types of violence. Typically, victim surveys show that men are far more at risk of violence than women, but there is a long-established critique that these surveys are particularly bad at uncovering the hidden rate of domestic and sexual violence committed against women, by men, in or around the family home (Coleman and Moynihan 1996; Maguire 2002). Even the local crime survey (Jones *et al.* 1986, Crawford *et al.* 1990; Kinsey 1985), which was designed in part to address the inadequacies of the national survey, only had limited success in achieving full disclosure from women about domestic and sexual victimisation. Yet despite this partial success, Jones *et al.* (1986) found that women were more likely to be the victims of crime than men. More feminist-informed research projects suggest vastly higher rates of rape and domestic violence than presented in any victim survey (Russell 1990; Painter 1991), though it is acknowledged that the definition of rape used by researchers can significantly influence the prevalence of victimisation (Walklate 2004).

Yet very little is known about the true extent of victimisation between the sexes. This is largely due to the high level of violent crime that goes undiscovered. Although there is an ongoing struggle to uncover the hidden rates of violence against women in the home (Yllö 1988; Stanko 1988, 1995), there is also an undiscovered rate of violence against men. This is the product of fighting that often takes place throughout many young men's lives, in the school playground, outside the pub or nightclub, between rival gangs and so on:

> Violence within the home, bullying at school or in the neighbourhood, courtship violence, gay-bashing, racial harassment and crime, sexual harassment and intimidation, 'fair' fights between adolescent men or women – little of which comes to the attention of the police or any official agency – are commonplace and rarely classified within the narrow confines of the criminal law. (Stanko 1994: 38)

Although some of these crimes of violence clearly lead to arrest and prosecution, many go unreported, seen as part of a wider culture of conflict where reporting such activity to the police would be considered a gross betrayal. Even in those instances of public violence where police are either called or on the scene, many conflicts are resolved by the intervention of a uniformed presence and do not result in arrest and prosecution (Reiner 2000). For many men these types of violent encounters are not even seen as forms of criminal victimisation, but as rites of passage, part of growing up, or even displays of prowess among peers. As Stanko and Hobdell (1993: 404) comment in their research into male victimisation: 'Negotiating physical violence while growing up was a backdrop to the men's lives.'

Thus, the comparative level of vulnerability between men and women in relation to the risk of victimisation is particularly hard to determine when so much violent crime remains invisible. Risk in relation to property crime is usually unaffected by gender, as burglary and theft from, or of, a vehicle rarely has a gendered dimension. However, it should be noted that in relation to the crime of theft from a person the statistics show that women are more likely to be victimised by a significant margin (Home Office 2006).

Using harm caused as the second measure of vulnerability, research demonstrates that the types of crime typically committed by men against women can have long-term consequences (Newburn 1993). The length and impact of this victimisation has been strongly linked to the prevalence of physical and sexual intimidation and harassment in the everyday lives of women (Stanko 1985; Dobash and Dobash 1992). Not only do women suffer from the physical trauma of such crimes, there can be ongoing emotional and behavioural consequences that impinge upon the quality of life. For example, Newburn (1993) points to sleeplessness, hypervigilance, not going out after dark, feelings of self-loathing and helplessness. Assessing the level of harm men feel as a result of victimisation is restricted by comparatively little research. A further complicating factor identified by Stanko and Hobdell (1993) is men's reluctance to acknowledge or express the harm caused to them by violent crime. However, Stanko and Hobdell (1993: 413) provide one of the few pieces of empirical research that explores how men are affected by physical assault:

> From this study, it appears that male victims of assault view their victimisation through a male frame, the essence of which sees victimization as 'weak and helpless'. This creates difficulties for men in expressing feelings, leaving them isolated and unable to ask for support. Moreover, men seem to be able to externalize blame, as opposed to women, who have a tendency to internalize blame when victimized. Feelings of anger are quite prominent in men and dealing with their anger is often a problem for others.

This suggests that men's attitude towards their own harm is a consequence of masculinity, where they feel uncomfortable identifying themselves as victims. This is perhaps a partial explanation for why they have received so little attention as the victims of violent crime. Newburn and Stanko (1994) continue this argument, suggesting that the failure of victimology to engage fully with men's victimisation is one that is grossly in need of redressing.

Although this may well be the case it also raises a wider question about how and why research into the harm caused by crime tends to be so selective. Feminist-inspired research into the extent and effects of hidden crimes in the home has been studied in depth, but this is clearly research that also fulfils a wider ideological goal, and is therefore deliberate in its choice of topic. This is not meant as a criticism of this type of research, merely an observation. This focus has provided the basis of an important antidote to a male-dominated criminology (Smart 1977) and a criminal justice system (Smart 1989) that has routinely ignored or marginalised these types of female victimisation. Moreover, the feminist methodologies that underpin much of this research provides a useful alternative lens from which to investigate the power dynamics between men and women that shape both meaning and experience in the social world (Yllö 1988). However, there is a danger that this perspective has been at the expense of research into wider dimensions of both male and female victimisation. If Newburn and Stanko's (1994) warning is to be taken seriously, victimology must take a leaf out of Stanko and Hobdell's (1993) research and expand its focus on gender to victimisation in its many different forms.

Vulnerability, ethnicity and harmful social conditions

Black and minority ethnic backgrounds are at greater risk of becoming victims of crimes than white people (Home Office 2004). The main reasons for this are their age structure, their socio-economic characteristics and the type of area they live in:

> The risk of victimization tends to be strongly associated with characteristics of the areas where respondents live, and after these area characteristics have been taken into account, the differences in risks between ethnic minorities and white people are considerably reduced. (Smith 1997: 115)

It can therefore be seen that the elevated rate of victimisation among black and minority ethnic groups arises, to some extent, because they fall into demographic groups that are at higher than average risk, and because they tend to live in areas where victimisation risks are relatively high. Findings from the British Crime Survey (Home Office 2004) corroborate this explanation to some extent. The younger age profile in particular plays an important part in why more black and minority ethnic people are victimised (Bowling and Phillips 2002). However, it should be noted that there are still some important variations in the risk of victimisation according to ethnicity. For example, black and minority ethnic groups are more likely to be the victims of personal crime than white people, but not property crime. People of mixed race are disproportionately victimised when compared to other black and minority ethnic groups. Even when allowing for the age demographic, mixed race people are more at risk of being victimised (Home Office 2004).

Of course, one of the most insidious trends in the victimisation of black and minority ethnic groups is the extent to which they are the victims of racially motivated offending. As would be expected, the levels of victimisation for this crime are significantly higher than for the white population (Home Office 2004). According to Bowling and Phillips (2002) racist incidents recorded by the police saw a massive rise between 1997 and 2000. This trend can be explained in three ways. First, there is a lot more racially motivated crime; second, victims have become more willing to report crimes than before; or third, the police have become more likely to record a crime as racially motivated. Which explanation is most likely, or carries the most weight, is a matter of conjecture. The police have certainly changed the way in which they count crimes and have also adopted a new, wider definition of a racially motivated crime since the Macpherson Report (1999). Regardless of how this trend is explained, what is clear is that national victim surveys show an even higher rate of racist victimisation than the police-recorded crime statistics. The 2000 British Crime Survey reported 280,000 racially motivated crimes and 2001/02 only slightly less at 206,000 (Home Office 2004). The 1988 and 1992 British Crime Surveys included 'booster' populations of African-Caribbeans and South Asians so that more reliable information could be gleaned about racially motivated offending. What these surveys demonstrated was that both African-Caribbeans and South Asians perceived that high levels of crimes committed against them were racially motivated (Aye Maung and Mirrlees-Black 1994). On average African-Caribbeans felt that 15 per cent of victimisation against them was racially motivated, whereas the figure reached 24 per cent for South Asians. The overall finding of this research was that South Asians were disproportionately the victims of racially motivated crime.

As with any other application of either police recorded crime or national victim surveys the data is somewhat limited when considering the extent of racist victimisation. Bowling and Phillips (2002) point to the process of racist victimisation and argue that the intimidation and harassment of black and ethnic minority groups in their everyday lives shapes their perceptions of security and provides a context in which more serious and violent offending is understood. In this way they draw a parallel with feminist research into women's experience of domestic and sexual violence as on a continuum from everyday harassment to extreme acts of violence (Stanko 1990). The pattern of ongoing and repeat victimisation in domestic violence is mirrored in racist victimisation (Sampson and Phillips 1992; Chahal 1992) and provides the cultural backdrop that shapes how safe black and minority ethnic groups feel in British society.

This is an important dimension when considering the level of harm caused to black and minority ethnic groups by victimisation. At the beginning of this discussion on ethnicity and vulnerability it was noted that higher rates of victimisation among black and minority ethnic groups could be understood in reference to their age, socio-economic circumstance and the type of area they live in. Of course this is true, but it begins to sound a little like a dismissal of discrimination – high levels of victimisation are nothing more than random bad luck. Nothing could be further from the truth. A cocktail of disadvantage and discrimination is often cited as the reason for the high levels of black and minority ethnic groups locked into deprivation (Rex and Moore 1967). Hence even the victimisation of black and minority ethnic groups that is obviously not racially motivated is part of a wider harm perpetrated by discriminatory values and policies in society. In other words, high levels of victimisation are rooted in what is currently thought of as institutional racism (Carmichael and Hamilton 1968; Smith 1989). Alongside this sits the direct harm caused by a pervasive undercurrent of harassment and intimidation that can significantly impinge upon well-being and quality of life of many tens of thousands of people:

> about a third of all people said they were constrained in the way they led their life because of fear of being racially harassed. The fear of being racially harassed affected the quality of life that many of these people could live. It was an important factor for some in deciding where to live. It placed a number of restrictions on their social lives with some not prepared to go out at night even in or near the area they lived; and some where not prepared to use public transport. (Virdee 1995: 47)

In this sense the harm caused by the victimisation of black and minority ethnic groups is something of a double whammy. Not only are there the direct consequences of individual acts of violence or theft, but there is also the indirect harm caused by wider inequalities that limit the capacity of black and minority ethnic groups to escape the social and economic conditions associated with high levels of criminal victimisation. Yet it should be noted that like age and gender, ethnicity is by no means the all-important variable when trying to understand levels of vulnerability. As Bowling and Phillips

(2002) assert, it is necessary to consider how ethnicity intersects with other important variables. The social reality of a working-class woman of African origin will be very different from a middle-class man of Indian origin. Yet vulnerability in relation to ethnicity is rooted not only in the high levels of risk and the harm caused by individual crimes, but more widely and pervasively in the power relations and social conditions that hinder the opportunities and security of black and minority ethnic groups in British society.

Vulnerability and economic status

Compared to gender, ethnicity or even age there seems to be comparatively little research that explores the relationship between economic status and vulnerability. The British Crime Survey uses various categories that could be considered indicative of economic status including household income, employment status, accommodation type and ACORN category. The findings from the most recent survey are somewhat mixed. In relation to violent crime the trend is clearest: those in the lowest economic bands are victimised most frequently. Looking at property crime suggests a more varied picture. Burglary rates tend to remain highest among the poorer groups, while car-related crime and vandalism has a higher incidence among the more affluent population. Yet it remains the case that economic status is one among the many factors that is likely to affect the risk of victimisation. The authors of the first Islington Crime Survey conclude that:

> Crime occurs for many reasons and one of them is the problem of poverty and unemployment. Burglary, sexual assault, inter-personal violence and racial attacks are all linked to the grave problems of economic deprivation within the inner city. (Jones *et al.* 1986: 203)

Further, given that there is an established link between those most at risk of offending and those most at risk of victimisation (Fattah 1989), the disproportional levels of offending among young, low-income males would seem to affirm the trend that low economic status leads to high levels of victimisation (Braithwaite 1979; Farrington 1989). Yet as Braithwaite (1979) demonstrates in his review of self-report studies, it is more accurate to say that young, low-income males commit more of those types of crime likely to be handled by the police. In other words, those types of crimes committed in high visibility public spaces such as street robbery, burglary and car crime. These sorts of crimes occupy a large part of police time and Maguire (2002) suggests that it may well be that crimes often hidden from the police, committed in the home or in the workplace, include a wider range of economic groups. In addition, evidence from self-report studies seems to demonstrate a much less clear relationship between offending and economic status (Graham and Bowling 1995; Wilson *et al.* 2006). Hence it becomes complicated to make inferences about the general level of victimisation among low economic groups by looking at offending rates.

Switching to harm as a measure of vulnerability by economic status reveals even less. There appears to be almost no research that considers the impact of crime or harm caused by crime in relation to economic circumstances. Newburn's (1993) overview of victims never really touches on vulnerability by income group and although he does discuss the financial effects of crime, he does not equate this with the vulnerability of any particular economic group. Similarly Spalek (2006), in her review of harm, talks about lower-income groups being less likely to have property insurance but beyond this statement of detail takes the point no further. Exploration of governmental organisations and charities that might legitimately have a mandate in exploring the harm caused by crime in relation to economic circumstances also bears no fruit. For example, the Social Exclusion Unit website advertises: 'Crime is also disproportionately committed by people from socially excluded backgrounds' (www.socialexclusionunit.gov.org). Yet there does not seem to be any corresponding message about the extent of victimisation among socially excluded groups. Therefore there seems to be something of a disturbing research vacuum about how crime affects different economic groups. Guesswork might lead to the conclusion that the impact of crime will be more severe the less well off you are, the less able you are to insure yourself against loss, the greater your loss to income in relation. Similarly, it could also be the case that injury leading to absence from work may lead to more severe economic consequences for people who are paid by the hour with very poor employment conditions. Yet this is all speculative. It may be that an affluent victim of property crime, perhaps more capable of coping with the financial consequences of crime, will be more severely emotionally or behaviourally affected. It seems that very few people are interested in talking about economic status and vulnerability.

Why might this be? One explanation lies with the work of Mawby and Walklate (1994), who argue that since the decline of the welfare state, victims have been reconstructed as consumers of criminal justice services. Like so many other groups, there can no longer be a presumption of universal state-provided welfare entitlements, instead there are services that you can choose either to access or not. Within this context the victim is construed as a neutral purchaser of services, and the state as the neutral provider. Hence, victims have been segregated from their social conditions. Yet this neutrality is only true insofar as it is presented in terms of an economic exchange. It is an illusion of neutrality, which according to Mawby and Walklate (1994) masks hidden economic and ideological agendas. This sounds very much like an attempt to reintroduce a notion of political economy into an analysis of victimisation. Where once Karl Marx (1867/1976) critiqued the work of Smith (1776) and Ricardo (1817) for failing to acknowledge the social and historical processes that underpin and shape value transactions in a capitalist system, so it appears Mawby and Walklate (1994) are arguing for a similar critical analysis of how these processes have helped shape victims and victim services.

Using this type of analysis it can be argued that the failure of research to engage with economic status and vulnerability is a product of a victimology that is itself shaped and directed by a governmental agenda. Hillyard *et al.*

(2004) make a similar point in relation to the wider discipline of criminology. This perhaps begins to explain why the types of victimisation explored in the British Crime Survey are predominantly the same ones which critical criminologists have argued have been defined by powerful groups interested in political and economic advantage:

> The official statistics on crime and criminals are deficient and biased. They over-represent the contribution to 'conventional' crimes of the lower class and or ethnically oppressed males. The also fail to reflect corporate and governmental crimes, including crimes committed by the State's agents of social control, such as the police. Finally, since they are based on a partisan legalistic conception of crime, the official data fail entirely to reflect the enormous amount of harm, injury and suffering caused by corporations and government when pursuing their sectional interests. (Box 1981: 88)

The logical corollary of this is that drawing attention to the suffering of such groups is unwise, and they are therefore omitted from the national victim survey. However, although this might explain why harm and economic status are largely missing from governmental surveys, it doesn't explain why gender and ethnicity, arguably in the same boat, have received far more research interest.

This difference can be understood in reference to wider shifts in the political and ideological landscape. As Levitas (1998) and Young and Matthews (2003) argue, the redistributive model of social justice has fallen by the wayside, replaced instead by a social integration model focused on employment as the route to social inclusion. Within this context it becomes easier to appreciate how economic status has fallen out of favour; it simply invites a solution that is perceived as both unfashionable and misguided – the eradication or reduction of economic disparities. Still another explanation for this omission can be located in the argument that society has moved to a neo-liberal, risk-obsessed focus on individual characteristics that ignore structural explanations for behaviour (Cohen 1985; O'Malley 2004). In these pervasive conditions it would also be concomitant that victims are also thought of in terms of individual characteristics and risk predisposers, rather than structural conditions. Yet it need not be so. Economic status refers to the affluent as well as to the deprived. Economic inequalities are a social reality and as such should be of legitimate interest to victimologists. Just because the ideology of redistribution appears to be bankrupt (Levitas 1998) does not mean that inequalities cannot be looked at through a different lens. Redistribution is an ideological perspective, but the study of economic forces, inequalities, power relations and how they are structured need not be rooted in the redistributive tradition.

Victims, victimology and the production of knowledge

What becomes apparent from looking at these four categories in relation to vulnerability is that each one is fraught with both shared and specific problems. There are well documented methodological issues for any crime statistic (Bottomley and Pease 1986; Coleman and Moynihan 1996) but there are more fundamental issues which greatly impact upon the available data. Each of the above four sections, whether about age, gender, ethnicity or economic status has sought to draw out a particular contextual dimension that has shaped, directed and to some extent limited research in that field. Of course this in itself is a highly artificial process, trying to distinguish between these four social groups is highly problematic. No one characteristic of an individual can shape their experience of victimisation. This point is made routinely by almost everyone who looks at victimisation (e.g. Bowling and Phillips 2002; Walklate 2004; Crawford *et al.* 1990):

> any attempt to reduce experience to solely one actor: gender, race, class or age, is doomed to failure. Such a reductionism simply ignores the wide variety of differences between the actually existing subgroups which are structured in terms of a combination of all these factors. (Crawford *et al.* 1990: 138)

Yet research continues to categorise experience in precisely the way everyone says it should not. So it becomes very difficult to break out of this mould and talk in new ways about victimisation. In the above discussion of vulnerability the aim has been to provide a very brief synopsis of vulnerability in terms of both risk and harm before considering how social and economic conditions can shape the research agenda. For age this was presented in terms of essentialism; for gender in terms of the narrow focus; for ethnicity in terms of a limited conception of harm and for economic circumstances the wider political and ideological vogue. Of course, each of these individual conclusions can be applied to all four categories but the overall point remains: to demonstrate how research knowledge about victims and vulnerability has to be understood within wider historical, social, ideological and economic conditions.

Once this is understood it becomes much more difficult to derive meaning from victim surveys. The British Crime Survey has now become an institution – not an alternative to official crime data, but part of it. Yet all it actually does is report the findings of the survey. It tells us next to nothing about how these trends can be explained and does not engage in any real form of interpretation of findings. An entirely positivist methodology without any apparent awareness of the methodological limitations of that perspective, the British Crime Survey cannot explain why some people are more vulnerable than others – just that they are. Even then, if you could ignore the methodological limitations and accept the predetermined categories, you still cannot find out easily what other factors influence the victimisation of particular groups. You cannot tell if the reason for high victimisation among young men is because they are also disproportionately in the low economic groups. Which means you also cannot tell who, if anybody, is immune from victimisation. (This resonates with the views of Hope expressed in Chapter 3.) What are the characteristics of a non-victim? How are they different from a routinely victimised person? How are the main trends understood? The British Crime Survey is bereft of any such insight.

This is by no means to say that the British Crime Survey is pointless. To do so would be to deny an invaluable source of information, which social scientists can ill afford to do. The problem is not with the survey itself, but with how it is used. Victimology has tended to absorb the positivist methods of the crime survey and correspondingly lowered its sights to simplistic empirical studies that describe the incidence of victimisation (Miers 1989, 1990). This is nothing more than the starting point, the easy bit. The British Crime Survey is a beginning from which to ask questions and advance ideas. The areas in which victimology appears to have been most successful in doing this is when it has been heavily influenced by methodologies and ideologies from other perspectives, namely feminist and ethnic minority research.

Hence the aim of this chapter is to conclude by presenting a model for understanding victims and vulnerability with reference to wider social conditions. This draws heavily on some of the analytical concepts employed by Karl Marx, but is not intended as a Marxist analysis. This is not a critique of capitalism, but an attempt to interpret how the social construction of vulnerability is shaped by market forces which help determine who and what an ideal victim is.

The ideal victim and the market place

As Taylor (1999) astutely argues in relation to offenders, victims are also now at the heart of the market economy, simultaneously producing and consuming services. As Mawby and Walklate (1994) argue, this conceptualises victims as a consumer unit, a neutral purchaser of goods, independent from the social processes that created them. This is a perspective that strongly resonates with Marx's (1867/1976) notion of fetishism, where being labelled a victim is assumed to be a naturally occurring state, rather than a product of social processes. Drawing on Marx's description of the alienation of labour, a parallel can be seen in the creation of the ideal victim. As the worker becomes enslaved to their labour under capitalism, so the victim becomes enslaved to the ideal victim. A process of objectification (Marx 1844/1970) occurs making victimisation something outside of, and beyond, the individual victim. The ideal victim is therefore turned into an objective unit to be bought and sold in the market place, regardless and irrespective of the actual conditions of people's experiences of victimisation. Within Marx's analysis of the alienation of labour this leads to the worker losing ownership of their labour. Using this analysis in relation to victims suggests that they too have been alienated from their victimisation. This would seem to sit comfortably alongside another of Christie's (1977) influential ideas regarding the theft of conflicts from victims. Christie's analysis is very much about professionals taking ownership of victimisation and denying individuals the capacity to determine their own responses to crimes. The following discussion begins to explore why this has happened and suggests that victims have been co-opted by economic and political forces in ways that have shaped our perceptions of both victimisation and vulnerability. The co-option of victims is not a new idea (Elias 1993; Williams 1999) but drawing upon Marx's theories about the relationship between economic systems and social processes will develop a new way of explaining how and why this process of co-option has occurred.

Borrowing an example from Taylor's (1999) discussion of Marx's writings on the productive forces of criminality a useful comparison with victims can be made:

> The criminal produces an impression, partly moral and partly tragic, as the cause may be, and in this way renders a 'service' by arousing the moral and aesthetic impressions of the public. He produces not only compendia on criminal law, not only penal codes and along with them legislators in the field, but also art, belles-lettres, and even tragedies … the criminal breaks the monotony and everyday security of bourgeois life. In this way he keeps it from stagnation, and gives rise to the uneasy tension and agility without which even the spur of competitiveness would be blunted. *Thus he gives a stimulus to the productive forces.* (Taylor 1999: 213–14, quoting Marx, *Theories of Surplus Value*, 1905–10)

In a similar fashion the same can be said for the victims of crime. An industry has built up around them. In recent years it often seems that they have surpassed offending behaviour in justifications for penal reform (Tonry 2004). Vested interests from politicians, pressure groups, charities, insurance companies, the security industry and housing developers all suggest that victims are one of the most recent groups to become subject to the logic of capitalism (Heilbroner 1985).

Victims, fear and the economic imperative

The contention here is that the victim of crime has become a commodity. He or she has an exchange value that exists outside of any actual experience of victimisation. This value is at the level of economic worth in the market place and political currency or power in society. As shall be seen, the two are intimately connected. Perceptions of vulnerability and levels of fear define this value. Actual victimisation is not a requirement of becoming a commodity; it is merely the potentiality of becoming a victim that provides value. It is therefore not a process of victimisation, nor any particular type of victimisation that is relevant here, but the conditions that give both political and economic meaning to the concept 'victim of crime'.

One major trend that seems to present itself regardless of which social group is studied is that the risk of victimisation does not seem to be strongly associated with perceptions of vulnerability. Young, low-income or unemployed men, often from black and minority ethnic groups, are routinely labelled as dangerous offenders rather than vulnerable, heavily victimised groups (Young 1971; Hall *et al.* 1978; Lea and Young 1984). Of course, in all probability both of these perceptions are equally valid when considering these social groups (Fattah 1989). This perhaps begins to explain why high levels of risk among these social groups do not result in victims with these characteristics being viewed as vulnerable. Instead it appears that either groups who are less victimised, or whose victimisation is less visible, attract more sympathy when they are harmed by crime. Children, the elderly and to some extent women are often viewed as vulnerable, but it appears that this is in reference to the harm caused to them, rather than their risk levels (which may be very high, but hidden). This is perhaps related to socially constructed notions of innocence or blamelessness that conform more closely to an ideal victim (Christie 1986).

Hence, the level of risk appears to play virtually no part in determining who is perceived as a victim. Harm is the benchmark. The more damage caused as a result of either personal frailty or type of offence leads to the application of the vulnerability label. It appears that the value of this type of vulnerability has not been lost on our politicians either. In the United States, Elias (1990, 1993) has commented on the political co-option of the victims of crime, in particular those politically 'safe' groups such as the elderly or children. Elias (1993) argues that both the Reagan and Bush administrations sought to align themselves with these types of vulnerable victims and Williams (1999) in the UK has also made similar points in relation to the political manipulation of crime victims. Thus the vulnerability label is reinforced by political rhetoric and support. Further, vulnerability to harm begins to have a value, a type of political currency that then begins to find a market value. The greater the level of harm likely to be suffered the greater the need to take preventative action, to purchase the security equipment that will protect you, the private health insurance that will heal you and the property insurance that will indemnify you. Alternatively, charitable organisations, quangos and pressure groups spring up on your behalf.

The fear of crime has been a recognised phenomenon for some time now (Hale 1996). Fear has been measured in relation to particular crimes, particular social groups and particular localities. Hale (1996: 95) argues that:

> At a common sense level people who feel unable to protect themselves, either because they cannot run fast, or lack the physical prowess to ward off attackers, or because they cannot afford to protect their homes, or because it would take them longer than average to recover from material or physical injuries might be expected to 'fear' crime more than others. Three broad groups have been identified as falling into this category: women, the elderly and the poor.

This perspective links up well with the above discussion of vulnerability. Thus the two concepts seem to sit side by side, the least powerful people in society suffering from the most harm and quite sensibly, therefore, the most fear. It is not the purpose of this discussion to provide a full analysis of fear here; in fact the discussion so far has been at pains to avoid slipping too much into a discussion of fear. Certain types of vulnerability may well engender fear, but vulnerability remains worthy of study in its own right, not just as an indicator of fear. Yet fear inevitably plays an important part in how people respond and adapt to their perceived level of threat. Although there is a lot of empirical research into the fear of crime, it generally does little more than tell us that to a greater or lesser extent people are afraid of being harmed. Some people fear more than others and this may lead them to take certain measures to limit their chances of being harmed in some way. Where this fear leads people to self-impose drastic restraints on their lives it is seen as an unhealthy social problem in need of a response (for a full review see Hale 1996 or Ditton and Farrall 2000).

Yet at a wider theoretical level fear has taken on a new dimension since the early 1990s, a dimension rooted in what Ulrich Beck (1992) has referred to as the risk society, where we are surrounded by large-scale natural and manufactured risks that threaten our safety and which we only partially comprehend. This type of world has been referred to more recently as reflexive modernity (Beck *et al*. 1994). Reflexivity refers to the capacity people have to reflect on their social conditions and thus transform them. However, this ongoing process of reflection and transformation also leads to uncertainty, which is anxiety-provoking. Bauman (2006) has most recently picked up on this uncertainty in his text about the many different causes of fear in contemporary society. Bauman (2006: 130) argues:

> It is our 'security obsession', and our intolerance of any minor – even the tiniest – breach in security provision which it prompts, that becomes the most prolific, self-replenishing and probably inexhaustible source of our anxiety and fear.

Bauman goes on to argue that it is due to this lack of security that people turn instead to the more achievable arena of safety, over which they can at least exercise some control:

> people tend to settle for the *security of their bodies and their extensions*: homes and their contents, streets through which bodies move, vulnerable and defenceless as they appear to be to blows that are particularly frightening and painful for being sudden and unexpected. But since it is the absence of 'existential security' (or the absence of confidence in its duration) that triggers the whole process, the safety concerns people 'settle for' are not the genuine cause of the troubles that prompt their feverish search for that settlement. (Bauman 2006: 138, emphasis in original)

Thus fear of crime is only part of the explanation. Fear is also of uncertainty, of global threats and natural disasters. Although contemporary British society is quite possibly one of the safest and most comfortable places to live in throughout history people remain fearful and anxious. This is because our expectations are not achievable and because we are more aware of the vast array of potential dangers that might harm us. Bauman goes on to argue that many of the 'safety panics' that frighten us (most recently about bird flu outbreaks in turkey factories) require a human 'villain':

> It is also humans – *other* humans, of course, cruel and selfish but either way unlike us – that in expert opinion and popular beliefs alike bear a large part of the responsibility for the pranks of nature and the vagaries of bodily health. (Bauman 2006: 131, emphasis in original)

Hence people remain anxious and fearful about their own safety in relation to a wide host of potential threats. Yet much of this fear is directed at individual perpetrators, not because any individual is necessarily responsible, but because it is far more comprehensible to believe it was a rogue person, dangerous and different, rather than corporate ambivalence about consumer safety. Bauman then asserts that 'The market thrives under conditions of insecurity; it capitalises on human fears and feelings of haplessness' (2006: 135).

This explanation argues that fear of crime is part of a wider fear about insecurity, which is sometimes misdirected towards individuals rather than more general threats to our safety. Alongside the decline of the welfare state the market provides the only source of safety that can be easily accessed, and the market responds accordingly. O'Malley (1996, 2004) makes a similar comment, pointing to the shift from social security to private security:

> Citizens are exhorted to minimise their risk of burglary or assault by identifying 'criminogenic' situations and avoiding or displacing them through routines of practice or the purchasing of security commodities. (O'Malley 2004: 72)

For O'Malley (2004) and Bauman (2006) the shift towards personal responsibility for our safety, and the provision of goods and services in the market place, is a consequence of wider social, economic and political conditions. Whether it be the pervasiveness of the neo-liberal agenda or the conditions of late modernity, it would appear that fear plays a central role in how we interact with the world around us, and it is increasingly in the market place that we find the apparent solutions to our vulnerabilities. Fear therefore feeds the market, providing a demand for security goods, private policing, gated communities, rape alarms, CCTV cameras, insurance companies and a whole host of new and improved technologies designed to minimise our chances of being injured.

Consequently, the concept of victim has been commodified; it has a value in the market place. This value is external to any actual process of victimisation; it is not individual victims that have been commodified, but the concept of victim. Figure 4.2 begins to map out the conditions under which this process occurs.

Within this diagram it is suggested that the transformation of the victim to commodity requires the intersection of three factors. The first factor is vulnerability, not the risk of victimisation, which appears to have only a peripheral relationship with both fear and idealness, but harm, or perceptions of harm. Vulnerability to harm appears to interact with Christie's (1986) notion of the ideal victim; the greater the level of harm, the less power a person has to resist harm, the greater the level of sympathy. Vulnerability to harm is therefore a type of currency: the more vulnerable you are, the greater the level of sympathy and the greater the need for security.

Fundamentally tied to vulnerability is the fear of crime. The more vulnerable a person feels the more likely they are to be afraid and vice versa. Fear provides the demand for security goods and support services. Thus, the greater the level of fear, the greater the demand levels will be. Without fear

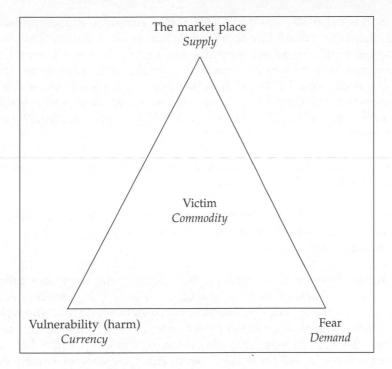

Figure 4.2 The commodification of crime victims

there is no reason for the consumption of goods or services. It should be noted that the relationship between vulnerability and fear is neither linear nor uniform. As has already been noted, fear appears to be condition of the risk society, not specifically fear of crime, but fear of harm in general. As a result many people will be afraid who are not necessarily part of those social groups generally thought to be more vulnerable to harm, but they will perceive themselves, their homes, and their families as being under threat. Reasonably affluent, well-educated and home-owning families will purchase home and private security products (Jones and Newburn 1998; Girling *et al.* 2000) regardless of either the rate of victimisation or their capacity to absorb any financial loss.

Finally, the marketplace provides a never-ending supply of goods and services for the victim. The market place is meant both in the direct economic sense – the businesses and companies that sell their wares for profit – and in a wider sense, the competition and jostling for resources among charities, quangos and pretty much anyone who wishes to secure resources in the name of the victim. These not-for-profit organisations have the same broad concern as those in the private sector: without demand from victims they become obsolete, lose resources and power, and end up defunct or bankrupt. As a result the marketing strategies of both sectors roughly correspond; they are keen to point out the potential threat to their customers. For example, it is not uncommon to see security firm websites that remind us:

You should also be considering the wider picture for your protection. What happens when I'm away on business or holiday? Do I want friends or family to attend if an alarm is signalled? Can I keep track on who comes and goes to the property – are the kids home from school? Is Mum back from the shops? Are there other ways to protect my family and possessions? Could I see who is at my front door and can I view my property with CCTV to my desk PC or video recorder? (www.defencehome.co.uk)

Charities pursue a not so different approach, though generally, as is the case here, for much more laudable goals:

Joan's story is difficult to hear but do try and listen to her. Joan's is just one of over 500,000 cases of abuse that are happening in the UK now. (www.helptheaged.org.uk)

The commodification of victims is thus contingent on vulnerability, fear and the market. Each of these is shaped by distinctive social and economic conditions which converge to transform the victim into a commodity. The value of the victim is determined by the level of their vulnerability and their fear. Thus there is an economic dimension to thinking abut what an ideal victim might be. Not only is it the personal characteristics so astutely outlined by Christie (1986), it is also the economic exchange value now invested in the victim identity.

Conclusion

What has become apparent during the course of this discussion is that risk is irrelevant to understanding what is actually going on with regards to victimisation. While risk assessment and actuarial justice may have infected the penal system (Feeley and Simon 1992) it seems less significant when thinking about the victims of crime. It is not risk that dictates our level of fear, or the harm we suffer. They are independent from each other. In this risk-obsessed age we have been diverted from the real issue, which is how our perceptions of victimisation are shaped by social, economic, historical and political forces. Risk governs neither how society or the state responds to victimisation, nor how we perceive our own likelihood of victimisation. These are instead ruled by social categories, power inequalities, personal characteristics and economic circumstances. Therefore, surveys that tell us how many men, women, children or black people have been victimised in any given year tell us very little about the actual experience of victimisation. They do provide a useful starting point to investigate victimisation, but the real job of work is to explore how society and individuals understand and give meaning to victimisation.

For example, what are the consequences of the commodification of victims? Everyone who is afraid of crime, everyone who feels they will disproportionately suffer from crime, will find themselves locked into a competitive market place trying to discern what goods or services are most likely to protect them. Each business or agency will compete for the attention of the victim; each will have a compelling statistic about the prevalence of crime that will play on existing fears and encourage people to buy their product. Which products or services should be bought? How much security is needed? Does the product work? These are the questions that will confront anxious consumers. Even worse, for those victims unfortunate enough not to be able to afford products or have a champion for their suffering, this situation will be doubly worrying. Their inability to provide security for themselves and their families will make them even more afraid because they are surrounded by so many businesses and pressure groups telling them that they need this or that protection. At the other end of the scale, for those for whom money is no object, there is a danger that the market will bleed them dry, slowly exploiting every single anxiety and fear until people retreat into their gated communities, terrified of everything unfamiliar or different (Bauman 2001).

Thus the market could simultaneously create and reinforce harms entirely separate from criminal victimisation, harms that affect wider social relations, our fear of others and our sense of safety. This is no different from any other arena, whether it is political, cultural or social; all have the capacity to cause harm and to repair it. As has been shown in the above discussion, this sometimes requires consideration of harmful events and conditions far outside of the narrowly defined crime context (Hillyard and Tombs 2004). Whether these harms are natural, cultural or economic, they all converge to affect levels of security and fear that are fundamental when considering well-being and quality of life issues in society. These concerns are surely the business of victimology; otherwise what is the point of studying victims at all?

Further reading

Bauman, Z. (2006) *Liquid Fear*. Cambridge: Polity. The third in Zygmunt Bauman's 'Liquid' series and as always a thought-provoking read.

Box, S. (1981) *Deviance, Reality and Society*. London: Holt, Reinhart and Winston. An absolute classic, though in this case Chapter 3 provides one of the best critical overviews of crime data. Not specifically about victims but an awful lot of relevant commentary that can and should be applied in this field.

Christie, N. (1986) 'The Ideal Victim', in E.A. Fattah (ed.) *From Crime Policy to Victim Policy: Reorienting the Justice System*. Basingstoke: Macmillan. This short but excellent chapter provides a superb discussion of how we continue to construct notions of victimhood that are wildly out of kilter with complicated social conditions.

Hillyard, P. and Tombs, S. (2004) 'Beyond Criminology', in *Criminal Obsessions: Why Harm Matters More than Crime*, Crime and Society Foundation, Monograph number 1. A really good discussion of the limits of criminology and why we should seek to develop a wider conception of what criminology should be about. The discussion is equally applicable to victimology and is a good source for the further exploration of the concept of social harm as the focus for criminology.

Spalek, B. (2006) *Crime Victims: Theory, Policy and Practice*. Basingstoke: Palgrave Macmillan. A recent textbook on victims that looks at both contemporary notions of the ideal victim and has an entire chapter devoted to the harm caused by crime.

References

Aitken, L. and Griffin, G. (1996) *Gender Issues in Elder Abuse*. London: Sage.

Anderson, S., Smith, C.G., Kinsey, R. and Wood, J. (1990) *The Edinburgh Crime Survey*. Edinburgh: Scottish Office.

Aye Maung, N. and Mirrlees-Black, C. (1994) *Racially Motivated Crime: A British Crime Survey Analysis*. London: Home Office.

Bauman, Z. (2001) *Community*. London: Polity.

Bauman, Z. (2006) *Liquid Fear*. Cambridge: Polity.

Beck, U. (1992) *Risk Society: Towards a New Modernity*. London: Sage.

Beck, U., Lash, S. and Giddens, A. (1994) *Reflexive Modernization: Politics, Tradition and Aesthetics in Modern Social Order*. Cambridge: Polity Press.

Bottomley, A.K. and Pease, K. (1986) *Crime and Punishment: Interpreting the Data*. Milton Keynes: Open University Press.

Bowling, B. and Phillips, C. (2002) *Racism, Crime and Justice*. Harlow: Longman.

Box, S. (1981) *Deviance, Reality and Society*. London: Holt, Reinhart and Winston.

Braithwaite, J. (1979) *Inequality, Crime and Public Policy*. London: Routledge and Kegan Paul.

Brogden, M. and Nijhar, P. (2000) *Crime, Abuse and the Elderly*. Cullompton: Willan Publishing.

Burgess, A.W. and Holmstrom, L.L. (1979) 'Adaptive strategies and recovery from rape', *American Journal of Psychiatry*, 136(10): 1278–82.

Carmichael, S. and Hamilton, C. (1968) *Black Power: The Politics of Liberation*. Harmondsworth: Penguin.

Chahal, K. (1992) *Hidden from View: A Study of Racial Harassment in Preston*. Preston: Preston Borough Council.

Christie, N. (1977) 'Conflicts as property', *British Journal of Criminology*, 17(1).

Christie, N. (1986) 'The Ideal Victim', in E.A. Fattah (ed.) *From Crime Policy to Victim Policy: Reorienting the Justice System*. Basingstoke: Macmillan.

Cohen, L.E. and Felson, M. (1979) 'Social change and crime rate trends: A routine activity approach', *American Sociological Review*, 44: 588–608.

Cohen, S. (1985) *Visions of Social Control*. London: Polity.

Coleman, C. and Moynihan, J. (1996) *Understanding Crime Data*. Buckingham: Open University Press.

Crawford, A., Jones, T., Woodhouse, T. and Young, J. (1990) *The Second Islington Crime Survey*. London: Middlesex Polytechnic.

DefenceHome website (2006) http://www.defencehome.co.uk/alarmsystems.html (accessed 12 February 2007).

Ditton, J. and Farrall, S. (2000) *The Fear of Crime*. International Library of Criminology, Criminal Justice and Penology. Aldershot: Ashgate.

Dignan, J. (2006) *Understanding Victims and Restorative Justice*. Maidenhead: Open University Press.

Dobash, R.E. and Dobash, R. (1992) *Women, Violence and Social Change*. Shepton Mallet: Open Books.

Elias, R. (1990) 'Which Victim Movement? The Politics of Victim Policy', in A.J. Lurigio, W.G. Skogan and R.C. Davis (eds) *Victims of Crime: Problems, Policies and Programs*. California: Sage.

Elias, R. (1993) *Victims Still: The Political Manipulation of Crime Victims*. London: Sage.

Farrington, D. (1989) 'Self-reported and Official Offending from Adolescence to Adulthood', in M.W. Klein (ed.) *Cross-national Research in Self-reported Crime and Delinquency*. Dordrecht: Kluwer.

Fattah, E.A. (1986) 'Prologue: On Some Visible and Hidden Dangers of Victim Movements', in E.A Fattah (ed.) *From Crime Policy to Victim Policy: Re-orientating the Justice System*. Basingstoke: Macmillan.

Fattah, E.A. (1989) 'Victims and victimology: The facts and rhetoric', *International Review of Victimology*, 1(1): 43–66.

Feeley, M. and Simon, J. (1992) 'The new penology: Notes on the emerging strategy of corrections and its implications', *Criminology*, 30(4): 449–74.

Girling, E., Loader, I. and Sparks, R. (2000) *Crime and Social Change in Middle England*. London: Routledge.

Graham, J.G. and Bowling, B. (1995) *Young People and Crime*, Home Office Research Study 145. London: HMSO.

Hale, C. (1996) 'Fear of crime: A review of the literature', *International Review of Victimology*, 4(3): 79–151.

Hall, S., Critcher, C., Jefferson, T., Clarke, J. and Roberts, B. (1978) *Policing the Crisis: Mugging, the State, and Law and Order*. London: Macmillan.

Heilbroner, R.L. (1985) *The Nature and Logic of Capitalism*. New York: W. W. Norton.

Help the Aged (2006) http://www.helptheaged.org.uk/engb/Campaigns /ElderAbuse/film/default.htm (accessed 12 February 2007).

Hillyard, P. and Tombs, S. (2004) 'Beyond Criminology', in *Criminal Obsessions: Why Harm Matters More than Crime*. Crime and Society Foundation, Monograph number 1.

Hillyard, P., Sim, J., Tombs, S. and Whyte, D. (2004) 'Leaving a stain upon the silence: Contemporary criminology and the politics of dissent', *British Journal of Criminology*, 33(3): 369–90.

Hindelang, M.S., Gottfredson, M.R. and Garofalo, J. (1978) *Victims of Personal Crime*. Cambridge, MA: Ballinger.

Holmstrom, L.L. and Burgess, A.W. (1978) *The Victim of Rape: Institutional Reactions*. Chichester: John Wiley.

Home Office (2004) *Ethnicity, Victimisation and Worry about Crime: Findings from the 2001/02 and 2002/03 British Crime Surveys*, Home Office Research Findings 237. London: Home Office.

Home Office (2006) *Criminal Statistics for England and Wales 2005/6*. London: Home Office.

Jones, S. and Newburn, T. (1998) *Private Security and Public Policing*. Oxford: Clarendon Press.

Jones, T., Maclean, B. and Young, J. (1986) *The Islington Crime Survey*. Aldershot: Gower.

Killeas, M. (1990) 'Vulnerability: Towards a better understanding of a key variable in the genesis of fear of crime', *Violence and Victims*, 5: 97–108.

Killeas, M. and Clerici, C. (2000) 'Different measures of vulnerability in their relation to different dimensions of fear of crime', *British Journal of Criminology*, 40(3): 437–50.

Kinsey, R. (1985) *The Merseyside Crime and Police Surveys: Final Report*. Liverpool: Merseyside Metropolitan Council.

Lea, J. and Young, J. (1984) *What is to be Done about Law and Order*. Middlesex: Penguin.

Levitas, R. (1998) *The Inclusive Society? Social Exclusion and New Labour*. Basingstoke: Palgrave Macmillan.

Lombroso, C. (1876) *L'Uomo Delinquente*. Turin: Fratelli Bocca.

Macpherson, W. (1999) *The Stephen Lawrence Inquiry: Report of an Inquiry by Sir William Macpherson of Cluny*, Cmd 4262–1. London: The Stationery Office.

Maguire, M. (2002) 'Crime Statistics, Patterns and Trends: Changing Perceptions and their Implications', in M. Maguire, R. Morgan and R. Reiner (eds) *The Oxford Handbook of Criminology*, 3rd edn. Oxford: Clarendon Press.

Maguire, E.M.W. and Bennett, T. (1982) *Burglary in a Dwelling: The Offence, the Offender and the Victim*. London: Heinemann Educational Books.

Marx, K. (1905–10/1969) *Theories of Surplus Value*. Moscow: Foreign Languages Publishing House.

Marx, K. (1844/1970) *Economic and Philosophic Manuscripts of 1844*. London: Lawrence and Wishart.

Marx, K. (1876/1976) *Capital: A Critique of Political Economy*, Volume 1. Harmondsworth: Penguin.

Mawby, R.I. (1979) 'The victimisation of juveniles: A comparative study of three areas of publically owned housing in Sheffield', *Journal of Crime and Delinquency*, 16(1): 98–114.

Mawby, R.I. and Walklate, S. (1994) *Critical Victimology*. London: Sage.

McCreadie, C. (1996) *Elder Abuse: Update on Research*. London: Age Concern Institute for Gerontology, King's College.

Miers, D. (1989) 'Positivist victimology: A critique, part 1', *International Review of Victimology*, 1(1): 3–23.

Miers, D. (1990) 'Positivist victimology: A critique, part 2', *International Review of Victimology*, 1(3): 219–231.

Muncie, J. (2003) 'Youth, Risk and Victimisation', in P. Davies, P. Francis and V. Jupp (eds) *Victimisation: Theory, Research and Policy*. Basingstoke: Palgrave Macmillan.

Newburn, T. (1993) *The Long-term Needs of Victims: A Review of the Literature*. Research and Planning Unit Paper 80. London: Home Office.

Newburn, T. and Stanko, E.A. (1994) 'When Men are Victims: The Failure of Victimology', in T. Newburn and E.A. Stanko (eds) *Just Boys Doing Business: Men, Masculinities and Crime*. London: Routledge.

O'Malley, P. (1996) 'Risk and Responsibility', in A. Barry, T. Osborne and N. Rose (eds) *Foucault and Political Reason*. Chicago: Chicago University Press.

O'Malley, P. (2004) *Risk, Uncertainty and Government*. London: Glasshouse Press.

Pain, R. (2003) 'Old Age and Victimisation', in P. Davies, P. Francis and V. Jupp (eds) *Victimisation: Theory, Research and Policy*. Basingstoke: Palgrave Macmillan.

Painter, K. (1991) *Marriage, Wife Rape and the Law*. University of Manchester: Department of Social Policy.

Reiner, R. (2000) *The Politics of the Police*, 3rd edn. Oxford: Oxford University Press.

Rex, J. and Moore, R. (1967) *Race, Community and Conflict*. London: Oxford University Press.

Ricardo, D. (1817) *On the Principles of Political Economy and Taxation*. London: Murrey.

Russell, D. (1990) *Rape in Marriage*. Bloomington: Indiana University Press.

Sampson, A. and Phillips, C. (1992) *Multiple Victimisation: Racial Attacks on an East London Estate*. Police Research Group Crime Prevention Unit Series Paper 36. London: Home Office.

Sheldon, W. (1949) *Varieties of Delinquent Youth*. New York: Harper.

Skogan, W.G. (1986) 'Methodological Issues in the Study of Victimisation', in E.A.Fattah (ed.) *From Crime Policy to Victim Policy: Reorienting the Justice System*. Basingstoke: Macmillan.

Smart, C. (1977) *Women, Crime and Criminology*. London: Routledge.

Smart, C. (1989) *Feminism and the Power of Law*. London: Routledge.

Smith, A. (1776) *An Inquiry into the Nature and Causes of the Wealth of Nations*. London: Routledge.

Smith, D.J. (1997) 'Ethnic Origins, Crime, and Criminal Justice in England and Wales', in M. Tonry (ed.) *Ethnicity, Crime and Immigration*. London: Chicago Press.

Smith, S.J. (1989) *The Politics of 'Race' and Residence: Citizenship, Segregation and White Supremacy in Britain*. Cambridge: Polity.

Social Exclusion Unit website (2006) http://www.socialexclusionunit.gov.uk/page. asp?id=3 (accessed 3 February 2007).

Spalek, B. (2006) *Crime Victims: Theory, Policy and Practice*. Basingstoke: Palgrave Macmillan.

Stanko, E.A. (1985) *Intimate Intrusions: Women's Experiences of Male Violence*. London: Routledge.

Stanko, E.A. (1988) 'Fear of Crime and the Myth of the Safe Home: A Feminist Critique of Criminology', in K. Yllö and M. Bograd (eds) *Feminist Perspectives on Wife Abuse*. London: Sage.

Stanko, E.A. (1990) *Everyday Violence*. London: Pandora.

Stanko, E.A. (1994) 'Challenging the Problem of Men's Individual Violence', in T. Newburn and E.A. Stanko (eds) *Just Boys Doing Business: Men, Masculinities and Crime*. London: Routledge.

Stanko, E.A. (1995) 'Women, crime and fear', *Annals, AAPSS*: 539: 46–58.

Stanko, E.A. and Hobdell, K. (1993) 'Assault on men: Masculinity and male victimization', *British Journal of Criminology*, 33(3): 400–15.

Taylor, I. (1999) *Crime in Context*. Cambridge: Polity.

Tonry, M. (2004) *Punishment and Politics*. Cullompton: Willan Publishing.

Virdee, S. (1995) *Racial Violence and Harassment*. London: Policy Studies Institute.

Walklate, S. (1989) *Victimology: The Victim and the Criminal Justice Process*. London: Unwin Hyman.

Walklate, S. (2004) *Gender, Crime and Criminal Justice*. Cullompton: Willan Publishing.

Williams, B. (1999) *Working with Victims of Crime: Policies, Politics and Practice*. London: Jessica Kingsley.

Wilson, D., Sharp, C. and Patterson, A. (2006) *Young People and Crime: Findings from the 2005 Young People and Crime Survey*. London: Home Office.

Yllö, K. (1988) 'Political and Methodological Debates in Wife Abuse Research', in K. Yllö and M. Bograd (eds) *Feminist Perspectives on Wife Abuse*. London: Sage.

Young, J. (1971) 'The Role of the Police as Amplifiers of Deviance, Negotiators of Reality and Translators of Fantasy', in S. Cohen (ed.) *Images of Deviance*. Harmondsworth: Penguin.

Young, J. (1988) 'Risk of Crime and Fear of Crime: A Realist Critique of Survey-based Assumptions', in M. Maguire and J. Pointing (eds) *Victims of Crime: A New Deal?* Milton Keynes: Open University Press.

Young, J. (1999) *The Exclusive Society*. London: Sage.

Young, J. and Matthews, R. (2003) 'New Labour, Crime Control and Social Exclusion', in R. Matthews and J. Young (eds) *The New Politics of Crime and Punishment*. Cullompton: Willan Publishing.

Part Two

Victims, Victimology and Feminism

Sandra Walklate

Introduction

As was highlighted in Chapter 2, feminism in its various guises has had a tremendous impact both on how understandings of who may or may not constitute a victim of crime and by implication what kinds of crimes they may or may not be victims of. In this section of the book the intention is to explore some aspects of this impact in greater detail, in the first instance by considering how responses to (in particular) violence against women have developed in recent decades and then by considering the wider implications that taking gender seriously has for victimology. All of these contributions have been, and are, differently informed by feminism, and it is to a consideration of the questions that feminism raised that we shall turn first of all.

As Chesney-Lind (2006) has observed, much of the focus given to violence against women over the last 25 years has its roots in what is referred to as second-wave feminism. Second-wave feminism, as articulated within the Anglo-American-European axis, took for granted that women had made gains in relation to civil rights but argued that these gains, while not inconsiderable, had not given women social rights. This lack of social rights demonstrated their unequal status *vis-à-vis* men and was particularly marked by women's experience of violence by men to them, and often by men that they knew. These experiences were the focal and vocal point of much feminist campaigning of the 1960s and 1970s, which, while frequently belittled by the terminology that was used to describe its voice (women's libbers), nevertheless has been sustained to the present day. The chapters in this section adhere to the profound questions to be learned from listening to women in different ways, and clearly articulate the different ways it is possible to move forward on the basis of that listening. They also reflect the different positions researchers and activists might adopt in relation to the 'woman' question. Kate Cook and Helen Jones remain committed to a primarily radical feminist stance which takes the organising principles of patriarchy as the central problematic for understanding women's lives. Carolyn Hoyle seeks to move beyond the restrictions that this agenda imposes on the ability to appreciate the diversity of women's lives and their experiences of male violence, complicated as it is by class, ethnicity, sexuality, etc. Pamela Davies exposes the way in which exploring the question of gender as the woman question, from whatever feminist perspective, limits our understanding of both men and women. Nevertheless each of them remain committed to the view that there is much to be learned from feminist work (whether that be radical, socialist, liberal, post-modern, or any other label that might lay claim to feminist heritage; for a fuller discussion of these different feminisms and their relationship with both criminology and victimology see Gelsthorpe 2002; Walklate 2004) for understanding both the nature and extent of criminal victimisation and responding to it. The chapters that follow all chart the changing nature of the feminist voice and also reveal some of the tensions that exist between feminism and victimology that Rock highlighted in Chapter 2. One of those tensions lies within the use of terminology so aptly articulated in the chapter by Kate Cook and Helen Jones: are women victims or survivors?

Spalek (2006) discusses a number of different ways in which the term victim can be defined, from the person injured or killed as a result of an event to the religious sacrificiant. However, it is not the definition of victim itself that concerns the feminist, it is the way in which the term is connoted that is seen to be problematic. The link between the passivity and powerlessness associated with being a victim and being female, does not for feminists capture how women routinely resist and manage their structural powerlessness, in other words, how they survive. Chapter 5 by Cook and Jones is certainly written in the spirit of this latter understanding. Moreover, the connotations associated with the term victim also conjure an 'ideal victim' (Christie 1986), discussed by Davies in Chapter 7. This ideal victim easily elides into notions of deserving and undeserving victims which are so readily identifiable in responses to the female rape victim alluded to by Cook and Jones, and as Davies discusses, is problematic for men as well as women. In addition, if the position taken by Rock is embraced it can be argued that the process of being assigned the victim label can be quite a complex one; so, for example, it is possible that at different points in time someone could be an active victim, a passive victim, an active survivor, a passive survivor, and all the experiential points in between. From this point of view this terminological debate seems a little sterile and Davies in her chapter explores the implications of this debate in considerably more detail. Yet the commitment of feminism runs somewhat deeper than this terminological debate implies, and that deeper commitment is reflected in all chapters in Part Two. This commitment is twofold: on the one hand it is a commitment of activism and on the other it is a commitment to knowledge, and as these chapters each differently demonstrate, these two aspects to feminism are not easily separable.

The commitment to activism is well illustrated by Cook and Jones. Their active involvement with and for women who have been raped, as volunteers, as campaigners, as part of the legislative consultative process and as teachers and researchers speaks volumes about their activist credentials, credentials which are differently shared with many campaigners in the victims' movement and which Fattah (1991) argued some time ago should be separated from the academic. Yet the commitment of feminists lies not just with the interests of the particular groups they campaign for, it also lies with a particular view of the process of knowing. So while it is possible to see that the campaigning stance of Cook and Jones is self-evident, as is their recognition that the desired policy implementation process to change things for women is fraught with difficulties, that self-evidence belies a deeper commitment to how it is possible to know things about the world. In different ways both Hoyle and Davies take up this knowledge question. Put briefly, as each of these authors develops this issue in different ways, while there are different feminisms, as suggested above, what these different feminisms do is make different claims to both what there is to be known about the world and how that knowledge can be accessed. What they have in common is a differently constituted challenge to 'malestream' knowledge – that is, knowledge that presumes that a male view of the world equates with all other views of the world.

Hoyle, for example, explores the problems and possibilities that have derived from the feminist input in relation to understanding and responding to domestic violence. She discusses in detail the methodological problems in measuring the nature and extent of domestic violence frequently articulated in the literature as the debate between whether or not such violence is symmetrical between the sexes (i.e. committed to the same extent by men and women) or asymmetrical (i.e. committed mostly by men against women). This is a very good example of the differential knowledge production process, referred to by Hope in Chapter 3 as the data generating process, that by implication raises very similar questions to the ones being posed here. Hoyle notes the achievements and challenges posed by radical feminism for how domestic violence has been understood, and goes on to examine how the dominance of the radical feminist view may not always result in advancement for the women it claims to have at its heart. This is particularly the case in the support given to arresting the offender for domestic violence that she goes on to demonstrate is not the only option. This ambivalence to this policy response is shared for different reasons by Chesney-Lind (2006). Hoyle thus makes an interesting case not only for resisting the malestream but also resisting any general claims to knowledge in a context as diverse and sometimes as subtle as responding to domestic violence and points to the intersectionality of vulnerability in the context of domestic violence that is alluded to by Hope in Chapter 3 and also discussed by Green in Chapter 4.

In a different though related way, Davies explores the conceptual knowledge problems posed for a victimology that fails to take account of the gendered base to some kinds of criminal victimisation so clearly demonstrated by Cook and Jones, and Hoyle. She encourages us to consider what victimology might take from a deeper understanding of the nature and impact of masculinity(ies) on victimology and what it takes to be its subject matter. She makes the case for a gender-wise victimology; a victimology that does not take gender as always being the salient variable in our understandings of criminal victimisation. She too makes the case for the need to be sensitive to the complex way in which other structural variables may intersect in people's everyday lives. However, it must be remembered that neither Hoyle nor Davies would have reached the point where their kind of analysis would be having the kind of impact that it has without the campaigning voices of people like Cook and Jones and many others before them. It may be that as Chesney-Lind (2006) has observed, second-wave feminism is currently being subjected to incorporation and co-option, some aspects of which are alluded to by Cook and Jones, but that co-option stands as testimony to both its achievements and its continued challenge to malestream thought. This does not mean that some problems do not remain.

As Davies clearly states, the misuse of the term gender in and of itself is becoming increasingly problematic. Even at this basic conceptual level there is a need for sustained vigilance. Moreover as Spalek has pointed out:

> Although some women are killed by men, and some feel that certain aspects of their lives have been completely ruined by violence, many women nonetheless manage to reconstruct their lives, emotionally, psychologically, and physically, and this kind of reconstruction should be acknowledged through the use of the word 'survivor' rather than 'victim'; *the same might also be said about all kinds of less powerful groups in society.* (Spalek 2004: 43, my emphasis)

So in addition there is a need for sustained vigilance over who is privileged and why, especially in the policy responses designed to make things better for people. There are three issues here: recognising what it is that people need and when (issues taken up by Dunn in Chapter 10), accepting that people do have their own personal coping strategies and may not want or need intervention (or at least not the kind on offer *qua* Hoyle), and recognising the importance of diversity. It is in this latter respect, as articulated in different ways in the chapters in Part Two, that feminism and feminists (along with other sectional interests) can come unstuck. As Hudson (2006: 30) states: 'Feminist and race critical criminologies have produced countless examples of the maleness and whiteness of criminal justice', and 'It has long been argued that the law in modern western societies reflects the subjectivity of the dominant white affluent adult male' (see also MacKinnon 1989; Smart 1989: Naffine 1990). Put simply the law cannot redress social inequalities: relationships of power that are socially and economically constructed. Yet Hudson (2003, 2006), along with the contributors here, suggests that the law can act as a catalyst for change, but only, in Hudson's view, if the law embraces a logic of discourse (that people can make claims in their own terms not in terms of the dominant discourse), is relational, and is reflective. Some of the problems and possibilities discussed by Cook and Jones in relation to rape and by Hoyle in relation to domestic violence connect with Hudson's view of the need for a reflective, relational discourse. Without this kind of stance, feminist campaigners in relation to the law will always be faced with the problem of universalism in law that contributes to the practical problems (including those of attrition discussed by Cook and Jones) of policy implementation. We shall return to the problem of universalism in the Conclusion. The problems and possibilities of policy implementation and development as part of a gender-wise approach are considered by Davies. However, her point is well made that victimology and victim-oriented policies have a long way to go before they match with her gender-wise agenda.

These three chapters taken together document both the fundamental and complex questions that feminism, and feminist work, has raised for victimology. They also demonstrate how much work there remains to be done in the academy, in policy and in politics, pointedly made in the publication of the HMIC/CPSI Report *Without Consent* (2007). Each illustrate how these various spheres of influence require continued vigilance if feminist voices are still to be heard. It is important, however, that those voices are not exclusive voices. They have been influential in placing other ways of knowing about the world to the fore. As a result, other voices can now also be heard. Such diversity raises all kinds of questions for policy and politics, as Hudson (referred to above) alludes to. The chapters in Part Three will consider the current policy state of play that endeavours to consider the victim of crime in general as opposed to just gendered experiences of criminal victimisation. All the chapters in this section agree that much remains to be done at every level to encourage a greater awareness of and sensitivity to the way in which structural variables impact upon people's everyday lives.

References

Chesney-Lind, M. (2006) 'Patriarchy, crime and justice: Feminist criminology in an era of backlash', *Feminist Criminology*, 1(1): 6-26.

Christie, N. (1986) 'The Ideal Victim', in E. Fattah (ed.) *From Crime Policy to Victim Policy*. London: Macmillan.

Fattah, E. (1991) *Understanding Criminal Victimisation*. Scarborough, Ontario: Prentice Hall.

Gelsthorpe, L. (2002) 'Feminism and Criminology', in M. Maguire, R. Morgan and R. Reiner (eds) *The Oxford Handbook of Criminology*, 3rd edn. Oxford: Oxford University Press.

Hudson, B. (2003) *Justice in a Risk Society*. London: Sage.

Hudson, B. (2006) 'Beyond white man's justice: Race, gender and justice in late modernity', *Theoretical Criminology*, 10 (1): 29–47.

MacKinnon, C. (1989) *Towards a Feminist Theory of the State*. Cambridge: Cambridge University Press.

Naffine, N. (1990) *Law and the Sexes*. London: Allen and Unwin.

Spalek, B. (2006) *Crime Victims: Theory, Policy and Practice*. London: Palgrave.

Walklate, S. (2004) *Gender, Crime and Criminal Justice*, 2nd edn. Cullompton: Willan Publishing.

Chapter 5

Surviving victimhood: the impact of feminist campaigns

Kate Cook and Helen Jones

And I want one day of respite, one day off, one day in which no new bodies are piled up, one day in which no new agony is added to the old, and I am asking you to give it to me. And how could I ask you for less – it is so little. And how could you offer me less: it is so little. Even in wars, there are days of truce. Go and organize a truce. Stop your side for one day. I want a twenty-four-hour truce during which there is no rape. (Dworkin 1984)

Introduction

This chapter is dedicated to the memory of one of the heroines of the feminist anti-rape movement, Andrea Dworkin, and as her words illustrate, radical feminism imagines a world free from sexual violation. This chapter is about rape and how we know about it, what we are currently doing about it, and where the future lies in striving for a world without rape. The focus is on women, not merely because so many more women are raped but because radical feminism has been centrally concerned with women, not men. It is women who are targeted by rapists; as women, as activists, and as academics (not mutually exclusive terms). This introduction aims to explain our position in relation to anti-rape theory and activism as well as providing an outline of what follows.

The gender dynamics of rape as a crime committed exclusively by men, almost exclusively on women, became a campaigning issue for feminists during the 1970s. The activists who first spoke out about rape during their consciousness raising meetings are now characterised as 'radical feminists', although they were known simply as 'feminists' at that time (Brownmiller 1999: 194). Bunch argues that radical feminist theory 'both grows out of and guides activism in a continuing spiralling process' (1983: 251) and as academics we have grown from, and continue to be guided by, feminist activism, our own activism and that of others. For us, the 'personal *is* political' and our theory follows from our practice and our experience. We have both worked in rape crisis centres and we continue to participate in anti-rape campaigning at local and national levels.

Many of the legal changes introduced in the past 30 years resulted from such feminist campaigning, which put pressure on the justice system to improve. During this time, feminist activism and academia have been closely linked. Bunch explains how this works. She saw the development of theory as taking four distinct but interrelated processes (1983: 251–3):

- describing and naming reality
- asking why the reality exists
- strategies for change
- constructing a vision for the future.

In this tradition, ideas for change are built from observations of 'reality' or, to put it another way, of women's lives. Theoretical visions come out of this practical process. This notion of theory developing from practice accords with MacKinnon's understanding of radical feminism, that it is 'first practice, then theory ... Feminism was a practice long before it was a theory' (1991: 13). Here, then, theory is made from the ground up. This is in stark contrast to other traditions, including those in law. MacKinnon argues that in 'legal academia you theorize, then try to get some practitioner to put it into practice ... The closest most legal academics come to practice is teaching' (1991: 13).

Although we are teachers (and one of us is a legal academic) we want to claim some distance from the last part of this observation. We are academics who teach but we are also feminist activists. This synthesis of practice and theory – a radical feminist praxis – underpins our theoretical base (and our teaching) as they are grounded in the experience of women's lives. Bunch's analysis of the development of theory moving from naming male violence against women to seeking a vision for a better future helps to guide this chapter together with our memories of Dworkin's tireless efforts.

Radical feminism sees social change at the heart of the political agenda on male violence against women. For this reason the chapter seeks to describe and name radical feminism and how it came to identify male violence against women as the key vehicle for oppressing women. Women always define rape more broadly than the law allows, and we begin our analysis with a discussion of the problem of definition. We consider feminist campaigning against sexual violence, further examining the concept of praxis and how academic and practitioner feminists (often but not always embodied in the same women) have worked to provide services, campaign for change and develop theoretical understandings. Our discussions draw on ideas from the US and Britain, but the legal content focuses on law reform in England and Wales (others also examine feminist anti-rape campaigns elsewhere: Matthews 1994 (the US); Department of Justice, Equality and Law Reform 1998 (Ireland); Sakshi 1996 (India)).

The chapter provides an overview of the influence of feminist campaigning on recent legislation such as the Youth Justice and Criminal Evidence Act 1999 and the Sexual Offences Act 2003. Working at local and national levels, feminists have participated in government consultations and committees, exhausted themselves in countless meetings, initiative launches and report writing and yet remained focused on the issue of confronting the extent of the violence. Such challenges have resulted in change in some areas such as the development of Sexual Assault Referral Centres (SARCs), specialist police officers and changes in court procedures and yet with a conviction rate of just 5.6 per cent (Kelly *et al.* 2005) there is still much to do. The chapter examines other efforts at effecting change, in the form of public awareness education work and other newer initiatives. It concludes by looking towards the future, although Dworkin's 24-hour truce as yet seems distant.

Definitions: identifying rape

A useful starting point is to ask a seemingly simple question, 'What is male violence against women?'. Walby (1990: 132) argues that 'Male violence exists in a myriad of forms', some of which may be named as: prostitution, pornography, rape, sexual assault, domestic violence, stalking, trafficking, purdah, female genital mutilation, forced marriage and murder. The focus of this chapter is on just one of these: 'rape', but since these violations are linked in many ways, it is important to acknowledge the connections between these 'myriad forms'. Kelly's continuum of violence provides a model for doing this within radical feminism, viewing all the forms of male violence as connected by their 'common character' (1988). The myriad forms of violation can all be understood as parts of a patriarchal structure which ensures women's continued oppression. From this perspective, the aim of a feminist praxis must be to end sexual violence.

'Rape' is at first glance a simple concept, yet the definition of rape is contested. Common sense might suggest a simple answer such as 'sex with a woman without consent' but this leaves the terms 'sex', 'consent' and 'woman' requiring further definition. For many 'women' the term 'sex' denotes something broader than the legal definition of the *actus reus* (guilty act) of rape and we return to this topic later, in evaluating changes within the Sexual Offences Act 2003. The concept of 'without consent' may appear straightforward to many women, but is fabulously convoluted in the hands of the adversarial legal system. Again, we revisit some aspects of this in later discussions.

In law, rape is a sexual offence. Feminist theory has struggled to explain the motivation for this offence and the literature contains conflicting opinions about whether rape is about sex, about violence or about both (Brownmiller 1976; Kelly 1988; MacKinnon 1989). Until recently, the law equated rape to acts of intercourse, utilising masculinist assumptions of what constituted 'rape'. The criminal offence was limited to penetration by a man's penis of a woman's vagina. This view was defined by heterosexual men, to describe sex with women, from their own subjective position. By extension, they defined the harm of rape on the same terms. This definition, which saw rape as intercourse without consent, used sex to mask the violent nature of the act and the elements of power and control that are inherent in sexual violence.

Rape defined by women clearly varies considerably from rape defined by the perpetrator, or from that defined by law. However, living within a patriarchal society, women's definitions are affected by many forces.

Cloaked in stigma, 'rape' is often a word that women find difficult to use in describing their own experiences (Kelly and Radford 1996). MacKinnon (1987: 105) argues that a woman understands her position by measuring 'against every rape case she ever heard about'. Media reporting of rape is frequently underpinned by patriarchal constructions of morality surrounding female sexuality constructing 'good' women as passive, malleable and obedient while 'bad' women are constructed as promiscuous, independent and rebellious. Popular culture feeds this dichotomy further, upholding the idea that (any) woman can say 'no' but mean 'yes'. In Mills and Boon romance novels the heroine is frequently reluctant but persuadable. In the cinema there are many examples: Rhett Butler, for instance, famously takes Scarlett O'Hara up the stairs as she protests, and in pornography, women frequently 'like' to be persuaded in a variety of ways.

In fact pornography goes much further than this, suggesting that women want to be raped. In pornographic stories women, subjected to appalling degradations, are described as being sexually excited, often becoming willing participants. It has also been suggested that news reports of rape cases use this type of titillation in a milder form. 'It is for the pleasure of the armchair rapist that detailed accounts of violent rapes exist in the media' (Griffin 1979: 7). Amid these confounding forces, the definition of rape has remained contentious. The law is built on a male-centred conceptualisation of rape. All of us are fed stories of rape, from the news media, pornographers and other fiction writers, and from each other. None of these help to reveal the reality of rape.

Understanding rape: radical feminism

Criminological theories have traditionally fed on mainstream ideas of rape, denying male responsibility for violence and minimising the impact of violence on women (Naffine 1997). Criminological responses to violence focused on men, often to the exclusion of women, yet the issue of masculinity remained largely invisible until the late 1980s (Connell 1987; Walklate 1995). Utilising traditional discourses, men have been able to excuse themselves as victims of their own sex drives and to blame women for stepping outside of accepted gender roles (Stanko 1990).

Before the radical feminist challenge, the assumption had been that violent men were different from ordinary men; that they were biologically defective in some fashion. Consciousness raising identified rape as commonplace (backed up by subsequent research, discussed in Brownmiller 1999) and feminist theory was then able to question whether so many women could be the targets of just a small group of pathologically deviant men. Wilson (1983) dismissed the 'few bad men' theory and the myth of the dangerous, sex-driven stranger, while Stanko (1990) has argued that the creation of the 'dangerous stranger' has hidden the more likely position that many men use violence as part of their 'normal' behaviour towards women. After many years of evidence gathering, the police and other state agencies now acknowledge the reality of radical feminist understandings:

> There is a general perception that the majority of rape offences are committed by a lone male against a female who is unlikely to be known to him. The reality is that this type of offence forms only a very small part of the overall total. (HMIC/HMCPSI 2002: 8)

The assumption that violent men were a small, unknown, deviant minority ignored the fact that one in every two girls experiences male sexual violence before they are 18 years old (Kelly and Radford 1987; Kelly *et al.* 1991). Feminist theory now accounts for rape and other forms of violence with alternative explanations. Wilson (1983: 12) argued that women's sexual lives exist on a continuum:

> Men whistle and call after us on the street. This is at the other extreme of the pleasure/danger continuum and is a more contradictory experience than the sheer terror of rape and mutilation ... Yet the daily control of women by sexual innuendo is not trivial.

Further development of this helped to identify Kelly's continuum of violence (Kelly 1988), placing 'everyday' violations (Stanko 1990) within a structural context. Mullender (1996: 36–7) indicates how men avoid self-blame: 'They blamed drugs, alcohol and uncontrollable anger ... abusive men will grasp at any excuse for their behaviour, and there are many half-baked theories of causation which give them ample scope.' Feminist theory is thus able to identify rape as one of a range of male behaviours which help to maintain patriarchal power. From this perspective the female definition of rape is clearly the form to prioritise. It remains crucial that, just as black people identify the scope and nature of racism, women define male violence.

This feminist critique of patriarchal rule did not occur without challenge. There have been suggestions that radical feminists' analysis and language 'transforms perfectly stable women into hysterical, sobbing victims' (Roiphe 1993: 112). A sceptical backlash in the 1990s argued that radical feminism encouraged women to label 'bad sex' as rape and see themselves as victims (Paglia 1992; Roiphe 1993; Wolf 1993).

Such criticisms and disagreements within feminism are nothing new. Bunch (1975) used the term 'victim' in her critique of the consciousness-raising exercises of the women's movement. She argued that some women became obsessed with their own personal experiences, wearing their victimisation as a 'chip on the shoulder, a cross to bear, or a badge of honor' (Bunch 1975: 95). hooks has made similar criticisms of the victim model (hooks 1984). Within activism, the term 'victim' was seen as reinforcing passivity and helplessness and so the term 'survivor' was adopted (Kelly 1988) as a stronger and more optimistic alternative.

In the 1990s backlash, however, the criticism was different. Rather than extending feminist theory, the accusation of 'victim feminism' threatened the years of feminist research and services for women. In her well-documented work responding to the backlash, US jurist Rhode charts 'the distance we yet have to travel' (1997: viii) to achieve equality, by cataloguing the range of ways in which the very existence of gender inequality is denied within American culture. Rhode outlines the backlash against feminist work on rape:

> critics often caricature antirape activists in far more extremist rhetoric than that used by the activists themselves. To commentators like Katie Roiphe, Camille Paglia, Mary Matalin, John Leo and Neil Gilbert, 'delusional' 'yuppie feminists[s]' with 'simpering prom-queen' sensibilities and 'neopuritan preoccupation[s]' are determined to transform the act of seduction into the crime of rape. (1997: 119)

To paraphrase the title of Burton Nelson's 1994 work, it does seem that the stronger women get the more men (and their cheerleaders) will play hardball. As Rhode demonstrates, according to this new orthodoxy of denial, feminists are evil. Feminists do not accept that equality has been achieved and the bad old days of unequal opportunities are over. The arguments of Gilbert *et al.* (discussed by Rhode) are dangerous since they can lead to stagnation and even to the loss of ground, in terms of public understandings of a feminist agenda. For the anti-rape movement this ridicule and rejection creates a new cultural story of rape, in which only certain women, who are characterised as sad, bad or mad, consider rape to be a major social problem.

In fact feminism has always been the subject of parody. From the earliest days the news media were happy to dismiss Women's Liberationists as 'Libbers' (discussed by Brownmiller 1999) so that to identify as a feminist today is to risk alienating any audience. Feminism is simultaneously dangerous, silly and outmoded. The story promulgated by the backlash (re)characterises rape as an aberration, which anyone can commit, and which only certain, foolish women consider a serious issue. It also led to a renewed tendency to assume that women make false allegations of rape.

Jordan (2004: 4) argues that it should not be of surprise that 'once the lid was lifted to expose the extent of sexual assault ... there would be some in society who would want to clamp the lid firmly back on the pot'. Her recent work challenges the myth of false reporting and clearly demonstrates the continuing need for a radical approach to challenge the notion that women lie about sexual violence:

> if there is any substantive truth in the statement that 'women lie about rape', it is most likely to be in underestimating the severity of what has happened, concealing the violation from those close to them, refusing to inform the police of its occurrence and colluding to protect the identity of the offender. (Jordan 2004: 55)

Radical feminism's core claim was that rapists were not monsters but 'ordinary' men. The backlash was about resisting this truth and in doing so constructed a new 'victim': the falsely accused man. Societal denial of the truth of sexual violence emerged because of the strength of radical feminist claims.

Such techniques of denial have been noted in response to other truth claims: 'Societies dissociate their knowledge of trauma – massive injustice, torture, genocide – preferring to live in the "bleached present" of conventional disbelief and logical denial' (Wylie in Enns 1996: 361). The 'bleached present' of the 1990s did give way to a mainstream acceptance of feminist understandings of rape which saw rape as the ordinary product of ordinary (male, heterosexual) behaviour. That helps to explain the emotiveness of the issue. It touches upon all our experiences, both male and female. 'It is its ordinariness which renders it so difficult to grasp and embrace' (Walklate 1995: 85). How radical feminism survived the backlash is part of the continuing story of campaigning against rape.

History: challenging rape

In 1975, Brownmiller was one of the first feminist writers to draw attention to the parallels between abusive male behaviour and 'normal', accepted, male behaviour. The exuberant rough and tumble of male football fans is one aspect of 'boys being boys'. Those same 'boys' also take their 'rough' behaviour home to 'their' female partners. Early writers highlighted how women's lives are more constrained than men's are because of everyday anxieties concerning male behaviour.

> At the age of eight, my suspicions were confirmed. My grandmother took me to the back of the house where the men wouldn't hear, and told me that strange men wanted to do harm to little girls. I learned not to walk on dark streets, not to talk to strangers, or get into strange cars, to lock doors, and to be modest. (Griffin 1979: 3)

Brownmiller and Griffin are both part of what has become known as the 'second wave of feminism' and many of the words and phrases used to describe male violence against women and its consequences stem from this second wave, which emerged in the 1960s and 1970s. This resurgence of feminism brought public attention to crimes of violence against women. As more became known, policies and practices came under challenge. However, developments in policy and practice did not spring from the altruistic benevolence of powerful decision-makers. The fight for women's rights has a long history, and similarly the struggle to put male violence against women on public and political agendas has not been easily won.

Women's resistance manifested itself first in finding the words to express and understand experiences and then in acquiring platforms from which to speak (Southall Black Sisters 1989; Bunch and Carillo 1992). Stanko (1994: 93) has suggested that whether as offenders or victims, women had been seen as 'heartless, helpless, hopeless, and/or in need of protection'. These stereotypes and norms enter the discourse of violence as a way of justifying male violence against women and second-wave feminism in the 1970s acted to highlight the language, policies and practices that legitimated such violence (Firestone 1970; Brownmiller 1975; Spender 1980).

Firestone (1970) was one of the early authors in this area who placed sexual oppression at the centre of her analysis (with Morgan 1970; Millett 1972). Firestone argued that the oppression of women (and children) was the prototype for all other forms of oppression. Firestone acknowledged the influence of dialectical materialism on her work – 'class analysis is a beautiful piece of work' (1970: 14) – but she remained critical. Discussing Engels, she insisted he 'acknowledged the sexual class system only where it overlapped and illuminated his economic construct' (1970: 15). The class-based theories of the past did not include women's experiences and women's voices. What emerged in the consciousness-raising sessions of the early 1970s was the theory that men of all classes abuse women, and while not all men abused, all men benefited from women's oppression:

> Everything from the verbal assault on the street, to a 'well meant' sexist joke your husband tells, to the lower pay you get at work (for doing the same job a man would be paid more for), to television commercials, to rock song lyrics, to the pink or blue blanket they put on your infant in the hospital nursery, to speeches made by male 'revolutionaries' that reek of male supremacy – everything seems to barrage your aching brain which has fewer and fewer defenses to screen such things out. (Morgan 1970: xviii)

Brownmiller (1975) described rapists as the 'shock troops of patriarchy', arguing that while not all men rape, all men benefit from the process of intimidation that keeps all women in a state of fear. She attacked men's silence about violence against women and also exposed the under-reporting of rape.

It has been argued that these early second-wave feminists conceptualised 'women' as a homogeneous group, and presumed that all women would understand and agree on the terms 'fear' and 'rape' in an unqualified manner. Feminists such as Firestone and Brownmiller used these terms as fundamental forms of oppression, understood by all women, at all times and in all cultures. Radical feminism now struggles to appreciate the diversity of women's experience and this oft-repeated criticism can hinder these attempts to include difference within our analysis. What the critics generally fail to appreciate is that this feminist 'meta-narrative' has given birth to networks of support which women, across our many differences, have been able to access.

Heidensohn (2000) suggests that feminism has raised the consciousness of women through transitions from being, acceptance and silence to knowing, resistance and voice. One part of this process in terms of rape emerged through the development of the rape crisis movement. In England the first Rape Crisis helpline opened in 1976, modelled on developments in the US where rape had been the defining issue for radical feminists (Brownmiller 1999: 218). Rape Crisis groups were typically independent collectives and avoided hierarchical structures. While there has always been some thirst for wider understanding of the radical feminist approach, this has not always been coupled with a wish for official recognition of feminist services. Relations with the state have generally been wary, at best:

When the London Rape Crisis Centre (LRCC) was opened in 1976, centre members' reluctance to become agents of the state was met with concern from official quarters about 'outsiders tampering with the normal course of the law' (Toner 1977: 182). The Home Office was distrustful of 'militant feminists' (Williams 1999: 69). Radical feminism, in challenging conventional arenas of politics, seemed to attack the traditional 'powerstructured relationships' (Millett 1972: 23) between the statutory and voluntary sector, avoiding co-option by (or into) a male dominated state. (Jones 2004: 56)

Supporting women: Rape Crisis centres

In England, Rape Crisis began as a disparate collection of independent feminist groups which quietly grew but which could not agree on any national grouping or affiliation, until the 1990s. Meanwhile, more centres opened during the 1980s and, despite concerns over co-option (see Smyth 1996: 69), these sometimes *did* receive some official funding, via their local councils. Bruegel and Kean (1995: 147) called the early to mid-1980s the 'moment of municipal feminism', charting the tensions and disagreements between feminists, local authorities and trade unions.

The political context of the 1980s brought some opportunities to feminist campaigners but they were faced with a situation where men were in the majority, which made it difficult to bring women's agendas to the fore. At all levels – discursive, legislative, policy-making and implementation – male definitions, explanations and solutions prevailed: 'minimal attention has been paid to how women define abuse and violence' (Kelly 1988: 139). As second-wave feminism began to lead to a slowly increasing female presence within the governance of town halls and trades unions some changes were seen.

> In the past 20 years, a different separatism has developed, this time within union structures ... this takes on many forms, such as women's officers, women's committees ... Women's self-organisation thus provides women with space and voice to debate women's concerns, develop consciousness, confidence and skills, to experience and acknowledge the diversity of priorities among women, formulate policies and practices and strategies to get these onto the trade union agenda. (Colgan and Ledwith 2000: 245)

It was not simply the increased presence of women in politics at the time that led this change, but rather their political and ideological beliefs (MacKay 1996). The 1980s saw the development of greater co-operation between statutory agencies, voluntary and charitable organisations and community groups. Official initiatives on violence against women stem from the challenges raised by women's groups, particularly criticisms of policing (Hanmer and Saunders 1984). Home Office Circular 69/86 *Violence Against Women* was followed in 1990 by Home Office Circular *Domestic Violence*, which recommended police participation in multi-agency initiatives. The feminist challenge was starting to influence legislation and policy.

It seemed that this trend would continue into the 1990s. At the end of the 1980s, the women at the voluntary group Rights of Women were spearheading a challenge to the antiquated laws on rape within marriage (Radford 1990). By the beginning of the 1990s this saw success in the House of Lords judgments in *R v R* [1991] 3 WLR 767. Meanwhile, the Rape Crisis Federation (RCF) was established in 1996 as a national co-ordinating body for the rape crisis movement in England and Wales (Jones 2004). The key aims of the organisation had been to secure a voice for the groups that constituted its membership, to lobby and campaign for changes in legislation on sexual violence and to secure statutory funding for rape crisis centres. However, it found itself in the paradoxical position of 'receiving state funding and developing an ever closer relationship with the state, [while] at a local level for the rape crisis movement there existed *no* state funding' (Jones 2004: 63 emphasis in original).

RCF was part of the feminist challenge that had, from the late 1970s onwards, begun to penetrate the state through political parties, local government and trade unions (Rowbotham *et al.* 1979). Another development during the 1990s was the formation of the optimistically named group Campaign to End Rape. This unfunded, voluntary organisation came out of a workshop run by Liz Kelly, Kate Cook and Jan Jordan at the 1996 Violence, Abuse and Women's Citizenship conference held in Brighton. It mounted a challenge to rape law, based on the evidence of attrition within the criminal justice system, which eventually resulted in the 2003 Sexual Offences Act.

Legislation: campaigning in earnest

These feminist groups were challenging an orthodoxy that found rape to be a crime committed by strangers, against virginal young women. This discourse was the root of the law which had once seen rape as a property crime committed against a man (see Griffin 1979) and which did not consider that rape could occur within the sanctity of marriage. Both of these constructions placed rape as a 'private' matter, something beyond the range of the criminal law which prosecutes matters in the 'public' sphere. The tendency to perceive gendered violence as a private affair, requiring limited state interference slowly but increasingly was being replaced by the recognition that the state had been failing rape victims.

Feminists sought legislative reform on a number of issues, including the marital rape problem already mentioned, a revision of the definitions of rape, consent and honest belief, and questioning the woman in court on her previous sexual history:

> Just as the defence can call evidence to establish that a woman is of 'notoriously bad character' so it has long been the law that she herself can be cross-examined to the same effect, because such evidence is relevant to the issue of consent, as showing a person more likely to consent to sexual intercourse. One of the earliest cases illustrating this principle is *R* v *Barker* where counsel was held entitled to ask the

celebrated question, 'Were you not, on [a date subsequent to the alleged offence] walking in the High Street at Oxford, to look out for men?'. (Home Office 1975: 17)

The newly formed Campaign to End Rape (CER) had a three-point action plan. These concerned the falling conviction rate, the approach to consent in rape and the proper prosecution of rape cases in court (Cook 1997). Other points of interest (seen as contributors to the attrition rate) were the handling of sexual history evidence in court and defendants who represented themselves in rape cases.

In 1998, amendments within the Youth Justice and Criminal Evidence Bill tried to tighten the position on the admissibility of sexual history evidence in court and to outlaw personal representation by rapists. The latter reform came about largely because of the courage of one rape survivor.

> The case which began to raise awareness took place in the summer of 1996 when Julia Mason was cross-examined, over a number of hours, by Ralston Edwards. Edwards even wore the same clothing that he had worn at the time of the rape. After his conviction Julia chose to speak publicly of her ordeal, since she did not want other women to have to go through the same humiliation. In fact other cases did follow, but the outcry was such that, despite Human Rights Act objections, the government felt compelled to act (Cook 1998) to prohibit future cross-examination in person. (Cook 2005)

CER, together with other feminists, tried to support Julia's claim and also lobbied to produce the clearest law on sexual history evidence. The resulting section 41 of the Youth Justice and Criminal Evidence Act 1999 does act to restrict the use of this evidence in court although the effectiveness of the provision in practice is still doubted (Cook 2005). Nevertheless, this campaigning success for CER as a radical feminist group was considered important. The trend was also continued when a representative (Sandra McNeill) was invited on to the External Reference Group (ERG) of the Sex Offences Review (SOR).

In 1999 Home Secretary Jack Straw set up the Sex Offences Review which comprised of a steering group of representatives from various governmental departments and an advisory group (ERG) which included representation from the Rape Crisis Federation, CER, Stonewall, MIND, Mencap, Barnados, religious groups, lawyers and other specialists including the feminist academics Temkin and Kelly. The terms of reference were:

> To review the sex offences in the common and statute law of England and Wales, and make recommendations that will: provide coherent and clear sex offences which protect individuals, especially children and the more vulnerable, from abuse and exploitation; enable abusers to be appropriately punished; and be fair and non-discriminatory in accordance with the ECHR and Human Rights Act. (Home Office 2000: iii)

The eventual review, entitled *Setting the Boundaries*, was published on 26 July 2000 and set out a new legislative agenda for sexual offences that culminated in the publication of the Sexual Offences Bill in January 2003. The Bill did not deliver the promise given in *Setting the Boundaries*, and feminist groups including CER and RCF, began to mobilise to lobby for change. RCF employed a lobbyist and, working with legal experts from CER, a concerted campaign was mounted including presenting evidence to a Parliamentary Select Committee where the deficiencies of the Bill and recommendations were made:

> RCF's support work reveals that many women who have been raped have little if any confidence in the present system of justice. This is hardly surprising when ... attrition ... continues ... Women either feel so discouraged that they fail to report the rape or they decide to withdraw their complaint: the corollary is that many rapists go unchallenged. It is clearly imperative that public confidence is restored through the implementation of sexual offences, which are coherent, clear and fair – to the complainant as well as the defendant. It is also imperative that the attrition rate is redressed. RCF and CER commend the government on many positive achievements within the Sexual Offences Bill and, in principle we welcome and support it with much enthusiasm. However, we regret that some of the clauses identified here remain unclear and ill-defined. (Select Committee Minutes 2003: Appendix 26)

The definition of rape in law was subsequently changed by the Sexual Offences Act 2003 which came into force on 1 May 2004. Section 1 extended the definition of rape to include the penetration by a penis of the vagina, anus or mouth. A new offence of sexual assault by penetration was also included, with assaults involving the insertion of objects, such as bottles, guns, knives, or other body parts, into the vagina or anus now attracting a potential life penalty. Thus rape remains a gender-specific offence which requires a penis for the commission of the *actus reus* (guilty act). The new section 2 offence allows other serious offences to be penalised appropriately, without compromising this important element of women's understanding of the concept of 'rape'. Thus an attempt was finally made to enact a survivor's understanding of the meaning of the term rape.

The Sexual Offences Act also limited the honest belief defence which had previously been available to defendants since 1975, when the House of Lords ruled in the case of *Morgan* [1976] AC 182, that a man's genuine belief in consent was a defence to a rape charge, even if the belief was unreasonable in the circumstances. Morgan had invited three men to have sex with his wife, telling them she liked to struggle. On a charge of rape these men then used this to claim that they believed the wife was consenting, notwithstanding her evident distress. The men were convicted but subsequently appealed and the House of Lords ruled that there could be no rape if a man honestly believed a woman had given her consent. His belief did not have to be reasonable. In the case of *Morgan* itself, the defendants were actually found guilty. However, the ruling caused a furore and feminists argued that it constituted a 'rapists' charter' (see Temkin 2002: 119–22). Any man charged with rape simply had to claim that he 'honestly' (i.e. subjectively, without any need for anyone else to take the same view) believed that the woman was consenting. This honest belief defence could potentially defeat any rape charge and women from CER and RCF considered that it was contributing to attrition. The honest belief defence was one of the most contentious issues tackled by Sexual Offences Review and the 2003 Act now requires that the belief in consent is subject to a test of reasonableness.

From the early 1980s, feminists have campaigned to improve legislation on rape. It might be assumed that the legislative framework is in much better shape now and that women are better protected by the law than ever before. However, as so few rapes result in a court case and so few of those result in conviction, feminist campaigning has also focused on the wider context of the policies and procedures of the criminal justice system and the public's understanding of rape.

Public awareness: advertising and other initiatives

While issue-led advertising campaigning has a long history in road safety and other areas, the issues around violence against women – domestic violence, rape, sexual assault and child abuse – were not among the topics traditionally prioritised by the state and indeed they were largely absent from UK policy debates in the 1970s and 1980s (Stanko 1990). Until the early 1990s, campaigns around male violence against women focused on crime prevention advice to women with suggestions including not travelling alone, particularly at night (see the Further Reading section below). As Stanko (1995: 52–3) argues:

> The popular signifiers of danger (dark alleys, open spaces, parks, and so forth) continually focus on public space – and on women in public. In spite of the police's own evidence that women overwhelmingly confront danger at home or in familiar locations such as work and usually at the hands of known men, the police advice continuously warns women of the dangers of public space.

Images used on such material typically illustrated and reinforced women's status as victim until the early 1990s when the Edinburgh-based Zero Tolerance campaign tackled these stereotypical 'victim' images of women head on (Foley 1993; Kitzinger and Hunt 1993; Stanko 1995).

MacKay (1996) discusses the genesis of the campaign, as a reaction to previous initiatives that saw responsibility for personal safety as lying with the woman. Zero Tolerance placed responsibility squarely on the shoulders of men and challenged the public's tolerance of male violence against women. The Zero Tolerance campaign designers recognised that if they were to move feminist ideas into mainstream thought, it was essential that the images used were not of battered, bruised and defeated women, but 'ordinary' women, women going about their everyday business. This refusal to use victim imagery was unprecedented, as was the dissonance between the images and the text. Instead of advertising products, when people read the text the words told them about women and children being beaten and raped. The Zero Tolerance campaign received much attention and provoked some controversy because of this break with normative expectations. Indeed, Warner (1995) likened the posters to wartime propaganda, as a 'Goebbels style exercise in hate propaganda'. His objection was that the 'Feminist Conspiracy' depicted all men as 'evil'. This type of criticism is an aspect of the power of feminist campaigning. When messages conform to normative expectations, the message is likely to have minimal impact. By violating the conventional norms, Zero Tolerance campaigns provoked response. For many women, the Zero Tolerance posters gave a feeling of empowerment. By using ordinary women in the posters, women could see 'that could be me' (Foley 1993).

Campaigns on male violence against women are no longer the preserve of women's groups. Many other agencies and organisations now share a sense of ownership; there is a cacophony of other voices around the table (see for example the recent campaign against male violence by Amnesty and recent police initiatives). These come from organisations that provide funding and other resources, organisations designing and producing campaign messages and materials, organisations providing research and evaluation and organisations involved in responding to the outcomes of campaigns. While some of these groupings may share the same political perspective, others may be there for very different reasons. There is some debate over whether this new diversity of campaign voices is a positive development. What is clear is that feminist activism started the movement towards such campaigns. Of major significance was the co-ordinated working between statutory and voluntary agencies which resulted through the campaigns. Awareness campaigns and their links to partnerships between statutory and non-statutory agencies highlight the changing relationship between feminism and the state (Cabinet Office/Women's Unit 1999; Heidensohn 2000; Kelly and Regan 2001).

The police advertising initiative referred to above demonstrates the ways in which advice given to women can still be premised on outmoded ideas about rape. Statistics demonstrate that reports of rape are rising. The 2001 British Crime Survey (BCS) interpersonal violence module (IPV) reported 190,000 incidents of serious sexual assault against women aged between 16 and 59 in England and Wales. Of these incidents, there were an estimated 80,000 rapes or attempted rapes in the year leading up to the research. The survey suggested that the majority of rape and sexual assault takes place in a domestic setting with 54 per cent of rapists current or former partners of the victim. A further 29 per cent were known to the victim and just 17 per cent of rapists were strangers. The survey also estimated that a small proportion of men – 0.2 per cent – had also been subject to sexual assault. In 2004–05, 14,002 rapes were reported to the police. The 2001 British Crime Survey interpersonal violence module found that only about 15 per cent of rapes came to the attention of the police. There is a clear dislocation between such statistical facts and how they are responded to (Kelly and Regan 2001). Despite the increasing political awareness of violence from known men, advice given to women on personal safety continues to focus on 'stranger danger' and the risk of being alone, on the streets, at night. In fact, there is so much information available to women suggesting that they are responsible for minimising the risk from any potential violence, that many feel that they are to blame:

> By the time they have reached adulthood, many women have developed an unconscious alarm system which monitors men's behaviour for possible danger. While each woman will devise her own way of using this information none the less, she knows before hand that it is she who is the cause of men's actions. When danger strikes, it is her behaviour that is scrutinised for its lure to men's physical and sexual aggressions. (Stanko 1990: 88)

Advertising then can still create problems, despite the availability of feminist understandings of rape. Indeed, the 'stranger danger' model could well be characterised as a continuing form of backlash, which aims to keep women oppressed by the fear of sexual violation. True public education could be put to good use in this arena, as the Zero Tolerance model demonstrates, and there is a telling need for real education about the law on rape and the provisions now in place to enable survivors to take cases to court: a need the current government seems reluctant to meet.

The present: where are we now with rape?

In the early years of the twenty-first century we have seen a growing number of legal and policy initiatives, in addition to the Sexual Offences Act 2003. Measures in the Criminal Justice Act 2003 aim to rebalance the legal system in favour of victims. Provisions from the Youth Justice and Criminal Evidence Act have finally come into force, allowing 'vulnerable witnesses' access to facilities for giving evidence via CCTV link and other protections in court. Initiatives such as the 2002 police Rape Action Plan have led to the setting up of more Sexual Assault Referral Centres across England and Wales. In 2001 the police also initiated 32 London rape centres, known as Sapphire units. Unfortunately these official initiatives have coincided with the loss of a number of rape crisis centres and with the closure of the original Rape Crisis Federation. Meanwhile, specialist training continues to be developed for police officers, and the Home Office, the Association of Chief Police Officers and the Crown Prosecution Service are jointly implementing the Rape Action Plan.

It is important to ask two questions here. First, would these initiatives have emerged without pressure from feminist campaigns, and second, what impact are they having? Certainly prior to the emergence of feminist campaigning in the 1970s, little was done by any agency of the criminal justice system to address rape. The second question is more difficult to answer. The statistics available on prevalence suggest that rape is not decreasing. Figures on reporting show a gradually increasing trend and so it can be said that rape survivors are more willing to trust in the criminal justice system to deliver some form of justice. Sadly, the conviction rate continues to fall, showing that trust to be horribly misplaced. In 2005 the Home Office report *A Gap or a Chasm?*, conducted by feminist researchers at London Metropolitan University, revealed that rape allegations resulting in a conviction had fallen to a record low from 24 per cent in 1985 to 5.6 per cent in 2002 with 11,676 rape cases resulting in just 655 convictions (Kelly *et al.* 2005). Of course, it may be argued that it is the very success of feminist campaigning on extending the remit of legislation beyond the formerly narrow remit of penile penetration of the vagina by an unknown man that has resulted in more reports of rape being made. However, such figures also point to the inability of the police or the courts to deal with cases effectively. In a report in the *Observer* (1 May 2005) an unnamed police officer claimed:

> After being created in a blaze of glory, the Met's dedicated rape units have been left without the funding or manpower to do the job demanded of them ... The burden on detectives is horrendous. On a murder or serious crime squad, senior detectives will have a team of detectives to delegate to, but in rape investigations each detective works mostly alone, responsible for every decision and every detail ... Nobody wants to work on the rape units any more. Even the trainees ordered in are not at the end of their training. They'll say they will not be in charge of investigations, but they are. I've seen them overwhelmed; good people, burnt out before their careers have even begun.

Furthermore, a recent report on the investigation and prosecution of rape cases found 'examples of lengthy delays' (HMIC/HMCPSI 2002: 19), with women from ethnic minority groups having 'particular difficulty in bringing offences against them to police notice' (2002: 19). The report provides examples of best practice across England and Wales but conceded that 'on some occasions, the social status of the victim, and/or the circumstances of the offence, determined the level of response' (2002: 31). This provides further indication that just as legislative change is not enough, changing procedures without challenging attitudes is unlikely to yield success. Despite changes in policing procedures, women who have been raped are often questioned on their behaviour; the assumption made is that they have somehow provoked an attack (Stanko 1994; Temkin 2000).

In their work on the court system, Gregory and Lees (1999: 100) argued that the court frequently had difficulty in bringing a guilty verdict if the complainant was seen as 'contributing to her own downfall by behaving inappropriately, by being in a nightclub at all or by wearing what is described as "provocative clothing"'. And yet there is no crime which can be likened to rape; no other crime where the complainant will have to undergo intrusive and intimate forensic examination, an experience that has been likened to a second assault (Gregory and Lees 1999). The majority of forensic medical examiners (FME) are male, there is evidence of a lack of 'harmonious' relations between police and FMEs, with women often having to endure 'lengthy delays' before examination (HMIC/HMCPSI 2002: 22). Following this, there is police questioning and, for the few cases that get to court, further difficult interrogation. Yet in the face of this, 'there appears to be a singular lack of curiosity about why women should make false allegations' (Gregory and Lees 1999: 61). The perception of a high prevalence of false allegations is unjustified and points more to the biases of the police and courts than to the actuality of women's behaviour (Jordan 2004).

Blaming the 'victim' is not only a useful strategy in diminishing individual men's responsibility for violence, it also provides a shield for inefficient and ineffective criminal justice systems. Smyth (1996: 56) has highlighted the 'paradoxical construction of women as simultaneously "victims" *and* as responsible for their own fate. *"She brought it on herself"'* (italics in original). Feminist campaigning in other countries reveals similar problems elsewhere (Kelly and Regan 2001). In Ireland and the Scandinavian countries there is the cultural norm of the strong, capable matriarchal figure. Within such discourses it is difficult to conceive of the woman as having been victimised (Ruuskanen 2001). This is useful in helping us understand victim-blaming in a context of cultural, gendered social roles and normalised behaviour. It is when the social role of the 'victim' falls outside that most usually associated with a 'battered wife' or a 'rape victim' that the person responsible for the violence becomes more visible. Blaming the victim is not a credible strategy when the victim is a very young child, a profoundly disabled women or a very old woman (Jones 2006). Because the wider society cannot think of a way of blaming these victims, the theory breaks down. There is still a need to move away from this culture of blame and feminist support models and campaigns are careful to avoid survivor criticism in their work. These can therefore provide practical models for a way forward.

The future?

A National Sexual Violence Action Plan (published late 2006) aims to set out broader partnership approaches to tackle sexual violence and joins a plethora of reports that have been published in recent years. However, Kelly (1999: 88) has argued that partnership is part of a soundbite politics. Together with 'multi-agency', 'community' and 'collaboration', partnership approaches to solving social problems have come to be regarded as a positive force for change. The development of feminist theories and effective challenges by women's organisations has resulted in changes to legislation, policies and procedures for responding to the problem of male violence against women. Ahmed *et al.* (2000: 1) have argued that 'feminism is driven by an imperative for change'. This is an ongoing project. Feminist groups continue to take alternative, direct action as well as continuing to participate in 'partnership' type approaches.

In the UK a feminist-led campaign group has been established to challenge the myths surrounding rape and sexual violence. The campaign is called The Truth About Rape and is supported by the Rape Crisis movement, the Campaign to End Rape and other women's groups (see 'Further Reading' below). The campaign, which launched in November 2002, highlights the nature of some of the commonly held beliefs surrounding rape. The campaign demonstrates the ongoing commitment of feminism to provide a challenge to traditional theories of violence, while struggling against the myths that deny the widespread existence of male violence against women which contribute to the commonly held beliefs, legal definitions and the constructions of violence depicted within the media (Stanko 1990; Walby 1990; Carter 1998; Berrington and Jones 2002).

At the time of writing we have services developed to serve the specific needs of women who have experienced male violence, yet there remains a need to acknowledge the complexities of struggles. Although acknowledging their different ethnic and class backgrounds, their differences in age and ability, what women have in common is a perception of the world that differs from that presented by men. This is where the concept of the continuum of male violence can be so useful as 'these are not isolated crimes, these are parts of the fabric of women's lives, and they all act to keep women, individually and collectively, under men's control' (Cook 1997: 23).

The feminist challenge to dominant theories of rape is more than the struggle of women for the right to define their own experiences. 'What we are fighting for is the privilege of interpretation, that we want to interpret our own lives and experiences. And we have not been allowed to' (Lundgren 1995: 39). Feminists are also fighting to uncover the institutionalised nature of violence against women and the injustice that is part of the fabric of the criminal justice system. With the highly publicised changes in legislation and the development of rape crisis, of Zero Tolerance and SARCs along with other initiatives, the perception may be that women who have been raped now find it much easier to get justice. At the same time, government figures confirm that rape convictions are at an all-time low and rape still goes largely unreported. Changing legislation and legal and judicial attitudes is a continuing struggle, however; the increasing legitimacy given to feminist analysis of male violence against women is an indication of the enormous impact feminism continues to have in the cultural domain. Inclusion of this chapter within a mainstream volume on 'victim'-ology is just another brick in a (very long) wall.

Further reading

Amnesty International UK: Stop Violence Against Women. On 5 March 2004 Amnesty International launched a global campaign to stop Violence Against Women (http://www.amnesty.org.uk/svaw/).

Department of Gender, Women and Health. Part of the World Health Organisation, this is responsible for 'researching and disseminating information on neglected topics directly pertaining to women's health, such as gender-based violence against women'. (http://www.who.int/gender/en).

Metropolitan Police (http://www.met.police.uk/sapphire/feature2.htm).

Rape Crisis (http://www.rapecrisis.org.uk).

Truth About Rape campaign (http://www.truthaboutrape.co.uk).

Zero Tolerance Trust (http://www.zerotolerance.org.uk/).

References

Ahmed, S., Kilby, J., Lury, C., McNeil, M. and Skeggs, B. (2000) *Transformations: Thinking Through Feminism*. London: Routledge.

Berrington, E. and Jones, H. (2002) 'Reality vs Myth: Constructions of women's insecurity', *Feminist Media Studies*, 2(3).

Brownmiller, S. (1976) *Against Our Will: Men, Women and Rape*. Harmondsworth: Penguin (originally published in the US in 1975).

Brownmiller, S. (1999) *In Our Time: Memoir of a Revolution*. New York: Dell Publishing.

Bruegel, I. and Kean, H. (1995) 'Gender and class in 1980s local government', *Critical Social Policy*, 15(2–3): 147–69.

Bunch, C. (1975) *Building Feminist Theory*. New York: Longman.

Bunch, C. (1983) 'Not by Degrees: Feminist Theory and Education', in C. Bunch and S. Pollack (eds) *Learning Our Way: Essays in Feminist Education*. New York: Crossing Press.

Bunch, C. and Carillo, R. (1992) *Gender Violence: A Development and Human Rights Issue*. Dublin: Attic Press.

Cabinet Office/Women's Unit (1999) *Living Without Fear. An Integrated Approach to Tackling Violence Against Women*. London: The Stationery Office.

Carter, C. (1998). 'When the "Extraordinary" Becomes "Ordinary"', in C. Carter, G. Branston and S. Allan (eds) *News, Gender and Power*. London: Routledge.

Colgan, F. and Ledwith, S. (2000) 'Diversity, identities and strategies of women trade union activists', *Gender, Work and Organisation*, 7(4): 242–57.

Connell, R.W. (1987) *Gender and Power*. Cambridge: Polity Press.

Cook, K. (1997) 'Raging against rape', *Trouble and Strife*, 35.

Cook, K. (1998) 'Rape and unrepresented defendants: The last straw, *The Criminal Lawyer*, Jul/Aug: 3–4.

Cook, K. (2005) 'Rape, the End of the Story: A Study of Rape Appeal Cases', unpublished PhD thesis, Manchester Metropolitan University.

Department of Justice, Equality and Law Reform (1998) *The Law on Sexual Offences: A Discussion Paper*. Dublin: Stationery Office.

Dworkin, A. (1984) 'I want a twenty-four-hour-truce during which there is no rape', *M.*, No. 13.

Enns, C. (1996) 'Counselors and the backlash: "Rape Hype" and "false memory syndrome"', *Journal of Counseling and Development*, 76: 358–67.

Firestone, S. (1970) *The Dialectic of Sex: The Case for Feminist Revolution*. New York: Bantam Books.

Foley, R. (1993) 'Zero Tolerance', *Trouble and Strife*, 27.

Gregory, J. and Lees, S. (1999) *Policing Sexual Assault*. London: Routledge.

Griffin, S. (1979) *Rape: The Power of Consciousness*. San Francisco: Harper and Row.

Hanmer, J. and Saunders, S. (1984) *Well Founded Fear: A Community Study of Violence to Women*. London: Hutchinson.

Heidensohn, F. (2000) *Sexual Politics and Social Control*. Buckingham: Open University Press.

HMIC/HMCPSI (Her Majesty's Inspectorate of Constabulary and Her Majesty's Crown Prosecution Service Inspectorate) (2002) *Joint Inspection into the Investigation and Prosecution of Rape Offences in England and Wales*. London: HMSO.

Home Office (1975) *Report of the Advisory Group on the Law of Rape*. London: HMSO.

Home Office (2000) *Setting the Boundaries: Reforming the Law on Sex Offences*. London: Home Office Communication Directorate.

hooks, b. (1984) *Feminist Theory: From Margin to Centre*. Boston, MA: South End Press.

Jones, H. (2004) 'Opportunities and obstacles: The Rape Crisis Federation', *The Journal of International Gender Studies*, 8(1&2): 55–71.

Jones, H. (2006) 'Visibility and Consent: The Sexual Abuse of Elderly Women', in J. Powell and A. Wahidin (eds) *Foucault and Aging*. New York: Nova Science.

Jordan, J. (2004) *The Word of a Woman? Police, Rape and Belief.* Hampshire: Palgrave Macmillan.

Kelly, L. (1988) *Surviving Sexual Violence.* Cambridge: Polity Press.

Kelly, L. (1999) 'What Happened To The "F" And "P" Words? Feminist Reflections on Inter-Agency Forums and the Concept of Partnership', in N. Harwin, G. Hague and E. Malos (eds) *The Multi-Agency Approach to Domestic Violence: New Opportunities, Old Challenges.* London: Whiting and Birch.

Kelly, L. and Radford, J. (1987) 'The Problem of Men: Feminist Perspectives on Sexual Violence', in P. Scraton (ed.) *Law, Order and the Authoritarian State.* Milton Keynes: Open University Press.

Kelly, L. and Radford, J. (1996) '"Nothing Really Happened": The Invalidation of Women's Experiences of Sexual Violence', in M. Hester, L. Kelly and J. Radford (eds) *Women, Violence and Male Power.* Buckingham: Open University Press.

Kelly, L. and Regan, L. (2001) *Rape: The Forgotten Issue? A European Research and Networking Project.* London: Child and Woman Abuse Studies Unit, University of North London.

Kelly, L., Lovett, J. and Regan, L. (2005) *A Gap or a Chasm? Attrition in Reported Rape Cases,* Home Office Research Study 293. London: Home Office.

Kelly, L., Regan, L. and Burton, S. (1991) *An Exploratory Study of the Prevalence of Sexual Abuse in a Sample of 16–21 year olds.* London: Child Abuse Studies Unit, Polytechnic of North London.

Kitzinger, J. and Hunt, K. (1993) *Evaluation of Edinburgh District Council's Zero Tolerance Campaign.* Edinburgh: Edinburgh District Council's Women's Unit.

Lundgren, E. (1995) 'Matters of life and death', *Trouble and Strife,* 31.

MacKay, F.S. (1996) 'Getting There, Being There, Making a Difference? Gendered Discourses of Access and Action in Local Politics', unpublished thesis.

MacKinnon, C. (1987) *Feminism Unmodified: Discourses on Life and Law.* Cambridge, MA: Harvard University Press.

MacKinnon, C. (1989) *Towards a Feminist Theory of the State.* Cambridge, MA: Harvard University Press.

MacKinnon, C. (1991) 'From practice to theory or what is a white woman anyway?', *Yale Journal of Law and Feminism,* 4: 13–22.

Matthews, N.A. (1994) *Confronting Rape: The Feminist Anti-Rape Movement and the State.* London: Routledge.

Millett, K. (1972) *Sexual Politics.* London: Abacus/Sphere.

Morgan, R. (ed.) (1970) *Sisterhood is Powerful: An Anthology of Writings from the Woman's Liberation Movement.* New York: Vintage Books.

Mullender, A. (1996) *Rethinking Domestic Violence.* London: Routledge.

Naffine, N. (1997) *Feminism and Criminology.* Cambridge: Polity Press.

Nelson, M.B. (1994) *The Stronger Women Get, the More Men Love Football: Sexism and the American Culture of Sports.* New York: Harcourt Brace.

Paglia, C. (1992) *Sex, Art and American Culture.* New York: Penguin Books.

Radford, J. (1990) 'Rape in marriage: Make it a crime!', *Rights of Women Bulletin,* Spring: 12–14.

Rhode, D. (1997) *Speaking of Sex: The Denial of Gender Inequality.* Cambridge, MA: Harvard University Press.

Roiphe, K. (1993) *The Morning After.* London: Hamish Hamilton.

Rowbotham, S., Segal, L. and Wainwright, H. (1979) *Beyond the Fragments: Feminism and the Making of Socialism.* London: Merlin Press.

Ruuskanen, M. (2001) 'The Good Battered Woman: A Silenced Defendant', in K. Nousiainene, Å. Gunnarsson, K. Lundström and J. Niemi-Kiesiläinen (eds) *Responsible Selves: Women in the Nordic Legal Culture.* Aldershot: Ashgate.

Sakshi (1996) *Gender and Judges: A Judicial Point of View.* New Delhi: Sakshi.

Select Committee Minutes (2003) Appendix 26. Available from: http://www. publications.parliament.uk/pa/cm200203/cmselect/cmhaff/639/639ap27.htm (accessed 2 June 2006).

Smyth, A. (1996) 'Seeing Red: Men's Violence Against Women in Ireland', in C. Corrin (ed.) *Women in a Violent World: Feminist Analyses and Resistance Across 'Europe'.* Edinburgh: Edinburgh University Press.

Southall Black Sisters (1989) 'Two Struggles: Challenging Male Violence and the Police', in C. Dunhill (ed.) *The Boys in Blue.* London: Virago.

Spender, D. (1980) *Man Made Language.* London: Pandora.

Stanko, E. (1990) *Everyday Violence.* London: Pandora.

Stanko, E. (1994) 'Dancing with Denial: Researching Women and Questioning Men', in M. Maynard and J. Purvis (eds) *Women's Lives from a Feminist Perspective.* London: Taylor and Francis.

Stanko, E. (1995) 'Women, crime, and fear', *Annals of the American Academy of Political and Social Science,* 539: 46.

Temkin, J. (2000) 'Prosecuting and defending rape: Perspectives from the Bar', *Journal of Law and Society,* 4(2): 219–48.

Temkin, J. (2002) *Rape and the Legal Process,* 2nd edn. Oxford: Oxford University Press.

Toner, B. (1977) *The Facts of Rape.* London: Arrow Books.

Walby, S. (1990) *Theorising Patriarchy.* Oxford: Blackwell.

Walklate, S. (1995) *Gender and Crime: An Introduction.* London: Prentice Hall.

Warner, M. (1995) *From the Beast to the Blonde: Fairy-Tales and their Tellers.* London: Vintage.

Williams, B. (1999) *Working with Victims of Crime: Policies, Politics and Practice.* London: Jessica Kingsley.

Wilson, E. (1983) *What's to be Done about Violence Against Women?* London: Penguin.

Wolf, N. (1993) *Fire with Fire: The New Female Power and How it Will Change the 21st Century.* London: Chatto and Windus.

Chapter 6

Feminism, victimology and domestic violence

Carolyn Hoyle

Introduction

The past few decades have witnessed a plethora of studies on domestic violence, particularly in the US and the UK. At first, research focused on the epidemiology of domestic violence, specifically on men's physical abuse of their female partners, but then critical attention was turned to the concepts of domestic violence: how should it be defined; who is likely to be a victim; how prevalent is it; is it a criminal or a psychological or a social problem; how extensive is the collateral damage; and who are the experts? Feminists, both activist and academic, became the authoritative voice on this emerging subject of public, political and academic concern. As with sexual violence against women and to a lesser extent child abuse, feminism found a niche in domestic violence. It sought to define the problem and prescribe the cures and in doing so it focused on the concept of patriarchy and, in particular, the imbalance in and abuse of power in many intimate relationships. Like many ideological positions that come to dominate a field, feminism laid itself bare to criticism of heavy determinism and being over-prescriptive in its claims about causes and solutions. Competition over the domain came from many directions and feminism responded. While power and control are still central to both feminist and mainstream understandings of domestic violence, some scholars have recently developed more nuanced understandings of the dynamics of abuse and begun to differentiate between types and experiences of violence, that has implications for policy responses to domestic violence. This chapter traces this movement, developing ideas about power and control and ends with a consideration of its impact on criminal justice policies today.

The rise of feminism, victimology and domestic violence

Modern feminism emerged in the late 1960s, in the same period as criminology's new sub-discipline, victimology. With its focus on women and victims[1] and the inequitable distribution of power, oppression and harm, it laid the ground for the recognition of the widespread problem of domestic violence and the motivation to challenge it. Feminists' concern with crimes against the powerless and their determination to expose not just the prevalence of abuse but also the experiences of those abused, led to the publication of numerous empirical and theoretical studies as well as powerful polemics on domestic violence. The pioneering work of a few academics (most notably, Edwards, the Dobashes, Smart, Stanko and Walklate) inspired an industry of academic and policy work on the subject, with currently no indication of diminishing interest. There are now academic journals dedicated to interpersonal and intimate violence and violence against women more generally, as well as countless monographs and edited collections and journal articles devoted to the subject. However, there have been and there remains, deep divisions within this body of work, reflecting the rifts between the different feminisms that emerged during the 1960s (Daly and Chesney-Lind 1988). In particular, mainstream and liberal feminists have been criticised for speaking only for people like them; typically white, middle-class, privileged women. As radical feminists[2] pointed out, not all disadvantaged groups are equally disadvantaged and women are not a homogeneous entity. Gender intersects with race, class and sexuality, among other variables, in ways that can doubly disadvantage people.

There are many areas of contention between different feminisms that it is not necessary to describe here, but a few words about the public/private distinction and its implications for the discussion about power and control may be helpful. Liberal feminism could not envisage the family as an institution of oppression and domination and hence placed value on the freedom of the family from illegitimate state interference. This position, it was argued by radical feminists, rendered abuse within the family invisible and beyond help. Radical feminists considered that all social institutions and relationships in both private and public worlds are characterised by a patriarchal power structure (Pateman 1987). Millett's *Sexual Politics* (1985), first published in 1970, established the foundations for a theory of patriarchy and a focus on the family as patriarchy's chief institution, that has been drawn on and developed by academic feminists since. Today, as is revealed below, there is still debate over the value of patriarchy as a core explanatory variable for domestic violence and the necessity and desirability of criminal justice intervention in family life. There have not only been divisions *within* feminism over how to define and respond to domestic violence, but also challenges from mainstream criminology and, in particular, victimology.

The contribution of victimology

For those who seek to understand domestic violence there are essentially two main bodies of research to draw on: predominantly survey research from victimologists, that can tell us a good deal about frequency and prevalence, as well as something about the distribution of domestic violence and relatively small, in-depth qualitative studies of the experience of domestic violence survivors carried out by those committed to feminist principles and methods. There have been clear tensions between feminism and victimology from the beginning; evidenced by the choice of language used by both groups, with victimologists' preference for 'victim' and feminists preference for 'survivor', and by the belief that feminism remains marginalised by victimology (Walklate 2004: 54).

Victimology has moved on dramatically from its early infamy brought about by the work of Von Hentig (1948), Mendelsohn (1956) and Wolfgang (1958) on victim precipitation and 'victim-proneness' and, most controversially, Amir (1971) who studied victim–offender interaction as a precipitating factor, blaming some victims in rape cases. Amir's work in particular attracted fierce criticism on methodological and ideological grounds (Morris 1987: 173–4; Walklate 1989: 4–5). Victimology was criticised for its assumptions about rationality and 'ideal' or 'normal' victims whose behaviour was judged by those who had the power to define what was appropriate – the male-dominated scientific academic community. This, it was argued, reflected 'a deeply embedded male view of the problem of victimisation' (Walklate 2004: 36–7).

Feminists also challenged the methodological limitations of highly quantitative survey data, typical of earlier victimology. Consequently, more recent surveys have sought to go beyond mere counting and measure victims' perceptions of crime and attitudes towards the criminal justice system. Victimologists have also undertaken smaller-scale, local surveys that have been able to document the uneven distribution of victimisation, by race, sex, age, class and locale. Their success in revealing differential patterns of victimisation has prompted changes also to the British Crime Survey (Percy and Mayhew 1997). Such studies have proven to be more sensitive to the prevalence of domestic violence and other interpersonal crimes than the larger-scale general victimisation surveys. For example, the most accurate national estimates of domestic violence today are provided by the 2001 British Crime Survey, that included a self-completion section on domestic violence and showed that 26 per cent of women and 17 per cent of men (aged 16–59) have experienced at least one incidence of domestic abuse since they were 16 (Walby and Allen 2004). However, surveys remain limited in the field of domestic violence because differences in approach, wording and categorisation of responses can generate widely differing estimates of victimisation. The sensitivity of survey questions and the approach and demeanour of the interviewer may also dramatically alter response rates. Such limitations led most feminist academics committed to empirical study of the experiences of vulnerable groups to favour in-depth qualitative work to describe and explain women's experiences of and responses to victimisation in the home.

Their choices of empirical methods speak to the divergence between the two approaches over what constitutes legitimate research. Victimology remains committed to objective and value-free social scientific method and its primary goal is academic not activist. Conversely, most feminists do not claim or even aspire to value-freedom. They are keen to establish, rather than deny, a relationship between the researcher and the researched, with a commitment to flexibility in interviews to encourage elaboration and empowerment of interviewees (Reinharz 1992). Furthermore, they are explicitly focused on changing the social world, not just recording and explaining it. Nonetheless, some challenges to feminist orthodoxies have come from victimology, especially from 'family violence surveys', and feminism has evolved in response.

Challenges to orthodoxies and the developing field

For a while orthodoxies about perpetrators, victims and motivations remained largely unchallenged in this field. To some extent, research was constrained within an ideological straitjacket that saw patriarchy as the only explanation and hence precluded serious consideration of violence that did not appear to take place within a patriarchal relationship or that seemed to be explained by more than just the unequal distribution of power and control. The strongest challenge to these prevailing attitudes came from family violence studies suggesting gender symmetry.

One of the most powerful orthodoxies to be established by feminist accounts of domestic violence, especially those of radical feminists, was that the family was a patriarchal institution and that women were almost exclusively the victims of domestic violence and men the perpetrators. This position was supported by a good deal of empirical evidence, especially studies of refuges and emergency medical facilities that show an overwhelming preponderance of female victims. Furthermore, it was argued that when men assaulted women this was to maintain the hierarchical nature of patriarchal domination, to maintain control over women, whereas if women assaulted their male partners this was almost always in self-defence (Saunders 1988). These orthodoxies have in recent years provoked fierce debate.

Since Steinmetz's (1977–1978) seminal paper on 'battered husbands', there have been a number of studies showing that men are also abused in the home and that they are less likely to report this abuse (Grady 2002; Felson 2006a), but the more provocative studies are those that suggest gender symmetry and that argue that domestic violence is not determined by gender or patriarchy (for recent examples see Felson and Pare 2005; Fergusson and Ridder 2005; Felson 2006b). Victimologists have produced more than one hundred studies suggesting that the rates of domestic violence by men and women are equivalent (Kimmel 2002). It is certainly the case that more women are being arrested for domestic violence than in previous decades (following the introduction of presumptive or mandatory arrest policies in many states in America; Miller and Meloy 2006) but it is argued that there is a significant amount of intimate violence perpetrated by women that is either never reported or does not result in any criminal sanction.

Victimologists such as Strauss, conducting large-scale US surveys, based on nationally representative samples and using 'conflict tactic scales' (CTS) to measure the violence (Straus et al. 1996), have presented a multifaceted view of partner violence, with women assaulting their partners at about the same rate as men and with diverse motives for both men and women. Straus's most recent research, using the revised Conflict Tactics Scales 2 (CTS2), provides further evidence for his claim that the predominant pattern of domestic abuse is one in which both partners are violent, with male-only violence being least likely in families where abuse takes places (Straus 2005). His data also challenge the belief that when women hit the motives are different and that male-dominance is the primary cause of partner violence (Straus 2006: 144). These data and other studies using the CTS and the CTS2 have been influential (although their challenges to feminist orthodoxy have provoked some academic ostracism and denial (Straus and Gelles 1990)). As Kimmel (2002) points out, the majority of empirical articles supporting gender symmetry in two meta-analytic reviews of the literature had used the CTS (Archer 2000; Fiebert 1997, 2004).

The CTS studies find high rates of domestic violence, low rates of injury, little or no escalation of violence and equal perpetration among men and women. Crime victimisation studies, using nationally representative samples of householders, seem to contradict the results of the studies relying on the CTS and uniformly find clear evidence of gender asymmetry in rates of domestic violence. They show that domestic violence is not so common, is serious and escalates over time and is predominantly perpetrated by men (Kimmel 2002: 1338–40). Furthermore, in-depth interview material elicited from a sample of men originally counted as 'male victims' in the Scottish Crime Survey shows that crime survey data overstate men's experiences of domestic abuse (Gadd et al. 2003). As Kimmel describes, the diverse types of data gathered by these different types of studies are the result of their distinct theoretical perspectives and data sources.

Family violence studies, that tend to use the CTS, provide valuable data for better understanding the rather common couple violence that takes place in many homes and affects men, women and their children. As Straus has argued, this research is useful in informing programmes of primary prevention, to help to prevent escalation towards serious physical assaults (1999: 39). The CTS is most helpful at showing the levels and types of aggression occurring when couples have arguments and that women and men may express their anger or frustration during an argument more equally than was traditionally thought. However, it tells us little about the ways in which partners use violence instrumentally to gain or regain control over the other partner. For this, crime victimisation studies or other types of empirical research are more valuable (Kimmel 2002). Studies that examine power and control-motivated instrumental violence – systematic violence, that is more likely to result in serious injury – show clear asymmetry, with more than 90 per cent perpetrated by men (Kimmel 2002: 1354–58; Walby and Allen 2004) and, furthermore, that when women abuse in relationships it is often in self-defence (Miller and Meloy 2006).

The relationship between definitions, methods and results

Dobash and Dobash provide a rigorous review of the apparently contradictory findings between family violence researchers and 'violence against women' researchers concerning gender and domestic violence. They show that family violence research uses a narrow, 'act-based' approach to the definition and measurement of violence. It is more likely to find gender equivalence because it conflates acts of violence and aggression (for example, slaps are treated in the same way as serious assaults) and does not examine the motivations, context or consequences associated with the aggression. The violence against women approach seeks to understand and control for this context and illustrates important differences between men and women in the perpetration of violence, as well as its consequences. These studies show that serious intimate violence is asymmetrical with men usually violent to women. Women's violence differs from that perpetrated by men in terms of nature, frequency, intention, intensity, physical injury and emotional impact. In their own in-depth study of 95 couples in which men and women reported separately upon their own violence and that of their partner, they show that women's violence does not equate to men's in terms of frequency, severity, consequences and the victim's sense of safety and well-being (Dobash and Dobash 2004: 324; see also Hamberger and Guse 2002).

Reviews of the scientific evidence for gender equality in rates of lethal and non-lethal partner violence show that these studies mostly exhibit certain methodological limitations; primarily the exclusion of questions about sexual abuse and stalking, the exclusion of separated couples and the omission of severity of injury from analysis. Many also rely on data from young people, such as college students or those in dating relationships, rather than older married couples. Straus's most recent research is based on student samples and relies on cross-sectional data, that may not reflect a cause–effect relationship between dominance and partner violence. Such studies can be limited by the way in which they frame questions about violence (Kimmel 2002: 1351). Saunders (2002) shows that studies without these problems confirm much higher rates of violence by men (thorough critiques of the CTS and CTS2 are provided by Kimmel 2002; Dobash et al. 1992; Currie 1998; DeKeseredy and Schwartz 1998). Clearly, it is crucial to consider carefully the context in which domestic abuse takes place and the motivations for and responses to violence in order to understand who is most seriously affected. Those who have sought to do so and have shown that not all violence is the same, have developed the field significantly.

Johnson (2000) has argued that in surveying the literature on domestic violence it is possible to distinguish four main patterns of partner violence: 'common couple violence'; 'intimate terrorism'; 'violent resistance'; and 'mutual violent control', that challenge the theory of gender symmetry. The distinctions can be recognised in general patterns of control that characterise relationships, in motivations for violence, rather than from one-off incidents. 'Common couple violence', typically revealed by family violence studies, is low in frequency and severity and is more likely to be mutual violence arising out of specific arguments. It is not characterised by a desire to control. 'Intimate terrorism' is more likely to be serious and to escalate over time and much less likely to be mutual. It is motivated by the desire to control a partner. It is, furthermore, almost entirely a male pattern of violence. Conversely, 'violent resistance' is primarily perpetrated by women. Attempts to resist violence do not manifest themselves only in fighting back or defending oneself, but also by seeking to escape the relationship. 'Mutual violent control', a rare and similarly under-researched category, describes partners who are both controlling and violent. Johnson sees this category as distinct from concepts of self-defence or mutual combat. He argues that the studies suggesting gender symmetry discussed above are measuring 'common couple violence' and not other, more menacing, types of domestic violence.

Dempsey (2006) has developed similar concepts, differentiating domestic violence in its 'strong sense' (corresponding to Johnson's intimate terrorism) and in its weak sense (corresponding to Johnson's situational couple violence and violent resistance). Her account explicitly examines the underlying conceptual elements that inform these distinctions: violence, domesticity and structural inequality. In its strong sense, domestic violence reflects the intersection of violence, domesticity and structural inequality whereas in its weak sense it reflects only the first two. In other words, in its weak sense domestic violence is not characterised by the two key concepts that underlie structural inequality: power and control.

The distinctions offered by Johnson and Dempsey are helpful as they encourage critical scrutiny of the nature, frequency and consequences of violence. In particular they are sensitive to the issue of power and control, central to many theoretical perspectives on domestic violence (Stets and Pirog-Good 1990; Winstok and Eisikovits 2006: 187; Kimmel 2002: 1352). Indeed Johnson has gone as far as saying that 'it is no longer scientifically or ethically acceptable to speak of domestic violence without specifying, loudly and clearly, the type of violence to which we refer' (2005: 1126). Surveys that do not or cannot distinguish between 'intimate terrorism' and 'violent resistance' or between 'strong' or 'weak' domestic violence, for example, will suggest that men and women are equally violent or even that women are more prone to domestic violence than men. Hence there is a need for more thorough empirical research, especially in-depth research employing qualitative methods that measure motivations and impacts (Saunders 2002). Furthermore, there is a need to take seriously sampling designs, as studies from refuges, hospitals, courts, college campuses, homes, etc. will likely reveal different levels and types of abuse. Quite simply who is asked what and where will, to some extent, determine findings on abuse.

Vulnerabilities: intersectional approaches to domestic violence

During the second wave of feminism gender was the primary defining variable; the explanation for power and control, for example, was found in patriarchy or gender role socialisation. In rejection of liberal feminism, that was thought to ignore the disparities in power and privilege between men and women, radical feminists advanced the 'dominance approach' to studying gender and have been credited with improvements in the criminal justice response to domestic violence (Barak *et al.* 2001). Although socialist and Marxist feminists considered the influence of class, the majority of mainstream feminists ignored this and other structural variables. Ultimately this myopia proved untenable. From the early 1990s feminists started to consider the dominance approach to be essentialist and reductionist (one voice, white heterosexual and privileged, speaking for all women) and this paved the way for intersectionality, what has been referred to as 'third-wave feminism' (Burgess-Proctor 2006: 28–31).

In recent years, the influence of postmodern feminism and socialist feminism has encouraged an intersectional approach to domestic violence that differentiates women's experiences, expands the definitions of those harmed by violence to include culturally specific forms of abuse, puts a greater emphasis on the structural causes of abuse and explores the complex role of culture in understanding domestic violence and our responses to it (Sokoloff and Dupont 2005: 40). Many researchers now explore how structural inequalities such as racism, class privilege and heterosexism, intersect with gender oppression and how women's experiences of violence are mediated through these structural forms of oppression (Sokoloff 2005; Sokoloff and Dupont 2005: 45). It is no longer acceptable to talk about 'battered women' as if this was an homogeneous group. The idea that domestic violence affects every person, across race, nationality and religious lines equally is 'not only a token attempt at inclusion of diverse perspectives but also evidence of sloppy research and theory building' (Kanuha 1996: 40). As Walklate (2004: 43) has argued, women and their experiences must not be undifferentiated and undifferentiable.

Sexuality

Academic research over the past decade or two has taken up the largely hidden phenomena of violence in same-sex relationships (Ristock 2002). A national survey in the US found that just over 11 per cent of women in same-sex relationships are raped, physically assaulted or stalked by their partner and 15 per cent of men report violence by male live-in partners (Tjaden and Thoennes 2000). The available research suggests that there are strong similarities between homosexual men and heterosexual women's experiences of domestic violence. For example, in both cases abuse is often motivated by the desire or need to control a partner (Ct-uz and Firestone 1998).[3] Other studies suggest that women are sometimes similarly driven. Before Renzetti (1992) wrote about lesbian violence in 1992 little was known about the dynamics of female-on-female intimate violence. Her research suggests that control and power were significant motivations for the psychological abuse and physical violence in these relationships, although in other respects there are differences, such as in help-seeking behaviour, that mean that assessment and intervention strategies must be specifically targeted at this population (McClennen 2005). Furthermore, the abuse takes place within the greater context of homophobia in society. Hence in this area of difference power and control is crucial to our understanding but the concept of patriarchy cannot explain abuse between women.

Age

Research, including the work of Straus and his colleagues, suggests that there is a good deal of domestic violence among young 'dating' couples. It is not clear the extent to which power and control plays a role in this violence, although it is certainly a feature of some of these violent relationships (Stets 1993). While there have been many studies of 'dating violence' and 'date rape' over the past decade or so, less research has been conducted on abuse of elderly women (Fisher 2003). What we know is that a relatively high proportion of older women experience abuse in the home. In one study of three European countries just less than 20 per cent of the sample of women older than 59 had experienced some form of domestic abuse and almost a quarter of these had been experiencing abuse over years (Ockleford *et al.* 2003). Elderly women remain in abusive relationships for many of the same reasons as younger women but feel even more trapped (Zink *et al.* 2003). Research reveals that the circumstances of abused elders are not uniform; as with all women, the type of abuse and service needs vary based on race and ethnicity (Grossman and Lundy 2003).

Ethnicity, religion and violence in different cultures

While there is a paucity of transnational and cross-cultural research on domestic violence (Cousineau and Rondeau 2004), we know that domestic violence is endemic across jurisdictions (Amnesty International 2005: 5) and partner violence accounts for a significant proportion of female murder victims (between 40 and 70 per cent in Australia, Canada, Israel, South Africa and America: Krug *et al.* 2002: 93). However, comparative research has revealed differences in women's experiences of abuse and has shown that power and control interact with other variables to leave some women more vulnerable to abuse and less likely to be able to escape. In some societies, rape victims and women suspected of engaging in premarital sex or adultery are murdered by their male relatives in 'honour killings' (in Pakistan more than 1,000 women every year; Coomaraswamy 2000; Warrick 2005) and acid attacks and even murder are a consequence of dowry disputes with alarming regularity in South Asia, although uncommon in the West. Yoshihama (1999: 873) has shown the limitations of mainstream definitions of domestic violence in Japan, where acts such as overturning a dining table or dousing a woman with liquid constitute abuse of a particularly insidious type. Such acts need to be seen within an understanding of the socio-cultural context.

A recent review of European and North American research on domestic violence suggests that differing prevalence rates across countries are explained by three factors that both resonate with but also challenge a narrow conception of patriarchy: deprived economic living conditions; traditional attitudes towards women and children; and a general tolerance of violent behaviour in a given society (Kury *et al.* 2004). Furthermore, cultural approaches confirm unique features, such as patri-lineal traditions of ancestor worship, Confucian virtues and conflict (Hester 2000; Rydstrom 2003).

Studies of the experiences of ethnic minority groups in the West have shown that race interacts with other sites of disadvantage. In the UK there is little variation in the prevalence of domestic violence by ethnicity (Walby and Allen 2004) but minority victims are less likely to report the violence or seek help from other sources (Parmar *et al.* 2005). Surveys in the US, however, suggest that domestic violence is higher among black couples than white and lowest among Asian communities (Tjaden and Thoennes 1999). It is not clear how to explain these data. They may reflect reluctance to reveal violence among Asian women. Eng (1995) found that Asian immigrant women had difficulty acknowledging domestic abuse as they felt ashamed; having been socialised to believe that marital failure is always the fault of the wife. Furthermore, the data might show differences in socio-economic status: some ethnic minorities in countries in the US might be trapped in violent relationships, without the resources to escape and therefore over time more likely to experience greater levels of domestic abuse.

Ethnicity intersects with sexuality, class and age, but also with other sometimes race-specific issues such as religion, culture, global politics or immigration. For example, socio-economic and cultural variables intersect in communities that have experienced the depredation of colonialisation and post-colonialist policies (see, for example, Brownridge's (2003) study of domestic violence against Aboriginal women in Canada). Such intersections make it difficult to disaggregate the various factors that may or may not account for apparently higher levels of domestic violence among some groups, producing findings that are contentious at the very least and may appear racist. For example, a national survey in Israel appears to show higher levels of domestic violence among Muslims and traditional Jews than among secular Jews, suggesting, according to its authors, a shared attitudinal orientation towards women in general and domestic violence in particular that legitimises such behaviour within these groups (Eisikovits *et al.* 2004). Further evidence may be provided by an attitudinal survey in Israel that found significantly more permissive attitudes to domestic violence among Arab respondents than among Jews (Herzog 2004) and a study showing significantly higher rates of intimate femicide among Arabs in Israel than among Jews (Landau and Hattis Rolef 1998). Hajjar's study (2004) of domestic violence in Muslim societies shows that it is not only religion that can trap women in abusive relationships, but the state's accommodation of or support for that religion. Her research shows that the use of Shari'a creates some commonalities in gender and family relations in Muslim societies, notably the sanctioning and maintenance of male authority over female relatives, but that different states vary in the extent to which they accept or accommodate interpretations of Shari'a that sanction or tolerate intra-family violence.

A review of the literature reveals little research on domestic violence among immigrant populations but suggests that cultural factors related to language, beliefs, traditional help-seeking behaviour and degrees of acculturation all influence how victims experience and respond to abuse. Their legal status can further increase their isolation and enable batterers to control them and create barriers to seeking and receiving help and support (Raj and Silverman 2002: 367; Bhuyan and Senturia 2005; Bui 2004). Furthermore, although there are similarities between groups, each community reveals particular details that make the women's experience unique (Bhuyan and Senturia 2005).

Race and class interact in particularly problematic ways, as it is still the case in the US and the UK that certain ethnic minorities tend to be in the lower socio-economic strata. Several studies show that black women are seriously abused and murdered at significantly higher rates than their representation in the population (Websdale 1999; Sokoloff and Dupont 2005). However, when socio-economic factors are controlled for, the racial differences largely disappear.

Class

Of the various intersections of oppression and domination, class analysis is the least developed in work on domestic violence (Sokoloff and Dupont 2005). One of the most persistent orthodoxies has been that all women are equally vulnerable to abuse. While it is true that women from all social classes can be victims, recent research suggests that those from lower socio-economic groups are significantly more likely to be victimised and that their victimisation and their needs are exacerbated by their poverty (Renzetti 2004; Sokoloff and Dupont 2005: 44). The US National Crime Victimisation Surveys show that very low-income households suffer about five times the amount of domestic violence as high-income families (Raphael 2002: 367).

Clearly some people are both more vulnerable to abuse and, when victimised, experience the abuse differently from others. In addition to the structural variables discussed above, other factors still under-researched, such as mental health disorders in late adolescence, increase vulnerability. For example, girls with behavioural problems, such as aggression and antisocial behaviour, are more likely to become involved with anti-social abusive partners (Ehrensaft 2006: 27). Dutton argues that domestic violence is better predicted by psychological rather than social-structural factors (especially personality disorders in either gender), particularly in cultures where there is relative gender equality (Dutton 2006). A broadening recognition of variance in women's experiences of abuse may threaten to undermine the patriarchal domination thesis. However, as Raphael argues, men in many different situations use violence to keep women controlled and can manipulate other vulnerabilities, such as poverty, to further abuse and control women (Raphael 2002: 368). Each disadvantage or site of oppression has the potential to aggravate the power imbalance or to render the victim even more vulnerable to abuse and to leave victims in greater need of support but less likely to benefit from available resources and services.

Responding to domestic violence: arrest is not the only option

There is a number of ways society can respond to incidents of domestic violence that can crudely be divided into three categories: legal interventions (including civil law, such as injunctions, and criminal law responses, such as arrest and prosecution); health care interventions (primarily emergency care, but including psychological support of both victims and perpetrators, and voluntary-attendance batterers' and victims' community programmes); and social service interventions (refuges and other victim services, including advocacy services). This section considers only the first of these, legal interventions, and then only one aspect of this, the criminal justice response, and does not aim to examine this in its entirety but to select a few types of responses and consider their potential efficacy.

Early feminist commentaries on domestic violence bemoaned the inadequate criminal justice response to domestic violence at a time when the police were too often reluctant to intervene, dismissing domestic violence as a social service matter. Their agitation did much to persuade criminal justice agents to take seriously violence against women and a new orthodoxy emerged that 'taking seriously' meant arresting, prosecuting and punishing perpetrators, as well as funding refuges for women to escape to. It also meant being clear who was the perpetrator and who the victim and separating the two for as long as possible.

The UK government has over the last few years made clear its intention to continue to take domestic violence seriously, with proposals to improve prevention, protection and justice and support for victims of intimate violence (Home Office 2003). The recent Domestic Violence, Crime and Victims Act (2004) provides the most significant overhaul of the law on domestic violence of the last few decades: it makes common assault and the breach of a non-molestation order arrestable offences; it enables courts to impose restraining orders when sentencing for any offence and on acquittal for any offence (or if a conviction has been overturned on appeal); it strengthens the civil law on domestic violence to ensure cohabiting same-sex couples have the same access to non-molestation and occupation orders as opposite-sex couples and extends the availability of these orders to couples who have never been married or lived together; and establishes a statutory basis for domestic homicide reviews. Although the Act also provides a Code of Practice that requires all criminal justice agencies to provide victims with adequate support, protection, information and advice (Home Office 2005), its main focus is on providing the police with more powers to arrest alleged perpetrators of domestic violence than ever before (Hoyle and Zedner 2007).

At the same time as legislation has provided police with more powers, the government has put further pressure on forces to increase arrest rates with the implementation of specific crime reduction targets. In the last few years the sanction-detection rate for domestic violence has been included in these police performance targets, leading to a top-down change in the police culture regarding domestic violence. In the Thames Valley police, for example, it is no longer typical or considered acceptable to take no action in domestic disputes where there has been a criminal offence.[4] Consequently, there has been a significant increase in the arrest rate for domestic violence: in all domestic violence cases in Thames Valley, it increased from 32 per cent in 2003–4 to 58 per cent in the following year. For those cases that are the subject of this chapter, domestic violence between intimate partners, the arrest rate has increased to approximately 84 per cent of cases where a criminal offence has been alleged. However, just when the feminist demand for the police to take seriously domestic abuse seems to have been met, or at least seems close to it, scholars are starting to question the efficacy of criminal justice: 'The chorus of critics of the current crime control focus of domestic violence policies is growing' (Coker 2004: 1349). Concerns about the perceived over-reliance on criminal strategies and sanctions in responding to domestic violence (Coker 2001, 2004; Maguigan 2002) have led some to ask, 'is the legal system so flawed that it hurts, rather than helps, victims of domestic violence?' (Goodmark 2004: 46).

The 'crime-centred' approach has been criticised for being paternalistic and limiting women's autonomy (Mills 1998); for having a disparate negative impact on ethnic minority men and women (Richie 2000); and for being ineffective at ending abuse (Hoyle 1998). Coker (2001) has shown the different ways in which state intervention can harm those who are already at increased risk of state interference: poor, black victims of domestic violence and in particular those with insecure immigration status or with a history of offending. These intersections can put victims at a high risk of having their children taken into care, being arrested themselves or being deported. This might be an acceptable risk if arrest and prosecution protected women from further abuse, but the evidence suggests it does not (Sherman 1992). Furthermore, women know this. A decade ago almost half of the victims in incidents that resulted in arrest withdrew support for prosecution after the arrest (Hoyle 1998: 183). Today, after significant improvements to the criminal justice system, still half of the victims whose cases were dealt with by one of the innovative specialist domestic violence courts chose to retract their statements and withdraw their support for prosecution, despite the courts' strong and supportive multi-agency partnerships ethos (Robinson and Cook 2006).

Given that victims are often the best judge of their safety, mandatory policies (implemented variably across different jurisdictions in the US) that ignore women's wishes are seen as particularly dangerous and ineffective (Hoyle and Sanders 2000; Buzawa and Buzawa 2003). They are also criticised for increasing the number of women who are arrested, including many who were acting in self-defence (Maguigan 2002; Coker 2004). Victimless prosecution avoids some of the problems of retaliatory violence that may result from victims testifying against their partners (Ellison 2003) but still rests on the assumption that victims are a homogeneous group that will experience violence in the same way and will benefit equally from the prosecution of the perpetrator. In fact, research suggests that such policies lead to discriminatory arrests against people because of their ethnicity or sexuality (Hirschel and Buzawa 2002) and that more vulnerable groups will not report to the police for fear of this.

Other concerns keep some minorities silent. For example, lesbians who do not wish to be open about their sexuality will not be keen to seek help for abuse (Ristock 2002) and some women may be reluctant to ask for help because their culture values family unity and the avoidance of shame over individual safety (Bui and Morash 1999). Ethnic minorities may fear that reporting violence to the police will leave their partners vulnerable to racist treatment or even deportation (Websdale 1999). In response to these concerns, some scholars have suggested context-sensitive policies that consider, for example, whether the violence is perpetrated in the context of a patriarchal and controlling relationship and is, in Dempsey's (2006) words, violence in the 'strong sense'; or whether women are at increased risk of deportation or losing their children if their partner is prosecuted. In other words, rather than following either a 'no-drop' or a victim-choice prosecution, there could be a middle ground: 'prosecution in context' (Epstein *et al.* 2002: 498). Others have looked beyond mandatory arrest to criminal responses based on a calculation of risk, or to voluntary or mandatory perpetrator treatment programmes, while others still have moved away from conventional criminal justice to more community-based responses, such as restorative justice. These alternatives have sprung not only from disillusionment with criminal justice but also from the evidence from cross-cultural and multicultural domestic violence studies that make clear that 'there is no one-size-fits-all explanation for domestic violence and that, consequently, solutions must reflect these differences' (Sokoloff and Dupont 2005: 50).

Targeting those at highest risk

Awareness that victims and perpetrators are not homogeneous groups has led criminal justice agents to consider how they might deploy their limited resources discriminately. In the last few years risk assessment models for domestic violence, such as the police-led SPECSS model developed in the Metropolitan Police service and adapted by Thames Valley police and the multi-agency risk assessment conferences (MARACs), have been developed as the latest tool in identifying, preventing and responding effectively to domestic violence (Richards 2003, 2004; Robinson 2004). The main purpose of risk assessment and management is to improve the protection of and interventions for families who are experiencing domestic violence and to target interventions on those who present the highest risk.

Studies from the US and the UK suggest a number of indicators can be identified as most appropriate to assessing risk of violence and homicide within the domestic setting. Previous physical assault by the suspect is one of the most robust and straightforward risk factors for domestic violence (Walby and Myhill 2001) (the British Crime Survey of 2000 found that 57 per cent of victims of intimate violence were repeat victims: Kershaw *et al.* 2000); and in the US 65 to 80 per cent of female domestic homicide victims were previously abused by the partners who killed them: Campbell 2004). Other risk factors include women's predictions of future risk and its likely severity; evidence of stalking; recent ending of a relationship instigated by the woman; access to/ownership of guns; displaying weapons such as knives within the household; threats with weapons; threats to kill; serious injury in a prior abusive incident; threats of suicide by male partner (in response to the woman's threats to leave); drug and alcohol abuse by the male partner; forced sex with the woman; and obsessiveness/extensive jealousy, extensive dominance (Brookman and Maguire 2003, drawing heavily on Campbell's Danger Assessment Scale: Campbell 1995).

As risk is necessarily an unknown, risk assessments are social constructs and yet they have significant practical and emotional implications for those deemed to be both at risk of being harmed and at risk of harming others. Therefore the efficacy of risk assessment and management tools deserves critical attention. There is currently very little empirical scrutiny of these processes but a suggestion that there is insufficient evidence that the tools are reliable indicators of risk, some concern that there is indefensible variability in the police use of such tools and that they are not sufficiently sensitive to changes in the victim or potential perpetrator's circumstances. Furthermore, they are based on presumptions about both victims' and perpetrators' behaviour and responses that may not be reliable. Finally, they may pose threats to proportionality in responding to offences when a perpetrator has previously been identified as 'at risk' (Hoyle 2006a). Until more reassuring data are produced, risk-assessment tools are unlikely to persuade those critics of criminal justice that a tailored arrest and prosecution response is the answer. They are, however, in line with the radical feminist position that seeks to criminalise potential as well as actual criminal behaviour and to erect barriers, both literal and metaphorical, between victims and perpetrators and therefore are likely to expand in the same way as feminist-inspired programmes of rehabilitation have, despite empirical challenges to their validity.

Rehabilitating abusers

Like mandatory arrest policies, court-ordered batterers' intervention program-mes have become a fairly common enforcement practice in the US and since the 1980s a relatively standardised form of intervention delivered by most probation services in the UK (Gadd 2004: 173). Despite ambivalence over their efficacy (Sartin *et al.* 2006), victims of domestic violence often express a desire for such interventions to help violent partners (Hoyle 1998; Ames and Dunham 2002) and they look set to stay: the Sentencing Advisory Panel (2006: Part 1) has recently given a cautious welcome to domestic violence programmes 'where the court is satisfied that the offender genuinely intends to reform his/her behaviour'.

The standard model in the US for batterers' programmes is based on the 'Duluth Model', established in 1981, in which intervention leaders attempt to educate violent men about their use of power and control strategies with women (Pence and Paymar 1993; Shepard and Pence 1999). The original Duluth model was an inter-agency strategy that co-ordinated health, criminal justice, welfare and educational services to enhance women's safety. However, it is the educative work with perpetrators that has attracted the most attention. The model stresses that violence is used by men as a form of power and control to shore up patriarchy (men are socialised to be dominant and women to be subordinate) and a 'power and control wheel' has become the prominent symbol for the model. The social learning theory that the re-education elements of the programme embrace suggests that men can learn to abandon their use of controlling behaviours and violence and move towards relationships based on equality.

The 'Duluth model' was imported into the UK by practitioners in Scotland; beginning with the CHANGE project in Stirling and the Lothian Domestic Violence Probation Project in Edinburgh. Both six-month court-mandated programmes, involving perpetrators in weekly sessions, were evaluated by Russell and Rebecca Dobash and their colleagues (1996). Their report was cautiously optimistic, suggesting that the programmes had been successful at reducing both the men's violence and their controlling behaviours (although see Mullender 2000 for a critique of the methodological limitations of their research). Following the apparent success of the model, many other British practitioners set up similar projects. There has been little subsequent research conducted on the effectiveness of these programmes in the UK and yet the government has supported their development (Gadd 2004), with new probation services' Integrated Domestic Abuse Programmes (IDAP) having recently been rolled out across the country. However, research in the US suggests that these programmes do not change batterers' attitudes nor do they reduce recidivism, which is typically high for those convicted of domestic violence (National Institute of Justice 2003). So, why does this model have only limited success? The answer would seem to be rooted in difference and diversity. The Duluth model is based on the traditional feminist notion of patriarchal power and control.

The influence of the power and control thesis

Power and control were for a long time the predominant explanations for the motivations and risk factors in domestic violence: men batter their female partners to exert power and control over them. More recently, researchers have begun to take a more nuanced perspective on power and control (for example Winstok and Eisikovits 2006) and, indeed, to look beyond it. Other variables, such as mental and personality disorders, that were excluded from consideration for fear that they would detract from batterers' accountability and criminality, are now being taken seriously and it is becoming possible to see partner violence as sometimes a dyadic problem, without being accused of blaming the victim (Rosenbaum 2006). The Duluth model might work well if all perpetrators were the same, if they were all defined only by their maleness and determination to preserve patriarchal authority at all costs. However, research over the last decade or so has confirmed what should have been obvious, that not all have the same personalities and motivations and not all exhibit the same behaviours (Dutton 1995; Saunders 1996; Gondolf 2002).

Accumulating data that challenges feminist orthodoxies on prevalence and aetiology, and may have more predictive power for partner abuse risk, do not seem to be breaking through the corpus of feminist doctrines and penetrating the field of treatment interventions. In particular, Duluth-based models eschew psychological treatment even of empirically established factors supporting habits of intimate abusiveness, in favour of a gender political model. This is despite research showing that a propensity for domestic violence is predictable in both genders during adolescence (Dutton and Corvo 2006). Ehrensaft (2006) shows that a development approach to partner violence is omitted from the field's mainstream lexicon; that the intersection of partner violence with other forms of family and non-family violence is under-represented; and that programmes to prevent partner violence are limited in their effects because they do not adequately integrate accumulating data on relevant risk factors (mental health, poverty, etc.), focusing instead on universal prevention programmes and gender-based intervention approaches. Her studies suggest that psychopathology competes with patriarchy as a persuasive explanatory variable for domestic violence. Not surprisingly, therefore, many practitioners' accounts suggest that the Duluth model lacks responsivity and that there is a greater need to engage with the emotional dynamics underpinning men's violent relationships (Gadd 2004: 189).

As Ehrensaft (2006) has argued, those devising programmes need to be cognisant of the multiplicity of risk factors to avoid the disconnect in the field between sound empirical data on aetiology and batterer programmes that focus on only power and control. In particular, programmes need to take into consideration the inter-generational aspects of violence; traditionally child abuse and domestic violence have been researched in isolation from each other, despite evidence of the correlation between the two and of the alarming rates of abuse towards children in the home (Straus and Gelles 1990).

The stranglehold on theory and policy development that the Duluth model exerts confounds efforts to improve treatment (Dutton and Corvo 2006: 478). Because it is theoretically rooted in the concept of patriarchy it takes a single-sex approach to treatment of men, ignoring the role of women in abusive relationships, explaining any female violence as self-defence. Research suggests that this approach is not empirically supported because both partners contribute to the risk of abuse and in some cases both should be treated (Ehrensaft et al. 2004). Indeed, several studies have found that controlling behaviour is common among both men and women in violent relationships and that levels of controlling behaviour differentiate distressed from non-distressed couples, rather than being specific to violent couples (Ehrensaft 2006).

Batterers, like victims, are clearly a heterogeneous group and, when it comes to intervening; one size does not fit all. Restorative justice is perhaps the only recent development for tackling domestic violence that does not assume that one blanket response will be effective for all; indeed, it aims to tailor responses specifically to each case by encouraging all parties to define for themselves both the problem and the possible solutions. It represents the first sign of policy wriggling out of the radical feminist ideological straitjacket.

Restoring relationships in the home

Over the last decade a minority of restorative justice advocates and scholars have argued persuasively for restorative approaches to domestic violence (Coker 1999; Strang and Braithwaite 2002; Hopkins et al. 2004; Mills 2006). Such processes, they claim, are more likely than traditional criminal justice to hold offenders to account for their behaviour; to make possible a range of support services to victims; to result in reparation or compensation to victims; to mobilise both support for offenders and monitoring of their future behaviour; and to challenge patriarchal attitudes amongst offenders and their families or friends that excuse or condone physical or emotional abuse.

Radical feminists, in speaking out for victims, have sought simultaneously to deny those victims a voice. They have fought hard to stop victims from influencing the criminal justice response to their victimisation even though studies suggest that victims improve their chances of recovery from crime when they play an active part in society's response to the crime (Mills 2006). Restorative justice provides the strongest challenge to this silencing of victims and therefore provokes fierce resistance among many feminists. It explicitly gives victims a voice and a chance to participate fully in the state and community response to their victimisation, including validation of their experiences and responses to those experiences.

Critics see many pitfalls in using restorative justice for domestic violence, with most concerns focusing on the power and control perpetrators have over their victims (for a thorough review of the criticisms see Morris and Gelsthorpe 2000). One of the main concerns is that restorative processes perpetuate power imbalances. It is thought that offenders will manipulate the informal process to diminish guilt, trivialise the violence or shift the blame to the victim. If the process permits power imbalances to go unchecked and reinforces abusive behaviour, it can reduce women's safety and put them at further risk of violence. Stubbs (2002) has argued that it is dangerous to assume that victims of domestic violence are able to assert their own needs and promote their own interests in the presence of perpetrators and that requiring such victims to participate may be disempowering and punitive.

While there is evidence that in some communities the ideals of womanhood create a mindset whereby women are reluctant to advocate for themselves (Goel 2005), many victims of domestic violence already feel disempowered by abusive relationships and the criminal justice system currently does little to empower them (Hoyle and Sanders 2000). Given that many become further disempowered and isolated by their partner's controlling behaviours, it may be that bringing friends, family and colleagues of the victim into the process, making them fully aware of the abuse and encouraging them to look out for the victim in future, might provide sufficient support to reduce the risk of re-victimisation and enhance the victim's feelings of safety – more than a fine or a court order (Hoyle 1998; Coker 1999). Furthermore, restorative processes may be able to facilitate repair of the relationship, if this is what both parties want and therefore might prove beneficial in cases where victims are currently unwilling to co-operate with a criminal prosecution because they do not wish to end the relationship (Hoyle 1998; Mills 2006).

Of course, restorative justice does not necessitate total rejection of criminal justice and its protections. Ultimately the restorative process may do little to change an offender's behaviour and there may be a need for a threat of further legal intervention in such cases. Braithwaite and Daly (1994) have proposed escalating responses to domestic violence, that might begin with a restorative conference but might ultimately lead to prison. Nancarrow's Australian research found support among Indigenous and non-Indigenous women for some sort of amalgamation of the criminal justice system and restorative justice to address inadequacies in each approach. Contrary to studies that suggest that restorative justice is most dangerous for minority women (Cameron 2006), Indigenous women in Nancarrow's study thought that restorative justice was the best primary response, on the condition that the processes were developed and controlled by local Indigenous communities,[5] whereas the non-Indigenous women thought the criminal justice system was the best primary response and that it should be the prominent partner in any amalgamation (Nancarrow 2006: 101).

Hudson has best conceptualised such an integrated response to domestic violence in her writings about the tension between the instrumental and expressive functions of punishment. As she argues, criminalisation and penalisation may not create communities that are safer for women but they do show that society is serious about condemning domestic abuse, emphasising that it is morally wrong (see also Coker 2004: 1349). Hence Hudson argues:

> If the aims and principles of retributive and restorative justice are integrated, with the targets of restorative justice (reintegration, empowerment of victims, reduction of offending, building of more cohesive, peaceful communities) being pursued within the constraints of due process safeguards and standards such as proportionality and equitable treatment, then a better justice will be possible. (2002: 631)

At times this would be more like restorative justice with safeguards and more focus on fair outcomes, but at other times it would look more like formal criminal justice with the ideals of reintegration securely embedded in the process (see also Hoyle 2006b). Either way the instrumental and expressive would be better catered for.

Even within such an integrated system cases would need to be selected carefully and would also need a great deal of preparatory and follow-up work. Coker helpfully describes the criteria that should be met before restorative processes go ahead: they should prioritise victim safety over batterer rehabilitation; offer material as well as social supports for victims; work as part of a co-ordinated community response; engage normative judgements that oppose gendered domination as well as violence; and not make forgiveness a goal of the process (Coker 2006: 67). Not all these criteria are as relevant in a process that is more criminal than restorative justice but most should be taken seriously in both systems.

Conclusion: a call for rigorous social science

The most important research on domestic violence over the last decade or so has explored differences; differences in types of domestic violence and the different experiences of those who do not fall into the category of white, middle-class, heterosexual, young woman. These studies show that neither power and control nor domestic violence is experienced uniformly across all populations at all times. There are differences in prevalence, frequency and in the impact of violence on families. Male victims, victims with insecure immigration status, or those in same-sex relationships are likely to react differently to violence in the home, to female or young heterosexual victims in particular in their preparedness to report to the police or even to seek support from a non-statutory agency. Furthermore, within these diverse groups there will be differences in experiences of violence, with some people experiencing repeat severe attacks, that render them debilitated by fear of a current or previous partner; while others are living in volatile relationships that are peaceful and even happy some of the time but characterised by mutual aggression or episodes of unilateral violence at other times. In other words, victims of domestic violence are not a homogeneous group but neither are black victims, or old victims or lesbian victims. There is structural and cultural heterogeneity.

Research now needs to be developed to take further account of these differences. Studies which produce prevalence rates among minority groups, for example, need to distinguish between 'intimate terrorism' and 'common couple violence' or between 'strong' and 'weak' forms of domestic violence, as this will provide the kind of detail we need to better respond to domestic violence across divergent groups. It is not easy to measure variance in prevalence rates across different populations as studies have tended not to employ consistent definitions of domestic violence (DeKeseredy and Schwartz 2001), so researchers need to co-operate in developing context-sensitive tools that can be used in different jurisdictions with all types of victims. The growth of comparative research will assist this enterprise. Rigorous qualitative research is also needed to better understand the explanatory power of patriarchy. Currently the concept of patriarchy seems to dominate policy responses to domestic violence. While it would be a step forward to encourage those agencies and organisations with a responsibility for protecting victims and dealing with perpetrators to take full account of the different experiences of black victims or older victims, it is not sufficient to simply add to the concept of patriarchy a list of structural variables. Instead, it is necessary to develop a fully integrated theory of domestic violence that takes account of the many ways in which various structural and cultural variables intersect with patriarchy and give meaning to the experiences of victims. This can only be achieved within an intellectual climate that is open to challenges to dominant orthodoxies. Theoretical perspectives on domestic violence need to be tested against reliable social science and this is not only dependent on rigorous research tools, but also on taking seriously findings that challenge prior assumptions or cut across political dogma. Domestic violence research still has some way to go in achieving this.

Feminism, particularly radical feminism, has done more to help those affected by domestic violence than any other movement. It is not an exaggeration to say that it has saved some women's lives. It was essential in alerting all of us, including those with the power to change policies, to take seriously the physical and emotional abuse that takes place within many homes. Radical feminism has had a greater impact on policy development in this field than any other movement, including mainstream or liberal feminism. This is partly because most activists working in the field were radical and they were able to present policy-makers with their evidence of the widespread pernicious abuse of women in the home. However, by and large, their experience was concentrated on a specific category of victims: those who sought refuge in shelters. These are not necessarily typical of all victims. They were women who had been very seriously abused, victims of what Johnson would call intimate terrorism and these activists had little or no contact with other victims of domestic violence. Hence, the experiences of just one type of victim have had a disproportionate impact on the development of theory and policy.

When radical feminists started their campaign to alert us to the extent and impact of domestic violence there was a dearth of rigorous empirical data to refute their claims about the aetiology of domestic violence and types and experiences of victims. Today this is no longer the case. Social scientific research on domestic violence has proliferated and we now have a more nuanced picture of the problem. There has been a lag, however, between new data and new ideas about responding to this apparently intractable problem, a lag that can be accounted for by the entrenched orthodoxies that developed over the last 30 years. Experiments with restorative processes for domestic violence suggest that this is now starting to change. To continue this process of change social scientists need to take seriously their responsibility to the academy and to policy-makers to provide rigorous data.

There is, or at least there should be, a difference between feminist activism and feminist-inspired social science. Criminologists and victimologists have a different role from feminist activists in the field of domestic violence. One of their most important roles is to provide rigorous scientific data to help policy-makers and practitioners to identify accurately and respond appropriately to the problem. As Hood has argued: 'the voices of criminologists will be heard only if they can speak in their "wider-ranging role" from a firm base of empirical research and research that can make claims to be scientifically rigorous, in the sense that it is repeatable, reliable and valid' (2002: 159).

Over the last decade concern has been voiced, primarily by those who do not consider themselves to be feminists (e.g. Dutton 2006; Straus 2006; Felson 2006a) but also by those who do (Mills 2003; Hoyle 2000), that the field of domestic violence has been constricted by an 'ideologically driven suppression of science, rational policy models and innovative, promising program development ... for the further criminalizing of deviance and an expansion of the power of the criminal justice system' (Dutton and Corvo 2006: 477). Dutton's (2006) research is an example of the recent and welcome trend for considering all evidence on domestic abuse from many disciplines, including social and clinical psychology, sociology, psychiatry, criminology and criminal justice research and rejecting politicised ideology unsupported by rigorous scientific data. He shows that treatment providers, criminal justice system personnel, lawyers and researchers have indicated the need for a new view of the problem – one less invested in gender politics and more open to collaborative views and interdisciplinary insights.

Criminal justice can provide solutions for some victims some of the time but we must take note of empirical studies that suggest that interventions are not effective for some victims and that they may have unintended and undesirable consequences and resist prescribing them universally for ideological reasons.

In other words, those who study domestic violence should adopt rigorous scientific methods and report accurately their findings, even when they cut across the hegemony of policy as established by radical feminism (Hoyle 2000). The research discussed above suggests that consideration of options for responding to domestic violence beyond arrest and prosecute, or the Duluth model of treatment, has been held back by the radical feminist commitment to a patriarchal view of society and of violence in the home that permits no consideration of the role women play in violent relationships and ignores various risk factors, including socio-economic disadvantage and psychological or psychiatric factors. Research shows that power and control are still crucial factors in our understanding of domestic abuse, but they are not the only factors and until full consideration is given to other variables responses to violence will likely be only partially successful. The focus should now be on developing theoretical and empirical work on domestic violence that takes account of dominant trends in domestic violence but also of divergence and that seeks to identify which responses, whether statutory or voluntary, work for whom and in what circumstances.

Further reading

The first section of Walklate's *Gender, Crime and Criminal Justice* (2nd edn, 2004) provides an excellent introduction to theories about gender and their impact on thinking about criminal victimisation. Loseke, Gelles and Cavanaugh's *Current Controversies on Family Violence* (2nd edn, Sage, 2005) is an interesting collection of essays that shows that experts do not agree about what should be studied, how violence should be defined and measured, who the main victims are, what the causes of violence are and what should be done to eliminate it. Dutton's (2006) *Rethinking Domestic Violence* critically reviews current research from various disciplines and arrives at controversial conclusions that contradict earlier views among researchers and policy makers. Sokoloff's *Domestic Violence at the Margins* (2005) focuses attention on the intersection of gender oppression with race, ethnicity, religion, sexuality and class. Strang and Braithwaite's *Restorative Justice and Family Violence* (2002) brings together writers who are both for and against the use of restorative justice for domestic violence, focusing attention on both feminist and indigenous concerns. *Domestic Violence* (3rd edn, 2003), by Eve and Carl Buzawa, is one of only a few books to focus on criminal justice responses and in particular on the victim's perspective.

Notes

1 Of course many feminists, especially from the early 1980s, would have rejected the term 'victims' for its implied passivity, preferring to emphasise women's strategies for coping and resisting violence by referring to them as 'survivors': (Kelly 1988: 27–8).

2 As with liberal and mainstream feminism, the label 'radical feminism' is used here to summarise the positions of a diverse range of theories.

3 Some research does not support this theory. For example, in one recent study of homosexual violent relationships, difficulties in conflict resolution and attachment fears appeared to better explain the occurrence of violence than did the intent to control one's partner (Stanley *et al.* 2006: 31–41).

4 Personal communication with DS Don Savage, Thames Valley Police Crime Programme Project Manager.
5 For indigenous women restorative practices would need to be tied to principles of self-determination because of historical and contemporary experiences of racism in established criminal justice practices (Daly and Stubbs 2006).

References

Ames, L.J. and Dunham, K.T. (2002) 'Asymptotic justice: Probation as a criminal justice response to intimate partner violence', *Violence Against Women* 8(1): 6–34.

Amir, M. (1971) *Patterns of Forcible Rape*. Chicago: University of Chicago Press.

Amnesty International (2005) *Amnesty International Report 2005: The State of the World's Human Rights*. London: Amnesty International Publications.

Archer, J. (2000) 'Sex differences in aggression between heterosexual partners: A meta-analytic review', *Psychological Bulletin*, 126: 651–80.

Barak, G., Flavin, J. and Leighton, P.S. (2001) *Class, Race, Gender and Crime: Social Realities of Justice in America*. Los Angeles: Roxbury.

Bhuyan, R. and Senturia, K. (2005) 'Understanding domestic violence resource utilisation and survivor solutions among immigrant and refugee women', *Journal of Interpersonal Violence*, 20: 895–901.

Braithwaite, J. and Daly, K. (1994) Masculinities, Violence and Communitarian Control', in T. Newburn and E.A. Stanko (eds) *Just Boys Doing Business? Men, Masculinities and Crime*. London: Routledge.

Brookman, F. and Maguire, M. (2003) *Reducing Homicide: Summary of a Review of the Possibilities*. London: Home Office.

Brownridge, D.A. (2003) 'Male partner violence against aboriginal women in Canada: An empirical analysis', *Journal of Interpersonal Violence*, 18(1): 65–83.

Bui, H. (2004) *In the Adopted Land: Abused Immigrant Women and the Criminal Justice System*. Westport: CT: Praeger.

Bui, H. and Morash, M. (1999) 'Domestic violence in the Vietnamese immigrant community: An exploratory study', *Women Against Violence*, 5: 769–95.

Burgess-Proctor, A. (2006) 'Intersections of race, class, gender and crime', *Feminist Criminology*, 1(1): 27–47.

Buzawa, E.S. and Buzawa, C.G. (2003) *Domestic Violence: The Criminal Justice Response*. Thousand Oaks, CA: Sage.

Cameron, A. (2006) 'Stopping the violence: Canadian feminist debates on restorative justice and intimate violence', *Theoretical Criminology*, 10: 49–66.

Campbell, J.C. (1995) 'Prediction of Homicide of and by Battered Women' in J.C. Campbell (ed.) *Assessing Dangerousness: Violence by Sexual Offenders, Batterers and Child Abusers*. London: Sage, pp. 96–113.

Campbell, J.C. (2004) 'Helping women understand their risk in situations of intimate partner violence', *Journal of Interpersonal Violence*, 19(12): 1464–77.

Coker, D. (1999) 'Enhancing autonomy for battered women: Lessons from Navajo peacemaking', *UCLA Law Review*, 47(1): 1–112.

Coker, D. (2001) 'Crime control and feminist law reform in domestic violence law: A critical review', *Buffalo Criminal Law Review*, 4: 801–60.

Coker, D. (2004) 'Race, poverty and the crime-centered response to domestic violence: A comment on Linda Mills's *Insult to Injury: Rethinking Our Responses to Intimate Abuse'*, *Violence Against Women*, 10: 1331–53.

Coker, D. (2006) 'Restorative justice, Navajo peacemaking and domestic violence', *Theoretical Criminology*, 10: 67–86.

Coomaraswamy, R. (2000) *Integration of the Human Rights of Women and the Gender Perspective: Violence against Women, Report of the Special Rapporteur on violence against women.* New York: United Nations, Economic and Social Council, Commission on Human Rights.

Cousineau, M.M. and Rondeau, G. (2004) 'Toward a transnational and cross-cultural analysis of family violence', *Violence Against Women*, 10(8): 935–49.

Ct-uz, J.M. and Firestone, J.M. (1998) 'Exploring violence and abuse in gay male relationships', *Violence and Victims*, 13(2): 159–73.

Currie, D.H. (1998) 'Violent Men or Violent Women? Whose Definition Counts?' in R.K. Bergen (ed.) *Issues in Intimate Violence.* Thousand Oaks, CA: Sage.

Daly, K. and Chesney-Lind, M. (1988) 'Feminism and criminology', *Justice Quarterly*, 5: 497–538.

Daly, K. and Stubbs, J. (2006) 'Feminist engagement with restorative justice', *Theoretical Criminology*, 10: 9–28.

DeKeseredy, W.S. and Schwartz, M.B. (1998) *Women Alone on Campus: Results from the Canadian National Survey.* Thousand Oaks, CA: Sage.

DeKeseredy, W.S. and Schwartz, M.D. (2001) 'Definitional Issues' in C.M. Renzetti, J.L. Edleson and R.K. Bergen (eds) *Sourcebook on Violence Against Women.* Thousand Oaks, CA: Sage, pp. 23–34.

Dempsey, M.M. (2006) 'What counts as domestic violence? A conceptual analysis', *William and Mary Journal of Women and the Law*, 12(2): 301–33.

Dobash, R.P. and Dobash, R.E. (2004) 'Women's violence to men in intimate relationships', *British Journal of Criminology*, 44(3): 324–49.

Dobash, R.E., Dobash, R.P., Cavanagh, K. and Lewis, R. (1996) *Re-education Programmes for Violent Men – An Evaluation*, Home Office Research Findings 46. London: Home Office Research and Statistics Directorate.

Dobash, R.P., Dobash, R.E., Wilson, M. and Daly, M. (1992) 'The myth of sexual symmetry in marital violence', *Social Problems*, 39: 71–91.

Dutton, D. (1995) *The Batterer: A Psychological Profile.* New York: Basic Books.

Dutton, D. (2006) *Rethinking Domestic Violence.* Vancouver: University of British Columbia Press.

Dutton, D. and Corvo, K. (2006) 'Transforming a flawed policy: A call to revive psychology and science in domestic violence research and practice', *Journal of Aggression and Violent Behavior*, 11(5): 457–83.

Ehrensaft, M.K. (2006) 'Intimate Partner Violence: Persistence of Myths and Implications for Intervention', Conference on Trends in Intimate Violence Intervention, New York University.

Ehrensaft, M.K., Moffitt T.E. and Caspi, A. (2004) 'Clinically abusive relationships in an unselected birth cohort: Men's and women's participation and developmental antecedents', *Journal of Abnormal Psychology*, 113(2): 258–70.

Eisikovits, Z., Winstok. Z. and Fishman, G. (2004) 'The first Israeli national survey on domestic violence', *Violence Against Women*, 10(7): 729–48.

Ellison, L. (2003) 'Responding to victim withdrawal in domestic violence prosecutions', *Criminal Law Review*, 760–72.

Eng, P. (1995) 'Domestic Violence in Asian/Pacific Island Communities' in D.L. Adams (ed.) *Health Issues for Women of Color.* Thousand Oaks, CA: Sage, pp. 78–88.

Epstein, D., Bell, M.E. and Goodman, L.A. (2002) '*Transforming Aggressive Prosecution Policies: Prioritizing Victims' Long-term Safety in the Prosecution of Domestic Violence Cases'*, Conference on Confronting Domestic Violence and Achieving Gender Equality (evaluating *Battered Women and Feminist Lawmaking* by Elizabeth Schneider). Washington, DC: American University.

Felson, R.B. (2006a) *'The Legal Consequences of Intimate Violence Vs. Other Violence'*, Conference on Trends in Intimate Violence Intervention, New York University.

Felson, R.B. (2006b) 'Is violence against women about women or about violence?', *Contexts*, 5(2): 21–5.

Felson, R.B. and Pare, P.P. (2005) 'The reporting of domestic violence and sexual assault by non-strangers to the police', *Journal of Marriage and Family*, 67(3): 597–610.

Fergusson, D.M. and Ridder, E.M. (2005) 'Partner violence and mental health outcomes in a New Zealand birth cohort', *Journal of Marriage and Family*, 67(5): 1103–19.

Fiebert, M.S. (1997) 'Annotated bibliography: References examining assaults on their spouses/partners', *Sexuality and Culture*, 1: 273–86.

Fiebert, M.S. (2004) 'References examining assaults by women on their spouses or male partners: An annotated bibliography', *Sexuality and Culture*, 8(3/4): 140–76.

Fisher, B. (2003) *Violence Against Women and Family Violence: Developments in Research, Practice and Policy*. Washington DC: US Department of Justice, National Institute of Justice.

Gadd, D. (2004) 'Evidence-led policy or policy-led evidence? Cognitive behavioural programmes for men who are violent to women', *Criminal Justice*, 4(2): 173–97.

Gadd, D., Farrall, S., Dallimore, D. and Lombard, N.I. (2003) 'Equal victims or the usual suspects? Making sense of domestic abuse against men', *International Review of Victimology*, 10(2): 95–116.

Goel, R. (2005) 'Sita's trousseau: Restorative justice, domestic violence and South Asian culture', *Violence Against Women*, 11: 639–65.

Gondolf, E. (2002) *Batterer Intervention Systems*. Thousand Oaks, CA: Sage.

Goodmark, L. (2004) 'Law is the answer? Do we know that for sure? Questioning the efficacy of legal interventions for battered women', *Saint Louis University Public Law Review*, 23: 7–48.

Grady, A. (2002) 'Female-on-male Domestic Abuse: Uncommon or Ignored?' in C. Hoyle and R. Young (eds) *New Visions of Crime Victims*. Oxford: Hart Publishing, pp. 71–96.

Grossman, S.F. and Lundy, M. (2003) 'Use of domestic violence services across race and ethnicity by women aged 55 and older: The Illinois experience', *Violence Against Women*, 9(12): 1442–52.

Hajjar, L. (2004) 'Religion, state power, and domestic violence in Muslim societies: A framework for comparative analysis', *Law Social Inquiry*, 29(1): 1–38.

Hamberger, L.K. and Guse, C.E. (2002) 'Men's and women's use of intimate partner violence in clinical samples', *Violence Against Women*, 8(11): 1301–31.

Herzog, S. (2004) 'Differential perceptions of the seriousness of male violence against female intimate partners among Jews and Arabs in Israel', *Journal of Interpersonal Violence*, 19: 891–900.

Hester, M. (2000) 'Domestic Violence in China', in J. Radford, L. Harne and M. Friedberg (eds) *Women, Violence and Strategies for Action: Feminist Activism, Policy and Practice*. Buckingham: Open University Press, pp. 149–66.

Hirschel, D. and Buzawa, E. (2002) 'Understanding the context of dual arrest with directions for future research', *Violence Against Women*, 8(12): 1449–73.

Home Office (2003) *Safety and Justice: The Government's Proposals on Domestic Violence*. London: The Stationery Office.

Home Office (2005) *The Code of Practice for Victims of Crime*. London: HMSO.

Hood, R. (2002) Criminology and Penal Policy: The Vital Role of Empirical Research', in A. Bottoms and M.H. Tonry (eds) *Ideology, Crime and Criminal Justice*. Cullompton: Willan Publishing.

Hopkins, C.Q., Koss, M.P and Bachar, K.J. (2004) 'Applying restorative justice to ongoing intimate violence: Problems and possibilities', *St Louis University Public Law Review*, 23: 289–311.

Hoyle, C. (1998) *Negotiating Domestic Violence: Police, Criminal Justice and Victims*. Oxford: Oxford University Press.

Hoyle, C. (2000) 'Being "a Nosy Bloody Cow": Ethical and Methodological Issues in Researching Domestic Violence', in R. King and E. Wincup (eds) *Doing Research on Crime and Justice*. Oxford: Oxford University Press, pp. 395–406.

Hoyle, C. (2006a) 'The Challenges of Risk Assessment and Management Tools for Domestic Violence', conference on Research and Theory: New Directions in Criminology, British Society of Criminology, Glasgow.

Hoyle, C. (2006b) 'Restorative Justice in Policing', in G. Johnstone and D. Van Ness (eds) *Handbook of Restorative Justice*. Cullompton: Willan Publishing.

Hoyle, C. and Sanders, A. (2000) 'Police response to domestic violence: From victim choice to victim empowerment?,' *British Journal of Criminology*, 40(1): 14–36.

Hoyle, C. and Zedner, L. (2007) 'Victims', in M. Maguire, R. Morgan and R. Reiner (eds) *The Oxford Handbook of Criminology*, 4th edn. Oxford: Oxford University Press.

Hudson, B. (2002) 'Restorative justice and gendered violence: Diversion or effective justice?', *British Journal of Criminology*, 42(3): 616–34.

Johnson, M.P. (2000) 'Conflict and Control: Images of Symmetry and Asymmetry in Domestic Violence' in A. Booth, A.C. Crouter and M. Clements (eds) *Couples in Conflict*. Hillsdale: NJ: Erlbaum.

Johnson, M.P. (2005) 'Domestic violence: It's not about gender – or is it?', *Journal of Marriage and Family*, 67(5): 1126–30.

Kanuha, V. (1996) 'Domestic Violence, Racism and the Battered Women's Movement in the United States', in J.L. Edelson and Z. Eisikovits (eds) *Future Interventions With Battered Women and their Families*. Thousand Oaks, CA: Sage, pp. 34–50.

Kelly, L. (1988) *Surviving Sexual Violence*. Cambridge: Polity Press.

Kershaw, C., Budd, T., Kinshott, G., Mattinson, J., Mayhew, P. and Myhill, A. (2000) *The 2000 British Crime Survey England and Wales*. London: Home Office.

Kimmel, M.S. (2002) '"Gender symmetry" in domestic violence: A substantive and methodological research review', *Violence Against Women*, 8(11): 1332–63.

Krug, E.G., Dahlberg, L.L., Mercy, J.A., Zwi, A.B. and Lozano, R. (2002) *The World Report on Violence and Health*. Geneva: World Heath Organisation.

Kury, H., Obergfell-Fuchs, J. and Woessner, G. (2004) 'The extent of family violence in Europe', *Violence Against Women*, 10(7): 749–69.

Landau, S.F. and Hattis Rolef, S. (1998) 'Intimate femicide in Israel: Temporal, social and motivational patterns', *European Journal on Criminal Policy and Research*, 6(1): 75–90.

Maguigan, H. (2002) 'Wading into Professor Schneider's "murky middle ground" between acceptance and rejection of criminal justice responses to domestic violence', *American University Journal of Gender Social Policy and the Law*, 11(2): 427–46.

McClennen, J.C. (2005) 'Domestic violence between same-gender partners', *Journal of Interpersonal Violence*, 20: 149–154.

Mendelsohn, B. (1956) 'Une nouvelle branche de la science bio-psycho-sociale: victimiologie', *Revue Internationale de Criminologie et de Police Technique*, 11(2): 95–109.

Miller, S.L. and Meloy, M.L. (2006) 'Women's use of force: Voices of women arrested for domestic violence', *Violence Against Women*, 12(1): 89–115.

Millett, K. (1985) *Sexual Politics*. London: Virago.

Mills, L.G. (1998) *The Heart of Intimate Abuse: New Interventions in Child Welfare, Criminal Justice and Health Settings*. New York: Springer.

Mills, L.G. (2003) *Insult to Injury: Rethinking our Responses to Intimate Abuse*. Princeton, NJ: Princeton University Press.

Mills, L.G. (2006) 'The justice of recovery: How the state can heal the violence of crime', *Hastings Law Journal*, 57(3): 457–508.

Morris, A. (1987) *Women, Crime and Criminal Justice*. Oxford: Blackwell.

Morris, A. and Gelsthorpe, L. (2000) 'Re-visioning men's violence against female partners', *Howard Journal of Criminal Justice*, 39(4): 412–428.

Mullender, A. (2000) *Reducing Domestic Violence ... What Works? Perpetrator Programmes*. Policing and Reducing Crime Briefing Note. London: Policing and Reducing Crime Unit, Home Office.

Nancarrow, H. (2006) 'In search of justice for domestic and family violence: Indigenous and non-indigenous Australian women's perspectives', *Theoretical Criminology*, 10: 87–106.

National Institute of Justice (2003) *Do Batterer Intervention Programs Work? Two Studies*. Washington, DC: Department of Justice.

Ockleford, E., Barnes-Holmes, Y., Morichelli, R., Morjaria, A., Scocchera, F., Furniss, F., Sdogati, C. and Barnes-Holmes, D. (2003) 'Mistreatment of older women in three European countries: Estimated prevalence and service responses', *Violence Against Women*, 9(12): 1453–64.

Parmar, A., Sampson, A. and Diamond, A. (2005) *Tackling Domestic Violence: Providing Advocacy and Support to Survivors from Black and Other Minority Ethnic Communities*. London: Home Office.

Pateman, C. (1987) 'Feminist Critiques of the Public/Private Dichotomy', in A. Phillips (ed.) *Feminism and Equality*. Oxford: Blackwell.

Pence, E. and Paymar, M. (1993) *Educational Groups for Men Who Batter: The Duluth Model*. New York: Springer.

Percy, A. and Mayhew, P. (1997) 'Estimating sexual victimisation in a national crime survey: A new approach', *Studies in Crime and Crime Prevention*, 6: 125–150.

Raj, A. and Silverman, J. (2002) 'Violence against immigrant women: The roles of culture, context and legal immigrant status on intimate partner violence', *Violence Against Women*, 8(3): 367–398.

Raphael, J. (2002) 'Battering through the lens of class', *American University Journal of Gender Social Policy and the Law*, 11(2): 367–76.

Reinharz, S. (1992) *Feminist Methods in Social Research*. Oxford: Oxford University Press.

Renzetti, C.M. (1992) *Violent Betrayal: Partner Abuse in Lesbian Relationships*. London: Sage.

Renzetti, C.M. (2004) 'Editor's introduction', *Violence Against Women*, 10(9): 958–60.

Richards, L. (2003) *Findings from the Multi-agency Domestic Violence Murder Reviews in London*. London: Metropolitan Police Service.

Richards, L. (2004) *'Getting Away With It': A Strategic Overview of Domestic Violence, Sexual Assault and 'Serious' Incident Analysis*. London: Metropolitan Police Service.

Richie, B.E. (2000) 'A Black feminist reflection on the antiviolence movement', *Signs*, 25(4): 1133–8.

Ristock, J. (2002) *No More Secrets: Violence in Lesbian Relationships*. New York: Routledge.

Robinson, A. (2004) *Domestic Violence MARACs (Multi-Agency Risk Assessment Conferences) for Very High-Risk Victims in Cardiff, Wales: A Process and Outcome Evaluation*. Cardiff: School of Social Sciences, Cardiff University.

Robinson, A. and Cook, D. (2006) 'Understanding victim retraction in cases of domestic violence: Specialist courts, government policy and victim-centred justice', *Contemporary Justice Review*, 9: 189–213.

Rosenbaum, A. (2006) 'Understanding Batterers: It's About Time', conference on Trends in Intimate Violence Intervention, New York University.

Rydstrom, H. (2003) 'Encountering "hot" anger', *Violence Against Women*, 9(6): 676–97.

Sartin, R.M., Hansen, D.J. and Huss, M.T. (2006) 'Domestic violence treatment response and recidivism: A review and implications for the study of family violence', *Aggression and Violent Behavior*, 11(5): 425–40.

Saunders, D.G. (1988) 'Other "truths" about domestic violence: A reply to McNeely and Robinson-Simpson', *Social Work*, 33: 179–83.

Saunders, D.G. (1996) 'Feminist-cognitive-behavioral and process-psychodynamic treatments for men who batter: Interaction of abuser traits and treatment model', *Violence and Victims*, 11(4): 393–414.

Saunders, D. (2002) 'Are physical assaults by wives and girlfriends a major social problem? A review of the literature', *Violence Against Women*, 8(12): 1424–48.

Sentencing Advisory Panel (2006) *Domestic Violence: The Panel's Advice to the Sentencing Guidelines Council*. London: Sentencing Guidelines Council.

Shepard, M. and Pence, E. (1999) *Coordinating Community Response to Domestic Violence: Lessons from the 'Duluth Model'*. Thousand Oaks, CA: Sage.

Sherman, L. (1992) *Policing Domestic Violence: Experiments and Dilemmas*. New York: Free Press.

Sokoloff, N.J. (2005) *Domestic Violence at the Margins: Readings in Race, Class, Gender and Culture*. Piscataway, NJ: Rutgers University Press.

Sokoloff, N.J. and Dupont, I. (2005) 'Domestic violence at the intersections of race, class and gender: Challenges and contributions to understanding violence against marginalized women in diverse communities', *Violence Against Women*, 11: 38–64.

Stanley, J.L., Bartholomew, K., Taylor, T., Oram, D. and Landolt, M. (2006) 'Intimate violence in male same-sex relationships', *Journal of Family Violence*, 21(1): 31–41.

Steinmetz, S.K. (1977–1978) 'The battered husband syndrome', *Victimology*, 2(3 Suppl. 4): 499–509.

Stets, J.E. (1993) 'Control in dating relationships', *Journal of Marriage and the Family*, 55(3): 673.

Stets, J.E. and Pirog-Good, M.A. (1990) 'Interpersonal control and courtship aggression', *Journal of Social and Personal Relationships*, 7: 371–94.

Strang, H. and Braithwaite, J. (eds) (2002) *Restorative Justice and Family Violence*. Cambridge: Cambridge University Press.

Straus, M. (1999) 'The Controversy over Domestic Violence by Women: A Methodological, Theoretical and Sociology of Science Analysis', in X.B. Arriaga and S. Oskamp (eds) *Violence in Intimate Relationships*. Thousand Oaks, CA: Sage.

Straus, M. (2005) 'Women's Violence Toward Men is a Serious Social Problem', in D.R. Loseke, R.J. Gelles and M.M. Cavanaugh (eds) *Current Controversies on Family Violence*. Newbury Park, CA: Sage, pp. 55–77.

Straus, M. (2006) 'Dominance and Symmetry in Partner Violence by Male and Female University Students in 32 Nations'. Conference on Trends in Intimate Violence Intervention, New York University.

Straus, M. and Gelles, R.J. (1990) *Physical Violence in American Families: Risk factors and Adaptations to Violence in 8,145 Families*. New Brunswick, NJ: Transaction.

Straus, M.A., Hamby, S.L., Boney-McCoy, S. and Sugarman, D.B. (1996) 'The revised conflict tactics scales (CTS2)', *Journal of Family Issues*, 7(3): 283–316.

Stubbs, J. (2002) 'Domestic Violence and Women's Safety: Feminist Challenges to Restorative Justice', in H. Strang and J. Braithwaite (eds) *Restorative Justice and Family Violence*. Cambridge: Cambridge University Press, pp. 42–61.

Tjaden, P. and Thoennes, N. (1999) *Extent, Nature and Consequences of Intimate Partner Violence: Findings from the National Violence Against Women Survey.* Washington, DC: National Institute of Justice/Centers for Disease Control and Prevention.

Tjaden, P. and Thoennes, N. (2000) 'Prevalence and consequences of male-to-female and female-to-male intimate partner violence as measured by the National Violence Against Women Survey', *Violence against Women*, 6: 142–61.

Von Hentig, H. (1948) *The Criminal and His Victim.* New Haven, CT: Yale University Press.

Walby, S. and Allen, J. (2004) *Domestic Violence, Sexual Assault and Stalking: Findings from the British Crime Survey.* London: Home Office.

Walby, S. and Myhill, A. (2001) 'Assessing and Managing Risk', in J. Taylor-Browne (ed.) *What Works in Reducing Domestic Violence? A Comprehensive Guide for Professionals.* London: Whiting Birch.

Walklate, S. (1989) *Victimology: The Victim and the Criminal Justice System.* London: Unwin Hyman.

Walklate, S. (2004) *Gender, Crime and Criminal Justice*, 2nd edn. Cullompton: Willan Publishing.

Warrick, C. (2005) 'The vanishing victim: Criminal law and gender in Jordan', *Law and Society Review*, 39(2): 315–48.

Websdale, N. (1999) *Understanding Domestic Homicide.* Boston, MA: Northeastern University Press.

Winstok, Z. and Eisikovits, Z. (2006) 'Motives and Control in Escalatory Conflicts in Intimate Relationships', conference on Trends in Intimate Violence Intervention, New York University.

Wolfgang, M. (1958) *Patterns in Criminal Homicide.* Philadelphia: University of Pennsylvania Press.

Yoshihama, M. (1999) 'Domestic violence against women of Japanese descent in Los Angeles', *Violence Against Women*, 5: 869–97.

Zink, T., Regan, S., Jacobson, C.J. and Pabst, S. (2003) 'Cohort, period and aging effects: A qualitative study of older women's reasons for remaining in abusive relationships', *Violence Against Women*, 9(12): 1429–41.

Chapter 7

Lessons from the gender agenda[1]

Pamela Davies

Introduction

This chapter is concerned with identifying what we know about how gender relates to the victimological enterprise. It is concerned equally to acknowledge that there are significant gaps in our knowledge about gendered patterns of risk to victimisation, fear of becoming victimised, experiences of and responses to victimisation. Moreover, as criminologists and/or victimologists we have a limited understanding and appreciation of how, when and where a gendered approach might be useful. In order to clarify some of these 'knowledge problems' in respect of women, men, gender and victimology the content of this chapter is organised around three main subject headings: gender and victimology; feminisms, gender and victimology; and masculinities, gender and victimology. Under these headings several key questions are considered. These include the following:

- What are the most significant features of the study of gender and victimology?
- What are the major achievements?
- What lies ahead for the future in terms of research and practice?

By focusing on these themes the chapter applauds the theoretical, policy, practice and research achievements relating to gender and victimisation and reveals details about the processes associated with victimisation. This organising framework also facilitates a reflexive discussion about these specific developments as well as the engendering of victimology. The main sceptical thread to the chapter ultimately queries whether gender deserves prioritising in the study of victimology and if so how and when. However, before becoming too engrossed in mapping out the rudiments of our victimological knowledge on the nature, extent and impact of gendered experiences of criminal victimisation in society, why a 'gender' agenda?

Gender and victimology

As indicated above, the bigger question of whether this chapter is right to prioritise gender as opposed to any other salient variable that might equally or more forcefully impact upon people's experiences of victimisation is one that is considered throughout the remainder of this chapter and conclusions are therefore reserved on this. Initially I am concerned with explaining what is meant by 'gender' and with exploring what gender does not mean and what it does encompass. In order to do this it is useful to consider how gender has come to be included in criminological and victimological inquiries from a historical perspective. The time-frame, however, is a relatively short one and can be briefly outlined.

Some enduring legacies persist in both the criminological and victimological enterprises. Several of these have a strong impact upon how a gendered approach has taken shape in these disciplines. In victimology these can be traced to the founders of the discipline in the 1940s and 1950s, and the 'domain assumptions' that can be associated with the victim typologies work of Von Hentig and Mendelsohn (Walklate 2007). Later developments saw the concept of 'risky lifestyles' introduced together with a focus on public spaces – as opposed to private ones such as the home – as locations for criminal victimisation. Also, since 1979 Amir has been associated with the controversial phrase 'victim precipitation', the legacy of which continues in connection to some women's experiences of rape. The work of these and a handful of authors writing in a similar vein (for example Hindelang *et al.* 1978) produced a domineering positivist framework for the consideration of victimisation which persists in the twenty-first century and impacts upon our understanding of how victimisation is researched, how it occurs, what form it takes, how often it happens, why it happens, when and where it takes place and who it happens to. While the positivist legacy has been strongly challenged it has not been extinguished. Some key features of this legacy are explored in other chapters of this volume. Some of those that impact upon a gendered victimology are summarised below.

First I return to what we can learn from the history of academic research. Lessons about women in the comparatively youthful sub-discipline of victimology are inextricably linked to the feminist critique of criminology which Smart initiated in the 1970s (Smart 1976). Pioneering work followed throughout the 1980s that had major implications in terms of understanding women as victims of violent and sexual abuse from men (see for example Brownmiller 1975; Dobash and Dobash 1979, 1998; Hanmer and Maynard 1987; Hanmer, Radford and Stanko 1989; Hanmer and Saunders 1984; Kelly 1988; Kelly and Radford 1987; Stanko 1985, 1988). This era of work from the late twentieth century also shaped our understanding of criminal women so that their criminality has been for the most part explained in terms of social and economic marginalisation and dependency. This has tended to have the effect of reframing criminal women as suffering at the expense of unjust, sexist, bias and patriarchal systems and institutions (for example Carlen 1983, 1985, 1988; Eaton 1986; Gelsthorpe 1989; Carlen and Worrall 1987). This too encouraged views of women as vulnerable and socially and culturally victimised. Thus criminal women might have been thoroughly explained as gendered economic victims (see Carlen 1983, 1985, 1988; Carlen and Worrall 1987) but not as comprehensively as perpetrators of economic crimes (Davies 2003a, 2003b) and as perpetrators of violent interpersonal crimes (Batchelor *et al.* 2001; Burman *et al.* 2001; Burman 2003). All of this has had an impact upon how a gendered perspective has been incorporated in the victimological enterprise, upon how victim research has been conducted and upon the choice of subject matter under investigation. Some of the consequences of this are summarised also below.

In terms of the history of gendered victim policies, the second wave of feminism and the political climate in the US and later in the UK fuelled radical and left unrest and activism. Radical and left realist scholarship was simultaneously published throughout the 1970s and 1980s, reflecting criminologically this changing political mood. This body of work challenged and critiqued conventional and traditional definitions of the crime problem and positivistic victimology. It also offered an alternative focus for the crime problem focusing upon the role of the state and also upon women's roles and experiences in public and private and in some cases a strong policy agenda for placing previously marginalised victims more firmly centre stage. This critique and the aims to incorporate lessons of feminism, together with political activities and initiatives, many of which were specifically aimed at providing a response to women's unmet needs, resulted in the formation of Women's Aid and Refuge provisions for female victims only of domestic abuse, rape crisis interventions and later rape suites, all of which helped put gender on to the victimological agenda (see also Chapters 5 and 6 in this volume). In addition to a whole variety of different social harms and injustices being highlighted, for a select few scholars (Pearce and Snider 1995; Perry and Dawson 1985; Szyockyi and Fox 1996) their victims became study-worthy and are sometimes included within the parameters of victimological study.

These historical developments within the academy and from political-social and economic pressures forced a proliferation of feminist ideas connected to both the criminological and the victimological enterprises. While a variety of feminist positions and feminisms are now evident, including liberal feminism, radical feminism, socialist feminism and postmodern feminisms, they all tend to have the so-called 'woman question' in common (for example Cain 1990; Carlen 2002; Harding 1987; Hudson 2000; Walklate 2000, 2001, 2003b, 2004). While all of this indicates an increased academic concern about victims generally as opposed to crimes and criminals, it also indicates a growing pro-women rather than fully gendered way of thinking. Considered within this historical context and against the political climate of 'equality for women', it is perhaps not surprising that studies of male and female crime and victimisation patterns have sometimes been conflated and confused with studies that are concerned with exploring how gender relates to criminological and victimological enquiries and enterprises. Indeed in much research in the fields of criminology, victimology, social psychology, economics and related disciplines this confusion is still clearly evident and the word gender is often inappropriately used as a substitute for sex. To clarify some of these confusions it is generally the case that in the context of policy issues gender-neutrality is wedded to the equality-based feminist positions while gender-specific policy advocates are wedded to difference-based perspectives (Daly 1994).

Philosophically feminists have warned that gender-neutrality simply equates to the male standard where masculinity and maleness are the yardsticks against which judgements of others are made (MacKinnon 1987). Furthermore and to clarify the sex/gender confusion, Walklate's observation is useful: 'sex differences, i.e. differences that can be observed between the biological categories, male and female: they are not necessarily a product of gender. Gender differences are those that result from the socially ascribed roles of being male or being female, i.e. masculinity and femininity' (Walklate 2004: 94). However, from the mid-1990s to date, it is fair to say that the victimological agenda has quickly gathered the impetus from developments within the criminological agenda and a preoccupation with sex rather than gender is no longer so dominant. Poor substitutes or proxies for gender now rarely invade the space of gendered inquiries. Androgynous or non-gendered beings are similarly rare although consequences of this remain problematic for translating into gendered policies. Daly pointed out over a decade ago: 'The equality-difference debate has haunted women activists for more than a century' (Daly 1994: 9), and when it comes to gender-wise policy, as this chapter will consider, transcending such dichotomies remains problematic.

The purpose of the above was not to provide a thorough chronological history of the development of victim perspectives, nor to provide any detailed critique of women and crime or the activities of the women's movement and how each of these relate to crime, criminology and victimology; these have been well documented elsewhere (see Marsh *et al.* 2004; Mawby and Walklate 1994). Rather, this selective potted history simply serves to provide a flavour of the context within which victimology has developed and how it has been shaped by questions tangentially related to gender issues. A second purpose is that it prepares the ground for the summary promised previously of some of the stereotypes, caricatures and conundrums that have come to be associated with gender and victimisation and that have yet to be unravelled by victimologists.

What then are some of the key features of the positivist legacy and how has a gendered perspective been incorporated into the victimological enterprise and with what consequences? Within the study of victimology women were originally characterised as victim-prone; indeed, women were generally ascribed ideal victim status (Christie 1986). Some women, however – for example those with risky lifestyles such as prostitution – were seen as culpable and precipitous victims. Women and particularly female children have tended to be visible and classically fragile and vulnerable as well as often passive victims (but only in public spaces and places). There has also been a presumption that all the victims of sexual violence are female and all perpetrators of it male and that all women are always fearful. However, the impact of feminism has been significant in that it has become clear that, for example, the private domain of the home as a potential site for criminal victimisation has been obscured, as have the risks of serious violence and abuse, particularly to those women and children who spend much of their time at home with those they know and often trust the most.

In contrast to this characterisation of women, are men. However, women are not simply the opposite to men, they are hierarchically subordinated to men. In particular white heterosexual men were the norm or 'gold standard' against whom the (irrational, fearful, victim-prone female) victim could be compared. Men have been largely exempt from victim status and have been rendered invisible as victims. Men and males are fearless criminals and there has been a presumption that all the perpetrators of sexual violence are male and all its victims female. These caricatures, myths and stereotypes have persisted despite clear and consistent evidence from survey-based research, such as the British Crime Survey, dating back to the early 1980s, that men are most at risk from almost all forms of criminal victimisation but especially those serious forms of interpersonal violence that occur on the streets and in public spaces. However, while risky places have been defined as those where men are, men have apparently refused to be fearful. And despite the feminist exposé of serious forms of victimisation behind closed doors, risky places tend not to be defined as those where women are frequently harmed. This has impacted upon the pace, standard, quality and availability of support for victims and upon appropriately gendered provisions in particular. Clearly this is not a neat and tidy picture where lessons for the gendering of victimology are concerned. Our victimological knowledge is fraught with stubborn and persistent legacies, unequal equations and paradoxes and contradictory sets of discourses. Unacknowledged experiences of victimisations remain in hidden locations and settings and between individuals and groups. These are victimological problems that do not fit the basic theoretical guidelines of victimology and that provide ambiguous and complex empirical data patterns.

Feminisms, gender and victimology

As briefly stated above, victimology has very rapidly learnt much from the developments following in the wake of the feminist critique within criminology and several feminist approaches to the study of crime and female victims rather than a unified 'sisterhood' can now be identified. Elsewhere, and by drawing upon a variety of different sources, I have suggested that some of the key characteristics of liberal, radical, socialist and postmodern feminisms as they relate to the study of victimology can be compared and contrasted according to six criteria (see Davies 2007). The criteria for comparison include the following:

- What each perspective argues against in the study of victimology.
- What each perspective argues for in the study of victimology.
- The theoretical approach each perspective chooses to focus upon.
- The policy issues that are promoted.
- The preferred methodological approach to the study of crime and victimisation.
- The political strategy adopted by each perspective.

While each of the feminist perspectives identifiable within victimology has significant differences according to each of these six criteria, they have two things in common. First, each challenges the conventional victimological agenda (Walklate 2000). Second, each has a common focus in asking the 'woman question' and thus in being oriented *for* rather than *on* women (Smith and Wincup 2000).

In exploring feminist approaches to the study of victims and victimology the example of rape is used to exemplify and illustrate some key themes and issues. In a recent newspaper article (*The Times* 2005) the headline read as follows: 'Women still held to blame for rape'. The clear message from this headline is that general opinion or common-sense beliefs subscribe to the view that women who are raped by men have only themselves to blame. The headline implies that such opinions are long-standing ones yet they ought perhaps to have changed. This is clearly a highly gendered headline implying several confusing and contradictory conventional wisdoms, in particular about women as victims but also about men as offenders. The article beneath the headline goes on to explain the research that uncovered these opinions, and also offers a variety of critical comments about the research and its findings derived from different bodies. Supplementary data is offered on the 'facts' relating to rape, on convictions for rape and on issues concerning the reporting of rape. Extracts related to these aspects of the report are reproduced below:

Findings from Amnesty International UK: research that prompted the headline referred to above showed:

- More than a third of people believe that a woman is totally or partially responsible for being raped if she has behaved in a flirtatious manner.
- 26 per cent of adults believed that a woman was partially or totally responsible for being raped if she was wearing sexy or revealing clothing.
- 22 per cent held the same view if a woman had had many sexual partners.
- 30 per cent said that a woman was partially or totally responsible for being raped if she was drunk.

Women's rights groups: 'said that they were astounded and saddened by the findings, which appear to reflect widespread misconceptions that women are sexually available and that some men simply cannot help themselves'.

Campaigners: 'also said that the survey provided a sobering insight into why the conviction rate for rape prosecutions at jury trial are falling at a time when the laws on rape and consent have been tightened'.

Vera Bird MP Fawcett Society, Commission on Women and the Criminal Justice System: 'We tend to blame the low conviction rate on failures in the police and judicial systems. But if juries are thinking like this then improving the procedures is not going to make much difference.'

Jenny Watson, Equal Opportunities Commission: 'There still seems to be an assumption that women are sexually available, so if a woman has gone out to have a good time, then she must want to have sex.'

Sheila Coates, Director of South Essex Rape and Incest Crisis Centre: 'victims – who often blame themselves – are reflecting the blame they can face from society'.

Data:

- 80 per cent of rapes are committed by someone known to the victim.
- The number of rapes reported to the police has gone up in recent years.
- The number of convictions for rape has remained constant in recent years.
- A drop in the conviction rate from 33 per cent in 1977 to just over 5 per cent today.

For the purpose of this chapter, one particular victimological question is raised by this article and is this: who knows what about how gender issues connect to crime and victimisation? The article suggests that public opinions of adults in Britain are out of touch with 'equal rights for women in the private field of sexual behaviour', ignorant of the unacceptably high number of women raped every year in the UK, and of the risks of non-stranger rape, and generally out of sync with women's rights groups, campaigners, equal opportunities and rape and incest crisis groups' aims, objectives and perspectives. All of this suggests a mismatch between the 'facts' about rape, scholarly research and policy and practice on the one hand and conventional, common-sense wisdoms on the other. While a simple solution would be to blame the way in which the press report crime and victimisation news stories, features and narratives, as well as other mediated versions of the crime problem where fact and fiction have become confused as infotainment (Jewkes 2005a), this is perhaps rather too simplistic and convenient a way in which to explain the disjunction between popular opinion and lived experiences of victimisation. The study of victims and victimology clearly still has many victimological oddities such as these to address and many lessons to learn and pass on before research is likely to find women no longer held to blame for rape.

As scholars of victimisation and victimology, what exactly do we know about gender and rape? We know that:

- Rape is an exception to the more general pattern of victimisation, which is usually higher for males than females.
- Rape is a highly gendered crime and type of victimisation.
- Age combined with sex renders some women more at risk to sexual violence.
- Gender and age structure women's fear of sexual violence with women being particularly fearful of violence from men.

- Women fear, perceive and deal with risk and experiences via different day-to-day coping strategies and support networks.

Feminist challenges to the conventional victimological agenda that have insisted on pursuing the 'woman question' have highlighted three significant features relating to gender and victimology. First, they have succeeded in establishing that women suffer almost exclusively from some forms of victimisation and disproportionately from others. Second, they have demonstrated a gender patterning to risk, fear and victimisation (see Pain 2001, for example). Third, they have pointed towards a gendered approach in responding to victimisation and supporting victims. In terms of major feminist achievements, feminism has put more emphasis on hidden processes, it has shown how the gender of the perpetrator has often been hidden (Morley and Mullender 1994), and as Goodey has stated 'feminist research has done much to recast women outside the stereotype of passive victims of male aggression' (Goodey 2005: 83). Perhaps most significantly, by employing the concept of 'survivor' rather than 'victim' (London Rape Crisis Centre 1984) feminists have made several points about the gendered nature of victimisation and its impact and about gender issues in the recovery from victimisation. The concept of 'survivor' challenges the ideologies and scientific basis of positivist victimologies and in particular public perceptions of the female victim as passive, helpless, powerless, blameworthy or victim-prone. Moreover, the concept carries with it positive connotations and is forward-looking. It signifies all of the negotiating and coping strategies women employ to live their daily lives. This latter point ties in with the second significant feature feminist perspectives revealed, as noted above, concerning irrational and rational fears.

In 1983 a debate was ignited about women's irrational and rational fears, as crime survey data appeared to prove that women's fear of victimisation from men was irrational. Four years later, and now almost 20 years ago, Stanko (1987, 1988) began to deconstruct women's irrational and rational fears of crime and victimisation. Several writers since have challenged the notion that all women are always afraid and are fearful of crime (Pearce and Stanko 2000; Walklate 2001) with Gilchrist and colleagues finding fearful men and fearless women (Gilchrist *et al.* 1998). As part of the counter-argument these writers have pointed out that if women are fearful they have just cause to be so and they remind us of the huge 'dark figure' of sexual crimes and domestic violence against women. Alternative data collection methods and techniques aimed at discovering the size of the 'dark figure' have found that women are subject to staggeringly high levels of violent victimisation in different settings. Venis and Horton claim that a man has physically or sexually abused one in five women at some time in women's lives (Venis and Horton 2002). The BCS estimates that 13 per cent of women had been subject to domestic violence, sexual victimisation or stalking in the 12 months prior to interview and states that 'women are the overwhelming majority of the most heavily abused group' (Home Office 2004). Women's Aid claims that every week two women are killed in domestic violence situations (Women's Aid 2003).

Other aspects of the counter-argument coalesce around the issue of women's rational response to victimisation. The ways in which women do rationality are as mediated by gender as any area of social activity. Walklate has argued that what a man may consider rational may not be considered so by a woman (Walklate 1995: 63). Drawing on feminist philosophers Harding (1986) and Ruddick (1990) and in the context of exploring and explaining the gendered nature of sexual violence, Lees has commented:

> It appears that there are different conceptions of rationality, which may be determined partly by the social and gendered background and experiences of individuals as well as the really different possibilities which exist between men and women. (Lees 1997: 139)

Philosophically it has been acknowledged that women's fears are not always unreasonable. Women's negotiation of risk points to their understanding of risk as gendered (Chan and Rigakos 2002) and further suggests that women know the risks they face and adapt their behaviour and lifestyles to minimise, negotiate and cope with these day-to-day living conditions. So in terms of supporting victims through experiences of victimisation, at one level women 'do it for themselves' by negotiating their own safety and minimising risks, they actively and routinely engage with and negotiate their own safety in their daily social life (Stanko 1990b). In other words, women rationally negotiate their own safety and rationally work through their experiences of victimisation and abuse. This can mean that women often stay in violent relationships (Mooney 2000) while others have shown how young women sometimes take an active role in either disrupting or stabilising the feeling of safety and order within communities (Pearce and Stanko 2000).

The above illustrates how gendered inroads have been made in the victimological enterprise. However, these developments also reveal gaps and omissions, and indicate where we might yet search in order to devise more gender-sensitive theories, polices, practices and research. We might, for example, impose a gendered insight and locate our research efforts into different locations and spaces, for example, in the home as well as on the street, at the workplace and at war, at school and in the playground as well as in institutions such as the care home, the hospital and the prison. Additionally, we have a scant level of understanding of the direct and indirect impacts of different types of victimisation on women in different settings. Thus we can identify some interesting and potentially fruitful avenues for further research *for* women (and *for* men) that might inform our gendered knowledge. Moreover, the omnipresence of the woman question should properly include all identities of women including, for example, immigrant women's experiences of victimisation and the suffering and harm experienced by the whole matrix of combined female identities. Thus young black/white women's experiences might be compared and contrasted with older white and ethnic minority women's experiences. I return to some of these complexities later in the chapter within a discussion of 'hate crimes'.

In order to be more comprehensive about understanding how gender variously connects to victimological questions, feminist scholars must face up to some very difficult questions. To illustrate this point I return to the victimological subject of sexual violence in order to consider what we have not cared to know about women as victimisers. While criminology has long downplayed the nature and extent of women's criminality and focused instead upon men as committers of crime and victimisers, this has contributed to popular and scholastic beliefs that women are generally law-abiding, not real criminals and do not generally or wilfully participate in interpersonal violence and abuse. Criminality is 'assumed to be a masculine attribute and women criminals are therefore perceived to be either "not women" or "not criminals"' (Worrall 1990: 31). Women are the criminal 'other'. It is easy to understand in this context how abusive women appears to be a subject too sensitive for feminist researchers in the field of crime and victimisation to take onboard. As Burman *et al.* (2001) have pointed out in relation to the absence of feminist studies of female violence, feminists, they suggest, have feared 'the potentially negative political and social costs for the feminist movement more generally' as well as the likelihood of a '"women blaming" backlash' (Burman *et al.* 2001: 74).

Some have started to brave this potential feminist disquiet and have recently asked some tricky questions. Walklate, for example, has raised several knotty problems including the construct of the 'white, heterosexual male as the Victimological Other: that which cannot be spoken' (Walklate 2007). I return to this subject in the next section. Walklate has also tackled the question of whether there can be a feminist victimology (Walklate 2003b), as well as broaching some of the questions associated with the broader concern of this chapter about the prioritisation of gender in the study of victims and victimology (Walklate 2003a, 2003b, 2004). In respect of 'economic crimes' there has been a reluctance to admit that women might mean to do property crime and that some of their motivations might be more aligned to economic greed than need (Davies 2003a, 2003b, 2005). Whether or not women mean to do crime raises the question of women's agency. Similar questions have arisen in connection with women doing robbery and other forms of violent crime, often in connection to drugs (Batchelor *et al.* 2001; Chesney-Lind and Pasko 2004; Sommers and Baskin 1992, Sommers *et al.* 1993; Miller 1998, 2001, 2002), while in Scotland, research by Burman and colleagues has carefully unpicked how girls too can behave not just badly, but violently (Burman 2003). Jewkes has similarly questioned mediated representations of women as victimisers (Jewkes 2005a) and the failure to adequately confront their potential and actual ability to inflict pain, harm and suffering:

> The simple truth that men are more aggressive than women not only encourages widespread cultural ignorance of the fact that women have the potential for violence, but it serves also to deny psychically the notion that women can kill *as women*. (Jewkes 2005a: 129)

In terms of women as doers of crime and therefore as victimisers inflicting harm and victimisation upon others, official and most other measures indicate a gender patterning of crime (Davies 2005). Women tend to specialise in crime differently from men and for the most part we do harm (but not as much as men) to the retail sector through customer theft. However, while women's contribution to the total volume of crime and victimisation is small compared with men's, it is not always petty or trivial and as indicated above we can point towards a number of significant and more serious aspects to women's offending that tend to be masked by general patterns. Few (Croall 2003 is an exception) have noted these anomalies or commented upon these concerns about women as perpetrators of street and conventional crimes and victimisations, workplace and occupational crimes and other hidden and invisible crimes 'behind closed doors' (Walklate 2005). Croall has pondered the scarcity of research and discussion of women's involvement in, and the gendered nature of, white collar, corporate, economic or business crime and victimisation. All of this potentially involves considering women seriously as active doers of crime, as victimisers capable of inflicting interpersonal violence and abuse as well as financial harm on others. Whether their crimes be hidden behind the domestic blind, and their physically, psychologically and emotionally abusive behaviour towards male and/or female partners and/or to male and/or female children is rendered invisible, or whether their crimes are committed in other locations – the street or the workplace for example – there are a vast range of opportunities to uncover the gendered nature and experiences of victimisation. There are some small pockets of innovative research that provide evidence in support of these hidden forms of victimisation. According to some recent research, woman-to-man and woman-to-woman interpersonal violence appear to be growth areas for criminological research (Abel 2001; Babcock *et al.* 2003; Bacon 2004; Grady 2002) and several surveys report significant levels of domestic violence perpetrated by women against men:

- A victimisation survey of female-perpetrated assaults in the UK found that men reported being victimised by females more than women and experiencing the more severe forms of assault (George 1999).
- The BCS (Home Office 2004) estimates 9 per cent of men had been subject to domestic violence, sexual victimisation or stalking in the 12 months prior to interview, although not all of these will have been female-to-male violence.

A select few offences have become known as traditional female crimes (despite there often being many more of these offences committed by men); these include prostitution and shoplifting but also infanticide and to a lesser extent filicide.

Infanticide, the murder of a new-born infant, is a highly gendered term that has achieved legal status by being written into defence arguments alongside the notions of diminished responsibility and post-natal depression. As such it is a defence appropriate for women only (Jewkes 2005a). This type of murderer, therefore, is always assumed to be a woman. Brookman (2004) has taken the challenge of exploring the facts and fiction of infanticide criminologically. She finds that recent statistics suggest that while homicide is predominantly a 'masculine' affair, female offending begins to parallel that of males in the instance of infanticide. Only a select few authors can be named in connection with research on feminal abuse and killing including femicide (Jamieson 1998; Lees 1997), homicide, neonaticide,[2] infanticide and other serious forms of violence. The subject of 'women who kill', while of recurring interest in mediated representations, has rarely been given any serious criminological or victimological space. There is some academic literature on these subjects although it tends to be researched and authored by scholars belonging to the fields of psychiatry, behavioural sciences, and mental and medical health (for example Eliott and Peterson 1993; Finkelhor and Russell 1984; Faller 1987; Wilkins 1990). This material is published and disseminated via disciplines that are extremely marginal to victimology and is not easily accessed by criminologists.[3] It remains a huge challenge to feminist criminological scholarship to consider women seriously as doers of crime rather than as the 'criminological other' and to take on the subject of women as perpetrators of child sexual abuse and infanticide in particular. Yet, women are very often primary carers, and whether as babysitters, child-minders, nannies, teachers, friends, relatives or mothers we have ample opportunity to perpetrate very serious forms of intra-familial abuse and victimisation.

Feminisms and the policy agenda

While victimology is concerned with research and explanation, it is also concerned with practical support provisions and policy developments for crime victims. One of the ways in which feminist influences have pervaded into the study of victimology is by extending the feminist critique to victim-oriented policies and initiatives. Feminist politics have illustrated how female victims have experienced how the 'man of laws masculinity' pervades victim-oriented policies that have evolved during the last 30 years or so. Thus while feminist influences have helped achieve certain 'landmarks' in respect of legislative provision, and have pioneered supportive policies and practices for women victims, they have simultaneously criticised and contested some of the major government-sponsored approaches to support for victims, suggesting they require systematically gender-proofing. Well into the decade of the 1990s Lees's research evidences how lawyers and judges operate within a legal system that is based on a male standpoint and on male interests (Lees 1997).

Some pro-women support system provisions and more social, fair and just legislative landmarks, rules, regulations and initiatives can now therefore be identified, some of which have been mentioned earlier in this chapter and are discussed in greater detail elsewhere in this book. Examples include domestic violence and child protection units; protective laws and policies including those relating to provocation; pro and mandatory arrest of male perpetrators of domestic violence against women; Women's Aid refuges and rape crisis centres; self-help groups. Additionally there are women-only organisations including Women Against Violence Against Women (WAVAW), National Coalition Against Sexual Assault (NCASA) and National Organisation of Women (NOW). There is clearly no unified approach to policy initiatives and responding to women's victimisation, and the variety of often competing voluntary groups and support networks, some with more radical roots and philosophies and some having achieved more mainstream and respectful status, are testament to this. However, they do all tend to have the 'woman question' in common. Such groups will often share a commitment to the notion of voluntarism, for example, and this signals other commonalities in respect of the healing and survivorship process. These usually but do not always include offering a service or system of support for women by women and an overwhelming pro-women and children approach, a commitment to the principles of self-help, mutual support and empowerment. Additionally, victim lobby and single-issue groups exist to support and promote the cause of certain victims. These include Support After Murder and Manslaughter (SAMM), where emotional support and victim advocacy is offered to those bereaved. Mothers Against Drink Driving (MADD), and Zito Trust, which highlights issues related to mental illness.

In addition to those lessons already discussed that derive from the gender agenda in criminology, there are other lessons from feminist commentators that might be adapted to achieve more gender-sensitive responses to victimisation, in particular more gender-sensitive restorative justice approaches involving both victims and offenders (Daly 2002, Hudson 2002). Pat Carlen (2002) has described how gender-sensitive responses to men and women in a Correctional Centre in Massachusetts, is achieved. With respect to the management of female inmates environmental features and approaches are more effective in this facility's mission to empower women. Lees (1997) has considered how best to seek gendered justice in the context of sexual violence. She suggests that in working towards the longer-term agenda, part of the piecemeal reforms involve developing a 'femocracy'. This involves feminists securing a powerful voice within (bureaucratic) state institutions thereby achieving a feminist agenda. Drawing upon the ideas of Pitch, Lees has also toyed with the notion of the 'feminisation of social control' to move towards a more gendered form of justice.

To summarise so far, it seems that a gendered approach to the study of victims and victimology, through the lens of feminism, has been occasionally useful and helpful as well as being often confusing. Social stereotypes and cultural expectations of femininity and motherhood have created a number of victimological conundrums and ambiguities. On the one hand criminal women are doubly deviant, have been doubly vilified and doubly punished, on the other hand the same social stereotypes have enabled women as victimisers to remain largely invisible, shielded from being suspected and accused by criminal justice and child protection agencies of the most serious forms of victimisation (Carrabine *et al.* 2004; Turton 2000). Meanwhile, women as victims are in a double bind. As Williams (2004) has observed, there are positive connotations attached to the term victim as well as negative ones. In conforming to the ideal-type female victim women can capitalise on these associations or they can suffer from them. In terms of surviving victimisation, it is important for women not to accept, collude and through surrendering to victimhood help reproduce gendered stereotypes and cultural expectations of femininity and prescriptive notions of the victim. However, if women fail to toe the line of doing-gender through victimisation in traditional criminal justice settings, if we appear to resist and deny labels and victimhood, we risk incurring harsher treatment and penalties, and in the case of victims, 'rough justice'.

A gendered approach has a tendency to overturn neat and tidy, oversimplified and unambiguous understandings of the nature, extent and impact of victimisation in society. Pro-women approaches to the study of victimisation have revealed neglected sites of abuse and suffering in the home, at work, at war, and harmful activities and products that appear to affect women and girls exclusively, all of which could appear to indicate that women bear the brunt of harm and suffering and victimisation (Davies 2007). Following feminist criminological theorising (Carlen 1988, Worrall 1990) on criminal women, this leads to a victimological dilemma for women who find themselves doubly victimised and doubly suffering (as well as doubly deviant and doubly suffering (Carlen 1988)). However, women cannot have it both ways and pro-women only approaches to victimology are not truly gender-sensitive. Feminist theorising does not need to be gender-equal but it could be more gender-friendly. This will involve considering both men as victims and women as killers and abusers.

Gender salience?

If a gendered approach is sometimes both useful and helpful as well as ambiguous and confusing, it is also questionable as to whether it is ever or always the key variable in understanding the relationship between women, crime and victimisation. I have briefly referred to how Walklate (2003b) has asked whether there can be a feminist victimology. Central to this question, she argues, are the tensions between conventional victimological concerns and a feminist-informed agenda. There are conceptual tensions, for example those discussed above, between the concept of victim and survivor and those surrounding what constitutes rational knowledge. A positive answer to Walklate's original question becomes increasingly unlikely and she poses the more gender-friendly question, can there be a feminist-informed victimology? (2003b: 38). Her conclusions centre around a focus on the interrelationship between agency and structure. So, to understand women's powerlessness and survivalism, the structural location of women and their negotiation of their structural location is key. She states: 'It is this kind of theoretical starting point, which neither treats gender as a variable nor locates it purely as a definitional category, which permits the inclusion of a critical edge of feminist work into victimology' (2003b: 41).

Arguments can be supported for giving at least equal priority to age in explaining and understanding victimisation and social harm in society. Goodey's research finds that gendered expressions of fear and vulnerability appear to show gender and age differences while class and ethnicity variables were held constant (Goodey 1997). Progressive research in the field of youth and crime has also recently taken steps to consider young people not only as perpetrators of crime and victimisation but as 'sinned against' (Brown 1998; Muncie 2004). The implications of this for the study of victims and victimology are enormous as we begin to digest the various ways in which young people experience victimisation from adults and other young people as well as from institutions, legislation and policies that also inflict punishment and abuse on young people.

Masculinities, gender and victimology

In early victim studies we are often presented with a homogeneous portrayal of the crime victim. Where gender distinctions were evident, however, there was often a homogeneous portrayal of who women are and an equally homogenised portrayal of who men are. These homogeneities are persistent and remain key obstacles to a more fully gendered understanding of victimisation. The same obstacles limit an improved understanding of masculinities, gender and victimology. Where women have been characterised as ideal victims, indeed as victim-prone and blameworthy, men have quite simply been characterised as victimisers. While this has not necessarily ensured that all female victims of all types of victimisations have been visible, and has not always corresponded with support provisions available to female victims, it has contributed to the continued and unchanging assumptions and presumptions about men as victimisers. It has also bolstered presumptions that all the victims of sexual violence are female (and all perpetrators male) and that men are never vulnerable, fearful or at great risk to victimisation. On the contrary, white, heterosexual, rational men have been the norm or yardstick against whom not only females but also all other victims could be compared. Men have not been ascribed legitimate or real victim status and have been largely invisible as victims.

Even with the advent of more sophisticated measurements of victimisation following the first British Crime Survey in 1982, and with the data we have accumulated since on risky places and venues, the ways of thinking about men and women that are illustrated above remain difficult for victimologists of the twenty-first century to dispense with. Men in self-report surveys continue to confirm lower levels of fear (Sutton and Farrall 2005). So, although risky places ought to have been redefined as those where men go and where women live, more innovative and imaginative research narratives indicate that there are still private experiences of victimisations in different locations and settings, between individuals and groups, that victimology has yet to properly contend with. There are several barriers that contribute to the difficulties in exposing and explaining these gendered experiences, risks and fears. Just a few suggestions as to what these barriers might be can be gleaned from a handful of research studies connected to a small selection of victimisations. Some of the general barriers, and some more specific ones, to exposing and explaining gendered experiences include the following:

- Obsessions with scientific and often empiricist quantitative research methodologies and techniques and the need to discover clear patterns and rates (this tends to obscure nuances and irregularities).

- Prejudices and constraints of time and resources militate against institutions and war crime investigators researching, investigating and documenting male sexual assault during war, preventing detection and punishment (Carlson 2006).

- Macho concealment of fear and socially desirable responses in surveys: it might be shameful and embarrassing for men to express fear and thus they may be unwilling to report it (Sutton and Farrall 2005).

- Hegemonic masculinities that suggest men aren't real victims; men and big boys don't cry (Goodey 1997).

- The stigma of male rape, men's fears that they will be considered to be homosexual, and myths regarding the promiscuity of gay men all conspire to prevent both heterosexual and gay men from reporting their experiences to the police (Gregory and Lees 1999).

- 'Men's hesitation to disclose vulnerability' (Stanko and Hobdell 1993: 400).

- Women who do not want to be portrayed as victims and who do not want always to feel vulnerable and in need of protection.

Victimology has therefore thought about men mostly as victimisers and has generally not contemplated men as victims. In discussing feminism, gender and victimology the historical developments have been very much associated with both the domain assumptions derived from the founders of victimology in the 1940s and 1950s as well as the feminist critique within criminology, which originated in the decade of the 1970s. This time-frame has produced many lessons for the study of victims and victimology in terms of understanding the nature and extent of women's experience of victimisation and how this might be accommodated in relation to criminal justice policy. The time-frame relating to the exploration of the nature and extent of understanding men's experience of victimisation is much shorter still, and in terms of the likely impact of this understanding and in particular how this might be accommodated in relation to criminal justice policy the lessons are perhaps still to come. Research on gender, masculinities and crime can be traced back only 20 or so years to the 1980s when new studies focused on criminal masculinities (Carrabine *et al.* 2004; Walklate 2004). These developments were inspired by feminist scholarship and initially the notion of masculinity was employed to help explain men's oppressive power over women and in particular men's violence against women. In this view violent men can be seen to be acting out, demonstrating and asserting their machismo. Thus this early application of the notion of masculinity emerged as a concern to explain and understand men as victimisers and women as victims and the concerns with masculinities grew out of women's and feminists' complaints about heterosexual men's sexual, domestic and economic violence (Groombridge 2001).

Once again we can highlight that it has been feminist challenges to the conventional victimological agenda, that have insisted on pursuing the 'woman question', that have made major achievements. They have been especially instrumental in bringing debates on masculinities, crime and victimisation into the arena of victim-centred research (Goodey 2005: 83). Since these early applications, theoretical considerations around masculinity and notions of masculinities took on greater significance in the social sciences generally. Connell's (1987) work on a tripartite structure of gender relations and the gender order was particularly influential, although Messerschmidt is credited with applying the concept of masculinities to the doing of crime by men and thereby importing the concept into criminology. Following this, masculinities emerged as a key theoretical concept in its own right (see McLaughlin and Muncie 2001).

So far this section on men, masculinities and victimology has considered some of the ways in which academic studies have considered men. It has discussed how there has been a shift from an overriding concern with men as offenders and perpetrators, to a focus on the maleness of perpetrators of crime, that is, as male criminals, men who have masculine identities. These identities are some of the most salient of all gender identities. This section has also made brief reference to the influential body of work that has prompted the suggestion that violent crime in particular can be understood as a product of masculinities and of men 'doing-gender'. Masculinities has not only evolved into a key theoretical concept and explanatory tool for understanding crime, but has also proliferated to the extent that there are journals, degree modules and books dedicated to it as a subject area in its own right.

So how might we think about the study of crime, criminal justice and victimisation from a masculinities perspective? A short quotation from Groombridge helps orient us in the right direction here. He suggests that we can now accept that 'while the problem may still be men, men still had problems' (Groombridge 2001: 261). We can briefly summarise what we now understand the concept of masculinities to encompass and what the study of masculinities within victimology might properly need to include. A simple summary list can be compiled of a number of key concepts and attributes. These include an understanding of:[4]

- essentialism
- masculinism, 'manliness', the 'hypermasculine' and machismo
- patriarchy, androcracy, fratriarchy
- hierarchies of domination and status, ritual, symbolism, difference
- hegemony and of male solidarity
- culture, identity, self-image and reputation
- manhood and male attributes, credentials and norms such as physical prowess, aggression, toughness and violence.

How all of these ingredients interact in very complex ways with femininity and sexuality might be particularly significant. Yet despite the recent emergence and fast-growing proliferation of academic materials relating to masculinities, few have cared yet to import the concept into the study of victims and victimology and therefore it is less easy to review in this chapter how victimisation might be understood as a product of masculinity. Studies that are beginning to broach this question are very much in their infancy. However, there does appear to be some potential for making sense of some of the less visible forms of victimisation that some men experience and suffer from, especially those forms of victimisation that are perpetrated by other men.

So, having made these advances in terms of understanding how gender might facilitate our understanding of victims and victimology we might ask some further questions. Can men now be victims? In the twenty-first century has the gender agenda fully incorporated men and masculinities? Is victimology up to the task of challenging established interpretations of who can be vulnerable, fearful and at risk? Clearly we know, as successive surveys have identified (British Crime Surveys from 1982 to 2004; George 1999), and qualitative studies have demonstrated, that men can be, are and always have been victims of crime. Sometimes men suffer from victimisation, whether it is murder, assault, sexual victimisation or stalking, from women, and sometimes they suffer similar forms of victimisation from other men. Walklate reminds us that 'it would be a mistake to presume that all the perpetrators of sexual violence are male and all its victims female' (Walklate 2004). However, as Goodey (2005) has pointed out the 'taboo' subject of female-on-male domestic violence does have an empirical basis, yet this has been downplayed (Gadd *et al.* 2003, Mirrlees-Black and Byron 1999) and the real impact this has on men's lives remains under-researched.

Exceptionally within the criminological domain, Lees (1997) has undertaken consultancy research on male sexual assaults on men (with Lynn Ferguson, the director of the Channel 4 *Dispatches* 1995 programme on male rape). Two surveys were conducted in 1995, one of male victims of rape and the first ever survey of police recording practices of rape of men by men. The criminological and victimological analysis focuses on men's experiences of sexual violence in the context of masculinity (see Lees 1997: 89–107 and Gregory and Lees 1999: 112–33). Lees presents a persuasive illustration of how hegemonic masculinity is a useful explanatory concept in this analysis:

> This chapter shows how this (hegemonic masculinity) seems to be the most feasible explanation for why sexual assaults on men are predominantly perpetrated by men who regard themselves as heterosexual in sexual orientation. It also explains why male rape so often takes place in all-male institutions such as prisons and the army. By sexually humiliating men who do not appear to live up to the dominant form of masculinity, the perpetrator's own masculinity is enhanced. (Lees 1997: 13)

In this extract Lees refers to a common and long known about experience peculiar to the imprisonment of men. Male rape and other experiences of mortification and brutality in men's prisons have been acknowledged criminologically since the classic study by Sykes in 1958. Although known about, however, the subject has been little cared about and victimologically men have not constituted real victims behind the closed doors of the prison. Men in prison who are subjected to aggression and violence are the victimological other twice removed or, contradictorily in the case of the rapist and paedophile, they are the deserving victim. Jewkes begins to shed light on the ways in which men behind bars do masculinity as an adaptation to imprisonment (2005b) although she does not discuss male rape as one of the overt manly or hypermasculine coping strategies used by inmates. So, while some brave scholars have dared to put women in the frame as perpetrators of crime and victimisers, others have chosen to put men in the frame as victims. Such approaches are only beginning to uncover the implications of the maleness of victimisation.

In terms of masculinities and the policy agenda there is very little to review to date. Having unearthed statistical data attesting to men's experiences of domestic violence, in 2003 the Home Office asked for views on how it should respond to the needs of this population (Home Office 2004). Few programmes or initiatives can be listed as appropriately gendered provisions for supporting men as victims in the same way as they can for women. Conversely, however, a number of programmes can be cited as suitable for men only as perpetrators and these are often connected to anger management and zero-tolerance towards domestic violence suffered by women. The gender agenda is still struggling to develop appropriately gendered responses and to construct a gendered policy agenda to crime and victimisation.

Gender salience?

As Walklate has queried elsewhere (2007), when is it that being masculine is the key variable in understanding the relationship between men, crime and victimisation, and when might other variables be more important? Hall and Winlow have similarly asked, in the context of high rates for crime, violence, corruption and terrorism, 'whether a culturalist-dominated gender studies continues to be useful to our political or pragmatic attempts to address these problems'. Indeed they have consistently asserted that men's and boys' violence is not best explained or likely to be reduced by focusing on the hegemonic masculinity thesis (Hall 2002; Hall and Winlow 2003a, 2003b). Together they argue that 'we need to relate violent crime and criminological theory to the economic principles that underpin culture and society' (Hall and Winlow 2003a). While their focus is on the perpetrators of violence and on men in particular, their arguments might similarly be employed in respect to victimisation. Arguments in support of prioritising other key variables might be equally applicable to the study of victims and victimology. From such a perspective victimisation needs to give precedence to the socio-economic. Borrowing once again from criminology, this resonates not only with Hall and Winlow but also with Davies's conclusions in respect of women who do crime for economic gain. It is women's needs and women's greeds that is key to understanding their doing of economic crime (Davies 2005). There are then some minor signposts that indicate dissenting voices over whether gender ought to always be omnipresent. This concurs with Walklate's conclusions for a critical victimology rather than a feminist victimology. She states that such a victimology 'demands an understanding of the processes of victimisation that is socio-economically and culturally situated' (Walklate 2003b: 42). Gender matters but 'doing-gender' ought not to always and necessarily to take precedence over economic and class explanations.

Gender, hate crimes and criminal justice policy

Some important issues concerning gender and hidden or invisible victimisations have already been examined above. This section specifically considers some of the less visible arenas of victimisation such as those associated with questions of sexuality, disability and in particular 'hate' crimes and the policy agenda. One of the lessons from connecting a gender agenda to the study of victimology, and one of the direct consequences of focusing upon specific victimisations such as domestic and racist violence, is that there is now a wider social and growing legal agenda to tackle hate crimes and victimisations.

A hate crime is one motivated by an offender's hatred of someone because of his or her race or religion, or sexual orientation, or disability. Crimes perpetrated in whole or in part due to any of these biases are a criminal offence and these can include a range of threats or actual physical attacks, verbal abuse or insults. Hate crimes can take place in traditional street settings, in public and private places and spaces, and also in cyberspace where it is called cyber-hate (Brown 2003). In addition to being closely linked with racist and homophobic harassment and prejudice (Mason 2005), hate crimes are often associated with right-wing extremists, xenophobic and anti-Semitic attitudes (Strobl *et al.* 2005). An alternative way of understanding hate crimes is to consider how hate groups characterise their victims by distancing 'them' from 'us' and by vilifying the 'other' so that 'minorities are portrayed in a very unsympathetic manner, as either animals, criminals, destroyers of civilisation, or financial liabilities' (Perry 2003: 306). Within the generic category 'hate crimes', there are many diverse hate groups and many diverse victim groups. For the purpose of this chapter the main reason for considering how the debates around hate crime have unfolded is to learn lessons for the gender agenda in victimology. At various points above I have paused to consider whether or not gender matters most and deserves being especially selected as a useful analytical concept. In the closing pages of this chapter I am particularly concerned with whether or not gender matters in responding to 'newer' or 'rediscovered' types of victimisation.

In the study of hate crimes, one of the key debates has been whether or not gender fits into the hate crime paradigm, and in the context of the United States, McPhail (2003) has usefully summarised the main arguments both for and against this. She suggests that there are numerous policy benefits of having gender included as a status within hate crime policy. Much benefit derives from having defined the victims as worthy of legal redress, which can mean new legal remedies and increased penalties. She lists three benefits of increasing public awareness of the seriousness of violence against women. These are:

1 It directs attention away from rape myths and on to motives of hate, power and control.
2 It shifts attention away from the victim and on to the motives and actions of the perpetrators.
3 It also moves attention away from the relationship and on to the violence.

It is also worth quoting from McPhail further to illustrate how policy solutions might flow more easily following the shift in focus on motivation from victim to perpetrator as indicated in each of the above points. This shift 'would change the questions asked of the victim "Why don't you leave?" and "What were you wearing?" to asking the perpetrator "Why did you target women?" and "What part does your misogyny play in this violence?"' (McPhail 2003: 273). Reframing the victimological gaze in this way fits snugly with the radical feminist agenda of explaining, conceptualising and responding to violence against women.

A gender-wise victimology?

This chapter has outlined and illustrated how the social relations of gender in the study of victims have very slowly been exposed during the last 30 years. In general terms it has illustrated that crime and the experience of victimisation occurs on a very complex gendered terrain. The arguments that follow from this additionally suggest that gender relations impinge on the experience and recovery from crime and victimisation. During the relatively short history of the discipline, we can identify achievements and there are several lessons for the study of victims and victimology. For example, the study of victims and victimology ought no longer to countenance mediated representations, research, policy, practice and theoretical approaches that assume an androgynous, sexually neutral, ideal victim, nor should it countenance a homogeneous gender-neutral or indeed a homogeneous female or male, victim. Differences between women's experiences ought to be respected and differences between men's experiences ought to be similarly respected not negated.

I have pointed out a number of examples and illustrations of how the study of victims and victimology might borrow from criminology with regard to becoming more gender-friendly and gender-sensitive. While these suggestions are potentially useful ones, that might ultimately improve our knowledge and understanding of victimisation in society, lead to advances in victimological research and improved support provisions and policies for victims, together with more appropriately tailored practices, this copy-cat approach is likely to be insufficient an effort in itself for constructing a gender-wise victimology. The more youthful discipline of victimology has already provided much of a spur to theoretical developments, as well as new policy, practice and research in criminology, and the passing on of knowledge is not just a one-way street between the overlapping disciplines.

While this chapter has illustrated how the social relations of gender in the study of victims are being increasingly exposed, criminologically there is still an apparent reluctance to consider women as real criminals (Heidensohn 1996; Davies 2003a, 2003b,) and this remains problematic for victimology. Victimologically there is an apparently similar reluctance to acknowledge the full extent and range of the victimisations that women suffer and consequently to appreciate and understand more comprehensively what constitutes victimisation. There are similar blockages to our understanding of men as gendered victims, preventing us from properly countenancing whether men yet count as victims.

In considering all of the above attention has inevitably focused upon the 'woman question' and how in turn this has had implications for our understanding of the 'man question'; femininities and masculinities; and ultimately the complete 'gender matrix' where women are victims and offenders and men are offenders and victims, where women victimise other women and (male and female) children and where men experience victimisation from women and other men. Moreover, they experience these victimisations in some instances due to their minority status and this has given rise to a discussion of hate crimes. McPhail (2003) concedes that gender interacts with other status categories and that people occupy multiple-status categories. Thus crime and the experience of victimisation occur on a very complex gendered terrain, and, as considered throughout this chapter and specifically in the section above, crime and the experience of victimisation is mediated by our very complex cultural identities. Gender matters but sometimes it might matter on a par with class-race-age. Alternatively, while gender matters it might not matter quite so much as class-race-age and it is more likely that we need to refine our social groupings of experiences of crime and victimisation so that they more sensitively reflect the very complex matrices of our identities. As I have been at pains to point out throughout this chapter, there are some strong voices of discontent as regards whether or not gender should be prioritised in order to better appreciate and understand criminality. This view could be equally relevant to a more informed appreciation and understanding of victimological issues. Alternative ways forward might consider how the intersectionalities of class-race-age-gender, or multiple inequalities (Daly 1993, 1997), variously combine 'as intersecting, interlocking and contingent' (Daly 1997: 33) to produce the very complex arrangements of matrices that shape our complex identities. Such ideas could be incorporated into a critical victimological perspective that is informed by feminisms and masculinities. For the most part, contemporarily, these are theoretical lessons and there remain very difficult and challenging debates as regards a gender agenda to future victim policies.

Further reading

Issue No. 53 of *Criminal Justice Matters* (2003) includes short articles on the subject of gender and crime. Contributors include Burman, who writes on girls and violence, and Hall and Winlow, on male violence; Croall addresses some gender questions about white collar crime and Gadd *et al.* discuss victims of domestic violence. Stanko has written extensively on violence against women; for example *Everyday Violence: How Women and Men Experience Sexual and Physical Danger* (1990), and a chapter entitled 'When Precaution is Normal' in Gelsthorpe and Morris (eds) (1994) *Feminist Perspectives in Criminology*. With co-authors/editors Stanko has also focused on men, masculinities, crime and victimisation; see *Just Boys Doing Business?* (1994) and 'Assault on men: Masculinity and male victimisation' in the *British Journal of Criminology* (1993). A provocative theoretical discussion can be found in Walklate, 'Can There be a Feminist Victimology?' in Davies, Francis and Jupp (eds) (2003) *Victimisation: Theory, Policy and Research*. Chapters by Davies ('Women, Victims and Crime') and Walklate ('Men, Victims and Crime'), in Davies, Francis and Greer (eds) (2007) *Victims, Crime and Society* foreground how theoretical developments around femininities and masculinities have shaped our recent understandings of men and women as victims.

Notes

1 The title of this chapter is adopted and adapted from a document entitled *The Gender Agenda* by the British Association of Women Police (BAWP).
2 Children killed in the first day or few weeks of life.
3 This suggests transgressive (Cain 1990) approaches for understanding women as victimisers might be useful to victimology.
4 As derived from the work of Brod 1990; Connell 1987, 1995; Jewkes 2005b; Jefferson 2001; Messerschmidt 1993, 1997; Remy 1990; Tolson 1977; Walklate 2004; West and Fenstermaker 1995; West and Zimmerman 1987.

References

Abel, E.M. (2001) 'Comparing the Social Service Utilisation, exposure to violence, and trauma symptomology of domestic violence female "victims" and female "batterers"', *Journal of Family Violence*, 16(4): 401–20.

Babcock, J.C., Miller, S.A. and Siard, C. (2003) 'Toward a typology of abusive women: Differences between partner-only and generally violent women in the use of violence', *Psychology of Women Quarterly*, 27: 153–61.

Bacon, B. (2004) 'Women's Violence Towards Intimate Partners: Intergenerational Explanations and Policy Considerations', paper presented to the British Criminology Conference, Portsmouth, July.

Batchelor, S., Burman, M. and Brown, J. (2001) 'Discussing violence: Let's hear it from the girls', *Probation Journal*, 48(2): 125–34.

British Association of Women Police (no date) *The Gender Agenda*.

Brod, H. (1990) 'Pornography and the Alienation of Male Sexuality', in J. Hearn and D. Morgan (eds) *Men, Masculinity and Social Theory*. London: Allen & Unwin.

Brookman, F. (2004) 'Infanticide: Fact and Fiction', paper presented to the British Criminology Conference, Portsmouth, July.

Brown, S. (1998) *Understanding Youth and Crime: Listening to Youth?* Buckingham: Open University Press.

Brownmiller, S. (1975) *Against Our Will: Men, Women and Rape*. London: Secker and Warberg.

Burman, M. (2003) 'Girls behaving violently?', *Criminal Justice Matters*, 53: 20–1.

Burman, M.J., Batchelor, S.A. and Brown, J.A. (2001) 'Researching girls and violence: facing the dilemmas of fieldwork', *British Journal of Criminology*, 41(3): 443–59.

Cain, M. (1990) 'Realist Philosophy and Standpoint Epistemologies or Feminist Criminology as a Successor Science?', in L. Gelsthorpe and A. Morris (eds) *Feminist Perspectives in Criminology*. Milton Keynes: Open University Press.

Carlen, P. (1983) *Women's Imprisonment*. London: Routledge.

Carlen, P. (1985) *Criminal Women*. Oxford: Polity.

Carlen, P. (1988) *Women, Crime and Poverty*. Buckingham: Open University Press.

Carlen, P. (ed.) (2002) *Women and Punishment: The Struggle for Justice*. Cullompton: Willan Publishing.

Carlen, P. and Worrall, A. (1987) *Gender, Crime and Justice*. Buckingham: Open University Press.

Carlson, E.S. (2006) 'The hidden prevalence of male sexual assault during war: observations on blunt trauma to the male genitals', *British Journal of Criminology*, 46(1): 16–25.

Carrabine, E., Iganski, P., Lee, M., Plummer, K. and South, N. (2004) 'Victims and Victimisation', in *Criminology: A Sociological Introduction*. London: Routledge.

Chan, W. and Rigakos, G.S. (2002) 'Risk, crime and gender', *British Journal of Criminology*, 42: 743–61.

Chesney-Lind, M. and Pasko, L. (2004) *The Female Offender: Girls, Women, and Crime*, 2nd edn. London: Sage.

Christie, N. (1986) 'The Ideal Victim', in E. Fattah (ed.) *From Crime Policy to Victim Policy*. London: Macmillan.

Connell, R.W. (1987) *Gender and Power*. Oxford: Polity.

Connell, R.W. (1995) *Masculinities*. Oxford: Polity.

Croall, H. (2003) '"Men's Business"? Some gender questions about white collar crime', *Criminal Justice Matters*, 53: 26–7.

Daly, K. (1993) 'Class-race-gender: Sloganeering in search of meaning', *Social Justice*, 20(1–2): 56–71.

Daly, K. (1994) *Gender, Crime, and Punishment*. London: Yale University Press.

Daly, K. (1997) 'Different ways of conceptualising sex/gender in feminist theory and their implications for criminology', *Theoretical Criminology*, 1(1): 25–51.

Daly, K. (2002) 'Sexual Assault and Restorative Justice', in H. Strang and J. Braithwaite (eds) *Restorative Justice and Family Violence*. Melbourne: Cambridge University Press.

Davies, P. (2003a) 'Is economic crime a man's game?', *Feminist Theory*, 4(3).

Davies, P. (2003b) 'Women and crime: Doing it for the kids?', *Criminal Justice Matters*, 50 (Winter).

Davies, P. (2005) 'Women and Crime for Economic Gain', unpublished PhD thesis, Northumbria University, Newcastle upon Tyne.

Davies, P. (2007) 'Women, Victims and Crime', in P. Davies, P. Francis and C. Greer (eds) *Victims, Crime and Society*. London: Sage.

Dobash, R.E. and Dobash, R.P. (1979) *Violence Against Wives: A Case Against Patriarchy*. Shepton Mallet: Open Books.

Dobash, R.P. and Dobash, R.E. (1998) *Rethinking Violence Against Women*. London: Sage.

Eaton, M. (1986) *Justice for Women?* Milton Keynes: Open University Press.

Elliott, A.J. and Peterson, L.W. (1993) 'Maternal sexual abuse of male children: When to suspect and how to uncover it', *Postgraduate Medicine*, 94(1): 169–80.

Faller, K.C. (1987) 'Women who sexually abuse children', *Violence and Victims*, 2(4): 263–76.

Finkelhor, D. and Russell, D. (1984) 'Women as Perpetrators: Review of the Evidence', in D. Finkelhor (ed.) *Child Sexual Abuse: New Theory and Research*. New York: Free Press, pp. 171–87.

Gadd, D., Farrall, S., Dallimore, D. and Lombard, N. (2003) 'Victims of domestic violence', *Criminal Justice*, 53: 16–17.

Gelsthorpe, L. (1989) *Sexism and the Female Offender*. Aldershot: Gower.

George, M.J. (1999) 'A victimisation survey of female-perpetrated assaults in the United Kingdom', *Aggressive Behaviour*, 25(1): 67–79.

Gilchrist, E., Bannister, J., Ditton, J. and Farrall, S. (1998) 'Women and the fear of crime: Challenging the accepted steroetype', *British Journal of Criminology*, 38(2): 283–98.

Goodey, J. (1997) 'Boys don't cry: Masculinities, fear of crime and fearlessness', *British Journal of Criminology*, 37(3): 401–18.

Goodey, J. (2005) *Victims and Victimology: Research, Policy and Practice.* London: Longman.

Grady, A. (2002) 'Female-on-Male Domestic Abuse: Uncommon or Ignored', in C. Hoyle and R. Young (eds) *New Visions of Crime Victims.* Oxford: Hart.

Gregory, J. and Lees, S. (1999) *Policing Sexual Assault.* London: Routledge.

Groombridge, N. (2001) 'Sexuality', in E. McLaughlin and J. Muncie (eds) *The Sage Dictionary of Criminology.* London: Sage.

Hall, S. (2002) 'Daubing the drudges of fury: Men, violence and the piety of the "hegemonic masculinity" thesis', *Theoretical Criminology*, 6(1): 35–61.

Hall, S. and Winlow, S. (2003a) 'Rehabilitating Leviathan: Reflections on the state, economic regulation and violence reduction', *Theoretical Criminology*, 7(2): 139–62.

Hall, S. and Winlow, S. (2003b) 'Culture, gender and male violence: A key problem', *Criminal Justice Matters*, 53: 14–15.

Hanmer, J. and Maynard, M. (eds) (1987) *Women, Violence and Social Control.* London: Macmillan.

Hanmer, J. and Saunders, S. (1984) *Well Founded Fear: A Community Study of Violence to Women.* London: Hutchinson.

Hanmer, J., Radford, J. and Stanko, E.A. (1989) *Women, Policing and Male Violence.* London: Routledge.

Harding, S. (ed.) (1986) *The Science Question in Feminism.* Milton Keynes: Open University Press.

Harding, S. (ed.) (1987) *Feminism and Methodology.* Milton Keynes: Open University Press.

Heidensohn, F. (1996) *Women and Crime*, 2nd edn. London: Macmillan.

Hindelang, M. J., Gottfredson, M. R. and Garofalo, J. (1978) *Victims of Personal Crime: An Empirical Foundation for a Theory of Personal Victimisation.* Cambridge, MA: Ballinger.

Home Office (2004) http://www.crimereduction.gov.uk/domesticviolence42.htm

Hudson, B. (2000) 'Critical Reflection as Research Methodology', in V. Jupp, P. Davies and P. Francis (eds) *Doing Criminological Research.* London: Sage.

Hudson, B. (2002) 'Restorative justice and gendered violence: diversion or effective justice?', *British Journal of Criminology*, 42(3): 616–34.

Jamieson, R. (1998) 'Towards a Criminology of War in Europe', in V. Ruggiero, N. South and I. Taylor (eds) *The New European Criminology: Crime and Social Order in Europe.* Routledge: London.

Jefferson, T. (2001) 'Hegemonic Masculinity', in E. McLaughlin and J. Muncie (eds) *The Sage Dictionary of Criminology.* London: Sage.

Jewkes, Y. (2005a) *Media and Crime.* London: Sage.

Jewkes, Y. (2005b) 'Men behind bars: 'Doing' masculinity as an adaptation to imprisonment, *Men and Masculinities*, 8(1): 44–63.

Kelly, L. (1988) *Surviving Sexual Violence.* Oxford: Polity.

Kelly, L. and Radford, J. (1987) 'The Problem of Men: Feminist Perspectives on Sexual Violence', in P. Scraton (ed.) *Law, Order and the Authoritarian State: Readings in Critical Criminology.* Milton Keynes: Open University Press.

Lees, S. (1997) *Ruling Passions: Sexual Violence, Reputation and the Law.* London: Sage.

London Rape Crisis Centre (1984) *Sexual Violence: The Reality for Women*. London: LRCC.

MacKinnon, C. (1987) *Feminism Unmodified: Discourses on Life and Law*. Cambridge, MA: Harvard University Press.

Marsh, I., with Cochrane, J. and Melville, G. (2004) *Criminal Justice: An Introduction to Philosophies, Theories and Practice*. London: Routledge.

Mason, G. (2005) 'Hate crime and the image of the stranger', *British Journal of Criminology*, 45(6): 837–59.

Mawby, R.I. and Walklate, S. (1994) *Critical Victimology*. London: Sage.

McLaughlin, E. and Muncie, J. (2001) (eds) *The Sage Dictionary of Criminology*. London: Sage.

McPhail, B. (2003) 'Gender-Bias Hate Crimes', in B. Perry (ed.) *Hate and Bias Crime: A Reader*. London: Routledge.

Messerschmidt, J.W. (1993) *Masculinities and Crime*. Lanham, MD: Rowman & Littlefield.

Messerschmidt, J.W. (1997) *Crime as Structured Action*. Thousand Oaks, CA: Sage.

Miller, J. (1998) 'Up it up: Gender and the accomplishment of street robbery', *Criminology*, 36(1).

Miller, J. (2001) *One of the Guys: Girls, Gangs and Gender*. New York: Oxford University Press.

Miller, J. (2002) The strengths and limits of "doing-gender" for understanding street crime', *Theoretical Criminology*, 6(4): 433–60.

Mirrlees-Black, C. and Byron, C. (1999) *Domestic Violence: Findings From the BCS Self-Completion Questionnaire*, Home Office Research Findings 83. London: Home Office.

Mooney, J. (2000) *Gender, Violence and the Social Order*. London: Palgrave.

Morley, R. and Mullender, A. (1994) *Preventing Domestic Violence to Women*, Crime Prevention Unit Paper 48. London: Home Office Police Department.

Muncie, J. (2004) *Youth and Crime: A Critical Introduction*, 2nd edn. London: Sage.

Pain, R. (2001) 'Gender, race, age and fear in the city', *Urban Studies*, 38/5–6: 899–913.

Pearce, F. and Snider, L. (eds) (1995) *Corporate Crime: Contemporary Debates*. Toronto: University of Toronto Press.

Pearce, J. and Stanko, E. (2000) 'Young women and community safety', *Youth and Policy*, 66: 1–18.

Perry, B. (2003) 'Defenders of the Faith: Hate Groups and Ideologies of Power', in B. Perry (ed.) *Hate and Bias Crime: A Reader*. London: Routledge.

Perry, S. and Dawson, J. (1985) *Nightmare: Women and the Dalkon Shield*. New York: Macmillan.

Remy, J. (1990) 'Patriarchy and Fratriarchy as Forms of Androcracy', in J. Hearn and D. Morgan (eds) *Men, Masculinity and Social Theory*. London: Allen & Unwin.

Ruddick, S. (1990) *Maternal Thinking: Towards a Politics of Peace*. London: Women's Press.

Smart, C. (1976) *Women, Crime and Criminology*. London: Routledge and Kegan Paul.

Smith, C. and Wincup, E. (2000) 'Breaking in: Researching Criminal Justice Institutions for Women', in R.D. King and E. Wincup (eds) *Doing Research on Crime and Justice*. Oxford: Oxford University Press.

Sommers, I. and Baskin, D. (1992) 'Sex, age, race and violent offending', *Violence and Victims*, 7(3): 191–201.

Sommers, I., Deborah, R. and Baskin, R. (1993) 'The situational context of violent female offending', *Journal of Research in Crime and Delinquency*, 30: 136–62.

Stanko, E.A. (1985) *Intimate Intrusions: Women's Experience of Male Violence.* London: Virago.

Stanko, E. (1987) 'Typical Violence, Normal Precaution: Men, Women and Interpersonal Violence in England, Wales, Scotland and the USA', in J. Hanmer and M. Maynard (eds) *Women, Violence and Social Control.* London: Macmillan, pp. 122–34.

Stanko, E. A. (1988) 'Hidden Violence Against Women', in M. Maguire and J. Pointing (eds) *Victims of Crime: A New Deal?* Milton Keynes: Open University Press.

Stanko, E. (1990a) *Everyday Violence: How Women and Men Experience Sexual and Physical Danger.* London: Pandora.

Stanko, E. (1990b) 'When Precaution is Normal: A Feminist Critique of Crime Prevention', in L. Gelsthorpe and A. Morris (eds) *Feminist Perspectives in Criminology.* Milton Keynes: Open University Press.

Stanko, E. and Hobdell, K. (1993) 'Assault on men: Masculinity and male victimisation', *British Journal of Criminology*, 33(3): 400–15.

Strobl, R. Klemm, J. and Wurtz, S. (2005) 'Preventing hate crimes: Experiences from two East German towns', *British Journal of Criminology*, 45(5): 634–46.

Sutton, R.M. and Farrall, S. (2005) 'Gender, socially desirable responding and the fear of crime: Are women really more anxious about crime?', *British Journal of Criminology*, 45(2): 212–24.

Szyockyi, E. and Fox, J.G. (1996) *Corporate Victimisation of Women.* Boston, MA: Northeastern University Press.

The Times (2005) 'Women still held to blame for rape', 21 November: 1.

Tolson, A. (1977) *The Limits of Masculinity.* London: Routledge.

Turton, J. (2000) 'Maternal sexual abuse and its victims', *Childright*, 165: 17–18.

Venis, S. and Horton, R. (2002) 'Violence against women: A global burden', *The Lancet*, 359/9313: 1172: 1235.

Walklate, S. (1995) *Gender and Crime.* London: Harvester Wheatsheaf.

Walklate, S. (2000) 'Researching Victims', in R.D. King and E. Wincup (eds) *Doing Research on Crime and Justice.* Oxford: Oxford University Press.

Walklate, S. (2001) 'The Victim's Lobby', in M. Ryan, S. Savage and D. Wall (eds) *Policy Networks in Criminal Justice.* Basingstoke: Palgrave.

Walklate, S. (2003a) 'Gender and crime: A red herring?', *Criminal Justice Matters*, 53: 6–7.

Walklate, S. (2003b) 'Can There be a Feminist Victimology?' in P. Davies, P. Francis and V. Jupp (eds) *Victimisation: Theory, Research and Policy.* London: Palgrave.

Walklate, S. (2004) *Gender, Crime and Criminal Justice*, 2nd edn. Cullompton: Willan.

Walklate, S. (2005) *Criminology: The Basics.* London: Routledge.

Walklate, S. (2007) 'Men, Victims and Crime', in P. Davies, P. Francis and C. Greer (eds) *Victims, Crime and Society.* London: Sage.

West, C. and Fenstermaker, S. (1995) 'Doing difference', *Gender and Society*, 9(1): 8–37.

West, C. and Zimmerman, D.H. (1987) 'Going gender', *Gender and Society*, 1(2): 125–51.

Wilkins, R. (1990) 'Women who sexually abuse children: Doctors need to become sensitised to the possibility', *British Medical Journal*, 300/3000: 1153–4.

Williams, K. (2004) *Textbook of Criminology*, 5th edn. Oxford: Oxford University Press.

Women's Aid (2003) Women's Aid Federation of England (http://www.womesaid.org.uk/about-wafe.htm).

Worrall, A. (1990) *Offending Women: Female Lawbreakers and the Criminal Justice System.* New York: Routledge.

Part Three

Victims, Policy and Service Delivery

Sandra Walklate

Introduction

The chapters in Part Two, while dealing in different ways specifically with the relationship between gender and criminal victimisation, by implication also raised more general questions pertaining to criminal justice policy and service delivery in relation to victims of crime *per se*. Women's experiences of the criminal justice process have historically pointed up the inadequacies in that process in responding to them as a specific group of victims. Yet as research as shown, aspects of their experiences are often shared with others as they negotiate their experience of criminal victimisation and their treatment by the criminal justice process. Indeed, as Rock documented in Chapter 2, particular studies in the UK, like those of Shapland *et al.* (1985) and Maguire and Bennett (1982), were influential in encouraging a closer look at the more ordinary and mundane experience of the criminal justice process for the victim of crime, from the response of the police to experience of giving evidence in court. In recent years much political and policy energy has been devoted to addressing these general experiences of the criminal justice system epitomised in particular by the government White Paper *Justice for All* published in 2002 and the Domestic Violence, Crime and Victims Act 2004. Indeed, the latter introduced some significant changes to how crime victims might be responded to. The Code of Practice for Victims of Crime, which was introduced as part of this legislation and became effective in April 2006, codifies all the expectations and obligations that a victim might have of the criminal justice system and sets targets for how and when the criminal justice agencies need to have responded to and/or delivered services to them.

The Code of Practice for Victims of Crime is discussed in detail in Rob Mawby's coverage of the current victim policy demands being made of the police, the probation service and of the Crown Prosecution Service in the court setting (Chapter 8). Indeed, this chapter provides an overview and framework for those that follow in this part of the book, as well as in Part Four. The changing focus of the work of these different branches of the criminal justice process marks just how far we have travelled from the idea that the victim is the 'forgotten party' of this process, a journey begun symbolically in the late nineteenth century, as Godfrey and Kearon argued in Chapter 1, and has to date culminated in what Mawby calls 'Labour's victim oriented justice'. Of course this journey has not only involved a reorientation in the service delivery of the state criminal justice system, it has also involved, and still does involve, the work of the voluntary sector. Brian Williams and Hannah Goodman, in Chapter 9, trace the role of the voluntary sector in the delivery of services to the victim of crime. As Cook and Jones in Chapter 5 have already intimated, the work of volunteers in the Rape Crisis movement has been, and continues to be, vital to the support of women who have been raped and/or sexually assaulted and want the kind of support that Rape Crisis has to offer. However, alongside this and the women's refuge movement, Victim Support has been an important and influential volunteer-based organisation, in lending a helping hand to victims of (all kinds of) crime. Williams and Goodman discuss the role of this organisation and point to the increasingly diverse range of organisations in the voluntary sector claiming to offer support to and for individuals and/or groups who have suffered from different kinds of victimisation. They illustrate that who gets supported for what is contemporarily quite a complex picture, and they situate this picture within a wider understanding of European framework agreements and networks. (The value and impact of such frameworks is an issue developed more fully in Chapter 14 by Van Dijk and Groenhuijsen). Williams and Goodman also raise the question of how well the voluntary and public sectors fit together in their delivery of services to the crime victim. This issue is also raised by Mawby, who goes on to suggest that the embrace of a new managerialism within the public sector of the criminal justice system has taken a particular toll on the relationship between the state and the voluntary sector, resulting in the latter being subject to closer scrutiny and tighter demands being made of it. Peter Dunn (Chapter 10) also alludes to the changing nature of this relationship in his more focused consideration of the problems of matching service delivery to victims' needs.

Chapters 8 and 9, while focusing on the question of different modes of service delivery to victims of crime and the quality of that delivery, each by implication address a deeper question: whether or not victims of crime have needs or rights. The Code of Practice for Victims of Crime, central to the discussion by Mawby, was heralded by the Home Office as providing the victim with rights. Yet that code, as Mawby illustrates, whilst extensive in its coverage, does not offer legal redress if anyone has a complaint about the service they have received. As a result it is difficult to see how this code does offer the victim legal rights as opposed to perhaps moral rights. Nevertheless many would argue that the transition of the crime victim from simply being the (forgotten) complainant in the criminal justice system, to being the consumer of services, to being an equal participant in that system is now complete. This is certainly the view of the Home Office. However, the debate as to whether or not victims have needs or rights has not been fully resolved by this kind of policy development. In Chapters 10, 11 and 12, the question of responding to victims' needs or harnessing victims' rights is addressed in three different ways. Walklate (2007) has labelled these as perpetuating welfare, moving towards allocution, and reorienting towards restorative justice; it is interesting that these three strategies presently coexist within criminal justice policy in England and Wales.

Chapter 10 by Peter Dunn clearly illustrates a version of the perpetuating welfare approach. He identifies, in the context of Victim Support as an organisation, just how complex meeting victims' needs might be. He also explores how the role of this organisation, whose initial focus was simply to lend a community-based helping hand to the victim of crime, has arguably suffered from both incorporation and co-option. The state has increasingly concerned itself with the victim, echoing some similarities with the position that feminists have found themselves in, commented on by Cook and Jones in Chapter 5. He discusses the complex and hugely variable impact that crime has on individuals, much of which is emotional in nature, and he argues for taking on board strategies both for assessing need and for the inclusion of users' views on service delivery. Dunn also points to the difficulties of separating needs from rights and what each of these might mean for the individual, the organisation offering a service, or indeed, the state. He suggests that the admixture of state and voluntary sector service delivery has taken its toll on the capability of Victim Support to retain its initial community-based focus on responding to victims' needs and has added to the difficulty of responding to those needs. Yet despite these problems, Dunn's own view is that it is important to work with and understand the interplay between needs and rights, focusing on the caring aspects of service delivery, and how best to respond to those who choose to access that service. This remains very much within a welfare model of dealing with the victim of crime.

In Chapter 11 Andrew Sanders and Imogen Jones explore the ways in which responding to the victim of crime in England and Wales, especially over the last ten years, have moved towards an allocution approach. This approach has become increasingly preoccupied with giving the victim a voice in court. Sanders and Jones discuss the pros and cons of these kinds of developments within the wider context of what is and is not possible within the adversarial as opposed to the inquisitorial criminal justice process. The right of the victim to be heard in court has certainly gained in political popularity despite the serious questions this raises about the central purpose of the adversarial system. The orality of the adversarial system is pointed to as being particularly problematic and demanding for those required to participate in it, whether as complainants or defendants, and Sanders and Jones question to what extent this demand can be lessened given its crucial role within the adversarial system. By implication this adds to the discussion of what can actually be expected of the Witness Care Units, discussed by Mawby, in securing the involvement of complainants within the criminal justice system and lessening their 'secondary victimisation' of it.

In Chapter 12, Jim Dignan discusses restorative justice. He explores the complexity of what 'restorative' might mean, in what kind of context, and points to the wide-ranging ways in which initiatives have come to carry the restorative justice label. The principle of returning the problem of crime to the people who own them – that is, the victim and offender – has grown enormously in popularity since Nils Christie's essay of 1977, 'Conflicts as Property', aided significantly by the work of John Braithwaite's (1989) *Crime, Shame and Reintegration*. However, the actual role afforded to the victim of crime in restorative justice is neither simple nor straightforward. As Dignan documents, what is meant by restorative justice can refer either to the processes of exchange that such initiatives involve, to the outcome of such processes, or to the values associated with them. In each of these instances he notes that there has certainly been a philosophical ambivalence towards the victim and an absence of the victim in restorative justice theory, as much of this work has been directed towards the offender. However, it is clear that while the victim certainly has a role to play in a wide range of restorative developments little attention has been paid in the evaluative findings as to whether or not the victim has been restored or healed. Dignan concludes by suggesting that despite all the interventions of this kind that have taken place in England and Wales since 1997, the victim remains, for the most part, peripheral to them.

As with the Victims' Code of Practice, many of the policy developments discussed in these three chapters do not offer the victim of crime legal rights. Indeed these interventions are often either optional for the victim or rely on the victim's willingness to participate, so articulating an ambivalent relationship to the idea of victim's rights that are claimable in law (see also Rock 2004). So despite political claims to the contrary, the case for victims' rights (that is, rights in law, with the notable exception of, for example, the protection of identity afforded to female victims of rape) appears to be as patchy as that of meeting victims' needs as illustrated by Dunn in Chapter 10.

A number of themes are brought to the fore in this section. The first is the increasingly complex way in which the public and voluntary sectors of the criminal justice process relate to each other and, moreover, the increasing influence that public sector policy provision seems to have over how the voluntary sector conducts its business. Little work has been conducted on the impact that new managerialism is having on the voluntary sector, but Mawby is right to point this up as an important area of consideration for the workings of voluntary organisations of all kinds. In addition that voluntary sector, in relation to the criminal justice system, has become more complex and more diverse. As new and often single-issue campaign groups have emerged, the influence and role of these groups both on policy formation and on service delivery has arguably shifted policies directed towards the victim of crime in ever more politicised ways, without necessarily improving the lot of the crime victim. The chapters in Part Three are clearly suggestive of the problems associated with this. This leads to the second theme that is implied in this section of the book: the role of emotion in criminal justice.

The changing way in which the emotional impact of criminal victimisation has been handled at the level of policy and politics is evidenced in a number of ways by the contributions presented here. As was intimated in the Introduction and Overview, the return of 'gothic horror' (Valier 2004) has made its presence felt in a number of ways since the early 1990s, nowhere more evident than in the sight of the screaming mob chasing the prison van containing the two boys convicted of the murder of James Bulger on Merseyside in 1993. Since that time, it has been the case that the media have been particularly prone to encouraging victims to say their piece outside the courtroom at the end of a trial whether or not a conviction has been secured. In some instances this is with the support of the investigating police officer or their solicitor. Giving voice to victims in this way, as an emotional appeal in the case of a missing child or relative, or subsequent to a court hearing, has been given an added dimension in the way the internet can be used to portray graphic images of events that more conventional media outlets eschew. Such processes, arguably, have provided politicians with the emotional capital with which to pursue policies. This is evidenced by their increasing willingness to listen to individuals who have been seen to suffer particularly at the hands of a criminal and/or the criminal justice system (as in the case of the parents of Sarah Payne, who had unprecedented access to the then Home Secretary in their campaign for a Sarah's Law, comparable with Megan's Law in the US) on the one hand, and the emotive language used to justify responses to the victims of terrorist activities on the other. No Home Secretary would now propose a change in criminal justice policy without invoking some emotionality with regard to the victim. In the contributions in Part Three we can see how some of those concerns have differently translated themselves into policy. From one point of view, all those initiatives concerned with the reorientation of the work of the criminal justice system are by definition geared towards making the victim feel better, exacerbating the worst effects of secondary victimisation (victimisation by the system itself). However, some of the policies discussed here go further that that. The use of Victims' Advocates in court, for example, discussed by Sanders and Jones, takes the issue of listening to the victim's voice much further, as the first statement of this kind, by Adele Eastman, published on 28 November 2006, illustrates. The use of statements of this kind is hugely contentious, as Sanders and Jones imply, not only in England and Wales but elsewhere in the Anglo-speaking world, as is demonstrated by Booth and Carrington in Chapter 15. Moreover, given the wider changing nature of service delivery in the criminal justice system, most notably policing, and given the continued gaps in provision alluded to here, alongside the increasing presence of emotionality and the use of emotional capital, a view worth considering might be that not only do we have a re-emergence of gothic horror, we are also witnessing a re-emergence of gothic justice intimated by Godfrey and Kearon in Chapter 1, innovations in restorative justice notwithstanding.

What the contributors also draw attention to in this part of the book is the importance of global policy transfer, which has influenced many of the contemporary policy developments in England and Wales, particularly in respect of victim impact statements/victim advocacy and the development of initiatives in restorative justice. United Nations and Council of Europe Framework agreements have also had their influence on developing responses to victims of crime. The influence of these transnational processes is taken up by the contributors in Part Four.

207

References

Braithwaite, J. (1989) *Crime, Shame and Reintegration*. Cambridge: Cambridge University Press.

Christie, N. (1977) 'Conflicts as property', *British Journal of Criminology*, 17: 1–15.

Maguire, M. with Bennett, T. (1982) *Burglary in a Dwelling*. London: Heinemann.

Rock, P. (2004) *Constructing Victims' Rights*. Oxford: Clarendon Press.

Shapland, J., Willmore J. and Duff, P. (1985) *The Victim in the Criminal Justice System*. Aldershot: Gower.

Valier, C. (2004) *Crime and Punishment in Contemporary Culture*. London: Routledge.

Walklate, S. (2007) *Imagining the Victim of Crime*. Maidenhead: Open University Press.

Chapter 8

Public sector services and the victim of crime

Rob I. Mawby

Introduction

In the 47 years that have elapsed since Steven Schafer (1960: 8) referred to the crime victim as the Cinderella of the criminal justice system, political (and academic) interest in the plight of victims has grown beyond recognition. While it is still true that the overwhelming amount of public funding goes on the police and penal system, in Britain, and many other western societies, victims have come to be accepted as significant actors on the criminal justice stage. Thus:

> The Government's vision is of a criminal justice system in which the needs and concerns of victims and witnesses, are central. (Home Office 2005a: 2)

However, there are marked differences in the part assigned to the victim in this new criminal justice production. The balance between victims as needing to be supported by the benevolent and caring state and victims as having rights to minimal levels of service is a delicate one, varying between countries, different points of time, and different services (Mawby 2007; Mawby and Walklate 1994). Leading on from this, appreciation of the precise services that victims should be offered is also subject to negotiation. Here, discussion broadly covers four levels of service: personal support for those who have been the victims of crime, primarily at the time of the offence but possibly through the trial and subsequently; financial compensation for victims or surviving family members; information, for example about the way the police are dealing with the case, or the way the suspect/defendant/offender is being processed; and involvement in making decisions about how the perpetrator is dealt with. Similarly, ideas about the roles of different agencies, particularly the balance between the public sector and NGOs, have varied over time and between countries.

Changes in the priority accorded to these different facets of victim services are illustrated by a review of government thinking over the past 40 years in Britain. This has seen a dramatic shift from a situation where the immediate needs of victims were gradually recognised, but where the voluntary sector was considered most appropriate for responding to those needs (Mawby and Gill 1987), to one where the public sector is seen as playing a key role in the delivery of a wide range of victims' rights and where voluntary agency involvement is expected to mirror that of the statutory sector with, for example, greater centralisation and the implementation of performance targets.

The 1960s were characterised by Mawby and Walklate (1994) as the decade of promise. The first formal measures aimed specifically at victims of crime were established in 1964 through the Criminal Injuries Compensation Board (CICB),[2] largely as a result of the campaign led by Margery Fry. This provided for victims of serious violent crime to claim compensation for the harm caused, but quite explicitly rejected the notion that victims had any right to compensation. Rather, so-called 'deserving victims' were seen as warranting sympathy that might be expressed through financial compensation from the state (Miers 1978; see also Chapter 13 in this volume). Despite extensions to the system, most significantly in 1978 and 1996, this principle remains (Home Office 2005b: 14–22). However, it is notable that even at this early stage a role for government agency involvement was established, with the CICB created by the then Conservative government and financed through the public purse. Today the CICA accounts for most of government expenditure formally allocated to victim services, with £200 million of the £230 million spent on support for victims assigned to the CICA (Home Office 2005b: 5), of which £170 million goes on compensation and the remainder on running the scheme (2005b: 15).

The 1970s promised more radical change (Mawby and Walklate 1994), partly through the creation of the National Association of Victim Support Schemes (later rebranded as Victim Support), more significantly through feminist-inspired services for female victims (or survivors) of partner violence and rape (see also Chapter 5 in this volume). These developments were noticeably located in the voluntary sector, but differed markedly in their philosophies. While Victim Support prioritised meeting the needs of victims for support in coping with their ordeal, and drew on multi-agency backing from the police, probation and judiciary, women's refuges and Rape Crisis centres espoused more political and educational aims, and in criticising the ways in which statutory services handled female 'victims'[3] tended to operate outside and in opposition to such services (Gill and Mawby 1990; Mawby and Walklate 1994). This initially tended to deter governments from investing in such services, although by 2005 over £10 million p.a. was being invested in a capital building programme (Home Office 2005a: 9).

The willingness of Victim Support to work constructively with statutory agencies was crucial in its expansion in the 1980s and beyond, with government funding increased against the general trend of the Thatcher government. This was perhaps not altogether surprising, given that as an NGO Victim Support epitomised the Thatcher government's commitment to enhance the role of the voluntary sector at the expense of state services. However, it has gained momentum under New Labour, with Victim Support currently enjoying some £30 million of state funding per year (Home Office 2005b: 5).

The commitment of successive governments to Victim Support is generally seen to epitomise the crucial role of the voluntary sector in victim services (see also Chapters 9 and 12 in this volume). However, two other policy developments in the 1970s and beyond illustrated the expectation of both Labour and Conservative governments that the public sector would take on a greater role in responding to victims. First, following the Advisory Council of the Penal System report in 1970 (Home Office 1970), the 1972 Criminal Justice Act introduced compensation orders to the courts, whereby courts had the powers to require offenders to pay compensation to their victims. These powers were subsequently extended in the 1982 and 1988 Criminal Justice Acts. Second, the concern of the Thatcher government to reconstruct those receiving public services as consumers, repackaged under John Major in the age of citizens' charters, placed a new and scarcely welcomed requirement on statutory authorities such as the police to demonstrate that they were providing crime victims with appropriate services and value for money.

This expectation that mainstream criminal justice agencies were in the 'victim business' was formally acknowledged in the first Victim's Charter (Home Office 1990). Published to a fanfare of publicity, this was described as setting out for the first time the rights and entitlements of victims of crime. It has been rightly pointed out that it did no such thing (Mawby and Walklate 1994; Williams 1999). Rather, with few exceptions it set out a code of good practice, listing the ways in which victims should be treated by both state bodies and NGOs. However, in this respect it was innovative in, for the first time, applying standards to agencies like the police, probation service and courts with respect to their treatment of victims. For example, the police would be expected to 'respond to complaints of crime with all due care and attention', the CPS should take into account the interests of the victim in deciding whether a prosecution is in the public interest, the courts should provide victims/witnesses with practical information on court layout and procedures, and the probation service should ideally inform victims when a life-sentence prisoner was due for release. Just how far these agencies were successful in attaining these standards were to be measured using consumer surveys charting victims' and witnesses' experiences and evaluations of services.

One such measure has been the British Crime Survey (BCS), which has traditionally asked victims to assess police performance and has more recently asked the public to rate their confidence in a variety of aspects of the criminal justice system (see, for example, Walker *et al.* 2006), while others include more specialist surveys of court users (Angle *et al.* 2003). The annual Witness and Victim Experience (WAVE) survey to assess victims' and witnesses' experiences of the criminal justice system 'provides an opportunity to highlight good and bad practice and ... to identify where we need to improve services' (Home Office 2005a: 10). Ironically, concern that such performance indicators may be of limited value or relevance encouraged a degree of self-regulation that incorporated further consumer surveys. For example, ACPO advised forces to ask victims/witnesses to rate their satisfaction with the performance of the police in relation to both 999 calls and services at police station enquiry counters, both additional to the more limited performance measures proposed by HMIC and the Audit Commission (Bunt and Mawby 1994).

The Victim's Charter was updated and extended in 1996 (Home Office 1996). The charter was set out in three sections, covering the services victims should expect, what should happen at different stages of the process, and how to complain if services were found wanting. For example, the prosecution system was expected to take victims' interests into account in arriving at its decisions and to provide information and support for victims in court. Help at court was then described as involving the CPS, Victim Support's Witness Service and court staff. Finally, the complaints system was detailed. The charter was then supplemented by specialist leaflets, including, among others, a *Charter for Court Users*, the *Code for Crown Prosecutors* and the *Going to Court* booklet. While these again appeared to be manuals for good practice, a Victim's Steering Group, based on the multi-agency partnership model, was established to monitor standards of service. Moreover, with new managerialism becoming a powerful driving force within government, the emphasis upon customer surveys became even more significant as the key mechanism for quality control and accountability (Williams 1999).

This gained increased momentum under New Labour, where victim-oriented justice has become the pivotal feature of Home Office thinking on crime and disorder, and a raft of discussion papers and policy documents have focused on victims' rights. Recent proposals relate to support services at the time of the offence and in court, including a comprehensive witness strategy (Home Office 2003a; 2005b), compensation (Home Office 2004), restorative justice (Home Office 2003b), post-court services for victims (HMIP 2000, 2003), and services for victims of domestic violence (Home Office 2003c). At the same time, moves to decentralise aspects of crime and disorder policy-making, with the introduction of Crime and Disorder Reduction Partnerships and Criminal Justice Boards, have placed emphasis upon local partnerships and multi-agency working.

Many of these initiatives are drawn together in the third, long-awaited reformulation of the victim's charter, *The Code of Practice for Victims of Crime* (Home Office 2005c), which describes the minimum level of services that victims should expect, and introduces a complaints system, culminating in the Parliamentary Ombudsman, should agencies fail to deliver an appropriate standard of service. Notably, and unlike earlier charters, the code focuses almost exclusively on public sector bodies. It spells out the services that should be provided by 11 statutory agencies and institutions:

- Criminal Cases Review Commission
- Criminal Injuries Compensation Authority
- Criminal Injuries Compensation Appeals Panel
- Crown Prosecution Service
- Her Majesty's Courts Service
- Joint police/CPS Witness Care Units
- All police forces for police areas in England and Wales, the British Transport Police and the Ministry of Defence Police

- Parole Board
- Prison Service
- Probation Service
- Youth Offending Teams

Ironically, the code does not apply to NGOs except where they are engaged in multi-agency partnerships such as YOTs, or where public sector bodies are required to liaise with, or refer victims to, NGOs like Victim Support.[4] On the other hand, the clear specification of the roles and responsibilities of these statutory agencies indicates the crucial place of public sector agencies in providing services for victims. In most cases, a time period is specified within which these requirements must be met.

The fact that the code of practice specifies the responsibilities of different agencies might be taken to imply that these are discrete. However, this has clearly never been the case. On the one hand, in many instances documentation identifies the need for agencies to co-operate in providing for victims. For example, while financial compensation has become the responsibility of the courts (regarding compensation orders) and the statutory Criminal Injuries Compensation Authority, other agencies such as Victim Support are expected to provide advice and support for victims in making their claims. On the other hand, many of the 'services' featured relate to the nature of interaction between the victim and statutory agencies. For example, since the emergence of Victim Support in England in the 1970s, there has been an explicit assumption that providing personal support for victims is a voluntary sector responsibility, but this is clearly not exclusively so, with the police expected to respond to victims with tact and sensitivity, perhaps best illustrated in innovations for dealing with rape victims.

Moreover, despite continued recognition that agencies like Victim Support have a crucial role to play in service delivery, it is clear that recent developments have framed this role in terms of the support they can give to the public sector. This chapter thus focuses on public sector involvement as heralding a new phase in state concern for victims. Because of the pivotal role of the police in responding to victims of crime, the next section of this chapter focuses on the police. The following two sections then cover court staff and the probation service as other examples of the public sector's developing involvement.

Police and victims

There are a number of reasons why it is important that the police provide a satisfactory service for victims. First, the police are highly dependent upon the public, and especially victims, for bringing crime to their attention and providing leads on the offender (Bottomley and Coleman 1976; Coupe and Griffiths 1997; Mawby 1979). Victims who feel that the police do not provide an appropriate response may fail to report crimes or even take unsanctioned vigilante action. Second, despite the emergence of victim assistance programmes in many countries, the police is still the main agency with which victims have contact. As a result, police response to victims may be the most significant post-crime experience. In this respect Joutsen (1987: 212) noted:

> They are generally the first representatives of the State to come into contact with the complainant. Furthermore their intervention will come at a time when the complainant is most likely to be suffering from the immediate shock of the offence. Their attitude will considerably influence not only what the complainant decides to do but also what impression he received of the administration of justice, and of how the community as a whole regards the offence.

Third, police forces in a range of countries traditionally have provided a very poor service for victims. Indeed, in many cases their response may have exacerbated the effects of the crime, promoting secondary victimisation rather than support:

> There is ample evidence from in-depth interviews that victims are particularly sensitive to the way they are personally approached by police officers. According to several researchers, many victims experience an acute need to be 'reassured' by the police. Others state that victims expect the police to recognise their status as someone who has been wronged by a fellow citizen. Many victims express dissatisfaction with police officers who are distrustful, callous or cynical. Such observations are often viewed as evidence of secondary victimisation ... Police officers must be taught that their deskside manners are as important to victims as bedside manners of doctors are to patients. (Van Dijk 1985: 154, 162)

Victims' perceptions of police services

Criticisms of the police have been expressed most forcefully in the case of their treatment of rape and domestic violence victims, but the point is no less relevant for victims of a range of property crimes. Nor is the problematic nature of police interaction with victims a recent one. Indeed, the advent of Victim Support was largely welcomed by the police as a means of referring on victim-oriented work to another agency. Mawby and Gill (1987: 156) quoted one senior officer in Devon and Cornwall as stressing that, 'We don't want police officers tied up with helping victims, they have not got the time.' The same study showed that operational staff routinely underestimated how much crime affected victims. Despite this, it seems that most crime victims in England and Wales consider the police deal with their crime satisfactorily, but a significant minority voice reservations. This is evident from both large-scale surveys such as the British Crime Survey (BCS) and International Crime Victim Survey (ICVS) and from more specialist, localised studies.

Official concern about victims' perceptions of their treatment by the police derives from a recognition that both public and victims' ratings of police performance have deteriorated in recent years, and that victims tend to be less positive in their views of the police than do citizens who have had no recent contact with them (Sims and Myhill 2001; Skogan 1995, 1996). Allen *et al.* (2006), analysing 2004/05 BCS data, found that victims' satisfaction had fallen between 1994 and 2000 but remained stable since. Overall, 58 per cent of victims described themselves as 'very or fairly satisfied', but the figure was less than this among lower-income households and black or Asian victims. Victims of burglary (63 per cent) and vehicle related thefts (58 per cent) were more satisfied than victims of violence (55 per cent) or vandalism (50 per cent). Victims of acquaintance violence expressed the lowest levels of satisfaction (46 per cent), suggesting that issues concerning police handling of domestic violence may apply equally to other sub-categories of violent crime.

However, it is less clear what victims want of the police, and how they rank the different services the police might provide. Traditionally, for example, there seems to have been an assumption that the priority is to clear up the offence, arrest a suspect and see the case through to conviction in court, with other support services for victims being accorded lower priority and hived off to other agencies such as Victim Support (Mawby and Gill 1987). More recently, the police have recognised that their responsibilities to victims extend a lot further. Nevertheless, it is clear that victims' dissatisfactions are wide-ranging (Allen *et al.* 2006; Ringham and Salisbury 2004). Most victims feel that the police have responded as quickly as possible, showed enough interest, and put in sufficient effort, although a minority do voice criticism. However, many feel that they are not kept informed of police progress (or lack of it). Thus in 2004/05 only 32 per cent felt they had been kept 'very or fairly well informed' (Allen *et al.* 2006), and this lack of further information applied to case details, support information, case progress and (where applicable) trial details (Ringham and Salisbury 2004). This raises questions about performance monitoring that are addressed in the next section.

A comparison of these findings with those from elsewhere in the world shows that while victims in England and Wales voiced fewer criticisms of the police than did victims from many other countries, their overall rating of police performance was relatively poor (see Table 8.1). In general, the national and international findings suggest that while many, if not most, victims are satisfied with the way the police respond, a sizeable minority express reservations. These relate to both police failure to conclude the case satisfactorily (no arrest made; no goods recovered) and to the ways in which the police treat victims. In the latter case, the police may be seen as not interested, impolite, slow to arrive or not providing sufficient information, either at the time the crime is reported or subsequently. Crime impacts upon victims. They therefore expect the police to recognise this and respond accordingly, by treating them with politeness, dignity and respect, and by accepting that they have a right to be kept apprised of the way the case is – or is not – progressing. However, it seems that the nature of policework, and particularly the ways in which the police interpret their jobs and the aspects of their work that they value, may mean that victim-oriented work is accorded less priority than crime-fighting, in much the same way that community policing is commonly undervalued. This raises the question of how policework can be reoriented to place victim services more centre stage.

Table 8.1. Percentage of victims of burglary/theft from cars and contact crimes who were satisfied with police service

	Burglary/Theft from vehicles	Contact crimes
Finland	73	76
Scotland	73	73
Denmark	81	63
Sweden	70	74
Canada	71	71
Switzerland	77	63
Australia	73	67
Northern Ireland	70	68
USA	68	60
England and Wales	68	60
Belgium	63	57
France	43	58
Poland	36	44
Japan	48	27
Portugal	31	33

Source: Van Kesteren *et al.* (2001: 70)

Improving police services for crime victims

Given the extent of victims' criticisms it is scarcely surprising that policies have been implemented in a number of countries aimed at improving police services. Approaches adopted by police services in the US (OVC 2001a, 2001b) include enhanced police training in victim-oriented work (Rosenbaum 1987) and enhanced police support (Skogan and Wycoff 1987). In the Netherlands, Winkel (1989, 1991) described a similar local initiative that incorporated both specialist training and additional support. Also in the Netherlands, a series of guidelines for police and prosecutors was issued, requiring the police to treat victims sympathetically, provide all the relevant information and, where necessary, refer them to other agencies, and victims now have a right to cite the guidelines should they subsequently take legal action against the police (Brienen and Hoegen 2000; Wemmers and Zeilstra 1991).

In England and Wales, the introduction of Victim Support was readily endorsed by the police, although there was some initial suggestion that grassroots officers were less enthusiastic than senior management (Mawby and Gill 1987). The referral system, whereby police routinely passed on victims' details to local Victim Support schemes, also provided a model of best practice. Victim Support has, in addition, provided a useful input to police initial training, although there has been no comprehensive evaluation of the impact of victim-oriented training on officers' attitudes and performance. Undoubtedly, though, the most significant policy initiatives have paralleled those in the Netherlands, with the victims' charters increasingly imposing requirements on the ways that the police deal with crime victims, and performance indicators, particularly consumer surveys – carried out both internally at force level (Bunt and Mawby 1994) and externally through the BCS and local surveys – used to monitor change.

The first Victim's Charter set the scene by reaffirming the police's responsibilities to victims on three levels: first, in the way they responded to the initial crime; second, by making them responsible for passing on details of victims' losses to the court or CPS in the event of a compensation order being imposed; and third by encouraging them to provide feedback on progress to the victim. The second Victim's Charter set this out in more detail, stressing their responsibility to respond quickly to the crime, investigate thoroughly, provide details of the investigating officer, pass on other relevant information to the victim, and relay victims' feelings to other agencies.

Subsequently, the introduction of victim statements of opinion (Victim Personal Statement Scheme) based on US victim impact statements (Mawby 2007), accorded the police additional responsibilities. A pilot scheme in 1996 in six areas of the country established a 'one-stop shop' where victims were kept up to date on the progress of their case by the police and where the police were responsible for helping victims to complete personal statements about 'their' crimes (Hoyle *et al.* 1999). Following a further review (Morgan and Sanders 1999), victim statements of opinion were introduced nationally, with the police charged with responsibility for helping victims make a statement (Home Office 2001a: 6). The same document made the police responsible for advising victims about claiming compensation from the offender (2001a: 8).

While victim-oriented policework has been formalised in other respects, including an involvement in restorative justice initiatives (Hoyle and Young 2003), current police responsibilities are most extensively detailed in the 2005 Code of Practice, where over four pages focus on the police's obligations (Home Office 2005c: 6–10):

- Where they consider that no investigation is appropriate, they must advise the victim of this as soon as possible and within five working days at the latest.

- In all other cases, the police must ensure that victims have access to information about local support services, for example by giving them a copy of the current local *Victims of Crime* leaflet in a language the victim can understand, within five working days of the crime being reported.

- They must clearly explain to victims[5] that their details will be passed on to Victim Support unless they ask the police not to, and then provide the local Victim Support Group with the victim's contact details no later than two working days after the crime is reported.

- The police must notify the victim on at least a monthly basis of progress in cases being actively investigated up until the point of closure of the investigation.

- Where an investigation into a serious crime remains undetected, the police must advise the victim (or victim's family in homicide cases), of this fact and the reasons for it. The possibility of the case being subject to periodic review must be discussed with the victim or family representative, who must be given the opportunity to decide whether they wish to be advised of any review procedures which take place. This decision must be recorded by the senior investigating officer at the time of the discussion. If the victim or family representative expresses a wish to be advised of any review procedures, the police must ensure that information about the review is passed on within one working day of the review procedure commencing. The victim or family must also be given the opportunity at this stage to say whether they wish to be advised of the reopening of the investigation due to new evidence or changes in forensic procedures. This decision must be recorded by the senior investigating officer at the time of the discussion. If an enquiry is reopened, the police must consider the expressed wishes of the victim or family before making contact with them and record the reasons for any decision made in this respect.

- Where a victim has died as a result of criminal conduct or suspected criminal conduct, the police must assign a family liaison officer to any relatives whom the police consider appropriate and make a record of the assignment. The police must also provide close relatives of the victim with the packs *Advice for Bereaved Families and Friends Following Murder or Manslaughter* or *Advice for Bereaved Families and Friends Following Death on the Road*, or their equivalents.

- If a suspect is arrested, the police must notify the victim of this within five working days.

- If the suspect is released with no further action being taken, the police must notify the victim of this and the relevant reasons for no further action being taken within five working days.

- Should the suspect be released on police bail, or police bail conditions subsequently altered, the police must notify victims of this, reasons for bail and any relevant bail conditions within five working days.

- Where a suspect is interviewed, the police must notify the victim of this fact and the fact that a file will be submitted for a decision on prosecution/ summons, within three working days of the suspect being interviewed and/or reported.

- When a summons is issued by the court, the victim must be notified of this fact and the date of the first hearing within five working days of the police being so notified.

- It will be the duty of the police to notify victims of all decisions to bring any criminal proceedings for a relevant offence. If the police decide not to prosecute the suspect, they are responsible for notifying the victim of this within five working days.

- When a suspect is charged with an offence, or a decision is taken that there is insufficient evidence to charge a suspect, it will be the responsibility of the police to notify the victim of this fact within five working days.

- If a suspect is charged with an offence in relation to relevant criminal conduct and released on police bail to appear at a court, the police must notify the victim of this event, the date of the court hearing and any relevant bail conditions within five working days.

- If bail conditions are amended by the police prior to the suspect appearing at court the police must notify the victim within five working days.

- Where the police successfully apply for the suspect to be remanded in custody, the police must notify the victim. If the police recommendation was rejected and the suspect was bailed, the police must also inform the victims and detail any conditions attached to the bail that relate to, involve or affect the victim, and what the victim can do if conditions are broken. This information must be provided within five working days.

- If a suspect is cautioned or given any other non-court disposal method, the police must notify the victim of this event within five working days.

- In cases where the offender is under the age of 18, the police must pass the victim's contact details to the Youth Offending Team (unless the victim asks the police not to) to enable victims to have access to reparation or other restorative justice type initiatives.

- The police must respond to requests for information from the CICA or the CICAP to enable a victim's claim for compensation to be assessed with the most accurate information available at that time.

- If a conviction or sentence in respect of relevant criminal conduct is being reviewed by the Criminal Cases Review Commission and, taking all the circumstances of the case into account, it is likely that the review will come to the victim's attention, the police must notify the victim no later than ten working days after the day the police receive notification of the review. If the Criminal Cases Review Commission decides not to refer a conviction or sentence in respect of relevant criminal conduct to the Court of Appeal or the Crown Court, and the victim has been informed of the review, the police must notify the victim no later than two working days after the day the police receive notification of the decision. If the Criminal Cases Review Commission decides to refer a conviction or sentence to the Court of Appeal or the Crown Court, the police must notify the victim no later than ten working days after the day the police receive notification of the decision.

- The police must take all reasonable steps to identify vulnerable or intimidated victims and take extra measures in such cases. This includes making information available to vulnerable victims more quickly, normally within one working day.

These requirements spell out in far more detail than before the precise police responsibilities for keeping victims informed of decisions taken at every stage of the process, from the point when an alleged crime is reported to the trial. At this stage, it becomes the responsibility of the CPS, the joint police/CPS Witness Care Unit and court staff to ensure that victims are kept informed. The fact that a time limit (i.e. normally within five working days) is imposed places additional responsibility on the police. It is, perhaps, ironic then that the Code of Practice, in placing the emphasis firmly on the provision of information, is largely silent on the question of how the police interact with victims. Even the limited aim of the second charter, to treat victims 'fairly and courteously' (Home Office 1996: 1) is not specified as a police requirement.

Discussion

Ideally police response to crime victims should encompass a service approach alongside a concern to do everything possible to clear up the crime. However, a traditional emphasis upon action, excitement and 'real' policework means that the police have often been criticised for their lack of concern for victims and – in the case of rape and domestic violence – an unwillingness to take the incident seriously. While these criticisms have been directed at the police in a number of societies, there is some evidence of recent improvements in police response. With regard to domestic violence and rape, for example, changes in police procedure have meant that in many cases the police are now more willing both to treat complaints as 'real' crimes and to place more emphasis on the service they provide to victims. With regard to property crimes, increased concern to monitor and evaluate police performance in England and Wales has in part led to a greater willingness to prioritise police *service*. Training and legislative control also provide partial means to effect changes in police response, but evidence from the USA and the Netherlands should caution us that they are no panacea.

However, this does not necessarily mean that victims' ratings of satisfaction with police response will improve. As is indicated in research in Central and Eastern Europe (Mawby 1998; Zvekic 1998), victims may appreciate the new service role adopted by the police but be highly critical of police failure to fulfil their more traditional functions. This at least serves as a warning against shifting the emphasis too far: the public does expect the police to investigate their crimes and make some effort to clear them up; indeed, not to do so is to undermine the notion that the police take victims' complaints seriously. But victims also expect the police to respond sympathetically, to treat them as people rather than crime numbers, to provide help or advice where necessary, and to keep them informed of any progress regarding 'their' crime. It is against these criteria, in addition to detection rates, that police services for crime victims need to be measured. The 2005 Code of Practice is a significant development in these respects, although it is regrettable that in focusing on the police as providers of information for victims and other criminal justice services, initial concerns over the manner of police interaction with victims seems to have been downplayed.

Court services

Courts are rarely victim-friendly places (see also Dunn, Chapter 10 in this volume). However, British courts have traditionally been even less victim-oriented than the courts in many other industrialised countries. Whereas in many countries on Continental Europe there was provision for the victim to be involved in the prosecution process, or in making a claim for compensation as part of the criminal trial, and in the USA court services for victims emerged in the 1970s as part of the Law Enforcement Assistance Administration's initiatives to encourage greater victim/witness co-operation (Mawby and Walklate 1994), in Britain court services were somewhat later arriving. Despite the involvement of court officials in the genesis of Victim Support, early initiatives focused on helping victims at the time of the offence rather than during the trial.

Research by Shapland, Willmore and Duff (1985; see also Shapland 1984) was extremely critical of the lack of information and support provided, noting that victims' perceptions of the way the criminal justice system responded to their problems became more negative as their cases progressed through the system. The Home Affairs Committee (1984) referred to their research and recommended that more attention should be paid to educating court staff and the physical design of courts, but devoted most of its attention to support at the time of the offence and compensation. A subsequent study by Shapland and Cohen (1987) reiterated these earlier findings and identified senior court officials as even less victim-minded than police managers (see also Raine and Walker 1990). In the light of these criticisms, Victim Support seized the initiative and set up a committee to consider the ways in which victims were treated in court. Established in 1986 and chaired by Lady Ralphs, herself a magistrate, the committee was highly critical of current practices, and made a wide range of recommendations on the information provided for victims/witnesses, the way they were treated in court, and the layout of court buildings (Ralphs 1988).

A number of initiatives flowed from these findings. On the one hand, the role of the voluntary sector, through Victim Support, was enhanced with the establishment of support services for witnesses in court, run by specialist units within local Victim Support schemes. Initially projects were piloted in seven Crown Courts (Raine and Smith 1991), before being introduced to all Crown Courts by the mid-1990s. By 2002 support services were also established in the magistrates' courts. As with Victim Support's community services, services were managed by staff employed by the charity on a full-time basis but involved volunteers who provided most of the direct contact with victims/witnesses. On the other hand, the importance of engaging the statutory sector in improving court services was acknowledged. One aspect of this was the expectation that the police and court officials would engage with Victim Support in producing and imparting to victims/witnesses information on how courts operated. Another was the assumption that court staff would modify their everyday practices to reduce the problems experienced by victims in court. This was reflected in the first Victim's Charter (Home Office 1990), which committed court staff to improve listing systems to cut down on the time witnesses had to wait before giving evidence and to provide practical information on court layout and procedures. The second Victim's Charter (1996) built on this, seeing the police, Witness Service, CPS and court staff as all providing a crucial service to victims/witnesses. However, the most significant developments have been more recent.

Recent developments

New Labour's court-based initiatives have to a large extent echoed US concerns, reflected in the 1970s LEAA programme, that conviction rates were being adversely affected by the reluctance of victims and witnesses to give evidence in court (Mawby 2007). If courts were radically altered so as to accommodate the needs of prosecution witnesses, the logic went, victims/ witnesses would be more willing to engage with the prosecution system. Improving the information provided for victims and prosecution witnesses prior to the trial, improving courtroom facilities during the trial, and enhanced feedback post-trial, were seen as essential ingredients that met the needs of both the victims and the state. The Code of Practice (Home Office 2005c) provides the most detailed account of what is expected of staff in and around the courts. While, as already noted, the police are seen as key providers of information at the early stages of the process, the roles of the joint police/ CPS Witness Care Units, CPS and court staff are seen as crucial where a case gets to court.

To date, the most significant manifestation of this commitment flowing from the 'No Witness No Justice' initiative has been new Witness Care Units, jointly run by the police and CPS (Home Office 2005b). Overseen by Local Criminal Justice Boards, but on a practical level 'line managed' by the police, the Witness Care Units work closely with Victim Support and the Witness Service. They provide a single point of contact for victims to allow earlier identification of victim and witness needs and enhanced co-ordination between the CPS and police. A needs assessment is carried out with all witnesses to identify problems that would prevent the witness attending court to give evidence, such as child-care or transport problems. The witness care officers then co-ordinate the support offered to the witnesses and manage any referrals to other agencies such as the Witness Service or Victim Support. They provide updates about the progress of the case and at the end of the trial they make sure that witnesses are told about the result and sentencing, and offer further support where appropriate. Notably, Witness Care Units are the responsibility of statutory agencies and work with Witness Support, which continues as a separate arm of Victim Support. This is a different model from that for Victims' Care Units proposed by the government and currently being trialled in North Yorkshire, Nottingham and Salford, which will be co-ordinated by Victim Support.[6]

The Code of Practice (Home Office 2005c) charges Witness Care Units with a number of tasks, including:

- Conducting a full needs assessment with all victims where a 'not guilty' plea is entered.

- Notifying victims where they are required to give evidence in court, and providing them with a copy of the *Witness in Court* leaflet (or equivalent).

- Informing victims of the date of all criminal court hearings.

- Where victims under the age of 17 are to be called as witnesses in cases involving sex, violence, or cruelty, ensuring that the victims and their parents or guardians are provided with the relevant *Young Witness* information pack (or equivalent).

- Notifying any vulnerable or intimidated victim of the outcome of all pre-trial hearings and the verdicts of the trial, including the sentence if the suspect is convicted, and other victims of the sentence (or any not guilty verdict).

- Explaining to victims the meaning and effect of the sentence given to the offender in their case, and responding to any questions the victim may have (if necessary referring the victim to the CPS).

- Informing victims of any appeal against conviction or sentence and the result of that appeal.

- In cases where an offender is convicted of a serious sexual or violent offence resulting in a sentence of imprisonment or detention of 12 months or more, providing a link between the victim and the probation service.

While this locates Witness Care Units at the hub of court-related services for victims and witnesses, the code continues by specifying the responsibilities of the Crown Prosecution Service, which is required:

- In liaison with the police, to inform victims of charging decisions.

- Where the prosecutor and CPS decide that it is inappropriate or unnecessary in the particular circumstances to notify the victim, to record the reasons for providing no information or only limited information.

- In cases involving a death, child abuse, sexual offences, racially and religiously aggravated offences and offences with a homophobic or transphobic element, and the CPS decides not to proceed with the case, to meet the victim personally to explain the decision.

- Where a victim witness has been identified as potentially vulnerable or intimidated, to ensure that systems are in place to consider the appropriateness of special measures under the 1999 Youth Justice and Criminal Evidence Act.

- To ensure that CPS or other prosecutors are available to introduce themselves to victims at court, and to answer any questions victims may have about court procedures and give an indication where possible of how long they will have to wait before giving evidence.

- In the event of delays to criminal proceedings, to explain the reason for the delay and, wherever possible, tell the victim how long the wait is likely to be.

- To arrange for victims' expenses to be paid promptly.

- Where the victim is referred to the CPS by the joint police/CPS Witness Care Units, to answer any questions the victim has about the sentence in their case.

- To provide the joint police/CPS Witness Care Units with copies of the List of Witnesses Attending Court as soon as these are finalised so that they can notify victims if they are required to give evidence.

- To respond to requests for information from the Criminal Injuries Compensation Authority or the Criminal Injuries Compensation Appeals Panel no later than 60 working days after the day on which the CPS receive the request.

Finally, court staff are required:

- To liaise with the joint police/CPS Witness Care Units, where it is necessary for information on appeals, amendments to sentence, court dates, adjournments or other court decisions to be passed on to victims.

- To ensure that, where possible, victims have, and are directed to, a separate waiting area and a seat in the courtroom away from the defendant's family or friends.

- Following the 1999 Youth Justice and Criminal Evidence Act, to ensure the availability of special measures for vulnerable victims to give evidence so far as is possible.

- To ensure, as far as is reasonably within their control, that victims/witnesses do not have to wait more than two hours before giving evidence.

- Where victims are due to appear as witnesses, to take contact telephone numbers for the victims so that they are able to leave the court precincts and be contacted when they are needed.

- To ensure, whenever possible, that there is an information point where all victims can find out what is happening in their case while their case is being heard in court.

Liaison with victims after the court hearing then becomes the responsibility of the probation service.

The probation service

Unlike the police, or even the prosecution system, the involvement of the probation service with victims is more tangential. Probation has, since its inception in the US and Britain, focused on the treatment of offenders, and largely excluded consideration of victims' needs or interests. Nevertheless, in both countries the possibility of compensation was provided for as a discretionary requirement of a probation order. Compensation was introduced as an optional condition of a probation order from its inception in the USA (Schafer 1960), and a similar requirement was included in the 1907 Probation Act and 1948 Criminal Justice Act in Britain. There is, however, little evidence that compensation featured significantly in probation requirements.

Despite this, probation officers played a key role in the development of victim services in England and Wales. They were instrumental in the establishment of the first victim support scheme in Bristol (Rock 1990) and a number of other areas. In Devon and Cornwall, for example, Mawby and Gill (1987) found that a sizeable minority of probation officers were actively involved with victim support schemes, while most were extremely positive about the importance of such schemes in meeting the needs of victims.

Many other developments have involved joint working with victims and offenders. John Harding (1982), for example, was an Assistant Chief Probation Officer when he wrote the first British text on restitution. Many smaller scale local initiatives have also been inspired by probation staff. In Plymouth, for example, the now defunct Victim/Burglar Group was managed by the probation service (Nation and Arnott 1991), providing a structured programme for convicted burglars subject to a probation order, part of which involved them in group discussions with burglary victims. This provided the opportunity for victims to express their anger and fears, albeit towards someone other than 'their' burglar, in a controlled environment. Feedback demonstrated that most felt they benefited from the experience. Additionally, being confronted by victims proved beneficial to offenders, who were forced to confront and re-evaluate their actions, enabling probation officers to challenge their 'techniques of neutralisation' (Sykes and Matza 1957). That is, burglars were less able to hide behind excuses that 'victims can afford it' or 'it didn't really affect the victim', and instead were left with the clear message that their actions had impacted on their victims.

Some of the more recent 'accredited programmes' offered by the probation service provide an extension of the offence-directed aspects of intensive probation and may also incorporate a victim-focus. Equally, probation has worked in partnership with other agencies on domestic violence and child protection issues where the needs of victims are to the forefront of policy initiatives (Barnish 2004; HMIP 2002, 2004).

Alongside these, New Labour's commitment to restorative justice provides alternative approaches to confronting offenders with the consequences of their crimes and thereby involving the probation service in work with victims. The use of mediation and/or reparation has been in existence for a considerable time (Johnstone and van Ness 2007; Miers *et al.* 2001; Umbreit 1999; see also Chapter 11 in this volume) but received new impetus in England and Wales through the 1998 Criminal Justice Act and 1999 Youth Justice and Criminal Evidence Act. The emphasis here has been on young offenders, where probation staff as members of local YOTs have become increasingly involved in assessing the needs of crime victims and addressing them in the context of the most appropriate ways of dealing with offenders (Crawford and Burden 2005; Dignan 2005; Miers *et al.* 2001). Arguably the most significant development in probation work with victims, however, relates to the post-sentence involvement of victims of serious crime.

Post-sentence involvement of victims of serious crimes

This requirement was introduced in the first Victim's Charter (Home Office 1990), whereby probation services were made responsible for establishing contact with victims of life-sentence prisoners (or in the case of homicides their close relatives), so that any concerns they might have about the release of the offender could be passed on to the prison and/or Parole Board. While on the face of it this suggested that victims needed to be kept informed, rather than drawn in to the decision-making process, the charter went on to suggest that the Parole Board might take victims' views into account in deciding whether or not to impose parole conditions, such as where the offender should or should not live. This introduced, for possibly the first time in recent history in Britain, the notion of victims having an influence on how offenders were treated. It also clearly repositioned the probation service: 'It was certainly the case that the Victim's Charter requirements altered the balance between the interests of offenders and those of victims in probation work' (Nettleton *et al.* 1997a: 207).

However, partly because the first Victim's Charter was advisory, partly because the recommendations were not supported by additional funding, and partly because of the degree of autonomy enjoyed by local probation services, many probation services ignored it (Johnston 1994; Nettleton *et al.* 1997b). Parole boards responded by becoming increasingly reluctant to grant parole (Nettleton *et al.* 1997b). Reacting to this impasse, the Home Office, through a combination of circulars, new national standards for the supervision of offenders in the community, the second Victim's Charter, discussions between the Association of Chief Officers of Probation and Victim Support, and a guidance document from the Association of Chief Officers of Probation, both clarified and extended expectations (ACOP 1996; ACOP/Victim Support 1996; Home Office 1995a, 1995b, 1996, 1997, 2001b). For example, there was the presumption that contact with victims would be made in all cases where offenders were sentenced to four years or more for serious sexual or violent offences and probation services were required to contact eligible victims within two months of sentence. The 1996 Victim's Charter stated that the probation service would contact victims of serious sexual or violent offences within two months of sentence to explain the meaning of the sentence and ask whether or not they wished to be kept apprised of release plans, and if so to take into account victims' concerns. Probation Circular 61/1995 (Home Office 1995a) also made clear the dual purpose of this contact:

> The purpose of making contact with the victim is twofold: to provide information to the victim about the custodial process, and to obtain information from the victim about any concerns he or she may wish to be taken into account when the conditions (but not the date) of release are being considered. (Home Office 1995a: 1)

The result is succinctly described by Crawford and Enterkin (2001: 709):

In sum, victim contact work operates around a two stage process – involving contact after sentence and during preparations for the offender's release – with three elements to it which, in the words of the ACOP/Victim Support joint statement (1996), constitute 'informing', 'consulting' (gathering information from the victim) and 'supporting' victims.

This dramatic shift in emphasis within probation reflected the repositioning of 'the work of the service as a public protection agency' (HMIP 2003: 13).

This was illustrated in a thematic inspection conducted by Her Majesty's Inspectorate of Probation in 1999–2000 (HMIP 2000). The report acknowledged that while the new duties required services to adopt a fundamentally different approach to work with offenders, limited attention had been given to implementing the new requirements by the Home Office Probation Unit. In particular, no additional funds had been made available. Moreover, although effective practice principles for work with offenders had been established, rather less attention had been devoted to establishing similar principles vis-à-vis victims. It therefore recommended further liaison with Victim Support; greater clarification of the categories of offenders where victims should be contacted; greater consistency in keeping records of contact, closure of cases, retention of information and confidentiality; ensuring that victims were informed of the use made of the information provided; and the extension of the scheme to victims of offenders sentenced to shorter prison terms (12 months). It also addressed the funding issue by recommending that victims should be included in the cash allocation formula for areas and that steps should be taken to assess the cost of victim contact work so that it might be adequately funded.

To some extent, these recommendations were superseded by the 2000 Criminal Justice and Court Services Act and Probation Circular 108/2000 (Home Office 2000). A single National Probation Service for England and Wales was created, comprising 42 probation areas, each with local governance, employer and service delivery responsibilities and being co-terminous with police service areas, and, through its Victims and Partnerships Policy team, allowed for the development of more coherent national standards. A Victims Central Lead Action Network, comprising police, probation practitioners and the voluntary sector, was established in 2001 to further enhance partnership work and 'joined-up thinking'.

Victim contact work was therefore placed on a statutory basis. The National Probation Service was required to contact the victims of serious sexual or violent offenders sentenced to 12 months or more and placed responsibility on local probation boards for different stages of work with victims:

- The local probation board for the area in which the offender is sentenced must take all reasonable steps to find out whether an 'appropriate person' wished to make representations about any conditions the offender should be subject to on release and to receive information about the requirements.

- Where the 'appropriate person' wished to make such representations, the relevant board must ensure that the person responsible for determining the conditions was informed accordingly.

- The local board where the victim lives would undertake the face-to-face contact work with the victim. Where the 'appropriate person' wished to receive information about any requirements to which the offender would be subject on release, the relevant board must take all reasonable steps to inform them of the nature of the conditions and provide them with relevant details, and any other information considered by the local board to be suitable in the circumstances of the case.

- The importance of creating systems to ensure relevant information could be routinely collected from local courts and the police was underlined.

The additional responsibilities for working with victims were funded nationally, with £6 million made available, but this funding did not cover work that was already in place.

Two further Probation Circulars were produced to clarify how local areas should implement the revised arrangements (Home Office 2001b, 2001c). These required areas to:

- Make a written offer of face-to-face contact between the victim (or family) and local probation area/victim contact unit, or its agent, within eight weeks of sentence.

- Provide information to victims (or family) about the criminal justice process, and keep victims informed, where victims so wished.

- Provide an opportunity for victims (or family) to give their views on proposed conditions surrounding the offender's release and include these in any pre-release reports, such as those to the Parole Board or prison governor. Victims should be allowed to see any part of the parole report that purported to represent their views.

- Inform the victim (or family) of any conditions of release that related to contact with the victim.

- Ensure that any information relating to victims (or family) is kept securely and separately from the offender's case record.

Following the establishment of the Home Office Justice, Victims and Witnesses Unit in 2003, a further thematic inspection was carried out to 'assess the extent to which the HMIP recommendations on victim contact had been implemented and look at the impact of the new duties outlined in the CJ&CSA 2000' (HMIP 2003: 19). This acknowledged that the National Probation Service had adopted victim work as a fundamental priority, but noted that there remained considerable differences between probation areas in the services provided to victims. It consequently recommended 'the setting of a new national standard for victim work to support and anchor the excellent and dedicated work seen during the inspection' (HMIP 2003: unpaginated foreword). This is developed further in the 2004 Domestic Violence, Crime and Victims Act and the 2005 Code of Practice (Home Office 2005c), which sets out the responsibilities of the probation service. These specifically apply in cases where the offender receives a sentence of imprisonment of 12 months or longer[7] after being convicted of a sexual or violent offence. In such cases the probation service is required to take all reasonable steps to establish whether a victim wishes to make representations about what licence conditions or supervision requirements (in the case of a young offender) the offender should be subject to on their release from prison and/or conditions of discharge from hospital and to forward these to those responsible for making decisions about the prisoner's or patient's release. It is also responsible for forwarding any requests for non-disclosure to those responsible for making decisions about the prisoner's or patient's release. It must also pass on any information to the victim about whether their offender will be subject to any conditions or requirements in the event of release or discharge and detail any that relate to contact with the victim or their family. The probation service is also responsible for providing victims with any other information that it considers appropriate: for example, a move to a lower category prison or a temporary release from prison on licence (Home Office 2005c: 15–16).

Key issues

Initially, national guidelines left probation service areas with considerable discretion over how to implement post-sentence contact with victims. Consequently, alternative arrangements were agreed in different areas prior to the creation of the National Probation Service, and despite attempts to standardise arrangements considerable variation still exist. Nettleton *et al.* (1997a, 1997b) distinguished three alternative models of structural response: 'we can handle it out there', 'third party', and 'specialist worker'.

'We can handle it out there'. In this model, throughcare officers contact the victim by letter outlining their responsibility, although making no reference to their role as the offender's officer. A response is invited if the victim would like to receive further information; lack of response is interpreted as declining further contact. According to this model, victim work is fully integrated into the supervisory role of the throughcare officer; it is not marginalised, nor delegated as an adjunct of everyday work, but is held to be complementary to existing tasks within the probation remit. This was the approach initially adopted in Devon and described by Rogers (1999) as favoured by probation officers, but has become less common. The 2003 thematic inspection noted that by that year only 11 areas in England and Wales relied on supervising probation officers (HMIP 2003).

The 'third party' model. In the second model an outside agency is used to initiate contact, offer information and record victims' wishes and concerns (see Johnston 1996). This means that the dilemma for the probation officer of separating both offender and victim issues and priorities is not faced. Here, a specialist worker, who is not a qualified probation officer but who possesses specific skills and training for this work, will collect information and report back to the probation throughcare officer. This model is distinctive in that victim contact work is separated from core probation tasks and is externalised. As a result, victim work is a peripheral task whose significance is felt vicariously rather than at first hand. The probation service maintains intact its primary focus on the offender, while exercising its new victim-oriented responsibilities at arm's length. This model was primarily associated with West Yorkshire, which had a history of mediation run through specialist victim–offender units (Crawford and Enterkin 2001).

The 'specialist worker' model. The third model identifies a probation officer or 'team' in the particular role of victim liaison: here, the work remains 'in-house' but it is clearly separated from offence work, with no confusion of roles apparent and with the relevant training attached. This was the approach adopted in the two probation areas reviewed by Newton (2003) and in Northumbia, the second area evaluated by Crawford and Enterkin (2001), and has become the preferred model nationally. Thus the 2003 thematic inspection noted that by then 31 areas in England and Wales used victim liaison officers, and acknowledged this to be the most effective approach, albeit there had not been any evaluation of the alternatives (HMIP 2003). This model enables a more consistent approach to be adopted and overcomes confusion of roles, while victim contact is developed as a specialism within probation, satisfying both the new dimension and focus within the service and the ambivalence noted in playing advocate to victim and offender simultaneously. However, it may restrict the extent to which victim-oriented work becomes fully integrated into probation.

A further variation relates to the extent to which Victim Support works with probation in making contact. While this appears to be widespread (Crawford and Enterkin 2001; Newton 2003), and is generally considered preferable, it is by no means standard practice (HMIP 2003), at least partly due to lack of central funding to involve Victim Support. However, Rogers' (1999) research in Devon, where visits were routinely carried out jointly by throughcare officers and Victim Support co-ordinators, found that victims valued the partnership approach, considering that the probation officer was there to provide the information and Victim Support the personal support they needed.

The role of the probation service in providing victim contact work is seen as valuable, partly in providing emotional support, partly in empowering victims, but primarily where victims seek further information:

> The research presented here suggests that victims of serious crime can benefit significantly from good quality, timely and well delivered information with regard to simple, factual information on the offender's custody; contextual information which would allow them to understand the conditions of the offender's custody; and explanations of criminal justice terminology and procedures. (Crawford and Enterkin 2001: 722)

Nevertheless, research suggests that a number of problems remain. From the perspective of the probation service and officers involved in this work, practical issues, involving for example the difficulty of making contact with victims and shortfalls in training and funding (Crawford and Enterkin 2001; Newton 2003; Rogers 1999) persist, as acknowledged by Her Majesty's Inspectorate of Probation (2003). More fundamentally, given that historically probation has been offender-oriented, integration of victim-work as core business continues to be problematical (Crawford and Enterkin 2001), although as one probation officer told Rogers (1999: 30), 'Victim consultation adds a new dimension to probation work, and when I see how easily and appropriately it fits into what we do, I cannot believe I once felt it was inappropriate.'

More important, perhaps, are problems raised by victims – the consumers – of the service, in whose interests it is justified. Some, for example, are reluctant to re-engage with the criminal justice process on the grounds that it forces them to revisit the trauma of the crime (Newton 2003), which partly explains the significant numbers with whom the probation service fails to make contact. Others feel that contact is made in the interests of offenders, not victims (Rogers 1999). Many of the issues raised surround the notion, ironically, that a measure aimed at least in part at empowering victims may in fact *dis*empower them. For example, where offenders are given access to victims' opinions and there is a possibility that they might retaliate (Crawford and Enterkin 2001; Rogers 1999); where they felt they were denied access to all the information available to the Probation Service (Crawford and Enterkin 2001; Rogers 1999); or where they felt that their views were subsequently ignored (Newton 2003). To quote from Rogers' (1999: 26) interviews with two victims:

Whatever you say gets told to him [the offender]. If I object to something, he finds out, but if he objects to something, I'm not allowed to know.

No disrespect to the probation officer, but she just couldn't tell me what I wanted to know. She kept saying 'Sorry, I can't tell you that.' I thought, what the bloody hell are you here for then?

Clearly progress has been made since the research reported here was concluded, and services to victims have improved. However, to echo (Crawford and Enterkin 2001: 723–4):

In integrating victims and taking account of their concerns within criminal justice, careful consideration needs to be given to the manner in which such initiatives may disturb the delicate balance between state and the offender and to ensure that victims' needs are not distorted by the needs and demands of criminal justice itself.

Summary and discussion

In an otherwise excellent review of the probation service's victim contact work, Crawford and Enterkin (2001: 709) suggest that NGOs, most notably Victim

Support, have become increasingly powerful in policy-making and service delivery: 'As such, it represents and reflects an increasing blurring of the boundaries between the state and civil society, as it has become incorporated in the task of delivering criminal justice.' On the contrary, I have argued that precisely the opposite has occurred. Traditionally, and accentuated by the moral and political philosophy of Thatcherism, the voluntary sector was accorded a central place in the provision of victim services. However, the state, principally through the police and financial support, also accepted a partial responsibility for service delivery, and in recent years this responsibility has been accentuated and the balance between public and voluntary sectors has correspondingly shifted.

There are a number of reasons for this, based around a gradual acceptance that victims' needs are too important to leave to NGOs (Mawby and Walklate 1994). One issue that is central to this is the injustice of geography that occurs within voluntary sector provision, with needs being greatest where voluntary sector provision was most problematic (Mawby and Gill 1987). Thus, rural areas and county towns with the least crime traditionally found it easiest to recruit Victim Support volunteers, while metropolitan high-crime areas struggled. Moreover Victim Support, used to competing with other criminal justice agencies deploying volunteers, like the police and probation service (Gill and Mawby 1990), found itself competing with a new wave of voluntary services including appropriate adults (Pierpoint 2004) and mediation and restorative justice programmes, with the result that the numbers of volunteers (as visitors or committee members) failed to keep up with increasing demand, especially as Victim Support took on court work and joint visits with the probation service.

Allied to this, the pressures of new managerialism have shifted government treatment of NGOs towards an assumption that they should operate according to the same 'rules of the game' as the public sector. Thus area differences in the way Victim Support schemes operate have been minimised through the imposition of a county structure, and ultimately, it seems likely, a national structure, and Victim Support has been required to account for the grants it receives and demonstrate good value. At the same time, rather than Victim Support being seen as the voice of victims, it appears that current government policy favours an expanded public sector responsibility for victim services, with Victim Support an aide where appropriate.

This is illustrated in Table 8.2, where the role of public sector services is compared with that of the voluntary sector at various stages of the criminal justice process:

- *At the time of the offence.* Perhaps the exception, the importance of Victim Support is maintained here and while the Code of Practice sets out the role of the police, this is described more in terms of their role in providing information, with the earlier emphasis on personal support less prominent. However, the fact that the new Code of Practice refers to public sector responsibilities means that Victim Support's role appears less central than as specified in the 1996 Victim's Charter. Moreover, the withdrawal of Victim Support's initial direct personal contact with victims, with a new reliance on letters and/or phone contact, means that in fact victims will in the future receive less *direct* personal help from the voluntary sector. Arguably, the new Victim Support-led VCUs will formalise the role of Victim Support. But the fact that police officers will be assigned to them will inevitably change the nature of the working relationship between Victim Support and police and reduce the traditional autonomy that Victim Support has enjoyed.

- *Progress of investigation.* In contrast, where earlier research identified Victim Support as playing a crucial role in building a bridge between the victim and the police, the Code of Practice sees liaison with and feedback to victims as a key responsibility of the police, continuing until the case reaches court.

- *Mediation/restorative justice.* Similarly, while earlier mediation initiatives were principally located in the voluntary sector, the formalisation of restorative justice programmes locates these more centrally within the YOTs, with NGOs playing a subsidiary role.

- *Claiming compensation.* Since its inception, Victim Support has built up considerable expertise in helping victims of violent crime to complete Criminal Injuries Compensation application forms, and in the absence of funding for legal advice Victim Support has established a key role in supporting victims throughout the process. This was acknowledged in the 1996 Victim's Charter. However, because the 2005 Code of Practice focuses on the public sector, this role is not re-endorsed and the code includes one page on the requirements of the CICA. Moreover, with regard to help with claiming compensation from the offender, Home Office (2001a) guidelines on making a Victim Personal Statement cite the police as responsible for advising victims.

- *Court/prosecution.* Here clearly the public-sector-managed Witness Care Units have taken over the principal responsibilities for supporting victims in court, with Witness Support servicing them. Additionally, the police are named as responsible for helping victims make a Victim Personal Statement (Home Office 2001a), a role that might previously have been accorded to Victim Support.

- *Post-sentence information.* This is clearly seen in the Code of Practice as a probation responsibility. While Victim Support may engage with probation in supporting eligible victims, there is no standard arrangement whereby this occurs, and Victim Support receives no dedicated funding for this. Further, paralleling the responsibility of the police for enabling victims to complete Victim Personal Statements, probation is assigned responsibility for relaying victims' views to the Parole Board.

The argument that Victim Support is becoming less significant a player in the 'victims' industry' is a contentious one. However, what is less contestable is the fact that as the public sector has been drawn into this industry and been required to tailor its services towards crime victims, so the balance of power has shifted. The public sector is undoubtedly more centrally involved in providing for victims than was the case even ten years ago, and the 2005 Code of Practice gives formal recognition to this. How successful it is, and how far the code ensures that victims do indeed receive a better deal depends on the ways in which the code is implemented.

Table 8.2 Model for victim services, England and Wales

	Public sector	NGOs
At the time of the offence	Police	Victim Support
Progress of investigation	Police	
Mediation/restorative justice	YOTs	Mediation schemes
Claiming criminal injuries compensation	CICA	Victim Support
Court/prosecution	Police/CPS/court staff	Witness Support
Post-sentence information	Probation	Victim Support

In this respect, the lack of government evaluation of its proposed policies is notable, particularly when compared with New Labour's evidence-based approach to probation and crime reduction initiatives. This reflects a long-term practice of introducing victim-oriented policies without first evaluating them, stretching back to the introduction of criminal injuries compensation. While some initiatives, like support for victims in court, or more recently the introduction of Victim Personal Statements, have been piloted, in the latter case policy appears to have been enacted despite rather than in line with the evaluation findings (Sanders *et al.* 2001).

This applies to both victim-oriented policies in general and to the greater involvement of the public sector. The impact of a given policy can be assessed both in terms of outputs (i.e. does the measure deliver what it aims to?) and outcomes (i.e. is it effective?). Thus, the 2005 Code of Practice might be evaluated in terms of whether or not it leads public sector agencies to act differently towards victims: for example, does the CPS, in liaison with the police, now routinely inform victims of charging decisions? And does this in fact result in victims perceiving the service they receive to be an improved one? In the broader context of the increased role accorded to the public sector, one might also ask, for example: how successful the probation service is in making contact with victims post-sentence; in what proportion of cases direct contact incorporates a joint communication/visit with Victim Support; and how victims perceived the contribution of probation and Victim Support? Given research evidence from the Netherlands that enforcing charters is fraught with difficulties, and from Devon that victims value the joint contribution of probation and Victim Support, it should not be taken for granted that policies will be necessarily either appropriately implemented or valued by the victim-consumer.

Recent government policy has undoubtedly intended to reposition public sector agencies, including the police, court services and probation, *vis-à-vis* their responsibilities towards victims. However, as yet we know little about how the working practices of these agencies have changed, or whether they have resulted in an improved service to victims. Ensuring that victims' needs are met without unjustifiably raising their expectations, empowering victims without returning to vigilante justice: these are key policy aims. Greater involvement of the public sector may be a means to achieve these, but it requires careful monitoring and critical external scrutiny.

Further reading

There are no texts, and little research material, focusing specifically on the role of the public sector in the provision of victim services, although some discussion has addressed the contribution of particular agencies, especially the police and probation services. More general texts, such as Goodey's (2005) *Victims and Victimology: Research, Policy and Practice* (Harlow: Longman) and Williams' (2005) *Victims of Crime and Community Justice* (London: Jessica Kingsley) do cover much of the ground, albeit in a less focused way, as does Mawby and Walklate's (1994) now dated *Critical Victimology*. The internet provides an excellent alternative, with Home Office material in particular readily available, especially: *Rebalancing the Criminal Justice System in Favour of the Law-abiding Majority: Cutting Crime, Reducing Reoffending and Protecting the Public* (2006); *Rebuilding Lives – Supporting Victims of Crime Consultation* (2005); and *Code of Practice for Victims of Crime* (2005). However, these documents reflect current government thinking and generally lack an outside critical edge.

Notes

1 I am grateful for the comments of my colleagues Steve Pearce and Jill Annison on an earlier draft of this chapter.
2 Subsequently renamed Criminal Injuries Compensation Authority (CICA).
3 Indeed, preference for the term 'survivor' rather than 'victim' is an indication of this more radical stance.
4 This was at least partly due to the reluctance of Victim Support to commit itself to national standards when its service was devolved to a county structure.
5 Generally excepting victims of vehicle crime and minor vandalism. The police should only pass Victim Support the details of victims of sexual offences or domestic violence or details of the relatives of homicide victims if the victims or relatives have given their explicit consent.
6 See www.cjsonline.gov.uk/the_cjs/whats_new/news-3428.html
7 Applies in some other cases such as where the offender receives a restricted hospital order.

References

ACOP (Association of Chief Officers of Probation) (1996) 'Probation Services and the Victims of Crime', position statement approved by ACOP National Council, February, Wakefield.

ACOP/Victim Support (1996) *The Release of Prisoners: Informing, Consulting and Supporting Victims.* London: ACOP & VS.

Allen, J., Edmonds, S., Patterson, A. and Smith, D. (2006) *Policing and the Criminal Justice System – Public Confidence and Perceptions: Findings from the 2004/05 British Crime Survey.* (Home Office Online Report 07/06) London: Home Office. (www. homeoffice.gov.uk/rds/pdfs06/rdsolr0706.pdf).

Angle, H., Malam, S. and Carey, C. (2003) *Key findings from the Witness Satisfaction Survey 2002*, Home Office Research, Development and Statistics Directorate, Findings 189. London: Home Office.

Barnish, M. (2004) *Domestic Violence: A Literature Review.* London: Home Office (www. homeoffice.gov.uk/hmiprobation/inspect_reports/thematic-inspections1.html/ thematic-dv-literaturereview.pdf?view=Binary).

Bottomley, A.K. and Coleman. C. (1976) 'Police statistics: The police role in the discovery and detection of crime', *International Journal of Criminology and Penology,* 4.

Brienen, M.E.I. and Hoegen, E.H. (2000) *Victims of Crime in 22 European Criminal Justice Systems: The Implementation of Recommendation (85) 11 of the Council of Europe on the Position of the Victim in the Framework of Criminal Law and Procedure.* Nijmegen, Netherlands: University of Tilburg (www.victimology.nl).

Bunt, P. and Mawby, R.I. (1994) 'Quality of policing', *Public Policy Review,* 2(3): 58–60.

Coupe, T. and Griffiths, M. (1997) *Solving Residential Burglary*, Crime Detection and Prevention Series Paper 77. London: Home Office.

Crawford, A. and Burden, T. (2005) *Integrating Victims in Restorative Youth Justice.* Abingdon: Policy Press.

Crawford, A. and Enterkin, J. (2001) 'Victim contact work in the probation service: Paradigm shift or pandora's box?', *British Journal of Criminology,* 41: 707–25.

Dignan, J. (2005) *Understanding Victims and Restorative Justice.* Maidenhead: Open University Press.

Gill, M. and Mawby, R.I. (1990) *Volunteers in the Criminal Justice System.* Milton Keynes: Open University Press.

Harding, J. (1982) *Victims and Offenders: Needs and Responsibilities.* London: NCVO/ Bedford Square Press.

Home Office (1970) *Reparation by the Offender: Report of the Advisory Council of the Penal System.* London: HMSO.

Home Office (1990) *Victim's Charter: A Statement of the Rights of Victims of Crime.* London: Home Office.

Home Office (1995a) *Probation Service Contact with Victims*, probation circular 61/1995. London: Home Office.

Home Office (1995b) *National Standards for the Supervision of Offenders in the Community.* London: Home Office.

Home Office (1996) *Victim's Charter: A Statement of Service Standards for Victims of Crime.* London: Home Office.

Home Office (1997) *Probation Service Contact with Victims*, probation circular 8/1997. London: Home Office.

Home Office (2000) *Criminal Justice and Court Service Acts 2000: Implementation of the New Statutory Duty on Probation Services in Respect of Victims of Serious Sexual or Violent Crimes*, probation circular 108/2000. London: Home Office.

Home Office (2001a) *Making a Victim Personal Statement.* London: Home Office (www. homeoffice.gov.uk/documents/victimstate.pdf?view=Binary).

Home Office (2001b) *Further Guidance on the National Probation Service's Work with Victims of Serious Crime*, probation circular 62/2001. London: Home Office.

Home Office (2001c) *Victim Contact Work – National Monitoring Arrangements*, probation circular 61/2001. London: Home Office.

Home Office (2003a) *A New Deal for Victims and Witnesses: National Strategy to Deliver Improved Services.* London: Home Office (www.cjsonline.gov.uk/library/pdf/18890_victims_and_witnesses_strategy.pdf).

Home Office (2003b) *Restorative Justice: The Government's Strategy Consultation Paper on the Government's Strategy on Restorative Justice.* London: Home Office (www.homeoffice.gov.uk/docs2/restorativestrategy.pdf).

Home Office (2003c) *Safety and Justice: The Government's Proposals on Domestic Violence.* London: Home Office (www.homeoffice.gov.uk/docs2/domesticviolence.pdf).

Home Office (2004) *Compensation and Support for Victims of Crime.* London: Home Office (www.homeoffice.gov.uk/docs2/victimscompensationconsultation.pdf).

Home Office (2005a) *Hearing the Relatives of Murder and Manslaughter Victims: Consultation.* London: Home Office.

Home Office (2005b) *Rebuilding Lives – Supporting Victims of Crime Consultation.* London: Home Office (www.jsonline.gov.uk/downloads/application/pdf/Rebuilding%20Lives%20supporting%20victims%20of%20crime.pdf).

Home Office (2005c) *Code of Practice for Victims of Crime.* London: Home Office (www.homeoffice.gov.uk/213275/victims-code-of-practice?view=Binary).

HMIP (2000) *Thematic Inspection Report: The Victim Perspective: Ensuring the Victim Matters.* London: Home Office (www.homeoffice.gov.uk/docs/themvict.html).

HMIP (2002) *Safeguarding children: The National Probation Service Role in the Assessment and Management of Child Protection Issues.* London: Home Office (www.homeoffice.gov.uk/hmiprobation/inspect_reports/thematic-inspections1.html/safeguarding_nps.pdf?view=Binary).

HMIP (2003) *Thematic Inspection Report: 'Valuing the Victim': An Inspection into National Victim Contact Arrangements.* London: Home Office (www.homeoffice.gov.uk/docs2/valuingthevictim.pdf).

HMIP (2004) *Reducing Domestic Violence: An Inspection of National Probation Service work with Domestic Violence Perpetrators.* London: Home Office (www.homeoffice.gov.uk/hmiprobation/inspect_reports/thematic-inspections1.html/thematic-domesticviolence.pdf?view=Binary).

Hoyle, C. and Young, R. (2003) 'Restorative Justice, Victims and the Police', in T. Newburn (ed.) *Handbook of Policing.* Cullompton: Willan Publishing, pp. 680–706.

Hoyle, C., Morgan, R. and Sanders, A. (1999) *The Victim's Charter – An Evaluation of Pilot Projects,* Home Office Research, Development and Statistics Directorate, Research Findings 107. London: Home Office.

Johnston, P. (1996) 'Probation contact with victims: Challenging through-care practice', *Probation Journal,* April: 26–8.

Johnston, P. (1994) *The Victims Charter (1990) and the Release of Life Sentence Prisoners: Implications for Probation Service Practice, Values and Management.* Cambridge: University of Cambridge, Institute of Criminology.

Johnstone, G. and Van Ness, D. (2007) *Handbook of Restorative Justice.* Cullompton: Willan Publishing.

Joutsen, M. (1987). *The Role of the Victim of Crime in European Criminal Justice Systems.* Helsinki: HEUNI.

Mawby, R.I. (1979) *Policing the City.* Farnborough: Saxon House.

Mawby, R.I. (1998) 'Victims' Perceptions of Police Services in East and West Europe', in V. Ruggiero, N. South and I. Taylor (eds) *The New European Criminology: Crime and Social Order in Europe.* London: Routledge.

Mawby, R.I. (2007) 'Criminal Justice and Crime Victims in Comparative Context', in P. Davies and P. Francis, (eds) *Victims in the Criminal Justice System.* Cambridge: Polity Press.

Mawby, R.I. and Gill, M. (1987) *Crime Victims: Needs, Services and the Voluntary Sector.* London: Tavistock.

Mawby, R.I. and Walklate, S. (1994) *Critical Victimology.* London: Sage.

Miers, D. (1978) *Responses to Victimization.* Abingdon: Professional Books.

Miers, D., Maguire, M., Goldie, S., Sharpe, K., Hale, C., Netter, A., Uglow, S., Doolin, K., Hallam, A., Enterkin, J. and Newburn, T. (2001) *An Exploratory Evaluation of Restorative Justice Schemes,* Crime Reduction Research Series Paper 9. London: Home Office.

Morgan, R. and Sanders, A. (1999) *The Uses of Victim Statements.* London: Home Office (www.homeoffice.gov.uk/rds/pdfs/occ-vicstats.pdf).

Nation, D. and Arnott, J. (1991) 'House burglaries and victims', *Probation Journal,* 38(2): 63–7.

Nettleton, H., Walklate, S. and Williams, B. (1997a) 'Three models of probation involvement with victims of crime', *Liverpool Law Review,* 19(2): 203–17.

Nettleton, H., Walklate, S. and Williams, B. (1997b) *Probation Training with the Victim in Mind: Partnership, Values and Organisation.* Keele: Keele University Press.

Newton, E. (2003) 'A study of the policies and procedures implemented by the probation service with respect to victims of serious crime', *British Journal of Community Justice,* 2(1): 25–36.

OVC (2001a) *Law enforcement,* New Directions from the Field, Bulletin 3 (www.ojp.usdoj.gov/ovc/new/directions/bulletins/welcome.html). (accessed 10 February 2007)

OVC (2001b) *First Response to Victims of Crime.* Washington DC, US Department of Justice (www.ojp.usdoj.gov/ovc/publications/infores/firstrep/2001/NCJ189631.pdf). (accessed 10 February 2007)

Pierpoint, H. (2004) 'A Survey on Volunteer Appropriate Adult Services', *Youth Justice,* 4(1): 32–45.

Raine, J.W. and Smith, R.E. (1991) *The Victim/Witness in Court Project: Report of the Research Programme.* London: Victim Support.

Raine, J. and Walker, B. (1990) 'Quality of services in the Magistrates' Courts – the user's perspective', *HO Research Bulletin,* 28: 42–8.

Ralphs, Lady (1988) *The Victim in Court: Report of the Working Party.* London: NAVSS.

Ringham, L. and Salisbury, H. (2004) *Support for Victims of Crime: Findings from the 2002/2003 British Crime Survey,* Home Office Online Report 31/04 (www.homeoffice.gov.uk/rds/pdfs04/rdsolr3104.pdf).

Rock, P. (1990) *Helping Victims of Crime: The Home Office and the Rise of Victim Support in England and Wales.* Oxford: Clarendon Press.

Rogers, G. (1999) 'Provision of post-sentence advice to victims of serious crime: Perceptions in one British probation service', *Crime Prevention and Community Safety: An International Journal,* 1(4): 21–34.

Rosenbaum, D.P. (1987) 'Coping with victimization: The effects of police intervention on victims' psychological readjustment', *Crime and Delinquency,* 33: 502–19.

Sanders, A., Hoyle, C., Morgan, R. and Cape, E. (2001) 'Victim impact statements: Don't work, can't work', *Criminal Law Review,* June: 447–58.

Schafer, S. (1960) *Restitution to Victims of Crime.* London: Stevens and Sons.

Shapland, J. (1984) 'Victims, the criminal justice system, and compensation', *British Journal of Criminology,* 24(2): 131–49.

Shapland, J. and Cohen, D. (1987) 'Facilities for victims: The role of the police and the courts', *Criminal Law Review,* January: 28–38.

Shapland, J., Wilmore, J. and Duff, P. (1985) *Victims in the Criminal Justice System.* Aldershot: Gower.

Sims, L. and Myhill, A. (2001) *Policing and Public: Findings from the 2000 British Crime Survey,* Home Office Research, Development and Statistics Directorate, Research Findings 136. London: Home Office.

Skogan, W. (1995) *Contacts Between Police and Public: Findings from the 1992 British Crime Survey.* Home Office Research Study 134. London: Home Office.

Skogan, W. (1996) 'The police and public opinion in Britain', *American Behavioral Scientist,* 39: 421–32.

Skogan, W.G. and Wycoff, M.A. (1987) 'Some unexpected effects of a police service for victims', *Crime and Delinquency,* 33: 490–501.

Sykes, G. and Matza, D. (1957) 'Techniques of neutralisation', *American Sociological Review,* 22: 664–73.

Umbreit, M.S. (1999) *Victim meets Offender: The Impact of Restorative Justice and Mediation.* New York: Criminal Justice Press.

Van Dijk, J.J.M. (1985) 'Regaining a Sense of Community and Order', in Council of Europe (ed.) *Research on Crime Victims.* Strasbourg: Council of Europe.

Van Kesteren, J., Mayhew, P. and Nieuwbeerta, P. (2001) *Criminal Victimisation in Seventeen Industrialised Countries: Key Findings from the 2000 International Crime Victims Survey* (www.minjust.nl:8080/b_organ/wodc/reports/ ob187i.htm).

Walker, A., Kershaw, C. and Nicholas, S. (2006) (eds) *Crime in England and Wales 2005/2006,* Research Development Statistics 11/05. London: Home Office. (www.homeoffice.gov.uk/rds/ pdfs06/hosb1206.pdf).

Wemmers, J.M. and Zeilstra, M.I. (1991) 'Victims' services in the Netherlands', *Dutch Penal Law and Policy,* 3. The Hague: Ministry of Justice.

Williams, B. (1999) 'The Victim's Charter: Citizens as consumers of criminal justice services', *Howard Journal,* 38(4): 384–96.

Winkel, F.W. (1989) 'Responses to criminal victimization: Evaluating the impact of a police assistance programme and some social psychological characteristics, *Police Studies,* 12(2): 59–72.

Winkel, F.W. (1991) 'Police responses aimed at alleviating victims' psychological distress and at raising prevention-awareness: Some grounded intervention programmes', paper to annual conference of Law and Society Association, Amsterdam.

Zvekic, U. (1998) *Criminal Victimisation in Countries in Transition.* Rome: UNICRI.

Chapter 9

The role of the voluntary sector

Brian Williams and Hannah Goodman

Introduction

This chapter examines the role of voluntary sector agencies which deliver services to victims of crime and campaign for their rights, in the UK and elsewhere. The relationships between different voluntary agencies are considered, along with their interactions with central government and with local state agencies. In some ways, the UK voluntary victim service sector is distinctive, and this is illustrated by comparison with similar provision elsewhere. The chapter concludes with a discussion of some possibilities for the future: the voluntary sector has increased its influence enormously over the past 35 years, gaining a central role in policy-making in the UK and in some other countries: can this continue?

The growth of voluntary sector work on victim issues

Voluntary sector involvement in issues relating to victims of crime began, like so many social movements, in the USA. Children as victims of physical abuse began to be defined as a social problem there in the late 1960s, and part of the response was the establishment of specialist children's bureaux within criminal justice agencies, along with the creation of shelters to house runaway children (Doerner and Lab 2002). Around the same time, North American feminists began setting up new institutions to provide practical protection to women victims, including rape crisis centres and shelters for physically abused women, run by new voluntary agencies set up for the purpose (see also Chapters 5 and 6 in this volume). These provided direct assistance to women and children in need, but they also collected information to substantiate feminist critiques of the discriminatory ways in which criminal justice and social welfare agencies worked with women as victims of male violence. This dynamic interaction between service provision and demands for legal and institutional changes has remained important throughout the history of victim services, although it can be difficult for agencies that are partly funded by the state to 'bite the hand that feeds them' by collecting evidence of the inadequacies of official responses to victims of crime and campaigning for change. (This is further complicated in the UK by the charity laws which constrain political action by registered charities.)

Awareness of violence and other abuse of women and children was also growing in other countries, helped by some of the research published in the US (Walklate 1989). Europe's first women's refuge was established in London in 1972 and the first Rape Crisis centre, also in London, was set up in 1976. The voluntary sector here did not follow the US example by founding shelters for children, because the statutory social services were more highly developed and were ready, at least to some extent, to take responsibility for dealing with child abuse (although this took some time to develop, and sexual abuse was recognised less quickly than physical abuse). The first national 24-hour telephone service for children, ChildLine, was launched in 1987 as the product of voluntary endeavour, in recognition of inadequacies in the official responses to various types of abuse and distress experienced by children, and has always been insufficiently resourced to deal with all the calls children attempt to make to it (McLeod 1996; ChildLine 2004; NSPCC 2006).[1] This is a common feature of voluntary sector services to victims of crime: the state has encouraged voluntary agencies to provide such services partly because they would be much more expensive if established on a statutory basis.

Analysis of ChildLine's work reveals that criminal victimisation forms a large proportion of its workload, but children and young people also frequently call to discuss issues such as family breakdown, relationship issues and bullying, and to seek advice about sexual health and the 'facts of life'. A smaller but significant number of calls relate to concerns about appearing in court as witnesses. Originally set up in response to public concern about child abuse, ChildLine responded to the issues raised by callers and campaigned on matters such as the difficulties involved for children in giving evidence in court, helping to make the case for changes, including the provisions for vulnerable witnesses in the Youth Justice and Criminal Evidence Act of 1999 (McLeod 1996; ChildLine 2006).

The voluntary sector: a 'victims' movement'?

Some writers, such as Zedner (2002), take for granted the notion of a *victims' movement*. While the range of voluntary sector organisations campaigning for victims' rights and providing services to victims of crime worldwide does have some characteristics of a social movement, it does not fit easily into other aspects of sociological definitions. As Zedner (2002: 432) notes:

In the United States, a strongly rights-based victim movement emerged in the 1960s and 1970s. Largely conservative in outlook, often seeking a more punitive response to offenders, it was in some states associated with demands for the retention or reintroduction of the death penalty.

In this context, it is easy to understand why the range of organisations active on victims' issues came to be seen as a movement: they shared a common ideological stance, although acting as a loose coalition rather than being centrally organised (see Byrne 1997). In other countries, there is less agreement among victims' groups, and less commitment to a political programme. Taking the UK as a case study, it is easy to see why these differences exist.

As noted above, voluntary organisations in the UK traditionally take advantage of the benefits of charitable status, and this restricts their ability to take overtly political positions.[2] They may also have other, more subtle reasons for avoiding political grandstanding. First, they may wish to give priority to first aid, to service provision aimed at alleviating victims' suffering. Second, they may (like Victim Support, the UK's largest national victims' organisation, for much of its history) deliberately decide to maintain a politically neutral position. On the one hand, this has enabled Victim Support to gain trust and considerable financial support from government departments. On the other, it has constrained its ability to criticise government policy publicly (Williams 1999: 91ff.).

But a single organisation rarely has a monopoly of work on victims' issues, and organisations may change over time. Since 1995, Victim Support has become much more of a campaigning organisation, while remaining well within the bounds of what is expected of a charitable body receiving large sums of government funding. Other groups are not constrained by either of these considerations, and feel free to take overt political positions and run controversial campaigns. Some were set up specifically as campaigning organisations, while others have always had a dual role. This range of bodies is not entirely new, but since the 1990s there has been a larger number of victims' organisations in the UK than in the past. Some such groups are transitory, while others have been in existence continuously since the 1970s. This variety and range of groups make the UK victim support scene look more like a social movement than it did in the early days when it consisted of a small number of relatively small organisations. All the same, victims of crime are difficult to corral into a movement, not least because many types of crime involve only transitory contact with any kind of criminal justice or voluntary agency.

It is also debatable whether people who come into contact with services involuntarily can be characterised as belonging to a movement. Interestingly, however, some victims of more serious crime have set up or joined groups such as Support After Murder and Manslaughter (SAMM) and Victim's Voice (formerly the Suzy Lamplugh Trust) which do depend upon people identifying themselves as victims/survivors over a period of time.

Different approaches to supporting victims and raising issues

The examples of SAMM and Victim's Voice demonstrate that some victims volunteer their time to self-help victims' groups. There may be many reasons for this. In some cases, people feel that they are regaining control of their lives by sharing their experience of victimisation with others who are new to the situation. Others are motivated by a desire to give something back in recognition of help they received when they needed it, or alternatively to ensure that a sympathetic service is available to others which was not available to them. Many survivors of serious crime (including the relatives of murder victims) want to see the ways in which victims and survivors are treated change, and they volunteer for victims' organisations with a conscious intention of becoming involved in campaigns. For some, this represents 'an effort to re-moralize a world that appears to have lost meaning' (Rock 2004: 333). Self-help groups such as SAMM consist mainly of people who have experienced victimisation themselves, along with those who are close to them. This range of motives is represented within each agency supporting victims: for example, some Victim Support volunteers are former victims, while some volunteers in many victim agencies are students, retired people or young professionals seeking an interesting way of meeting others and, for some, of enhancing their CVs. The more a victim support group identifies itself as a self-help organisation, however, the more likely it is to become involved in political campaigning. Victims' of severe crimes sometimes see themselves as having been transformed by the experience, and they may feel that this confers on them a unique 'existential legitimacy' (Rock 2004: 333), a view that in some cases leads them to take on a role as representing victims to the mass media.

Domain expansion and specialisation

There has been competition for resources between victim support agencies within the UK in the period since the 1980s, and at times it has made relationships between them difficult at both the national and the local level. Victim Support is the largest and best resourced of the organisations concerned, and it has grown by developing a strong and stable relationship with central government and with the local arm of the state, as well as by a strategy of gradual domain expansion.

In this context, domain expansion refers to organisations' need to evolve and expand in response to a changing context, but the broader meaning of the term is also relevant: social movements grow by identifying and defining new social problems that require their attention (Durand and McGuire 2005; Jenness 1995). As part of this process, Victim Support has expanded onto 'turf' that was previously the undisputed territory of other, specialist agencies. While in the 1970s it dealt predominantly with victims of domestic burglaries and emphasised that its volunteers were not qualified counsellors (unlike some in other support agencies), Victim Support has expanded its remit and improved the training of its volunteers so that many of them now routinely work with the victims of serious crimes of violence and of rape and sexual assault. This has naturally led to competition for resources between Victim Support and other agencies such as Rape Crisis and Refuge. Victim Support has been the undoubted victor in this competitive environment, as the figures relating to central government grants demonstrate. SAMM, on the other hand, has been taken under the wing of Victim Support to a certain extent: the two organisations now share premises, and both have service level agreements with the Home Office.

Victims of certain types of crime may ultimately find that there is less choice when they seek assistance: those who are sufficiently well informed (probably a small minority) currently have access to more than one voluntary agency in the case of offences such as murder, rape and 'domestic' violence. While Victim Support offers a relatively uniform, national service, the less well-resourced agencies such as Rape Crisis and Refuge have more of a political analysis of violence against women and do more in terms of public education, crime prevention and political campaigning. This diversity is healthy, especially if the different agencies work well enough together to refer individuals between them in appropriate cases, as they now generally do. Sadly, the comparatively apolitical approach of Victim Support may make it more attractive to local and national government when it comes to providing funding, and this weakens the other agencies, not least because it means that they have to spend more of their time fund-raising.[3]

Paradoxically, the growth of Victim Support has meant that it is more capable of exercising political influence than in the past, and it has perhaps become correspondingly confident in doing so. Since 1995 it has published a number of documents overtly critical of government policy, for example the various attempts to rein back the cost of the statutory compensation scheme for victims of violent and sexual crime. It has also increasingly employed a discourse of victims' rights rather than solely emphasising their needs (Williams 1999).

As the nationally recognised agency supporting victims, Victim Support has also been able over the years to expand its activities to encompass a range of new categories of crime victims: for example the Witness Service, providing support to victims in court, evolved from 1991 to 2003, the national telephone helpline was established in 1998, and the campaigns to obtain funding to expand the agency's work with rape victims and child victims began in 1996. Hate crime and 'domestic' violence victims increasingly receive services from Victim Support through the normal route of crimes referred to local schemes by the police.

Its dominant position has also meant that Victim Support has achieved a 'quasi-official status' (Goodey 2005: 105) which guarantees it a place at the table when changes to national government policy touching upon victims are being discussed (see Rock 2004). Largely because of the reputation and work of its first director, Helen Reeves (who retired in 2005), Victim Support has also become increasingly influential in Europe: for example, it was involved in drafting the EU Framework Directive Decision on the Standing of Victims' in Criminal Procedure, published in 2001 (Rock 2004).

Small and specialist victim support agencies

There is a wide range of small and specialist victim support agencies, some of which have already been mentioned earlier in this chapter. To give only a few examples, the Zito Trust campaigns on the inadequacy of community care arrangements for people with mental health difficulties, and offers advice and support to 'victims of community care breakdown'. It was set up in 1994 after the murder of Jonathon Zito by someone with schizophrenia, and was for a time supported financially by Eli Lilly, the drug company (Zito Trust 2006).

RoadPeace has been in existence since 1992, and exists to support 'bereaved and injured road crash victims', as well as campaigning for the inclusion of such victims in policies and provisions relating to crime victims. In recent years, government consultations about victim policies have begun to address the issues raised by RoadPeace; it has had a remarkable amount of success given its small size, although the Victims' Code of Practice relates only to victims where an offender has been prosecuted (RoadPeace 2006).

Mankind UK provides a telephone helpline and a counselling service to adult male victims of sexual assault, rape and sexual abuse and their families and friends. Action on Elder Abuse provides information and assistance to people at risk of abusing older people, and to the victims themselves. The Network for Surviving Stalking and the National Association for People Abused in Childhood provide the services suggested by their names. The Roofie Foundation campaigns for the recognition of drug rape as a major crime problem and provides a 24-hour helpline to victims. All have easily accessible websites.

For historical reasons, Northern Ireland has a substantial number of victim support organisations – at least 40 of them (Deloitte and Touche 2001). These range from generic organisations such as Victim Support Northern Ireland (funded by the Northern Ireland Office, and therefore independent of, but closely linked to, Victim Support in London) to the very specialised Psychotherapy and Counselling Network which provides advice and training for 'marginalized people who have undergone trauma' (CAIN 2006). Voluntary agencies have thrived partly because in recent years government funding has been made available to some of them, and also because of a desire to ensure that appropriate help is made available to members of both communities in Northern Ireland. Many small victim support agencies are also involved in publicising paramilitary and state violence and their impact or working for peace, and there is distrust in some communities of statutory provision. Assisting victims (of the 'Troubles' and of ordinary crime) is seen as part of the peace process, but some have argued that the large number of small voluntary agencies is unnecessary; it has led to competition for victims to support in some areas (Deloitte and Touche 2001: 11). Meanwhile, the role of the respective statutory victims' agencies is not well known among the general public, and there is a confusing overlap in titles and functions.[4] This is a legacy of more than 30 years of inter-communal conflict, and it seems likely that not only the trauma, but also the range of provision for dealing with it, will continue for some considerable time.

The UK government and voluntary sector victim support agencies
Specialist agencies can be influential in their own way. There are signs that central government is increasingly turning to them for expertise, and offering

them greater opportunities to provide services. This can perhaps be traced to the establishment of what became the Interdepartmental Working Group on Vulnerable or Intimidated Witnesses shortly before the election of the Labour government in 1997. This was in part a response to an event the previous year which had been widely discussed during the General Election campaign: a woman had been required to give evidence in a rape trial in which the accused had represented himself, and he had subjected her to six days of cross-examination (Rock 2004: 349). Not surprisingly, victim groups had called for a change in the law (eventually achieved in the form of sections 34–40 of the Youth Justice and Criminal Evidence Act 1999). The new government implemented a manifesto commitment by extending the remit of the previous working group on cross-examination of rape victims by unrepresented defendants to cover all vulnerable and intimidated witnesses.[5]

The working group consulted a wide range of disability, civil liberties and women's organisations about how to implement its brief, and 'the definition of who composed the universe of proper "stakeholders"' (Rock 2004: 366) expanded as other organisations representing child victims and the victims of hate crime made approaches to the officials involved. The working group also commissioned a literature review on the issues involved, and this was completed in 1997. A version of it was also included in the working group's final report, which was circulated very widely (Home Office 1998) and was the subject of a three-month consultation period. The voluntary victim support sector took full advantage of this opportunity, and 140 responses were received. Despite some opposition from the judiciary, the consultation led to the government putting forward the Youth Justice and Criminal Evidence Bill, which became law in 1999. It was an important achievement: it not only outlawed defendants cross-examining complainants in person in rape cases – indeed, that was arguably one of its least important provisions. It introduced 'special measures' for vulnerable witnesses aimed at making giving evidence a much less fraught experience, and it began a process of change in the culture of the criminal justice system in relation to victims and witnesses that will probably prove to be irreversible. While there may be situations in which government consultation with stakeholder groups is tokenistic, this was not such a case: the voluntary victim support agencies had spoken with something close to a single voice in response to the consultation, and this apparently gave the Home Office the courage to put forward proposals known to be opposed by senior judges, in the knowledge that elements of public opinion were behind them (Rock 2004).

The nature and extent of voluntary agencies' links with government began to change after 1997. The government provided short-term funding to the Rape Crisis Federation for the first time, although when this expired in 2003 the national federation collapsed. However, the establishment of the Victims' Fund in 2005 provided a way of funding such agencies at arm's length: the political stances taken by many voluntary victim support agencies make it difficult for the government to provide direct financial support. The Victims' Fund consists mainly of cash recovered from offenders, the proceeds of crime which are seized, and the income from the surcharge on criminal convictions and fixed penalty notices. It is perhaps significant that the Victims' Fund is presented in government press releases as relating mainly to organisations supporting victims of sexual crime (Home Office 2005a), which tend to be feminist-inspired and to espouse an analysis of sexual offending as relating to abuse of male power; consequently they also tend to be very critical of central government policies on crime. Maguire and Shapland (1990: 212) held the view that Rape Crisis was 'radicalizing' victims and this may have made it more unlikely that they would receive funding from central government in the past. In fact the Victims' Fund can also make grants to organisations supporting other types of victims, as advised by the Victims' Commissioner. Where Rape Crisis is concerned, the fund has provided vital (if small) funding to a considerable number of local projects (Rape Crisis 2005). It has also made grants to Women's Aid refuges, the national Rape Crisis Co-ordination Group (which replaced the federation), telephone helplines and other projects. At the time of writing, however, no grants have been made to specialist groups catering for the needs of abused women and children from ethnic minorities.[6]

The recognition that groups which are at times critical of government nevertheless have a useful contribution to make is evident also in relation to other victim support organisations. Support After Murder and Manslaughter (SAMM) has received an annual grant from the Home Office since 2000,[7] which is administered by the national office of Victim Support and linked to a service level agreement requiring the production of a regular newsletter and the provision of training to police and CPS staff as well as providing support to families bereaved through homicide (SAMM 2005). In effect, this pays the salaries of SAMM's two staff, and this is likely to alter the dynamics of the relationship between the organisation and the Home Office at least to some extent. Such an organisation has considerable potential to embarrass the government, especially in high-profile cases, and the annual grant of £100,000 brings with it a degree of accountability to the Home Office. The specialist support provided to victims of homicide, and the training provided to police officers and prosecutors, come quite cheaply. Specialist organisations such as Respond also receive government funding. Respond supports both victims and perpetrators of sexual abuse and bullying who have learning difficulties, as well as providing staff training, and it receives funding from the Department of Health as well as from charitable trusts (Respond 2006).

Agencies supporting victims elsewhere in Europe

Services across Europe did not develop along the same lines as those in the UK. Maguire and Shapland (1990: 203) state that the development of the victim movement in Europe was reactive, 'encouraged by a number of international initiatives, such as a convention and two important recommendations by the Council of Europe, in 1983, 1985, and 1987 (on, respectively, state compensation, the position of the victim in the criminal justice system, and on assistance to victims)' rather than proactively as a need was identified by criminal justice professionals or feminists, as took place in the UK.

The development of services may also be affected by cultural and historical factors. Mawby (2003: 165) argues that in former communist countries, volunteering is seen as a throwback to communist times, and that many people need to have two jobs to make a living, which leaves little time for voluntary work on top. Non-state organisations were frowned upon in other Eastern-bloc countries, and voluntary entities had to be registered with the government. For these reasons, victim organisations in Europe are often younger than the UK (1974) and German (1976) agencies. For example, victim support in Slovakia was set up in 1999; in Finland it was established in 1994, and in the Czech Republic in 1991 (Studies in Crime Prevention and Urban Victimisation 2002: 180–1).

A European Forum for Victim Services was created in 1990. This aims to promote the rights and services for victims of crime. It was set up by national organisations working with victims of crime in Europe. The Forum produced a 'Statement of Victims' Rights to Standards of Service' in 1999. This states that victims have a right to free, independent, confidential services offered by trained staff (European Victim Services Forum website). Overall, the Forum is concerned with ensuring that victims have high-quality services available to them. The UK is represented on the Forum by Victim Support, although the extent to which VS can speak for all victim agencies in the UK is limited. This therefore suggests that there is a wide range of local and national services that are not signed up to an organisation that exists with a view to control the quality of victim services. Services can take different forms across Europe: for example, in Germany services are offered by the Weisser Ring. This was set up by a journalist who after making a programme about the criminal justice system felt that victims had been forgotten in the process. The Weisser Ring operates out of 400 offices across Germany and is funded from donations, membership fees and fines (Studies in Crime Prevention and Urban Victimisation 2002; Weisser Ring website). In contrast to this, the Ecole Nationale de la Magistrature states that services for victims are a more recent creation within France. Services in France may be overseen by INAVEM, an administrative centre for victim agencies that does not in itself offer a direct service but instead monitors service quality of over 150 victim agencies (Ecole Nationale de la Magistrature website).

Organisations may also have different definitions of who is a victim of crime. Victim Support in the UK offers a service to 'anyone who has been affected by crime and who wants support'. For Victim Support, Ireland, a victim is 'somebody affected by crime as it relates to the criminal justice system'. For the Associação Portuguesa de Apoio à Vítima in Portugal, it would be 'anyone who has been affected by any act liable to be punished in accordance with the penal code' (Studies in Crime Prevention and Urban Victimisation 2002: 194). Wilson stated that for Northern Ireland: 'Victims were defined as "those directly affected by acts of violence, rather than indirectly affected by the troubles in general"' (quoted in Knox 2001: 184). Knox goes on to argue that a 'victim may include, where appropriate, the immediate family or dependants of the direct victim and others who have suffered harm in intervening to help victims or prevent victimisation' (2001: 184). Victim status is not conferred automatically in any country. This means that the availability of services can be limited. For example, in the UK under the Victims' Code of Practice (Home Office 2005b) services are provided to the victim, or to the victim's family or representative in the case of a fatal incident, but there is no statutory duty to provide a service to a victim *and* their family *and* those who have suffered harm, as in Knox's definition.

Funding for victim agencies in Europe also comes from many sources. For example, the Finnish Victim Support Service, set up in 1994, has received funding from the Slot Machine Association (Victim Support Finland 2003). Victim Support Germany receives funding from donations, memberships and fines imposed on offenders in court. In Slovakia, funding is given by NGOs, grants, but also additional funding is gained through membership fees (Studies in Crime Prevention and Urban Victimisation 2002: 186).

Victim Support in the UK has a service level agreement with the Home Office which it needs to meet as a condition of its funding. Other victim organisations in Europe also have ties to government departments, for example in Belgium, the SAW victim department is involved in 'meetings and negotiations' with the government (2002: 191). In other countries, victim agencies feel that being independent allows them to advocate more freely on the behalf of victims. Victim Support in Germany claim that by remaining independent 'we are free to take our own decisions and do not have to rely on state funding' (2002: 192).

Provision of services to victims of crime

With such a wide range of victim services available, funded from different sources and provided by both professionals and volunteers, service delivery takes many different forms. Support to victims may include emotional support such as a trained volunteer to talk to, face to face or over the telephone. Other agencies such as Respond and Rape Crisis offer services by trained counsellors or psychotherapists (Respond website). Discussing the number of agencies that have been set up in Northern Ireland offering counselling services for victims, O'Hara (2006) questions whether these services always meet the needs of victims. She talked to staff in cognitive behavioural centres who had clients come to them after accessing counselling saying that this had made them feel worse. This may not be due to the quality of the service offered, but that the victims had not accessed the correct form of support to meet their needs. Access to services may also be limited by referral procedures, for example Child Victims of Crime (CVOC) receives referrals from police officers (CVOC website). The impact of this is that crimes that are not reported, or where children are not seen as being affected by them, will not result in a service being offered.

National organisations such as Rape Crisis may also offer different services in different parts of the country depending on the funding that is available within an area. Harne (2002) discusses how Rape Crisis provision may range from a telephone helpline service, survivor groups, to in some areas counselling or services for partners of rape victims. So it seems that victims also face a postcode lottery that governs what services are available to them.

Quality of services to victims of crime

Guidelines exist that offer a definition of 'quality' services for victims (such as the European Forum for Victim Services 1999 Standards); however, signing up to these is optional. There are also specific forums that concentrate on particular offences, for example the Rape Crisis Network Europe (RCNE), which brings together services from 30 countries and has a remit to offer training for volunteers and staff, and to lobby for legal changes for the position of victims (RCNE website).

In some countries, for example France and the United States, national organisations have a supervisory role for smaller victim agencies, rather than offering a service in themselves. NOVA was formed in 1975 by representatives of 'law enforcement victim assistance programs, victim witness service programs, academia, rape crisis and battered women's centers, and victim compensation programs' (Young 2001a: 2). NOVA has set out to increase the professionalism of services that are provided to victims, both by paid and unpaid workers. Young includes in this 'training, ethics and accountability' (2001b: 2). These networks may take a political stance: for example, NOVA often supports campaigns for harsher sentences for offenders.

Victim Support in the UK operates to the following standards (Viney 1999: 2):

- Understanding of the effects of crime
- Independent structure of the organisation
- Confidentiality for the individual victim
- Time to listen
- Knowledge of the criminal justice system
- Partnership with other agencies

For smaller agencies, although there may be standards of service, it can be difficult to know who is responsible for ensuring that these are met, or for knowing what would happen if they were not.

Conclusions and likely future implications

The voluntary sector has different traditions and dominant ideologies in different countries. This is likely to mean that international organisations will be able to share good practice, but not easily to enforce minimum standards for victim care, because victim organisations differ in their emphasis. Some are fiercely independent, while others are largely government-funded; some are primarily service providers, but others concentrate to a greater or lesser extent upon campaigning activities. There are undoubtedly 'turf wars' going on within individual countries where no organisation has a monopoly in providing services to victims of crime.

However, organisations that work directly with victims may have unique moral legitimacy, and thus they are hard to ignore, politically (see Goodey 2005: 128–31). Increasingly, this political role is backed up by the work of international organisations on issues relating to the treatment of victims. While the UN Declaration of Basic Principles of Justice for Victims of Crime and Abuse of Power of 1985 has only persuasive power, it has undoubtedly been influential internationally (and it takes a much wider view of victimisation than most victim support organisations providing direct services). In Europe, however, Framework Decisions promulgated by the Council of the European Union are legally binding (and, as Goodey notes, they are thus correspondingly narrowly-worded). All the same, the 2001 Framework Decision on the Standing of Victims in Criminal Proceedings set out expectations that member countries are taking increasingly seriously. Victims throughout the growing European Union can expect to be provided with (Goodey 2005 130):

- Compassionate and respectful treatment
- Information on the legal proceedings and on their rights
- The presentation of their views to decision-makers
- Legal aid
- Swift case processing
- Protection of their privacy and identity in appropriate cases
- Protection from retaliation and intimidation where required
- Court-ordered and state compensation
- Special treatment to reflect special needs

We know that countries in Europe and elsewhere are at very different stages in terms of meeting these aspirations (see Brienen and Hoegen 2000), but in Europe they have legal force and individual victims have, at least theoretically, means of redress if their rights are not recognised and met. Increasingly, pan-European co-operation will help to ensure that minimum standards are implemented everywhere. This will doubtless be assisted by the involvement of people who can represent the whole of the voluntary victim support sector in their respective countries.

Victim Support in the UK is an example of an organisation that encompasses both service provision and campaigning roles. The balance between the two has altered over the years, and it is more of a campaigning body now than it was in the mid-1990s. The balance is a delicate one, particularly for an organisation that is so dependent on public funding. However, its growth and its increasing influence have given it a 'back-room' influence, and a formal role in public policy-making, which make this less of a problem than perhaps it once was (Rock 2004). There is no directly comparable organisation elsewhere (and there are intriguing differences between the separate but linked Victim Support organisations in England and Wales, Scotland and Northern Ireland: devolution of political power has strengthened the independence of such organisations). However, Victim Support may provide a model for developments in other countries.

The service-providing and campaigning victim support agencies that are not at the negotiating table when policy in relation to victims of crime is made have greater freedom to criticise whatever arrangements are put into place, but this is often at the expense of secure funding – and anyone who has been involved in voluntary agencies knows how dispiriting it is to be preoccupied with fund-raising at the expense of getting the core work done. However, one strong negotiating card held by voluntary victim support agencies is that they provide services at much lower cost than the state could ever hope to do, and for this reason it is in governments' interests to prevent such organisations from going under.

Further reading

For readers wishing to understand the politics of victim support in England and Wales, Paul Rock's masterly *Constructing Victims' Rights: The Home Office, New Labour, and Victims* (Oxford University Press, 2004) is a fascinating and invaluable source. A more general text with a European reach which pays appropriate attention to women's issues is Jo Goodey's very readable *Victims and Victimology: Research, Policy and Practice* (Longman, 2005). Two other recent books are also useful. Brian Williams' *Victims of Crime and Community Justice* (Jessica Kingsley, 2005) looks at recent developments in criminal justice policy from a victim point of view. Sandra Walklate's excellent *Imagining the Victim of Crime* (Open University Press, 2007) is more theoretical, situating victims within a sociological understanding and building upon the author's 20 years of work in this area.

Notes

1 ChildLine merged in 2006 with the National Society for the Prevention of Cruelty to Children, a larger charity, with a view to providing an improved service. In just under 20 years prior to the merger, it worked with almost two million children.
2 The law does, however, allow charities to work alongside closely related campaigning organisations.
3 Victim Support in England and Wales received £29m in central government funding in 2004/05. Rape Crisis operates as a federation of local groups and received no central government funding, except in Scotland where under the National Strategy to Address Domestic Abuse in Scotland ten local Rape Crisis centres received £50,000 per year from 2004/05, as well as £100,000 towards funding the central federation. When the Victims' Fund established under the 2004 Domestic Violence, Crime and Victims Act came into effect in 2006, £1.25m was put aside in 2006/07 to support the victims of rape and sexual assault, and Rape Crisis groups are likely to be among the voluntary organisations bidding for this cash.
4 The Northern Ireland Memorial Fund has a small grants scheme for the benefit of individuals; the Victims Unit at Stormont co-ordinates activity relating to victims of the 'Troubles'; the Victims Liaison Unit supports implementation of the Bloomfield Report on victims of the 'Troubles'; Trauma Advisory Panels are multi-agency panels in each Health and Social Services Board area which co-ordinate the provision of services for victims in response to local need.
5 The working group was also given the task of finding ways to implement the recommendations of the Pigot report on video evidence and a Police Research Group study on witness intimidation: see Home Office 1998: 1.

6 Such groups include Apna Ghar (a domestic violence shelter serving primarily Asian women and children), the Chinese Information and Advice Centre, Jewish Women's Aid, the Muslim Women's Helpline and Southall Black Sisters.

7 One-off grants had been made since 1998 (Rock 2004: 69).

References

Brienen, M.E.I. and Hoegen, E.H. (2000) *Victims of Crime in 22 European Criminal Justice Systems*. Nijmegen: Wolf Legal Productions.

Byrne, P. (1997) *Social Movements in Britain*. London: Routledge.

CAIN (2006) 'List of some of the groups providing support to victims of "the Troubles" in Northern Ireland', http://cain.ulst.ac.uk/issues/victims/victimgroups. htm (accessed 8/5/06 May 2006).

ChildLine (2004) *Championing Children: 18 years of listening to young people*, www. childline.org.uk (accessed 27 January 2006).

ChildLine (2006) *Child Witnesses in Court: What ChildLine's callers have told us about being a witness in court*. www.childline.org.uk (accessed 27 January 2006).

Child Victims of Crime (2006) http://www.cvoc.org.uk/content/aboutus/whatwedo. htm (accessed 25 May 2006).

Deloitte and Touche (2001) *Evaluation of Services to Victims and Survivors of the Troubles: Summary Report*. Belfast: Deloitte and Touche.

Doerner, W.G. and Lab, S.P. (2002) *Victimology*, 3rd edn. Cincinnati, OH: Anderson.

Durand, R. and McGuire, J. (2005) 'Legitimating agencies in the face of selection: The case of AACSB', *Organisation Studies*, 26(2): 165–96.

Ecole Nationale de la Magistrature website: http://www.enm.justice.fr/centre_de_ ressources/dossiers_reflexions/oeuvre_justice/aide_psy.htm (accessed 25 May 2006).

European Victim Services Forum website: www.euvictimservices.org (accessed 22 March 2006).

European Victim Services Forum (1999) *Statement of Victims' Rights to Standards of Service*, www.euvictimservices.org/EFVSDocs/service_Standard_rights.pdf (accessed 22 March 2006).

Goodey, J. (2005) *Victims and Victimology: Research, Policy and Practice*. Harlow: Longman.

Harne, L. (2002) 'The problem of rape and supporting victims', in *Journal of Family Planning and Reproductive Healthcare*, 28(3): 120–2.

Home Office (1998) *Speaking up for Justice: Report of the Interdepartmental Working Group on the Treatment of Vulnerable or Intimidated Witnesses in the Criminal Justice System*, London: Home Office.

Home Office (2005a) 'More support for victims of sex crimes', press release, 24 November, http://press.homeoffice.gov.uk/press-releases/more-supp-for-vic-of-sex-crimes? (accessed 8 May 2006).

Home Office (2005b) *The Code of Practice for Victims of Crime*. London: Home Office.

Jenness, V. (1995) 'Social movement growth, domain expansion, and framing processes: The gay/lesbian movement and violence against gays and lesbians as a social problem', *Social Problems*, 42(1) February: 14–70.

Knox, C. (2001) 'The "deserving" victims of political violence: "punishment" attacks in Northern Ireland', in *Criminal Justice*, 1(2): 181–99.

Maguire, M. and Shapland, J. (1990) 'The "Victims Movement" in Europe', in R.C. Davies, A.J. Lurigio and W.G. Skogan (eds) *Victims of Crime: Problems, Policies and Programs*. California: Sage, pp. 205–25.

Mawby, R. (2003) 'The Provision of Victim Support and Assistance Programmes: A Cross-National Perspective' in P. Davies, P. Francis, and V. Jupp (eds) *Victimisation: Theory, Research and Policy*. Basingstoke: Palgrave Macmillan, pp. 148–71.

McLeod, M. (1996) *Talking with Children about Child Abuse: ChildLine's first ten years*. London: ChildLine.

NSPCC (2006) *ChildLine Set to Join NSPCC*. www.nspcc.org.uk/html/home/nesandcampaigns/childlinesettojoinnspcc.htm (accessed 27 January 2006).

O'Hara, M. (2006) 'Peace of mind', *Guardian*, Society, 29 March, pp. 1–2.

Rape Crisis (2005) 'Victims Fund', www.rapecrisis.org.uk/victimsfund.html (accessed 8 May 2006).

Rape Crisis Network Europe website: www.rcne.com (accessed 25 May 2006).

Respond (2006) www.respond.org.uk (accessed 8 May 2006).

RoadPeace (2006) www.roadpeace.org (accessed 8 May 2006).

Rock, P. (2004) *Constructing Victims' Rights: The Home Office, New Labour, and Victims*. Oxford: Oxford University Press.

Studies in Crime Prevention and Urban Victimisation (2002) Lisbon: Associação Portuguesa de Apoio à Vítima.

Support After Murder and Manslaughter (2005) 'SAMM and the Home Office funding', *SAMM Newsletter*, Summer: 4.

Victim Support Finland (2003) http://www.rikosuhripaivystPs.fi/en/etusivu/index.php (accessed 25 May 2006).

Viney, A. (1999) *Victim Support: The UK Experience*, http://www.aic.gov.au/conferences/rvc/viney.pdf (accessed 25 May 2006).

Walklate, S. (1989) *Victimology: the Victim and the Criminal Justice Process*. London: Unwin Hyman.

Weisser Ring Website http://www.weisser-ring.de/bundesgeschaeftsstelle/kontakt/international/english/index.php (accessed 25 May 2006).

Williams, B. (1999) *Working with Victims of Crime: Policies, Politics and Practice*. London: Jessica Kingsley.

Young, M.A. (2001a) *The Victims Movement: A Confluence of Forces*, http://www.trynova.org/victiminfo/readings/VictimsMovement.pdf (accessed 25 May 2006).

Young, M.A. (2001b) *Standardisation of Victim Service Practices*, http://www.trynova.org/victiminfo/readings/StandardsofVictimServicesPractices.pdf (accessed 25 May 2006).

Zedner, L. (2002) 'Victims', in M. Maguire, R. Morgan and R. Reiner (eds) *The Oxford Handbook of Criminology*. 3rd edn. Oxford: Oxford University Press.

Zito Trust (2006) www.zitotrust.co.uk/about.html (accessed 26 January 2006).

Chapter 10

Matching service delivery to need

Peter Dunn

Introduction

During the 1970s, awareness of the impact of crime on victims, their need for support in dealing with that impact, and their rights to freedom from further victimisation began to emerge. This growing awareness is reflected, in the UK, by the establishment of Victim Support in 1974, the opening of the first women's refuge in London in 1972, and first Rape Crisis centre in 1976. It is also evident in a range of criminal justice reforms in the past three decades that the current UK government now describes as putting victims at the heart of the criminal justice system. But the stimuli behind these initiatives were very different. The establishment of Victim Support was prompted by concerns of people working in offender-focused organisations such as NACRO, the police and the probation service that very little was being done to help victims. They saw that victims were adversely affected by their victimisation, and that they needed help in recovering. Rape Crisis and the start of the women's aid movement reflected more radical feminist concerns about the oppression of women and the complicity of the state in that process. It was based less on concepts of needs, and more on the notion that victims had rights to receive redress and protection from further victimisation (Mawby 1988).

Because this chapter is concerned with matching service delivery to the needs of victims of crime in general, it will address:

- Some of the difficulties inherent in the concept of need, and in assessing it.

- The development of victim services – those of Victim Support in particular – and the extent to which these have been effective in meeting victims' service needs, with reference to the work of other organisations.

- How victim services can involve service users in developing effective practice with victims and witnesses.

What is meant by needs and effectiveness?

Establishing victims' needs, and how effective support organisations are in meeting those needs, is not at all straightforward. Drawing on the work of Armstrong (1983), Newburn argues that the concept of victim need is highly problematic because defining it is bound to be subjective, and there is the question of whose needs are being identified – those of victims, or those of the state and the criminal justice system? (Newburn 1993; Spalek 2006).

When thinking about victims' needs, it is helpful to have in mind:

- The wide variety of human experience of crime and reactions to it. Victims of similar crimes may experience their victimisation completely differently and will have very diverse needs as a result of it. Reactions to crime are affected by a range of factors such as gender, race, culture, sexuality, class, disability, poverty, age, and health. Many of the assumptions that might be made by service providers on the basis of a superficial awareness of these factors are just as likely to be incorrect as correct. An example of this would be the assumption that an elderly woman is likely to be more profoundly affected by the burglary of her home than a young man would be, and the prioritisation of her referral over others that might result from this assumption.

- That some victims underestimate the extent to which they are affected by crime. Claiming to be unaffected can in itself be a coping mechanism.

- That many needs arising from the experience of victimisation are beyond the scope of support services to meet. Someone who has experienced a serious assault may, most of all, want to get away for a good holiday as soon as they have physically recovered from their injuries. It is unlikely that this need could be met by a support service.

- There are difficulties in reliably assessing need, particularly when many victims do not get access to support services. They include victims of corporate crime and victims who do not report crime to the police. Some needs may not emerge until a long time after the event, such as those that would be indicated by a diagnosis of post-traumatic stress disorder. There is also the tendency of some people to overstate their needs, or to conflate needs with wants, while others understate them. Some victims may not be able to articulate their needs and might opt for services on a 'why not?' basis.

- How basing service provision for victims on the basis of needs alone ignores the fact that, to ensure equal justice, victims should be entitled to services, redress, and protection from further victimisation on the basis of rights as well. Otherwise, victims who do not articulate their needs, or who cannot gain satisfactory access to services, are ignored.

For these reasons, the concept of need is problematic and for the purpose of this discussion, it might be helpful to conceptualise needs as service needs. The concept of service needs should reflect a combination of what victims and witnesses want, and what help they might expect to receive to enable them to get over the effects of the crime; underpinned by the principle of victims having a range of rights. These should include rights to fair and respectful treatment, to compensation, to support services, to protection from further victimisation, and to some form of restitution for their loss.

It is also important to be able to describe what is meant by effectiveness. Organisations that support victims may be tempted to see effectiveness in terms of people's satisfaction with the services they provide, whereas measurement of outcomes might be a more valid indicator. But in this context, outcomes are difficult to measure. The best outcome, for a victim, might be the successful prosecution of the offender, no further incidents of victimisation, and adequate recompense for losses. These might all be beyond the scope of a support organisation. Or, the best outcome might be a move to a different area, well away from the offender, with no further involvement in criminal justice processes. A dictionary definition of the term 'effective' is 'having the power to produce, or producing, a desired result' (*Chambers*), so the effectiveness of Victim Support might be determined from the extent to which its services meet outcomes described in its strap-line: 'helping people cope with crime'. But the effectiveness of the organisation varies according to whose interests are the subject of its work. Victim Support's major source of funding, the government, would want it to be effective in contributing to public confidence in the criminal justice system and bringing more offenders to justice by supporting victims and witnesses through the criminal justice process. This might not necessarily be the best outcome for victims, or a suitable imperative for an independent voluntary organisation. Rock describes the difficulty in measuring the cost-effectiveness of victim services: indicators 'would be near to void unless it was known what condition victims were in before they received support, and how long after the event, if ever, recovery could be said to have taken place' (Rock 2004: 56).

Early research on effectiveness and victim satisfaction

An early study of the extent to which Victim Support was effective in meeting victims' service needs was conducted by Maguire and Corbett in 1987. They interviewed 156 victims of burglary, assault and snatch theft who had been visited by Victim Support volunteers. Two-thirds of the people visited said they felt the support they had received had made 'some difference' and 12 per cent said it had made a 'big difference' to the way in which they coped with the emotional aftermath of the crime. Very few criticisms of Victim Support volunteers were recorded, and a group of victims who had received support appeared to have recovered better than a similar group of victims who had not been supported. People liked the element of outreach – the fact that Victim Support had taken the trouble to contact them rather than wait for them to seek support (by this time, it had been demonstrated that victims do not usually, of their own accord, ask for help). Corbett and Maguire described the offer of help in itself as valuable because it demonstrated that someone cared and because 'it was clear that most of those who needed and benefited from the support would not have sought it on their own initiative. Without the visit they would simply have suffered in silence' (Corbett and Maguire 1988: 29). This is consistent with Walklate's view that emotional support is very difficult to quantify: 'human beings are not necessarily very good at identifying the links between their feelings and events which they have experienced' (Walklate 1989: 134). This, combined with a sense of guilt that many victims describe experiencing, is why outreach – offering a service to victims rather than waiting for them to seek it out – is of central importance in effective service provision.

Unfortunately, though, Maguire and Corbett's research, while revealing high levels of satisfaction with Victim Support's service, and which subsequent research has to some extent replicated, does not necessarily show that the service is effective in meeting victims' service needs. This requires more than just indicators of user satisfaction.

What is known about the impact of crime and victims' needs?

Janoff-Bulman and Frieze (1983) reviewed existing research on reactions to victimisation and they suggested that psychological distress in victims results from the shattering of three basic assumptions that most people hold about themselves and the world around them. These are:

- Personal invulnerability, and the sense that we have autonomy.
- A perception that the world is meaningful and ordered.
- A view of the self that is positive.

They argued that 'coping with victimisation is ... a process that involves rebuilding one's assumptive world' and they noted that 'even relatively "minor" victimisations can result in a great deal of suffering and disruption' (Janoff-Bulman and Frieze 1983: 1–2). They found that common emotional reactions to victimisation include shock, confusion, helplessness, anxiety, fear, and depression; and that victimisation can cause post-traumatic stress disorder (PTSD).

According to Janoff-Bulman and Frieze, assumptions are shattered and victims no longer see the world as being a safe place. Victims are confronted with the reality of human malevolence and their own vulnerability, and this can be paralysing. The trauma of victimisation activates a negative self-image. Recovery from victimisation involves 're-establishing a conceptual system that will allow the victim to once again function effectively' (1983: 7). This involves coming to terms with the fact that bad things happen, but that does not mean the world is all bad. They suggested that victims can be helped to:

- Redefine the event to minimise the threat to the assumptive world.

- Make sense of it. This includes finding some purpose in the victimisation or attributing the victimisation, in part, to personal behaviour which can be changed in future as a means of regaining autonomy and control.

- Engage in preventive behaviour, like fitting better home security, moving house, not going out alone late at night, or getting a new unlisted phone number.

This conceptualisation of the impact and effects of criminal victimisation had a major influence on the development of Victim Support's services. The Victim Support handbook *Helping People Cope with Crime* states that:

> most [crimes] have been deliberately caused by another person who has wilfully intruded into the victim's life. As a result, many victims feel they have suffered a fundamental loss of control ... as well as losses of confidence in society, self esteem, or loss of faith in others. (Spackman 2000: 4)

While many of Janoff-Bulman and Frieze's findings have been supported by later research, particularly concerning victims' immediate responses to victimisation, there are a number of problems with their conceptualisation of the shattering of basic assumptions, and the measures that victims can take to regain a sense of autonomy. Their analysis appears based on middle-class, European approaches to how society is ordered and how it functions. There is no recognition that the very many women whose lives are completely controlled by men will have never had the opportunity to feel a sense of autonomy, or the fact that people who have lived in places where violent conflict is a fact of daily life are unlikely to have ever perceived the world as a meaningful and ordered place. For example, Spalek (2006) quotes research from the USA in 2000 that found black people surveyed had the lowest scores for the 'belief in a just world' whereas white males of low socio-economic status showed greater support for the concept. Drawing on the work of Bowling and Phillips in the UK on the impact of racist victimisation, Spalek comments that 'services supporting the victims of crime, developed largely from these mainstream analyses, will insufficiently help victims who belong to minority ethnic communities' (2006: 86). She argues that the secular nature of victim services, which do not address spiritual needs, makes services less attractive to some minority ethnic communities for whom religious affiliation is a fundamental aspect of their self-identity.

Mawby and Walklate (1994) reviewed existing research on the impact of crime, pointing out that assessing emotional effects raises numerous methodological difficulties. They ask, 'how ... does one distinguish between the victim who is unaffected, the victim who experiences emotion but does not express it, and the victim who expresses his or her emotions in privacy?' (1994: 35). They describe US studies that list the emotional effects of crime as being fear, nervousness, anxiety, depression, confusion and paranoia; evident in nightmares, sleep disruption, and difficulty in functioning at work and socially. Rape is identified as likely to have the most serious and long-lasting effects, followed by aggravated assaults, molestation and burglary. Some research in the UK has addressed the added impact of secondary victimisation through the police investigation and court processes, which are shown to add to the emotional effects (Williams 1999). There is evidence that financial losses decrease over time, while physical, social and psychological effects may persist. They cite evidence from the British Crime Survey that personal crimes such as robbery, wounding, burglary and threats affected a larger proportion of victims than did other crimes. Of significance to the question of assessing victim need is the finding that 'supposedly less serious personal crime, incorporating many incidents that have traditionally been "no-crimed"[1] by the police, have a greater impact than do serious household crimes' (Mawby and Walklate 1994: 42).

Evidence of the greater impact on victims of hate crime than other, non-hate motivated crimes is discussed by Hall (2005). Victim Support's 2006 research report on hate crime described effects on victims of constant victimisation to include depression, physical illness, loss of income and employment (due to chronic illness or having to dispose of businesses that became unviable due to frequent attacks). Not surprisingly, what victims most wanted, from police and support organisations, was intervention to prevent further victimisation (Victim Support 2006a).

The emotional impact of rape can be particularly severe, with the primary reaction being fear – at the time of the rape, this can include fear of death: and fear of offender retaliation. Such fear is often long-lasting. Studies also report the extent of depression among rape victims, and the development of phobias that are related to the offence (Newburn 1993). A feminist analysis might argue that effects such as prolonged fear and phobias are not necessarily unhealthy, but are instead a logical, self-protective response to women's experience of male sexual violence.

Morgan and Zedner have documented the effects of crime on children in detail, including the findings of their study of 212 families affected by a range of crimes from theft to rape. They found that 'psychological distress is clearly the predominant reaction of all victims to crime' (Morgan and Zedner 1992: 53), with some children having quite severe reactions to even minor crimes like theft of a bicycle. A boy assaulted in the street was shocked that passers-by failed to help him. They wrote that 'where … adults around fail to stop a crime as it occurs, children are likely to be deeply shaken' (1992: 54). Children living in homes that had been burgled were similarly affected. They felt their home was no longer a safe place. Children who had witnessed a violent assault of another family member were particularly badly affected.

Discussing the impact of repeat victimisation, Shaw (2001) uses the Kübler-Ross bereavement model to illustrate the serious consequences of repeat and chronic victimisation. This is particularly relevant to the impact of hate crime. Shaw's research suggests that people who are repeatedly victimised experience a sense of loss of their normal life so powerful that it is like bereavement. Because victimisation for them is constant, they never get the chance to work their way successfully through the four phases of bereavement that Kübler-Ross identified. The loss they experience is the loss of their life as it was, and the loss of their life as it should be. Discussing Tom, a victim of racist crime who was victimised almost daily, Shaw writes:

> although he speaks of a property crime, this incident affected his fear for his personal safety. The loss is in both material and emotional terms. This

is the nature of the bereavement suffered through chronic victimisation … There appears to be no boundary to his perception of what he could potentially be a victim of and by whom he could be victimised. This creates despair as the whole perception of life is changed. (Shaw 2001: 177)

Mezey's research into links between traumatic victimisation and post-traumatic stress disorder demonstrates the serious emotional effects of bereavement by homicide: 'in particular, high rates of post traumatic stress disorder were identified' (Mezey *et al.* 2002: 65). She found that 37 per cent of relatives of murder victims had started psychotropic medication since the murder and 27 per cent had given up work (Mezey *et al.* 2002). Victim Support's 2006 research into the needs of people bereaved by homicide describes how the effects of traumatic bereavement are made worse by bereaved people's contact with the criminal justice system, whose processes tend to be re-victimising. It shows the crucial role played by the police in either mobilising support services for bereaved people, or – by sometimes making assumptions about who might or might not benefit from support – unwittingly denying access to them (Paterson *et al.* 2006).

Mawby and Walklate (1994) reviewed research on the impact of rape, including on rape victims' partners. Victims reported relationship problems of communication, sexual difficulties, and the need to control emotions. Effects on partners include disbelief, concern, shame, anger, guilt, betrayal and the likelihood of some partners developing post-traumatic stress disorder.

The 1988 British Crime Survey asked about effects of burglary on children in the household and children reported similar problems to adults, with insomnia, nightmares, and bed-wetting experienced by many. Yet, as Morgan points out, 'routine acts of minor violence committed against children, whether by other children or by adult family members, remain resistant to being defined as criminal acts' (Morgan 1988: 81). She cites US Department of Justice research that shows children report higher rates of victimisation than adults (when they are given a chance to report it) and that they have higher levels of fear of crime.

What victims want and need from victim services

Maguire (1985) has reviewed existing research evidence about victims' needs and identified three areas of need:

- Information, including information about progress in police investigation and court processes (if the crime has been reported), and information about crime prevention and insurance. He suggested all police should carry a card with information about services for victims and that the police should have a duty to inform every victim about the outcome of investigations.

- Practical help, including short-term financial support, lock-fitting, claiming insurance or compensation, etc.

- Emotional support, which as we have already noted is an evident need, but difficult to quantify. Two years later, Maguire and Corbett attempted to assess victims' emotional needs based on their understanding of the impact of the event and they concluded: 'about 1 in 4 of the crimes (excluding rape) found to have the greatest emotional impact – i.e. burglary, robbery, snatch thefts and serious assault – and in 1 in 10 of all recorded offences against individuals, can be shown to "need" a visit from a volunteer to provide some form of psychological support or reassurance. Among these victims … will be different levels of need according to their social characteristics' (Maguire and Corbett 1987: 77).

Meanwhile, Shapland conducted a longitudinal study of crime victims over a period of three years in England. She noted the 'persistence and consistency of physical, social and psychological effects over time, compared to the low level and decrease of financial loss'. She noted that 'suffering an effect does not necessarily imply the existence of a need for any particular kind of support' and that it is 'impossible to measure "actual" need' (Shapland 1986: 219). She recommended that a victim-centred assistance scheme should:

- Provide immediate payment for loss of earnings and expenses incurred in connection with the crime.
- Provide a system for practical help and emotional support, co-ordinating the delivery of services and providing information.
- Involve the increased use of compensation by the courts.
- Provide state compensation as a back up.

An important source of data about people's experience of crime and the criminal justice process in the UK is the British Crime Survey, run by the Home Office at regular intervals from 1982 and now conducted annually involving doorstep interviews with up to 40,000 respondents. The Home Office explains that it:

> measures the amount of crime in England and Wales by asking people about crimes they have experienced in the last year. The BCS includes crimes which are not reported to the police, so it is an important alternative to police records. Victims do not report crime for various reasons. Without the BCS the government would have no information on these unreported crimes.[2]

The BCS also asks respondents about other crime-related issues.

In 2002–3 the BCS included questions on support for victims of crime. It found that in the majority of incidents (75 per cent) victims did not want any help or advice. When victims did want help, most wanted information from the police, protection from further incidents, or 'moral' support in the form of someone to talk to. Of respondents who recalled contact with Victim Support, 64 per cent of them rated it as very or fairly helpful. For those who wanted help, someone to talk to was the type of help most often provided (48 per cent received this), whereas fewer people received practical help such as clearing up after the offence (29 per cent) or protection from further victimisation, which 13 per cent of people who wanted such help received. While there was no significant demographic differences in victims' satisfaction with Victim Support services (by ethnic origin and gender), the survey showed that Asian and black people are far less likely to know about Victim Support than white people. While 82 per cent of white people knew of Victim Support, only 47 per cent of Asian people and 66 per cent of black people were aware of it (Ringham and Salisbury 2004).

The BCS findings reported above illustrate an important distinction between user satisfaction and effectiveness. While most people were very or fairly satisfied with Victim Support's services, and most white people knew about Victim Support (and would therefore have the opportunity to use its services), less than half of the Asian people interviewed were aware of Victim Support, and would not therefore have the opportunity to benefit from it. Services that are not readily (and equally) accessible cannot be said to be effective in meeting victims' service needs. However, this does need to be seen in the context of Victim Support being a hard-pressed voluntary organisation that applies most of its resources to service delivery rather than to marketing and self-promotion.

In some ways, the BCS encapsulates many of the difficulties inherent in researching the extent and effects of crime. Currently, it does not include young people under 16. Yet other research suggests that victimisation of young people might be more widespread than victimisation of adults (unpublished NOP survey for Victim Support Week 2003; Morgan and Zedner 1992; Anderson *et al.* 1994). There are considerable methodological problems in gaining information from people on their doorsteps about their experiences of victimisation. People may have different definitions of crime, they may fear, and be affected by, other local problems that they would not describe as crime, or they may experience so much victimisation that they forget the details of individual incidents (Walklate 1989; Hollway and Jefferson 2000); or people may not mention victimisation because they are ashamed about it. The 1996 BCS contained a computerised self-completion questionnaire designed to elicit information about people's experience of domestic violence. The validity of the results – 4.2 per cent of both male and female respondents reported having experienced domestic violence (Mirrlees-Black 1996) – were criticised by other researchers who argued that male respondents in particular had misunderstood questions about their experience of domestic violence, and some had claimed to be victims when they were in fact perpetrators (Gadd *et al.* 2002).

However, these indicators also suggest that organisations who support victims, if they want to be effective in meeting victims' expressed service needs, should:

- Provide interventions that can help protect people from further victimisation – particularly with domestic violence, hate crime and burglary. Following their study of repeat victimisation, Farrell and Pease argued that 'the historical separation between crime prevention and Victim Support seems misguided, even tragic' because of the potential for the likelihood of further burglaries to be reduced by the well-targeted intervention of support combined with crime prevention advice and practical help (Farrell and Pease 1997).

- Provide more practical help and information.

- Market their services to minority communities, who may not know about and feel confident in using mainstream services.

Newburn (1993) draws attention to the lack of research evidence about the needs of victims of crime: if more research existed, the development of support services would be better informed. Similarly, there has not been much research into the effectiveness of support for victims, and most of what is available focuses on interventions with victims of rape, sexual assault, child abuse and domestic violence. Marandos reviewed 20 studies that attempted to measure the effectiveness of programmes designed to help victims recover from criminal victimisation. Outcome measures included PTSD symptom scales and depression inventories. While some of the studies concerned victims of a range of crimes, eight addressed only sexual offences, and nine included only female victims. Ten studies evaluated short-term interventions delivered by counsellors, volunteers, or police officers. In nine of these, there was no reduction in psychological symptoms. Marandos concluded that 'this group of studies did not support the effectiveness of short term interventions' (Marandos 2005: 54); though she noted that methodological flaws including the lack of baseline measures might partly account for this finding. Longer term, highly structured interventions based on the principle of treatment integrity, where they are carried out by trained practitioners, managed effectively, and implemented strictly according to the original design of the programme, did appear to be effective in reducing adverse psychological symptoms. She concluded that 'while (crisis intervention) services may be beneficial for the majority of victims, more intensive and professional services are potentially beneficial for victims who demonstrate high levels of psychological symptoms relating to a criminal victimisation experience' (Marandos 2005: 56). However, this finding contradicts research quoted by Newburn (1993), which indicated the value of informal social support in speeding the recovery of rape victims.

Gaining user feedback about the service they have received is problematic for organisations that support victims. This is because:

- Services have very limited resources that they want to apply to service delivery. There are fears that because getting feedback is time-consuming and expensive, service delivery will suffer as a result.

- The imperative to help victims move on from victimhood has the effect of deterring service providers from wanting to talk to them afterwards about their experience of support, in case this might somehow fix them in a permanent state of victimisation.

- Supporters worry that asking victims to be interviewed by a researcher will somehow be re-traumatising, despite evidence that many people value the opportunity to recount their experiences and comment on the service they have received (Morgan and Zedner 1992; Plotnikoff and Woolfson 2004).

- There may be a fear that finding out what people really think of the service is risky because the organisation might not have the skills or resources to make the improvements indicated.

- Smaller voluntary organisations may not have the skills or resources to undertake complex evaluations, including devising surveys.

This is a serious set of shortcomings because, as Shapland points out, services that have not evaluated, and taken user feedback into account as part of evaluation, run into difficulty because 'when the service hits some crisis (funding changes or dries up, the nature of the need changes, the service needs to undertake a major territorial or organizational expansion) it is extremely difficult for the service (and its funders) to know what it has done or where it is going' (Shapland 1993: 245).

The use of victim satisfaction surveys can provide valuable data about the extent to which services are successful in meeting users' expectations. Since 2004, Victim Support has developed and piloted a victim satisfaction survey that consists of a postal survey, sent to a random sample of victims who have been offered support in the previous few months. It asks about satisfaction with the timing and method of the initial contact, and about the quality of the emotional support, practical help, and information provided by Victim Support personnel. In the 2006 round of the survey 22,505 surveys were sent out and 12 per cent of these were completed and returned. It does not ask questions about people's experience of Victim Support's Witness Service, which has been the subject of recent government research on court user satisfaction (see Angle *et al.* 2003).

The majority of respondents (82 per cent) were satisfied with the first contact made by Victim Support. Those who had been contacted at first by telephone were more satisfied than those who had been sent a letter. In one area, victims were much more satisfied with their contact with Victim Support than in the other areas (91 per cent). Respondents were asked whether they had received emotional support: 45 per cent had, and 42 per cent said they had not. Twelve per cent of respondents reported not having received emotional support, but said they would have liked it. Victims of violent crime or burglary were the most likely to have had emotional support. Respondents were asked whether, and how, the emotional support had helped them: 47 per cent said that the feeling of being understood was the best way of describing the effect of receiving emotional support; 35 per cent felt reassured, 32 per cent felt less anxious, and 23 per cent referred to experiencing an increase in confidence as a result of the emotional support they received; 21 per cent felt less angry about the crime.

The survey form includes space for making written comments. The sense of being listened to and the fact that the supporter was neutral were seen by respondents as important. Respondents wanted more face-to-face contact, and they wanted Victim Support to be more proactive in offering further contact at a later date. In terms of the emotional support they received, 91 per cent of respondents were satisfied. Regarding overall satisfaction with all aspects of the service (emotional support, practical help and information), 78 per cent were satisfied. There were no significant differences in the satisfaction levels of black and minority ethnic respondents, though the sample was small, with only 5 per cent of respondents describing themselves as being of BME (black and minority ethnic) origin.

This survey, and other recent Victim Support research, indicates high levels of satisfaction with the emotional support provided. Respondents tend to be slightly less satisfied with practical help and information, and this might be explained by the fact that the provision of practical help requires greater resources (such as, for example, fitting locks) and the provision of information is often dependent on the response of other criminal justice agencies such as the police. The survey is useful because the data:

- Provides evidence about the way in which victims like to be contacted in the first instance.

- Shows that in general Victim Support meets most service users' expectations – particularly where emotional support is concerned.

- Demonstrates that the quality of practical help and information provided by Victim Support could be improved; and that there is a continuing demand for this service despite recent criminal justice reforms designed to improve the performance of statutory criminal justice agencies in providing information.

- Suggests that people find emotional support in particular to be helpful, and that it may help them cope better with victimisation.

- Suggests that people would like more, not less contact with Victim Support.

- Generates a small amount of qualitative data from respondents, in written comments, that helps inform service development.

- Provides an opportunity for victims who are strongly dissatisfied to request that they are re-contacted by the local Victim Support service.

However, the victim satisfaction survey has a number of limitations. These include the possibility that people who are satisfied may be more inclined to complete and return the survey, though some people who responded took the trouble to write critical comments, too. It is not a complete indicator of service effectiveness – it does not attempt to follow people up over a period of time to ask if recovery is sustained. Nor is it sent to victims who were unable to obtain a service because they were not referred, did not know about Victim Support, or did not perceive the organisation to be relevant to their needs. To work effectively, victim satisfaction surveys require adequate resourcing; in particular, skilled survey design and the availability of staff to input returned questionnaires.

The impact on victims and witnesses of attending court

Elsewhere, Eric Shepherd and I have described some of the emotional impact of giving evidence in court (Dunn and Shepherd 2006).[3] The effects of the court experience are likely to be particularly difficult for witnesses who may be vulnerable or intimidated, such as children, victims of rape, or disabled people. Witnesses' anxiety about attending court is a major source of attrition in rape trials in particular. The NSPCC/Victim Support research study *'In Their Own Words'* found alarming levels of intimidation of young witnesses by lawyers at court, behaviour that was described as 'bullying' by some of the young witnesses' supporters. Most of the young people and their carers reported very high levels of anxiety in the months – or longer – leading up to them giving evidence. For some young people, this resulted in bed-wetting, nightmares, poor school attendance, and being prescribed tranquillising or anti-depressant medication. Asked by the researchers what they would like to say to criminal justice staff about their experience, it was noted that one young witness wanted to tell the judge to 'intervene to make sure things are fair in court, when lawyers intimidate people and witnesses get confused' (Plotnikoff and Woolfson 2004: 7). While anxiety about giving evidence is normal and cannot be avoided, high levels of distress, disturbance, and bullying by lawyers cannot possibly serve the interests of justice and is clearly damaging to witnesses, especially children.

Summary: victims' needs and what works in meeting those needs

Before going on to describe some examples of initiatives designed to help victim services be more effective in meeting service needs, it may be useful to draw together some of the research evidence on the impact of crime, review some of the difficulties inherent in assessing need, note some of the difficulties involved in determining effectiveness, and remind ourselves of the context in which most victim services operate.

Impact and effects of crime are varied, wide and unpredictable. One person may be relatively unaffected by crime, whereas another victim of a similar crime may experience overwhelming loss, fear and depression, perhaps sustained over a long period of time, from which they struggle to recover. Emotional effects are likely to persist longer than practical and financial effects. Extreme emotional effects, such as post-traumatic stress disorder, may not become apparent for a long time after the crime. Crimes that might be described as 'minor' can have a devastating effect on victims who experience them regularly, for example hate-motivated harassment. Many victims and witnesses find that contact with the criminal justice system is a source of re-victimisation. The fact that there are distressing effects arising from victimisation does not necessarily imply that victims need (or want) to receive a service to help them cope with those effects. Most victims may not want to receive a service; but many victims tend to underestimate the emotional effects of victimisation, perhaps as a means of coping with those effects.

Need is a problematic concept and needs are difficult to establish. Many of the needs that arise from victimisation would be beyond the capacity of support organisations to meet. Services to victims of crime should not be based solely on the concept of need, but designed to uphold victims' rights as well. 'Needs' should be conceptualised as service needs, which take into account people's expressed needs, shaped by their expectations, and assessed with a view to what is effective in meeting those needs. This conceptualisation is helpful as a way of not setting services up for failure in attempting to meet potentially unlimited need. The service needs of many victims tend to be overlooked and are under-researched. Quoting Lipsky (1982), Soetenhorst wrote: 'need becomes a tricky issue when related to a quota of help or support to be offered. The type of assistance offered often defines the need' (Soetenhorst 1989: 116).

Effectiveness is about more than service user satisfaction. Establishing effectiveness should include considerations of equal accessibility, relevance to all victims and communities, and the ability of a service to help victims achieve desired outcomes. Services that are attractive or accessible only to particular sections of the overall community cannot be considered effective. Effectiveness depends on being able reliably to assess people's service needs and provide services that are based on evidence gained from scientific research. But the practical difficulties in establishing evidence-based practice are great.

The context in which victim services operate is an important consideration in trying to assess effectiveness. Mawby and Walklate point out that in most countries, victim services are based in the voluntary sector. They rely heavily on volunteers and there are wide implications of this. Funding is often short term and can be withdrawn in the event of a change in the political climate. Or it may be short term in the expectation that the organisation will find ways of becoming self-funding. Victim and witness services have to compete with other voluntary organisations to attract personnel from a limited pool of potential volunteers, and they may have to spend more time on fund-raising than on supporting victims.

Effective services to victims of crime

So, is Soetenhorst's suggestion that 'the type of assistance offered often defines the need' correct? Is it unfortunately true of victim services that 'the public wants what the public gets', as The Jam, in their hit song 'Going Underground',[4] described the general state of affairs in 1980s Britain? To look at the extent to which services are effective in meeting the service needs of victims and witnesses, it would be helpful to explore first, the extent to which victim services make individual assessments of need before delivering a service; and second, ways in which services consult service users and involve them in managing and developing their services.

Maguire wrote in 1985 about victims' need for emotional support, practical help and information; and those are the main components of Victim Support's service. Victim Support's original purpose was to mobilise resources in the community to help victims of crime, not necessarily to meet all victims' service needs itself. This marked an acceptance that an organisation with insecure and very limited funding could never hope to meet every type of need arising from victimisation. It was also in recognition that it would be wasteful to try to replicate services that are already available in the community. It upheld the principle that statutory organisations such as the police and health service had responsibilities towards victims of crime and they should be held to account for delivering, not excused from it. For those reasons, Victim Support does not see itself as an advice organisation or a counselling service (counselling should be available from the National Health Service for people who have been traumatised through victimisation). But for years, there have been tensions developing for victim services.

These tensions have been described by Newburn (1993), who pointed out that there is a conflict between the original support role, based on short-term intervention by 'good neighbour' types of people, who have basic skills in listening, empathising and signposting; and the demands of the more intensive, long-term work that organisations like Victim Support are increasingly doing. This is occasioned by the continuing increase in the proportion of victims supported who have experienced more serious types of crime, such as assault, rape and robbery, or who have been bereaved by homicide. Since 2001, Victim Support's referrals of victims of violent crime have risen from 352,000 to 538,000, while referrals of non-violent crime have declined very slightly (Victim Support 2006b). Victims of violent crime are likely to need longer-term work that may demand greater competence in the supporters who deliver it. Newburn considers that, with continuing resource limitations, there is a need to decide how to handle this tension, or the service to victims of 'less serious' crime will suffer (though the meaning of 'less serious' is difficult to specify).

To some extent this tension is played out in the current debate in Victim Support about counselling. Victim Support's *National Standards* discourage local Victim Support services from offering counselling as it is beyond the scope of the 'core' service. This is because it requires high levels of specialist competence in the personnel delivering it and in the staff who supervise them; and because it should be the responsibility of local health services to provide counselling. Yet, many local Victim Support services end up offering counselling: because they find it is not readily available locally; because the distinction between emotional support and counselling is difficult to establish; and because staff and volunteers, some of whom are counselling students or ex-counsellors, like to be thought of as 'counsellors' rather than 'supporters' – it sounds more professional and it helps confer a sense of enhanced status. At some point, victim services will have to resolve these types of tensions because people who use services are likely to have their expectations raised as the government publicises its agenda for 'putting victims at the heart of the criminal justice system', creating more informed demand for services that in turn raises expectations.

Assessing service needs

Almost all the available literature on assessing victims' needs concerns assessments made, by professionals in criminal justice agencies or support organisations, of general victim need. Some of the literature refers to victimisation surveys that are a useful indicator of impact of crime and of needs, on which the development of new services can be based (and there are difficulties with victimisation surveys, described earlier in this chapter). There seem to be very few examples of individual needs assessment tools in use with victims of crime. This suggests that there is a real problem in matching service delivery to need. How can we determine what type of service we should be offering a victim if we have not properly assessed their service needs?

This section describes two initiatives that attempt to fill this gap: the Victim Support *Young People's Support Pack* and the Victim Care Unit assessment tool.

Young people's support pack

This was devised by Victim Support in 2002 to help with the development of services to young victims of crime. It was originally envisaged as an assessment tool, but during its development it became clear that what was needed most was a means of enabling better communication between supporters and young people, that should in turn contribute to the achievement of an accurate assessment of service needs. Many children and young people are reticent about describing highly personal events, and younger children, in particular, may find it hard to articulate their feelings about painful experiences. The pack consists of nine components:

- *An infant activity sheet*, designed to help young children aged up to 8 years to express their feelings about the crime. There are pictures of faces which suggest a range of feelings associated with victimisation. Children can point to the face that matches their feelings, and they are invited to draw a picture of what happened or write a story.

- *A junior activity sheet for children aged 8 to 11.* This has a similar purpose to the infant activity sheet, but is more appropriate for older children. As well as enabling them to talk about how they feel, it encourages them to describe things they like doing, who is important to them, and what would help them feel better.

- *A senior activity sheet, for teenagers.* This uses sentence completion exercises like 'This is how I felt at the time ...' and 'The things I would like to happen now are ...' It enables young people to think about previous difficult events, and how they have dealt with them. All three activity sheets are designed as discussion starters, to help the child or young person conceptualise how they feel about what has happened to them, articulate that to their supporter, and think about what might help them feel better. It also encourages them to decide who else in their life might be able to help them (parents, teachers, friends, siblings, etc.) and what they would like from Victim Support. Supporters are trained not to question young people, nor to attempt to interpret what younger children might draw on their activity sheet. Completed activity sheets remain the property of the young person.

- *Case record sheet*. This records all the contact details of the young person, with information about the offence, and a list of actions that the supporter and the young person will take together in the support process.

- *Assessment of competence*. This is used when a young person under the age of 16 requests a service without parental involvement, and there is a need to assess their competence to receive support in these circumstances. If they are assessed as competent, i.e. mature enough to be able to receive support independently, they will be supported. If not, they are signposted to other sources of help and support.

- *Child protection form*. This is used in the event of there being any child protection concerns, as a means of recording the nature of the concerns and the action to be taken by the service manager. This would normally involve referral to social services.

- *Indirect victims checklist*. This helps the volunteer to ensure that if other members of the household have been affected by the crime, they can be offered a service too.

- *Checklist for parents or carers*. This reminds the volunteer to ask a short set of questions about the service needs of their child.

- *A guidance booklet* to help people use the pack correctly.

The *Young People's Support Pack* was independently evaluated by a young people's organisation as part of the piloting process. The evaluators tested it with groups of young people in schools and other settings, and they held interviews with staff and volunteers who had used it. Young people generally liked the activity sheets, which they thought were aimed well at their particular age group. They were thought suitable for both males and females, and for different ethnic groups. They thought the activity sheets were accessible, clear and easy to understand. They did not like the fact that they were asked to write their name on it, which made them worry about confidentiality. Space to record names will be deleted when the pack is revised. Staff and volunteers also liked the activity sheets. These were highly regarded for their ability to help structure support sessions, for being compatible with other tools such as toys, and their ability to enhance the quality of work with young people.

Victim Care Unit assessment tool

In April 2006 the UK government published its proposals for a restructuring of services to victims of crime in England and Wales through the establishment of Victim Care Units (VCUs).[5] Four models were proposed, all involving the receipt of referrals from the police, a basic needs assessment, and the commissioning of a service from local service providers, using a case management approach. The government envisages that Victim Support will have a central role in the provision of VCUs. At the time of writing, VCUs are being piloted in three areas and part of the piloting involves the use of initial needs assessment tool, devised by Victim Support. The three page form will be used by VCU staff when making their first contact with a victim and it will determine the nature of the initial response. It incorporates a case record form, a means of monitoring outcomes, and a reminder to re-contact the victim at a later date to repeat the offer of support – something that recent research suggests will be valued by some victims who decline the first offer of support.

Involving service users in service development

The involvement of service users has been achieved to a greater extent in services for victims of domestic violence than in general victim services, reflecting perhaps the different philosophy from which domestic violence projects have grown. This involves a feminist approach that emphasises the rights of women to be free from male violence, and incorporates an understanding of the dominant nature of male violence in society and the lack of coherent challenge to it by state institutions. This section also describes some recent service-user consultation carried out by Victim Support to help establish more effective ways of engaging with young victims of crime.

Women's Aid

The Women's Aid guide to user participation, *Professionals by Experience*, opens with some quotes from women who have experienced domestic violence and tried to get help. Two of these are: 'How do they know what to do if they don't ask women in the situation? It doesn't make sense, does it? It's stupid if they go and set up things up without women knowing about it and without asking women what they need ...'; and 'Women should be involved so agencies can be more effective. So women who have had all their power taken away can have a voice' (quoted in Hague *et al.* 2002: 4). They show how service-user participation can operate at four levels:

- User consultation: service users are consulted but little changes as a result.
- User influence: where service users can influence the policy-making and service provision of the agency.
- User power, where service users have real power to make decisions and to participate in the decision-making processes.
- User control, where service users control and run the service.

Hague *et al.* argue that service user involvement is all the more important in domestic violence work because the experience of many women referred to mainstream services is that they have to search around a variety of services before they receive help. When they do receive it, that help is often inadequate or unsafe, and their experiences of public sector services are that they are generally patchy and judgemental. Community or service-user consultation is therefore not only good practice, it is also a requirement now in UK legislation such as the 1998 Crime and Disorder Act; and the need for meaningful, effective consultation is often specified in performance indicators. Where domestic violence is concerned, being part of that process can lead to the 'collective empowerment' of women.

Without attempting to write an inevitably unsatisfactory summary of the Women's Aid guide here, it seems important to mention the key principles for service-user involvement that Hague *et al.* (2002) describe:

- Equality and diversity – the importance of making sure that those being consulted are a diverse range of people, not just those who are articulate, white, and middle class.

- Safety – for women who are victims of domestic violence, the most unsafe time for them is just after they have split up with their partner. This has implications for confidentiality, safe venues for consultation meetings, safe transport to venues, etc. Current service users may not have sufficient energy to contribute to consultation if they are still in a state of crisis.

- The importance of supporting the work properly – consultation can be hard work for those involved. Service users should be paid for their time, and supported through the process.

Involving one or two service users in forums or management meetings run by professionals often does not work, due to different communication styles, official language, and procedures that might be alien to service users. As one service user said: 'It's hard for survivors to attend meetings, however welcoming they try to be. You still feel small and as though you shouldn't be there when they are all professionals. It's probably best to consult survivors in other ways' (quoted in Hague *et al.* 2002). The 'how to do it' section of the guide provides detailed advice on how to set up and manage consultation processes, using a range of different methods.

Victim Support

Victim Support's work with young people has been helped by consultation in schools and other young people's venues. This is part of a wider project to produce guidance for local Victim Support's services on stakeholder consultation. The guidance will define stakeholders as 'anyone with a reasonable interest in what we do and how we do it' and the first step in consultation is to identify who these stakeholders are. At the very least, they consist of service users, members of local communities (who are indirect beneficiaries of Victim Support's work, and who are also potential service users and volunteers); criminal justice agencies, other statutory organisations; voluntary organisations with whom we work in partnership; the media; regulatory bodies such as the Charity Commission; and Victim Support volunteers, staff and trustees. The benefits of stakeholder consultation are:

- It is an opportunity to listen, first hand, to real needs and expectations.

- It establishes the credibility of the organisation and its services by demonstrating user involvement in planning, targeting and delivery of services. This is particularly important when competing for scarce resources.

- It is an opportunity to learn about others' experience and priorities, and promote development. This is particularly important where there is a lack of research evidence about people's service needs.

- The principle of consultation complements the principle of victims and witnesses having the right to expect the highest standards of service provision, and it meets the imperative of working in partnership with others.

The benefits of stakeholder consultation are that it stimulates ideas, which helps to create variety and innovation in services (subject to the resources being available to provide them). By obtaining information about need, it enables more effective targeting of services, and it gives more accountability to stakeholders.

There are other imperatives for involving young services users. The British government's Green Paper *Every Child Matters*, which has shaped children's policy and the provision of statutory services since 2003, specifies that services should involve children and families in putting together the picture of their needs and in designing the service to meet those needs. For all these reasons, victim services must be willing to change the way that decisions are made to enable the participation and influence of all stakeholders.

Victim Support has consulted with young people in schools and other venues including youth clubs, holiday activity schemes and pupil referral units.[6] This programme of consultation was initiated in response to the findings of research in 2003 for Victim Support by NOP. As well as revealing high levels of victimisation among young people, it showed that 60 per cent of young people had not heard of Victim Support but that almost all thought they would find the type of services the organisation provides helpful if they were victimised.[7] There was a need to establish how young people perceived Victim Support and what type of help they would want if they were victims of crime. Getting young people to think about how crime victims feel was not difficult: many of them had experienced victimisation in the form of theft, assault, bullying and even robbery. Significantly, not many described these as 'crimes', which they thought was a term applicable to only the most violent or extreme forms of victimisation such as armed robbery, murder and rape. This has implications for crime surveys because it shows how important it is to check people's definitions of concepts such as crime before attempting to ask them if they have ever been affected by it (see Hollway and Jefferson 2000).

Victim Support staff, teachers and youth workers held focus groups with young people where they asked them for their reactions to various key words – including 'victim', 'support' and 'crime' – as well as to logos that a support organisation might use. Most young people perceived the word 'victim' to have negative connotations of weakness with which they would not want to be associated. The word 'support' was viewed much more positively. Despite this mixed response to the terms, young people wanted a logo that looks 'cool' but also conveys a sense of what the organisation actually does. For this reason they were still in favour of the name 'Victim Support'.

Concerning young people's service needs, participants were asked to write on self-adhesive notes what the effects of crime are for young people, and to stick these inside the outline of a young person drawn on a big sheet of paper. They were then asked to write down things that might help a young victim, and stick these on the outside of the outline. Perceived needs included talking and being listened to; friends and family; diversion; justice and recompense; practical solutions; stopping the victimisation; understanding why it happened; and getting information. These points covered much that Victim Support already provides, which was useful in validating the existing service model, but it also suggested a number of new areas of service provision. These included a young people's website; the option to make initial contact via texting, freephone and e-mail; and individual support through a choice of locations, including school drop-in sessions. Contact details need to be easy to remember and one young person suggested the Victim Supportline phone number should be '0800 ROBBED'. Building young people's confidence and trust was seen to be vital. They suggested this should be done through personal recommendation and sponsorship, and through more awareness raising work in schools. Above all, the young people suggested the service should be free, flexible, responsive to their needs, informal, non-judgemental; and that it should feature work in the long term using diaries, plans, and follow-up contact to see how things are going.

Finally, there is value in involving service users in working groups and forums that are concerned with service development, provided that the principles of service user consultation as described by Hague *et al.* (2002) are upheld. However, one individual cannot hope to provide the range of diverse feedback that is needed, and should not be expected to try to speak for all. Victim Support involved an 18-year-old member of the UK Youth Parliament, who had experienced both racist and homophobic crime, in its young victims project steering group. Rather than being a sole representative of all young people's views, his insight as a victim of crime combined with his expertise in suggesting ways of effectively engaging with and consulting young people was of great help to the project.

Evaluating the effectiveness of victim services and victims' movements

Writing in 1981, Salasin suggested that existing barriers to the delivery of services to victims were societal attitudes towards them (which include a view that victims are somehow to blame for their victimisation); the hegemony of the criminal justice system in the victim domain; and the organisational capacities of mental health service providers to respond to victims' needs. In her chapter in the same book, Chelimsky wrote that the most important challenge to victim services will be to:

develop a network of caring people who can muster the public and private support required, develop the services which give victims the help they need, but also keep the agencies charged with delivering those services and that help firmly focused upon their task. (Chelimsky 1981: 95)

So, what has changed since 1981 and has the challenge described here been met?

Evidence of some of the barriers being overcome and the challenges having been met to some extent is provided by increased general awareness of the damaging impact of crime, and the ability of the thinking encapsulated in Mawby and Walklate's (1994) concept of critical victimology to combat the predominance of earlier notions of victim precipitation. The capacity of the mental health system to support victims of crime has probably not changed significantly since the 1980s. It has not needed to, because support organisations have developed to meet those needs and health services have been able to avoid developing large new areas of service provision to reduce the effects of victimisation. Even Victim Support, which is not a counselling organisation, has in many areas stepped in to provide counselling for victims of crime whose health might be further affected if they have to wait six months or more for a counselling referral via their doctor. The inadequacy of health provision for victims of crime is described in *Criminal Neglect*, which states that:

waiting times for counselling … are a frequent problem, especially when many would benefit from an immediate intervention. We believe that people who have been victims of crime should not have to pay for the services they need simply to get help more quickly. (Victim Support 2002: 8)

The hegemony of the criminal justice system in the victim domain has reduced as victims' organisations have increased in number and scope. This has prompted the UK government, for example, to try to reclaim that hegemony in its efforts to present the police, Crown Prosecution Service, etc. as the primary provider of services to victims and witnesses. 'We're reforming the justice system so that the needs and rights of victims and witnesses are placed at the heart of what we do', proclaims the Home Office website.[8] This is being worked towards partly by the requirement that criminal justice agencies operate to a Code of Practice[9] for victims and witnesses that makes requirements as to the standards of services that such agencies provide. The Home Office information about it omits all but the briefest mention of Victim Support. This, and the claim to put victims and witnesses at the heart of what they do, illustrates how the UK government has sought to claim for itself the credit for supporting victims. Many of the requirements in the Victims' Code of Practice are about increasing public confidence in the criminal justice system and bringing more offenders to trial by ensuring victims report crime and turn up at court to give evidence. This is not the same as ensuring that support is available to all victims, including those who do not have the confidence to report crime in the first place, and victims of corporate crime that is rarely subject to prosecution, such as pension fraud. The individualisation of victims' experience, and the construction of victims as individual consumers of the criminal justice system, masks any recognition of the structural or corporate components of victimisation. It thereby impedes effective challenges to established, oppressive structures. As Spalek points out:

> although victims' needs are acknowledged, they are framed and used according to the bureaucratic and political goals that prevail. As a result, the help that is afforded to victims is limited, and this has important consequences for individual victims as well as for the wider gender, class, ethnic, religious and other group collectivities they may belong to. (Spalek 2006: 116)

Driven by the need to survive financially, organisations involved in supporting victims inevitably get drawn into focusing primarily on the needs of victims and witnesses who play their part as 'active citizens' and as consumers of criminal justice.

The bureaucratic and political goals that Spalek refers to are set out in detail by Rock (2004). He argues that during the 1990s in Britain the government conceptualised victims not as citizens (who as citizens would have rights) but as consumers or customers of a new, business-like and managerialist criminal justice system. Through a range of criminal justice system charters and service standards, victims could be presented as being at the heart of the criminal justice system, without being accorded rights to be a party in legal proceedings, have a role in court, or participate in decision-making: 'victims were, in effect, to be contained within a political *cordon sanitaire*' (Rock 2004: 19). This culture of consumerism has wide implications for victim services, whose 'customers' will want their expectations met through services that are effective in achieving the outcomes they want.

Williams points out that 'while undoubtedly at the "respectable" end of the spectrum of victims' organisations, Victim Support has been very effective in raising public and political consciousness of victims' issues without undertaking much overtly political campaigning' (Williams 1999: 92). However, much of the credit in terms of raising public and political consciousness should also go to organisations who might not wish to be seen as so respectable. These include feminist organisations that have challenged the male-centred consensus that accounted for notions of victim precipitation; groups of victims who are brought together by their mutual anger at their treatment by the criminal justice system; black and minority ethnic, disabled, and gay and lesbian writers and organisations who have drawn attention to the way in which the state often tacitly condones the victimisation of people who experience disadvantage and discrimination; and self-help organisations whose members feel their needs have not been met by mainstream provision for victims and witnesses.

Matching service delivery to need: summary

In trying to draw the various threads in this chapter together, I hope that what is emerging is that, in the UK at least, victim services have achieved some success in matching service delivery to need, but that success is qualified by some significant areas of difficulty that present major challenges in developing supportive interventions that are fit for the first decade or two of the twenty-first century.

These areas of difficulty include:

- The distinction between wants, needs and expectations, and the requirement that these are understood before service needs can be properly assessed or planned for; being affected by victimisation does not necessarily mean people need or want support.

- While Victim Support's service model is based on the three categories of need – emotional support, practical help and information – that were identified by Maguire and Corbett's research in 1987, there have been only very limited achievements since then in refining needs assessment methods or in demonstrating the effectiveness of services in meeting identified needs.

- The tendency of victim services to not respond adequately to the particular needs of minority groups. Examples of this failure include continuing to offer the service by letter to asylum-seekers who don't speak English, or failing to promote diverse and inclusive images that might enable lesbians, gay men and transgender people to feel confident in approaching the service for help.

- The relative newness of service-user consultation in victim services and the difficulties caused when evidence as to the unsuitability of a service calls for an about-turn. Such change, in organisations that are under-funded and lightly managed, is hard to achieve.

- The failure of victim services to orchestrate adequate protection from further victimisation for those who are most vulnerable.

- The inaccessibility of established services to some victims, which makes those services completely ineffective for those victims.

- The volunteer-led ethos which, while having tremendous benefits in terms of providing value for money and fostering community responsibility for tackling the effects of crime, can work against the achievement of quality standards, the involvement of service users, and the adoption of treatment integrity and evidence-based practice.

The effectiveness of victim services in the UK, and elsewhere, has been evident in propelling governments into accepting responsibility for promoting a better response to the needs of some victims of some crimes, through funding victim services and through reforming the criminal justice system to make it less re-victimising; and in developing services that meet some of the needs of some victims. The next challenge is to refine and improve assessment methods, ensure service provision is more evidence-led, and begin to address the legitimate needs and rights of people whose victimisation is ignored, who do not get access to the criminal justice system, and who are currently not served by established provision.

Acknowledgements

I am grateful to Alison Walker, Research and Development Administrator at Victim Support National Office for conducting the initial literature search on assessing victims' needs. I also very much appreciated the improvements suggested by Professor Paul Rock who read the first draft of this chapter.

Further reading

Davies, P., Francis, P. and Jupp, V. (eds) (1996) *Understanding Victimisation*. Northumbria: Social Science Press.
Davies, P., Francis, P. and Jupp, V. (eds) (2003) *Victimisation: Theory, Research and Policy*. Basingstoke: Palgrave Macmillan.
Goodey, J. (2005) *Victims and Victimology: Research, Policy and Practice*. Harlow: Pearson Education.
Kemshall, H. and Pritchard, J. (eds) (2000) *Good Practice in Working with Victims of Violence*. London: Jessica Kingsley.
Rock, P. (1990) *Helping Victims of Crime: The Home Office and the Rise of Victim Support in England and Wales*. Oxford: Clarendon Press.
Wortman, C. (1983) 'Coping with Victimisation: Conclusions and implications for further research', *Journal of Social Issues*, 39(2): 195–221.

Notes

1 Not recorded by the police as a crime.
2 Home Office website: www.homeoffice.gov.uk/rds/bcs1.html.
3 For information about the experience at court of people bereaved by homicide, see Paterson *et al.* (2006).
4 The Jam, 'Going Underground', track 12 on their 1983 album *Compact Snap!* (Polydor, London).
5 http://press.homeoffice.gov.uk/press-releases/Compensation-victims-crime?version=1.
6 Where children who are excluded from mainstream schools are educated.
7 NOP telephone poll commissioned by Victim Support for Victim Support Week, February 2003.
8 http://www.homeoffice.gov.uk/crime-victims/victims/Victims-rights/?version=2
9 The Victims' Code of Practice has now replaced the Victims' Charter.

References

Anderson, S., Kinsey, R., Loader, I. and Smith, C. (1994) *Cautionary Tales: Young People, Crime and Policing in Edinburgh.* Aldershot: Avebury.

Angle, H. Malam, S. and Carey, C. (2003) *Key Findngs from the Witness Satisfaction Survey 2002.* London: Home Office.

Chelimksy, E. (1981) 'Serving Victims: Agency Incentives and Individual Needs', in S. Salasin (ed.) *Evaluating Victim Services.* Beverly Hills, CA: Sage.

Corbett, C. and Maguire, M. (1988) 'The Value and Limitations of Victim Support Schemes', in M. Maguire and J. Pointing (eds) *Victims of Crime: A New Deal?* Milton Keynes: Open University Press.

Dunn, P. and Shepherd, E. (2006) 'Oral Testimony from the Witness's Perspective – Psychological and Forensic Considerations', in A. Heaton-Armstrong, E. Shepherd, G. Gudjonsson and D. Wolchover (eds) *Witness Testimony: Psychological, Investigative and Evidential Perspectives.* Oxford: Oxford University Press.

Farrell, G. and Pease, K. (1997) 'Repeat Victim Support', *British Journal of Social Work*, 1 (Februry): 101–13.

Gadd, D. *et al.* (2002) *Domestic Abuse Against Men in Scotland.* Edinburgh: Scottish Executive Central Research Unit.

Hague, G., Mullender, A. and Aris, R. (2002) *Professionals by Experience: A Guide to User Participation and Consultation for Domestic Violence Services.* Bristol, Women's Aid Federation of England.

Hall, N. (2005) *Hate Crime.* Cullompton: Willan Publishing.

Hollway, W. and Jefferson, T. (2000) *Doing Qualitative Research Differently: Free Association, Narrative and the Interview Method.* London: Sage.

Janoff-Bulman, R. and Frieze, I. (1983) 'A theoretical perspective for understanding reactions to victimisation', *Journal of Social Issues* 39(2): 1–17.

Maguire, M. 'Victims needs and victim services', *Victimology*, 10.

Maguire, M. and Corbett, C. (1987) *The Effects of Crime and the Work of Victims Support Schemes.* Aldershot: Gower.

Marandos, O. (2005) 'Assessing the effectiveness of interventions designed to support victims of crime: A systematic review of psychological outcomes', in 'The Development of a Psychometric Scale for the Assessment of Emotional Vulnerability in Victims of Crime', unpublished doctoral dissertation, University of York.

Mawby, R. (1988) 'Victims' needs or victims' rights: alternative approaches to policy making', in M. Maguire and J. Pointing (eds) *Victims of Crime: a New Deal?* Milton Keynes: Open University Press.

Mawby, R. and Walklate, S. (1994) *Critical Victimology: International Perspectives.* London: Sage.

Mezey, G., Evans, C. and Hobdell, K. (2002) 'Families of homicide victims: Psychiatric responses and help-seeking', in *Psychology and Psychotherapy: Therapy, Research and Practice*, 75: 65–75.

Mirrlees-Black, C. (1996) *Domestic Violence: Findings from a new British Crime Survey self completion questionnaire.* London: Home Office.

Morgan, J. (1988) 'Children as victims', in M. Maguire and J. Pointing (eds) *Victims of Crime: A New Deal?* Milton Keynes: Open University Press.

Morgan, J. and Zedner, L. (1992) *Child Victims: Crime, Impact and Criminal Justice.* Oxford: Clarendon Press.

Newburn, T. (1993) *The Long-term Needs of Victims: a Review of the Literature.* London: Home Office.

Paterson, A., Dunn, P., Chaston, K. and Malone, L. (2006) *In the Aftermath: The Support Needs of People Bereaved by Homicide.* London: Victim Support.

Plotnikoff, J. and Woolfson, R. (2004) *In Their Own Words: The Experiences of 50 Young Witnesses in Criminal Proceedings*. London: NSPCC and Victim Support.

Ringham, L. and Salisbury, H. (2004) *Support for Victims of Crime: Findings from the 2002/2003 British Crime Survey*. London: Home Office.

Rock, P. (2004) *Constructing Victims' Rights: The Home Office, New Labour, and Victims*. Oxford: Oxford University Press.

Salasin, S.E. (1981) 'Services to Victims: Needs Assessment', in S. Salasin (ed.) *Evaluating Victim Services*. Beverly Hills, CA: Sage.

Shapland, J. (1986) 'Victim Assistance and the Criminal Justice System: The Victim's Perspective', in E.A. Fattah (ed.) *From Crime Policy to Victim Policy: Reorienting the Justice System*. Basingstoke: Macmillan.

Shapland, J. (1993) 'Monitoring Victim Needs and Victim Programmes', in A. Alvazzi del Frate, U. Zvekic and J.J.M. Van Dijk (eds) *Understanding Crime: Experiences of Crime and Crime Control*, Acts of the International Conference, Rome, 18–20 November 1992. Rome: UNICRI.

Shaw, M. (2001) 'Time Heals all Wounds?', in G. Farrell and K. Pease (eds) *Repeat Victimisation*, Crime Prevention Studies vol. 12. Monsey, NY: Criminal Justice Press.

Soetenhorst, J. (1989) 'Victim Support Programs: Between Doing Good and Doing Justice', in E.C. Viano (ed.) *Crime and Its Victims: International Research and Public Policy Issues*. New York: Hemisphere.

Spackman, P. (ed.) (2000) *Victim Support Handbook: Helping People Cope with Crime*. London: Hodder and Stoughton.

Spalek, B. (2006) *Crime Victims: Theory, Policy and Practice*. Basingstoke: Palgrave Press.

Victim Support (2002) *Criminal Neglect: No Justice Beyond Criminal Justice*. London: Victim Support.

Victim Support (2006a) *Crime and Prejudice*. London: Victim Support.

Victim Support (2006b) *Victim Support Community Service 2005/6 Statistical Report* (www.victimsupport.org.uk).

Walklate, S. (1989) *Victimology: the Victim and the Criminal Justice Process*. London: Unwin Hyman.

Williams, B. (1999) *Working with Victims of Crime: Policies, Politics and Practice*. London: Jessica Kingsley.

Chapter 11

The victim in court

Andrew Sanders and Imogen Jones

Introduction

For many people, appearing in court is, or would be, a frightening prospect. Many people have never spoken in public, let alone been challenged in public. For victims of crime, the pain of victimisation will often be accentuated by both this prospect and the experience of giving evidence. A survey of witnesses in 2000 found that almost a fifth felt intimidated by the process, and in a further survey in 2002 33 per cent said they did not want to testify again (Whitehead 2001; Angle *et al.* 2003). Appearing in court can, in other words, amount to secondary victimisation. On the other hand, many victims want to tell their story and see 'their' offenders publicly brought to justice. If this does not happen then there may, again, be secondary victimisation. The problems that arise can be categorised as follows:

- How to give victims a voice or influence in the handling of their cases
- How to enable victims to give a full and accurate account of their evidence
- How to make court buildings and courtrooms non-threatening, while still enabling the accounts of victims to be challenged fairly.

In this chapter we discuss these problems and recent attempts to overcome, or at least to alleviate, them. Special attention is given to 'vulnerable' victims, for whom all these problems will be more intense. Victims of rape and of domestic violence are important sub-groups of the 'vulnerable' victim category. These sub-groups face particular difficulties, to which there have been important policy and legal responses of various kinds; but these are not covered in detail here as they are the subjects of Chapters 5 and 6.

The key issue throughout this chapter is how far the criminal justice system can be made as fair as possible for victims without becoming more unfair to accused people. All too often the rights of the accused are portrayed as obstacles in the way of fair treatment for victims. It is true that some aspects of criminal justice involve a trade-off from one to the other, and we acknowledge when this is so. But some reforms are possible that enhance the victim experience without undermining the rights of the accused, and such reforms may even be positive for both. The more that criminal justice can develop these 'win-win' processes, and move away from what is currently a 'lose-lose' situation in many respects, the better for victims in particular and justice as a whole.

An important background point is that most crimes are not dealt with in court. Substantial numbers are 'diverted' from court – they become the subject of no further action or official warnings from enforcement agencies such as the Health and Safety Executive (HSE), police, and CPS. Victims of health and safety offences, in particular, suffer from a prosecution rate of probably less than 1 per cent, despite these offences being arguably as serious as 'normal' offences prosecuted by the police and CPS (Hawkins 2002; Sanders and Young 2006: chapter 7). As this chapter is concerned with the court, we do not pursue this point. But the problem of victims lacking voice or influence in relation to 'their' cases in court, and attempts to alleviate this, are similar to those in relation to the earlier stages of investigation and detection.

The problem of adversarialism

Like other common law jurisdictions, such as most of the USA, Australia and Canada, England and Wales has an adversarial system. In adversarial systems there are just two parties to criminal disputes: the prosecution and the defence. Although the prosecution acts on behalf of the victim in some respects, this is almost incidental to the fact that, in both formal and substantive terms, the prosecution acts on behalf of the state – or, in the language used in the Code for Crown Prosecutors, the 'public interest'. The theoretical safeguard for victims is that they can prosecute privately, but this is very rarely a practical option, and the CPS can, in any event, take over private prosecutions and then drop them (Sanders and Young 2006: chapters 7 and 13).

Decisions may be taken, for example, to not prosecute, to accept guilty pleas on relatively minor charges, to drop some or all charges, and so forth, regardless of the views or interests of victims. In the inquisitorial systems that are usual in European jurisdictions, by contrast, there may be any number of parties to the dispute, and victims are usually recognised as one of them. This does not necessarily give them control of 'their' cases – in fact it rarely, if ever, does so – but it gives them a place at the virtual table. Because common law systems require enforcement agencies to act in the 'public interest' those agencies tend to have more discretion in these adversarial systems than they do in most inquisitorial systems. The latter tend to be based on the 'legality' principle that greatly restricts discretion (Tak 2005). The common law approach enables large numbers of 'detected' cases to be diverted away from courts, although diversion is increasingly a feature of other systems, too, and 'regulatory' offences (such as against health and safety) are almost universally dealt with less punitively than 'normal' crimes (see for example Gobert and Punch 2003).

Victims in court and adversarialism

Adversarial systems affect witnesses in court in two different ways. Paradoxically, one is the failure to recognise victims as parties, while the other puts them arguably overly centre-stage. Taking the latter first, one of the central principles of adversarialism is that of orality. Unlike in inquisitorial systems, that make considerable use of written evidence gathered in advance in the form of dossiers, in adversarial systems most evidence must be given orally in court and be open to challenge. Thus victims, and their evidence, may be challenged more directly and robustly in adversarial systems than in other systems. We shall examine these differences, and their implications, later.

The failure to recognise victims as parties is particularly problematic in relation to the 'mass production' of guilty pleas – perhaps the most striking characteristic of adversarial systems. Inquisitorial systems generally require full hearings in all or most cases, bringing offenders to justice publicly and generally allowing victims a role in this. The principle of orality makes adversarial trials much longer than inquisitorial trials, thus creating pressure to avoid them. For these and other reasons defendants in most cases are encouraged to plead guilty. This is done by offering one or more of: reduced sentences, less serious charges, and fewer charges. There is therefore usually no trial. Because victims are not parties, these decisions, which many victims object to, are taken on the basis of the 'public interest' (which usually means saving the resources that would otherwise be expended on a long and uncertain trial) rather than the interests of the victims (Fenwick 1997).

Sometimes the trial 'cracks' at the last moment, adding to the distress of the victims. In *Peverett* ([2001] 1 Cr App R 416), for example, the five victims who turned up expecting to give evidence at what they thought would be a trial were said to be stunned when they were told they would no longer be allowed to tell their story, and by the non-custodial sentence that was the state's end of the bargain; and so, many charges were dropped resulting in no convictions being recorded in respect of four of the victims (*Guardian*, 30 October 2000). Further, in *Bargery* ([2004] EWCA Crim 816) serious violence charges were reduced to 'threatening behaviour', even though the two victims alleged that they were kicked and beaten when lying on the ground, leading to another non-custodial sentence. Cases like this, and *Peverett* in particular, led to such public disquiet that the Code for Crown Prosecutors now states that the interests and views of victims should be taken into account in plea bargaining, but 'the decision rests with the Crown Prosecutor' (para. 10.2) (all these developments are discussed further in Sanders and Young 2006: chapter 8).

Another problem with guilty pleas is that the hearings consist of a brief statement of facts by the prosecutor followed by a usually more lengthy statement of mitigation by the defence. Victims have no opportunity to challenge this mitigation – which may blame the victim for the offence or impugn the victim's character – nor to highlight what they may see as the crucial facts, because they have no formal role in court hearings. In rape cases, for example, the violence that accompanies sexual assault is often overlooked (Kelly *et al.* 2005: 75), and when charges are reduced, as in the cases discussed above, the violence that is put to the court cannot be greater than fits the reduced charges. This is a particular concern in racially aggravated and domestic violence offences (Burney and Rose 2002; Burney 2003; Gus John Partnership 2003; HMCPSI/HMIC 2002, 2004).

The Code of Practice for Victims of Crime

As a result of not being parties to hearings, victims have traditionally not even known when 'their' cases were being heard – or even that they were coming to court at all – apart from in contested cases. But as we have seen, few cases are contested, and even then victims were involved only when they were required to give evidence. Thus for the last 20 years or so of the twentieth century it was commonly said that victims were marginalised, ignored or silenced. This has now changed to some extent. We have seen that Crown prosecutors are now obliged to consult victims about plea bargaining. But a prerequisite for this, and for any other involvement in their cases, is being given information about them. The Code of Practice for Victims of Crime (and its predecessor, the Victim's Charter of the 1990s – see also Chapter 8 in this volume) is intended to ensure that victims are no longer ignored and need no longer be silent. Whether they do, or should, remain marginal or influential – or, more precisely, in what respects they should be influential – is another matter to be discussed later. The governments of the new millennium have been strong in rhetoric about putting victims at the centre of the system, and 're-balancing' it in their favour, but we shall see that the reality is another matter.

The Domestic Violence, Crime and Victims Act 2004 created the Code (OCJR 2005), with oversight from a Commissioner for Victims and Witnesses.[1] The police should provide information to victims such as whether a suspect has been arrested (and if so what happened subsequently) and, where applicable, whether a defendant has been given bail (para. 5.9–26); police/CPS Witness Care Units should provide information and support to victims in contested cases (para. 6); and the CPS should provide information about decisions for which it is primarily responsible, such as plea bargaining or dropping cases altogether. Prosecutors should also offer to meet victims in particularly serious cases (para. 7), although this is currently rare.[2] The result should be better information for victims of crime than was previously provided. But, as in the past (Hoyle et al. 1998), many victims are not told why decisions were taken that they might not agree with, and so there is no 'right to understand'. The Code also provides 'enhanced' service rights for vulnerable and intimidated victims (see later).

No rights in any real sense are provided by the Code, because these provisions are not enforceable in the courts. The Code states: 'Where a person fails to comply with this Code, that does not, of itself, make him or her liable to any legal proceedings ... Breaches of this Code should be referred initially to the service provider(s) concerned' (para. 1.3 and 1.4). If that does not lead to a satisfactory result, the case can then be referred to the Parliamentary Ombudsman who can award a 'consolatory' (not compensatory) payment. Not only is the Code weak in this respect, it only applies to offences dealt with by the police and CPS. In other words, the victims of health and safety offences, identified earlier as being the most shabbily treated group of victims, remain out of the loop. It is as though government is in denial about the hundreds of homicide victims, and thousands of criminally maimed victims, literally lying on the floors of factories and building sites around the country.

In conclusion, adversarialism leads not only to a minority of victims having 'their' cases dealt with in court, but to just a minority of that minority having any role to play in those decisions and in those cases that do come to court. But at least the side-effects of adversarialism are now ameliorated to the extent that most victims in cases that do come to court do at least now know what is going on, and there is the potential for some of them to be more supported and/or involved than they were.

Preparing for court

We observed earlier that adversarialism has a paradoxical double-effect on victim-witnesses: in failing to recognise them as parties to 'their' cases, thus refusing to accord them specific participatory rights or assistance; and in putting them centre-stage in the witness box. Thus at one and the same time they are put under pressure by cross-examination (and the fear of it) and denied help in coping with it. All witnesses might find this double-effect difficult, but it is particularly problematic for many victim-witnesses. For it is precisely the (often distressing) crimes to which they fell victim, and for which many will have no support, about which they will be cross-examined. For many years even counselling in respect of the crime itself was denied to victims who would be giving evidence, in case this could be construed as 'coaching' for the eventual trial (Sanders *et al.* 1997). This was rightly criticised in *Speaking up for Justice* (discussed later) (Home Office 1998: recommendation 28). There is still a cautious attitude towards counselling because of the risk that the defence will claim that the victim's evidence has been contaminated by it, but CPS guidance should now ensure that counselling is not routinely withheld any more.[3]

When victims are contacted by Victim Support (see Chapters 9 and 12 in this volume), they are now made aware that counselling is available to help them deal with the effect of the crime. If the victim requests counselling, Victim Support writes to the CPS informing them of this, and in any event, the topic of the counselling will be limited to the impact of the crime on the victim and not the details of the crime. For particular categories of victims the provision of counselling will be routine, for example, by Sexual Assault Referral Centres (SARCs) for rape victims.

Only a system in which the orality principle is central would go to the extreme and unnecessary lengths that our system has done in the past in order to avoid contamination of oral testimony. The problems have been acknowledged and partially (though separately) addressed in the last few years.

First, vulnerable and intimidated witnesses (VIWs) are identified as a group with particular needs by the Youth Justice and Criminal Evidence Act 1999 (YJCE) and by a range of administrative measures following on from *Speaking up for Justice*, the Home Office (1998) report that laid the foundations for this legislation. The YJCE categorises vulnerabilities according to either the nature of the crime itself (primarily sexual offences and domestic violence), objective characteristics of the victims (youth, old age, mental illness or disability) or actual or feared intimidation.[4] This categorical approach fails to recognise that vulnerability is on a spectrum (rather than yes/no) and that it is personal to individuals: for example, a person who is 'normal' in most contexts may be particularly frightened of public speaking and/or of speaking in court in particular; and a young person may be unusually confident and not 'vulnerable' in this sense at all. However, to allow victims to self-identify would lead to huge numbers that would overload the limited services available for 'vulnerable' victims, while relying on police or other services to use sophisticated judgements to identify relevant vulnerabilities would be unwise when, at present, they do a poor job of identification (on both points, see Burton *et al.* 2006b).

Thus while victims are still not recognised as a legal category, some help is available at least to those most likely to find court processes an ordeal. We shall see in the next section that this help takes a variety of forms in court. But the prior step is getting victims to court. *Speaking up for Justice* recognised that the more vulnerable the victim the less likely, in the absence of help, they are to be prepared to give evidence, to be seen as credible and reliable by the police and CPS, and indeed to be credible and reliable (particularly in the face of robust cross-examination) in court. Much can be done to prepare witnesses (particularly vulnerable witnesses) for court, which should not only help them to give the best evidence they can, but also reduce the fear, apprehension and, in some cases, trauma brought by the contemplation of giving evidence (and, indeed, even of court cases where they do not have to give evidence, but where they wish to attend despite having to see the defendant). This all has the added benefit of increasing the confidence of the police and CPS in the victims' ability and willingness to give evidence, making 'their' case more likely to go ahead.

Second, witnesses are recognised as an administrative category in need of assistance (although less extensive assistance than is available to vulnerable victims), as are victims.[5] The Code of Practice for Victims of Crime makes special provision for vulnerable victims (para. 1.6 and para. 4). Pre-trial familiarisation and preparation, like counselling, has caused difficulties, although (again like counselling) it is now restricted only to the extent that preparation might constitute coaching.[6] It has great value in helping to conquer the fear of the unknown (Burton *et al.* 2006a: chapter 5). American research on rape victims has shown the particular value of pre-trial preparation (Konradi 1997; also, in the European context, see Bacik *et al.* 1998), although this goes further than is currently regarded as proper in the UK. All victim-witnesses should therefore be offered pre-trial familiarisation visits (Code, para. 1.6) and be supported by police/CPS Witness Care Units. These units are part of the Home Office 'No Witness, No Justice' initiative (see PA Consulting 2004 for an interim evaluation). They must carry out a 'needs assessment' (para. 6.2) – for example, on the need for an escort to and/or from court, for intimidated witnesses particularly. Further, when cases do come to trial, prosecutors should introduce themselves to victims at court and answer any reasonable questions they might have (para. 7.9). Court staff must ensure that 'where possible' at criminal proceedings, relevant victims have a separate waiting area and a seat in the courtroom away from the defendant's family or friends (para. 8.4).

We can only speculate on how effective the Code will be. It should certainly lead to some benefits as on many of these points victims have not been well treated. Research on vulnerable and intimidated witnesses (VIWs) found that pre-trial familiarisation visits and escorts were probably the most useful services that could be offered, yet they frequently were not offered (Burton *et al.* 2006a: chapter 5). The needs of vulnerable victims with mental or learning disabilities were particularly neglected (but also see Plotnikoff and Woolfson 2004 in relation to child witnesses). Overall, nearly half of all VIWs in an extensive survey seemed to want (more) help and support (Hamlyn *et al.* 2004: chapter 2).

Facilities in court have been traditionally poor. Improvements have been made in recent years but many of the concerns reported in the mid to late 1990s (Shapland and Bell 1998; Plotnikoff and Woolfson 1998) remained some years later. Witness satisfaction surveys conducted in 2000 and 2002 (Whitehead 2001; Angle *et al.* 2003) found that the most important unmet needs of witnesses concerned lack of information and separate waiting areas. A major problem for VIWs, in particular, once they arrive at court, is the possibility of coming face to face with the defendant, and delays or having to wait before giving evidence (Burton *et al.* 2006a: chapter 6). However, Hamlyn *et al.* (2004: chapter 3) found that the provision of separate entrances and waiting areas did not necessarily prevent defendants and VIWs seeing each other – in toilets, outside the courtroom and so forth – which was upsetting for many VIWs. Thus while the finding of Burton *et al.*, that in the Crown Courts surveyed in 2003–04 virtually all had separate waiting areas, is welcome, the finding that little over one-quarter had separate entrances and that hardly any had separate toilet facilities, are not. And facilities in magistrates' courts still lag far behind those of Crown Courts.

But even this does not get to the heart of the problem. In all of the four areas in the study by Burton *et al.* (2006a) the courts had separate waiting facilities for prosecution and defence witnesses. However, many witnesses were ambivalent about this, and felt that separation was more like 'segregation'. They were therefore reluctant to use the specially designated area even though they were uncomfortable with the prospect of seeing the defendant and their supporters in the shared waiting areas. Some felt that separate waiting facilities for prosecution witnesses sent a distorted message about whose side the court was on when the defendant is, quite properly (when on bail), free to roam the court building, yet the prosecution witness is invited or discouraged from doing so. They felt that the defendant should be 'separated' rather than them.

Keeping the defendant and their supporters out of the main court waiting areas is arguably not feasible or desirable. But helping prosecution witnesses keep out of court buildings except when they are needed is. They could be 'summoned' by pager or mobile phone. Hamlyn *et al.* (2004: chapter 6) found that while this was not done at all, VIWs overwhelmingly supported the idea: 64 per cent said that this would have been useful (for further discussion see Burton *et al.* 2006a). The Code now provides, in a welcome response to these findings, that witnesses should not have to wait for hours in court to give evidence, and – if there is a delay – to be able to leave court and be contacted (e.g. by mobile) (para. 8.6 and 8.7).

The establishment and expansion of the Witness Service (WS), initially in the Crown Court only, but now across the whole network, has been an important development of the last decade or so (Riding 1999).[7] In most of the respects discussed above – pre-court familarisation visits, witness care in court, and even the identification of witnesses as vulnerable in many cases – the WS is now crucial. Indeed, of all the criminal justice agencies, the WS seem to be the most highly regarded by witnesses (perhaps not surprisingly, as their duty is to witnesses alone instead of being split across several groups) (Hamlyn *et al.* 2004: chapter 7; Hunter *et al.* 2004).

Coping with testimony

Cross-examination

In an adversarial system it is essential that the defence be allowed to test prosecution evidence; and if there is reasonable doubt about its strength, there should be an acquittal. This is true in inquisitorial systems too: article 6 of the ECHR (guaranteeing a fair trial) enshrines the right of defendants to examine, or have examined, witnesses against them. However, the interests of witnesses, as well as defendants, are incorporated into the concept of a fair trial (Jackson 2005), allowing limits to be set on the way witnesses are treated. But drawing the line between what is robustly fair and what is viciously destructive of the character of the witness is often difficult. Judges may stop oppressive cross-examination, and have been encouraged to do so more readily (Royal Commission on Criminal Justice 1993: 122; discussed in Sanders and Young 2006: chapter 10). But they are reluctant to do this, because a consequent conviction could be overturned on the ground that judges did not give the defence lawyer a full opportunity to cross-examine (Davis *et al.* 1999; Burton *et al.* 2006a).

We have seen that the Witness Service, and the assistance it can facilitate (especially pre-court familiarisation), has helped alleviate many of the problems faced by victims in court, and that the WS is greatly appreciated by witnesses. However, traditionally witnesses are on their own once they get to the witness box, which can still be terrifying, no matter how much the WS and pre-court services prepare them for this and reduce their anxiety (Riding 1999). Many witnesses find cross-examination, and sometimes questioning from the judge, upsetting and challenging. Vulnerable witnesses, and victims of sexual offences in particular, are more upset and stressed by cross-examination than anything else that happens in relation to their cases (Hamlyn *et al.* 2004). Several examples are given by Burton *et al.* (2007). Advocates are poor at modifying their questioning styles when dealing with witnesses with learning disabilities (and, by implication, with other vulnerable or nervous witnesses: Kebbell *et al.* 2004). The effects of this on witnesses can ruin an otherwise strong case as well as weak cases. Aggressive and humiliating questioning in court is therefore a major cause of attrition (Kelly *et al.* 2005). It is sometimes hard for magistrates, judges and juries to know whether testimony lacks credibility because it really is untrue or mistaken, or because questioning unfairly tripped up or confused the witness.

There is no official guidance as to what level of aggression a lawyer can use when cross-examining a witness. Whether a line and style of questioning is deemed acceptable is only subject to the opposing counsel's right to object and the trial judge's discretion to intervene. Basic guidance is provided in the Code of Conduct of the Bar (Bar Council 2004: para. 708). It obliges lawyers to make the court aware of legal decisions or statutes that are relevant to the current case, and not to make scandalous statements or those which are simply intended to annoy the witness or suggest that victim or witness is guilty of a crime or any misconduct unless the allegations go to an issue in the case. No guidance is given on what kind of tone of cross-examination is acceptable. The Code is therefore an inadequate safeguard against unduly distressing cross-examination.

Many people, including members of juries, believe that they can tell when a person is lying, despite research evidence to the contrary (Riding 1999). Thus the behaviour and performance of witnesses may be as important as the substance of what they have to say, even though psychological research 'shows that confidence is not an indicator of reliability, that inconsistency is not conclusive of inaccuracy, and that a witness may appear nervous not because she is lying but because she is stressed' (McEwan 1995). These problems are often exacerbated by the practice of giving witnesses their 'statements' to read in advance. These statements are often couched in 'police language', and therefore unfamiliar. Moreover, a surprisingly large number of people are to a greater or lesser degree illiterate, but hide this, so when they are given 'their' statements they cannot understand them, but do not admit to this. They are then often tripped up in the witness box when what they say in court is inconsistent with what they allegedly said to the police (Sanders and Young 2006: chapter 6; Burton *et al.* 2007).

Vulnerable and intimidated victims and witnesses

There have in recent years been several new measures aimed at alleviating these problems. However, most of them have been directed at 'vulnerable' witnesses, primarily through the YJCE 1999.[8] 'Vulnerability' is a misleading catch-all term. Different people, even those with ostensibly similar vulnerabilities (such as youth or learning disability) have diverse concerns about court and respond differently to the variety of measures to alleviate these concerns (Burton *et al.* 2006a). The police and CPS should therefore assess every individual's particular needs, in 'early strategy meetings' where necessary. Research has found shortfalls here (see for example Cooper and Roberts 2005). Also, many vulnerable witnesses are not identified as such until 'spotted' by the WS (Hamlyn *et al.* 2004; Burton *et al.* 2006a, 2006b). Whether or not the Code's requirements and the new Witness Care Units will make a difference remains to be seen. For the problem is not so much a lack of will as limited resources and skills training – problems that cannot be wished away by legislative *fiat* (let alone the quasi-legislative *fiat* of the Code).

What kind of 'needs' are being assessed? We saw earlier the importance of pre-testimonial needs such as for familiarisation/preparation and escorts. As far as giving evidence is concerned, there are several different 'special measures' (a technical term used in the YJCE: see Ellison 2001). Originally limited to Crown Courts, but now being introduced in magistrates' courts as well, they include screens (to shield witnesses from defendant(s) and vice versa); video-recorded evidence-in-chief (recorded by the police soon after the crime is reported, requiring the police to correctly identify the witness as vulnerable at that stage); live television link (allowing the witness to give evidence in a separate room or even a separate building); clearing the public gallery; removal of wigs and gowns; and the use of communication aids. Video-recorded pre-trial cross- and re-examination and the use of intermediaries are at varying stages of development (see later).

Different measures will suit different witnesses. They therefore need to be properly informed about how these measures work if they are to express an informed view on what might help them, but VIWs currently rely heavily on the police to give them this information. Currently the police often recommend the use of a live television link in preference to screens, for example, without consulting the witness, despite the statutory obligation, in some types of case, to do so. Court staff have observed that the police are often badly informed about the facilities of the court and how special measures work in practice, and therefore the witnesses are also often badly informed and disabled from making informed choices (for further discussion see Burton *et al.* 2007). Nonetheless, these measures do generally seem to help victims and witnesses (Hamlyn *et al.* 2004; Cooper and Roberts 2005), and we can only expect them to do so even more in future as officials become more skilled in matching what is needed with what is available, and in guiding people accordingly.

Two developments are yet to be implemented and/or evaluated. The first relates to cross-examination. Pre-recorded examination-in-chief helps vulnerable witnesses to the extent that they spend less time in the witness box and can relate their version of events while their memories are clear and fresh. But then being cross-examined in court, weeks or months afterwards and without getting 'warmed up' by giving evidence first, takes away many of these benefits, even if the cross-examination is done over CCTV. It has long been hoped that cross-examination and (where needed) re-examination could all be done in advance, but this is not a straightforward matter and may never take place (Cooper 2005).

The second development is the provision for 'intermediaries' to 'translate' questioning for witnesses who cannot cope (YJCE, s29). However, this too presents formidable problems as the nature of adversarial cross-examination has been given insufficient attention thus far (Ellison 2002). Pilot schemes are now taking place. It is reported that 'In at least 20 trials, the courts have now listened to and accepted the evidence of witnesses who would never otherwise have been heard' (Wurtzel 2006). Not only can intermediaries 'translate' for witnesses and courts, but they can participate in pre-trial planning. Whether the problems that rightly concern Ellison are being overcome remains to be seen.

For victims of sexual offences, and those of certain other crimes, the YJCE prevents defendants cross-examining in person and restricts the use of certain types of evidence (on the witnesses' sexual history in particular) being elicited. But while the defendant's belief in consent, which is often impossible to disprove (Harris and Grace 1999; HMCPSI/HMIC 2002), remained a defence to most sexual offences, the rate of acquittals and secondary victimisation of witnesses in court was inevitably higher than in most other offences. Perhaps changes to the substantive law, particularly on consent in the Sexual Offences Act 2003, will make these provisions more effective (McEwan 2005).

These measures will not solve the problems that vulnerable victims have with the criminal justice system. That is not because of a lack of will on the part of government or criminal justice agencies, or (primarily) a lack of resources. The problem is that vulnerable victims are in structurally weak positions in society. Social and cultural change might alleviate this for the victims of sexual offences and domestic violence, but not for the aged and mentally vulnerable. Legal solutions to social problems can only ever be partial solutions.

If we do not remember that these problems are not completely solvable, we are likely to go to more and more extreme lengths, with harmful consequences, to try to solve them. People with very low actual or mental ages, for example, simply have less comprehension than other people. There comes a point when a witness has to be regarded as not competent to give evidence or, in some cases, not competent to give evidence on matters of detail or in relation to forgotten events.[9] It may be tempting in future to allow witnesses who understand very little of what is happening to give evidence, or to restrict cross-examination further. But this would erode the rights of suspects and defendants even further than has already happened over the last few years, increasing the risks of conviction of innocent defendants. It hardly needs to be said that not all alleged victims and witnesses, whether vulnerable or not, tell the truth (for example, see Sanders and Young 2006: chapter 13); not all are correct in their beliefs and recollections; and some defendants are innocent even when victims tell the truth if, for example, a defence is proved or there is a lack of *mens rea*. As things stand, however, most of these measures give genuine help to victims without significantly jeopardising the rights of defendants. Only the sexual history provisions curtail the rights of one party in order to improve those of the other. On this issue there is no getting away from the fact that one person's freedom is another's jeopardy.

Victim impact statements

We have seen that one consequence of adversarialism is that victims are not parties to, and therefore have traditionally had no rights in relation to, 'their' cases, and that they were therefore often silenced. The new Code is the most recent recognition by government that this was unfair (see Rock 2004 for the development of policy since 1997). We have already briefly discussed new obligations to inform victims about 'their' cases and to consult them in relation to plea bargaining (that is, to go further than simply giving information to victims in these cases).

We have also seen that the problem of adversarialism goes further than plea bargaining. The mass production of guilty pleas means that most cases are not heard fully in court and the victim's perspective, in particular, is omitted. Victim impact statements and schemes attempt to remedy this and to involve victims in these cases.[10] Involvement can, in principle, take various forms – an opportunity to discuss, to be consulted, or to actually participate in decision-making. Whatever type of involvement is provided, it can take place at one or more of various stages of the criminal process: in particular, the decision to prosecute, bail/remand decisions, decisions to reduce or drop charges, sentencing, and early release from prison. In this section we are primarily concerned with the sentencing stage, but similar issues apply to all the stages.

The experimental schemes

In the USA, where the victims' movement took off earlier than in the UK, victim involvement usually takes the form of making a victim impact statement (VIS) to police or probation officers (if they wish), who relay the information provided by the victim in the VIS to the court and/or the prosecutor. The idea was taken up in England and Wales in the 1996 version of the Victim's Charter, which announced some experimental schemes on these lines (Scottish experiments began later: Scottish Executive 2003). The VIS supplements the original witness statement with another written statement detailing the medical, psychological, financial and emotional harm caused by the crime. Only facts are sought, not the opinions of victims about what should happen to offenders (*Practice Direction (Victim Personal Statements)* [2001] 4 All ER 640). This is, in other words, not a consultative process. Victims' interests are to be taken into account but not their views about what is in their interests. By contrast, in some states in the US victims give *opinion* statements even in capital punishment cases where juries, who in some states decide for or against the death penalty, can be influenced by emotive appeals from victims' families (Sebba 1994; on the USA in general, see Erez 1994).

The experimental schemes in England and Wales were evaluated by Hoyle *et al.* (1998) and Morgan and Sanders (1999), who found that many victims who opted to make a VIS were disappointed. Many who said at the start of their case that they were pleased that they were participating, said at the end that they no longer felt this way. Expectations were raised and then dashed. Despite this, Erez claims on the basis of her research that making a VIS is good for victims, because it 'empowers' them by making them visible to criminal justice officials who can thus no longer ignore their interests (Erez 1999; Erez and Rogers 1999). This claim is evaluated later.

The Victim Personal Statement (VPS) scheme

Despite the discouraging evidence, and strong arguments against the principle of victims influencing sentencing decisions (e.g. Ashworth 2000; Edwards 2002; Sanders *et al.* 2001; Sarat 1997), VIS (now relabelled VPS) schemes have been introduced nationwide. The statement is taken by the police at the same time as the witness statement, with the opportunity to add to it at a later point (Home Office 2003). This remedies one defect of the experimental scheme, which required the police to return to victims in cases where there was to be a prosecution to see if they wanted to make a VPS. But now that all victims are asked if they wish to make a VPS, the percentage take-up is so low that a planned statistical survey had to be abandoned in favour of a study of just 28 participants (only 22 of whom actually completed a VPS: Graham *et al.* 2004). Effort is being put into increasing the take-up rate. On a small sample taken in 2004, it rose from 2 per cent to 19 per cent (CPS per cent ACPO 2004: 9). But whether such a relatively high rate can be sustained when unusually strenuous efforts are not applied is doubtful. The very low numbers of victims wanting to make a VPS casts doubt on how far this is an initiative sought by victims, or whether it is something that politicians realise that potential victims, more than actual victims, think they will want (Sanders 2002). The 'right to information' provisions in the Victim's Charter, now strengthened by the Code, by contrast, were far more popular. They evidence an apparent desire on the part of many victims to know what is going on without, in most cases, a desire to influence events.

Generalisation is difficult from a small study such as by Graham *et al.* (2004). For what it is worth, as in the earlier research, some victims were unhappy because they did not know what use, if any, had been made of the VPS, and felt that they had been sidelined, and some would not have made a VPS had they understood the scheme at the time (e.g. some had thought it would help secure a conviction). Less dissatisfaction is reported from a much larger evaluation of the Scottish scheme, although 38 per cent of these victims said that making the VPS did not help them feel better even though this was the main reason for doing it in most cases; and, again, a substantial number wrongly thought that the VPS would assist conviction. A higher proportion of Scottish respondents knew that their VPS had been used in court than was the case in the first English evaluation. This might explain greater satisfaction in Scotland than in England, although Scottish prosecutors and judges appeared to take as little notice of the VPS as their counterparts in England and Wales (Leverick *et al.* 2006).

The Victims' Advocate scheme

Justice for All? confirmed the government's dedication to 'rebalancing the criminal justice system in favour of the victim' (Home Office 2002). A symbolically important step in realising this reshaping of the criminal justice system for victims following the introduction of VPS and the Victims' Code of Practice was to give selected victims of crime the right to make, or have made, an oral statement in court about the effects of the crime on them, akin to some forms of VIS in the USA.

In September 2005 the government published the consultation paper *Hearing the Relatives of Murder and Manslaughter Victims* (DCA 2005). Lord Falconer introduced the consultation saying:

> Victims need a voice. Victims are at the heart of our criminal justice system. Our vision is a criminal justice system in which the needs and concerns of victims, and witnesses, are central. Since coming into government, we have modernised and rebalanced the criminal justice system in order to place victims and witnesses at its centre ... But giving victims a voice is vital. Vital for justice, vital for fighting crime – but most of all, vital for the victims themselves. Victims and their families need to be heard. Their case needs to be put. Victims need a voice. We are determined as a government to make sure that their voice is heard. (DCA 2005: 3)

After the consultation process the government announced that the Victims' Advocate scheme, applicable to the families of murder and manslaughter victims, would be piloted in five Crown Court centres from April 2006. The scheme relies upon the police family liaison officer (FLO) to explain the process to the bereaved families. In addition to the right to make a VPS, those qualifying for the scheme are further entitled to make an oral statement, get free legal advice if they choose to make the statement and take additional legal advice on personal and social matters arising from the death.

Relatives who choose to make the statement, called a family impact statement (FIS), have three options of how to make it: a written statement that would be read by the judge but not read out loud in court (like the VPS); a written statement that would be read out loud in court; and an oral statement to the court. Relatives who choose to make statements personally in court may elect to do this with the help of a CPS lawyer or an independently appointed lawyer, who will talk them through the statement as if it were evidence-in-chief.[11] Relatives who choose to have their statements read out in court on their behalf have the option of this being done by a CPS lawyer, an independently appointed lawyer or (with the leave of the court) a lay person with whom the relative is close.

Initially, the FLO will record what the family says about the effect the death has had on them and submit this to the prosecution, defence and judge. Once the chosen relative has decided by which method they wish their FIS to be delivered, if at all, to the court, the FLO should inform the CPS of this decision. The CPS will then apply to have the statement admitted into court in a pre-trial hearing. The FIS can be updated and the new version shown to all parties involved before admission. Of course, the FIS is only actually heard if, and after, the defendant is found guilty of the charge.

Like the VPS, the content of the FIS should be limited to the effect that the death has had on the family, not their opinions on suitable punishments. Harriet Harman QC, a minister in the Department of Constitutional Affairs, noted that the statement made by the mother of Anthony Walker, a teenager who was axed to death in an unprovoked attack, was the kind she envisaged being admissible under the scheme. This statement, read after Anthony's killers were convicted read: 'Anthony was a wonderful young man who had everything to live for. His murder has subjected my family to a living nightmare. The world is a worse place without my son' (Gibb 2005).

Appraisal

One argument against VIS schemes is that, as we have seen, most victims do not want to participate. Against this it could rightly be said that they cater for those who do, and do no harm to those that do not. But arguably it is not the best use of resources to cater for such a small minority in this way, when far more want – yet are inadequately provided with – information about their cases. It comes down in part to just how valuable they really are for victims who participate in VIS schemes.

Erez argues that the form of 'empowerment' embodied in VIS has two benefits. First, that it is cathartic for victims. Her findings and those of Hoyle *et al.* are partially reconcilable in that for some victims they are cathartic; but Hoyle *et al.* found this was so more at first than at the end of the case. As one victim put it: 'It was worthwhile at the time because it made me feel better but it was obviously ignored so it was a waste of time' (Morgan and Sanders 1999: 32). For others they are not cathartic at all. Whether, on balance, they produce a net cathartic benefit is hard to say.

The second beneficial consequence claimed by Erez is that VIS can influence sentencing decisions. Morgan and Sanders found that VIS, in the Victim's Charter schemes at any rate, had virtually no effect on sentencing – or, in fact, on any other pre-trial stages such as bail. Again, there is little contradiction here, as Erez concedes that most research, including her own, found the effect to be slight. This partly explains why VIS is so unsatisfactory for so many victims. They expect their statements to make a difference, and when they do not they are disappointed. Expectations are raised and then dashed. Victims remain ignored even if not forgotten. Morgan and Sanders found that few prosecutors, judges or magistrates were willing to take any notice of a VIS even though most of them articulated the rhetoric of victims' rights. For if the VIS gave information of an unexpected and significantly aggravating kind – such as a lasting impact of an assault on the victim's health – a medical report was expected anyway. And if a lasting impact was claimed without any supporting medical or psychological evidence, this was 'taken with a pinch of salt' for it was feared that the victim might be exaggerating. Indeed, in the USA it was found that in one area a large number of impact statements were neither read nor, if read, put in the prosecution file (Henley *et al.* 1994). Being treated like this hardly restores the self-respect of victims or reduces their secondary victimisation.

The complaint used to be that victims were used by the system: their witness statements were taken and then they were ignored. And now under the VPS scheme? Two statements are taken (witness and personal), and then they are both ignored. The Victims' Advocate scheme could lead bereaved families to make three statements, all of which are likely to be ignored. As Erez herself complains, the limited use of VIS represents a compromise between supporters and opponents of victims' rights, 'maintaining the time-honoured tradition of excluding victims from criminal justice with a thin veneer of being part of it' (Erez and Rogers 1999: 234–5). This is not empowerment, and for many victims it is the reverse.

Sentencing has always taken account of the physical and financial harm done by crimes. Many courts have been receiving such information, such as in the form of medical reports referred to above, in serious cases for years (Sanders and Young 2006: chapter 13). The question is not whether such information should be available to courts, but how it should be provided – and the VIS is a poor method. Whether sentencing should also take account of emotional and psychological harm (which is far more subjective than physical and financial harm) is more debatable; but, again, if it is to do so, it should be via expert evidence, not the personal statements of victims, who not only vary unpredictably in their reactions to victimisation, but who are liable to over or under-state these reactions in statements of the VIS kind. The Victims' Advocate scheme, in particular, could encourage highly emotionally charged views to be expressed in some cases that should not influence courts (Edwards 2005). If they do, offenders are treated unequally; if they do not, victims will feel, as discussed earlier, that they are being ignored.

The main problem with VIS schemes, from the point of view of victims, is that they are *statement* schemes that have been grafted on to existing adversarial frameworks. They do not, therefore, facilitate discussion or real involvement, and they are poor ways of ensuring that relevant information is transmitted. For example, we identified real problems from the point of view of victims with the way guilty plea cases are often presented to court. One might have thought that VIS schemes deal with these problems by allowing victims' understanding of their cases to challenge, where applicable, those of defendants. But the VPS and FIS is made well before the final hearing, and so instead of a genuine engagement between victims and offenders, courts are presented with competing accounts between which they will rarely be able to adjudicate.

Just as VIS schemes do not allow victims to engage with offenders' presentations of cases, so also, in practice, they do not allow offenders to engage with the victims' presentations of cases in their impact statements. In theory, defendants can challenge their content, but Morgan and Sanders (1999) found that this never happened, as defence lawyers feared that it would anger courts and make matters worse for their clients. This is all as likely to be true of the Victims' Advocate scheme as it is of the VPS scheme. For example, the defendant in an Irish case pleaded guilty to the manslaughter of his young neighbour. The victim's mother gave a VIS, the text of which had been agreed with the defence in advance. However, she departed from this, saying 'our doctors have told us to try and get on with our lives but how can we, knowing that there was semen found on our son's body?' (*Irish Times* 25 January 2006; McGowan 2006). To challenge this in court would inflame the court and upset the relatives, but clearly the mother was desperate to make the point. We shall look at better ways of engaging victims, promoting dialogue, and of transmitting information later in the chapter.

VIS schemes also wrongly discriminate between different types of victim. As we saw earlier, the VPS is available only for certain types of crime. Health and safety offences are a major omission. Victims of these offences are airbrushed out of existence as 'victims' in general and in the new Code in particular. Technically, relatives of people killed when companies or company personnel are charged with manslaughter will be eligible for both VPS and the Victims' Advocate schemes, but in reality this will hardly ever happen. For manslaughter charges in these circumstances are vanishingly rare – as they are when suspects and prisoners die in custody – even when there are prosecutions under the Health and Safety at Work Act (Sanders and Young 2006, chapters 7 and 12). Thus the massive inequity in the way bereaved families in different circumstances are treated will be exacerbated by VPS and FIS schemes.

A further inequity is created by the limited application of the Victim Advocate scheme to only the relatives of victims of murder or manslaughter. For example, a number of offenders were convicted for the murder of teenager Mary Ann Leneghan and the attempted murder of her friend during 2006. While Mary was stabbed, her friend was shot in the head, but miraculously survived. There was little to separate the two offences apart from this small wonder. If the FIS scheme had been operating in the Crown Court at which the defendants were tried, and they had all pleaded guilty, we could have been faced with the situation where the deceased victim was represented, and the living victim having no 'voice' at court (Spencer 2006). One could also foresee uneven application to the victims of a mass murderer or terrorist bomb, where the families of the deceased would have a 'voice' but those who survived would not.

Inquisitorial alternatives

Caution must be exercised that one does not overgeneralise about the nature of inquisitorial systems. The term is applied to systems of adjudication in many different countries, and inevitably there are significant differences between different systems. However, certain procedural themes run throughout most such jurisdictions. In particular, the prosecuting authorities, as well as the police, are involved in investigating offences. Furthermore, once the case file is compiled it will be passed on to a lower judicial figure, such as a magistrate, who compiles a written dossier of the evidence, based upon not only police evidence (including evidence such as DNA results, etc.) but also upon witness testimonies based on oral questioning of the witnesses (including the victim and defendant) by the magistrate in private. This forms a substantial aspect of the evidence considered at trial. If insufficient evidence is available to proceed at this stage, the case may be dispensed here (Spencer 1994: 33; Hodgson 2002).

Trial hearings are not based upon pleas of guilt or innocence but upon a search for the 'truth'. This is perhaps the stage that most shocks proponents of the adversarial model. The trial judge will conduct the proceedings, not only as an arbitrator of law but one of fact too. He/she will conduct most questioning with the prosecution, defence and victim's lawyers playing a relatively passive role. Yet, perhaps surprisingly, confessions are much more common in inquisitorial systems, with some suggesting that the French system amounts to a 'religion of confession' (Hodgson 2005: 62), such evidence being regarded as just one form of evidence of guilt. Indeed, traditionally there is no such thing as a 'guilty plea' (though abbreviated hearings are increasingly used in less serious cases like the 'composition pènal' in France: Hodgson 2005: 59). There is always a hearing, and so there is always the opportunity for the victim to be heard. The prosecutor is generally obliged, in theory, to collect and present any evidence that exonerates the accused as well as evidence that suggests his guilt (Feest and Murayama 2000: 55). Finally, there is no distinction between evidence that goes to guilt and that which goes to sentencing (Moskovitz 1995).

We noted above that adversarial systems embody the principle of orality, but there is not the same mistrust of written evidence in inquisitorial systems. This is because of the overriding 'truth'-finding objective, rather than a contest between those who can best 'manipulate witness testimony in such a way that victory is made more likely' (Doak 2005: 298). Indeed, Moskovitz suggests that the prosecution and defence do not view the outcome of the proceedings in terms of 'winning' or 'losing' at all (Moskovitz 1995). Thus, evidence is not so restricted, witnesses being allowed to tell the narrative of their account rather than being led by a barrister who wishes to elicit the best account to suit the purpose of their account of events. Documentary and other 'untestable' prejudicial evidence is freely admitted because of a more relaxed concept of relevance governing the admission of evidence. If the evidence has been obtained improperly or may be relevant to the circumstances of the crime, then it can be considered relevant to finding out the truth of the matter. The presence of the judicial figure(s) as part of the fact-finding panel should prevent such evidence being given undue weight because they can explain the appropriate weighting to any lay adjudicators.

Victim participation

The German system encapsulates what is perhaps the most far-reaching official role of the victim within a criminal prosecution without the victim himself being the main prosecutor. There are three main ways in which the victim may, in certain circumstances, participate in the German system: as a civil claimant; an auxiliary prosecutor; and as a witness. Private prosecution is also possible in restricted circumstances.

The victim becomes a civil claimant though the 'adhesion' procedure, whereby he may make a claim for compensation for damages arising from the crime during any stage of the proceedings, right up until the closing statements are made. This is not an automatic right and leave has to be sought from the judge to join the proceedings in this way, who can refuse permission without giving reasons beyond a statement that the application was inadmissible (Brienen and Hoegan 2000: 365; Doak 2005: 308). This is perhaps the most common mechanism of formal victim participation across the various inquisitorial systems, often referred to under the French name for such a role of a *'partie civile'* (Spencer 1994: 39). This has benefits in jurisdictions such as France and Belgium because the victim is afforded the right to initiate a prosecution and be heard as well as seeking damages. This could have advantages over the auxiliary prosecutor role because it enables the victim to be a totally separate party to the trial (Doak 2005: 310). While participation is limited to the pursuit of a civil claim, this can be coupled with the right to examine witnesses and submit evidence, as in France.

Victims of more serious offences such as sexual offences, assault, kidnapping, attempted murder and manslaughter, and family members of murder victims, may make a public claim to their right to act as an auxiliary prosecutor. Here, while the public prosecutor still bears the burden of proving the case, the victim is formally aligned through a declaration of solidarity with the public prosecutor and as such enjoys substantial procedural rights. These are the right to be present during the hearing (even if he is a witness too), to object to a judge or expert witness, question witnesses, object to the decisions of the presiding judge, offer evidence, make statements and appeal judgements. This, of course, is coupled with a right to legal representation, meaning it may not be the victim himself who intervenes in these ways.

Finally, victims are likely to appear as prosecution witnesses. Here they also have the right to legal representation, who can be present when the witness is questioned, and be heard by the court or prosecutor. This is not available to witnesses in general. Victims can also criticise questions put to them by the judge or counsel. The victim also has the right to ask for a confidant to be present.

This may appear to be vastly better for victims than the adversarial system. But the more laborious pre-trial stages of case preparation mean that victims are often subjected to numerous sessions of cross-examination. Not only do the police interview as they do here, but the public prosecutor and the magistrate are also likely to. Victims are more frequently summoned to testify at trial and also at any appellate hearings. Furthermore, in cases of sexual assault, victims are often asked to complete a psychological examination to prepare a statement on their credibility (Brienen and Hoegan 2000: 383). While the victim at trial can be assisted by a lawyer, this does not mean that the cross-examination will not be aggressive or disturbing, although measures similar to those in the YJCE are available where applicable. Victims and relatives do not need VIS schemes when this kind of involvement is accorded to auxiliary prosecutors. This is even more so given that evidence as to guilt and that which goes to sentencing are not separated. As the method through which evidence is given is more relaxed, the victim will be more likely to have their interests represented at the trial.

Is this any better?

It was suggested that the judiciary are, in theory, meant to act as independent and impartial adjudicators. While prosecutors are very active in the pre-trial phases, they are far more submissive during the trial stage, this being where the adjudicative judge takes over. But this separation of roles may not be as clearly defined as the theory suggests. For instance, in the German example described above, judges and prosecutors receive the same training, have offices in the same building, meet frequently and may share a common attitude towards offenders and appropriate sanctioning. In the face of such shared experience, it is not surprising that once a case goes to trial it is very likely that a conviction will be gained, undermining the pillar stones of the protections offered by the impartial judge (Feest and Murayama 2000: 60). This has to be put against a background of a history which affords much more trust in the pre-trial stages to weed out weak cases, and in the trial judge to be impartial, originating in the Napoleonic era and the perceived need to separate the judiciary from the state. If it is successful in doing so, then victims benefit from not only a right to be heard because cases will not usually be dispensed with through guilty pleas or charge bargains, but also because there is a lesser chance of them finding that the wrong person has been convicted of 'their' crime (for examples of the anguish caused to victims of crimes in which there are wrongful convictions, see Sanders and Young 2006, chapter 1). Inversely, if it fails in this task and the judiciary and prosecutor do not pursue exonerating evidence as intently as they do incriminating evidence, while the defence lawyer remains relatively inert, the chances of wrongful conviction are potentially increased. Furthermore, it has been argued that the procedures in the pre-trial phases of inquisitorial investigations are far less respectful of a defendant's human rights than our adversarial alternative. This leads to questioning how reliable the regularly obtained confessions during this period are (Hodgson 2005: 214–19). While such confessions do not exclude trials, they constitute heavily weighted evidence of guilt. If we must be more cautious about the reliability of these confessions than we are about those made in our own system, and have mind to the relaxed view of evidential 'reliability' and 'relevance' in inquisitorial systems, we may be further concerned that having 'their' day in court does not bring benefit for victims if this too may lead to miscarriages of justice.

The potential pitfalls of this model of victim participation are not restricted to procedural and structural concerns. While the rights to meaningful participation may appear to be far more substantial, like with the VPS in England and Wales, take-up of these rights is patchy. In a study conducted in 1989/90 in Germany, it was found that auxiliary prosecutors appeared in 14.3 per cent of cases where the right was available. They played a passive role, intervening only to request additional evidence or a procedural decision. However, those victims who did exercise this right felt it had a positive effect upon their position in the system (Kaiser 1991). The reason for this low uptake appeared to be the lack of information provided to victims about their participatory rights provided by the prosecutors. Kury and Kaiser (1991) found that 28.6 per cent of victims would have liked to have participated in the trial had they been aware of the right to do so. This take-up rate does increase for victims of sexual offences, with roughly 50 per cent taking up the right. It seems that take-up is not low because the idea is unappealing to victims; instead, it is due to resistance from the legal profession (Bacik *et al.* 1998). Indeed, victims take on the role of civil claimant attached to the criminal trial far more frequently (Frase 1990).

Overall, victims can assist in the overarching aim of truth-finding in inquisitorial criminal proceedings (Doak 2005). This of course has to be placed against the background that what is being sought is the truth, not legal guilt, and not a winning outcome for one 'side'. In an adversarial system we have to ask ourselves different questions, namely, who are the appropriate adversaries? One of these is clearly the defendant, and at present the other is the state. It is difficult to find room in such a contest for the formal involvement of the victim as another formal party to the proceedings. The inquisitorial model is based upon completely different foundations, not only about the role of the victim, but also that of the judiciary, lawyers, evidence and sentencing. Within this system it is far easier to place the victim as a formal participant in the trial without offending the basic principles upon which the system is based.

Conclusion

As in other areas of the criminal justice system, victims are now treated far better in court than was true for the whole of the twentieth century. Equally important, the run-up to court is recognised both as an important stage in itself and as vital in structuring the experience of the court stage. The special attention now given to vulnerable victims is also welcome, even though operationalising the new measures is only partially successful, despite (and to some extent because of) mechanistic and legalistic legislative definition of 'vulnerability'.

Political rhetoric often presents the rights of the accused and those of victims as mutually exclusive. All too often the latter are used as an excuse to erode the former. The CJA 2003 contains several provisions (e.g. relating to hearsay and 'bad character') that were justified by government on these spurious grounds. This chapter has shown that there need be no clash of rights most of the time. The new Code should therefore be welcomed, as all the new pre-court developments, such as the end to unnecessary restrictions on counselling, pre-court familiarisation, and prosecutor–victim meetings, are beneficial for victims, do not undermine the position of the accused, and could be valuably made more available to victims who seek them. This is true also of most of the measures used to help witnesses cope with cross-examination – available only for 'vulnerable' witnesses but arguably extendable to all witnesses who could benefit from them. It is also true of the WS and measures to separate prosecution and defence witnesses and to reduce the time witnesses need spend in the court building.

There are two main clashes of rights. First, in relation to evidence, particularly cross-examination. The more robustly the defendant challenges the victim, the more the victim suffers. The more the victim is protected, the more the rights of defendants are undermined. There is no easy answer to this within an adversarial system that places so much emphasis on oral confrontation in court. Second, there are VIS schemes. They have the potential to escalate sentences, to the detriment of offenders, and to do so inconsistently, to the detriment of broader notions of justice. To the extent that they do not have this effect, victims are being hoodwinked. But here the clash of rights is more apparent than real, as VIS schemes have little other benefit to most victims who use them. And it is not self-evident that victims benefit from higher sentences anyway. The determination of government to establish VIS schemes despite the arguments against them, coupled with the cynical way the 'victim card' is played in other respects, highlighted in this and other chapters, leads one to question how deeply committed government really is to helping victims. The desire appears to be genuine, but only up to a point. The scandalous air-brushing from view of victims of health and safety offences is further evidence of this.

VIS schemes respond to a need, among some, for involvement, but do not fulfil that need. Inquisitorial systems have little or no need of VIS schemes, and have fewer problems with cross-examination. This is because guilty pleas are used in minor cases only, victims can be parties in the case (or, at least, can often have legal representation), and there is less reliance on oral evidence. Restorative justice (RJ) has not been discussed here (it is the subject of the next chapter) but is capable of paying heed to the needs and wishes of both victims and offenders far more satisfactorily in most cases than can adversarial systems (see chapter 12 in this volume). Unfortunately, that minority of cases that is contested often involves the most distressing processes (particularly cross-examination) and RJ has not yet provided a satisfactory way of dealing with contested cases.

The term 'rights' has been used loosely in this conclusion for victims as well as for the accused. However, as observed earlier, none of the 'rights' of victims discussed here are legally enforceable. The denial of 'rights' set out in the Code may, at best, attract consolation payments (not compensation). This does not put victims at the centre of the criminal justice system, nor even on a par with the accused. It might therefore be argued that victims are still not given due respect. On the other hand, rights to compensation (along with VIS schemes) may not be a good use of limited resources, and one could question whether a 'compensation culture' should be further encouraged among victims. More fundamentally, victims cannot be made central without displacing the accused, which would breach much of the ECHR. We do not try to resolve these questions here, but simply flag them up.

We have seen that in a few respects the rights of the accused and victims are irreconcilable. Inquisitorial and restorative approaches would do a lot to alleviate the situation. But for the foreseeable future we are stuck with the adversarial system for most cases that come to court. Much more can be done within that system to help victims in court, by making the new reforms work better, before we need to tamper further with the rights of the accused or import systems with very different histories and cultures. We will be left with the rights of victims being less entrenched and less enforceable than those of the accused. This, however, is only as it should be. Victims have, regrettably, already suffered the losses associated with being victimised. The accused stands to lose as much or more if convicted of the crime. This may be appropriate – but only if the accused is indeed the criminal. The rights of the accused are designed to ensure, as far as is reasonably practical, that only guilty people are convicted. It does victims no good if the real criminal is left free while innocent people are convicted. Only rarely is the accused's loss the victim's gain.

Further reading

Burton, M., Evans, R. and Sanders, A. (2007 forthcoming) 'Vulnerable and intimidation witnesses and the adversarial process in England and Wales', *International Journal of Evidence and Proof.*

Doak, J. (2005) 'Victims' rights in criminal trials: Prospects for participation', *Journal of Law and Society*, 32(2): 294–316.

Hamlyn, B., Phelps, A., Turtle, J. and Sattar, G. (2004) *Are Special Measures Working? Evidence from surveys of vulnerable and intimidated witnesses*, Home Office Research Study 283. London: Home Office.

Hodgson, J. (2005) *French Criminal Justice: A Comparative Account of the Investigation and Prosecution of Crime in France.* Oxford: Hart Publishing.

Sanders, A. and Young, R. (2006) *Criminal Justice.* Oxford: Oxford University Press, chapter 13.

Notes

1 Ss 32, 48–53 and Sched 8. No Commissioner had, by December 2006, yet been appointed, although the Code came into operation in April 2006.

2 Guidance is elaborated in CPS's, *Witnesses and Best Evidence – Meeting the CPS Prosecutor.* Available on the CPS website: (http://www.cps.gov.uk/) (discussed in Burton *et al.* 2007).

3 See various documents on the CPS website (http://www.cps.gov.uk/): *Provision of Therapy for Vulnerable or Intimidated Adult Witnesses Prior to a Criminal Trial; Provision of Therapy for Child Witnesses Prior to a Criminal Trial.*

4 The legislation is too complicated to cover in detail here. For details see Ellison 2001.

5 A distinction is drawn between 'administrative' and 'legal' categories because no legal implications flow from the recognition of victims and witnesses in the Code: as observed earlier, the 'rights' and obligations it sets out are unenforceable.

6 Following a Court of Appeal judgement, the Bar Council (2005) issued guidance to be found at: (http://www.barcouncil.org.uk/document.asp?languageid=1&documentid=3386).

7 Witness Services are established under the Victim Support umbrella. For details see (http://www.victimsupport.com/).

8 Much of this was prompted by a Council of Europe policy, and now an EU Framework Decision, leading all EU members and CoE signatories to have a similar set of measures.

9 The YJCE tries to deal with this problem more intelligently than the law used to do, by providing for a new 'competence' test of 'understanding' (s53).

10 They are not restricted to guilty plea cases, but it is in such cases where victims are most silenced.

11 A consequence of this is of course that the defence may cross-examine the relative if they feel a false impression is given, which may be distressing for the relative. The normal rules pertaining to the protection of vulnerable witnesses described above apply to reduce the intimidation felt by the witness.

References

Angle, H., Malam, S. and Carey, C. (2003) *Key Findings from the Witness Satisfaction Survey 2002*, Home Office Findings 189. Home Office Online Report 19/03.

Ashworth, A. (2000) 'Victim's Rights, Defendant's Rights, and Criminal Procedure' in A. Crawford and J. Goodey (eds) *Integrating a Victim Perspective Within Criminal Justice*. Aldershot: Ashgate.

Bacik, I., Maunsell, C. and Grogan, S. (1998) *The Legal Process and Victims of Rape*. Dublin: Dublin Rape Crisis Centre and School of Law, Trinity College.

Bar Council (2004) *Code of Conduct*.

Brienen, M. and Hoegen, E. (2000) *Victims of Crime in 22 European Criminal Justice Systems*. Nijmegen: Wolf Legal Productions.

Burney, E. (2003) 'Using the law on racially aggravated offences', *Criminal Law Review*, 28.

Burney, E. and Rose, G. (2002) *Racist Offences – How is the Law Working?* London: Home Office Research, Development and Statistics Directorate.

Burton, M., Evans, R. and Sanders, A. (2006a) *Are Special Measures for Vulnerable and Intimidated Witnesses Working?* Home Office Online Report 01/06.

Burton, M., Evans, R. and Sanders, A. (2006b) 'Implementing special measures for vulnerable and intimidated witnesses: The problem of identification', *Criminal Law Review*, 229.

Burton, M., Evans, R. and Sanders, A. (2007 forthcoming) 'Vulnerable and intimidation witnesses and the adversarial process in England and Wales', *International Journal of Evidence and Proof*.

Cooper, D. (2005) 'Pigot Unfulfilled: Video-recorded Cross-Examination Under s 28 of the YJCEA 1999', Crim LR 456.

Cooper, D. and Roberts, P. (2005) *Special Measures for Vulnerable and Intimidated Witnesses: An Analysis of CPS Monitoring Data*. London: CPS.

CPS/ACPO (2004) *No Witness, No Justice Pilot Evaluation*, Executive Summary.

Crawford, A. and Goodey, J. (eds) (2000) *Integrating a Victim Perspective within Criminal Justice*. Aldershot: Ashgate.

Davis, G., Hoyano, L., Keenan, C., Maitland, L. and Morgan, R. (1999) *An Assessment of the Admissibility and Sufficiency of Evidence in Child Abuse Prosecutions*. London: Home Office.

DCA (2005) *Hearing the Relatives of Murder and Manslaughter Victims*. London: Office for Criminal Justice Reform.

Doak, J. (2005) 'Victims' rights in criminal trials: Prospects for participation', *Journal of Law and Society*, 32(2): 294–316.

Edwards, E. (2005) 'A genuine voice?', *New Law Journal*, 155: 1341.

Edwards, I. (2002) 'The place of victims' preferences in the sentencing of "their" offenders', *Criminal Law Review*, 689.

Ellison, L. (2001) *The Adversarial Process and the Vulnerable Witness*. Oxford: Oxford University Press.

Ellison, L. (2002) 'Cross-examination and the intermediary: Bridging the language divide?', *Criminal Law Review*, 114.

Erez, E. (1994) 'Victim participation in sentencing: and the debate goes on', *International Review of Victimology*, 3: 17.

Erez, E. (1999) 'Who's afraid of the big bad victim? Victim impact statements as victim empowerment *and* enhancement of justice', *Criminal Law Review*, 545.

Erez, E. and Rogers, L. (1999) 'The effects of victim impact statements on criminal justice outcomes', *British Journal of Criminology*, 39: 216.

Feest, J. and Murayama, M. (2000) 'Protecting the Innocent Through Criminal Justice: A Case Study from Spain, Virtually Compared to Germany and Japan', in D. Nelken (ed.) *Contrasting Criminal Justice*. Aldershot: Ashgate, pp. 47–75.

Fenwick, H. (1997) 'Charge bargaining and sentence discount: The victims' perspective', *Int. Rev. Victimology*, 5: 23.

Frase, R. (1990) 'Comparative criminal justice as a guide to American law reform: How do the French do it, how do we find out and why should we care?', *California Law Review*, 78: 538.

Gibb, F. (2005) 'Judges set against plans for Victims' Advocates', *The Times*, 14 December.

Gobert, J. and Punch, M. (2003) *Rethinking Corporate Crime*. London: Butterworths.

Graham, J., Woodfield, K., Tibble, M. and Kitchen, S. (2004) *Testaments of Harm: A Qualitative Evaluation of the Victim Personal Statements Scheme*. London: National Centre for Social Research.

Gus John Partnership (2003) *Race for Justice: A review of CPS decision making for possible racial bias at each stage of the prosecution process*. London: CPS.

Hamlyn, B., Phelps, A., Turtle, J. and Sattar, G. (2004) *Are Special Measures Working? Evidence from Surveys of Vulnerable and Intimidated Witnesses*, Home Office Research Study 283. London: Home Office.

Harris, J. and Grace, S. (1999) *A Question of Evidence? Investigating and Prosecuting Rape in the 1990s*, Home Office Research Study 196. London: Home Office.

Hawkins, K. (2002) *Law as Last Resort*. Oxford: Oxford University Press.

Henley, M., Davis, R. and Smith, B. (1994) 'The reactions of prosecutors and judges to victim impact statements', *International Review of Victimology*, 3: 83.

HMCPSI/HM IC (2002) *A Report on the Joint Inspection into the Investigation and Prosecution of Cases Involving Allegations of Rape*. London: HM CPSI.

HMCPSI/HMIC (2004) *Violence at Home: Joint Thematic Inspection of the Investigation and Prosecution of Cases Involving in Domestic Violence*. London: HMCPSI.

Hodgson, J. (2002) 'Hierarchy, bureaucracy, and ideology in French criminal justice: Some empirical observations', *Journal of Law and Society*, 29(2): 227–57.

Hodgson, J. (2005) *French Criminal Justice: A Comparative Account of the Investigation and Prosecution of Crime in France*. Oxford: Hart Publishing.

Home Office (1998) *Speaking up for Justice: Report of the Interdepartmental Working Group on the Treatment of Vulnerable or Intimidated Witnesses in the Criminal Justice System*. London: Home Office.

Home Office (2002) *Justice For All?* London: HMSO.

Home Office (2003) *Making a Victim Personal Statement*. London: Home Office.

Hoyle, C., Cape, E., Morgan, R. and Sanders, A. (1998) *An Evaluation of the One-Stop Shop and Victim Statement Pilot Projects*. London: Home Office.

Hunter, C., Nixon, J. and Parr, S. (2004) *What Works for Victims and Witnesses of Anti-Social Behaviour*. London: Home Office.

Jackson, J. (2005) The effect of human rights on criminal evidentiary processes: towards convergence, divergence or realignment', *Modern Law Review*, 68(5): 737.

Kaiser, M. (1991) 'The Status of the Victim in the Criminal Justice System According to the Victim Protection Act', in G. Kaiser, H. Kury and H.-J. Albrecht (eds) *Victims and Criminal Justice: Legal Protection, Restitution and Support*. Freiburg: Max-Planck-Institute for Foreign and International Law.

Kebbell, M., Hatton, C. and Johnson, S. (2004) 'Witnesses with intellectual disabilities in court: What questions are asked and what influence do they have?', *Legal and Criminological Psychology*, 9: 23.

Kelly, L., Lovett, J. and Regan, L. (2005) *A Gap or a Chasm? Attrition in Reported Rape Cases*, Home Office Research Study 293. London: Home Office.

Konradi, A. (1997) 'Too little, too late: Prosecutors' pre-court preparation of rape survivors', *Law and Social Inquiry*, 22: 1.

Kury, H. and Kaiser, M. (1991) 'The Victim's Position within the Criminal Proceedings – An Empirical Study', in G. Kaiser, H. Kury and H.-J. Albrecht (eds) *Victims and Criminal Justice: Legal Protection, Restitution and Support.* Freiburg: Max-Planck-Institute for Foreign and International Law.

Leverick, F., Chalmers, J. and Duff, P. (2006) 'An evaluation of the pilot victim statement schemes in Scotland', (unpublished).

McEwan, J. (1995) 'Adversarial and Inquisitorial Proceedings', in R. Bull and D. Carson, (eds) *Handbook of Psychology in Legal Context.* Chichester: John Wiley.

McEwan, J. (2005) 'Proving consent in sexual cases: Legislative change and cultural evolution', *International Journal of Evidence and Proof*, 9: 1.

McGowan, L. (2006) 'When victims attack', *New Law Journal*, 156: 574.

Morgan, R. and Sanders, A. (1999) *The Uses of Victim Statements.* London: Home Office.

Moskovitz, M. (1995) 'The O.J. inquisition: A United States encounter with continental criminal justice', *Vanderbilt Journal of Transitional Law*, 28: 1121.

Office of Criminal Justice Reform (OCJR) (2005) *Code of Practice for Victims of Crime.* London: HMSO.

PA Consulting (2004) *No Witness, No Justice – National Victims and Witness Care Project* (available on the Home Office and PA Consulting websites).

Plotnikoff, J. and Woolfson, R. (1998) *Witness Care in Magistrates' Courts and the Youth Court*, Home Office Research Findings 68. London: Home Office.

Plotnikoff, J. and Woolfson, R. (2004) *In Their Own Words: The Experiences of 50 Young Witnesses in Criminal Proceedings.* London: NSPCC.

Riding, A. (1999) 'The Crown Court Witness Service: Little help in the witness box', *Howard Journal*, 38(4): 411–420.

Rock, P. (2004) *Constructing Victims' Rights.* Oxford: Oxford University Press.

Royal Commission on Criminal Justice (1993) *Report.* London: HMSO.

Sanders, A. (2002) 'Victim Participation in an Exclusionary Criminal Justice System', in R. Young and C. Hoyle, *New Visions of Crime Victims.* Oxford: Hart.

Sanders, A. and Young, R. (2006) *Criminal Justice.* Oxford: Oxford Unviersity Press.

Sanders, A., Crearon, J., Bird, S. and Weber, L. (1997) *Victims with Learning Disabilities: Negotiating the Criminal Justice System.* Oxford: Centre for Criminological Research.

Sanders, A., Hoyle, C., Morgan, R. and Cape, E. (2001) 'Victim impact statements: Don't work, can't work', *Criminal Law Review*, 447.

Sarat, A. (1997) 'Vengeance, victims and the identities of law', *Social and Legal Studies*, 6: 163.

Scottish Executive (2003) *Making a Victim Satement: Guidance for Victims.*

Sebba, L. (1994) 'Sentencing and the victim: The aftermath of *Payne*', *International Review of Victimology*, 3: 141.

Shapland, J. and Bell, E. (1998) 'Victims in the magistrates' courts and Crown Court', *Criminal Law Review*, 537.

Spencer, J. (1994) 'French and English Criminal Procedure: A Brief comparison', in B. Markesinis (ed.) *The Gradual Convergence.* Oxford: Oxford University Press, pp. 33–46.

Spencer, J. (2006) 'Victim advocates and victim care – The place of the victim in the criminal process' *Magistrates' Courts Practice*, 10: 4.

Tak, P. (ed.) (2005) *Tasks and Powers of the Prosecution Services in the EU Member States, Vol I and II*, Nijmegen: Wolf Legal Producions.

Whitehead, E. (2001) *Witness Satisfaction: Findings From the Witness Satisfaction Survey 2000*, Home Office Research Study 230. London: Home Office.

Wurtzel, D. (2006) 'Victims and witnesses: The system already rebalanced', *Counsel*, August 2006: 5.

Chapter 12

The victim in restorative justice

James Dignan

Introduction

'Restorative justice' is a peculiarly imprecise and contested concept, which makes it difficult to define, analyse and evaluate. Likewise, the place of the victim in restorative justice theory, practice and policy-making is by no means straightforward and has been the subject of considerable debate. Historically, the attitude of many early restorative justice advocates was profoundly ambivalent towards victims (see Dignan 2005: 105). At a theoretical level also, the main focus has been directed towards restorative justice's capacity to prevent reoffending and the shaming and reintegrative mechanisms by which this might be achieved (Braithwaite 1989; Scheff and Retzinger 1991).

Attempts to assess the role of victims within restorative justice processes are bedevilled by the sheer variety of restorative justice practices, while efforts to evaluate those processes in terms of their potential benefits for victims are hampered by the wide range of contexts in which they operate. As a rapidly evolving international phenomenon restorative justice initiatives have been adopted in many different countries encompassing a variety of legal jurisdictions and widely differing cultural contexts. The way restorative justice relates to the wider criminal justice system within such settings, which is the main focus of this chapter,[1] provides yet another set of potentially confusing variables. The range of offence types and categories of offenders for which they cater also differ markedly from one restorative justice scheme to another. Indeed, much the same point could be made in respect of individual victims, including the type and degree of victimisation they experience and also the way they respond to it. An additional problem is that the evaluation of restorative justice is still in its infancy, of very variable quality and again still has a tendency to focus primarily on offenders and reconviction rates rather than specifically victim-related concerns.

From a policy-making perspective, victims and their needs now feature prominently in political rhetoric about the need to reform the wider criminal justice system, but often seem to have a much lower profile in shaping specific restorative justice initiatives. Last, but by no means least, the concept of 'the victim' is no less problematic in a restorative justice context than in many other criminal justice and victimological settings.[2]

Faced with such a litany of problems, the task of providing a coherent and meaningful account of 'the victim in restorative justice' is unusually challenging. I begin by considering why the term 'restorative justice' has proved so difficult to define, and propose a different way of approaching the task that avoids some of the problems that have been encountered. I then examine the somewhat limited extent to which victim-related concerns have featured within the three main intellectual traditions that have helped to shape the restorative justice movement in recent years. What restorative justice might potentially have to offer to victims is then assessed in the light of those theoretical developments that are more relevant from a victim perspective. The next section addresses the varying role and prominence that is accorded to victims within each of the main types of restorative justice practice that are likely to be encountered in contemporary criminal justice settings. I then examine the progress that has been made in evaluating restorative justice initiatives from a victim perspective before attempting to summarise some of the main empirical findings. The place of the victim in English restorative justice policy-making is examined in the final section, which also comments on some of the main problems of implementation that have impeded the take-up of restorative justice initiatives by victims.

What is restorative justice?

One of restorative justice's more unfortunate shortcomings is that its leading proponents have been unable to agree on a working definition of the concept itself (McCold 1998: 200), which makes it difficult to pin down and also very much harder to evaluate. Though embarrassing, this failure is not altogether surprising. After all, the restorative justice movement draws, as we shall see, on a rather disparate collection of intellectual currents. The term itself has been applied to a bewilderingly wide range of practices operating in a variety of different contexts. And while some view restorative justice rather narrowly, as simply an alternative way of responding to criminal wrongdoing, others see it as a far more radical and potentially transformative social movement. Perhaps the mistake lies in the quest for an exact word or phrase that would encompass all these elements, which probably is impossible. In which case, a more productive response might be to abandon the quest for a traditional 'stipulative' definition in favour of a more discursive one that sets out simply to describe the term according to its main essential properties.

Three such sets of properties can be derived from the literature, which relate respectively to restorative justice processes, outcomes and values. *Restorative justice processes* seek to provide an opportunity for those with an interest in a particular offence to deliberate together on the most appropriate way of responding to it. Victims who have been harmed by an offence clearly have an interest in how it should be resolved. Indeed, some forms of restorative justice process such as mediation can only take place where the victim is willing to participate. This can take the form of a face-to-face dialogue with the offender in the presence of a neutral mediator or, alternatively, the latter may act as a go-between to facilitate the communication of information, questions and answers from one party to another; or to convey attitudes and feelings including apologies and expressions of forgiveness. Central to the process is the opportunity it provides for an *exchange* of dialogue between the parties, and it is for this reason that one-sided forms of communication such as victim impact statements or simple letters of apology are best differentiated from restorative justice processes (Dignan and Cavadino 1996: 157–60; Shapland *et al.* 2004: 2). Other people may also have an interest in how an offence is resolved apart from the direct victim, and other restorative justice processes such as conferencing provide a forum within which they too may participate. Unlike mediation, the direct victim may not necessarily have any involvement in such proceedings. And even where they do participate, the involvement of other interested parties means that the range of interests that is likely to be addressed within such a forum will tend to extend beyond those of the immediate victim.

Restorative justice outcomes are best thought of as those emanating exclusively from one of the various restorative justice processes; otherwise the term restorative justice itself is liable to become a catch-all that is devoid of specific content. Some such outcomes may arguably help to 'restore' victims in the aftermath of an offence, as where an offender agrees to apologise, to provide more tangible forms of reparation for or on behalf of their victim, or to take constructive steps to prevent a repetition of the offence in the future. Other kinds of victim restoration are also possible, whether in the form of court-ordered or state-funded compensation, victim assistance, insurance or medical care; but once again for analytical purposes it is sensible not to lump these together with restorative justice outcomes. Not all restorative justice outcomes are victim-focused, however. Some may be more offender-focused by seeking to (re)integrate them as law-abiding members of the community; others are more community-focused by seeking to revitalise informal deliberative mechanisms and so strengthen community solidarity.

A number of core *restorative justice values* inform the writings of many restorative justice theorists and underpin the approach of many restorative justice practitioners. They include the principle of inclusivity that seeks to engage all the relevant stake-holders in the restorative justice process; an attempt to balance the different sets of interests that are known to be affected when an offence has been committed; a commitment to the principle of 'non-coerciveness'; and a problem-solving orientation (Dignan and Lowey 2000: 1; see also Van Ness and Strong 2006: 48–50). When it comes to implementing restorative justice practices within a criminal justice context, however, difficult choices often have to be made that may require some of these aspirations to be sacrificed or at least compromised. Some forms of restorative justice practices, for example, seem to favour community empowerment at the expense of victim participation, as will be evident in a later section. It is also difficult to sustain a commitment to voluntary participation, at least on the part of offenders, within the inescapably coercive context of a criminal trial and sentencing process. Nevertheless, the values that underpin restorative justice theory and procedures represent a coherent set of aspirations that should serve as a lodestar for those engaged in the difficult business of turning principles into practice.

Although it is unrealistic to expect a concept as complex and nuanced as restorative justice to be encapsulated in a single pithy definitional phrase, it is nevertheless possible, as we have seen, for it to be delineated precisely enough for analytical purposes. Even when this is done, however, the place of the victim in restorative justice essentially remains uncertain and contingent whatever perspective is adopted, as is seen in the following sections, starting with the historical origins of the concept itself.

Ambivalence towards victims in restorative justice's philosophical precursors

Credit for coining the term 'restorative justice' itself is usually given to Albert Eglash (1977), who characterised it as a particular form of restitution. Over the last three decades it has drawn specifically on at least three distinct philosophical and intellectual strands, which I have summarised elsewhere as the 'civilisation thesis', the 'moral discourse' thesis and the 'communitarian thesis' (Dignan 2005: 95ff.). As Daly and Immarigeon (1998) point out, however, its roots were also undoubtedly nurtured by a variety of cognate social movements including the civil rights and women's movements of the 1960s. One of the most notable features of all three inspirational strands is that they are profoundly ambivalent in their attitudes towards victims.

The 'civilisation thesis' stems from a strong belief that the criminal justice system is barbaric in its treatment of offenders. Many of its most prominent advocates (e.g. Cantor 1976 and also Eglash himself) have argued forcefully that the most effective way of ameliorating this would be to replace the current system of draconian criminal penalties with civil law remedies such as restitution and reparation. Although this approach might help to repair the harm inflicted on victims, such benefits are liable to be seen as incidental gains, or mere 'salubrious by-products' in Cantor's (1976: 113) own words, as opposed to desirable goals in their own right; though not all supporters of the thesis adopt this line. Schafer (1960 1968 1970) and Wright (1982), for example, do place greater emphasis on the importance of meeting victims' needs.

The 'moral discourse thesis' is closely associated with Anthony Duff's communicative theory of punishment, which argues that a more effective way of responding to wrongdoing may be to engage offenders in normative or moralising dialogue instead of simply punishing them in more conventional ways (Duff 1986, 2001, 2002, 2003). As such, it is also primarily offender-focused, even though victims may themselves have an interest in ensuring that offenders are less likely to victimise them or others again in the future.

As for the 'communitarian thesis', one of its principal advocates, Nils Christie (1977), has castigated the conventional criminal justice system in part for its neglect of victims. At the same time, he also sees the community itself as a principal stakeholder and participant in the kind of informal dispute-settlement processes that he favours in preference to professionalised trial-based processes, partly because they provide a means of reinvigorating local communities. Crawford (2000: 290) has perceptively outlined the dual significance of communities within Christie's writing, pointing out that they are valued both for their role in informal dispute settlement processes and also as an instrument of social control with the capacity to help prevent and reduce the incidence of victimisation. However, the introduction of another discrete stakeholder into restorative justice processes such as conferencing also injects an element of tension between the interests of victims and those of the community and, at the same time, a degree of uncertainty as to which set of interests will prevail when they are in conflict.

This ambivalence towards victims within the three main philosophical strands that have helped to nurture and sustain the concept of restorative justice as a discrete response to criminal wrongdoing does not necessarily mean that the approach is detrimental to the interests of victims. But it does mean that it would be unwise to simply assume that it is beneficial without a careful assessment of the available empirical evidence (see below).

The victim in restorative justice theory

At a more theoretical level also, the focus has again mainly been directed towards restorative justice's potential to reduce repeat offending, as reflected most notably in John Braithwaite's (1989) criminological theory of reintegrative shaming. This has been augmented and supplemented by other scholars drawing on psychological understandings derived from 'affect theory'[3] (e.g. Scheff and Retzinger 1991; Nathanson 1992). A more tangential contribution has come from Tyler's (1990) work on procedural justice. In marked contrast to this, restorative justice's potential to 'restore' victims has received scant attention from criminological theorists. Victims scarcely featured at all in Braithwaite's groundbreaking work *Crime, Shame and Reintegration*, and were not even mentioned in a passage setting out a restorative justice conference style process for dealing with offenders (1989: 173–4). Indeed, it was only as Braithwaite's theory came to be elaborated in the light of practice developments in Australia and New Zealand that the approach's potential relevance for victims was spelt out (see, for example, Dignan 1992: 469, 1994; and in the USA Van Ness 1993).

There have been theoretical developments that could help to explain why restorative justice encounters might be beneficial for victims, but for the most part these have come from disciplines other than criminology. A useful distinction to bear in mind when assessing restorative justice's potential benefits for victims is between those that are reciprocal in the sense that they depend on some form of mutual interaction between the parties and those that are unilateral or one-sided in their impact.

Of the reciprocal benefits, the ones that have received most attention, particularly from sociological theorists, are those associated with the giving of an apology by an offender. If accepted by the victim, and particularly if it elicits an expression of forgiveness, it is often argued that this can help to bring about a sense of 'closure'. Nicholas Tavuchis's sociological account of the process highlights in the following terms the seemingly miraculous effect that a successful apology can have: 'no matter how sincere or effective, [an apology] does not and cannot *undo* what has been done. And yet, in a mysterious way and according to its own logic, this is precisely what it manages to do' (Tavuchis 1991: 5; also cited by Bottoms 2003: 95).[4] If it can be successfully accomplished, the giving and acceptance of an apology can have a healing and cathartic effect on both parties and, in principle, can offer the basis for a reconciliation between the parties and the resumption of a relationship they may previously have experienced. As such, the apology has been identified as the social mechanism that lies at the heart of what has been described as 'the core sequence' in a successful restorative justice encounter (Retzinger and Scheff 1996: 321). Tavuchis's analysis of the apology is extremely illuminating, and there can be no doubting the potential importance of apologies, in theory at least, in contributing to the restoration of victims, offenders and also their communities.

Notwithstanding its potential value, the practical significance of the apology may be limited in part by the fragile nature of the process that it entails. Tavuchis (1991: vii) himself describes it as a 'delicate and precarious transaction' that depends on the negotiation of a series of emotionally fraught moves by each of the parties. Indeed, his analysis raises some interesting questions concerning the value and importance that victims place on the tendering of an apology. Is this one of the things they are looking for when they agree to take part in a restorative justice encounter? And are they willing to trust in the sincerity of offenders who tender an apology to them? Another question it raises is whether the essentially dyadic or two-party exchange that lies at the heart of the process can be replicated in the context of a restorative justice encounter. For, whatever form it takes, this will invariably involve at least one additional party and, in the case of conferencing, possibly several others. Perhaps the biggest question of all is whether the theoretical benefits of an apology can be elicited in circumstances where the parties may not have experienced any prior relationship of any kind and, indeed, may not even belong to the same moral or social communities (Bottoms 2003: 98).

An alternative and more recent theoretical analysis also from a sociological perspective accords a somewhat less pivotal role to the apology (though this is still seen as symbolically very important) and places correspondingly greater emphasis on the overall context of a restorative justice event. Collins (2004) has characterised this as a form of 'interaction ritual' in which people are physically brought together to participate in a shared social encounter. According to Collins, the intensity of the emotions that may be unleashed during such an encounter – anger, fear, shame or empathy – may have a contagious effect that could unite the participants in a shared sense of righteous indignation at the offence. In the right circumstances this can in turn help to restore the self-identity of the victim and to reaffirm the group's commitment – including that of the victim – to a collective set of moral principles. For Collins, the tendering of a sincere apology by the offender plays a central role in affirming this sense of collective solidarity. However, it is also conceivable that the emotional response of *other* participants, including, for example, the family of the offender, could in principle help to restore a victim's sense of self-identity as having been unjustly wronged, even in the absence of a sincere apology from the offender.

If successful, one outcome that might be anticipated from a restorative justice encounter is a victim's acknowledgement that it has helped them get over the offence and put it behind them. An additional hypothesis that has been suggested by Sherman *et al.* (2005) is that victims will feel less vengeful towards offenders since their own commitment to the community's shared sense of morality should also have been reaffirmed by the process. Like Tavuchis's analysis of the apology, however, Collins' account also appears to assume that restorative justice's ability to restore victims is necessarily and inextricably contingent on the actions or emotional responses of others. But is this the case; or might it be possible for restorative justice encounters to confer certain benefits on victims unilaterally and irrespective of any reciprocal behaviour on the part of other participants?

The social science literature relating to 'narrative theory'[5] offers an alternative response suggesting, as it does, that a variety of practices such as 'story-telling', dramatisations and account-making may have therapeutic value in helping people to come to terms with distressing events that they may have experienced. Participating in such a process could plausibly help to 'restore' victims in a variety of ways quite apart from the possibility of receiving an apology or some other form of reparation from offenders, or an acknowledgement by others that the victim has been undeservedly wronged. For example, it could conceivably help victims to reframe their own experiences, thereby making sense of, and possibly coming to terms with them, or even to begin to re-assert control over their own destiny and self-perception. For some victims the opportunity to participate in such an encounter may enable them to 'face the demons' of their anxieties and nightmares and thereby, conceivably, to face them down (Gehm. 1998: 26).

From a rather different perspective, some of the psychological literature on cognitive behavioural therapy provides a more scientific explanation of some of the mechanisms that could be involved in such a process. One form of cognitive behavioural therapy programme is informed by assumptions about the way fear is generated and countered that are derived in turn from conditioning theory (Foa and Kozak 1986). In essence, this involves the deliberate exposure of victims within safe settings to the same kind of fear-provoking stimuli that are likely to be associated with the original offence. As well as helping to desensitise victims to the emotional trauma associated with the event itself, the process can also entail a cognitive element by helping victims to understand how the traumatic event may have come about. This could help to counter a self-perception that they may somehow have contributed to it or even brought it upon themselves. It is also possible that a restorative justice encounter may likewise help the victim to neutralise the trauma associated with the original offence. They may also gain reassurance from being told, as is usually the case, that they happened to have been unlucky in being targeted, as opposed to being deliberately singled out.

In addition to these rather more subtle processes, there are also other more obvious ways in which restorative justice could, in theory at least, help to 'restore' victims in the aftermath of a criminal offence. For some victims this could involve some form of reparation from their offender; others might conceivably derive comfort from an offender's agreement to take appropriate action to reduce the likelihood of them reoffending in the future. Before going on to assess the empirical evidence relating to restorative justice's ability to deliver the various restorative outcomes for victims, it may be helpful to examine the role and prominence of victims in the different forms of restorative justice practice.

The role and prominence of victims in restorative justice processes

Once the focus switches from restorative justice theory to the way it might operate in practice, another important distinction needs to be drawn between 'restorative justice processes' and 'restorative justice programmes'. The term 'restorative justice process' is applied here exclusively to the three main *procedural approaches* that have come to be associated with restorative justice: victim–offender mediation, conferencing, and healing or sentencing circles. Attempts to *implement* these approaches – whether by means of legislation or less formal strategies – are referred to here as 'restorative justice programmes'. The distinction is not entirely watertight, and it can sometimes be difficult to determine whether a certain aspect or feature is intrinsic to a particular type of restorative justice process or is a consequence of the way it has been implemented. As far as possible, however, this section will focus primarily on the procedural aspects that are associated with restorative justice processes, while the empirical evidence relating to the outcomes that are associated with such processes is examined in the next section. The variable impact that restorative justice programmes can have on victims will be specifically addressed in the final section, on restorative justice policy-making.

Of the three main types of restorative justice processes, victim–offender mediation is unique inasmuch as victim participation forms an integral part of the process itself, though there is some flexibility in the precise form this can take. This is not to say that victims' interests necessarily take precedence over those of offenders, or even that mediation is likely to be more accessible to victims than are other forms of restorative justice.[6] It is simply that without *any* form of victim participation there can be no mediation. The two main variants involve either a face-to-face encounter between victim and offender in the presence of neutral third party mediator or, alternatively, the two main parties may conduct an indirect dialogue through the medium of the mediator. The latter then acts as a go-between or conduit in relaying views, questions or answers for parties unwilling or unable to meet face to face.

Compared with other restorative justice processes, mediation often entails a greater degree of initial preparation in order to explain what is involved, allay any concerns, identify the main issues and expectations for each party and generally seek to maximise the prospects for a direct and meaningful exchange between them (Umbreit 1994, 1997). In addition, mediation tends to have a much narrower focus, concentrating mainly on the harm suffered by the victim together with the most appropriate form of reparation or redress, though in practice much is likely to depend on the operational context. Likewise mediation might appear – in the absence of other stakeholders – to offer the greatest scope for active and intensive participation on the part of both the main protagonists, though again much may depend on the context, degree of preparation, characteristics of the parties and also the attitude of the mediator.

It is even more difficult to generalise with regard to the role and prominence of victims when it comes to conferencing, since there are at least two quite distinct conferencing variants; these are normally referred to as family group conferencing and police-led conferencing. Family group conferencing, which originated in New Zealand, is the more restrictive of the two in terms of the range of people who are entitled as of right to attend and participate, which generally tends to be limited to offenders and direct victims (Morris and Maxwell 2000: 215). Supporters of both parties may also be invited, though their role is likely to be less prominent, at least in the preliminary phase of the discussions. Police-led conferencing tends to be somewhat more inclusive both with regard to the categories of victims who may be entitled to attend, and also in its more relaxed attitude towards participation by members of the wider community. A third conferencing variant known as the community reparation panel takes this a step further by actively encouraging participation by members of the general community who may have no direct interest in any of the offences being discussed. This particular variant will be discussed more fully in the section on restorative justice policy-making.

One attribute that is common to all forms of conferencing, however, is that none of them are dependent on the participation or, indeed, even the presence of victims. This raises important questions about the relative importance that is attached to meeting the needs and concerns of victims on the part of those responsible for convening such conferences. Indeed, such questions are still pertinent even when victims do participate in conferencing, given the presence and active involvement in the process of a variety of other stakeholders.

As for the *role* of victims in conferencing, it is again difficult to generalise. Victims are seen as having an important part to play in family group conferencing, one of the main aims of which is described in terms of meeting their needs (Morris and Maxwell 2000: 211). Among the benefits that Morris and Maxwell identify are making victims feel better about what has happened to them, fostering reconciliation between the parties, facilitating reparative outcomes (whether symbolic or actual) and reconnecting both parties with their communities. The role of the victim in police-led conferencing is rendered rather more problematic by the focus on the 'reintegrative shaming' of offenders that is seen as being a central part of the process, in which all parties – including victims – are said to play a part. Critics object that this makes reconciliation between the parties less likely (Morris and Maxwell 2000: 216; Young 2001: 201), and even that it manipulates victims in order to reduce offending, which Ashworth (2000: 186) describes as a form of 'victim prostitution'.

There are also important procedural differences between the two conferencing models, which again have important implications for victims. The most important of these differences from a victim perspective is that in a family group conference victims are obliged to withdraw from the deliberations once the focus turns from the effects of an offence to the action that might be considered appropriate on the part of the offender. Responsibility for formulating the action plan rests exclusively with the offender and their family, who discuss the matter in private, though the resulting proposals are then put before the whole conference, which gives the victim and the police an opportunity to veto plans that they find objectionable. In police-led conferencing, however, victims are not excluded in this way from the decision-making process.

With regard to healing and sentencing circles, it is even more difficult to generalise, partly because the processes draw much more heavily on traditional ritual procedures that developed within Canadian first nation communities, which can thus vary from one to another. There is also a difference between sentencing circles and healing circles. The former operate in the context of a regular criminal trial and often involve the judge, who alone is authorised to pronounce the final sentence. The latter tend to operate outside the criminal justice system and can involve a wide variety of non-criminal disputes. There is scope for victims to be involved in sentencing circles. Indeed, a separate circle may often be convened specifically for the victim, and another for the offender, before the entire sentencing circle meets to formulate a consensus as to what happened and what needs to be done about it. Circles embrace the notion of community participation and can involve community elders, kinship groups and others, which again raises concerns over possible conflicts of interests between their concerns and priorities and the needs and wishes of victims (LaPrairie 1995). Another set of concerns relates to the tension that exists between a desire to deal with even serious offenders in the community and concerns over victim safety, particularly in small-scale isolated communities where victims lack anonymity and can be extremely vulnerable (Crnkovich 1993; cited in Lilles 2001: 171). Moreover, both sets of concerns are exacerbated by the fact that indigenous communities are often characterised by acute power imbalances along generational, gender and kinship lines (Griffiths and Hamilton 1996).

Restorative outcomes for victims? Key empirical findings

The evaluation of restorative justice initiatives is still in its infancy and much of it is of uneven quality. Most funded research has been predominantly offender-oriented, with a particular focus on the impact that restorative justice might have on reconviction rates. Much less emphasis has been placed on its possible impact on victims when formulating research strategies, and most studies to date have concentrated on a fairly narrow range of issues relating broadly to 'victim satisfaction' ratings. Methodologically speaking, much restorative justice research has been of variable quality, which means that many of the findings need to be treated with caution. Some attempts are now being made to test its theoretical potential to 'restore' victims more rigorously and systematically, though in the main these mostly comprise follow-up 'adjuncts' to wider evaluations that were initially prompted chiefly by offender-oriented considerations. Moreover, the measures they use are rarely comprehensive or optimal in assessing the restorative impact of restorative justice processes on victims. One partial explanation for this is that some of the theoretical developments referred to above have appeared on the scene too late to influence the design of the current generation of restorative justice evaluations. When assessing the significance of restorative justice research from a policy-making perspective more generally, one of the biggest challenges is to determine the extent to which the 'outcome' findings can be attributed to the restorative justice process itself as opposed to factors relating to the 'programme context' (see next section).

In this section I start by drawing attention to some general 'attitudinal surveys' that shed some light on victims' willingness in principle to take part in restorative justice encounters. (Victim participation rates in specific restorative justice programmes tend to vary widely in response to a variety of contextual factors and, for this reason, these are discussed in the next section on restorative justice policy-making.) I then review the main reasons victims give for taking part in restorative justice encounters before turning to the empirical findings, concentrating on those that relate to the theoretical potential of restorative justice in helping to 'restore' victims.

Victim surveys have shown that around one in two victims would be willing in principle to meet with their offender in the context of a restorative justice encounter. The 1998 British Crime Survey found that 41 per cent of victims would have been willing to participate in such a meeting (Mattinson and Mirrlees-Black 2000: 40–4).[7] A slightly differently worded question in the 1984 survey yielded a positive response from 51 per cent of victims (Maguire and Corbett 1987: 227–31). Similar findings were reported by the 1999 Canadian victim survey, with 24 per cent of victims expressing a strong interest in mediation and 27 per cent indicating that they were somewhat interested (Tufts 2000; reported by Wemmers 2003). Such findings suggest that, were they to be made more widely available, there would be a reasonably high take-up rate for restorative justice meetings on the part of victims, but they also highlight the fact that they would not necessarily appeal to all victims.

Those victims who do agree to take part in restorative justice encounters tend to give a variety of reasons for doing so. In a recent study that is still ongoing, four main sets of reasons were cited (Shapland *et al.* 2004; see also Strang 2002: 122).[8] Most victims (66 per cent) agreed to take part largely for expressive reasons; they welcomed the opportunity to participate and wanted to have a say in how the problem was resolved. A similar proportion were also motivated by altruistic considerations, though this was less likely to be a 'very important' factor for them, and for one in four victims it was not at all important. Another significant factor (expressed by just over half) was a sense of duty, though there was very little indication that they felt under any kind of compulsion to attend. Just under half of all victims (42 per cent) were motivated by a desire to receive reparation.

One of the most constant and consistent sets of findings from restorative justice research is that participants – both victims and offenders – experience a strong sense of procedural justice that stems from being heard with respect and treated fairly (Daly 2005; Strang 2002: 122ff.). They also welcome the chance to have a say in the deliberations. Moreover, a recent meta analysis[9] of 13 studies that incorporated an experimental research design suggests that victims who participate in restorative justice processes express significantly higher satisfaction ratings than those who experience the conventional court process (Latimer et al. 2001: 910).

Whether restorative justice can actually help to 'restore' victims (as opposed to treating them fairly and with respect) is a question that very few studies have set out to systematically investigate, and most attempts suffer from methodological shortcomings that constrain their validity. In this section I concentrate on research findings that appear to have a bearing on the theoretical benefits for victims that were set out in a previous section, starting with the findings relating to apologies.

Three sets of studies are of particular note in this regard. The first is an evaluation of the South Australian Juvenile Justice (SAJJ) family group conferencing scheme conducted by Kathy Daly (2001, 2005), which was one of the first to highlight the important distinction between 'procedural justice' outcomes and those relating to more substantive (and elusive) forms of victim restoration. The second is a police-led conferencing scheme known as RISE (the Reintegrative Shaming Experiment) which is based in Canberra, the findings of which are summarised in Strang (2002). This is one of the few restorative justice evaluations to have utilised an experimental research design (devised and operated by the Justice Research Consortium) involving the random allocation of cases to either treatment or control groups. Because the primary aim of the research has been to investigate the impact of restorative justice on reoffending rates, however, the unit of allocation is based on offenders rather than victims. So, from a victim perspective the approach does not technically constitute a randomised control trial and is more accurately described as a 'quasi-experimental comparison of victims whose offenders were randomly assigned to either court or conference' (Strang 2002: 74). The third study, which is still ongoing, is a Home Office-funded evaluation of three separate restorative justice schemes in England, one of which uses the same experimental methodology as the RISE experiment. The Justice Research Consortium is also responsible for conducting the randomised control trials within this latter scheme, and has reported on some of its preliminary findings (see Sherman et al. 2005; Strang et al. 2006). However, the overall evaluation of all three schemes, including the one being conducted by JRC, is being undertaken by a team based at the University of Sheffield and is still ongoing (see Shapland et al. 2004, 2006).

Strang's (2002: 114) findings highlighted the importance of receiving an apology in the eyes of the great majority of victims, irrespective of whether they were dealt with by means of a conference or a conventional court hearing. Interestingly, however, as we have seen, this tends not to feature among the reasons victims give for taking part in a restorative justice encounter. Her study also showed that conference victims were far more likely to receive an apology than those whose cases went to court (see also Sherman *et al.* 2005: 387). This is not altogether surprising, however, given that so few victims are present in court when 'their case' is being dealt with.

What is less clear from the research findings is whether an apology that victims may receive in the course of a restorative justice encounter actually helps to 'restore' or 'heal' them, as postulated in the theoretical accounts. Thus it is relatively rare for victims to explicitly forgive offenders in the course of a restorative justice encounter (Shapland *et al.* 2006: 57), even after receiving an apology, though it can happen in some instances. This does not preclude the possibility that victims may come to feel more forgiving towards their offenders over time, and some of the JRC findings suggest that this could be the case. Overall, the findings are rather inconsistent, however, and offer only weak support for the hypothesis that victims who take part in restorative justice encounters are more likely to feel 'restored'.

Remarkably high levels of forgiveness (averaging 75 per cent) were reported in the JRC London sample (Sherman *et al.* 2005: 389). Indeed, the 'forgiveness rate' of London victims was almost twice as high as that recorded for Canberra victims, even though the offences in the London sample were far more serious than in Canberra. When compared with the control sample, however, which was only done for London, the differences in forgiveness rates were somewhat inconsistent across the different offence types and much less pronounced overall, the weighted average being described as 'barely significant'. These somewhat equivocal findings do little to counter the doubts that Bottoms (2003) and others have expressed regarding the extent to which apologies may be capable of routinely realising their healing potential in the context of contemporary social settings.

What of the theoretical claim that restorative justice encounters can function as 'interaction rituals' that can indirectly help to restore victims by mobilising social solidarity and helping to overcome some of the negative effects of victimisation (see above)? Sherman *et al.* (2005: 388) have argued that this hypothesis is strongly supported by their findings that across all the sites in which their random allocation experiments have been conducted conference victims are consistently far more likely to feel that the apologies they received were genuine than are court victims. However, these results are sharply at odds with Daly's (2001: 77) findings that most conference victims doubted the sincerity of their offender's apology, and that only 27 per cent believed that the main reason why the offender said sorry was because they really felt that way. In the absence of a control group it is impossible to compare the perceptions of Daly's conference victims with those of victims who go to court. Nevertheless, her conclusion that there may be limits on victims' willingness to see offenders in a positive light calls into question the JRC contention that restorative justice helps to mobilise social solidarity in this way.

One possible explanation[10] for these incompatible findings is that the JRC trials fail to account for the very different context in which apologies are likely to be delivered in conferences as compared with courtroom settings. In the former they are likely to be relatively explicit, to come directly from the offender and to be directed at the victim. In the latter they are far less likely to be forthcoming at all, and even when they do materialise they are more likely to be delivered by the offender's legal representative (not the offender) to the court (as opposed to the victim) by way of mitigation in the hope of reducing the severity of the sentence. In circumstances such as these it is hardly surprising that in a controlled experiment conference victims would be *relatively* more likely than court victims to believe in the sincerity of any apology that might be forthcoming. In view of Daly's findings, however, it would be unwise to accept this as necessarily confirming restorative justice's capacity to routinely promote empathy and mobilise social solidarity on the part of conference participants.

Given the difficulty of devising a controlled experiment that is based on a true 'like for like' comparison with regard to feelings of forgiveness, it might be better to find other more appropriate ways of testing restorative justice's ability to function as an interaction ritual that could help to 'restore' victims. Studies conducted by the JRC have shown that conference victims tend to feel less afraid of their offender, less angry and also more sympathetic towards them once the conference has been concluded (Strang 2002; Strang *et al.* 2006). However, as these are based on simple before/after comparisons without any randomised control procedures it is impossible to determine whether these positive changes are causally attributable to the conferencing process itself. Daly (2003: 229) recorded that victims' self-reported recovery rate was higher in cases where the offender had completed a reparation agreement than in cases where this was not the case. This is consistent with the proposition that restorative justice can aid victim recovery, but again the research design lacked a controlled experimental methodology, so we cannot be sure that this is the case.

The strongest support to date for the proposition that restorative justice is capable of functioning as a successful interaction ritual comes from the JRC research team's comparison of conference victims and court victims with regard to their desire to avenge themselves against their offender. This is based on a randomised trial methodology across a range of sites and catering for a variety of offence categories in two separate jurisdictions, and shows that the desire for revenge is strongly and consistently reduced in respect of victims whose cases are dealt with by conferencing. Given that the categories of victims and offenders may be less blurred and dichotomised than is commonly supposed (Dignan 2005: 20), this finding suggests that restorative justice processes could well help to reduce the risk of future retaliatory offending by crime victims.

Turning now to the final theoretical claim – that restorative justice is capable of assisting in the restoration of victims by providing them with 'unilateral' benefits that do not necessarily depend on the reciprocal actions of others – few attempts have yet been made to put this to the test. Perhaps not surprisingly, such findings as are available are somewhat inconclusive, therefore. As part of its randomised control trials the JRC has obtained and analysed measures of post-traumatic stress symptoms for victims, but only in respect of the London samples and not the Canberra ones (Angel 2004; Sherman *et al.* 2005: 372). The JRC team surmise that restorative justice encounters could be functionally equivalent to cognitive behavioural therapy sessions in their impact on victims. If so, one possible indicator of recovery from post-traumatic stress that could be indicative of a restored sense of personal equilibrium is a reduction in victims' propensity to blame themselves for what had happened. When put to the test as part of its randomised allocation experiments, however, no consistent differences in levels of self-blaming were found with respect to any of the variables: offence type, gender or locality. An alternative approach would be to conduct a before and after comparison of PTSD symptoms experienced by victims in respect of both treatment and control group samples, though a recent attempt to do just this failed because of access difficulties (see Boriboonthana 2006).

Until now, attempts to put restorative justice's theoretical potential to 'restore' victims to the test have been fairly rudimentary; and because they have mainly been tacked on as an afterthought the measures that have been adopted are far from ideal. This state of affairs is likely to change quite rapidly for a number of reasons: recent theoretical developments, renewed interest on the part of empirical researchers and the increasing salience of victims (at least at a rhetorical level) within penal policy-making circles, which is the subject of the next section. Although the results of the available findings from the relatively limited number of empirical studies to date are indicative rather than conclusive, they are nevertheless reasonably propitious and afford grounds for cautious optimism that methodologically more sophisticated studies may well prove yet more rewarding.

The victim in English restorative justice policy-making

In recent years the government has continually trumpeted its professed aim of rebalancing the criminal justice system in favour of victims, witnesses and communities (Home Office *et al*. 2002). All this talk has been backed by some action in the form of victim-focused reforms that are discussed elsewhere in this volume (see in particular Chapters 8, 9, 10 and 11; and see also Dignan 2005: esp. chapters 2 and 3). When it comes to restorative justice policy-making, however, the government's rhetoric on this issue has not been matched by a comparable commitment to promote the development of restorative justice initiatives specifically for the benefit of victims. In short, the government's approach has been characterised by a lack of strategic direction, a confused and pusillanimous approach to restorative justice policy-making and a persistent refusal to address known obstacles that have constrained the level of victim participation in those limited restorative justice processes that have been made available. In this section I will discuss each of these shortcomings in turn.

In 2003, the government published a consultation document setting out its restorative justice strategy (Home Office 2003; see also Home Office 2004). This wide-ranging document brought together a number of disparate initiatives including restorative justice in policing and community safety, restorative justice as a diversionary mechanism plus various reparative and victim–offender contact developments. It also addressed a number of more thematic concerns relating broadly to the relationship between restorative justice and the wider criminal justice system. As a restorative justice *strategy*, however, the document was disappointing in a number of important respects.

First, it seems to view restorative justice simply as a diverse range of supplementary and mostly peripheral interventions that might or might not be applicable at different phases of the criminal justice process. A more strategic alternative to this rather piecemeal perception would have been to characterise restorative justice as a coherent approach underpinned by a principled value base that should inform the activities of *all* criminal justice agencies and personnel. Restorative justice, in other words, could provide the basis for a more defensible and far less controversial rebalancing of the criminal justice system to take account of the needs and interests of victims, offenders and the wider community without playing one set of interests off against another.[11]

Second, the strategy lacked a clear vision of what a restorative justice approach might have to offer *victims* at every stage of the criminal justice process, which could then act as a navigational aid for criminal justice strategists and policymakers. Without such a focus there is a danger that restorative justice initiatives that seek to engage victims in deliberations about how their offence should be dealt with may be seen as interchangeable with purely reparative initiatives or attempts to engage the wider community in criminal justice decision-making.

Third, the strategy offered an exceedingly tentative, disjointed and per-missive restorative justice reform agenda that contrasts sharply with the much bolder, more coherent, integrated and directive blueprints that have been adopted in other jurisdictions, not just overseas but also in other parts of the UK. Thus, much of the detailed strategy set out in the document consists of merely *facilitating* greater use of restorative justice processes by the police and others by means Codes of Practice and guidelines. Several sets of initiatives relate to the introduction of purely reparative measures that are more concerned with community reparation, and are therefore of only marginal relevance for direct victims themselves. Much of the strategy is aimed at piloting new measures (such as adult-based restorative justice interventions), but without any longer-term commitments to adopt them. This exceedingly cautious stance contrasts with the government's decision to press ahead with its youth justice reform programme of 1998 well before the pilot evaluation had been completed. Moreover, the only new measure to be implemented, the conditional caution, is being phased in gradually.

As for the recent history of restorative justice policy-making, three main types of restorative justice interventions have been introduced in England and Wales over the last decade, though they draw on a rather eclectic mixture of approaches (Bottoms and Dignan 2004). The first is based on the police-led and facilitated scripted conferencing model that was pioneered in Australia before being adopted and developed by the Thames Valley police. Although initially introduced as an alternative to old-style police cautions, police forces across the country are now encouraged, but not obliged, to use this approach in connection with the statutory reprimand and final warning system when dealing with young offenders under the 1998 Crime and Disorder Act.

Victims can be invited to attend such conferences, or they may be invited to a mediation meeting, together with their offender, as part of a 'change programme' that can accompany a final warning. In practice, however, very few victims participate in such restorative justice encounters: 14 per cent in the case of Thames Valley-style restorative cautions (Hoyle *et al.* 2002: Table 1); and fewer than 4 per cent in the case of mediations conducted in connection with final warnings (Holdaway *et al.* 2001: 72–80).

The second main type of restorative justice intervention operates as an alternative to prosecution for most young offenders who appear in court for the first time, provided they admit their offence. They are referred instead to a youth offender panel (or YOP) which is conducted by a member of the local youth offending team and two community representatives. This initiative draws on a disparate range of precursors including Vermont-style Community Reparative Panels, New Zealand-style family group conferences and Scottish Children's Hearings. Victims may again be invited to attend the panel meetings, but the pilot evaluation found once again that disappointingly few victims (13 per cent) did so (Newburn *et al.* 2002: 41).

The third main type of restorative justice intervention is based on the practice of victim–offender mediation, which victims can also be offered if young offenders are sentenced to certain penalties such as a reparation order or action plan order[12] after being convicted. These penalties were introduced under the 1998 Crime and Disorder Act but, as with the other two sets of measures, the pilot evaluation found that only a small minority (9 per cent) of cases resulted in mediation between victims and offenders (Dignan 2002: 80).

This eclectic mixture of restorative justice approaches raises serious doubts about the overall *coherence* of the government's restorative justice strategy. Moreover, the extremely low rates of victim participation for all three sets of initiatives raises equally pressing questions concerning the depth of the government's commitment to promote the use of restorative justice for the benefit of victims. The government's rather confused and timid attitude towards restorative justice stands in marked contrast to the much more ambitious and coherent approach adopted in other jurisdictions such as New Zealand and, more recently, Northern Ireland.[13] In both these countries family group conferencing is now a routine response for young offenders and their victims, both as an alternative to prosecution and in place of the traditional sentencing process. Moreover, victim participation rates of 50 per cent in New Zealand (Maxwell and Morris 1993) and 69 per cent in Northern Ireland (Campbell *et al.* 2006: 141) have been recorded.

The disappointingly low level of victim participation in almost all the English restorative justice initiatives is well known, as are the reasons for it. One of the main problems relates to the 1998 Data Protection Act, enacted in the same year as the legislation introducing the early restorative justice measures: the Crime and Disorder Act. The former Act requires the consent of data subjects to be sought before personal information can be passed on by authorised data holders to other parties. The latter Act imposes a duty on youth offending teams to consult with victims, and gain their express consent to taking part in a restorative justice encounter or receiving direct reparation from an offender. In practice this usually means that a victim's consent has first to be sought by the police, who are authorised data holders, before their name and contact details can be passed on to the youth offending team worker who would be responsible for assessing the prospects for any restorative justice intervention. However, the police, who are responsible for first raising the possibility of a restorative justice encounter, may have neither the time nor the experience to advise on the potential benefits to be gained from such an approach. An additional complication is that the process of obtaining consent and assessing the prospects for a restorative justice encounter can be quite time-consuming, whereas courts are now less inclined to order adjournments in order to facilitate such consultation than they were in the past, in part because the government has also been pressing them to speed up the processing of offenders.

The government had an opportunity to resolve the problem when it enacted the Domestic Violence, Crime and Victims Act in 2004, but chose not to do so. While making provision for organisations that are bound by the Code of Practice for Victims to share information so that they can comply with their obligations, the Act specifically says that this does not override the Data Protection Act. Consequently, it is still necessary for organisations to set up administrative protocols to enable the exchange of information, and the same bureaucratic obstacles still stand in the way of a speedy and efficient victim consultation procedure.

Other problems include cultural resistance on the part of some YOT staff who are so used to acting on behalf of offenders that they are reluctant to accept their newly imposed responsibilities with regard to victims (Holdaway *et al.* 2001: 87). In addition, it is likely that the speed and complexity of the youth justice reform programme, combined with a lack of resources, compounded the difficulty of establishing an effective victim consultation procedure, at least in the early days.

None of these implementational problems should be insurmountable. Indeed, Shapland *et al.* (2006: 43) found that where agencies are willing to persevere in their attempts to engage victims, a substantial proportion are willing to participate in restorative justice processes even where the offences are quite serious and committed by adult offenders.[14] But in the absence of much stronger government support, the place of the victim in restorative justice is likely to remain tenuous, while the place of restorative justice within the wider criminal justice system seems destined to remain somewhat peripheral despite the various reforms that have been introduced since 1997.

Further reading

Crawford, A. and Goodey, J. (eds) (2000) *Integrating a Victim Perspective within Criminal Justice.* Aldershot: Ashgate Dartmouth.

Daly, K. (2005) 'A Tale of Two Studies: Restorative Justice from a Victim's Perspective', in E. Elliott and R.M. Gordon (eds) *New Directions in Restorative Justice: Issues, Practice, Evaluation.* Cullompton: Willan Publishing.

Dignan, J. (2005) *Understanding Victims and Restorative Justice.* Maidenhead: Open University Press.

Strang, H. (2002) *Repair or Revenge: Victims and Restorative Justice*. Oxford: Clarendon Press.

Walklate, S. (2006) 'Changing Boundaries of the "Victim" in Restorative Justice: So Who is the Victim Now?', in D. Sullivan and L. Tifft (eds) *Handbook of Restorative Justice*. London: Routledge.

Notes

1 Restorative justice is by no means confined to criminal justice settings, however. Others include schools, child welfare decision-making, interpersonal relationships within familial, occupational or community contexts and also deep-seated inter-communal conflicts on a national or even supra-national scale.

2 Space precludes a discussion of this topic in this chapter; but see Dignan (2005: 167–78); Walklate (2006).

3 'Affect theory' has to do with the study of emotions (including that of shame) that lie behind action and that may predispose people to behave in certain ways. One of the pioneers in this field was Sylvan Tomkins (1962) whose ideas have been developed by Donald Nathanson (1992).

4 Tony Bottoms' very thorough and illuminating assessment of the significance of Tavuchis's work within a specifically restorative justice context provides a clear account of the potential role of apologies within restorative justice processes, and also their strengths and limitations in contemporary social settings.

5 See, for example, White and Epston (1991) and, within a specifically restorative justice context, Gehm (1998); Winslade and Cotter (1996). See also the somewhat analogous, though less public and interactive notion of 'account-making', as discussed by Orbuch (1997).

6 Mediators have been criticised by some for being excessively 'protective' in only granting access to the process in the most favourable of circumstances irrespective of the wishes or, in some cases, needs of the parties themselves (e.g. Hagley 2003: 250ff.). Other forms of restorative justice processes in England and Wales have also been criticised for their failure to empower victims (Stahlkopf 2005: ch. 6; Zernova 2005: 291ff.).

7 A somewhat higher proportion – 58 per cent – would have accepted reparation from their offender.

8 The findings reported here relate to a small preliminary survey of 37 victims and 44 offenders. They were interviewed prior to conferencing in one of the study sites being evaluated as part of a much larger study being funded by the Home Office under the auspices of the Crime Reduction Programme.

9 Meta analysis is a technique for recording and analysing the aggregated statistical results from a collection of discrete empirical research studies.

10 I am indebted to Joanna Shapland (personal communication) for this suggestion.

11 The sense of strategic drift with regard to restorative justice's potential role in assisting crime victims is heightened by the fact that a subsequent 54-page policy document focusing specifically on proposals to provide further support for crime victims contains only two brief references to restorative justice (Home Office *et al.* 2005).

12 Although these particular penalties are only available for young offenders, it is also possible for restorative justice encounters involving adult offenders and their victims to be set up, for example when an offender is sentenced to a new-style generic community order under the 2003 Criminal Justice Act.

13 Differences in restorative justice policy-making with regard to juvenile offenders in the constituent parts of the UK are examined by Dignan (2007).

14 The proportion of victims who were willing to participate in restorative justice encounters ranged from 30 per cent in adult probation cases and 36 per cent of prison cases to 56 per cent of London Crown Court burglary cases and 89 per cent of referral order youth offender panel cases (Shapland *et al.* 2006: Table 3.3).

References

Angel, C. (2004) 'Crime Victims Meet their Offenders: Testing the Impact of Restorative Justice Conferences on Victims' Post Traumatic Stress Symptoms', paper presented to the American Society of Criminology, Nashville, TN, 17 November.

Ashworth, A. (2000) 'Victims' Rights, Defendants' Rights and Criminal Procedure', in A. Crawford and J. Goodey (eds) *Integrating a Victim Perspective within Criminal Justice.* Aldershot: Ashgate Dartmouth.

Boriboonthana, Y. (2006) 'The Effect of Restorative Justice Practices on Crime Victims: A meta-analysis', unpublished PhD thesis, University of Sheffield.

Bottoms, A.E. (2003) 'Some Sociological Reflections on Restorative Justice', in A. von Hirsch, J. Roberts, A.E. Bottoms, K. Roach and M. Schiff (eds) *Restorative Justice and Criminal Justice: Competing or Reconcilable Paradigms?* Oxford: Hart Publishing.

Bottoms, A.E. and Dignan, J. (2004) 'Youth Justice in Great Britain', in M. Tonry and A.N. Doob (eds) *Youth Crime and Youth Justice: Comparative and Cross-National Perspectives*, Crime and Justice: A Review of Research, Vol. 31. Chicago and London: University of Chicago Press.

Braithwaite, J. (1989) *Crime, Shame and Reintegration.* Cambridge: Cambridge University Press.

Campbell, C., Devlin, R., O'Mahony, D., Doak, J., Jackson, J., Corrigan, T. and McEvoy, K. (2006) *Evaluation of the Northern Ireland Youth Conference Service*, NIO Research and Statistical Series Report No. 12 (also available at: (http://www.nio.gov.uk/evaluation_of_the_northern_ireland_youth_conference_service.pdf).

Cantor, G.M. (1976) 'An end to crime and punishment', *The Shingle (Philadelphia Bar Association)*, 39(4): 99–114.

Christie, N. (1977) 'Conflicts as property', *British Journal of Criminology*, 17: 1–15.

Collins, R. (2004) *Interaction Ritual Chains.* Princeton, NJ: Princeton University Press.

Crawford, A. (2000) 'Salient Themes and the Limitations of Restorative Justice', in A. Crawford and J. Goodey (eds) *Integrating a Victim Perspective within Criminal Justice.* Aldershot: Ashgate Dartmouth.

Crnkovich, M. (1993) *Report on the Sentencing Circle in Kangiqsujuaq.* Ottawa: Justice Canada.

Daly, K. (2001) 'Conferencing in Australia and New Zealand: Variations, Research Findings and Prospects', in A.M. Morris and G. Maxwell (eds) *Restorative Justice for Juveniles: Conferencing, Mediation and Circles.* Oxford: Hart Publishing.

Daly, K. (2003) 'Mind the Gap: Restorative Justice in Theory and Practice', in A. von Hirsch, J. Roberts, A.E. Bottoms, K. Roach and M. Schiff (eds) *Restorative Justice and Criminal Justice: Competing or Reconcilable Paradigms?* Oxford: Hart Publishing.

Daly, K. (2005) 'A Tale of Two Studies: Restorative Justice from a Victim's Perspective', in E. Elliott and R.M. Gordon (eds) *New Directions in Restorative Justice: Issues, Practice, Evaluation.* Cullompton: Willan Publishing.

Daly, K. and Immarigeon, R. (1998) 'The past, present and future of restorative justice: Some critical reflections', *Contemporary Justice Review: Issues in Criminal, Social and Restorative Justice*, 1(1): 21–45.

Dignan, J. (1992) 'Repairing the damage: Can reparation be made to work in the service of diversion?', *British Journal of Criminology*, 32(4): 453–72.

Dignan, J. (1994) 'Reintegration through Reparation: A Way Forward for Restorative Justice?', in A. Duff, S. Marshall, R.E. Dobash and R.P. Dobash (eds) *Penal Theory and Penal Practice: Tradition and Innovation in Criminal Justice*. Manchester: Manchester University Press, pp. 231–44.

Dignan, J. (2002) 'Reparation Orders', in B. Williams (ed.) *Reparation and Victim-Focused Social Work*, Research Highlights in Social Work. London and Philadelphia: Jessica Kingsley.

Dignan, J. (2005) *Understanding Victims and Restorative Justice*. Maidenhead: Open University Press.

Dignan, J. (2007) 'Juvenile Justice, Criminal Courts and Restorative Justice', in G. Johnstone and D. Van Ness (eds) *Handbook of Restorative Justice*. Cullompton: Willan Publishing.

Dignan, J. and Cavadino, M. (1996) 'Towards a framework for conceptualising and evaluating models of criminal justice from a victim's perspective', *International Review of Victimology*, 4: 153–82.

Dignan, J. with Lowey, K. (2000) *Restorative Justice Options for Northern Ireland: A Comparative Review*, Review of the Criminal Justice System in Northern Ireland Research Report 10. Belfast: Criminal Justice Review Commission/ Northern Ireland Office.

Duff, R.A. (1986) *Trials and Punishments*. Cambridge: Cambridge University Press.

Duff, R.A. (2001) *Punishment, Communication and Community*. Oxford: Oxford University Press.

Duff, R.A. (2002) 'Restorative Punishment and Punitive Restoration', in L. Walgrave (ed.) *Restorative Justice and the Law*. Cullompton: Willan Publishing.

Duff, R.A. (2003) 'Restoration and Retribution', in A. von Hirsch, J. Roberts, A.E. Bottoms, K. Roach and M. Schiff (eds) *Restorative Justice and Criminal Justice: Competing or Reconcilable Paradigms?* Oxford: Hart Publishing.

Eglash, A. (1977) 'Beyond Restitution: Creative Restitution', in J. Hudson and B. Galaway (eds) *Restitution in Criminal Justice*. Lexington, MA: D.C. Heath and Company.

Foa, E.B. and Kozak, M.J. (1986) 'Emotional processing of fear: Exposure to corrective information', *Psychological Bulletin*, 99: 20–35.

Gehm, J.R. (1998) 'Victim–offender mediation programs: An exploration of practice and theoretical frameworks', *Western Criminology Review* (available online at: (http://wcr.sonoma/edu/v1n1/gehm.html).

Griffiths, T. and Hamilton, R. (1996) 'Sanctioning and Healing: Restorative Justice in Canadian Aboriginal Communities', in B. Galaway and J. Hudson (eds) *The Practice of Restorative Justice*. Monsey, NY: Criminal Justice Press.

Hagley, L. (2003) 'Disempowerment in Victim Offender Mediation', unpublished PhD thesis, University of Birmingham.

Holdaway, S., Davidson, N., Dignan, J., Hammersley, R., Hine, J. and Marsh, P. (2001) *New Strategies to Address Youth Offending: The National Evaluation of the Pilot Youth Offending Teams*. RDS Occasional Paper 69. London: Home Office (also available at: (www.homeoffice.gov.uk/rds/index.html).

Home Office (2003) *Restorative Justice: The Government's Strategy*. London: Home Office.

Home Office (2004) *Restorative Justice: The Government's Strategy – Responses to the Consultation Document*. London: Home Office.

Home Office, Department of Constitutional Affairs and Attorney General (2005) *Rebuilding Lives – Supporting Victims of Crime*, Cm 6705. London: HMSO.

Home Office, Lord Chancellor's Department and Attorney General (2002) *Justice for All*, Cm 5563. London: The Stationery Office.

Hoyle, C., Young, R. and Hill, R. (2002) *Proceed with Caution: An Evaluation of the Thames Valley Police Initiative in Restorative Cautioning*. York: Joseph Rowntree Foundation.

LaPrairie, C. (1995) 'Altering course: New directions in criminal justice and corrections: Sentencing circles and family group conferences', *Australian and New Zealand Journal of Criminology*, Special Issue: Crime, Criminology and Public Policy, December: 78–99.

Latimer, J., Dowden, C. and Muise, D. (2001) *The Effectiveness of Restorative Justice Practices: A Meta-Analysis*. Ottawa: Department of Justice.

Lilles, H. (2001) 'Circle Sentencing: Part of the Restorative Justice Continuum', in A.M. Morris and G. Maxwell (eds) *Restorative Justice for Juveniles: Conferencing, Mediation and Circles*. Oxford: Hart Publishing.

McCold, P. (1998) 'Restorative Justice: Variations on a Theme', in L. Walgrave (ed.) *Restorative Justice for Juveniles: Potentialities, Risks and Problems for Research*. Leuven: Leuven University Press, pp. 185–200.

Maguire, M. and Corbett, C. (1987) *The Effects of Crime and the Work of Victim Support Schemes*. Aldershot: Gower.

Mattinson, J. and Mirrlees-Black, C. (2000) *Attitudes to Crime and Criminal Justice: Findings from the 1998 British Crime Survey*, Home Office Research Study 200. London: Home Office.

Maxwell, G. and Morris, A.M. (1993) *Family, Victims and Culture: Youth Justice in New Zealand*, Wellington, NZ: Social Policy Administration and Victoria University of Wellington.

Morris, A.M. and Maxwell, G. (2000) 'The Practice of Family Group Conferencing', in A. Crawford and J. Goodey (eds) *Integrating a Victim Perspective within Criminal Justice*. Aldershot: Ashgate Dartmouth.

Nathanson, D.L. (1992) *Shame and Pride: Affect, Sex and the Birth of the Self*. New York: Norton.

Newburn, T., Crawford, A., Earle, R., Goldie, S., Hale, C., Masters, G., Netten, A., Saunders, R., Sharpe, K. and Uglow, S. (2002) *The Introduction of Referral Orders into the Youth Justice System*. Home Office Research Study 242. London: Home Office (also available at: http://www.homeoffice.gov.uk/rds/index.html).

Orbuch, T.L. (1997) 'People's accounts count: the sociology of accounts', *Annual Review of Sociology*. 23: 455–78.

Retzinger, S.M. and Scheff, T.J. (1996) 'Strategy for Community Conferences: Emotions and Social Bonds', in B. Galaway and J. Hudson (eds) *Restorative Justice: International Perspectives*, Monsey, NY: Criminal Justice Press, pp. 17–36.

Schafer, S. (1960) *Restitution to Victims of Crime*. London: Stevens & Sons.

Schafer, S. (1968) *Victimology: The Victim and his Criminal*. Reston, VA: Reston.

Schafer, S. (1970) *Compensation and Restitution to Victims of Crime*. Montclair, NJ: Patterson Smith.

Scheff, T.J. and Retzinger, S.M. (1991) *Emotions and Violence*. Lexington, MA: Lexington Books.

Shapland, J., Atkinson, A., College, E., Dignan, J., Howes, M., Johnstone, J., Pennant, R., Robinson, G. and Sorsby, A. (2004) *Implementing Restorative Justice Schemes (Crime Reduction Programme): A Report on the First Year*, A Report on the First Year, Home Office Online Report 32/04. London: Home Office (also available at: http://www.homeoffice.gov.uk/rds/pdfs04/rdsolr3204.pdf).

Shapland, J., Atkinson, A., Atkinson, H., Chapman, B., Colledge, E., Dignan, J., Howes, M., Johnstone, J., Robinson, G. and Sorsby, A. (2006) *Restorative Justice in Practice: The Second Report from the Evaluation of Three Schemes*. Sheffield: Centre for Criminological Research (also available at: http://www.shef.ac.uk/ccr/).

Sherman, L.W., Strang, H., Angel, C., Woods, D., Barnes, G.C., Bennett, S. and Inkpen, N. (2005) 'Effects of face-to-face restorative justice on victims of crime in four randomized controlled trials', *Journal of Experimental Criminology*, 1: 367–95.

Stahlkopf, C. (2005) 'Rhetoric or Reality: Restorative Justice in the Youth Justice System in the United Kingdom', unpublished PhD thesis, University of Oxford.

Strang, H. (2002) *Repair or Revenge: Victims and Restorative Justice*. Oxford: Clarendon Press.

Strang, H., Sherman, L.W., Angel, C., Woods, D., Bennett, S., Newberry-Birch, D. and Inkpen, N. (2006) 'Victims of face-to-face restorative justice conferences: A quasi-experimental analysis', *Journal of Social Issues*, 62(2): 281–306.

Tavuchis, N. (1991) *Mea Culpa: A Sociology of Apology and Reconciliation*. Stanford, CA: Stanford University Press.

Tomkins, S. (1962) *Affect/Imagery/Consciousness*. New York: Springer.

Tufts, J. (2000) 'Attitudes du public face au systeme de justice penale', *Juristat*, 20(12). Centre canadien de al statistique juridique.

Tyler, T.R. (1990) *Why People Obey the Law*. New Haven, CT: Yale University Press.

Umbreit, M.S. (1994) *Victim Meets Offender: The Impact of Restorative Justice and Mediation*. Monsey, NY: Criminal Justice Press.

Umbreit, M.S. (1997) 'Humanistic mediation: A transformation journey of peace-making', *Mediation Quarterly*, 14(3): 201–13.

Van Ness, D.W. (1993) 'New wine and old Wineskins: Four challenges of restorative justice', *Criminal Law Forum*, 4(2): 251–76.

Van Ness, D.W. and Strong, K.H. (2006) *Restoring Justice: An Introduction to Restorative Justice*, 3rd edn. London: LexisNexis/Anderson Publishing.

Walklate, S. (2006) 'Changing Boundaries of the "Victim" in Restorative Justice: So Who is the Victim Now?', in D. Sullivan and L. Tifft (eds) *Handbook of Restorative Justice*. London: Routledge.

Wemmers, J.-A. (2003) 'Victims' Perspectives on Restorative Justice: How Much Involvement are Victims Looking For?' XIth International Symposium of Victimology, Stellenbosch, South Africa, 13–18 July.

White, M. and Epston, D. (1991) *Narrative Means to Therapeutic Ends*. New York: Norton.

Winslade, J. and Cotter, A. (1996) 'Moving from Problem Solving to Narrative Approaches in Mediation', in G. Monk, J. Winslade, K. Crocket and D. Epston (eds) *Narrative Therapy in Practice: The Archaeology of Hope*. San Francisco: Jossey-Bass.

Wright, M. (1982) *Making Good*. London: Sage.

Young, R. (2001) 'Just Cops Doing "Shameful" Business? Police-led Restorative Justice and the Lessons of Research', in A.M. Morris and G. Maxwell (eds) *Restorative Justice for Juveniles: Conferencing, Mediation and Circles*. Oxford: Hart Publishing.

Zernova, M. (2005) 'Restorative Justice: Aspirations of Proponents and Experiences of Participants in Family Group Conferences', unpublished PhD thesis. University of Hull.

Part Four

Comparative Perspectives

Sandra Walklate

Part Four examines some of the issues and policy developments addressed in Part Three by placing them in a comparative perspective. Some time ago Nelken (1994) argued that the future of criminology (and by implication here, victimology) lay with the importance of comparative research. The essence of his argument was that with the increasing importance of transnational crime more needed to be known about how different countries operated legally, politically and culturally, before any strategy to prevent this kind of crime could be implemented. Of course, alongside the increase in transnational crime there has been a rise in the number of victims of such crime, the most telling of which have arguably been those who died and have since suffered as a result of the events in Bhopal in 1984, and more recently those who have suffered as a result of terrorist activity. While events such as these stand out both in their impact and in the memories that they conjure, individuals can also be victimised in different countries in the same way that they are at home, that is from the more routine and mundane events like car crime and street robbery. However, comparisons are not problem-free and can be summarised in one question: what are we comparing? Do we compare concepts of justice; systems of justice; cultures of justice; to name just a few of the possible comparisons that can be made. These difficulties notwithstanding, it is evidently the case, as demonstrated by the contributions in Part Three, that policies, and research methodologies, relating to victims of crime have travelled from country to country, with very little detailed consideration as to the efficacy of those policies in the different legal, social, and political contexts in which they are being operationalised. The authors here endeavour to put some of that detail in place for us.

In Chapter 13 David Miers discusses the development of the criminal injuries compensation scheme in England and Wales. He traces this development from its first formation as the Criminal Injuries Compensation Board in the 1960s to its present format and discusses some aspects of its operational problems. The key to understanding how this scheme operates lies with the notion of the innocent and blameless victim and the distinction that it encourages in compensation terms between the deserving and the undeserving victim. This distinction, of course, flies in the face of what is known about victims and offenders, that is, they share in very similar characteristics. However, delinquent victims, to use the term that Miers adopts, implicated as they are in what happened to them, are either barred from compensation or receive less compensation on the grounds of their delinquency. This distinction, as Miers documents, fuels the discussion on what kind of injuries are considered for compensation as well as how much people might receive and under what circumstances. He goes on to discuss the extent to which the events of 7 July 2005 acted as a catalyst for the UK government to review the operating practices of the scheme, this has led to a reconsideration of the kinds of injuries the scheme might compensate and under what circumstances. Miers goes on to explore the main differences and similarities between the scheme in England and Wales with that of Northern Ireland and also draws on some examples from Europe, North America and Australasia, in this exploration. Here the point is well made about the problems of comparison alluded to above. While there have been a number of European directives setting standards for such schemes, their actual operation is clearly very variable. Miers asks whether or not, if such schemes did not exist, it would be necessary to invent them. This is an intriguing question, given the cultural changes that have occurred since the inception of the CICB in 1964. Commentators like Furedi (2002) would argue that we now live in a compensation culture, and the question is perhaps not an easy one to answer. However, Miers seems to suggest that the existence of such schemes constitutes a means whereby expression is given to the idea of 'civic trust'. In other words it seems reasonable that when the assumption of an ordered social life is fractured by events beyond an individual's control, governments step in and make good that fracture in some way. This position, of course, still embraces the notion of the deserving victim and all the operational problems that this entails. The nature and impact of European directives is taken up by Jan Van Dijk and Marc Groenhuijsen in the following chapter.

Chapter 14 reports on data gathered by the International Criminal Victimisation Survey, with which Jan Van Dijk has been associated since its inception in 1989. In this chapter they use data from the most recent sweep of this survey as a way of monitoring the effectiveness of European directives on the treatment of victims of crime. This data illustrates the variable levels of reporting crime from country to country which as the authors suggest is clearly the first barrier to monitoring the effectiveness of victim policies. Reasons for non-reporting also vary but the most common are familiar to us all: thinking that the crime was not serious enough to report and believing that the police would not do anything about it if it was reported. Echoing Chapter 8 in this volume, these authors focus a good deal of attention on victims' satisfaction with the police response to them, concurring with Mawby on the importance of the nature and quality of the initial police response to the victim. The data here reports a downward trend in satisfaction with the police response to victims especially in countries where these policies have been particularly promoted, most notably the Netherlands and the UK.

There are different possible explanations for this: one might be that this is a result of raised victim expectations following from the promotion of victim policies. Whatever the explanation, they go on to document significant gaps between the demand for and the supply of victim services across Europe, and by implication point to the difficulties in presuming, what, if anything, European directives can offer in countries on quite different trajectories in the development of their victim policies. Indeed, as their data elucidates, even those with quite advanced victim-oriented services still have some way to go. In Chapter 15 Tracey Booth and Kerry Carrington document some aspects of these different policy trajectories.

Chapter 15 complements those chapters in Part Three that concerned themselves with the development of public and voluntary sector policy delivery for the victim of crime. As was suggested in those contributions, and as has been alluded to above, the question of policy transfer has become an increasingly prominent feature in the criminal justice arena over the last ten years. How such processes of transfer actually work is varied and variable (for a fuller discussion of this see Sparks and Newburn 2002), but what is evident is that within the Anglo-speaking world particular policies seem to have acquired a passport, and Booth and Carrington document the influence of that passport. They situate their analysis within an appreciation of the different and differential role that the victims' movement, including the feminist movement, has had in different countries, thus echoing some of the observations already made by Williams and Goodman in Chapter 9. They point out that the victims' movement is much more politicised in some countries than in others (a dynamic that is clearly a variable in understanding the likely success or otherwise in travelling victim-oriented policy) and particularly point to the way in which the terrorist attacks of 9/11 gave some leverage to victims' movements in the United States. They go on to consider the various ways in which efforts have been made to improve victim participation within different criminal justice systems from their role in sentencing, victim impact statements (which are discussed in detail, thus developing the analysis offered by Sanders and Jones in Chapter 11), and victim involvement in parole decisions. As the question of restorative justice is discussed in detail by Dignan in Chapter 12, this issue is not addressed here explicitly but is set within a wider analysis of Indigenous and customary law and the role of specialised courts. The latter has been embraced in the context of domestic violence in England and Wales (see Cook *et al.* 2004). As Booth and Carrington observe, all of these initiatives arguably endeavour to move the role of the victim in the criminal justice process from one of passivity to one of activity, and it remains a moot point as to both the viability of these policies and their efficacy.

What is particularly interesting about the material presented by Booth and Carrington is the amount of time and effort that appears to have been dedicated in Australia in particular in testing the efficacy of the interventions that have been put in place and assessing what their impact has been, if any, on the victims' perceptions and experience of the criminal justice system. It is evident from their analysis that the results of this are not clear or straightforward, since even in Australia the different territories can and do implement different interpretations and practices in respect of the same policy. The result is that the questions of what works, where, when, how, and for whom are quite complex. Booth and Carrington's analysis is very sensitive to the way in which local difference can impact upon the policy intention. If this is the case in the local national context of Australia, how much more complex might the picture be if the question of policy transfer was considered in this detailed way across national, legal, social and cultural borders, raising all kinds of questions about why and how policies addressed here and in the previous section have had such a global impact. Jones and Newburn (2002, 2005) have engaged in this kind of analysis in relation to zero tolerance policing and private prisons utilising a framework that involves understanding both policy process and policy level, lending some weight to the view of O'Malley (2002) that globalisation was not taking its toll on all criminal justice systems in the same way. In a similar vein I have argued (Walklate 2005) that there is obviously some mileage in understanding which local political, social and cultural conditions are, for example, facilitative of restorative justice initiatives, and which are not, and what the reasons for those differences might look like. Taken together, the contributors here lend considerable support to the value that such work, which places the problems of comparison and policy transfer at its centre, might provide.

References

Cook, D., Burton, M., Robinson, A. and Vallely, C. (2004) *Evaluation of Specialist Domestic Violence Courts/Fast Track Systems*. London: Crown Prosecution Service/Department of Constitutional Affairs, London.

Furedi, F. (2002) *The Culture of Fear*. London: Continuum.

Nelken, D. (ed.) (1994) *The Futures of Criminology*. London: Sage.

Jones, T. and Newburn, T. (2002) 'Policy convergence and crime control in the USA and the UK: Streams of influence and levels of impact', *Criminal Justice*, 2(2): 173–205.

Jones, T. and Newburn, T. (2005) 'Comparative criminal justice policy making in the United States and the United Kingdom: The case of private prisons', *British Journal of Criminology*, 45(1): 58–80.

O'Malley, P. (2002) 'Globalising risk: Distinguishing styles of "neo-liberal" criminal justice in Australia and the USA', *Criminal Justice*, 2(2): 205–22.

Sparks, R. and Newburn, T. (eds) (2002) 'How does crime policy travel?', *Criminal Justice*, 2(2), special issue.

Walklate, S. (2005) 'Researching restorative justice: Politics, policy and process', *Critical Criminology*, 13: 165–79.

Chapter 13

Looking beyond Great Britain: the development of criminal injuries compensation

David Miers

Introduction

For some years a central claim of criminal justice policy has been to 'make sure that the victim's voice is heard at the heart of Government' (Home Office 2005: 8; see generally Rock 2004: chapter 10). Not the least of the reasons that has accompanied its restatement has been the perceived need to redress the system's balance in the victim's favour. The use of this metaphor is a contentious matter that goes beyond this chapter's scope (Henderson 1985; Wood 2005), but it figured prominently in the 1960s when the Criminal Injuries Compensation Scheme ('the Scheme') was first introduced in Great Britain. The massive changes that have taken place over the past 40 years in the relationship between victims of crime and the criminal justice system are well documented (Sanders 1999; Hoyle and Zedner 2006).[1] Of particular note are the government's efforts to give meaning to the principle that as the guilty party is the offender, 'in an ideal world, it should be the offender who compensates the victim' (Home Office 2005: 14). The making of compensation orders against offenders as an element of or possibly the only sentence may in part satisfy that idealism, as may such long-standing devices as restitution and reparation,[2] and its more recent promotion of restorative justice (Miers and Semenchuck 2005). Within this response, the Scheme, which was placed on a statutory footing in 1995, now constitutes a central feature (Home Office 2005: 6–12). The Criminal Injuries Compensation Authority currently awards around £170 million a year (CICA 2003: 9; 2006b: 5), and since 1964 more than £3 billion has been awarded to approximately 960,000 successful applicants under the Scheme's various terms.

This chapter comprises three sections. The first traces the development of the Scheme. It focuses on the Home Office's justification for its introduction and remarks on one of the structural tensions that has always troubled the implementation of this taxpayer-funded arrangement, dealing with delinquent victims. The second describes the Scheme's operation and remarks on those of its aspects that were the subject of a fundamental review in 2005/06.

This section also briefly remarks on developments in Northern Ireland. The third comments on the underlying uncertainties that concern the Scheme's future scope and on the gradually sharpening European focus on crime victim compensation. The chapter uses examples from North America and Australasia to highlight particular points, and it concludes by remarking on the shift in the purpose of compensation that is evident in a number of countries, including Great Britain.

The development of the Criminal Injuries Compensation Scheme: establishing the scheme

The original, non-statutory, Scheme was established in 1964, administered by the Criminal Injuries Compensation Board ('the Board'). It was based on recommendations that were the product of a shift in governmental concern about the place of the victim in the criminal justice system (Home Office 1961, 1964).[3] The critical response to the liberal ideology that informed penal and criminal justice policy during the 1960s politicised the experience of personal victimisation as a means of questioning that policy's integrity and credibility (Miers 1980; Elias 1983). Part of this politicisation focused on the apparent discrepancies between the state's treatment of offenders and of their victims. Nor was this criticism confined to criminal justice policies in Great Britain. Many of the compensation schemes introduced in other common law jurisdictions at this time were preceded by public campaigns to correct what their critics saw as a similar imbalance.[4] There were and continue to be deep-rooted concerns about secondary victimisation that require attention, if for no other reason than that victims' alienation from the system means that prosecutions, especially of sexual offences, fail (Hoyle and Sanders 2000). Whatever their substance, the perceived discrepancies between the state's treatment of offenders and of victims was, and continues to be, a powerful rhetorical device (Ashworth 2000: 186; Garland 2001: 143).[5]

If critics were quick to compare the state's treatment of offenders with that of victims, neither were those responsible for formulating policy slow to recognise the political capital that could be made from such comparisons. The White Paper that put forward many of the reforms of the 1960s observed:

> The assumption that the claims of the victim are sufficiently satisfied if the offender is punished by society becomes less persuasive as society in its dealing with offenders increasingly emphasises the reformative aspects of punishment. Indeed in the public mind the interests of the offender not infrequently seem to be placed before those of the victim. This is certainly not the correct emphasis. (Home Office 1959: 7)

This observation was cited with approval in the 1964 White Paper, which included the specific proposals that became the Scheme. The key point is that the Scheme made *unique* provision for victims of personal crime by comparison with victims of other disabling injuries, for example at work or on the road, and in so doing also visibly differentiated them from any resources directed *to* offenders. For this, victims would themselves need to be visibly different *from* offenders: they would need to be 'innocent'. We return to the implications of this core requirement later in this chapter.

Justifying state compensation for victims of crime

When it was introduced the Scheme was one of many being established throughout the common law world. Notable at this time was their promoters' recurring efforts to justify the allocation of public funds to meet the gap between the 'ideal world' and the reality of the victim's theoretical civil remedy,[6] a gap that continues to be a matter of official comment. '[Offenders] are not always caught or even identified, and may lack the means to pay compensation to the victim' (Home Office 2005: 14). Clearly the victim of violent crime is at a disadvantage in these respects, but so too are the victims of property offences, white collar crime and a whole range of regulatory offences. The difficulty with the argument that the state should stand behind the offender is that it argues too much. When it accepted the desirability of making financial provision for the victims of violent crime the Home Office was emphatic that there was no question of its extension to theft and criminal damage, still less that victims enjoyed a right to compensation (Home Office 1961: para. 17).

Among other possible justifications, their promoters sought to locate the juridical basis of a compensation scheme in doctrinal arguments based on contract and state liability. The contractarian argument (that in consideration for citizens giving up the right to the private use of force, the state will protect them) fails because it is plainly fictitious. Citizens gain far more than they lose as a result of the state's monopoly over law enforcement (Ashworth 1986), and it overstates the force of recognising citizens' rights. Allowing that the state has an obligation to protect its citizens says no more than that it should provide a fair share of what might reasonably be allocated to such public goods as health care or education, or law enforcement. Neither does it follow that its failure to meet that obligation in any case should carry a right to damages as measured in the law of contract (Haldane and Harvey 1995).

The state liability argument posits the state as a tortfeasor where its negligence in preventing criminal activity causes citizens to be injured. As a general proposition, the common law does not support this. The Home Office's long-held position is entirely consistent with the courts' repeated decisions that in the absence of a 'special distinctive risk' of harm to the victim, it would not be fair, just or reasonable to impose liability for another's offences on a police authority.[7] This argument assumed fresh significance in the context of the United States' federal government's enactment of a Victim Compensation Fund to compensate the survivors of, and dependants of those killed by, the terrorist crimes in the United States on 11 September 2001 (Goldscheid 2004). The Fund was an eleventh-hour afterthought to the Air Transport Safety and System Stabilisation Act 2001, which exempted the airlines and various other bodies from liability in tort for any negligence on their part (Alexander 2004; Issachoroff and Mansfield 2006: 284–320). But there is substantial doubt as to whether the survivors would have been able to establish liability as a matter of law (Diller 2004: 721–22; Sebok 2004: 501–17).

Even as it has always denied that the state has any legal liability for criminal injuries, the Home Office has repeatedly affirmed that the government recognises that the public feels a sense of responsibility for, and sympathy with, the innocent victim of a crime of violence. It is 'simply right' that these sentiments are given financial expression.[8] Underlying this simple moral assertion is a more powerful argument that draws on elements of these doctrinal arguments. This is that to experience crime is to experience a failure in civic trust; that is, in the trust that citizens have (and are encouraged to have) in the capacity of the criminal justice system to protect them. 'Civic trust' is a condition of social justice (de Greiff 2006: 461–4). It describes, first, the trust that citizens have of one another in a society that is predominantly well ordered, and in which most social interactions are successfully (non-violently) mediated between them and not by law. Second, it describes the trust that citizens have in the legal system to respond to offensive conduct. This trust may be thought to require that the law ought not only show a concern for the victim's injury but also take concrete measures to restore the harm done to public trust and confidence.

The further argument, which continues to figure as a justification for their special financial recognition, is that what differentiates victims of crime from victims of other disabling events is that they have suffered a distinctive harm. Unlike other forms of hardship such as those caused by road accidents, industrial accidents and diseases, congenital disabilities, or even another's negligence, crime victims have, stereotypically, suffered injuries that were inflicted 'deliberately', or more precisely, intentionally or recklessly. The injuries they sustain may be as unexpected, severe or disruptive of their lives as an accident at work, but unlike them, they were, in the paradigm case, the result of being the target of another's ill-will and not just of another's inadvertence. This also differentiates them from the victims of property crime precisely because the offender's ill-will is in those cases (primarily) directed against an inanimate object. It is this feature of personal animus that makes the defendant's behaviour morally objectionable and that justifies treating the offence as a public wrong and as the occasion for public censure. But for the Scheme's promoters it is not enough that the impact of violent crime should be met from social welfare, available to all who suffer financial hardship, or that the moral balance that the offender disturbed is corrected only by the mobilisation of the criminal justice system against him. What is also required is the public recognition of the disruption to the victim's moral right as an individual to the quiet enjoyment of her membership of her community; that is, as a citizen. This is made explicit in the particular cases of sexual offences and homicide. Here, the Home Office argued, the public find sexual offences 'especially repugnant' and the circumstances of homicide 'particularly horrific and the trauma to the victim's family [...] severe'. A financial award 'is society's way of acknowledging the harm that has been done to the victim as a representative of the community' (Home Office 2005: 14, 21; Duff 1998).

The legal system both depends on citizens' generalised norm-compliance (else it could not cope) and more particularly relies on the trust that they have in the system if it is to respond effectively. Citizens' willingness to report offences rests upon their trust that the system will reliably produce the outcomes they can reasonably expect; that is, efficient crime prevention measures and the investigation and prosecution of offences. The initiatives that the Home Office proposed in 2005 are, as has been the case in the past, designed to restore that trust. The Scheme may be seen as a long-standing element in that design (Home Office 2005: 23–34). But this does not address what would constitute 'appropriate amounts' of compensation to those victims to be included in it (Home Office 2005: 18). In particular, it is not obvious why the British taxpayer should be expected to bear the costs of compensating the victim for future loss of earnings or the cost of long-term care, in addition to an amount payable for the injury itself; and, so far as they are not deductible under its provisions, these costs will exceed what victims of other disabling life events will recover under the social security system. We return later to the more particular issue of what ought to be the Scheme's scope.

Innocent, blameless victims

Victims who have significant criminal records or whose own conduct contributed to their injuries present both policy and operational difficulties. The policy difficulties stem from the observable fact that delinquent victims resemble offenders too closely, and may have been formally so defined in the past (Miers 2000). The possibility that they might receive compensation therefore both subverts one of the Scheme's prime objectives, to distinguish victims from offenders, and threatens the stereotype of the 'innocent' victim. The politicisation of crime victims requires that the taxpayer be asked to compensate only those who present 'deserving' characteristics. These are the 'ideal' victims, stereotypically children, the elderly and the law-abiding, whose lives are disrupted by predatory (young and typically male) offenders (Christie 1986). These stereotypes are just that: but they play a powerful role in populist demands for 'justice' for victims of crime, and equally powerfully require the exclusion of delinquent victims from the Scheme's provisions.

Broadly speaking, this exclusion addresses two forms of delinquency. The first comprise cases in which the victim's own behaviour contributed to the incident in which he was injured. Provisions that disentitle applicants in such cases are ubiquitous in the common and the civil law world. All of the United States' schemes permit the denial or reduction of benefits to people who are injured while committing crimes or engaging in substantial misconduct contributing to their victimisation. These provisions routinely pose operational questions, such as determining the extent of the victim's contribution, and on occasion questions concerning the implementation of the policy, such as what kind of conduct should be taken into account, but in general they are uncontroversial.

By contrast, the exclusion of those with a history of offending behaviour, but which has no causal relationship with the injury, is. The exclusion of claimants with 'live' criminal records has been an article of faith for the Scheme and is justified by the same policy that excludes victims on the ground of their conduct. Prior to and since its inception, both the agency and the Home Office have repeated that the Scheme applies to the 'blameless' victim (CICA 2004: 4; Home Office 2005: 15). But 'blame' in this context does not refer to a victim's actions in respect of the criminal injury, but to his or her moral worth as a person who should properly be the beneficiary of public money. The Home Office recognised that 'opinions are sharply divided' between those who believe that although the conviction is unspent, the offender's sentence has been served, and those who consider it unacceptable that claimants with unspent convictions for serious offences should be compensated by the taxpayer (Home Office 2005: 21). This division of opinion is reflected in North America, where a minority of schemes permit reduction or denial, and at the European level, where a comparative analysis of 16 European schemes found that some did and some did not contain such a provision (Greer 1996: 707).[9] The operation of the Scheme's provisions is examined later in the chapter.

Current arrangements in Great Britain and in Northern Ireland

In describing the Scheme that has been operating in Britain since the mid-1990s this section has a broader purpose. This is to identify the main parameters of *any* such scheme; for example, as is required by Article 12.2 of the European Union's Council Directive of 2004 for the 'fair and appropriate' compensation of victims of 'violent intentional crimes' (European Union 2004). Where relevant I note the standards set by the *Convention on the Compensation of Victims of Violent Crime* (Council of Europe 1983), and comment on the detailed changes proposed by the Home Office in 2005.

The British Scheme

Structure

The present Scheme was made under section 1 of the Criminal Injuries Compensation Act 1995, coming into force on 1 April 1996. This followed a Home Office review which, while making radical changes to the non-statutory Scheme that had been in operation since 1964, retained many of its aspects, in particular those concerning the scope of compensable injuries and the conditions of eligibility (see Miers 1997, 2001; Padley and Begley 2005).

The primary substantive change was the substitution of a tariff for the common law basis for the assessment of general damages, but there remained significant similarities to the primary incidents of personal injury and Fatal Accident Act actions in respect of the assessment of special damages. The major formal change was the creation of two new non-departmental public bodies replacing the Criminal Injuries Compensation Board to deal respectively with initial decisions, the Criminal Injuries Compensation Authority (CICA), and appeals against those decisions, the Criminal Injuries Compensation Appeals Panel (CICAP). Following a further review a number of changes were introduced with effect from 1 April 2001 (Home Office 1999). In what follows I footnote some references to the two latest reports of the Criminal Injuries Compensation Authority that illustrate the detailed application of the Scheme's provisions.

Criminal injuries: definition

The Scheme applies to three broad categories of criminal injury causing personal injury or death (Scheme 2001: para. 8). The first is a crime of violence, which the Scheme does not define, but may be taken to include any offence against the person that may be committed intentionally or recklessly, but not negligently. Given its centrality, the lack of definition, which maintains the position under the pre-1996 Scheme, might be thought surprising. However, the vast majority of applications raise no issue on this matter and where it has been judicially tested the courts have treated its definition as a question of fact. Equally, there may have seemed little point in endeavouring to undertake what is a problematic exercise: attempts to define 'a crime of violence' are likely to result either in over- or under-inclusion of offences. By contrast, jurisdictions such as Canada with Criminal Codes typically tie their schemes to specified Code offences. The omission of a definition in the Scheme means that 'crime of violence' has always been stipulated to cover the offences of arson and poisoning.[10] Injuries caused by traffic offences continue to be excluded, unless there is evidence that the vehicle was deliberately used to cause injury.

The second category of offence comprises injuries arising from an offence of trespass on a railway. This can include injuries sustained by train drivers and their passengers caused by acts such as leaving objects on the tracks or throwing objects at the train. But its primary beneficiaries have been train drivers who suffer psychiatric injury as a result of dealing with suicides and attempted suicides on the railway. Its formalisation in the pre-1996 Scheme was a tribute to the political influence of the railway trade unions. The third category comprises accidental injuries arising from activity 'directed to containing, limiting or remedying the consequences of a crime', but only where the victim was, at the time he sustained the injury, taking an exceptional risk which was justified in all the circumstances (Scheme 2001: para 12). This will cover 'good samaritans' who go to the assistance of persons injured by criminal violence; for example following the bombings in London in July 2005. Its primary beneficiaries have been the emergency services, notably the police. When considering such claims CICA will apply different standards between different rescuers; what is exceptional for citizens may not be for police officers.

The Home Office for some time regarded these two categories as anomalous provisions of the Scheme, both of which go beyond the EU Council Directive's requirement to provide for the victims of intentional violent crime. Its 2005 Consultation Paper once again proposed their exclusion; indeed, it went further, proposing the exclusion of all employees criminally injured in the course of their duties, typically teachers, medical and prison staff (Home Office 2005: 21). Altogether, they account for awards totalling £11.6 million a year, 85 per cent of which are made to public sector employees. The government's intention was that such injuries should be met by the victims' employers, whether public or private sector. As expected, the proposals generated strong opposition, not least, and unsurprisingly, from the constituency that benefits most, the police, who accounted for 48 per cent of the awards made in 2004/05, 77 per cent of which were for accidental injuries while taking an exceptional risk (Home Office 2005: Annex 3, para. 28). There was similarly fierce opposition from the business community who naturally resented the inevitable increase in their insurance premiums.

Criminal injuries: proof

It is for the applicant to make out her case, to which, as section 3(2) of the Criminal Injuries Compensation Act 1995 provides, 'the standard of proof shall be that applicable in civil proceedings'; that is, the balance of probabilities.

The Scheme does not require that the offender be convicted of an offence; indeed, convictions have figured in slightly less than half of the applications received. Proof that the injury was caused by a criminal offence *may* be demonstrated by a conviction, but even here CICA must exercise its own judgement in the matter. Neither, save in the case of domestic violence, need the offender be identified and prosecuted, or even, as in the case of young children, amenable to conviction.[11] Nor is acquittal fatal to an application. Where there is no conviction, the usual question for the Scheme is whether the requisite fault and external elements of a crime of violence can be inferred from the facts as reported to and verified by the police or from other cogent evidence.[12] In answering those questions CICA is bound to follow the courts' interpretation of the relevant criminal law. In some instances there may, on the facts, be no issue. In the case of the suicide bombings in July 2005, the Authority publicly stated that it would not be necessary for claimants to establish that a crime of violence took place, as 'this [was] all too obvious' (CICA 2005: para. 26).

One of the requirements to make out the case effectively imposes on the victim a personal duty to report the injury as soon as possible, normally to the police (Scheme 2001: para. 13(a)). Failure to do so may result in refusal or reduction of an award. Only where there are very good reasons why the victim did not make his own report will reporting via a third party be acceptable. These typically include cases where the victim had been knocked unconscious, is a young child or is disabled in some way.[13]

A connected ground on which an award may be refused or reduced is where the applicant failed to co-operate with the police or other authority in attempting to bring the assailant to justice, or with the Authority in connection with the claim. These too are obligations to which the Scheme has always attached considerable importance. Given that in many applications no offender was identified, they comprise the main safeguards against fraud.[14]

Criminal injuries: limitation of actions

The claim for compensation must be made within two years of the incident. Paragraph 17 gives CICA discretion to waive this condition where it is reasonable and in the interests of justice to do so, taking into account such factors as the applicant's age, medical condition and availability of contemporaneous police records. The two-year time limit can create particular difficulties for claims relating to sexual abuse against the applicant when a child. There are a number of important considerations in these cases, not least the need for sensitivity to victims who may have experienced difficulty in coming to terms, in particular, to being sexually abused by their parents or close relatives. There are also likely to be problems with the verification of the incident(s), which becomes progressively difficult over time, and with delay in the appearance of any injury subsequent to the incident, in particular mental injury.

Criminal injuries: the financial threshold

A universal feature of criminal injury schemes is a financial threshold below which awards will not be made.[15] For many, this will, as in the Scheme, where it was set in 1996 at £1,000, be expressed in money terms, but for others comprise a means test. This is particularly so in the United States, where compensation schemes supplement the social security systems that generally address financial hardship caused by disabling injuries. This principle of social policy stands in contrast to the essentially bureaucratic reason for the inclusion of a minimum in the British Scheme, that the payment of small sums will be administratively more expensive than their substantive value.[16] But thresholds can also be used (and raised) as a means of reallocating the available budget to more serious injuries, as the Home Office did in the past and considered during 2005.

Compensable injuries

Compensable injuries are personal injuries, which include 'physical injury (including fatal injury), mental injury (that is, temporary mental anxiety, medically verified, or a disabling mental illness confirmed by psychiatric diagnosis) and disease (that is, a medically recognised illness or condition)' (Scheme 2001: para. 9). The Scheme is confined (unlike compensation orders) to personal injury. No award can be made for any loss of or damage to property, or for any injury arising from the commission of such an offence. A person who suffers mental trauma as a consequence of returning home to find it burgled and seriously damaged does not sustain an injury under the Scheme.

Physical injuries and disease

The kinds of injury that constitute 95 per cent of claims have arisen from the most common offences against the person such as assault occasioning actual bodily harm, wounding, and causing grievous bodily harm.[17] Where these result in a physical injury that exceeds the financial threshold the victim will be eligible for an award based on the tariff. Derived initially from common law values applied in personal injury actions and revalued in 2001, the tariff is the Scheme's substitute for general damages that are payable in a personal injury action.

All tariff awards include an (unquantified) element representing the mental anxiety normally associated with a physical injury. This may additionally be taken to address the sense of insecurity or lack of confidence that victims, especially the elderly, may experience, and may be important where as the result of a sexual offence, the victim is fearful that s/he has contracted a sexually transmitted disease. Where the victim is infected with HIV/AIDS, the tariff makes express provision.[18] Many common assaults result only in minor injuries which, valued individually, would not meet the threshold. The Scheme addresses this by providing that victims who sustain three 'minor injuries', such as cuts and grazes, bruising, black eyes and bloody noses, will qualify for compensation where the residual effects were significant and required repeated medical attention. As we shall see later in the chapter, in 2005 the Home Office proposed a radically different way of responding to these 'minor' but often psychologically debilitating effects of being a victim of crime.

Mental injury

Claims for mental injury are potentially complex. Broadly speaking, they fall into two types. The first comprises claims for mental injury accompanying the victim's physical injury. Where it satisfies the definition, the mental injury is compensable under the tariff, according to its severity.[19] The second comprises claims by victims who did not suffer any physical injury but who were traumatised by the events or their immediate aftermath and seek compensation for that mental injury alone. Here the Scheme requires some interpretation.

Paragraph 9 specifies four categories in which compensation will be payable for mental injury without physical injury, but in each case imposes restrictions. First, victims of sexual offences may recover, but not in cases where as a matter of law they were unable to give consent (for example, because of their young age), they consented in fact. This would be irrelevant for the purpose of determining the offender's guilt, but it disqualifies the victim from an award. The second permits recovery to railway employees who witnessed or were closely involved in the immediate aftermath of a physical injury arising from an offence of trespass on a railway.

The other two are of more general application, and mirror the common law's approach in personal injury actions, which seeks to restrict defendants' liability for psychiatric injuries caused by their negligence. The third category comprises what the common law calls 'primary' victims, being a victim immediately injured by the victimising event, which may be a physical, fatal or a mental injury. Where the primary victim sustains a mental injury only, he is eligible for compensation only 'if he was put in reasonable fear of immediate physical harm to his own person' (Scheme 2001: para. 9(a)). The victim of an attempted robbery who subsequently developed mental anxiety or illness would qualify under this heading. So would a person who was present during the robbery of another, but *only* if she was put in fear of physical harm to herself; it is not enough that she was put in fear for the safety of that other person. The provision is also applicable to a person who is stalked, subjected to silent phone calls or other forms of harassment. Whether the victim was put in 'reasonable' fear of 'immediate' harm is a question of fact that turns on the applicant's own characteristics, such as age, gender, physical and mental capacity.

The fourth category comprises 'secondary' victims, persons who are mentally injured by the fact of a criminal injury to a primary victim. They will qualify if they meet two conditions. The first is that they must have had a close relationship of love and affection with the primary victim which subsisted (except in fatal cases) at the time of the claim. Whether there is such a relationship is a question of fact. The second condition is that the applicant must have either witnessed and been present on the occasion when the primary victim was injured, or have been closely involved in the immediate aftermath. An example of the first alternative is a parent who suffers mental injury as a result of witnessing her son being physically injured or killed, as by the bomb blast on the bus in Tavistock Square, London on which they were travelling on 7 July 2005. An example of the second is a parent who suffers mental injury when, being in his office near Tavistock Square, responded to a mobile phone call from his daughter by going at once to the scene where he finds that she had been physically (or mentally) injured by that explosion.[20]

Uncompensable persons

As noted above, there are two aspects to Scheme's exclusion of delinquent victims.[21] We consider here key points in their operation.

The victim's conduct

Paragraph 13(d) provides that an award may be refused or reduced because of the applicant's conduct before, during or after the events giving rise to the application. The issue that arises is the scope of that disentitling conduct. Typical are cases in which the victim displayed a willingness to engage in violent confrontation, such as an agreement to take part in a fight, striking the first blow, or aggressive or threatening behaviour. This is, of course, conduct exhibited by offenders, and it may be a matter of chance as to which of the two protagonists ends up in hospital. A second, more controversial, case arises where the victim was at the time of injury under the influence of alcohol or illegal drugs. In many cases there will be a mix of violent conduct and the consumption of alcohol; but the question is whether merely *being* drunk at the time should disadvantage the claim. Following proposals for 'cutting out drunks' (Home Office 1999: para. 50),[22] a new paragraph 14 was introduced. This gives the claims officer discretion to refuse or reduce an award 'where he considers that excessive consumption of alcohol or use of illicit drugs by the applicant contributed to the circumstances which gave rise to the injury.'

The essential difference between the Scheme and the common law, under which delinquent claimants who sue their offenders may also fail or have their damages reduced because of their conduct, is that the Scheme is publicly funded. The examples above do not, as the 1961 White Paper put it, constitute behaviour in which 'innocent' victims engage: it is not behaviour in respect of which the state may owe them any moral obligation, 'at least in the form of compensation for that injury' (Home Office 1961: para. 31). Indeed, while there may be a causal link between the victim's use of offensive language and the injury he sustained, the provision does not require it. Conduct subsequent to the injury that is wholly unrelated to it that results, for example, in the victim being convicted of an offence, will also trigger its application.[23]

The victim's character

More controversial is paragraph 13(e), which permits the Authority to refuse or reduce an award because of the applicant's character as shown by his criminal convictions (excluding spent convictions) or by evidence available to the claims officer. This can comprise cautions registered against the applicant, or, indeed, police evidence that they are aware of his criminal activity, but have been unable to bring a prosecution. The provision does not require any relationship to exist between the victim's criminal record and the events giving rise to the injury. Moreover, in a claim arising from a fatal injury the victim's bad character may be equally fatal to his dependant's claim, no matter how 'blameless' that person's character may be.

The Scheme does not apply to convictions that are spent under the Rehabilitation of Offenders Act 1974 (Scheme 2001: Guide, para. 8.15). CICA uses a system of 'penalty points' for live convictions, based in part upon the rehabilitation periods in the 1974 Act and in part on the period of time between the imposition of the sentence and the receipt of the application. Although the calculation of the applicable penalty points in any case may prove difficult, the intended transparency of the new Scheme in this regard is a clear improvement on its predecessor. In general, the calculation gives increasing credit as the period of time between the original sentence and the application to the Authority increases; in this way the 1996 Scheme formalises its predecessor's recognition of an applicant's efforts to go straight. Conversely, the shorter the time between the sentence and the application, the greater the degree of reduction. The table of penalty points ensures that applications from claimants who have pursued a life of crime, or otherwise reoffend will always be subject to the scale of percentage reductions. Part of its 2005 consultation invited views about the detail of this sliding scale, but the government also indicated that it was not minded to change the basic proposition (Home Office 2005: 21).[24]

Compensable persons

The Scheme applies without discrimination as to the nationality of the victim. In this respect the United Kingdom has, for as long as it has been in operation, been compliant with Article 12.2 of the EU Council Directive. By contrast, British citizens criminally injured in countries that have no such arrangements are not covered by the Scheme, and will be uncompensated. This was the case with British citizens killed or injured in New York on 9/11 and in the Egyptian resort of Sharm-el-Sheikh in July 2005. The government's response was to make small payments available to them not exceeding £3,000, to assist their immediate medical and other practical needs. But the demands that it should develop a long-term policy on criminal injuries sustained by British citizens abroad raise 'a number of complex issues' that remain unresolved.[25]

Survivors

The compensation that is payable under the Scheme falls broadly into two categories. The first is the 'standard amount' determined by reference to the nature of the injury (the tariff). This comprises 467 descriptions of injury differentiated according to their seriousness among 25 award levels, from £1,000 to £250,000 (the maximum award for any single injury). In the case of multiple injuries each of whose tariff value exceeds the minimum payment, CICA can award a proportion of the standard amount payable for the second and the third most serious injuries: these are respectively 30 per cent and 15 per cent.

The second is an 'additional amount' payable where the effects of the injury have lasted for longer than 28 weeks. This is payable in respect of loss of earnings and/or earning capacity, and/or as special expenses for continuing medical or other care, including alterations to accommodation and the like.[26] This can include compensation for loss of or damage to property or equipment on which the applicant relied as a physical aid (such as spectacles or a hearing aid), reasonable private medical expenses, and compensation for long-term care.

Fatalities

The Scheme makes threefold provision for cases in which the victim dies as a result of the victimising event. It provides, first, for an award for 'bereavement'. Where there is only one qualifying claimant, this is £11,000; where there is more than one, each receives £5,500. Second, a qualifying claimant who was under 18 years of age at the date of the parent's death will receive a payment for loss of parental services of up to £2,000 a year. This award is quite separate from any compensation under the third head, the loss of support (dependency) payable to the victim's dependants.

Assessing compensation

The assessment of the award for 'additional compensation' and for loss of dependency is based closely on the methods followed for the calculation of these sums at common law and under the Fatal Accidents Act 1976. They are too complex a matter to pursue here (see Padley and Begley 2005), but two matters may be mentioned.

Financial limitations

So far as tariff awards are concerned, the applicant's financial circumstances are entirely irrelevant. Rich or poor, the only consideration is whether the victim's injury is valued at least at the £1,000 minimum. There is a maximum amount for any single tariff award (£250,000), and an overall limit on the total compensation payable of £500,000.[27] This upper limit attracts criticism, but it may be noted that the vast majority of successful applicants receive awards no higher than £5,500.[28] The Home Office's 2005 proposals, discussed below, both envisaged a reallocation of the Scheme's budget from minor to 'serious' injuries and reflected a more fundamental rethinking about the Scheme's purpose.

On the other hand, there has always been a limit on the basis on which the calculation of compensation for loss of earnings or earning capacity will be made. This is restricted to 1.5 times gross average industrial earnings (Scheme 2001: para. 34). Its purpose is to limit the compensation payable by the taxpayer for the benefit of the better-off, who it is assumed will have also made private insurance and pension provision for serious injury.

Other sources of income[29]

The underlying policy in respect of other sources of income that are payable to the victim consequent on the injury is that there should be no betterment at the taxpayer's expense. The operation of this policy is, however, not always simple.

It is uncontroversial that any amount that the victim recovers from the offender under a compensation order (or a civil action) should be fully deductible from any award. History suggests that such payments will be limited; it is unlikely that CICA will make much use of the subrogated right to pursue the victim's civil action against the offender.[30] Second, since the Scheme is funded by the taxpayer, it follows that state benefits payable for loss of earnings or disability should be deducted. An important consideration concerns the purpose of particular elements of the award. Where taxpayer-funded benefits are deductible, it might be thought correct that they should only be deducted from those elements that are themselves awarded for the same purpose as the benefit. A state disability pension should not, for example, be deducted from a payment for pain and suffering. The Scheme has over time operated both total and focused deduction. Collateral payments were originally, with few exceptions, deductible from the total award, not just from the head of damage to which they referred. In recognition of its disengagement from the common law assessment of general damages for personal injury, the 1996 Scheme provides that deductions shall *not* be made from their equivalent, the tariff-based awards, but only from any award of additional compensation for the same contingency.

A more difficult area concerns payments made under occupational and private insurance and pensions. The contributions in these cases have come from their employers and from the victims themselves and for this reason it might be thought unfair that these benefits should be deducted. But they do serve to reduce the victim's loss, and for that reason the taxpayer ought to be relieved from over-compensating the claimant. This stands in contrast with the common law, which generally takes the view that the claimant's financial prudence (even though it may in the case of occupational pensions be compulsory) ought not to decrease a guilty defendant's liability to pay damages (even though they are almost invariably met by insurance). The Scheme pursues an equivocal path here. Some such payments (for example in respect of private health treatment) are to be deducted; otherwise insurance and private pensions that were entirely funded by the claimant escape.

A fourth collateral benefit that creates further complexity as to fiscal equity between victims and taxpayers comprises charitable donations. Their treatment became an issue in the United States following the acts of terrorism on 11 September 2001 (Abraham and Logue 2004; Katz 2004). The question was whether the Federal Victim Compensation Fund should deduct them from its awards. As in the case of insurance the common law permits the charitable windfall to benefit the claimant, even if that leads to over-compensation, rather than to reduce the extent of the defendant's liability to pay damages. But where the award comes from public funds, the question whether it is better that the victim benefits twice than that the taxpayer's burden is reduced becomes more difficult where there is a third party, the donor, whose own interests in contributing to charity deserve consideration. The answer, which was also adopted in Britain concerning the London Bombings Relief Charitable Fund, was to leave the payments untouched. Whether the donors (many of whom would also have been taxpayers) were content with this is unknowable. But allowing *some* victims of crime (of 9/11 or 7/7 and possibly other terrorist bombings) to benefit twice because they happen to be the objects of charity, while 'ordinary' victims of violent crime benefit only once, raises as yet unanswered issues of equity as between similarly placed victims.

Northern Ireland

The Scheme described above applies to England, Scotland and Wales, but not to Northern Ireland. For much of the twentieth century compensation was payable via a civil court procedure to the victims of collective violence, the awards levied on the police authority. This was a legacy of arrangements from the previous century whose purpose was to place the responsibility for the financial consequences of unlawful assemblies and riots, to both persons and property, on the community within which the offenders were assumed to live. These arrangements were replaced in 1968 by the Criminal Injuries to Persons (Compensation) (NI) Act 1968 which introduced a statutory version of the Scheme then operating in England and Wales. Following the escalation of terrorist violence during the 1970s and the introduction of direct rule, the 1968 Act was replaced in 1977 by an Order in Council, itself amended by the Criminal Injuries (Compensation) Order 1988.

Together these introduced a number of restrictions that both reflected this escalation and sought to reduce the cost to the taxpayer. In particular, the definition of mental injury was tightened in 1977 to filter out the many hundreds of less serious claims for nervous shock, some of which were bogus. These arrangements remained in force until 2001 when, following a review (Bloomfield *et al*. 1999; and see Greer 1996), a tariff scheme modelled on that introduced in Great Britain was introduced by the Criminal Compensation (NI) Order 2002.

Beyond Great Britain and beyond compensation: rethinking the British Scheme

On 7 July 2005 four suicide bombers exploded their bombs on the London Underground and on a bus in Tavistock Square. Fifty-six people were killed and 746 were injured. These events gave urgency to an unresolved policy issue concerning the level of compensation that ought to be made, more broadly, to any victim of violent crime. They also revived some equally long-standing issues concerning delay in delivering compensation and led directly to the publication of the Home Office consultation paper, *Rebuilding Lives* (Home Office 2005).

Delay, that is, the lapse of time between an application and its resolution, has always been a vexed issue.[31] CICA sought to pre-empt the inevitable pressure to resolve the 7 July claims quickly: it announced that it would fast-track them and issued a Guide (CICA 2005). But giving priority to one group prompted criticism of the justice of differentiating between crime victims according to some factor such as the scale or impact of the event, or the offender's motivation (Miers 2006: 709). Operational decisions carry the potential for the divisive treatment of similarly placed victims, and it is present also in the more fundamental question, what level of compensation ought crime victims to receive? As we saw earlier, even where a notion such as civic trust may provide a justification for a compensation scheme, it does not answer the question, how much? The British Scheme's answer was, even following the 1996 changes, to a significant extent based on what a successful claimant in a civil action against the offender would receive by way of damages. In the same way as its tenuous control over expenditure led the Home Office to introduce the tariff in 1995, so financial pressures led to the 2005 proposals to rethink the Scheme's purpose. In practice, this meant focusing on 'serious' injuries at the expense of the majority of the 'less serious'. More fundamentally, it meant distancing the Scheme from its residual common law characteristics and thus from the inevitable (frustrated) expectation that it would deliver 'full' compensation.

Complexity and delay are endemic in the common law's method of dealing with the financial consequences of serious injury. The simplification that the government sought was to be achieved, first, by disengaging less serious cases from the Scheme, which would be dealt with otherwise than by a monetary response. Second, claims for loss of earnings and earning capacity and long-term care in 'serious' cases would not be individually calculated, but be resolved by reference to a further set of standardised payments for particular injuries. As with the 1996 tariff, there would therefore be no need to account for state benefits, which would remove a substantial element in the calculation of additional compensation. The tariff value of these new designated injuries would exceed the present cap of £250,000 per injury, and the overall cap of £500,000 would be lifted to a higher ceiling. These radical steps would mean that the Scheme would be able to deliver compensation to the seriously injured more quickly. The savings that would be made from the exclusion of work-related injuries and of less serious injuries would in turn be sufficient both to compensate the most serious injuries and to fund nonfinancial responses that are 'timely, practical and local' for all crime victims. At the time of writing, the government had made no announcements about the Scheme's future structure.

Europe and beyond

European attention to crime victim compensation took substantial shape in the Council of Europe's 1983 *Convention on the Compensation of Victims of Violent Crime* (Miers 1985). During the 1990s the European Union published consultation papers and funded reviews of victim compensation provision (Mikaelsson and Wergens 2001: 169–75; Commission of the European Communities 2001), whose conclusions culminated in the 2004 EU Council Directive (European Union 2004), Article 12.2 of which provides that

> All Member States shall ensure that their national rules provide for the existence of a scheme on compensation to victims of violent intentional crimes committed in their respective territories, which guarantees fair and appropriate compensation to victims.

The 2004 directive required member states to establish their national schemes by 1 July 2005. Many were already compliant at the date of the directive, but the obligation posed considerable difficulties for the ten accession states that became Members of the European Union on 1 May 2004. For them, crime victim compensation was only one issue within a much broader agenda concerning their criminal justice systems' compliance with European Union standards.[32] In December 2005 the 13 states (of the total of 25) having schemes was entirely composed of existing member states.[33]

However, merely to count the number of schemes currently operating in Europe says nothing of their scope or operation. There continue to be important differences of detail between them in respect of such matters as the range of victimising events, compensable persons and injuries, heads of damage and their financial limits. These were comprehensively reviewed in Mikaelsson and Wergens (2001: 176–250). The fundamental point is that whatever these differences, each scheme constitutes an answer to the same set of basic questions for the design of *any* scheme (see also Alexander 2004: 629). These are: which victims are to be compensated to what level of compensation for what injuries arising from what crimes, and under what conditions can their eligibility be lawfully limited or denied, by what agency and subject to what appeal mechanism?

These are therefore the questions that were asked in respect of the schemes established in Australasia, Canada and the United States in the 1970s and thereafter. As in Europe, the answers differ; but in the United States they also disclose a different orientation concerning their schemes' underlying philosophy. California established the first compensation scheme in 1965, followed by five others over the next three years. By 1980 28 states had introduced them, and by the turn of the century they had been introduced in all 50, plus the District of Columbia, the Virgin Islands and Puerto Rico. Like those elsewhere, these schemes sought to respond to the victim's experience, but were introduced to perform an essentially social welfare function.[34] They focus on the direct expenses that victims incur as a result of their injuries, providing financial support only as a last resort. All collateral sources of payment to the victim, such as medical or auto insurance, employee benefit programs, social security, and Medicaid, must be accessed *before* the schemes will consider payment. And they are characterised by payments conditional upon proof of need; by contrast the Scheme was founded on the notion of loss.

Although there are some detailed differences between them, the United States' schemes, taken as a whole, present a very different picture from that under the CICS. This is starkly revealed by their respective expenditure figures. In 2005 the total of payments made by all schemes in the United States was close to $265 million to just over 115,000 successful applicants. In the same period, the Scheme made payments of around £170 million to 33,330 claimants. A crude comparison, ignoring both the differing terms of the two countries' schemes and their crime and application rates, shows that the United States' schemes averaged £1,360 per applicant compared with £5,150 in Britain.[35] If the number of awards in the United States bore the same ratio to its population as does the Scheme's to the population of Britain, the total would be closer to 165,000 claimants, at an annual cost of £244 million ($380 million).

The proportionately lower payment levels nevertheless do follow from the much narrower scope of and, compared with Britain, the much lower upper limits contained in the US schemes.[36] Taken as a whole, the United States' schemes cover the same major types of expense: medical expenses, mental health counselling, lost wages for victims unable to work because of crime-related injury, lost support for dependants of homicide victims, and funeral expenses. Three states compensate for pain and suffering,[37] but the vast majority makes no provision for an award for the injury itself. Some make some provision for replacement services for work that the victim is unable to perform because of crime-related injury (primarily child care and housekeeping), rehabilitation, which may include physical therapy and/or job therapy, and modifications to homes or vehicles for paralysed victims. However, the maximum benefits are generally very low by comparison with the Scheme. Although a few states have higher maximums, they typically range between $10,000 (£5,882) and $25,000 (£14,706); the Scheme's maximum for a single tariff payment is £250,000 ($425,000) and for any award £500,000 ($850,000).

Schemes in the United States are funded from a number of different sources, including the Federal Government.[38] By contrast, while it funds its Department of Justice's Victims of Crime Initiative, the Canadian Federal Government has no responsibility for compensation schemes, which are a matter for provincial and territorial governments.[39] Canada also differs from the United States in that some of its schemes, at least when they were first introduced, more closely resembled the 'offender surrogate' model that was adopted in Britain in 1964 (Burns 1992). This remains the case in Ontario, Prince Edward Island and New Brunswick,[40] all of which compensate for pain and suffering (to a limited extent in the latter case), and to a lesser extent in Alberta, Manitoba and Saskatchewan, which are confined to special damages. In all cases, the awards they are able to make are subject to much lower limits than in Britain.[41]

By 1983 all of the Australian states and territories had enacted schemes that, while imposing upper limits, provided compensation for special, and elements of general damages. But like Britain, the financial pressures occasioned by both the level of awards and the schemes' administrative costs drove many of them to introduce tariffs or to make substantial reductions in their scope and compensation levels.[42] These retrenchments were accompanied by greater emphasis on recovery from the offender (Freckelton 2001 2003).[43] In contrast, the scheme in Western Australia continues to cover both pain and suffering and loss of the enjoyment of life, while also *increasing* in 2003 the maximum award payable to AUS$75,000.[44] None of these changes was, however, as radical a departure from the offender surrogate model as occurred in New Zealand. Having established the first scheme in 1963, in 1972 it was repealed when New Zealand enacted its omnibus no-fault scheme, which subsumed criminal injuries.

Beyond compensation

Compensation schemes that seek to stand in for the offender, even where there are upper limits on awards that would be inapplicable in a civil action, inevitably suffer from many of its disadvantages. Delay (encouraging compensation neurosis), complexity in the calculation of awards, and the generation of unrealistic expectations about their amount, are, as noted earlier, long-standing issues. Such schemes also perpetuate a more profound philosophy: that postponed awards (however hard the scheme's administrators seek to decide claims quickly) are an appropriate response to personal victimisation.

As noted, budgetary considerations led to a radical reduction in the scope of a number of the Australian schemes during the 1990s. But these changes were also the product of a change in policy, shared by some Canadian schemes, that there were more effective responses to the here-and-now of victimisation than delayed compensation. In 1996 Victoria and in 2002 British Columbia shifted the focus of their schemes from financial compensation to benefits targeted to victims' immediate needs. Established in 1972, the British Columbia scheme had addressed primarily male victims concerned about the loss of wages following a criminal injury.[45] But 'today, many victims, especially children and women, need financial support as well as assistance to aid in their recovery from the physical and psychological effects of their victimisation'.[46] This was likewise the motive behind the Victims of Crime Assistance Act 1996 in Victoria, which provides limited compensation for medical expenses and loss of earnings, and vouchers for psychiatric counselling. In these respects these new schemes are similar to those in the United States, all of which enable the victim to recover, subject to varying limits, the expense of obtaining mental health counselling. This is included in a number of the Canadian schemes, and in the case of Nova Scotia, is entirely confined to it.[47] In addition, most provide 'clean up' compensation and reimbursement for expenses incurred in repairing broken windows and doors.

This shift was also evident in the Home Office's 2005 Consultation. Like these other schemes, victims of 'non-serious' crimes would no longer be the recipients of state compensation, but would instead be eligible for a 'menu' of services to be delivered by Victim Care Units. This menu would comprise two elements. The first is the provision of emotional support. This might include reassurance that the crime was not the victim's fault, help in understanding the feelings they are experiencing, support in the choices they make, and professional counselling where appropriate, including help with post-traumatic stress. The 'practical support' menu addresses more immediate needs, including hardship payments, vouchers for taxis to work where the injury leaves the victim unable to drive, cosmetic surgery, personal alarms and target-hardening the victim's house following a burglary (Home Office 2005: 27–8). As will be clear from earlier sections, these last go beyond the Scheme's current scope, which is limited to compensation for personal injury.

If the Scheme did not exist, would the Home Office feel the need to invent it? The pragmatic answer is that it is politically inconceivable that some version of the Scheme will not continue to be a part of the criminal justice system's response to violent crime. But that does not mean that 40 years on the Scheme should stay the same, or that if the Home Office were to invent it anew it would start from where we are now. Equally pragmatic are the financial limits on what the Home Office can budget for victim support in general and the Scheme in particular. Targeting particular injuries may be seen as a cynical device for reducing state expenditure, as Freckleton (2003) argued in the case of the changes introduced in the State of Victoria. But it was clear from the Home Office consultation in 2005 that there was no additional money but only proposals to spend it differently.

The less cynical response is to acknowledge what the research overwhelmingly confirms, that victims of crime principally value personal attention in the form of information, immediate practical help and someone to talk to. Most personal crime does not result in life-threatening or even serious physical or mental injury, but it does result in inconvenience, despair, anger, loss of confidence, anxiety, and a debilitating constraint on victims' sense of security and freedom to go about their lives. There may remain a good case for payments (but not necessarily 'compensation' as understood in law) directed to serious injuries (if not simply by virtue of the EU Directive). But there may be greater gains for the maintenance of civic trust if, beyond compensation, the state deals efficiently and effectively with the majority of victims.

Further reading

For their application of the British Scheme, see the annual reports of the Criminal Injuries Compensation Authority and the Criminal Injuries Compensation Appeals Panel. At the time of writing these were Criminal Injuries Compensation Authority *Annual Report and Accounts 2004/05* (2006, London: The Stationery Office, HC 1427) and the Criminal Injuries Compensation Appeals Panel *Annual Report and Accounts 200/06 2/03* (2006, London: The Stationery Office, HC 1428).

Notes

1 See 'the victim's walk through' at www.cjsonline.org/.
2 It has long been the case that the court may defer sentencing an adult offender in order for him to make reparation. This is now provided by section 278 of and Schedule 23 to the Criminal Justice Act 2003. The confiscation of an offender's assets under the Proceeds of Crime Act 2002 that are then allocated to the Home Office's Victims' Fund may also be seen as indirect reparation. The Fund is used to support Rape Crisis and other interventions (Home Office 2005: 11).
3 The influential Quaker reformer, Margery Fry, had independently argued the case (Rock 1986: 50–9). An early comparative study is Schafer (1970).
4 In his account of the rise of the 'victim movement', Rock cautions that general shifts in social values are generally not attributable to single events (Rock, 1984: 79–99). It may however be noted that some of the campaigns in favour of introducing compensation schemes were specifically tied to instances of violent or sexual offences against vulnerable or altruistic victims (Miers 1978: 57–8).
5 For example, the Victims of Crime Trust (http://news.bbc.co.uk/1/hi/uk/3659675.stm).
6 Special issues of three law journals published at this time contain the full range of these justifications (*Symposia* 1959, 1960, 1970).
7 *Hill v Chief Constable for West Yorkshire* [1989] A.C. 53, *Brooks v Commissioner of Police for the Metropolis* [2005] UKHL 24. *Van Collee v Chief Constable of the Hertfordshire Police* [2006] EWHC 360 was an action under section 7 of the Human Rights Act 1998 for breach of the victim's Article 2 and 8 Convention rights. The court found that such a risk did exist where the police had failed to protect a witness who was murdered by the man against whom he was to give evidence. Cox J. held that as a general proposition, liability at common law and under the Act were based on similar principles [75–76].
8 The Home Secretary introducing the Criminal Injuries Compensation Act 1995; H.C. Debates, vol. 260, col. 734, 23 May 1995. 'Its [CICA's] aim is to provide victims with material recognition of their pain and suffering and to allow society to express its sympathy for what they have been through' (CICA 2006b: 4). An ethical stance associated with sympathy (identifying with another's loss) is empathy (understanding another's loss), which underpinned the Council of Europe's 1983 thinking, that compensation was a matter of social solidarity (Council of Europe 1983: Preamble; Buck 2005: 150–4).
9 Curiously, an EU-funded survey conducted during 2000/01 did not ask for any information on this issue (Mikaelsson and Wergens 2001). Five of the United States' schemes authorise denial based on prior criminal activity, and in Canada, the Alberta scheme provides for reduction or refusal under the headings both of the victim's conduct and of his criminal record, while Manitoba and Ontario are confined to the former.
10 The crime of violence may be directly caused by an animal whose owner intentionally or recklessly causes it to attack the victim (CICA 2006b: 7).
11 Compensation shall be awarded in the above cases even if the offender cannot be prosecuted or punished (Council of Europe 1983: Article 2.2).
12 CICA 2006a: 8.

13 CICA 2006b: 7. In 2004/05 2,379 (7 per cent) of the disallowed 33,847 applications were rejected because the applicant did not comply with this reporting requirement (CICA 2006b: 6). Many schemes in the United States impose a 72-hour reporting requirement.

14 CICA 2006a: 8. In 2004/05 7,803 (23 per cent) of the disallowed claims were rejected because the applicant failed to co-operate with the police (CICA 2006b: 6).

15 'The compensation scheme may, if necessary, set for all or any elements of compensation ... a minimum threshold below which compensation shall not be granted' (Council of Europe 1983: Article 5).

16 CICA 2006b: 8. In 2004/05 9,120 (27 per cent) of the disallowed claims were rejected because the injury was valued at less than this minimum (CICA 2006b: 6).

17 Sections 47, 20, and 18 respectively of the Offences against the Person Act 1861.

18 CICA 2006a: 7.

19 The Scheme imposes some conditions that are too complex to explore here; see Scheme (2001: Note 5 of the General Notes to Tariff of Injuries).

20 A full account of the difficulties to which the interpretation of para. 9(b)(ii) gives rise is beyond the scope of this chapter. But it may be noted that CICA made awards to applicants located in Britain who were speaking to their spouses by phone when the second plane struck the World Trade Center on 9/11, or who saw the impact on television knowing that their spouses were there. In this case the applicants witnessed the events as they happened, and were 'immediately', though they were not 'closely', involved in their aftermath (see Miers 2006: 701–3).

21 Compensation may be reduced or refused on account of the victim's or the applicant's conduct before, during or after the crime, in relation to the injury or death. Compensation may also be reduced or refused on account of the victim's or the applicant's involvement in organised or his membership of an organisation which engages in crime of violence. Compensation may also be reduced or refused if an award or a full award would be contrary to a sense of justice or to public policy (*ordre public*) (Council of Europe 1983: Articles 8(1)–8(3)).

22 CICA 2006a: 7. The cost of 'public house related incidents' was estimated to be around £10 million a year.

23 Compare the decision of the Supreme Court of Kansas, which held that a causal link between the victim's conduct and the injury sustained is a necessary element in a finding of 'contributory misconduct'. *Fisher v Kansas Crime Victims Compensation Board*: www.kscourts.org/kscases/supct/2005/200515209/93701.htm.

24 In 2004/05 3,629 (11 per cent) of the disallowed claims were rejected because of the applicant's conduct and 3,470 (10 per cent) because of the applicant's criminal record (CICA 2006b: 6). An applicant was awarded compensation notwithstanding that the penalty points would have required a reduction, as he was injured while going to another victim's aid (CICA 2006a: 7).

25 The caution was expressed by the Home Office (2005: 21), and it is therefore something of a surprise to find that the government's position on immediate help in these circumstances lies within the Department for Culture, Media and Sport. See http://www.culture.gov.uk/what_we_do/Humanitarian_assistance/.

26 'Compensation shall cover, according to the case under consideration, at least the following items: loss of earnings, medical and hospitalisation expenses' (Council of Europe 1983: Article 4).

27 'The compensation scheme may, if necessary, set for all or any elements of compensation an upper limit above which ... compensation shall not be granted' (Council of Europe 1983: Article 5).

28 In 2004/05 56 per cent of the successful applicants (35,446) received awards between £1,000 and £2,000; 89 per cent receive awards under £5,500 (CICA 2006b: 6; Home Office 2005: 16).

29 'With a view to avoiding double compensation, the State or the competent authority may deduct from the compensation awarded or reclaim from the person compensated any amount of money received, in consequence of the injury or death, from the offender, social security or insurance, or coming from any other source' (Council of Europe 1983: Article 9).

30 Section 57 of the Domestic Violence, Crime and Victims Act 2004 gives the Authority power to recover some or all of the compensation from a person convicted in respect of the injury.

31 The number of applications has, surprisingly, been falling over the past few years, from 78,282 in 2001/02 to 66,290 in 2004/05 (CICA 2006b: 9; Home Office 2005: 19). Its *Victim's Charter* objective that 90 per cent of cases should be resolved within 12 months of receipt has become increasingly unrealistic. The actual performance against this target over the past four years has been around 76 per cent, dropping in 2004/05 to 73 per cent. Other aspects of its claims processing have improved (CICA 2006b: 9).

32 This drive to convergence in the provision of European-wide crime victim compensation is reflected in other 'third pillar' matters, notably the EU Council's Framework Decision of March 2001 on the *Standing of Victims in Criminal Proceedings* (European Union 2001; see Wergens 1999 and Brienen and Hoegen 2000). The same drive can be seen in the development of restorative justice; see Miers and Willemsens (2004).

33 Austria, Belgium, Denmark, Finland, France, Germany, Ireland, Luxembourg, Netherlands, Portugal, Spain, Sweden, and the United Kingdom (the Scheme, plus the Northern Ireland scheme).

34 See Edelhertz and Geis (1974). On the social welfare function of the 9/11 Fund see Diller (2004).

35 Exchange rate of $1.70:£1.00.

36 The National Association of Crime Victim Compensation Board's Program Directory helpfully summarises, to a common template, the key features of all 52 schemes (www.nacvcb.org/progdir.html). The summary is drawn from the NACVCB's *Crime Victim Compensation Overview* (www.nacvcb.org/articles/Overview-prn.html). See further the NACVCB's Crime Victim Compensation Quarterly, available on its website.

37 Hawaii, Rhode Island and Tennessee.

38 More than four-fifths derive funds from levies imposed on offenders; a smaller number are funded from state taxation. They are all also eligible for federal funds payable under the Victims of Crime Act (typically 20–25 per cent of the state's total compensation budget). To be eligible, the state must meet minimum conditions concerning compensable persons and injuries. The VOCA grant programme is administered by the Office for Victims of Crime in the United States Justice Department.

39 www.justice.gc.ca/en/ps/voc/funding.html

40 Ontario: Compensation for Victims of Crime Act 1990 (www.cicb.on.ca/en/fact1.htm). PEI: Victims of Crime Act 1989. New Brunswick: Victim Services Act 2002 (www.gnb.ca/0276/corrections/vicser-e.asp).

41 Alberta: Victims of Crime Act 1997 (www.solgen.gov.ab.ca/victim). Manitoba: Compensation for Victims of Crime Program; www.gov.mb.ca/justice/victims/victimsindex.html Saskatchewan: Victims Compensation Program (www.saskjustice.gov.sk.ca/VictimsServices/programs/compensation.shtml).

42 For example the Victims Compensation Act 1996 in New South Wales, which substantially reduced its scheme's former upper limits.

43 In excluding pain and suffering, the Victims of Crime Assistance Act 1996 of the State of Victoria provided that the court may make an order against the offender for such compensation. Its Victims of Crime Assistance (Amendment) Act 2000 made a partial reinstatement of pain and suffering to a limit of AUS$7,500. In Tasmania the Victims of Crime Assistance Act 2005 provides financial assistance to enable victims to sue their offenders (see www.justice.tas.gov.au/victims/).

44 From AUS$50,000. Criminal Injuries Compensation Act 2003 (see www.justice. wa.gov.au).

45 Claims under the Criminal Injuries Compensation Act 1972 were administered by the Workers' Compensation Board, which also dealt with industrial injuries.

46 Crime Victim Assistance Act 2002 (www.pssg.gov.bc.ca/victim_services/cva/index. htm)

47 Criminal injuries counselling program (www.gov.ns.ca/just/PolVS/programs. htm).

References

Abraham, K. and Logue, K. (2004) 'The genie and the bottle: collateral sources under September 11th Victim Compensation Fund', *De Paul Law Review*, 53: 591–626.

Alexander, J. (2004) 'Procedural design and terror victim compensation', *De Paul Law Review*, 53: 627–718.

Ashworth, A. (1986) 'Punishment and Compensation: Victims, Offenders and the State', *Oxford Journal of Legal Studies*, 6(1): 86–122.

Ashworth, A. (2000) 'Victims' Rights, Defendants' Rights and Criminal Procedure', in A. Crawford and J. Goodey (eds) *Integrating a Victim Perspective in Criminal Justice*. Aldershot: Ashgate, pp. 185–206.

Bloomfield, K., Gibson, M. and Greer, D. (1999) *Criminal Injuries Compensation in Northern Ireland. A Report to the Secretary of State for Northern Ireland*. Belfast: Northern Ireland Office.

Brienen, M. and Hoegen, E. (2000) *Victims of Crime in 22 European Criminal Justice Systems*. Nijmegen: Wolf Legal Productions.

Buck, K. (2005) 'State compensation to crime victims and the principle of social solidarity', *European Journal of Crime, Criminal Law and Criminal Justice*, 13(2): 148–78.

Burns, P. (1992) *Criminal Injuries Compensation*, 2nd edn. Canada: Butterworths.

Christie, N. (1986) 'The Ideal Victim', in E. Fattah (ed.) *From Crime Policy to Victim Policy*. London: Macmillan, pp. 1–17.

CICA (2003) *Criminal Injuries Compensation Authority Annual Report and Accounts 2001/02*, HO 450. London: The Stationery Office.

CICA (2004) *Criminal Injuries Compensation Authority Annual Report and Accounts 2002/03*, HC 451. London: The Stationery Office.

CICA (2005) *Criminal Injuries Compensation Authority Compensation for the Victims of the London Bombings of 7 July 2005*.

CICA (2006a) *Criminal Injuries Compensation Authority Annual Report and Accounts 2003/04*, HC 1196. London: The Stationery Office.

CICA (2006b) *Criminal Injuries Compensation Authority Annual Report and Accounts 2004/05* HC 1427. London: The Stationery Office.

Commission of the European Communities (2001) *Compensation to Crime Victims* COM (2001) 536 final, 28 September 2001 (http://europa.eu.int/comm/justice).

Council of Europe (1983) Convention on the Compensation of Victims of Violent Crime, Strasbourg, 24 November.

Diller, M. (2004) 'Tort law and social welfare principles in the Victim Compensation Fund', *De Paul Law Review*, 53: 719–68.

Duff, P. (1998) 'The measure of criminal injuries compensation: political pragmatism or dog's dinner?', *Oxford Journal of Legal Studies*, 18(1): 105–42.

Edelhertz, H. and Geis, G. (1974) *Public Compensation to Victims of Crime*. New York: Praeger.

Elias, R. (1983) *Victims of the System*. New Brunswick, NJ: Transaction Press Publishers.

European Union (2001) Council Framework Decision 2001/220/JHA of 15 March 2001 on the standing of victims in criminal proceedings, OJ L 082/1 22 March 2001.

European Union (2004) Council Directive 2004/80/EC of 29 April 2004 relating to compensation to crime victims, OJ L 262, 06/08/2004, p. 15.

Freckelton, I. (2001) *Criminal Injuries Compensation: Law, Practice and Policy*. Sydney: The Lawbook Company.

Freckelton, I. (2003) 'Compensation for Victims of Crime: Health and Financial Considerations', paper given to the XIth International Symposium on Victimology, Stellenbosch, South Africa.

Garland, D. (2001) *The Culture of Control: Crime and Social Order in Contemporary Society*. Oxford: Oxford University Press.

Goldscheid, J. (2004) 'Crime victim compensation in a post 9/11 world', *Tulane Law Review*, 79: 166–233.

Greer, D. (ed.) (1996) *Compensating Crime Victims: A European Survey*. Freiburg: Max-Planck-Institut.

de Greiff, P. (2006) 'Justice and Reparations', in P. de Grieff (ed.) *The Handbook of Reparations*. Oxford: Oxford University Press, pp. 451–77.

Haldane, J., and Harvey, A. (1995) 'The philosophy of state compensation', *Journal of Applied Philosophy*, 12: 273–82.

Henderson, L. (1985) 'The wrongs of victims' rights', *Stanford Law Review*, 37: 937–000.

Home Office (1959) *Penal Practice in a Changing Society*, Cmnd 645. London: HMSO.

Home Office (1961) *Compensation for Victims of Crimes of Violence*, Cmnd 1406. London: HMSO.

Home Office (1964) *Compensation for Victims of Crimes of Violence*, Cmnd 2323. London: HMSO.

Home Office (1999) *Compensation for Victims of Violent Crime: Possible Changes to the Criminal Injuries Compensation Scheme*. London: The Stationery Office.

Home Office (2005) *Rebuilding Lives: Supporting Victims of Crime*, Cm 6705. London: The Stationery Office.

Hoyle, C. and Sanders, A. (2000) 'Police response to domestic violence: From victim choice to victim empowerment', *British Journal of Criminology*, 40(1): 14–36.

Hoyle, C. and Zedner, L. (2007) 'Victims, Victimisation and the Criminal Process', in M. Maguire, R. Morgan and R. Reiner (eds) *The Oxford Handbook of Criminology*, 4th edn. Oxford, Oxford University Press.

Issachoroff, S. and Mansfield, A. (2006) 'Compensation for the Victims of September 11', in P. de Grieff (ed.) *The Handbook of Reparations*. Oxford: Oxford University Press, pp. 284–320.

Katz, R. (2004) 'Too much of a good thing: When charitable gifts augment victim compensation', *De Paul Law Review*, 53: 547–90.

Mikaelsson, J. and Wergens, A. (2001) *Repairing the Irreparable*. Umea, Sweden: Crime Victim Compensation and Support Authority, Swedish Ministry of Justice.

Miers, D. (1978) *Responses to Victimisation*. London: Professional Books.

Miers, D. (1980) 'Victim compensation as labelling process', *Victimology*, 5(1): 3–17.

Miers, D. (1985) 'The provision of compensation for victims of violent crime in Continental Europe', *Victimology*, 10(4): 662–71.

Miers, D. (1997) *State Compensation for Criminal Injuries*. Oxford: Oxford University Press.

Miers, D. (2000) 'Taking the Law into their own Hands: Victims as Offenders', in A. Crawford and J. Goodey (eds) *Integrating a Victim Perspective within Criminal Justice*. Aldershot: Ashgate, pp. 77–95.

Miers, D. (2001) 'Criminal injuries compensation: The new regime', *Journal of Personal Injury Law*, 371–95.

Miers, D. (2006) 'Rebuilding lives: Operational and policy issues in the compensation of victims of violent and terrorist crimes', *Criminal Law Review*, 695–721.

Miers, D. and Semenchuck, M. (2005) 'Victim–Offender Mediation in England and Wales', in A. Mestitz and S. Ghetti (eds) *Victim Offender Mediation with Youth Offenders in Europe*. Dordrecht: Springer, pp. 23–46.

Miers, D. and Willemsens, J. (eds) (2004) *Mapping Restorative Justice: Developments in 25 European Countries*. Leuven: European Forum for Victim–Offender Mediation and Restorative Justice.

Padley, C. and Begley, L. (2005) *Criminal Injuries Compensation Claims*. London: Law Society.

Rock, P. (1984) *A View from the Shadows*. Oxford: Oxford University Press.

Rock, P. (1986) *Helping Victims of Crime*. Oxford: Oxford University Press.

Rock, P. (2004) *Constructing Victims' Rights*. Oxford: Oxford University Press.

Sanders, A. (1999) *Taking Account of Victims in the Criminal Justice System: A Review of the Literature*, Social Work Research Findings 32. Edinburgh: Scottish Office Central Research Unit.

Schafer, S. (1970) *Compensation and Restitution to Victims of Crime*. Montclair, NJ: Patterson Smith.

Scheme (2001) *The Criminal Injuries Compensation Scheme 2001*, TSI (Issue Number One 4/01). London: Home Office.

Sebok, A. (2004) 'What's law got to do with it? Designing compensation schemes in the shadow of the tort system', *De Paul Law Review*, 53: 501–26.

Symposium (1959) 'Compensation for victims of criminal violence: A round table', *Journal of Public Law*, 8: 191–253.

Symposium (1960) 'Compensation to victims of crimes of personal violence', *Minnesota Law Review*, 50: 221–310.

Symposium (1970) 'Governmental compensation for victims of violence', *Southern California Law Review*, 40: 1–121.

Wergens, A. (1999) *Crime Victims in the European Union*. Umea, Sweden: Crime Victim Compensation and Support Authority, Swedish Ministry of Justice.

Wood, J. (2005) 'In whose name? Crime victim policy and the punishing power of protection', *National Women Studies Association Journal*, 17(3): 1–17.

Chapter 14

Benchmarking victim policies in the framework of European Union law

Jan Van Dijk and Marc Groenhuijsen[1]

Introduction

The Framework Decision of the European Union on the Standing of Victims in Criminal proceedings of 2001 lays down minimum standards for treatment of crime victims. This Decision has made mandatory for EU member states basic principles of justice for victims developed over the past 20 years by the international community. The new EU standards build on earlier international codification efforts of the United Nations (GA Declaration of 1985) and the Council of Europe (Recommendation 1985/11). The EU Framework Decision is unique by making a comprehensive set of victim-friendly principles of justice legally binding for its 27 member states.

Politically important as these international legal instruments may be, they are far from executing themselves. The first necessary follow-up is incorporation of the standards in domestic legislation and regulation. A status report of the European Commission published in 2004 showed that even in this elementary respect much more needs to be done (Commission 2004). In none of the member states the Framework Decision had been fully transposed into national legislation (Groenhuijsen and Letschert 2006)

Compliance with international legal instruments requires more than adaptation of domestic legislation. Implementation must be followed up in case law and in operational activities such as the provision of resources, tools, skills and training. In the final analysis what really matters is the impact of implementation efforts on the key client groups, in this cases the victims of crime.

Brienen and Hoegen (2000) have looked at legislative compliance with Council of Europe Recommendation 85/11, including its follow-up in case law, instructions as well as training programmes for police officers and prosecutors. They made an overall assessment of the stage of implementation of these guidelines per country. Substantively the EU Framework Decision of 2001 closely resembles the COE Recommendation. The findings of Brienen and Hoegen on the implementation of the COE Recommendation therefore provide a rough assessment of compliance of European countries with the EU Framework Decision as well. In the next section we discuss the methodology of Brienen and Hoegen and subsequently present a ranking of EU countries, based on their 'scorecards' of the extent of socio-legal compliance with the international standards.

In this contribution the findings of legal desk research on compliance are supplemented with empirical data on the impact of domestic victim policies as perceived by actual victims. Data is presented based on standardised victimisation surveys carried out in 18 EU member states in 2005 (EU/ICS), co-funded by the DG research of the EC as well as in Bulgaria, Iceland, Norway, Turkey and Switserland (Van Dijk *et al.* 2007). The analysis focuses on the percentages of persons victimised by serious crimes between 2000 and 2005 who have reported their experience to the police, the rate of satisfaction among those reporting victims and the percentages of reporting victims of serious crimes who have received specialised help. Combining results on these 'performance indicators' of domestic victim policies, a composite victim satisfaction index is presented.

In the concluding section the results of the socio-legal analysis and of the victim-centred impact evaluation will be related to each other. From these combined results some general conclusions about the state of implementation of the EU Framework Decision across the member states of the Union will be drawn.

Measure of implementation of the COE recommendations

In the introduction we referred to the evaluative study by Brienen and Hoegen and the so-called 'scorecard methodology' they have used in order to assess any progress made in implementing the Council of Europe's recommendations on victims' rights. The method – and the results it has yielded – can be summarised as follows.

The authors argue that compliance with the standards set by the recommendation can best be measured not by taking a snapshot view of the relevant jurisdictions, but by reviewing the dynamics of the criminal justice systems involved regarding victim rights. In order to do so, they have introduced the concept of a 'developmental model' of implementation. The basic idea behind this is to look for *changes* within the system, for actual *reform* in the direction of the aspirations contained in the recommendation. The analysis takes place at three levels. One is the level of legislative initiatives, where new victims' rights are being incorporated in criminal procedure. The second level concerns daily practice: the number of times or the percentage of cases in which the legal rights are actually applied. And the third layer is of a more qualitative nature. It is about best practice on the basis of so-called 'genuine progress indicators' which are regarded as concrete signs of development and sophistication.

Brienen and Hoegen have calculated all legislative reforms in the 22 jurisdictions between 1985 and 1999 (formal implementation) and have collected data on compliance with the new standards (actual implementation).

In both categories (formal and actual), the 'developmental model' distinguishes four ratings. They range from 'poor' to 'adequate' and then on to 'good' and 'excellent'. Obviously, 'poor' means that the recommendation is not complied with either by legislative provisions or in actual practice. 'Adequate' reflects partial conformity, whereas 'good' indicates that the requirements are generally being met. Some jurisdictions even go beyond the standard set by the recommendation; in those instances the score excellent is awarded. For the purposes of this rating procedure, the various parts of the Council of Europe recommendation have been grouped into three areas: informational rights for victims; restitution/compensation; and treatment and protection.

Besides the quality of legislation Brien and Hoegen looked, as said earlier, at practical implementation measures. Just to illustrate how illuminating this layered approach is, we mention some of the more remarkable findings. The table about supplying information on the rights of the victim during the procedure shows a significant discrepancy between the law in books and the law in action, that is to say, in the opposite direction from what one would expect. In quite a few countries (Belgium, England and Wales, Ireland, Luxembourg, the Netherlands, Scotland, Sweden and the Swiss canton of Zürich) the actual level of transferring information goes beyond the requirements of the recommendation and is classified as 'excellent', while the rating of the formal legislation on this item is of a lower category (either adequate or even poor). This confirms that countries sometimes can achieve compliance without adapting their Code of Criminal Procedure or similar legislative instruments. In the area of treatment and protection, a striking research finding is that in many score boxes the rating indicates that compliance is 'adequate', meaning more or less at the level required by the recommendation. As an exception to this rule, on the very basic provision that police officers have to be trained to deal with victims in a sympathetic, constructive and reassuring manner, the majority of jurisdictions is rated 'poor' while only a single one (Denmark) has the score of 'excellent'.

Acording to the assessment, the outcomes on compensation and restitution are downright disappointing. All across Europe, it proves to be much easier to provide victims with information and to secure dignified treatment and protection than it is to award victims financial redress for the harm they have suffered. For instance, if compensation/restitution is a penal sanction, the recommendation requires that it should be collected in the same way as fines and take priority over any financial sanction imposed on the offender. Many countries fail to comply with this basic standard; only few jurisdictions (England and Wales, Norway, Scotland and Sweden) are rated as 'good' in this respect.

Then there is the assessment of progress on the basis of genuine progress indicators (best practices). The authors have identified six genuine progress indicators.

1 The creation of *opt-in information systems*. These are more effective than general, formal commitments, because it logically leads to the installation of an information infrastructure for the authorities to monitor the victims' expressed wishes to be informed of events during the entire proceedings.

2 Enforcement of compensation or restitution orders on behalf of the victim, both when the order is a penal sanction and when it is emanating from an adhesion procedure.

3 Judicial review of the final decision not to prosecute a case.

4 Protection of the personal details of the victim, by withholding them from the offender during the criminal procedure.

5 Provision of information on the offender's release from custody.

6 The existence of a regular flow of victimological research and evaluative studies of legal reform and new policies.

It is neither possible nor useful to elaborate on the exact status or nature of these instruments. Let it suffice to observe that the indicators have proved to be significant discriminating factors in determining the overall emancipation of the victim in a given criminal justice system.

Based on this three-tier system, the scorecard methodology led to the following composite conclusion. When all ratings of the legislative initiatives, other indicators and best practices were taken into account, the countries that rank in the top are Belgium, England and Wales, Ireland, the Netherlands and Norway. Below them, with medium rating, come Austria, Denmark, France, Germany, Scotland, Sweden and Switzerland. Lowest scores were given to Greece, Iceland, Italy, Luxembourg, Portugal, Spain and Turkey. From the countries that were included in the International Crime Victims Survey which will be discussed in the following sections, Estonia, Finland, Hungary and Poland were missing in the Brienen and Hoegen evaluation of the implementation of the Council of Europe recommendation.

Victim-based performance indicators

In 1987 the initiative was taken by a group of European criminologists involved in national crime surveys, to launch a fully standardised survey, called the International Crime Victims Survey, to further comparative criminological and victimological research. In 1989 the first ICVS was carried out in 13 countries, mainly from Western Europe and North America (Van Dijk et al. 1990). The fifth survey was carried out in 2005 in over 30 countries including 22 European countries. Surveys in 18 European countries were co-funded by the Directorate General for Research of the European Commission (under the acronym EU/ICS). Reports on the EU and on global results are forthcoming (Van Dijk et al. 2007; Van Dijk 2007). In this chapter results are presented regarding the treatment of victims in 25 different European countries, including in England/Wales, Scotland and Northern Ireland separately.

The EU/ICS interviews samples of households from national populations about their recent experiences with the most frequently occurring types of conventional crime (volume crime). Samples include at least 2,000 respondents who are generally interviewed with the CATI (Computer Assisted Telephone Interview) technique. In countries such as Bulgaria and Turkey where this method is not applicable because of insufficient distribution of landline telephones, face-to-face interviews are conducted, generally with samples of

1,000–1,500 respondents. In Finland an additional sample was drawn from mobile-only users.

The EU/ICS provides an overall measure of victimisation in the previous year by any of the 11 'conventional' crimes included in the questionnaire. A first group of crimes deals with the vehicles owned by the respondent or his/her household; a second group refers to breaking and entering (burglaries); and a third group of crimes refers to victimisation experienced by the respondent personally, including robbery, pickpocketing, assault and sexual offences. The analysis focuses on repondents who have been victimised during the last five years. This means the reference period of the experiences is 2000–05. In this period victims can be expected to undergo the impact of official victim policies that were in place in 2000.

To assess the impact of EU victim policies as implemented in individual EU countries on experiences and perceptions of victims, data were analysed regarding reporting behaviour, satisfaction with reporting, need and reception of specialised victim support. To increase comparability of results the analysis of reporting behaviour was limited to victims of five types of moderately serious crime: theft from motor vehicles, burglary, robbery, threat/assault and sexual offences. Analyses of the need of and reception of specialised victim support were limited to only four types of crime: burglary, robbery, sexual offences and threat/assault.

In each country an average of 400 respondents had been victimised by one of the five types of crimes. With such sample sizes, national population rates vary within confidence limits of approximately 3 to 4 per cent. In the case of a reporting rate of 50 per cent, there is a 90 per cent certainty that the true rate among the national population lies in the range between 46 and 54 (for more information on confidence intervals see Van Kesteren *et al.* 2000).

Reporting rates

Percentages of serious crimes reported to the police vary greatly across world regions. Figure 14.1 shows results from the ICVS 2000–05 for seven world regions.

Reporting rates are the highest in Western Europe, Australia/New Zealand and USA/Canada. Reporting to the police is least common in Latin America and Asia. Reporting rates in Central and Eastern Europe are much lower than in Western Europe. When data on Central and on Eastern European countries are dissegregated, rates of some Eastern European countries appear to be as high as those in Western Europe. This is clearly the case with Hungary (58 per cent). Poland, Bulgaria and Estonia show moderately high rates around 40 per cent. Within Western Europe reporting rates vary between 40 and 70 per cent. Lowest rates are found in Iceland (40 per cent), Finland (48 per cent), Greece (49 per cent) and Portugal (51 per cent). The highest rates are found in Austria and Belgium (68 per cent). Table 14.1 provides details of these figures.

There is no evidence that reporting rates for the five types of crime have changed much over the years in European countries. Noteworthy seem the

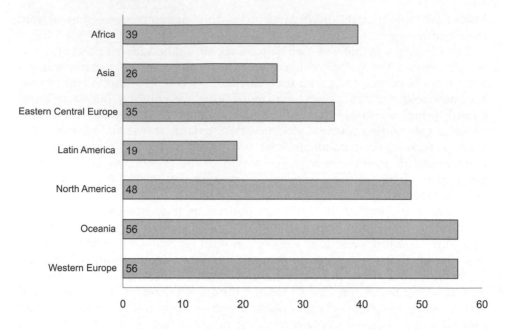

Figure 14.1 Percentages of victims of five types of serious crime who say they reported to the police in seven world regions (results of EU/ICS/ICVS 2005)

Table 14.1 Percentages of victims of five types of serious crime who say they reported to the police in 25 European countries (results of EU/ICS, 2005)

Rank		Percentage	Rank		Percentage
1	Austria	70	14	Ireland	51
2	Belgium	68	15	Portugal	51
3	Switzerland	63	16	Italy	50
4	Sweden	64	17	Greece	49
5	Scotland	61	18	Finland	48
6	Germany	61	19	Luxembourg	48
7	England and Wales	61	20	Spain	47
8	Denmark	60	21	Poland	46
9	Nothern Ireland	59	22	Turkey	44
10	Netherlands	58	23	Estonia	43
11	Hungary	58	24	Iceland	40
12	France	54	25	Bulgaria	36
13	Norway	53			

incremental increases in reporting since 1996 among victims in Poland and Estonia. This result may point at a more general upward trend in reporting in Eastern Europe, reflecting increased confidence in the integrity and competence of the police.

The decision to report victimisation experiences to the police is determined by a variety of considerations. Most frequently mentioned reasons in previous sweeps of the ICVS were 'should be reported', 'retribution', to 'recover property', to 'stop it', 'insurance reasons' or 'to get help' (Van Dijk 1999; Van Kesteren *et al.* 2000). There are distinct differences between the reporting motivations of victims of property crimes and of contact crimes. Victims of property crimes more often mention to report to recover property or to satisfy insurance. Victims of contact crimes more often mention that they want the victimisation to stop or to receive help (Van Dijk 1999). Victims in the more affluent countries are more likely to report for insurance reasons (Van Dijk 1999). One explanation for higher reporting rates in Western Europe is the higher proportion of households covered by insurance for losses from property crimes.

Victims who have not reported are asked to give their reasons as well. Most frequently mentioned reasons are 'not serious enough', 'police could do nothing' and 'police won't do anything'. The reason 'not serious enough' is more often mentioned in the more affluent regions of the world in cases of property crime.

Special victim policies by law enforcement and judiciary authorities as promoted in the EU Framework Decision can only be applied when the majority of victims are ready to report their victimisations to the police. Sufficiently high reporting rates can be seen as a precondition for the implementation of such policies. There is some evidence that the way victims are treated by the police by itself affects the readiness to report. Previous analyses of ICVS data have shown that repeat victims of property crimes are less likely to report incidents to the police, presumably because earlier experiences as reporting victims had been unsatisfactory (Van Dijk 2000). If victims expect to receive better services, including referrals, reporting rates may go up. However, other factors such as perceived effectiveness and integrity of law enforcement as well as administrative insurance requirements also determine reporting rates (Goudriaan 2006). Reporting rates can in our opinion better be used as indicators of overall police performance than as indicators of the adequacy of special victim policies.

Victim satisfaction

The EU/ICS asks reporting victims whether, on the whole, they were satisfied with the way the police dealt with the matter. In developing countries satisfaction tends to be higher among victims of contact crimes than of property crimes. This is probably because in developing countries victims of property crimes are often disappointed that the police had failed to recover their property. In developed countries satisfaction levels of victims of different types of crime show much less variation. In contrast to elsewhere victims of burglary in developed nations show slightly higher rates of satisfaction (see also Allen *et al.* 2006). This is probably because these victims are satisfied with having secured the documents required by insurance and have few other demands. Figure 14.2 shows how Western Europe compares to other world regions in terms of victim satisfaction. It shows that the mean rate of victim satisfaction of Western European countries lies slightly below that of Australia/New Zealand and USA/Canada but is almost twice as high as elsewhere in the world. Especially noteworthy is the low level of victim satisfaction in Eastern/Central Europe.

The contents of Table 14.2 show that in Europe victim satisfaction rates vary around a mean of 57 per cent. Of the old 15 member states of the EU lowest rates are found in France, Italy and Greece. In Greece very few victims are satisfied with their treatment by the police. Newer members (Hungary, Poland, Estonia) as well as Bulgaria and Turkey also show rates significantly below the European mean.

Rates of satisfaction among victims of serious crimes show a remarkable downward trend in several countries. Between 1996 and 2005 victim satisfaction went down from 72 per cent to 62 per cent in England and Wales, from 71 per cent to 62 per cent in The Netherlands, from 74 per cent to 67 per cent in Sweden and from 67 per cent to 61 per cent in Scotland. Nation-specific crime victim surveys in England/Wales and The Netherlands, using much larger samples, have also registered a decline in satisfaction in recent years. In England/Wales satisfaction dropped in 2000 to its current level (Allen *et al.* 2006). In the Netherlands satisfaction dropped in 2002 and has since remained stable (Veligheidsmonitor 2006). The ICVS has observed similar drops in satisfaction in the USA and Canada.

This downward trend cannot be explained by a different profile of crime, for example a smaller proportion of burglary victims among reporting victims than before.[2] It cannot be a result of lower perceived effectivenesss of the police either since clearance rates have not declined further and perceptions of police effectiveness have actually gone up across Europe (Van Dijk *et al.*

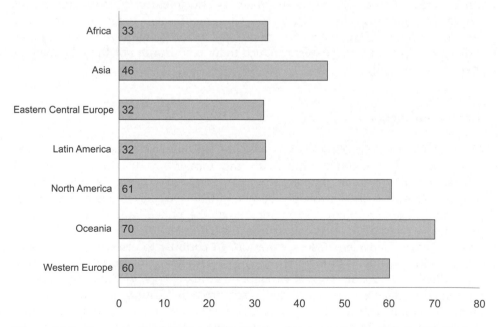

Figure 14.2 Percentages of victims of five types of serious crime satisfied with the way their complaint has been handled by the police per world region (results of EU/ICS/ICVS 2000–05)

Table 14.2 Percentages of victims of five types of serious crime satisfied with the treatment of their complaint by the police (results of EU/ICS 2005 for 25 European countries)

Rank		Percentage	Rank		Percentage
1	Denmark	75	14	Northern Ireland	61
2	Finland	72	15	Portugal	58
3	Luxembourg	70	16	Norway	55
4	Scotland	70	17	Iceland	55
5	Switzerland	69	18	France	53
6	Austria	68	19	Italy	43
7	Sweden	67	20	Bulgaria	41
8	Germany	67	21	Hungary	41
9	Spain	65	22	Poland	46
10	Belgium	65	23	Turkey	33
11	Netherlands	62	24	Greece	28
12	England and Wales	62	25	Estonia	17
13	Ireland	61			

2007). Reduced victim satisfaction seems to genuinely reflect more negative evaluations by victims of their reception by the police. Paradoxically, such deterioration is most pronounced in countries where services for victims are most advanced.

This intriguing result can be interpreted in different ways. One explanation is that in countries such as the United Kingdom and the Netherlands victims are treated as professionally as before or even better but that expectations among victims have risen even more. Expectations could perhaps have been raised in particular regarding the provision of information. Another, competing interpretation is that in some of the countries spearheading more rights and services for victims, police forces may feel that victim needs are duly met if a referral is made to a specialised victim support organisation. Police forces in the United Kingdom and the Netherlands may have started to suffer from 'victim fatigue'.

There is some empirical evidence to support the latter interpretation. Three out of the top five countries in terms of victim satisfaction with the treatment of their complaint by the police did not have a fully functional independent national victim support organisation in place during the time-frame covered by the survey. Switzerland and Luxembourg, placed at fifth and third respectively, both had an NGO in place named the 'Weisse Ring', which at the time suffered in terms of credibility with the police. For Luxembourg, the situation turned so serious that the Weisse Ring was expelled as a member from the European Forum for Victim Services, the umbrella organisation for national victim support organisations. There were strong pressures in that jurisdiction to create new facilities for victims from within the police forces. In Switzerland, tensions did not run that high, but in the late 1990s it was far from clear whether the Weisse Ring would continue to be considered by the police as the natural focal body providing dedicated support to victims of crime.[3] Denmark, in its turn (at first place in the satisfaction table), is yet another story. In 1999, victim support was still regarded as 'still mainly a grass-roots local or regional service' (Brienen and Hoegen 2000: 1000). There was no way of comparing the situation there with the much more advanced independent organisations in England and Wales and in the Netherlands, which at the time were national in nature, had national coverage, offered specialised assistance and were actively involved in policy-making at the governmental level. Only later, well into the new millennium, did the Danish NGO develop into a mature national organisation which was then admitted as a member to the previously mentioned European Forum for Victim Services.[4] All of this could help to explain why the police in Denmark, Luxembourg and Switzerland felt they had a special responsibility in treating reporting crime victims in a sympathetic way, which could not be left to an outside agency to which the victims were simply referred.

More generally, in recent years priorities in policing may have shifted towards terrorism prevention and better enforcement of laws and bylaws and away from service-delivery[5] including for victims. The upshot of the finding remains that fewer victims than before are satisfied, in particular with the information received.[6]

Main reasons of dissatisfaction are that the police 'did not do enough', 'were not interested', 'did not find the offender', 'did not recover goods', 'gave no information' or were 'impolite'. These opinions suggest that victim satisfaction is determined by both the outcome of the investigation (arrest of offender, compensation) as by the quality of services delivery to victims (expression of real interest, provision of information and respectful treatment).

British research has found some indications that victims are less satisfied when a known offender is not charged and/or no property is recovered (Allen et al. 2006). The main source of dissatisfaction, however, appeared to be that insufficient information had been given (Sims and Myhill 2000). Regardless of outcomes, older, middle-class victims in England/Wales tend to be more satisfied than victims belonging to ethnic minorities (Nicholas and Walker 2004). In an in-depth evaluation of victim satisfaction in the Netherlands victims were asked to rate several aspects of police performance (Winkel et al. 2006). Multivariate analyses showed that victim satisfaction was more strongly related to the quality of the reception/treatment than by outcomes (arrests, charges or the arrangement of compensation). Taken together these findings suggest that victim satisfaction to a large extent reflects how victims have experienced the quality of the reception/treatment by the police. This finding suggests that victim satisfaction as measured in surveys can be used as an indicator of the implementation of EU guidelines concerning the respectful and considerate treatment of victims and the duty to provide relevant information.

In countries such as France, Italy and Greece implementation of this part of the Framework Decision leaves much to be desired. This is also the case with several of the newer members or accession countries. Paradoxically, levels of satisfaction in some of the other countries have gone down in recent years rather than up.

Demand and supply of specialised victim services

The EU/ICS questionaire asks victims of four types of serious crime (burglary, robbery, sexual offences, threat/assault) whether they have received support from a specialised victim support agency. Victims of contact crimes are generally twice as likely to receive help than victims of burglary. Those who had not received any help were asked whether they would have appreciated help in getting information, or practical or emotional support. Figure 14.3 shows the rates of victims receiving specialised assistance in world regions.

The results indicate that the need of help among victims of serious crime is widespread but not universal. In developed nations only three or four in ten express such needs. The distribution of the need of help across regions is the reverse of that of its actual reception. In developing countries many more victims would have wanted such help. This is partly caused by the fact that in those countries such help is rarely offered and fewer general provisions and social services are available.

The comparison between the regional percentages of victims of serious crimes who had received assistance and of those who would have appreciated receiving such assistance indicates a gap between supply and demand of such services. Even in countries where victim support has become more common, the need for such help is still largely unmet. Victim support was received most often by victims in New Zealand (20 per cent). In Western Europe, Australia and North America this is around 9 per cent. In other regions including Eastern/Central Europe, provision of specialised help is still a rare occurrence.

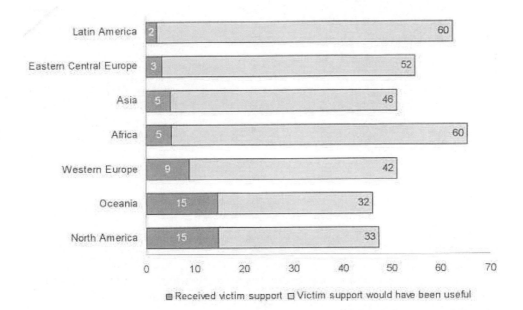

Figure 14.3 Percentages of victims of serious crimes who have received or would have considered useful specialised victim support, by world regions (EU/ICS/ICVS 2005)

To assess the take-up rate of victim support organisations in European countries we have calculated what proportion of victims wanting specialised support have actually received it per country. Figure 14.4 shows the results. In five countries (Scotland, Austria, Northern Ireland, the Netherlands, England/Wales) one in three victims of serious crimes wanting specialised support actually receive it. In another five countries one in four receive the specialised support they need. Elsewhere in Europe current provisions for victim support meet less than 15 per cent of the demand.

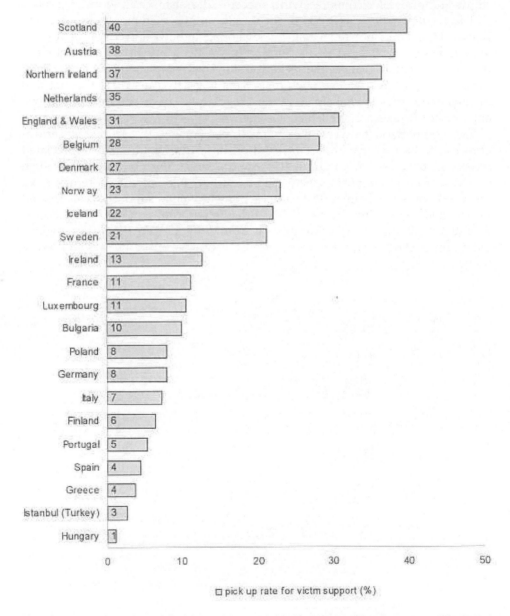

□ pick up rate for victm support (%)

Figure 14.4   Proportion of those wanting support who received it per country (EU/ICS/ICVS 2005)

In several EU countries, take-up rates of victim support have gone up since 1996 and/or 2000 (Austria, Belgium, Denmark, the Netherlands, Northern Ireland and Scotland). In other countries, including England and Wales and Sweden, the expansion of victim support seems to be stagnant in recent years.

Obviously, the EU guideline on the provision of victim support is far from satisfactorily implemented. In all countries organisations responsible for victim support should analyse why most victims of serious crimes in need of their services are not reached. In consultation with donors, plans should be made to significantly expand the coverage of victim support in the coming years.

A composite index of victim satisfaction

The level of satisfaction of victims with the way the police handle their reports and the extent to which the demand for victim support is actually met, are both important indicators of the implementation of the EU Framework Decision. The take-up rate of victim support is partly determined by the need for such services, which is dependent on external factors such as availability of general services for victims. The percentages of all victims of serious crimes who received such support seems a straightforward indicator of the extent to which specialised support is made available. A comprehensive index of victim satisfaction was constructed by averaging the percentages of victims of serious crimes satisfied with the police and percentages who received victim support. Figure 14.5 shows the ranking of European countries on this index.

Victim policies in Scotland, Denmark and Austria show the best results, closely followed by the Netherlands, England/Wales, Sweden, North Ireland, Luxembourg and Belgium. In the medium range are Finland, Norway, Spain, Ireland, Germany and Iceland. Least effective policies seem to be in place in Portugal, France, Italy, Greece, Turkey, Hungary and Bulgaria.

Discussion and policy implications

The study of Brienen and Hoegen allows a crude ranking of European countries in terms of their compliance with the COE Recommendation and EU Framework Decision. The composite victim satisfaction index allows a ranking of countries in terms of the perceived impact of these policies on actual victims of serious crime. For 18 countries rank numbers on both variables are available. The legal and victimological rankings were found to be fairly strongly correlated ($r=0.60$; $n=18$; $p<.05$).

Countries that perform poorly according to the legal scorecard (Greece, Turkey, Italy, Iceland, Luxembourg, Portugal and Spain) all belong to the group countries with the lowest scores on victim satisfaction, with the exception of Luxembourg. Almost all countries that came out favourably in the legal assessment (the Netherlands, England/Wales, Norway, Belgium and Denmark) show comparatively high or medium-high scores on victim

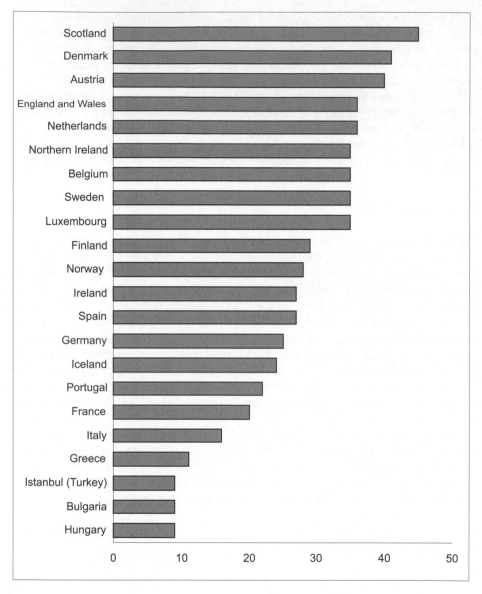

Figure 14.5 Ranking of countries on composite index of victim satisfaction

satisfactions as well. Countries such as Germany and France feature in the medium range in both classifications.

This fairly high measure of concurrence can be seen as a cross-validation of both measures. The formal compliance of domestic laws and regulations with international standards is apparently not without consequences for the satisfaction of actual victims about the way they are treated or serviced. By interviewing victims of crimes about their experiences, a rough assessment can be made of the extent to which actual policies of the member states comply with the EC Framework Decision.

However, the association between legal assessment and victim satisfaction is far from perfect. One of the most striking incongruencies are the top positions of Scotland, Denmark and Austria on the victim satisfaction index. One possible explanation is that in these countries improvements have recently been introduced in victim policies that are not yet reflected in the legal assessment. For example, in Austria new legislation has been passed to offer better protection to victims of domestic violence. It would seem useful if the Brienen and Hoegen study of 2000 were repeated across the current member states of the EU.

Worth mentioning is furthermore that according to Brienen and Hoegen Denmark, together with the Netherlands, Belgium, Luxembourg and Norway, boasts the most comprehensive regular training programme for police officers on victim reception and treatment. The intensity and quality of training of relevant officials may well be the critical success factor in the operational implementation of victim policies.

A remarkable and disappointing finding of our evaluation is the declining satisfaction with the police of victims in several countries at the forefront of the victims movement, such as the United Kingdom and the Netherlands. Raised expectations may have played a role but it seems equally likely that in these countries police forces have started to relegate victim services to existing, well-functioning victim organisations. If such a trend is indeed emerging, it means that extra efforts are needed to maintain high-quality police services for victims when referral to outside organisations becomes routine. Initiatives seem required to counter the unintended negative side-effects of well-functioning victim support organisations on the victim-centred performance of the police.

Further reading

J. Goodey (2005) *Victims and Victimology: Research, Policy and Practice.* Harlow: Pearson.

Commission of the European Communities, *Report from the Commission on the basis of Article 18 of the Council Framework Decision of 15 March 2001 on the standing of victims in criminal proceedings*, Brussels 03.03.2004, COM(2004)54 final.

M.E.I. Brienen, M.S. Groenhuijsen and E.H. Hoegen (2000) 'Evaluation and meta-evaluation of the effectiveness of victim-oriented legal reform in Europe', *Criminologie*, 33(1): 121–44.

M.S. Groenhuijsen (1999) 'Victims' rights in the Criminal Justice System: A Call for More Comprehensive Implementation Theory', in J. Van Dijk, J. Wemmers and R. Van Kaam (eds) *Caring for Crime Victims.* Monsey, NY: Criminal Justice Press.

J.J.M. Van Dijk (2007) *World of Crime: Breaking the Silence on Crime, Justice and Development Across the World.* Thousand Oaks, CA: Sage.

Notes

1 We want to express our gratitude to John Van Kesteren of Intervict for his assistance in the data analysis.

2 In all countries satisfaction levels went down in equal measure among victims of burglaries and of contact crimes.
3 In the – generally optimistic – overview *Opferhilfe in der Schweiz. Erfarungen und Perspektiven* (Victim Support in Switzerland. Experiences and Perspectives), Bundesambt für Justiz, Bern/Stuttgart/Wien 2004, there is hardly any reference to a single NGO offering nationwide services to all categories of crime victims.
4 Visit www.euvictimservices.org.
5 The Dutch crime victim survey shows, for example, that the provision of crime prevention advice to reporting victims has gone down significantly since the 1990s.
6 A general factor behind the drop in satisfaction may be the gradual increase of victims reporting by phone or via internet. There is some evidence that since 2002 victims who have no face-to-face contact with the police are somewhat less satisfied (Allen *et al.* 2006, 2005). Older sweeps of the BCS, however, showed no such difference (Sims and Myhill 2000).

References

Allen, J., Edmonds, S., Patterson, A. and Smith, D. (2006) *Policing and the Criminal Justice System – Public Confidence and Perceptions: Findings from the 2004/2005 British Crime Survey*, Online report 07/06. London: Home Office.

Allen, J., El Komy, M., Lovbakke, J. and Roy, H. (2005) *Policing and the Criminal Justice System – Public Confidence and Perceptions: Findings from the 2003/04 British Crime Survey*, Online Report 31/05. London: Home Office.

Brienen, M.E.I. and Hoegen, E.H. (2000) *Victims of Crime in 22 European Criminal Justice Systems*. Nijmegen: Wolf Legal Productions.

Commission of the European Communities (2004) *Report on the basis of Article 18 of the Council Framework Decision of 15 March 2001 on the Standing of Victims in Criminal Proceedings*. Brussels: 3 March.

Goudriaan, H. (2006) *Reporting Crime*. Leiden: NSCR.

Groenhuijsen, M. and Letschert, R. (2006) 'Reflections on the Development and Legal Status of Victims' Rights Instructions', in M. Groenhuijsen and R. Letschert (eds) *Compilation of International Victims' Rights Instruments*. Nijmegen: Wolf Legal Publishers, pp. 1–18.

Nicholas, S. and Walker, A. (2004) *Crime in England/Wales 2002/2003: Supplementary Volume 2: Crime, Disorder and the Criminal Justice System – Public Articles and Perceptions*, Statistical Bulletin 02/04. London: Home Office.

Sims, L. and Myhill, A. (2001) *Policing and the Public: Findings from the 2000 British Crime Survey*. Home Office Research Findings 136. London: Home Office.

Van Dijk J.J.M (1999) 'The Experience of Crime and Justice', in G. Newman (ed.) *Global Report on Crime and Justice*. United Nations Office for Drug Control and Crime Prevention, Centre for International Crime Prevention. New York: Oxford University Press.

Van Dijk, J.J.M., Mayhew, P. and Killias, M. (1990). *Experiences of Crime Across the World: Key Findings from the 1989 International Crime Survey*. Deventer: Kluwer Law and Taxation Publishers.

Van Dijk, J.J.M. (2000) 'Implications of the International Crime Victims Survey for a Victim Perspective', in A. Crawford and J. Goodey (eds) *Integrating a Victim Perspective within Criminal Justice*. Aldershot: Ashgate/Dartmouth.

Van Dijk, J.J.M. (2007 forthcoming) *World of Crime: Breaking the Silence on Levels of Crime, Justice and Development across the World*. Thousand Oaks, CA: Sage.

Van Dijk, J.J.M., Manchin, R., Van Kesteren, J. and Hideg, G. (2007) *The Burden of Crime in the European Union*, Research Report: A Comparative Analysis of the European Crime and Safety Survey (EU ICS) 2005. Gallup/Europe (www.intervict.nl).

Van Kesteren, J.N., Mayhew, P. and Nieuwbeerta, P. (2000). *Criminal Victimisation in Seventeen Industrialized Countries: Key Findings from the 2000 International Crime Victims Survey*, Onderzoek en beleid, No. 187. The Hague: Ministry of Justice, WODC.

Veiligheidsmonitor Rijk (2006) Voorburg/Heerlen: Centraal Bureau voor de Statistiek.

Winkel, F.W., Spapens, A.C. and Letschert, R.M. (2006) *Satisfaction of Victims with the Administration of Justice and Victim Support* (Tevredenheid van slachtoffers met 'rechtspleging' en slachtofferhulp) (in Dutch with an English summary). The Hague: WODC.

Chapter 15

A comparative analysis of the victim policies across the Anglo-speaking world

Tracey Booth and Kerry Carrington[1]

Introduction

The last three decades have seen an unprecedented rise in interest in the victim by politicians, criminal justice policy-makers and a diverse range of scholars in feminism, criminology, victimology, sociology, law and public policy (Zedner 2002; Garland 2001; Young 2002; Rock 2005). As this interest has been an international phenomenon, this chapter provides a comparative analytical overview of these developments across a number of Anglo-speaking countries from the northern and southern hemispheres.

The heterogeneity of victim movements

Organised victim movements began to appear in the UK, the US, Canada, Australia and New Zealand between the 1970s and early 1980s (Rock 2005: 2). Many were spawned by a disgruntlement that victims were either neglected or mistreated by the criminal justice system. Victims were the forgotten non-persons of the system (Rock 2005: 2). Historically, the role of victims in an adversarial system of justice has been limited to an instrumental one as a witness for the Crown. Confined to this role, victims were largely silenced in the criminal process and had no role in critical threshold decisions such as whether or not to proceed with criminal proceedings against alleged offenders. They were rarely informed about delays, decisions to drop charges or to accept a lesser charge in exchange for a guilty plea (Zedner 2002: 436).

One defining aspect of the victim movements is their sheer diversity and fragmentation. Victim movements in England and Wales, for instance, include groups representing the victims of road trauma, murdered children, and sufferers of specific disasters or violent events (Rock 2005: 6). Even in the United States, where victim groups have been aligned with punitive political groups supporting the death penalty, a variety of victim groups coexist. These differences were most poignant in the aftermath of the September 11 terrorist attacks when counter-posing victims groups formed – one explicitly to rally against punitive sanctions such as the death penalty and one to call for the death penalty for all terrorists.

Another defining aspect of victim support services and groups is that many in the field of sexual and domestic violence have been inspired or instigated by feminists. Feminists working in victim support services in the UK, US, Australia, New Zealand and other parts of the world have played a key historical role in elevating the needs of women and children as victims, assisting the emergence of victim support agencies and services such as women's refuges and sexual assault centres and lobbying for legislative reform, such as the introduction of apprehended violence orders.

There appears to be wide variation in the effectiveness of victim movements to influence policy outcomes. Victim movements in the United States appear to have had the most purchase on policy development, with all states having passed legislation to support and compensate victims and more than half recognising victims' rights in legislation (Young 2001a). The executive director of National Organisation for Victim Assistance (NOVA), Marlene Young, boldly claims that 'The movement has redefined laws affecting victim participation in the system, definitions of who is a victim and what the effects of victimisation are' (Young 2001a: 1). The victims' movement began as a confluence of loosely organised groups (child victim advocates and advocates for the victims of violent crime and violence against women) who in 1975 formed NOVA (Young 2001b: 2).

No single victims group or movement in Australia has been able to monopolise government patronage in the way that Victim Support has in the UK (for a description of this monopoly see Rock 2005: 10–11) or NOVA has done in the US. Rather a variety of victim groups currently occupy a tangential role in the criminal justice system through the provision of state-supported victim services. Those officially recognised by the NSW government, for instance, include Enough is Enough, the Homicide Victims Support Group and Victims of Crime Assistance League (VOCAL). VOCAL has now spread to other jurisdictions with groups in the Northern Territory (www.nt.giv.au.pfes/police/community/guides/victims-of-crime.html). These homicide support groups have been associated with political campaigns calling for more rights for victims. Enough is Enough was formed in 1994 by Ken Marslew, whose son Michael was murdered during an armed hold-up of a Pizza Hut earlier that year. Ken Marslew has been a long-term advocate and campaigner for victims' rights in Australia. Like the formation of victim groups elsewhere, his motivation was based on a deep cynicism that the criminal justice process, as is evident in the following comments:

> There is no justice in our system… We are living in an offender friendly society where the spirit of justice is dead. Laws are not administered within the spirit with which they are written, principles, equality and ethics (as well as truth) are not part of our legal process, and this is a catalyst for violence. (Marslew 1998: 2)

Interestingly Ken Marslew does not just seek vengeance and is a strong advocate of violence prevention, mediation and restorative justice (Marslew 1998: 3).

Like victim movements in the northern hemisphere, in Australia this movement emerged from an array of interest groups: through the refuge movement, women's support organisations, the women's electoral lobby, Aboriginal and community legal services, and sexual assault and advice centres. The victims championed by these diverse interest groups include child and adult survivors of sexual assault and domestic violence who rarely rate a mention in law and order political agendas (Hogg and Brown 1998). While these loose-knit groups are not usually associated with punitive calls for heavier penalties for offenders, feminist activists have been fairly strident in their critique of the Australian justice system's failure to adequately address the needs of victims of domestic or sexual violence. Many argue that at best the criminal justice system inadequately addresses the needs of victims, and at worst re-victimises the victim (Carmody and Carrington 2000).

The UK has a similar umbrella organisation to NOVA called Victim Support. However it does not appear to have anything like the extent of resources and policy reach that NOVA enjoys in the US. Victim Support, as the single national provider in the UK, receives significant annual government funding, yet according to Rock it is a 'pygmy' of an institution, swamped by the power and influence of much bigger players in the criminal justice system. It has not yet been able to effectively negotiate mandated victim support beyond minimal counselling, information and advice (Rock 2005: 12).

One reason perhaps is that victim support groups in the UK appear to have been less politicised than in Australia and the US although equally as diverse (Rock 1990). The original Victim Support service, established in Bristol in 1974, focused mainly on victims of property crimes such as burglary, and homicide (Rock 1990). Alongside this, support for the victims of sexual assault and domestic violence grew out of the women's refuge movement and the Rape Crisis centres which began to emerge in Britain in the 1970s (Zedner 2002: 434) (see also Chapters 5 and 6 in this volume). Victim movements are consequently heterogeneous in their character and aims, making it a mistake to characterise these movements as singularly motivated by vengeance or punitiveness.

The politicisation of the victim

My administration has made the fight against crime a top priority. But when a crime does occur, I am dedicated to providing assistance and comfort to victims and to ensuring that the rights of victims are protected. At the time of their great trauma, crime victims deserve nothing less than our complete support. (President George Bush, Press Release, 27 April 2002)

... the prime minister [Tony Blair] has said the rights of suspects must not 'outweigh' those of the 'law-abiding majority'. (BBC News, 23 June 2006)

'Victims have to be paramount'. (Tony Blair, 10 Downing Street News Room (http://www.number10.gov.uk/output/page9274.asp))

Supporting the victims of crime has become a mantra of most major political parties in Australia and other western nations over the last 15 years (Hogg and Brown 1998).[2] During the 1990s much of this political discourse privileged an idealised version of a victim – the vulnerable, elderly, victim of vicious assaults or attacks by strangers. Since September 11 2001 the political discourse has broadened to include the victims of terror. The talk about getting tough on crime and taking victims' concerns seriously has heightened suspicions especially among criminal defence lawyers that the elevation of the role of the victim in the criminal process is at the expense of the rights of the accused. Some criminologists have also complained that the elevation of the long-neglected victim is symptomatic of a punitive turn in the last decade of the twentieth century (Garland 2000; Loader 2005). However, it is a mistake to assume that all victims seek punitive retribution, or that the motivation for seeking victims' rights has to be at the expense of offenders' rights. Rather, as illustrated above, a more diverse collection of groups have lobbied various governments over the last 30 years on behalf of victims seeking redress for a range of different needs and concerns.

The politically popular support for victims in a law and order electoral climate has also led to the dramatic expansion of victim services. For instance after winning the Victorian state government election from the conservative Liberal government in 2004, the Bracks' Labor government announced an overhaul of victims' services and an additional commitment of AUS $12.8 million in victim support over the next three years. In announcing the overhaul the attorney-general said:

> The Bracks' government understands its responsibility to the victims of crime ... When this government came to office victims of crime services were in a shambles ... Under the old system, services were fragmented and uncoordinated ... The needs of the victims are at the heart of this new system. (Rob Hulls, Attorney-General and Minister for Community Services, media release, 16 September 2004)

Given the politicisation of the victim, one of the central initiatives undertaken by Anglo-speaking governments has been to incorporate the demands of victims' rights groups into their policy platforms and political agendas. Some governments have gone as far as to officially incorporate victim movements into the criminal justice system, either as volunteers, information or support agencies (as in NSW through the establishment of a Victims Bureau in 1996; in the UK through mandating Victim Support as the official provider of services; in the US through mandating NOVA as the recognised body to provide victim support) or as advisers to victim units and ministries (as in the Victims' Advisory Panel established in the UK in 2003, see Rock 2005: 18). These groups have also been given recognition and 'voice', through the adoption of an array of instruments variously referred to as victims' charters, protocols, codes or guidelines, depending on jurisdiction. Below we compare some of these measures across the Anglo-speaking axis.

Victims' charters

Victims' charters of various kinds have been adopted across the US, UK, Europe, Canada, Australia and New Zealand as a means of setting minimal standards for the treatment of victims and witnesses (Zedner 2002: 436). In most jurisdictions these charters are not legally binding, some are expressed as statutory instruments which prescribe minimum standards (such as in NSW), while others are expressed as loose guides or protocols (in the current Northern Territory Charter, and the 1990 Victim's Charter in UK). The major import of these charters is symbolic in that they acknowledge the role of the victim, and the suffering or harm caused, encourage the sensitive treatment of victims within the criminal justice system and seek to ensure that victims have better access to information, support services, witness support and protection. The emphasis is on the provision of information, not services. Indeed there is still little by way of mandated services available to victims, such as the provision of free professional counselling or crisis accommodation. These charters have been criticised as policy instruments that do not provide any substantive rights for victims but are an unenforceable set of minimal standards (Zedner 2002: 436), implemented in an *ad hoc* manner without much state-funded support (Rock 2005).

Australia has eight different jurisdictions, making generalised statements about the implementation of these charters or protocols difficult. All jurisdictions have introduced some variation of a victims' charter, with the exception of Victoria which released a draft victims' charter for community consultation in 2005. NSW introduced its Charter of Victims Rights a decade ago in 1996, Western Australia in 1994, South Australia in 2001, the ACT in 1994, and Queensland in 1995. Tasmania and the Northern Territory both have victims' charters, but neither are prescribed as statutory provisions. In no Australian jurisdiction are victims' rights legally binding (Manning and Griffith 1996). The Western Australian policy recognises 'the unique needs of victims in regional and remote areas where the provision of victim support services are restricted by distance from population centres large enough to provide such supports' (Department of Attorney-General, WA 2003: 2). The various Australian charters contain similarly worded motherhood statements that encourage courtesy and respect of victims' rights or needs; that stress the importance of victims' access to information about services, remedies, the role of the witness in court, the custodial status of the accused, and the criminal process from reporting a crime to police, through to bail, committal and trial hearings. These charters also elevate the security concerns of victims as witnesses throughout the process, calling for protection of victims where a reasonable apprehension exists. Some also allow for extra provisions for vulnerable and intimidated witnesses, as does the UK Code of Practice for Victims (see Section 4 of the Code; see also Sanders and Jones in this volume). Victims' charters promote the continuing role of the victim in post-trial processes, such as applications for probation and parole, and victims' compensation and in some instances victim–offender mediation or conferencing loosely modelled on the principles of restorative justice. This may involve the victim in a pre- or post-release reparative conference with the offender.

Access to information, services, and compensation are the critical components of these various charters or guidelines.[3] The Northern Territory Department of Justice sums up what their charter means for victims in its jurisdiction in these terms:

> The Charter sets out the way you as a victim of crime should be treated in the criminal justice system. You can expect to be treated in a sympathetic, constructive and reassuring manner. The Charter ensures that victims, their circumstances and their rights are acknowledged, respected and protected. This may help to repair some of the harm and distress suffered by victims of crime in our community. (www.nt.gov.au/justice/crimvict/ntcharter.shtml)

The UK introduced its first Victim's Charter in 1990, a revised version in 1996 and in 2005 launched a Code of Practice for Victims of Crime. Like most charters elsewhere in the world, the UK code is not legally binding (Home Office 2006: 1). The policy document prescribes a minimum set of standards relating to victim support and access to information. Agencies expected to deliver these minimum standards include the Criminal Cases Review Commission, the Criminal Injuries Compensation Authority, the police, the Crown Prosecution Service, Her Majesty's Courts Service, Witness Care Units, the Parole Board, the prison service, the probation service and youth offending teams (2006: 2). The code embodies a similar set of minimal expectations about victim support, protection and compensation through civil proceedings. Key elements of the code include access to timely information, a complaint process, victim support (provided entirely through volunteer agencies and charitable bodies), special services for vulnerable or intimidated victims (www.homeoffice.gov.uk/crime-victims/victims/victims-rights) and the right to privacy especially in cases involving minors and sexual assault. Like Australia, the emphasis is on information and co-ordination of service providers, rather than services *per se*. The code is largely symbolic.

The expansion of victim support

Initiatives to introduce victims' rights in Australia preceded the 1985 UN declaration Basic Principles of Justice for Victims of Crime and Abuse of Power. The South Australian government was the first Australian jurisdiction to introduce measures to redress complaints by victims about their disadvantaged status in the criminal justice system, following an inquiry into the victims of crime established in 1979, by a forward-looking Labor government led by Don Dunstan. That committee made 70 recommendations, nearly all of which were implemented prior to the 1985 declaration (Eres *et al.* 2006). The major exception was the recommendation to allow victim impact statements (VIS) to be tendered to courts. The introduction of the VIS in Australian jurisdictions has been a more controversial issue, which we consider in detail later.

South Australia has the most developed victim support services in Australia, offered in country and metropolitan population centres across a number of portfolios. A 65-page booklet outlines the SA government's support for victims. The booklet is even available in Aboriginal English. The Department of Public Prosecutions offers witness support through a system of court companions, interpreter services, and practical assistance with writing victim impact statements, as well as legal advice about the victim's role in the criminal justice process. Victims are also offered pre- and post-court support through the Victims Strategy of the SA police department. The SA Department of Correctional Services maintains a Victims Register. Before any prisoner in that state can be released from jail or community programmes, the department has to consult any registered victim. A registered victim is entitled to information about sentence details, security classification and reclassifications, prison transfers, escapes and the details of the release of the offender on bail, home detention, parole or pre-release community service programme. Only after the expiry of parole of the offender will the victim's name be removed from the register and the responsibilities of the state cease. The SA government also offers specific support services and crisis accommodation for victims of sexual assault and domestic violence. To co-ordinate this vast array of victim support services, the SA government employs Victims Support Co-ordinators to ensure a 'seamless' holistic government approach to victim support.

All Australian jurisdictions provide for criminal injuries compensation and a range of extensive victim support services such as counselling and mediation services. NSW has a designated Victims of Crime Bureau which co-ordinates a range of support and services for the victims of crime including counselling, a 24-hour hotline, compensation, assistance with completing victim impact statements, referral to other agencies, and ensuring that other agencies observe the Victims Charter (http://www.lawlink.nsw.gov.au/lawlink/victimsservices/ll_vs.nsf/pages/VS_index).

Tasmania has a Victims Assistance Unit. The unit provides a range of similar services in country and metropolitan areas. There are Victim Support Units in the Northern Territory, South Australia, Western Australia and a Victims Support Agency in Victoria. Most jurisdictions also provide free counselling to victims of crime regardless of whether they reported the crime to police. In NSW around 4,000 victims each year since 2001 have received two free hours of counselling (Victims Compensation Tribunal 2005: 20). Of those who received counselling in the year ending 30 June 2005, 98 per cent said they found their counsellor supportive and helpful and 92 per cent said it helped them cope better (Victims Compensation Tribunal 2005: 21). Some coroner's courts also make provision for counselling for the relatives of homicide victims, such as the Coroner's Counselling Service in WA. By comparison the UK Code only allows for advice and support provided by charitable bodies, and entitlements to victim support are dependent on having first reported the alleged crime to the police (Home Office 2006: 3 section 3.11). However, Victim Support, the national charity that provides free support to the victims of crime, claims it does provide support 'whether or not you report the crime' (www.victimsupport.org.uk).

Other initiatives on the agenda of most Australian jurisdictions include the expansion of VIS to parole hearings (Black 2003), the establishment of victims registers and special units to support vulnerable witnesses such as child witnesses, and the expansion of Indigenous models of justice that involve the victims of family and sexual violence in Indigenous communities.

Through Victim Support, the UK Home Office has established an elaborate network of volunteer organisations spread across the country to provide victim support services. However, little is provided by way of direct support for victims through counselling, protection and crisis accommodation. Victim Support, the national charity auspiced by the Home Office to provide victim support in the UK, is limited to providing free 'practical' and 'emotional' support to victims. This organisation's promotional literature emphasises the information needs of victims and encourages victims to report crimes to the police. It is uncritical and conservative in outlook, stays out of politics, presents itself through a calm rational discourse, unlike the angry victim organisations associated with Rape Crisis centres. This is why, argues Rock, Victim Support has been the major beneficiary of government patronage and funding (Rock 2005: 10). The emphasis of UK policy is on access to information, through initiatives such as the interactive victim's walkthrough (http://www.cjsonline.gov.uk/victim/walkthrough/index.html), not access to services which require continuing funding. By contrast, while all Australian jurisdictions emphasise access to information they also provide direct support by way of state-funded services to victims such as counselling, mediation, offender–victim mediation and repatriation schemes, crisis accommodation, witness protection and security. The Western Australian government even provides direct funding to a number of victims' rights groups (Department of Attorney-General, WA 2003: 3).

The United States provides a stark contrast to the UK system of victim support, particularly for a country that has a minimalist welfare system. The United States has an elaborate nationwide system for supporting the victims of crime. All 50 states have passed legislation supporting the victims of crime and over half have legislation that protects victims' rights in legislation. Under President Reagan's leadership the US Congress passed the 1984 Victims of Crime Act which established a fund for compensating victims through the collection of federal fines (Young 2001: 2). The Federal Office for the Victims of Crime was established in 1988 by an Amendment to the Victims of Crime Act 1982. The office provides training, produces publications, runs public education campaigns, supports projects promoting victims' rights and organises a victims' rights week every April (http://www.ojp.usdoj.gov/ovc/publications/factshts/what_is_ovc/fs_000307.html#1).

The National Organisation for Victims Assistance (NOVA), which lobbied long and hard for recognition of victims' rights, is funded by the US government to provide a range of services and supports for victims (www.trynova.org). Unlike its UK counterpart Victim Support, NOVA appears to have had more success in shaping US public policies and programmes.

The strategic leverage of victims' movements in US seems to have been boosted by terrorist attacks on US citizens and the subsequent war on terror. For instance, in the wake of the 1995 Oklahoma bombing, the US federal government established a number of new measures and policy devices to address the needs of 'mass victimisation and trauma' created by events such as these. As a US Department of Justice report explains: 'It created mass casualties and injuries, affecting not only the immediate victims, survivors and the Oklahoma City community but also the entire nation' (US Department of Justice 2000: 1).

Oklahoma was followed by the 1996 bombing of US military offices in the Khobar Towers in Saudi Arabia, and the 1998 bombing of US embassies in Kenya and Tanzania. A US government inquiry into these bombings made a number of recommendations about the practical delivery of victim support on a mass scale, such as the establishment of compassion centres designed to provide relatives of victims with immediate, accurate and timely information about their relatives in a way that is caring and protects their privacy (US Department of Justice 2000: recommendation 3). In the wake of these bombings the US broadened its support to terror victims. This policy initiative encompassed a range of programmes designed to respond to the needs of terror victims in the immediate, medium-term and long-term aftermath of the event. The provision of court and witness support and counselling to terror survivors and their families throughout the lengthy prosecution over the Oklahoma bombing is an example of the kind of long-term support provided by the Office for Victims (US Department of Justice 2000: 13).

After the September 11 terrorist attacks the US Department of Justice set about developing an even more nationally comprehensive policy of victim support in response to mass criminal victimisation. The US Congress made the largest ever monetary commitment to the Office for Victims for Crime, committing $68.1 million in funding for victim support in the 2002 financial year (US Department of Justice 2003: 2). A further $2.4 million was committed to support victims throughout the trial of alleged terrorist Zacarias Moussaoui (2003: 1). The funds assisted 22,000 victims, crisis support workers and family members (2003: 1).

In addition the US Congress created and funded the Terrorism and International Victim Assistance Services Division 'to address emerging issues related to serving victims of violent crime, mass victimization, and terrorism both in the United States and abroad' (www.ojp.usdoj.gov/ovc/ publications/factshts). The Office for Victims is authorised to commit up to $50 million for this purpose (US Department of Justice 2003: 3). Most significantly the division administers the Antiterrorism and Emergency Assistance Program. This programme provides US nationals, soldiers, civilians and government employees who are the victims of terrorism or international crimes anywhere in the world to a range of victim services. The division provides funding for the reimbursement of funeral, burial, medical, accommodation and transport expenses of victims or their relatives. This relatively new initiative acknowledges the international and global nature of victimisation, extends the ambit of the US Crime Victims Act to victimisation that occurs outside US borders, and acknowledges the collective victimisation of communities wrought by terrorist activity (US Department of Justice 2006). The US Department of Justice describes this initiative thus:

> Over the year, hundreds of US nationals, officers and employees of
> the US government have been killed or injured in international acts of

terrorism occurring outside United States ... While victims of acts of international terrorism abroad have much in common with victims of other types of violent crime, they face some unique challenges based on the nature, extent, and location of the crime. (US Department of justice 2006: 3)

This policy measure extends the concept of victimisation to any US national or any officers or employee to acts of terrorism occurring outside US borders. The contentious decision as to whether or not the act (such as an attack on US military deployed in Iraq) is an act of terror is determined by the US Attorney General (US Department of Justice 2006: 5). The 2006 Report to Congress conflates a long list of civilian and military victims of international terrorism by referring to victims of the Pan Am Flight 103 over Lockerbie in 1988; victims of attacks on American embassies and military barracks on Kenya, Tanzania and Yemen in 1998 and 2000; the victims of attacks in Bali in 2002; and terrorist attacks in Afghanistan, Iraq, Egypt and London in 2004 and 2005 (US Department of Justice 2006: 3). Curiously there is no reference to the war on terror or deployment of US military troops in any one of these locations. By using the language and policy measures designed originally to address the needs of domestic victims of crime, the Bush administration has cleverly orchestrated a simple but effective dyad that associates any US combatant deployed in the war on terror as a terrorist victim and not a casualty of war. US enemies are unequivocally constructed as terrorists with seemingly little appreciation of the complex and blurred boundaries of shared victimisation between warring nations or parties. Whether either of the other two major parties to the coalition of the willing – that is the UK or Australia – head down this path of expansive victim support services to military personnel deployed to 'fight the war on terror' is yet to be seen.

Participation by victims in legal proceedings

Reforms that aim to provide pertinent information, victim assistance and compensation for victims of crime, like those discussed above, have been generally welcomed as appropriate mechanisms through which to acknowledge victims and express the community's concern and compassion for crime and victimisation. More controversial have been those legislative reforms providing victims with opportunities to become active participants in criminal justice proceedings with the potential to influence the severity of punishment through submissions to sentencing courts and, more recently, to parole decision-making processes. The following section considers these more controversial aspects of victim participation in detail.

The sentencing process

It is a well-accepted sentencing principle in common law jurisdictions that the penalty imposed must be proportional to the objective seriousness of the offence;

offence seriousness is measured according to the culpability of the offender and the harm caused by the offence. Thus, harm sustained by a victim as a result of an offence and foreseeable by the offender is relevant to the formulation of penalty at common law. In *R v P* the Australian Federal Court said:

> There is no question that increasing public concern about the position of victims of crime in the criminal justice system has been accompanied by repeated instances of judicial recognition that loss or damage suffered by a victim is a factor to be taken into account in the sentencing process ... [T]hat reliable information of that nature should be presented is in the public interest, not only in the interest of the injured victim ... since a proper sentence should not be based on a misconception or ignorance of the salient facts.

Australian legislative sentencing regimes make provision for harm sustained by crime victims to be taken into account as a discrete factor in the formulation of penalty. In certain circumstances, harm sustained by a victim can also amount to an aggravating factor. For instance, section 21A(2)(g) of the NSW Crimes (Sentencing Procedure) Act 1999 provides that 'substantial injury, emotional harm loss or damage' caused by an offence can aggravate the penalty.

Given the adversarial nature of the criminal hearing the crime victim is not a separate party to the proceedings. At best the victim will be a witness, and in the sentencing process the victim has no role at all. Because victims have had no standing in the sentencing process, information regarding the impact of the crime on victims has generally been presented to the court in an *ad hoc* manner by the prosecution, either directly or in pre-sentence reports prepared by various criminal justice agencies. However, the prosecutor's responsibility is to the state to act in the public interest and assist the court in reaching the most appropriate decision, and not to the victim and what are perceived as private interests. Accordingly concerns have been expressed that 'the gathering and presentation of evidence of the effect of the crime on the victim tends to undermine the actual and perceived independence of counsel for the prosecution by identifying counsel with the victim' (Burchett, Miles and O'Loughlin JJ in *R v P* at 545).

Victim impact statements

As noted above, increasingly crime victims have become pivotal to contemporary crime and justice policy in common law jurisdictions (Garland 2001). Beginning in the United States in the late 1970s and most recently as a pilot scheme in Scotland in 2003–05, reforms have been introduced to provide victims with a role in sentencing proceedings. Consequently, victims of crime now generally enjoy limited participatory rights in the sentencing process through the submission of victim impact statements (VIS) to the court between conviction and sentence.[4] The VIS is a well-entrenched feature of criminal justice policy in Australia and currently all Australian jurisdictions other than Queensland[5] have statutory regimes incorporating VIS into the sentencing process.

McLeod (1986: 508) has astutely observed in the US context that implicit in the use of the phrase 'victim impact statements' is a general agreement as to the 'substance, preparation and presentation' of VIS. However, she argues that a review of the various legislative models in the US reveals 'minimal consensus' as to a variety of matters including definition of the victim, contents of the VIS, methods of presentation and the procedural basis for submission of VIS (1986: 508). Except for the fact that VIS are not mandatory in any Australian jurisdiction, a review of law and practice in Australia also indicates little uniformity on a variety of issues including definition of victim, offence and harm, contents of VIS and procedural and evidential matters. However, despite significant variations in legislative frameworks with regard to the definition of 'victim', all bar two Australian statutory models extend the right to submit a VIS to not only the direct or primary victim of the offence but also to the primary victim's family, in cases where that victim has died as a result of the offence (the 'family victim').[6] Sentencing courts in the remaining two jurisdictions, Victoria and South Australia, have interpreted the statutory definition of victim to include the victim's family in death cases (*R v Birmingham No. 2, R v Miller*). Exceptionally, Victoria also extends the definition of 'victim' to include a 'body' as a well as a person (section 95A, Sentencing Act 1991, Victoria).

The NSW statutory model expressly extends the definition of victim who may submit a VIS to include a witness to the offence who has suffered harm as a result of the offence (section 26, Crimes (Sentencing Procedure) Act 1999, NSW). Similarly, in recent terrorism cases in the United States, the sentencing courts have extended the scope of 'victim' beyond family and friends of the deceased to allow VIS from rescuers (*United States v McVeigh*) and, in the most recent case of *United States v Moussaoui*, also the mayor of New York, to be presented to the sentencing court. This expansion in legal recognition of the concept of victim is consistent with the expansion of US victim support already described, to encompass the collective nature of victimisation wrought by terrorism. Where large numbers of people have died as a result of the act of terrorism, a contentious issue has been the selection of those victims that may submit a VIS since realistically the court does not have time to hear hundreds of victims. Allegations were made in both the McVeigh and Moussaoui cases that only those family victims in favour of the death penalty were chosen to submit a VIS to the sentencing court (Lithwick 2006).

Of the Australian statutory regimes, only Victoria, Western Australia and the Northern Territory do not limit those crimes to which the victims' rights to submit VIS attach.[7] Thus, a victim of any crime may submit a VIS in those jurisdictions. Tasmania, South Australia and the Australian Capital Territory[8] limit those crimes to 'indictable' offences. NSW employs a more narrow approach and confines the victim's participatory rights to offences of violence or threatened violence (including sexual assault offences), driving offences causing actual physical bodily harm or death and breaches of the relevant occupational health and safety legislation that cause actual physical bodily harm or death (section 27, Crimes (Sentencing Procedure) Act 1999, NSW).

As a result, victims of property offences or so-called white collar crimes may not submit a VIS. Current victim policy in NSW effectively excludes victims' voices in the context of white collar crimes and promotes a 'criminology of the other' that justifies punitive treatment of violent offenders and renders 'white collar' offenders invisible to the community (Garland 2001; Edwards 2001; Sanders 2002).

Typically the content of a VIS is limited to details of the harm victims have suffered as a result of the offence and, in the case of family victims, the impact of the death of the deceased (the primary victim) upon them. Most of the Australian jurisdictions employ broad definitions of harm including physical, emotional and financial effects of the crime.[9] NSW has restricted the contents of a VIS from a primary victim to details of 'personal harm', actual bodily harm, mental illness and nervous shock, and from a family victim to the impact of the death of the deceased upon them (section 26, Crimes (Sentencing Procedure) Act 1999, NSW). In a marked departure from the common law, the statutory models of both Victoria (section 95A, Sentencing Act 1991) and Western Australia (section 24, Sentencing Act 1995, Western Australia) provide that the injury, loss or damage caused by the offence to the victim need not have been reasonably foreseeable by the offender. Such a provision demonstrates a significant shift in sentencing policy emphasising the harm caused by the offence in the assessment of criminal responsibility at the expense of the culpability of the offender; the offender's criminal responsibility may in part depend upon individual characteristics of the victim that were neither known nor foreseeable by the offender and therefore a product of moral luck (O'Malley 1993).

Only the Northern Territory and a few US jurisdictions permit victims to express an opinion as to the penalty that should be imposed in their VIS.[10] According to the common law, the attitudes of the victims should not be allowed to interfere with the proper exercise of the sentencing discretion, whether the attitude is one of forgiveness or vengeance (*R v Palu*, *Coulthard v Kennedy*). A sentence is intended to reflect various and often conflicting purposes of punishment and the attitudes of the victim are but one aspect of the circumstances of the offence. It is important that penalties imposed accord with community values and express the community's disapproval of particular crimes. For instance, in the case of a grave and serious crime, the need for deterrence and denunciation may be more pressing than formulating a penalty to suit the wishes of the victim. Furthermore, it is often the case that victims express forgiveness of the offender and ask for a more lenient penalty in situations involving domestic violence and incest. In such cases there is the danger of the 'prospect of pressures, crude or subtle, on victims to plead for mercy; pressures that emanate from another member of the family' (*The Queen v Helmut Mueller*).

Statutory requirements with regard to the form of written VIS also vary among the Australian jurisdictions. Provisions range from the requirement of a statutory declaration, using a prescribed form or simply imposing a page limit of six A4 pages. However, similar to the position in Canada and most US jurisdictions, VIS can also be presented orally to the sentencing court by the victim or, in certain circumstances, a representative of the victim.[11]

In late April 2006, a 12-month pilot project commenced in selected courts in England and Wales allowing family victims to present a family impact statement (FIS) orally to the sentencing court in murder and manslaughter cases. Interestingly this pilot also introduces the concept of a victim's advocate, a lawyer, to represent the victim and assist the family victim to present the oral FIS to the court (Protocol 2006) (see also Sanders and Jones in this volume).

Oral presentation of VIS, or allocution, is viewed as problematic by some commentators and the oral FIS pilot in the United Kingdom was strongly resisted by lawyers and judges. Allocution requires a degree of confidence on the part of the family victim and the general wherewithal to speak publicly. It is argued that allocution increases pressure on victims and furthermore that not all family victims will be in a position to exercise this opportunity. However, there are also disparities between victims in the presentation of written VIS[12] and all Australian jurisdictions operate victims' services which provide assistance to victims preparing VIS (Booth 2001). An important equity concern raised by the Witness Assistance Service in NSW (WAS) is that victims from regional centres may not have the opportunity to present their VIS orally to the court if to do so means that they would have to travel to another region, most likely metropolitan Sydney in serious matters. Witness expenses are not available to victims to provide the court with VIS and many regional victims do not have the resources to travel.[13] To date there has been little, if any, research in this area but a perusal of sentencing judgements and anecdotal evidence in NSW suggests that a significant majority of victims do opt to read their VIS aloud to the court. Indeed, within days of the commencement of the British pilot in April 2006, it was reported in the *Guardian* that a family victim had read his VIS to the court that was sentencing offenders for the murder of his son and significant extracts from that statement were also published in the report (Lewis 2006). Such reporting, it is argued, leads to 'sensationalism' of these matters, particularly in homicide cases where the tabloids are likely to report this angle of the sentencing process because it is 'sexy' or appealing. Of course, many aspects of homicide matters attract prominent media coverage and it seems a little disingenuous to isolate reports of reading VIS aloud to the court in this context (Booth 2004: 255).

Purposes of victim impact statements

The purposes of VIS in the sentencing process are usually expressed in instrumental terms. From an instrumental perspective, VIS are said to enhance particular purposes of sentencing, retribution and rehabilitation, as well as serve public policy concerns related to the alleviation of victim dissatisfaction with the criminal justice system. As a mechanism for making information available to the court detailing the harm suffered by the victim as a result of the offence, a VIS is said to provide the sentencing judge with a more accurate basis for the determination of the seriousness of the offence, make an informed sentencing decision and enhance proportionality and accuracy in sentencing (*R v P*).

Most of the Australian statutory models provide a role for VIS in the sentencing process as a factor to be taken into account in the formulation of penalty, although there is no indication of the weight to be afforded to VIS in any given case. In addition, each jurisdiction operates a victims' services unit that provides victims with information and assistance in relation to VIS in sentencing. The Victorian, South Australian and Western Australian statutory frameworks assign a role to the VIS to 'assist the court' in determining the sentence to be imposed. Subject to a copy of the VIS being made available to the offender beforehand, the sentencing courts in the Northern Territory and the ACT are required to consider the VIS in deciding how an offender is to be sentenced. By way of contrast, the NSW legislation preserves judicial discretion in deciding whether VIS will be taken into account in sentencing. In that jurisdiction, a sentencing court may receive and consider a VIS from a primary victim if it considers it appropriate to do so. With regard to family victims, the NSW sentencing courts *must* receive a VIS from a family victim; if tendered, it must be accepted by the court but it is still a matter for the court to consider whether it is appropriate to take that VIS into account for the purposes of determining the penalty. On the other hand, the Tasmanian statutory model does not specify a role for a VIS submitted to the sentencing court although practice indicates that a VIS tendered in a particular matter is taken into account by the court as a factor in the sentencing process (*R v Dowlan*).

Despite the fact that there is no relevant legislation in Queensland which expressly provides for the submission and consideration of VIS in the sentencing process, general sentencing provisions provide that the sentencing court must have regard to the physical and emotional harm done to the victim and more generally the injury, loss or damage caused by the offence. Practice in that jurisdiction indicates that a VIS is often the vehicle used to establish such victim harm. Similarly, the general sentencing provisions of the statutory models in Victoria, South Australia, the Northern Territory and the ACT, provide that sentencing courts must consider the injury, loss or damage caused by the offence. Of the remaining Australian jurisdictions, the NSW sentencing provisions provide that harm sustained by a victim of crime may be an aggravating factor to be taken into account in sentencing. The Tasmanian model has no similar provisions although the prevailing common law would require that harm caused to the victim by the offence would be relevant to the sentencing process.

With regard to the rehabilitation of the offender, it has been argued that a VIS disclosed in court directly confronts the offender with the effects of the crime on the victim and this effect might be enhanced in circumstances where the VIS is presented to the court orally (NSW 1996). Offender recognition of the wrongfulness of the crime and its human consequences may lead to repentance and more readily promote accountability and responsibility on the part of the offender (Roberts and Erez 2004). Certainly the positive effects of confrontation with the results of crime victimisation on offenders have been noted in the restorative justice context (Daly 2005).

Another instrumental purpose of victim impact evidence is located in the impact of consumerism over the last three decades which has transformed the criminal justice system into a 'service to be measured and consumed' (Ryan 2003: 131). Dissatisfaction of victims of crime with the criminal justice system has been well documented and current government policy actively seeks to remedy victim discontent, increase victim satisfaction with criminal justice processes and restore the dignity of crime victims (Erez 2000). Thus, through providing victims with a 'voice' or role in sentencing proceedings, VIS can redress the perceived imbalance between the offender and the victim in an offender-oriented criminal justice system (Erez 2000).

When introducing the new oral FIS pilot for family victims in England, Harriet Harman, Minister for Constitutional Affairs, made it plain that her government was seeking to reduce public dissatisfaction of family victims. She was reported by the BBC as saying: 'Rather than making someone wait until after the sentencing on the windswept steps of the court, they can actually have a dignified moment in court if they want to' (BBC 2006). Undoubtedly, in an era of much public complaint about sentencing, governments are very keen to avoid statements from unhappy victims on windswept steps expressing dissatisfaction with criminal justice processes. Therefore, important aims of VIS are increased victim satisfaction and greater co-operation with criminal justice processes.

The controversial nature of VIS

Aside from the more general administrative and managerial concerns about the costs and burdens imposed on the criminal justice system, much of the controversy surrounding VIS has centred on the integrity of the sentencing process (Ashworth 1993; Erez 1999; Booth 2000). It is argued that taking account of victim impact evidence introduces a high degree of emotionalism into an otherwise rational sentencing process (Booth 2000, 2001). Inevitably victim impact evidence is highly subjective, describing intensely personal responses to the crime and frequently expressed in emotive and evocative language (Booth 2001; Hinton 1996). The emotional nature of victim input has fostered concerns that sentencing judges might be distracted from the rational, objective sentencing approach that is required by the law and fundamental sentencing principles will be undermined. How can judges avoid their own humanity and remain immune from the emotional impact of such evidence, particularly where it is presented orally to the court? (Booth 2004). Indeed, but similar concerns will also apply to judges' responses to other aspects of the matter before them and, furthermore, it can be argued that there is nothing inherently wrong with incorporating emotion in legal proceedings in any event (Booth 2004). Judicial experience, objectivity and common sense are unlikely to be unduly swayed by the emotional impact of victim impact evidence (Corns 1994; Garkawe 1994; Erez 2000).

Victim impact evidence is frequently described as superfluous because details of the harm caused by the offence are already before the court in evidence presented by the prosecution. Additionally, the effects of an offence, particularly the emotional impact, will in large part depend upon personal characteristics of the victim that were unknown or unforeseeable to the offender. Consideration of such evidence is regarded as unfair to the offender and will cause similar offences to be penalised differently according to the vagaries of 'moral luck' (O'Malley 1993). Nor are VIS mandatory and together with the selective presentation and variable quality of VIS in any event,[14] sentencing principles such as parity, uniformity and predictability are possibly jeopardised. Ultimately, as a sentencing tool, VIS skew the retributive focus of sentencing and overemphasise victim harm at the expense of offender culpability when assessing the seriousness of an offence. Consequently, VIS might become the catalyst for more severe penalties and are designed, in reality, to serve punitive government policies (Elias 1993; Ashworth 1993; Sanders 2002).

Despite these concerns, empirical research in various jurisdictions including Australia, Canada, the United States and the United Kingdom during the last 15 years suggests that VIS appear to have had no significant effects upon sentencing outcomes, court processes and on sentencing patterns generally (Erez et al. 1994; Erez 2000; Roberts 2003). A major study conducted in South Australia concluded that VIS had not undermined fundamental principles underlying the criminal justice system; victims had not been transformed into parties to the proceedings and nor had victim participation compromised defendant's rights (Erez et al. 1994).

If this is the case, however, it appears that VIS may fail to achieve other instrumental purposes of reducing victim dissatisfaction and alienation. Given the research findings, VIS can be characterised as symbolic or token rather than meaningful and victims of crime submit their VIS usually with false expectations. Critics point to studies indicating that victims, who understand the purpose of VIS in instrumental terms, are disappointed when their VIS does not appear to influence the sentence (Erez and Tontodonato 1989; Hoyle et al. 1998; Erez and Roberts 2004). Consequently, VIS are viewed as being counter-productive, as likely to cause further trauma for victims and certainly not a mechanism by which to increase levels of consumer satisfaction with the criminal justice system.

However, this argument assumes that victims of crime submit VIS primarily for the purpose of influencing the penalty imposed but this image of the vengeful victim is not reflected in the research and it would be erroneous to assume a generic victim response, as argued in the introductory section on the heterogeneity of victims and victim movements. Victims submit VIS for a myriad of reasons: to take the opportunity to speak, to influence penalty, to be heard and to be acknowledged as stakeholders in the process (Erez 1999; Sebba 2001; Booth 2001; Strang 2002), not necessarily to enhance penalties. Indeed these concerns of victims are recurrent themes in restorative justice models and discourses. Moreover, victim disappointment stemming from false expectations can be avoided by explaining the sentencing processes. Prior to submitting VIS, victims should be told that VIS are only one factor that a court will consider when determining the type and severity of penalties. All Australian jurisdictions have established and maintained agencies providing victim assistance and support whose responsibility is to provide such information.

There are, nonetheless, significant procedural and evidential difficulties associated with using VIS to provide evidence of harm sustained by victims. Problems arise in relation to non-compliance with the rules regarding the content of VIS. Many victim authors do not restrict themselves to the effects of the offence and include irrelevant information such as characterisation and opinions of the offender and the offence, views on the criminal justice process and, in the case of family victims, photographs and other memorabilia relating to the deceased victim (Booth 2001). Although it is likely that the sentencing court will accede to a motion to rule such evidence inadmissible, challenges to VIS are more likely to be avoided as often as possible.

Particular difficulties arise because VIS from crime victims are often unsworn and, although there appears to be nothing in the various statutory models to prevent it, the practice appears to be that victim-authors are not cross-examined about content in Australia (*R v Wilson*). Victoria and Western Australia have made explicit provision in their statutes for the cross-examination of victims, but in practice such cross-examination would be tactically unwise for an offender, especially one who hopes to be regarded as remorseful. Indeed, there may be a tactical advantage in not pursuing a cross-examination. For instance, in *Waye v R* the sentencing judge in a Northern Territory court gave the offender credit for not cross-examining the victims over their VIS (at age 14). Undoubtedly, the stressful experience of cross-examination could also have a 'chilling effect' on the victim-author particularly in cases where the offender is unrepresented (*R v Shaban*). Nor is it likely that cross-examination of victims would be considered by the community at large as facilitating justice. Indeed, such a legal event would be likely to end up on the front page of the local tabloid as yet another example of appalling sentencing procedure in our courts. However, a failure to cross-examine could be seen as acceptance of what might in the circumstances be an excessive or exaggerated response with no recourse on appeal. In these circumstances as suggested by Sperling J in *R v Slack*, substantial weight should not be given to an account of harm in an unsworn statement which was untested by cross-examination and 'in the nature of things, far from being an objective and impartial account of the effect of the offence on the victim'.

Also problematic is the conceptualisation of harm in victim impact evidence and the potential for the offender's criminal responsibility to be a function of unknown and unforeseeable effects of the crime on the victim. Where harm sustained by a victim can amount to an aggravating factor, the sentencing court must begin with an idea of the level of harm, particularly of an emotional nature, that would ordinarily be sustained by a victim of a particular crime. What will be the assumed level of harm that a victim will ordinarily suffer as the result of an offence? When will the harm suffered by a victim be substantial or of an aggravating nature? Consideration of victim harm in this manner may lead to the assumption of a *de facto* 'ideal victim' or concept of proper victimisation (Christie 1986; McCarthy 1994) and invites the court to focus on the harm caused by the crime rather than the culpability of the offender.

One way to resolve this issue is to take account of victim impact evidence in circumstances where there is a compelling link between the harm sustained by victims and the culpability or blameworthiness of the offender (Wasik 1998). For example, in *R v Lewis*, the NSW Court of Criminal Appeal found that the murder of a woman was a more serious crime because the offender knew that she was the mother of five children. The focus of the penalty was the culpability of the offender, in particular his knowledge that he had organised the killing of a mother of five children, rather than the personal status and characteristics of the victim.

Particular problems of VIS in homicide cases

A particularly controversial issue has been the status of VIS from family victims in the sentencing of homicide offenders. The nature of the harm suffered by family victims and disclosed in a VIS is emotional distress as a result of the impact of the deceased's death on the deceased's family and inevitably the impact of the deceased's death will be a function of the value and worthiness of the deceased (Booth 2001). Logically, the more valuable and loved the deceased, the greater the impact of the deceased's death and the greater the harm suffered by the family victim. Taking account of such VIS from family victims is problematic because if the greater the harm means the greater the penalty, according to the NSW Supreme Court such a result would offend fundamental concepts of equality and justice (*R v Previtera*). Unlike other Australian jurisdictions, the NSW statutory model provides that it is up to the sentencing court to decide whether it is appropriate to take account of VIS from family victims, and to date the NSW Supreme Court has refused to take account of such evidence, [15] for reasons explained by Adams J in the NSW Court of Criminal Appeal in *Dang*:

> Assume the deceased was friendless; assume the deceased had no family. It would be monstrous to suggest that that meant for some reason killing her should attract a lesser penalty than would be the case if, as is the situation here, she had a loving family and grieving relatives. Essentially then, the reason that victim impact statements in cases involving death are not taken into account in imposing sentence is that the law holds, as it must, that in death we are all equal and the idea that it is more serious or more culpable to kill someone who has or is surrounded by a loving and grieving family than someone who is alone is offensive to our notions of equality before the law. (at [25])

On its face, this is a compelling argument. However, it has not prevented sentencing courts in other Australian jurisdictions from taking account of VIS from family victims. Although those sentencing courts acknowledge the principle that justice requires all victims to be treated equally, few Australian sentencing courts have actually directly confronted the difficulties expressed by the NSW Supreme Court. One court that has done so is the South Australian Supreme Court in *R v Birmingham No. 2*. In that case Perry J said that while it was 'unquestionably right, not only as a philosophical proposition but for the purposes of the law, that courts should not put a greater value on one human life as opposed to another' taking account of victim impact evidence from family victims represented no breach of this principle (548). According to his view it was a matter of perspective: 'it is not a matter of valuing one life more than another. Rather it is a question of having regard to the totality of the "injury, loss or damage" which may include [that] suffered by "family victims"' (548).

The United States Supreme Court has also grappled with this issue in the context of capital sentencing where generally it is the jury that decides whether the death penalty should be imposed. In *Booth v Maryland* the court considered that victim impact evidence from family victims was inadmissible in such cases because it did not relate to the culpability of the offender and there was a significant danger of an arbitrary and capricious result. During the course of judgement the court said: 'we are troubled by the implication that defendants whose victims were assets to their community are more deserving of punishment than those whose victims are perceived to be less worthy'. However, in a newly constituted US Supreme Court some three years later, in *Payne v Tennessee* the court reversed this ruling and said that taking account of VIS from family victims is not about comparing victims: 'it is designed to show instead each victim's "uniqueness as an individual human being"' (at 2607).

Is the argument that it is contrary to concepts of equality and justice an accurate reflection of the law and current policy? Common law has traditionally recognised crimes involving 'vulnerable' victims as being more serious and penalties imposed accordingly. Vulnerability in this context includes age, the elderly or the very young, and those with disabilities. Modern statutory sentencing models reflect policy trends to impose greater penalties where the victim of an offence falls into a particular category of victim such as police officer, emergency services worker or judicial officer.[16] Sebba describes this is as a form of 'social accounting' rather than 'moral' accounting (Sebba 1994: 155). For example, is the murder of a heart transplant surgeon a worse crime than killing an anonymous citizen? Intuitively not all crimes are the same; it is possible to distinguish between victims and reasons why crimes involving some victims are more serious than others and therefore should attract a higher penalty. Of course, this is not to say that the process is value-free – after all, who is to decide the social value of particular victims? (Christie 1986; Sebba 1994).

Shifting the debate

There is no doubt that taking account of victim impact evidence in sentencing is problematic, and more recently the debate has shifted from the instrumental to what are described as the expressive and communicative purposes of VIS (Booth 2004; Roberts and Erez 2004). Expressive and communicative purposes are served in two significant ways. First, as a device to provide victims with a 'voice', the VIS enables victims to communicate directly with the court and the offender. Through VIS, victims are able to recount their experiences, express their feelings about the harm they have suffered as a result of the crime and be involved in the sentencing experience. Often, a VIS is the only opportunity that victims have to communicate directly with the offender and the court and it is a particularly effective mechanism where the victim impact evidence is presented orally. Research has demonstrated that a majority of victims of crime wish to participate and provide input, even when they think their input might be irrelevant for sentencing purposes (see Roberts and Erez 2004).

In recent years common law jurisdictions have witnessed a shift from a conventional model of criminal justice to an increasingly popular restorative approach to criminal justice. This shift reflects a concern for victims and acknowledgement of the legitimacy of the crime victims' interest in the process. Communication between the victim and the court and between the victim and the offender is said to introduce a restorative element to the sentencing proceedings without undermining the traditional form of adversarial criminal proceedings (Roberts and Erez 2004: 227). The restorative elements are located in hearing and listening to the victims tell their story and the court's overt acknowledgement of victim experiences (*R v Beckett*).

Second, the expressive function of VIS is part of the communicative or emotive function of punishment more generally. By acknowledgement of VIS and reference to the victim's words in the course of judgement, courts are able to communicate a message that is overtly responsive to the legitimate interests of victims and reflects the community's changing sensibilities in this context. The court communicates both a message of sympathy and clear recognition that these victims have been wronged. In several common law jurisdictions, judges are taking the opportunity to refer to the victim in their sentencing remarks and such developments are appreciated by victims (Booth 2004; Roberts and Erez 2004: 231). The relevance and purpose of VIS from this perspective is to give the court scope to express changing values and expectations of the community and also victims of crime generally. That punishment reaffirms public sentiments of normality and thus reinforces a sense of collective solidarity is a quintessential Durkheimian thesis (see Durkheim 1895/1938: 61) to which VIS give concrete effect. In this sense all forms of punishment can be seen as being emotionally or morally driven. Why should the VIS be singled out by critics as any more or less emotive than other discourses at work in the punishment process?

Although the use of VIS in the formulation of penalty in Australia remains controversial, there is little doubt that VIS are well established in Australian criminal justice policy and will be retained. Perusal of sentencing judgements and anecdotal evidence suggests that a significant majority of victims elect to tender a VIS and increasing numbers are utilising the opportunity to read their VIS aloud to the court. Such a level of participation, despite the fact that most would be made aware that their VIS will have little influence on the ultimate penalty, demonstrates that victims want this chance to be heard, to recount their experiences and be involved in the sentencing process. Through acknowledgement of VIS, the sentencing courts are able to communicate a message that encompasses the wider interests of crime victims and expresses the changing values and expectations of the community. It is important to remember that sentencing is as much about process as it is about outcome (Vincent 2006).

Victim participation in the parole decision-making process

Parole is the means whereby prisoners are released into the community to serve the remainder of their sentence in accordance with the penalty imposed subject to any conditions set by the relevant parole board (Black 2003).[17] Generally, Australian state and territory parole boards are chaired by a judicial officer and are made up of various community representatives, victim representatives, correctional officials, police officers and other experts (Black 2003: 1). Recent legislative amendments in NSW require that at least one community member must be a 'person who in the opinion of the Minister has an appreciation of the interests of victims of crime' (section 183(2A), Crimes (Administration of Sentences) Act 1999, NSW). According to the NSW Law Reform Commission (NSW 1996: 11.3) 'parole reflects the philosophy of rehabilitation, and recognises the advantage to both the community and the individual offender of conditional release from custody occurring in a supervised and supported manner conducive to rehabilitation' and also with a view to reducing recidivism (Simpson 1999). The prospect of parole is likely to provide prisoners with an incentive for rehabilitation and foster better prisoner discipline (Simpson 1999; NSW 1996). The basis for granting parole varies among the jurisdictions. In certain cases it may be an automatic entitlement, but more commonly a prisoner must be assessed by a parole board before a decision is made to release him or her into the community.

Victim participation in parole decision-making processes has increased markedly over the last decade in Australia and although the Australian statutory models vary, generally one or a combination of the following features is included (Black 2003; Bernat *et al.* 1994):

- The right to be informed of matters concerning prisoners including parole applications and forthcoming hearings.
- The right to make submissions to the parole decision-making process.
- The right to have those submissions considered in the parole decision-making process.

Information about applications for parole is usually subject to victim registration for this purpose. During the last decade, most Australian jurisdictions have established and maintained a victims' register. Victims of crime are able to register their interest in receiving information regarding the prisoner whose offence victimised them. Four Australian jurisdictions – NSW, Queensland, Northern Territory and Victoria – limit the eligibility of those victims who can join the register to victims of particular types of crime, such as acts of violence and murder.[18] Generally across the jurisdictions, registered victims are entitled to information pertaining to applications for parole, release, leave and escapes of the relevant prisoner. Access to the benefits of victim registration depends on individual victims being both informed of their rights and proactive in securing registration; only those victims who apply and meet the criteria will be registered. Privacy considerations dictate that unregistered victims will not automatically receive any information or be notified when the prisoner has applied for parole.

In most jurisdictions, victims are given the opportunity to make submissions to the relevant parole board when the prisoner makes an application for parole.[19] Submissions must be in writing and, in a few jurisdictions, provision can also be made for these submissions to be presented orally to the parole board. However, the provisions regarding content of victim submissions vary markedly. In NSW, victims are notified when the parole board has formed an initial intention to make a parole order for a serious offender and victims may apply to the parole board for the matter to be reconsidered (section 145(2)(c), Crimes (Sentence Administration) Act 1999, NSW). No statutory guidance is provided for the content of victim submissions, although according to the NSW Department of Corrective Services the purpose of those submissions is to inform the parole board of the ongoing impact of the offence, feelings and any fears concerning the release of the offender and any particular conditions a victim would like considered if parole is granted; new allegations or evidence and comments regarding the perceived in adequacy of the sentence are excluded (Milner 2006). Nor is such guidance available in the Northern Territory (section 3GB (3)(b), Parole of Prisoners Act, NT).

Victims in Tasmania are directed to provide a statement detailing any injury, loss or damage suffered by the victim as a direct result of the offence and the effects of the commission of the crime on the victim (section 72(2B), Corrections Act 1997, Tasmania). In the ACT, victims' submissions to the parole board may include the likely effect on the victim if the prisoner is released on parole or any concern that the victim might have about the need for protection from violence or harassment by the prisoner (section 46 (3)(b), Rehabilitation of Offenders Act 2001, ACT). The Victorian statutory model provides that submissions from a victim must address the effect of the prisoner's release on the victim and any terms and conditions that the victim wishes to have attached to the parole order (section 74A, Corrections Act 1986, Victoria). A wider approach is utilised in the South Australian legislation, which provides for the registered victim to make 'such submissions to the Board as he or she thinks fit' (section 77(2)(ba), Correctional Services Act 1982, SA). Statutory bodies charged with victim support and information in the Australian jurisdictions have compiled information packages providing considerable assistance on the content and writing of such submissions. However, evidence in NSW suggests that despite this information, many victims do not understand the nature of the parole process (NSW Ombudsman 2005).

Although terminology differs, the duty of a parole board is generally to consider whether release of the prisoner into the community is in the public interest, a task that increasingly receives a significant degree of public attention and scrutiny (Bernat et al. 1994: 123). Factors to be taken into account in deciding whether release of a prisoner is in the public interest range over a wide spectrum in Australia and the comprehensive list provided in the Tasmanian legislation is typical of those matters that will be considered by parole boards (Black 2003). Section 4 of the Tasmanian Corrections Act 1997 provides that the parole board is to consider:

- The likelihood of the prisoner reoffending.
- The protection of the public.
- The rehabilitation of the prisoner.
- Any remarks made by the court in passing sentence.
- The likelihood of the prisoner complying with the conditions.
- The circumstances and gravity of the offence for which the prisoner was sentenced to imprisonment.
- The behaviour of the prisoner while in prison.
- The behaviour of the prisoner during any previous release on parole.
- The behaviour of the prisoner while subject to any court order.
- Any report tendered to the board relating the social background of the prisoner, the psychological condition of the prisoner.
- The probable circumstances of the prisoner after release from prison.
- Any statement provided by a victim of the offence.
- Any other matters that the board thinks are relevant.

Significantly, information from the victim is a factor to be taken into account in deciding whether it is in the public interest to release a prisoner on parole and this is consistent with other Australian statutory models. However, there is no indication as to the weight to be afforded to this information and generally Australian statutory models do not indicate how submissions from victims are to be utilised in the parole decision-making process. Presumably the information will be used to address matters that the parole board is required to take into account, such as the nature and circumstances of the offence to which the offender's sentence relates, the likely effect on any victim or the victim's family of the prisoner being released on parole and any terms and conditions that may be appropriately attached to the grant of parole (section 135(2), Crimes (Sentence Administration) Act 1999, NSW). According to the NSW Department of Corrective Services, the role of victims' submissions is to clearly advise the parole board in relation to the likely effect on any victim of the offender and to assist the parole board in determining appropriate conditions to impose on an offender who is being released on parole (Milner 2006). By way of contrast, the Victorian legislation does set out comprehensive provisions as to how the parole board may deal with submissions from victims although it directs that the board 'may, in its absolute discretion, give that submission such weight as the board sees fit in determining to make a parole order' (section 74B, Corrections Act 1986, Victoria).

Arguments in support of consideration of victim submissions in parole decision-making processes echo similar considerations to those canvassed above in relation to VIS. From the perspective of the victim, it is contended that a voice in parole decision-making will offer therapeutic benefits such as enhanced victim well-being and healing as well as increased satisfaction with criminal justice processes (Moriarty 2005; Polowek 2005). The restorative potential of an apology from the prisoner that might be forthcoming in the process should also be recognised as a benefit to participating victims (Roberts

2001). In addition, victims can bring any concerns about future harassment or violence to the attention of the board and seek appropriate conditions to be attached to any grant of parole. A study of the victim submissions to the Parole Board in Tasmania found that most victims were not seeking vengeance but merely wanted the offender located in some place where he or she would not have contact with the victim (Black 2003: 4).

The few studies that have been done in the US reveal only modest victim satisfaction from participating in parole decision-making (Moriarty 2005: 385). To date there has been little research into the number of victims that become registered and/or exercise the right to make submissions to parole boards in Australia (Black 2003). As at 31 December 2005, in NSW there were 245 serious offenders on the victims' register and some 853 victims registered (Milner 2006). However, the NSW Parole Authority does not keep records about how many victims make submissions nor the characteristics of those victims that make submissions (NSW Ombudsman 2005: 39). Statistics available from the Victims Assistance Unit in Tasmania estimate that there are some 35 per cent of registered victims of serious offences and further, that some 95 per cent of those registered victims make submissions to the board (Black 2003: 4). Anecdotal evidence in NSW suggests that family victims who were unable to submit a VIS to the sentencing process in homicide matters before legislative reform in 1997, are particularly keen to have their say before the parole board.[20] Likewise, research in New Zealand suggests that having a voice in parole proceedings is of paramount importance to many victims who had made little contribution to the sentencing of the offender in the first place (Ball 2006). Of concern, though, are the impressions from NSW Parole Authority members suggesting that it is uncommon for people from a non-English-speaking or Indigenous background to make submissions (NSW Ombudsman 2005: 39).

From the perspective of the decision-maker, it is argued that victim submissions may provide the board with information that it does not have and thereby assist the board in its assessment of the matter (Polowek 2005: 65–6). For instance, victim submissions may provide further details of the offence that the board can use to assess the prisoner's understanding of the offence and also his or her responsibility for the events (Polowek 2005: 66). The importance of this information is demonstrated by section 135A of the NSW Crimes (Administration of Sentences) Act 1999, which requires probation and parole reports to cover the 'offender's attitude to any victim of the offence to which his or her sentence relates, and to the family of any such victim'. Furthermore, it is contended that information regarding the continuing effects of the crime can assist the parole board to determine the appropriate punishment for the crime committed that is the actual period that should be served for the crime (Polowek 2005). However, this latter point is less persuasive, as arguably such a consideration is irrelevant to the question of whether the prisoner is a parole risk and outside the parole board's terms of reference (Polowek 2005: 70).

Like the debate surrounding VIS, arguments opposed to the consideration of victim submissions in parole decision-making processes focus on concerns about the integrity of the process. As noted above, because the criteria governing victim submissions does not provide much, if any, guidance as to the weight of information from victims, it is feared that decision-makers, who are generally not trained to consider only relevant evidence objectively, might be unduly swayed by irrelevant information from victims (Polowek 2005: 70). Potential consequences include the over-weighting of victim information, inconsistent decision-making and higher rates of parole denial for those applications where there are submissions from victims.

Certainly the few studies of the influence of victim submissions on parole decisions suggest a disparity in the treatment of prisoners according to whether there are victim submissions available to the parole board. Contrary to research findings regarding the influence of VIS on sentencing, results from the small number of studies that have been done in the US indicate that victim participation has a significant effect on the decision of parole boards (Morgan and Smith 2005). A study done in Pennsylvania in 1989 found that victim submissions had a significant effect on parole outcomes; parole was refused to 43 per cent of the group of inmates where victim submissions were received, but was refused to only 7 per cent in the group where no victim submissions were received (Parsonage et al. 2002). In that state, the law required that victim submissions were to be taken into account in the decision-making process but with no indication of the weight to be given to them. The researchers further analysed the content of the victim submissions and found that the victims described the nature and extent of their victimisation and the continuing impact of the crime upon them (Parsonage et al. 2002). A study of parole decisions for violent offenders in the mid-1990s in Alabama found that the percentage of cases in which parole was denied was significantly greater where there were victim submissions (Morgan and Smith 2005). Although the researchers could not separate the relative importance of written submissions as opposed to oral presentation by victims, they did find that attendance at parole hearings was strongly associated with parole application outcomes (Smith et al. 2005: 72).

Whether or not the results of these studies can be generalised to other geographical locations, it appears that victims are having a significant impact at this stage of the criminal justice process. Research on victim participation in the parole decision-making process is scanty in Australia; only the Tasmanian Parole Board publishes its decisions and there is no indication of the weight that is given to victim input. According to research by the Australian Institute of Criminology, the Tasmanian Parole Board's view is that in nearly all cases it would be wrong to refuse parole solely because of the objection of a victim (Black 2003). However, the recent *Esho* case in NSW indicates the importance of victim submissions and also the significant extent of public attention that parole decisions receive in Australia. Clearly, there is a need for further research on this aspect of victim participation in criminal justice processes.

Enhancing the role of the victim in the justice system: from passive to active participants

Clearly the adversarial system is limited in its capacity to allow for an active role for the victim, beyond that of being a witness or more recently by supplying a VIS in a sentencing or parole hearing. Even where VIS are permissible the impact of these is in most instances largely irrelevant to the sentence or the outcome. The treatment of witnesses in an adversarial court process, regardless of the extra provision of support to intimidated and vulnerable witnesses, can still amount to a secondary victimisation, especially in sexual assault and family violence cases, deterring many from wishing to give evidence or process matters through the courts. The frustration with the limits of an adversarial system of justice has led some scholars and policy-makers to look to alternative models of justice, inspired by principles of restorative justice, customary and Indigenous law.

As restorative justice is considered at length by Dignan in Chapter 12, we concentrate below on customary law, Indigenous justice and demands for specialised courts for children and victims of sexual assault. It is worth noting, however, that restorative justice has had little purchase in the administration of criminal justice in adult matters, and there is a debate about whether restorative justice promotes victims' rights or is driven by other imperatives, such as cost-effectiveness, cultural appropriateness, crime prevention, restoring community values, and reducing reoffending (Cunneen and White 2002). Juvenile justice systems in Australian, Canadian and New Zealand jurisdictions have introduced alternatives to the children's court modelled loosely on restorative justice principles such as those embodied in youth justice conferencing (Maxwell and Morris 2002; Daly 2001). None stands alone or apart from the existing criminal justice system. Indigenous young offenders – due to their early and repeated contacts with the justice system – are less likely to be referred to a youth conference (Cunneen and White 2002: 377). For a case to be referred to youth conferencing the offender must plead guilty and meet other eligibility criteria as established by legislation. Hence victim participation in youth conferences is dependent on the type of crime committed and the type of offender being prosecuted, circumscribing the victim's role to a limited number of cases.

Indigenous justice and customary law

In settler societies such as New Zealand, Canada and Australia, much of the inspiration for creating a more inclusive and active role for the victim, the victim's family and community members has come from customary forms of justice, such as circle sentencing and family conferencing (Maxwell and Morris 1994). By contrast, alternatives to adversarial justice in the UK have grown out of offender–victim mediation programmes that have operated largely on a voluntary basis during the post-trial or pre-release stages of criminal justice from around the 1970s (Zedner 2002: 444).

Since the 1991 Royal Commission into Aboriginal Deaths in Custody, recourse to formal and informal customary practices has been increasing in Australian jurisdictions. Examples include the circle sentencing trials in Nowra, Walgett and Armidale NSW (based on circle sentencing models in Canada), the Nunga and Aboriginal courts in South Australia, the Koori courts in Victoria and the Murri courts in Queensland (Marchetti and Daly 2004: 1).

The first formal inclusion of customary law into an Australian jurisdiction occurred with the implementation of the Nunga court in South Australia in 1999 (Marchetti and Daly 2004: 2). Victoria is the only jurisdiction to enact legislation to validate its customary law in the Magistrate Court (Koori Court) Act 2002. There is considerable variation in how these customary practices operate. The urban court model, such as the Nunga court, conduct their deliberations in a magistrate's court, involve Aboriginal case workers and elders, allow for the offender to have a support person by their side and generally entail far less formality than a normal magistrate's court. For instance the presiding magistrate wears casual clothing and sits at the same level as the defendant. However, the power to make decisions still resides with the magistrate who takes advice from elders (Marchetti and Daly 2004: 3) and the role of the victim is still largely limited to that of witness, unless they are invited to speak from the gallery of the courtroom.

Circle sentencing by comparison allows for the victim and their supporters to be fully included in the process. All participants sit inside a circle and actively participate in the process. Victims are central to the process, being called upon to describe how the crime has affected them, in their own voice and their own time. Unlike witnesses under cross-examination, victims' views on sentencing and punishment are elicited and considered by the circle alongside other factors such as severity of the crime, degree of offender reparation and remorse and importantly the wider impact on the community of these types of crimes. These models of reparation between victims and offender and community representatives have found expression in indigenous models of justice – such as the Maori family conferencing trialled in the 1980s (Maxwell and Morris 1994), circle sentencing in Canada (Stuart 1996), and circle sentencing available in parts of Australia for indigenous offenders (Aboriginal Justice Advisory Committee 2000). Victim participation is still limited to only those victims where the Indigenous offender meets the criteria of eligibility. While enhancing the participation of victims in criminal justice, these new initiatives based on customary justice are not necessarily driven by enlarging victim's rights. The overwhelming imperative may be to restore the authority of elders; to enhance the cultural appropriateness of the criminal justices system and to enhance the authority of a legal system imposed upon Indigenous peoples dispossessed of their land by invasion. By far the most important driving force underlying circle sentencing is the reduction of the over-representation of Indigenous offenders in the formal end of the criminal justice system (see Chantrill 1998).

Specialised courts

Feminists have long argued that the special needs of the victims of domestic and sexual assault are not afforded the dignity, respect or protection they deserve in a legal system, designed primarily around the interests of men (see Cook and Jones, and Hoyle in this volume; Department of Women 1996; Heath and Naffine 1994; Mason 1995; Smart 1989; Carrington 1997; Carmody and Carrington 1998; Young 1998; Fitzgerald 2006). Nowhere is this more apparent than with the way the sexual assault complainant is positioned in a way to silence, discredit and impugn her, through damaging insinuations about her character and motive (Young 1998: 444–5). Not surprisingly, sexual assault cases have the highest rate of attrition for any crime in Australian jurisdictions (Fitzgerald 2006), prompting calls for an entirely separate sexual assault court to deal with sexual assault matters (Criminal Justice Sexual Offences Taskforce 2006).

Perhaps one of the most interesting developments in the administration of criminal justice is the proposal to specialise courts to hear matters relating specifically to sexual assault matters and family violence. The Criminal Justice Sexual Offences Taskforce (2006) recommended that NSW trial a separate court for sexual matters. Court staff would be trained specifically to handle victims more sensitively while respecting the rights of the accused. Special closed circuit television and other technologies will be maintained and readily available. Sexual assault matters will not be rescheduled and interrupted by other criminal matters heard in the same courts. Victims as witnesses will be provided with additional witness support throughout the hearing. The trial is loosely modelled on the Family Violence Court in Winnipeg which began hearing cases in 1990 (Criminal Justice Sexual Offences Taskforce 2006: 155–7). Evaluations of the Winnipeg Family Violence Court in Canada found that victims are more confident about processing their complaints through the special court system and more satisfied with the court process and outcome (Ursel 2002). Ursel argues that much of the success is due to the change in court culture, making it more sensitive to the needs of victims while maintaining a rigorous approach to prosecution (Criminal Justice Sexual Offences Taskforce 2006: 157). Specialised courts have also been introduced in England and Wales and are currently being considered for extension (see Cook *et al.* 2004).

Conclusion

An expansion of policies and services designed to meet (or at least appease) the victims of crime has occurred over the last 30 years in response to lobbying by an eclectic mix of loosely organised victim movements in Anglo-speaking countries such as Australia, the UK and the US. The politicisation of victims during elections, and more recently during the war on terror, is no doubt a crucial underlying factor in the expansion of policies and programmes aimed at ameliorating the concerns of victims, mass victims and more recently terror victims. From the evidence we have been able to gather, the degree of recognition of victims' rights differs by jurisdiction but appears most widespread in the United States where all states provide victim support and compensation and around 30 states have mandated victims' rights. The US government has taken an extraordinary step of extending this mandatory support to US citizens who are the victims of terror in and outside its borders. However, when it comes to actively including victims in the justice process, circle sentencing of Indigenous offenders of the kind established in Canada and now widely used in Australia provides the greatest scope yet for the involvement of victims in the actual criminal process. In juvenile justice systems across the Anglo-speaking axis the increasing use of youth conferencing and restorative models of intervention have also enhanced the role of selected victims in the justice process. Specialised courts designed to inculcate a court culture sensitive to victims is the newest measure being considered for implementation in the UK and for trial in Australia. The emergence of victim's charters, victims' registers and the use of victim impact statements in sentencing, probation and parole hearings have also extended the role of the victim in the administration of criminal justice around the Anglophone world. While all these are welcome developments, according to our analysis, most of these measures are still limited, embryonic or symbolic.

Further reading

Black, M. (2003) 'Victim submissions to parole boards: The agenda for research', *Trends and Issues in Crime and Criminal Justice*, 251.

Bernat, F.P., Parsonage, W.H. and Helfgott, J. (1994) 'Victim impact laws and the parole process in the United States: Balancing victim and inmate rights and interests', *International Review of Victimology*, 3: 121–40.

Edwards, I. (2004) 'An ambiguous participant: The crime victim and criminal justice decision-making', *British Journal of Criminology*, 44(6): 946–67.

Erez, E. (2000) 'Integrating a Victim Perspective in Criminal Justice through Victim Impact Statements', in A. Crawford and J. Goodey (eds) *Integrating a Victim Perspective Within Criminal Justice*. Aldershot: Ashgate.

Marchetti, E. and Daly, K. (2004) *Indigenous Courts and Justice Practices in Australia*, Trends and Issues in Criminal Justice, No. 277. Canberra: AIC.

Morgan, K. and Smith, B. (2005) 'Victims, punishment, and parole: The effect of victim participation on parole hearings', *Criminology and Public Policy*, 4(2): 333–61.

Moriarty, L. (2005) 'Victim participation at parole hearings: Balancing victim, offender, and public interest', *Criminology and Public Policy*, 4(2): 385–91.

Parsonage, W.H., Bernat, F. and Helfgott, J. (1992) 'Victim impact testimony and Pennsylvania's parole decision-making process: A pilot study', *Criminal Justice Review*, 6.

Roberts, J. and Erez, E. (2004) 'Communication in sentencing: Exploring the expressive function of victim impact statements', *International Review of Victimology*, 10: 223–44.

Rock, P. (2005) 'Victims' Rights in the United Kingdom', paper presented to the Australian Institute of Criminology Occasional Seminar Series, 24 August (www. aic.gov.au/confernces/occasional/2005-08-rock.html).

Ursel, J. (2002) '"His Sentence is My Freedom": Processing Domestic Violence Cases in the Winnipeg Family Violence Court', in L. Tutty and C. Goard (eds) *Reclaiming Self: Issues and Resources for Women Abused by Intimate Partners*. Halifax: Fernwood Publishing.

Notes

1 This chapter has been equally jointly co-authored.
2 The Australia Labor Party has a policy that if elected to office it will develop national model legislation for the delivery of services and supports for crime victims (www.alp.org.au/platform/chapter-06.php, ALP p. 94, accessed 18 May

2006). Currently the seven jurisdictions of Australia have a varying array of different provisions and standards.

3   NSW Charter of Victims Rights, Northern Territory Charter for Victims of Crime; Tasmania has not adopted the Victims Charter into legislation but uses it as a guide the provision of services through the Victims Assistance Unit. In 2005 Victoria released for community consultation a Victims Charter.

4   Victim impact statements are also known as victim personal statements in England and Wales and victim statements in Scotland.

5   While Queensland law lacks an explicit statutory basis upon which a victim of crime may rely to submit a VIS, a combination of statutory provisions dealing with matters to be taken into account in sentencing and a charter of victim's rights has led to a practice whereby VIS submitted by victims of crime are accepted by sentencing courts (Thomas 1999).

6   Sections 26 and 28, Crimes (Sentencing Procedure) Act 1999 (NSW), s81A, Sentencing Act 1997 (Tasmania), s24, Sentencing Act 1995 (WA), s106A, Sentencing Act (Northern Territory), s47, Crimes (Sentencing) Act 2005 (ACT).

7   Sentencing Act 1991 (Victoria), Sentencing Act 1995 (Western Australia), Sentencing Act (Northern Territory).

8   Section 81A, Sentencing Act 1997 (Tasmania); s7a, Criminal Law (Sentencing) Act 1988 (South Australia); s48, Crimes (Sentencing) Act 2005 (ACT).

9   Section 95B, Sentencing Act 1991 (Victoria), s24, Sentencing Act 1995 (Western Australia), s81A, Sentencing Act 1997 (Tasmania), s7A, Criminal Law (Sentencing) Act 1988 (SA), s106A, Sentencing Act (Northern Territory), s47, Crimes (Sentencing) Act 2005 (ACT).

10 Section 106B(5A) of the Northern Territory Sentencing Act provides that 'A victim impact statement or victim report may contain a statement as to the victim's wishes in respect of the order that the court may make in relation to the offence referred to in the statement of the report.'

11 Section 30A, Crimes (Sentencing Procedure) Act 1999 (NSW), s95B, Sentencing Act 1991 (Victoria), s81A, Sentencing Act 1997 (Tasmania), s7A, Criminal Law (Sentencing) Act 1988 (South Australia), s25, Sentencing Act 1995 (Western Australia), s106A, Sentencing Act (Northern Territory), s50, Crimes (Sentencing) Act 2005 (ACT).

12 Studies have revealed that whether or not a victim will submit a VIS depends on particular characteristics of the victim including class, gender, cultural background, level of literacy, costs of reports and the assistance that is made available for this purpose (Booth 2000).

13 Discussion with witness assistance officers at the Witness Assistance Service in the NSW Office of the Director of Public Prosecutions 2005.

14 Whether or not a victim will submit a VIS may depend upon particular characteristics of the victim, including gender, class, cultural background, level of literacy, costs of reports and the assistance that is made available for this purpose (Richards 1992: 133; Hall 1991: 233).

15 The statutory provisions require the sentencing court to accept and acknowledge receipt of a VIS from a family victim and perhaps also comment on it. However, the court need only take account of that VIS in the determination of penalty if it considers it appropriate to do so.

16 For an example, see 21A (2)(a) Crimes (Sentencing Procedure) Act 1999 (NSW).

17 For convenience, the phrase 'parole board' will be used to refer to parole decision-making bodies generally in this chapter but it is important to note that various terminology is used in Australia including the 'State Parole Authority' in NSW, the

'Community Corrections Board' in Queensland and the 'Sentence Administration Board' in the ACT.

18 Sections 142 and 145, Crimes (Administration of Sentences) Act 1999 (NSW), s3GB, Parole of Prisoners Act (Northern Territory), s30A, Corrections Act 1986 (Victoria), Corrective Services Act (Queensland). Interestingly, despite the legislative provision, the NSW Department of Corrective Services extends the right of registered victims of a serious offender to make submissions to the parole board to all victims of crime (Milner 2006).

19 Western Australia is the exception. The Northern Territory Parole Board may invite submissions from the members of the victim's family where the board is considering the release on parole of a prisoner who is serving a term of imprisonment for life for the crime of murder – s3GB, Parole of Prisoners Act. In Queensland, registered concerned persons can make submissions to Community Corrections Boards in writing. However, the Corrective Services Bill 2006 is currently before the Queensland Parliament and one of the provisions of this Bill enables victims to have a say about parole.

20 Personal communication with the Director of the Homicide Victims Support Group, Martha Jabour on 11 April 2006.

References

Aboriginal Justice Advisory Committee (2000) 'Circle Sentencing in Aboriginal Communities in the Sentencing Process', discussion paper.

Ashworth, A. (1993) 'Victim impact statements and sentencing', *Criminal Law Review*, 498.

Australian Labor Party (2006) Policy Platform, Chapter Six, Community Security and Access to Justice (www.alp.org.au/platform/chapter-06.php).

Ball, W. (2006) 'The Role of Victims in the Parole Process: New Zealand', paper presented at the Parole Authorities Conference, Sydney, 10 May.

BBC (2006) 'Family voice in trials to begin', 24 April www.news.bbc.co.uk/1/hi/wales/4937746.stm (accessed 23 May 2006).

Bernat, F., Parsonage, W. and Helfgott, J. (1994) 'Victim impact laws and the parole process in the United States: Balancing victim and inmate rights and interests', *International Review of Victimology*, 3: 121–40.

Black, M. (2003) *Victim Submissions to Parole Boards: The Agenda for Research*, Trends and Issues in Criminal Justice, No. 251. Canberra: AIC.

Booth, T. (2000) 'The dead victim, the family victim and victim impact statements in NSW', *Current Issues in Criminal Justice*, 11(3): 292–307.

Booth, T. (2001) 'Voices after the killing: Hearing the stories of family victims in NSW', *Griffith Law Review*, 10(1): 25–41.

Booth, T. (2004) 'Homicide, family victims and sentencing: Continuing the debate about victim impact statements', *Current Issues in Criminal Justice*, 15(3): 253.

Bush, G. (2006) National Crime Victims' Rights Week 2002, press release, 27 April, The White House, President George Bush, homepage.

Carmody, M. and Carrington, K. (2000) 'Preventing sexual violence?', *Australian and New Zealand Journal of Criminology*, 33(3): 341–61.

Carrington, K. (1998) *Who Killed Leigh Leigh?* Sydney: Random House.

Chantrill, P. (1998) 'Community Justice in Indigenous Communities in Qld: Prospects for keeping young people out of detention', AIC Conference presentation.

Christie, N. (1986) 'The Ideal Victim', in E. Fattah (ed.) *From Crime Policy to Victim Policy*. London: Macmillan.

Cook, D., Burton, M., Robinson, A. and Vallely. C. (2004) *Evaluation of Specialist Domestic Violence Courts/Fast Track System*. London: Crown Prosecution System/Department of Constitutional Affairs.

Corns, C. (1994) 'The Sentencing (Victim Impact Statement) Act 1994', *Law Institute Journal*, 68: 1054.

Criminal Justice Sexual Offences Taskforce (2006) *Responding to Sexual Assault: The Way Forward*. Sydney: Attorney-General's Department of NSW.

Cunneen, C. and White, R. (2002) *Juvenile Justice: Australian Perspectives*. Melbourne: Oxford University Press.

Daly, K. (2001) *Restorative Justice and Conferencing in Australia*, Trends and Issues in Criminal Justice No. 186. Canberra: Australian Institute of Criminology.

Daly, K. (2005) Remarks to Victims Support Agency Forum, 'What does a modernised justice system mean to women?', 14 September, Melbourne Town Hall.

Department for Women (1996) *Heroines of Fortitude: The Experiences of Women in Court as Victims of Sexual Assault*. Sydney: NSW Government.

Department of Attorney-General, Government of South Australia (undated) *Information for Victims of Crime* (www.voc.sas.gov.au, accessed May 2006).

Department of Attorney-General, Government of Western Australia (2003) *Justice for All: A Policy for Victims of Crime*.

Durkheim, E. (1895/1938) *The Rules of Sociological Method*. Chicago: University of Chicago Press.

Edwards, J. (2001) 'Victim participation in sentencing: The problems of incoherence', *Howard Journal*, 40(1): 30–54.

Elias, R. (1993) *Victims Still: The Political Manipulation of Crime Victims*. Thousand Oaks, CA: Sage.

Erez, E. (1999) 'Who's afraid of the big bad victim?', *Criminal Law Review*, 545.

Erez, E. (2000) 'Integrating a Victim Perspective in Criminal Justice through Victim Impact Statements', in A. Crawford and J. Goodey (eds) *Integrating a Victim Perspective Within Criminal Justice*. Aldershot: Ashgate.

Erez, E. and Roberts, J. (2004) 'Communication in sentencing: Exploring the expressive function of victim impact statements', *International Review of Victimology*, 10: 223–44.

Erez, E. and Tontodonato, P. (1990) 'The effect of victim participation on sentence outcomes', *Criminology*, 28: 451.

Erez, E., Roeger, L. and Morgan, F. (1994) *Victim Impact Statements in South Australia: An Evaluation*. South Australian Attorney-General's Department.

Fitzgerald, J. (2006) *The Attrition of Sexual Assault Offences from the New South Wales Criminal Justice System*, Contemporary Issues in Crime and Justice, No. 92. Sydney: NSW Bureau of Crime Statistics and Research.

Garkawe, S. (1994) 'The role of the victim during court proceedings', *University of New South Wales Law Journal*, 17(2): 595.

Garland, D. (2000) 'The culture of high crime societies: Some preconditions of recent "Law and Order" policies', *British Journal of Criminology*, 40(3): 347–75.

Garland, G. (2001) *The Culture of Control*. Oxford: Oxford University Press.

Heath, M. and Naffine, N. (1994) 'Men's needs and women's desires: Feminist dilemmas about rape law reform', *Australian Feminist Law Journal*, 3: 30–52.

Hinton, M. (1996) 'Guarding against victim-authored impact statements', *Criminal Law Journal*, 20: 310.

Hogg, R. and Brown, D. (1998) *Rethinking Law and Order*. Sydney: Pluto Press.

Hogg, R. and Carrington, K. (2006) *Policing the Rural Crisis*. Sydney: Federation Press.

Home Office (2006) *Code of Practice for Victims of Crime*. London: Home Office.

Hoyle, C., Cape, E., Morgan, R. and Sanders, A. (1998) *Evaluation of the 'One Stop Shop' and Victim Statement Pilot Projects*. London: Home Office.

Lewis, P. (2006) 'Former cricketer condemns drunken gang for beating his son to death', *Guardian* 3 May.

Lithwick, D. (2006) 'Do Death Sentences Really give Victims Relief?' http://www.slate.com/id/2138638/?nav=tap3 (accessed 4 July 2006).

Loader, I. (2005) 'Fall of the Platonic guardians: Liberalism, criminology and political responses in England and Wales', *British Journal of Criminology*, 46: 561–86.

Manning, F. and Griffith, G. (1996) *Victims Rights and Victims Compensation: Commentary on the Legislative Reform Package*. Briefing Paper, NSW Parliament, Sydney.

Marchetti, E. and Daly, K. (2004) *Indigenous Courts and Justice Practices in Australia*, Trends and Issues in Criminal Justice, No 277. Canberra: AIC.

Marslew, K. (1998) 'Why and how ENOUGH IS ENOUGH ANTI-VIOLENCE MOVEMENT was formed', paper presented at Partnerships in Crime Prevention Conference, Hobart, 25–27 February.

Mason, G. (1995) 'Reforming the Law of Rape: Incisions into a Masculinist Sanctum', D. Kirkby (ed.) *Sex, Power and Justice*. Melbourne: Oxford University Press, pp. 50–67.

Maxwell, G. and Morris, A. (1994) 'The New Zealand Model of Family Group Conferences', in C. Alder and J. Wundersitz (eds) *Family Conferencing and Juvenile Justice: The Way Forward or Misplaced Optimism?* Canberra: Australian Institute of Criminology.

Maxwell, G. and Morris, A. (eds) (2002) *Restorative Justice for Juveniles: Conferencing, Mediation and Circles*. Oxford: Hart.

McCarthy, T. (1994) 'Victim impact statements: A problematic remedy', *Australian Feminist Law Journal*, 3: 175.

McLeod, M. (1986) 'Victim participation in sentencing', *Criminal Law Bulletin*, 22: 501.

Milner, K. (2006) 'The Role of Victims of Crime in the Parole Process', paper presented at the Australian Conference of Parole Boards and Parole Authorities, Sydney May.

Morgan, K. and Smith, B. (2005) 'Victims, punishment, and parole: The effect of victim participation on parole hearings', *Criminology and Public Policy*, 4(2): 333–61.

Moriarty, L. (2005) 'Victim participation at parole hearings: Balancing victim, offender, and public interest', *Criminology and Public Policy*, 4(2): 385–91.

New South Wales (1996) *Sentencing*, Law Reform Commission, Discussion Paper No. 33.

New South Wales Ombudsman (2005) *Review of the Crimes (Administration of Sentences) Amendment Act 2002 and the Summary Offences Amendment (places of Detention) Act 2002*, Discussion Paper, March.

O'Malley, T. (1993) 'Punishment and moral luck: The role of the victim in sentencing decisions', *Irish Journal of Criminal Law*, 40.

Parsonage, W.H., Bernat, F. and Helfgott, J. (1992) 'Victim impact testimony and Pennsylvania's parole decision-making process: A pilot study', *Criminal Justice Policy Review*, 6: 187–206.

Polowek, K. (2005) 'Victims' Participatory Rights in Parole: Their Role and the Dynamics of Victim Influence as seen by Board Members', unpublished PhD thesis, Simon Fraser University.

Protocol for Victim Advocate's Pilot (2006) Queen's Bench Division.

Richards, C. (1992) 'Victim's rights wronged', *Alternative Law Journal*, 17: 131.

Roberts, J. (2001) 'Public Opinion, Sentencing and Parole: International Trends', in R. Roesch, R. Corrado and R. Dempster (eds) *Psychology in the Courts*. New York: Routledge.

Roberts, J. (2003) 'Victim impact statements and the sentencing process: Recent developments and research findings', *Criminal Law Quarterly*, 47: 365–96.

Roberts, J. and Erez, E. (2004) 'Communication in sentencing: Exploring the expressive function of victim impact statements', *International Review of Victimology*, 10: 223–44.

Rock, P. (1990) *Helping Victims of Crime*. New York: Oxford University Press.

Rock, P. (2005) 'Victims' Rights in the United Kingdom', paper presented to the Australian Institute of Criminology Occasional Seminar Series, 24 August (www. aic.gov.au/confernces/occasional/2005-08-rock.html).

Ryan, M. (2003) *Penal Policy and Political Culture in England and Wales*. London: Waterside Press.

Sanders, A. (2002) 'Victim Participation in an Exclusionary Criminal Justice System', in C. Hoyle and R. Young (eds) *New Visions of Crime Victims*. Oxford: Hart Publishing.

Sebba, L. (1994) 'Sentencing and the victim: The aftermath of *Payne*', *International Review of Victimology*, 3: 141–65.

Simpson, R. (1999) *Parole: An Overview*. NSW Parliamentary Briefing Paper.

Smart, C. (1989) *Feminism and the Power of Law*. London: Routledge.

Strang, H. (2002) *Repair or Revenge: Victims and Restorative Justice*. Oxford: Clarendon Press.

Stuart, B. (1996) 'Circle Sentencing in Canada: A partnership of the community and the criminal justice system', *International Journal of Comparative and Applied Criminal Justice*, 20: 291–309.

Thomas, M. (1999) 'They Do Things Differently There: Issues Arising from the Queensland Experience of Victim Impact Statements', paper presented at the Restoration for Victims of Crime Conference, Australian Institute of Criminology, Melbourne.

Ursel, J. (2002) 'His Sentence is My Freedom': Processing Domestic Violence Cases in the Winnipeg Family Violence Court', in L. Tutty and C. Goard (eds) *Reclaiming Self: Issues and Resources for Women Abused by Intimate Partners*. Halifax: Fernwood Publishing.

US Department of Justice (2000) *Responding to Terrorism Victims: Oklahoma City and Beyond*, Office for Victims of Crime (www.ojp.usdoj.gov/ovc/publications/infores/respterrorism).

US Department of Justice (2003) *Meeting the Needs of the Victims of the September 11th Terrorist Attacks: Department of Defense Appropriations Act of 2002*. Washington: Office for Victims of Crime.

US Department of Justice (2006) *International Terrorism Victim Expense Reimbursement Program*, Report to Congress, April, Washington.

Victims Compensation Tribunal, Chairpersons Report 2004/05. Sydney: NSW Government.

Vincent, Mr Justice (2006) 'Judge's Attitudes and Perceptions towards the Sentencing Process', paper presented at the National Sentencing Conference, Canberra, February.

Wasik, M. (1998) 'Crime Seriousness and the Offender–Victim Relationship in Sentencing', in A. Ashworth and M. Wasik (eds) *Fundamentals of Sentencing Theory*. Oxford: Clarendon Press.

Young, A. (1998) 'The waste land of the law, the wordless song of the rape victim', *Melbourne University Law Review*, 22(2): 442–65.

Young, J. (2002) 'Critical Criminology in the twenty-first century', in K. Carrington and R. Hogg (eds) *Critical Criminology: Issues, Debates and Challenges*. Cullompton: Willan Publishing.

Young, M. (2001a) 'The Victims Movement: A Confluence of Forces', National Organization of Victims' Assistance, publication an address delivered to the first National Symposium on Victims of Federal Crime, 10 February 1997, Washington DC (www.trynova.org/victiminfo/readings/).

Young, M. (2001b) 'Victim Rights and Services: A Modern Saga', a version of this paper originally appeared as a chapter in R.C. Davis, A.J. Lurigio and W.G. Skogan (eds) (1997) *Victims of Crime*, 2nd edn. Thousand Oaks, CA: Sage (www.trynova.org/victiminfo/readings/).

Zedner, L. (2003) 'Victims', in M. Maguire, R. Morgan and R. Reiner (eds) *Oxford Handbook on Criminology*, 2nd edn. Oxford: Clarendon Press.

Case list

Booth v Maryland (1987) 482 U.S 496

Coulthard v Kennedy (South Australia Supreme Court) BC9200437

Dang [1999] NSWCCA 42

Esho v Parole Board Authority of New South Wales [2006] NSWSC 304

Payne v Tennessee (1991) 111 S. Ct. 2597

The Queen v Helmut Mueller Queensland Court of Appeal BC9603449

R v Beckett [1998] VSC 219

R v Birmingham No. 2 [1997] 96 A Crim R 545

R v Dowlan *BC9700239*

R v Lewis [2001] NSWCCA

R v Miller [1995] 2 VR 348

R v P 111 ALR 541

R v Palu [2002] NSWCCA 381

R v Previtera (1997) 94 A Crim R 76

R v Shaban [2004] ABQB 558 at [20]

R v Slack [2004] NSWCCA 128

R v Wilson [2004] NSWSC 597

Waye v R [2000] NTCCA 5

United States v McVeigh 940 F. Supp. 1571, 153 F.3d 1166 (10th Cir. 1998)

United States v Moussaoui Criminal No. 01-455-A (United States District Court, Eastern District of Virginia)

Part Five

Other visions of victims and victimology

Sandra Walklate

Introduction

In these final three chapters we explore some of the continuing absences from and newer presences on the victimological agenda. Goodey's chapter continues the comparative perspective developed in Part Four as she discusses the increasing contemporary concern with victims of racially and religiously motivated crime both in the UK and Continental Europe. As with Miers' discussion of criminal injuries compensation in Chapter 13, England and Wales has led the way in formulating responses to this kind of victimisation, though as Goodey's chapter elucidates the influence of this response and its ability to travel to other jurisdictions is not even or consistent (a theme also addressed by Van Dijk and Groenhuijsen in Chapter 14). The variable impact that responding to such victimisation has had is analysed by Goodey in a number of different ways, from the problem of data collection – which the French would argue are by definition discriminatory criteria (hence no data) – to the more familiar (in the UK context at least) problems of identification, reporting and recording racially and religiously motivated incidents. It is crucial, of course, to set the rising recognition of this kind of victim problem within the wider social, political and economic changes that have accrued consequent to the growth and development of the European Community and the associated economic migration. In addition, it is also important to note the impact that both local and global terrorist activities have had on the growing political preoccupation with racial and religiously motivated crime, concerns that Booth and Carrington document in Chapter 15 in their more general analysis of victim policy in the Anglo-speaking world. Interestingly the question of terrorism is also a theme addressed by Mythen in Chapter 18. Goodey proceeds to develop her analysis of xenophobia with a useful discussion of the problems associated with the concept of 'hate' crime. The difference between law in books and law in action acts as a constant barrier to what she would call the delivery of 'joined-up justice' pointing to, in a different way, one of the inherent problems of the victims' rights stance discussed in several contributions in Part Three. Goodey never loses sight of the fact that more often than not the people most likely to be subjected to racial and religiously motivated crime are also the most vulnerable in society. Green introduced the concept of vulnerability in Chapter 4 and it is a concept that Whyte also draws upon in his discussion of one of the continuing absences from the victimological agenda: victims of corporate crime.

Situated squarely within what has been called radical victimology emanating from, among others, the work of Quinney (1972) and Elias (1986, 1993), Whyte explores the lack of fit between Christie's (1986) 'ideal victim' and the victim of corporate crime (a conceptual vehicle that was also used by Davies in Chapter 7). Matching the view developed by Godfrey and Kearon in Chapter 1, Whyte points to the variable symbolic use of the crime victim within the political and policy domain. Whyte argues that what underpins this symbolic use of the ideal imagery of the crime victim are the central presumptions of neo-liberal democracy that valorise property. Interestingly that same imagery also, in Whyte's words, acts as an alibi to the extension of state control and the associated processes of governance. Who could argue against enhanced protection for the innocent? However, this innocent victim, normally the victim of unprovoked interpersonal violence, is not the victim of corporate crime. Hence the victim of corporate crime has had a varied, variable and rather marginal presence on the victimological agenda, the empirical efforts of, for example, Pearce (1990) and Slapper and Tombs (1999) and theoretical considerations of Kauslarich *et al.* (2001) notwithstanding. Yet as Whyte observes there has been increasing interest in the idea of the victimised state in terms of crime committed against businesses: an interesting twist in the victim story. He goes on to observe that crimes committed by corporations receive relatively little attention as a result of two related processes: lack of criminalisation (a product of neo-liberal democratic capitalism) and a resultant lack of data. However, with effort, some data on the impact of corporate crime can be produced as Whyte illustrates more than convincingly through his example of corporate killing. Again the concept of vulnerability emerges in tracing the impact of this kind of corporate crime. The social inequalities associated with criminal victimisation documented by Green in Chapter 4 are overlaid by the global inequalities exploited by business corporations, and Whyte clearly demonstrates that the variables of class, race and gender again become self-evident. However, Whyte also points to the role of victimology itself in contributing to the variable presence of corporate crime on the victimological agenda. Employing Mathieson's (2004) concepts of 'silencing' and 'pulverisation', he examines the neatness of fit between the victimological agenda and neo-capitalism, a neatness of fit that is not perfect as the existence of various campaign groups, that have succeeded in at least getting the issue of corporate killing on the policy agenda, illustrates. Nevertheless the point is well made that the academic agenda too carries with it political implications: a different take on whether or not it is possible to separate the academic from the activist (Fattah 1991) that we came across in Part Two of this book.

Chapters 16 and 17 each in their different ways are suggestive of the inherent possibilities for the victimological agenda. Goodey traces the further influence of appreciating diversity and its relationship with criminal victimisation, while Whyte traces the continuity of sameness and its relationship with criminal victimisation. Each of these differing visions of the victim of crime have been differently constituted within wider social, political, legal and economic processes by each of these authors. However, what has also been evident over the last 25 years in relation to the increasing political and policy preoccupation with the crime victim has been the role of culture. In Chapter 18 Mythen explores what the possibilities might be for a cultural victimology.

While much has been made of Garland's (2001) seminal work *The Culture of Control* and its relevance for understanding the cultural context of the increasingly punitive stance towards offenders that has been embraced particularly in the UK and the USA, little effort, to date, has been made to explore the relevance of the 'cultural turn' (which seems to have captured the imagination of some criminologists) for victimology. Mythen endeavours to do this. In an exploratory discussion of the question of culture for victimology, Mythen asks us to consider whether or not the cultural turn within criminology is pertinent for victimology. In outlining two major contributors to the contemporary preoccupation with culture, that of Beck and Furedi, Mythen points out that the theoretical work of Beck (while having little to say about crime and victimisation *per se*) encourages a vision of the 'universal victim' (we are all equally at risk from universal goods and bads); while the more discursive approach of Furedi offers a vision of the 'faux victim' (we are all exposed to the compensation-oriented victim culture). In other words, rather in contrast to the visions of victimhood offered in the chapters by Green, Goodey and Whyte, for Beck and Furedi there are no longer degrees of victimhood: we are all (equally) victims. Moreover, as Mythen argues, as a consequence the work of Beck inadvertently sits rather well with the extending processes of governance and control of which Garland (2001) speaks. Using the relationship between the pre-eminent concerns about terrorism and how this concern has been embraced to fuel the politics of fear and victimisation as an example, Mythen examines how the notions of 'all' and 'us' have become both inclusionary and exclusionary at the same time in this current climate of fear. In this way he illustrates not only the importance but also the relevance of the cultural (alongside the social, political, economic and legal) for victimology. This importance lies in our developing an understanding not of how 'we are all victims now' but of how the processes that encourage a belief in the view that we are all victims masks, in Mythen's words, the fact that 'the real sufferers are silently crushed elsewhere' and 'over-surveyed citizens are indelicately classified as either offenders or victims'. The question remains: what message(s) do these other visions of crime victims and victimology imply for this area of analysis?

By implication, Mythen's consideration of the possibilities for a cultural victimology returns us to the general question posed by Rock in Chapter 2: what is the state and status of theory in this area of analysis; with a corollary being, if theory has some status here, from where should that theory be drawn? Mythen's answer to this question is clearly a holistic one. In other words, it makes little sense to lay claim to some special disciplinary status for victimology when as an area of public and policy concern it is clearly best understood by appreciating how the cultural, the social, the legal, the economic, the political and the psychological intertwine, to render some issues problematic and not others. It is clear from his analysis, though, that part of the conceptual assemblage for victimology is culture. Moreover, as Whyte illustrates, this conceptual assemblage should also include an appreciation of the nature of neo-liberal capitalism and its global interconnection. However, such interconnections are not only economic in form, they are also increasingly legal, as is illustrated in the chapter by Goodey and also intimated in the chapters in Part Four. Understanding the complexity of the cross-cultural legal networks that make demands on nation states is increasingly problematic for those proclaiming an interest in the victim of crime and/or victimology. Not only does that complexity raise the problem of law in books and law in practice, as Goodey articulates, it also raises the problem of sameness and difference. This is an empirical question: who is a victim of what and when and what does the impact of that victimisation look like? This is a practical question: how do you formulate policies that adequately respond to who is a victim of what and when, when the impact of that victimisation might look quite different on an individual-by-individual basis? (This problem is raised by implication in Goodey's critical assessment of the problem of 'hate crime'.) Moreover, this is also a theoretical, political, and legal question: how is it possible to manage the tensions between sameness and difference; between universalism and individualism? Mythen points to one way of thinking about the ways in which this tension is being managed culturally through the political manipulation of what is understood by 'all of us'; but does this offer a sufficient road map for offering a new (better?) direction for concerns about the victim of crime? We shall revisit this question in the Conclusion.

Taken together, these chapters illustrate not only what remains to be understood about the nature and extent of criminal victimisation but also what remains to be embraced by a victimological agenda. They each raise questions of theoretical, empirical and a policy nature that could take the victimological agenda in a number of directions. Those directions, arguably, might be best served by thinking critically about the current shape and form of victimology itself. Such a critical evaluation of this area of concern returns us to the questions that Rock (Chapter 2) so aptly asked about its status as a discipline and the consequent theoretical apparatus it might have at its disposal, along with Hope's challenge to us that in order to appreciate the victim condition it is also necessary for us to understand the non-victim condition. Moreover, as many of the other contributions have demonstrated either implicitly or explicitly (though rather more explicitly in the case of Whyte in Chapter 17), it is difficult to separate out national concerns about criminal victimisation from international concerns and the subsequent implication of victimology, whether academic or activist in those developments. Nevertheless, Part Five raises some important questions concerning how best to understand this particular moment for the victim of crime. This issue will be pursued in the Conclusion.

References

Christie, N. (1986) 'The Ideal Victim', in E. Fattah (ed.) *From Crime Policy to Victim Policy*. London: Macmillan.

Elias, R. (1986) *The Politics of Victimisation*. Oxford: Oxford University Press.

Elias, R. (1993) *Victims Still*. London: Sage.

Fattah, E.A. (1991) *Understanding Criminal Victimisation*. Scarborough, Ontario: Prentice Hall.

Garland, D. (2001) *The Culture of Control*. Oxford: Polity.

Kauslarich, D., Matthews, R.A. and Miller, W.J. (2001) 'Towards a victimology of state crime', *Critical Criminology*, 10: 173–94.

Mathieson, T. (2004) *Silently Silenced*. Winchester: Waterside Press.

Pearce, F. (1990) 'Commercial and Conventional Crime in Islington', in A. Crawford, T. Jones, T. Woodhouse and J. Young (1990) *The Second Islington Crime Survey*. London: Middlesex Polytechnic Centre for Criminology.

Quinney, R. (1972) 'Who is the victim of crime?', *Criminology*, 10: 309–29.

Slapper, G. and Tombs, S. (1999) *Corporate Crime*. Harlow: Longman.

Chapter 16

'Race', religion and victimisation: UK and European responses

Jo Goodey

European Union Agency for Fundamental Rights (FRA), Vienna, previously the European Monitoring Centre on Racism and Xenophobia (EUMC)

Disclaimer – The views expressed in this chapter are those of the author and not those of the FRA or the EUMC.

Introducing a historical and contemporary problem

'Racist crime', which is used in this chapter as shorthand to include racially, ethnically and religiously motivated crime, has a long history in Europe. The Holocaust and, more recently, 'ethnic cleansing' during the civil war in the former Yugoslavia, symbolise the most extreme manifestations of ethnically and religiously motivated 'hate' crimes that Europe has witnessed. Yet, these most heinous of crimes, which are marked by their scale and *modus operandi*, reflect one end of a spectrum that can range from genocide through to racist harassment and graffiti (Bowling 1998; Bowling and Philips 2002).

In the aftermath of the Second World War, European countries ratified a range of legislation recognising racist and religious discrimination, and racist and xenophobic crime. These legal responses variously reflect historical developments in individual countries, and can be characterised broadly under three main headings:[1] (1) legislation that sets out to combat National Socialist/fascist/neo-Nazi ideologies, which is particularly important in countries that have suffered under dictatorships; (2) anti-discrimination legislation, which has its origins in the United Nations 1969 International Convention on the Elimination of all Forms of Racial Discrimination (ICERD); and (3) 'hate crime' legislation, which currently exists in some form in many member states, but which is not as wide-ranging as 'hate crime' legislation in the US. In the area of racist and religiously motivated crimes, many European countries can be characterised as embracing a hybrid legal response that incorporates elements of the above approaches.

Given the weight of historical and contemporary legislation in Europe to specifically address the problem of racist crime, it becomes apparent, when looking at criminal justice data on racist crime, that many EU member states' legislation is not being implemented in practice. In other words, the 'law in the books' does not reflect the 'law in action'. Reports by international bodies such as the Council of Europe's European Commission against Racism and Intolerance (ECRI)[2] and the European Union's European Monitoring Centre on Racism and Xenophobia (EUMC), which became the European Union Agency for Fundamental Rights (FRA) on 1 March 2007, alongside that of major NGOs such as the European Network against Racism (ENAR), indicate beyond any doubt that racism and racist crime are significant problems in many European countries. However, as a significant social 'ill', it is clear that racist crime is not afforded the attention it deserves in some EU member states.

Focusing on criminal justice data collection as a symbol of individual states' recognition of and response to the problem of racially and religiously motivated crime, this chapter examines what we know about racist crime in Europe, and specifically in England and Wales. The chapter asks why criminal justice data collection in this area is limited in the mainstay of European Union member states, and critiques the non-application of the law in practice. With this critique in mind, the chapter is divided into three parts; the first presents an overview of human rights, and other legislative and policy responses to racist discrimination and racist crime: the second and main part of the chapter critiques existing criminal justice mechanisms for data collection on 'racist crime' in the EU, and explores the challenges faced when attempting to compare diverse data sets; and the third part critically examines the hate crime model for its potential to respond effectively to racist crime in Europe. The chapter concludes by looking at the need for 'joined-up justice' that is able to promote the application of the law in practice, and to see it reflected in criminal justice data collection.

Contextualising legislative and policy responses

A number of international bodies exist that recognise and seek to counteract the problem of racism and xenophobia, including violence and crime. In Europe, a triumvirate of three bodies has stewardship of the main international legal instruments and initiatives in this area; namely: the United Nations (UN); the Council of Europe (CoE); and the European Union (EU). Parallel to the work of these three, the Organisation for Security and Cooperation in Europe (OSCE), through its Office for Democratic Institutions and Human Rights (ODIHR), has developed some programmes in Europe that specifically promote recognition and policing of 'hate crime' – based essentially on a US model (OSCE/ODIHR 2005).

International human rights legislation – originating from the UN – forms the backbone of anti-discrimination legislation. The United Nations Universal Declaration of Human Rights, which was adopted by the UN General Assembly in December 1948, is the legal basis for recognising that all persons are entitled to human rights 'without distinction of any kind, such as race, colour, language, religion, political or other opinion, national or social origin, property, birth or other status'.[3] In turn, the United Nations International Convention on the Elimination of all Forms of Racial Discrimination forms the cornerstone of many EU member states' legislation that specifically relates to racial discrimination and racist crime;[4] with Article 4(a) indicating that States:

> shall declare an offence punishable by law all dissemination of ideas based on racial superiority or hatred, incitement to racial discrimination, as well as actions of violence or incitement to such acts against any race or group of persons of another colour or ethnic origin, and also the provision of any assistance to racist activities, including the financing thereof.

At the European level, the Council of Europe (CoE) bases its work in the area of combating racism and intolerance on human rights standards set out by the UN Universal Declaration of Human Rights and the Council's own European Convention on Human Rights,[5] which was adopted in 1950 and came into force in 1953. While the CoE has not included a Convention specifically addressing racial discrimination and racism, the Council established the European Commission against Racism and Intolerance (ECRI) in 1993. This is an independent monitoring body that addresses all necessary measures to 'combat violence, discrimination and prejudice faced by persons or groups of persons on grounds of race, colour, language, religion, nationality and national or ethnic origin'.[6] In turn, the Council's Framework Convention for the Protection of National Minorities,[7] which was adopted in 1994, incorporates a dimension to address racism and intolerance.

At the level of the European Union, 1997 was a year in which a range of initiatives were adopted to combat racism and intolerance; namely, 1997 was declared the European Year Against Racism; the European Monitoring Centre on Racism and Xenophobia was established as an independent agency of the EU;[8] and the Treaty of Amsterdam was agreed, which includes provisions under Article 13 on non-discrimination based on racial or ethnic origin, religion or belief. In 2000, the implementation of these provisions emerged in the form of two Directives: the Racial Equality Directive 2000/43/EC,[9] 'implementing the principle of equal treatment between persons irrespective of racial or ethnic origin', and the Employment Equality Directive 2000/78/EC,[10] 'establishing a general framework for equal treatment in employment and occupation'. In addition, the Community Action Programme that followed in the footsteps of the 2000 Race Directive had, as one of its principle objectives, the goal to promote data collection on, among other things, ethnic and racial discrimination,[11] and the anti-discrimination directives themselves require the establishment of specialised bodies in each member state to monitor cases of discrimination.

Specifically, with respect to the area of racist *crime*, the Council of the European Union forwarded a Proposal for a Framework Decision on Combating Racism and Xenophobia in 2001 COM (2001).[12] In April 2007, the Council of the European Union finally reached a general approach on the Framework Decision, the text of which can be adopted after some parliamentary scrutiny reservations have been lifted, thus offering scope for approximation of laws in EU member states concerning certain racist and xenophobic offences. The Framework Decision also establishes that conduct it prohibits is punishable with a maximum of at least one to three years imprisonment.[13]

Although a plethora of international legislation exists to combat racist and religiously motivated discrimination and crime, to which all EU member states are signatories (Nickel 2003), these legislative 'gold standards' are not backed up by policy and practical initiatives in many EU member states for collecting data on the extent and nature of racist and religiously motivated crime (Dummett 1997; Witte 1996), nor is there provision for monitoring the implementations of legislation in practice. This theme will be returned to later in this chapter, suffice to say that legislation – or the law in the books – is not supported by criminal justice data collection that might hint at the nature and extent of racist and religiously motivated crimes – the law in practice.

Responding to 'racially' and religiously aggravated crimes: England and Wales

Turning to the case of England and Wales, legislative and policy responses to racial discrimination and, specifically, racist crime, have developed over the course of the last four decades. While England and Wales is a signatory to foundational international legal instruments such as the Universal Declaration of Human Rights and the European Convention on Human Rights, legislation in England and Wales took its own form and momentum from the mid 1960s to focus on discrimination as it specifically relates to 'race'; the 1965 Race Relations Act, although severely limited in its scope, came into force on 8 December 1965 (a few days before, on 21 December 1965, the United Nations International Convention on the Elimination of all Forms of Racial Discrimination was adopted, and finally ratified in January 1969).

More recently, the Crime and Disorder Act 1998 was important for its creation of 'racially aggravated' offences for specific crimes, such as malicious wounding and aggravated assault, with corresponding provisions for tougher sentencing. In 2001, the Anti-Terrorism, Crime and Security Act amended the 1998 Crime and Disorder Act to include provision for enhanced sentencing options for religiously aggravated offences, increasing the maximum penalty for racially and religiously aggravated offences from two to seven years. These powers were also enhanced by section 153 of the Powers of Criminal Courts (Sentencing) Act 2000, which imposes a duty on courts to treat evidence of racial or religious hostility as aggravating factors when deciding on the sentence for *any* offence that is not specifically stated under the Crime and Disorder Act 1998. Still more recently, the Racial and Religious Hatred Act 2006, which in its very title shows the shift towards consideration of 'hate crime' by legislators in England and Wales, creates specific legislation relating to incitement of hatred against a person on the grounds of their religion. These various laws have not developed in isolation, but have been accompanied by a range of practical and policy initiatives in criminal justice – most notably in the area of policing ethnic minority communities. These practical initiatives have served to both bolster and challenge the application of the law in practice.

In England and Wales, policy initiatives to combat racism and xenophobia, specifically with respect to racist violence and crime, have often emerged as a direct response to inter-community conflict and, in particular, poor community–police relations. One such catalyst for change was the 1981 Brixton riots, which erupted in the largely Afro-Caribbean London district of Brixton, and were followed by riots in other UK cities where ethnic minority communities were concentrated in deprived urban areas. The Scarman Inquiry into the Brixton riots attributed their cause largely to the police's overuse of stop-and-search powers against the Afro-Caribbean community. Among a number of recommendations, the inquiry called for an emphasis on community policing and recruitment of ethnic minority police officers. Although the riots were not directly related to racist crime, they drew attention to the policing of ethnic minority communities, and the need for improvements in police–community relations.

In the 1990s, police mismanagement of the investigation into the racist murder of Afro-Caribbean teenager Stephen Lawrence resulted in the Macpherson Inquiry (1999); the findings of which formed the basis of many reforms in England and Wales concerning the policing of racist crime. One of the most notable developments to emerge from the report was the adoption of its working definition of a 'racist incident', as 'any incident which is perceived to be racist by the victim or any other person'. Before this definition, police forces were collecting information on racist incidents on the basis of a 1985 Association of Chief Police Officers (ACPO) definition, which reads: 'any incident in which it appears to the reporting or investigating officer that the complaint involves an element of racial motivation; or any incident which includes an allegation of racial motivation made by any person'.[14] With the adoption of the Macpherson Report's definition of a racist incident, the justice system in England and Wales moved from a criminal justice-centred definition of a racist incident, where the 'racist' attribute of a crime was primarily the decision of a police officer, to a victim-centred definition.

These legislative and policy responses to racist and, latterly, religiously motivated crime in England and Wales have been driven to a large extent by particular events, and the adoption of recommendations that have emerged from inquiries in the aftermath of these events. At the same time, the integration of ethnic minorities into British life has been addressed proactively, to greater or lesser degrees by successive governments, through a range of non-discrimination initiatives that emerged via 'race relations' and, more recently, 'multiculturalism' and the language of 'diversity' (Home Office 2004). In turn, the evolving victims' movement of the 1970s and 1980s leant support to the recognition of people's experiences as victims – including victims of racist violence and crime. From here, the movement towards 'victim-centred' justice gained momentum in the UK and has remained at the top of governmental and non-governmental concerns to date (Goodey 2005).

In comparison with the UK, in much of the rest of Europe the idea of victim-centred justice is, as yet, some way off (Brienen and Hoegen 2000; Crawford and Goodey 2000; Wergens 1999). This situation partly reflects lower crime levels in some parts of Western Europe, when compared with the UK, and the role played by less adversarial criminal justice systems that do not serve to pitch offender and state against victim – a criticism that has been at the heart of many calls for criminal justice reform in England and Wales (Fyfe 2001; Lees 1997). Also, when one considers the specific recognition of racist victimisation in Europe, member states' different histories of and responses to immigration need to be taken into account. In this regard, the particular needs and rights of immigrant communities, including their experiences of racist discrimination and crime, have been able to develop over a longer period in the UK when compared with many other European countries, some of which are only now beginning to experience immigration – both legal and illegal – on a significant scale.

And last, but not least, the conclusions and recommendations of the Scarman and Macpherson inquiries has meant that the police in England and Wales have had to drastically improve their response to racist crime, which they have only been able to pursue, with varied success, with the support of minority communities in the context of enhanced police–community relations (Rowe 2004). An academic and policy 'culture of critique' has built up around policing in the UK and, specifically, around policing of racist crime (Holdaway 1999). Yet, looking elsewhere in Europe serves to cast UK-policing in a more favourable light than is sometimes the case if we remain with a UK based critique. In this regard, the EUMC's report on *Policing Racist Crime and Violence*, which compares policing responses to racist crime in twenty-five EU member states, has this to say about the UK (Oakley 2005: 42):

> Only the United Kingdom [among the EU25] appears to have developed a comprehensive and systematic approach in which addressing racist crime and violence is seen at policy level as an integral part of policing a multi-ethnic society, although everyday policing needs to be monitored to ensure that this is followed up in practice.

This EUMC report goes on to note that the police in France, Germany and Sweden have also 'demonstrated a serious commitment to address issues of racist crime and violence in recent years, even if their focus and/or range of activities have not been as comprehensive'. However, it remains the fact that most EU member states are lagging behind the UK in fundamental areas with respect to the development of effective policing responses to racist crime.

These particular histories of 'victim recognition' help to explain the divergent status of data collection on racist crime in Europe. What we do and do not know about racist crime reflects the importance that individual countries within Europe have assigned to criminal victimisation in general, and racist victimisation in particular (Lentin 2004); and whether, in turn, they choose to collect and make publicly available data on criminal and racist victimisation.

The limitations of data: what we (don't) know

Although it can be said that racist and religiously motivated crimes have existed throughout Europe's history, this statement is difficult to substantiate in the absence of comprehensive evidence in a number of European countries. As an illustration: the UK's generous working definition of a racist incident, which has been accompanied by a top-down emphasis for the police to record all reports of racist incidents, currently means that the police in England and Wales record more racist incidents than the *combined* recording of racist incidents, or crimes, in the 24 other member states of the EU.[15] For the 12-month period 2004–05, the police in England and Wales recorded 57,902 'racist incidents' (with 54,286 incidents recorded in the previous period 2003–04). In comparison, Germany reported 15,914 politically motivated right-wing 'crimes' in 2005 (12,533 in 2004), Sweden recorded 2,383 'incidents' in 2005 (2,414 in 2004), and France recorded 974 racist 'acts and threats' in 2005 (1,574 in 2004). In turn, a number of member states only make information available on racist crimes that have reached the final stages of the criminal justice process and are prosecuted under specific pieces of legislation. For example, in 2004 Lithuania registered five crimes relating to incitement to national, racial, ethnic or religious hatred, two crimes relating to disturbance from performing a religious act of worship or ceremony, and two crimes for keeping or disseminating hate material. If reporting only on court cases appears limited, it should be noted that five of the 25 EU member states – Cyprus, Greece, Italy, Malta and Spain – did not make *any* data on racist incidents or crimes available in the public domain during the reporting period 2004–2005.[16]

This information is striking for two basic reasons. First, there is tremendous variation between countries in the extent of their collected data, which ranges from the very high figure for England and Wales through to non-existent data collection in some member states. Second, the nature of what is being counted differs widely between each member state; with some only counting successful prosecutions under specific legislation and others counting 'incidents' reported by the public that have yet to be officially recognised as crimes by the criminal justice system.

Looking at countries with similar majority and immigrant and/or ethnic minority populations – such as France and the UK – the disparity between the officially recorded data appears remarkable (EUMC 2005). Obviously, we cannot take this official criminal justice data at face value; in other words, we cannot read this data as indicating that one country has a greater problem with racist crime than another. If this were the case we might conclude that five countries, with no available data, currently have no problem with racist violence and crime. At the same time, it is problematic to attempt to make direct comparisons between countries with very different data collection mechanisms. Instead, comparisons of recorded racist crime in different years can be made for the same country. However, while recognising that officially recorded crime only touches the tip of the iceberg when it comes to the actual extent of crime, trends analysis is a useful tool with which to map out patterns in officially recorded crime in the absence of robust alternative sources (EUMC Annual Report 2006). At the same time, looking at individual countries' patterns in data collection on racist crime can be used as an indicator of whether criminal justice agencies are responding seriously to the problem from one year to the next – with increases in data collection also reflecting improvements in recording practices.

Comparing the incomparable

The EUMC, which was transformed into the EU's Agency for Fundamental Rights (FRA) on 1 March 2007, was given the mandate to provide the European Community, the European Parliament and its member states with objective, reliable and comparable data and information on racism and xenophobia in five core areas, including racist violence and crime.[17] The FRA, continuing the work of the EUMC, collects official criminal justice data and unofficial reports of racist violence and crime through its National Focal Points (NFPs), with one NFP in each member state. The above figures illustrate the kind of data, and often the absence of any data, with which this EU agency has to work. The essential challenge for the FRA is to try and make sense of data that is not directly comparable between member states – because it is based on different legislation, and different data collection systems and norms. However, while the information the FRA has to hand is not directly comparable, it can be comparatively analysed (without claims to its direct comparability (Wrench 2005)) for what it tells us about the nature of each Member State's data collection mechanisms for recording racist violence and crime.

The different nature of every country's legal, criminal justice and data collection systems means that racist violence and crime is defined, prosecuted and recorded differently (Brienen and Hoegen 2000). These differences serve to reveal the particular concerns and histories of some member states to prohibit and prosecute certain crimes. For example, as reported in the EUMC's Annual Report 2006, Germany, Austria, France and Sweden all record and make available information on anti-Semitic crimes. Germany has a particularly well-developed system for recording anti-Semitic crimes and other specific 'racist offences', which are categorised as 'politically motivated right-wing' crimes; official criminal justice data for 2005 indicates that, of the 15,914 crimes registered under the general heading of 'politically motivated right-wing', 1,682 were anti-Semitic, of which 49 were violent anti-Semitic crimes. Likewise, 2004 data for France indicates that of the 1,574 reported 'acts' and 'threats' of a racist, xenophobic or anti-Semitic nature registered by the state, 970 were classified as anti-Semitic (200 violent acts and 770 threats). However, while recording of anti-Semitic crimes is well developed in some EU member states (as a reflection of European history), recording crimes against other vulnerable social groups – such as Muslims or homosexuals – has only emerged recently as a possible area of police concern in a couple of EU member states; Sweden and the UK (see the EUMC 2007 report on *Muslims in the EU: Discrimination and Islamophobia*).[18]

Legislation in England and Wales can now distinguish between racially and religiously aggravated offences, but Home Office published data does not disaggregate information relating to these different crime types, and instead puts them together under a general heading (Home Office 2006). In comparison with French data collection on religiously motivated crimes against *specific* communities, official data collection is relatively under-developed in this area in England and Wales; disaggregated data on recorded incidents and crimes against specific religious communities is simply not available. Only limited Crown Prosecution Service figures provide some indication of who the victim or victims were with respect to their religion in particular cases. Even the London Metropolitan Police Service's regular weekly bulletins on the number of reported 'faith hate' crimes in the aftermath of the 7 July 2005 bombings did not separate anti-Muslim crimes from the generic counting of faith-hate crimes. To this end, while legislation in England and Wales has now developed to recognise religiously aggravated offences, the mechanisms for distinguishing between racist incidents and faith hate incidents – let alone between specific faith incidents against certain communities – has still some way to develop (Home Office 2006). However, where criminal justice data collection in England and Wales is relatively sophisticated compared with other member states is in its ability to document detailed victim characteristics, including ethnicity, through the British Crime Survey, a theme that will be addressed below.

Where the state falls down on specific data collection, non-governmental organisations (NGOs) often step in to fill this gap. In the case of the UK, the Community Security Trust publishes a comprehensive annual report on anti-Semitic hate crimes,[18] and other NGOs – such as the Islamic Human Rights Commission, the Muslim Youth Helpline, and the Forum against Islamophobia and Racism (FAIR) – collect specific information on anti-Muslim or Islamophobic incidents. In other EU countries where there is no publicly available official criminal justice data on racist and religiously motivated crime, NGOs play a vital role in collecting and publishing information; examples include SOS Racismo and the Movimiento contra la Intolerancia in Spain, Antigone in Greece, and COSPE (Cooperazione per lo Sviluppo dei Paesi Emergenti) in Italy. Yet NGO data is often by its very nature sporadically collected, and therefore it is difficult to draw any conclusions about the nature of racist violence and crime in and between countries on the basis of this 'unofficial' data alone. Having said this, the current absence or limited extent of official data collection on racist crime in many European countries means that unofficial data is all there is concerning information about vulnerable populations' experiences of victimisation.

Ethnic monitoring, data protection and data collection

One stumbling block to more detailed data collection on racist crime is the tradition and resistance in most EU member states to collecting data on 'ethnicity' (Krizsán 2001). Given that the police are the first stage in the criminal justice system for identifying racist crime, the absence of reporting procedures for identifying a victim's ethnicity would seem to preclude the accurate registration of certain crimes. As a result, detail about who is victimised is lost in the criminal justice process, and police intelligence gathering on the nature of racist crime is under-developed.

Among the EU25, the UK has the most well-established system for data collection on ethnicity, with the census now routinely collecting information about the ethnicity of British citizens. In the UK, the idea of ethnicity data collection is wedded to the historical development of 'race relations', and is seen as a means for assessing the extent to which certain groups in society are under- or over-represented in different sectors of social and economic life, from job recruitment to housing allocation. Like the UK, some other (typically 'Anglo-Saxon') countries – such as the United States, Canada and Australia – have developed a range of data collection mechanisms that record people's ethnicity, and which are used by governments as indictors of both 'discriminatory' and 'good' practices concerning certain segments of the population (Simon 2005). To this end, data collection on ethnicity is seen as a way of measuring discrimination and, ideally, this information can be used to promote policy responses for combating racist discrimination against ethnic minorities. At the same time, according to writers like Simon (2005), ethnic monitoring is the practical recognition that the state and society need to redress past discriminatory (racist) practices, which were often ingrained in law. Nowhere is this need for redress more evident than with the example of affirmative action policies in the US.

In comparison with the UK, the historical legacy of many EU countries, which have suffered under dictatorships, means that data collection on ethnicity has traditionally been viewed with suspicion because of the sinister purposes to which it was used in the past. The oft-heard objection to ethnic data collection is that it was used to identify Jews during the Nazi reign in Europe. In an inverted reading of the 'historical debt' argument that spurred affirmative action in the aftermath of slavery and years of discriminatory treatment of African-Americans in the United States, a number of European countries do not collect ethnic/religious data in recognition of the great harm to which it was put against Europe's Jewish population. In turn, another central argument against ethnic data collection, which is essentially a French one, is that the principle of equality of citizenship is undermined by the collection of data that deliberately seeks to classify citizens differently (Bleich 2003). This practice is deemed discriminatory in itself. For these reasons a number of member states specifically prohibit the collection of ethnic data, including data on religious affiliation, in their legislation and even their constitutions. What this means in practice is that censuses and other population registers do not collect information on ethnicity, and the police and other criminal justice agencies do not record victims' ethnicity.

The EUs 1995 Directive on Data Protection[20] is often cited in support of prohibitions on ethnic data collection. It indicates that use of personal information where individuals are identified or can be identified is prohibited, and, therefore, is regularly held up as a reason for not collecting sensitive information, including information about individuals' ethnicity or religion. However, the Directive specifically exempts data collection where the individual is made anonymous and can no longer be identified (Goldston 2001). In support of this, the Council of the European Union's Racial

Equality Directive (Race Directive)[21] states that information about indirect discrimination can be gathered for statistical purposes – so indicating that data collection on ethnicity, providing the individual cannot be identified, is possible, and lending support to the 1995 Data Protection Directive's reference to anonymous data collection.

Aside from the objections that are offered in a number of European countries against ethnic data collection, the mainstay of member states *do* collect data on people's nationality (when they are not citizens), their country of birth, and/or the country of birth of their parents, which could be used as a proxy indicator for ethnicity. In this way, countries are able to distinguish between nationals (citizens) and non-nationals (non-citizens), and are able to categorise non-nationals according to their land of emigration. But what this data collection does not facilitate is an examination of people's differential treatment, including their experiences of criminal and racist victimisation, on the basis of their *ethnicity*. This means that nationals of a particular country are treated as one homogeneous group when it comes to distinctions based on ethnicity.

In sum, arguments for and against data collection on ethnicity appear to fall into two camps: one that sees data collection in this area as discriminating against certain groups, and the other that sees data collection for the uses to which it can be positively put to fight discrimination. The extent of objections against ethnic data collection reflect each country's particular history and how governments and their statistical agencies decide, or decide not to, monitor contemporary society in all its variations. The impact of having one stance or the other can be felt sharply with respect to ethnic data collection in the area of criminal justice statistics.

Ethnic data collection and criminal justice statistics: England and Wales

In countries like the UK where data collection on ethnicity exists, statistics on ethnicity and criminal justice are, arguably, the most contentious area in which ethnic data collection is currently put to use. In England and Wales, section 95 of the Criminal Justice Act 1991 introduced the collection of criminal justice data on race for the purpose of (a) enabling persons engaged in the administration of justice to become aware of the financial implications of their decisions; or (b) facilitating the performance of such persons of their duty to avoid discriminating against any persons on the ground of race or sex or any other improper use.

The results of this data collection are published in the Home Office's 100-page plus annual report on *Statistics on Race and the Criminal Justice System*. In the 2005 edition (published in 2006), one of 12 chapters, looks at 'Victims and Homicide', and the remainder focus predominantly on statistics related to race and offending in relation to different stages of the criminal justice system. Reflecting the misplaced way in which new 'managerialist-speak' has been adopted by the Home Office, the publication's summary introduction refers to black and minority ethnic groups as 'users' of the criminal justice system when, essentially, meaning offenders. The summary states: 'At a general level, all Black and Minority Ethnic (BME) groups have a higher representation as users of the Criminal Justice System (CJS) when compared to their representation as members of the population as a whole' (Home Office 2006: vi). It goes on to qualify this statement with some examples of these 'users' different uses of the criminal justice system; for example, the fact that black defendants are more prominent in the Crown Court caseload because they tend to elect for jury trial more than other ethnic groups, including the white majority. However, what the report does not do, and arguably because this goes beyond its narrow remit under section 95, is look at the processes by which BME groups enter the criminal justice system in the first place; processes that can include multiple layers of discrimination from education onwards.

The report's findings on the over-representation of BME people in the criminal justice system could be put to misuse by those seeking to benefit from an uncritical reading of the figures. But the Home Office's publication of extensive statistics on ethnic minorities and offending is offset by its equally extensive data collection on ethnicity and victimisation, which includes data collection on racist victimisation. The government has gained some legitimacy, although not without criticism, in collecting figures on race and justice as a result of the country's long history of having developed a legislative and policy response to racist discrimination and, specifically, racist victimisation. This is reflected in the annual publication of criminal justice data on the number of recorded racist *incidents* (57,902 in the 12-month period 2004–05) and the number of racially and religiously aggravated *offences* (37,028 in 2004–05).

In turn, the British Crime Survey (BCS), which since 1988 has included a question on respondents' ethnicity, contains invaluable information about different groups' experiences of crime in general, and racist crime in particular. According to Jansson (in an online Home Office report[22]), 1 per cent of the total number of BCS crimes where the victim was white were thought to be racially motivated, compared with 11 per cent of BCS crimes where the victim was from a BME group. Extrapolating the BCS findings, the Home Office estimates that there were 179,000 racist incidents in England and Wales during the reporting period 2004–05 – 121,000 more incidents than are reported by the public to the police.

Yet, when one compares the level of public reporting to the police in England and Wales with other countries with similar populations, the figures for England and Wales are phenomenal. Although there is some indication that these reports often emanate from the majority white population and, therefore, might hint at the misuse of legislation that was intended to serve vulnerable minority groups, the fact that the police go on to record a significant number of racist offences would suggest that the legitimacy of public reporting should not be under-stated. What this high level of reported and recorded incidents tells us is a number of things: first, that mechanisms are in place for the public to be able to report racist crime and for the police to record it; second, that this implies that the public has developed a certain degree of trust in the state to encourage such a high level of reporting. Without public trust in state institutions, and the ends to which they will put sensitive data, the collection of information relating to ethnicity cannot be legitimated by the state. Hence the continuing concerns in many European countries.

If the criminal justice system is viewed as a *public service*, then anonymous data collection that is able to examine people's treatment at the hands of that system, according to their ethnicity, would seem a desirable goal. Yet in many countries the accountability of the criminal justice system to the public, let alone minority members of that public, is often lacking, and effective mechanisms are not in place that could begin to do this job. As a result, the publication of something nearing the Home Office's report, *Statistics on Race and the Criminal Justice System* or the British Crime Survey's results on ethnicity and victimisation are, at present, a long way off for most member states. Unfortunately, this means that the extent and nature of racist crime is an unknown quantity and, therefore, a little understood phenomenon in many member states.

Against this backdrop, there are indications that an alternative criminal justice approach to monitoring racist violence and crime is being promoted in some EU member states through the adaptation of the US 'hate crime' model. Yet this initiative, too, is often not based on solid data or police intelligence that can inform policy-makers about where legislation and reform should be directed, and where it is most needed. Again, the disjuncture between the law in the books and the law in action is evident.

The 'hate crime' model: the 'place' of hate crime in Europe

As stated at the beginning of this chapter, legislative responses to racism in Europe generally come under one of three broad approaches: (1) legislation that sets out to combat National Socialist/fascist/neo-Nazi ideologies; (2) anti-discrimination legislation; and (3) hate crime legislation.

In some member states individual laws exist that might be described as hate crime legislation because they focus on prohibition of incitement to violence, hatred and discrimination in relation to 'race', ethnicity and nationality. Some member states have more generous legislation in place that encompasses incitement to discrimination, hate or violence in relation to a range of demographic variables and group characteristics – not just race, ethnicity or nationality. For example, Chapter IV, Section 1 of the Spanish Criminal Code refers to 'incitement to discrimination, hate or violence against groups on the basis of their religion or belief and other ideologies, family situation, belonging to an ethnic group or race, nationality, sex, sexual tendency, illness or disability'.[23] Nevertheless, having the most generous laws in place, as in the example of Spain, is no indication that the policing of prohibited acts will be followed through in practice. However, among the EU25, Sweden offers perhaps the clearest exception to this general rule, as the policing of hate crimes is proactively pursued at a number of levels in the criminal justice system – from the introduction of a clause in the Penal Code in 1994 for enhanced sentencing provisions for hate crimes, through to the provision of a liaison officer in every police authority with specific training on hate crimes, and the annual Police Board conference on hate crimes.

In comparison with Sweden, in England and Wales the legislative and criminal justice emphasis has been on prohibition and punishment of *racist* criminal acts against black and minority ethnic groups, and latterly against religious groups; with the language used referring to 'hostility' rather than 'hate' (Crime and Disorder Act 1998). But with the enactment of the Racial and Religious Hatred Act 2006, and the introduction of definitions of 'hate incidents' and 'hate crimes' by the Association of Chief Police Officers in 2000 and again in 2005, which has been accompanied by specific action concerning hate crime by individual police forces, legislation and criminal justice policy responses in England and Wales appear to be shifting their focus to 'hate' (Croall and Wall 2002). Yet the term 'hate' remains ill-defined in legislation in England and Wales, with the Racial and Religious Hatred Act 2006 simply referring to it as 'hatred against a group of persons defined by reference to religious belief or lack of religious belief'. Weak definitions of difficult concepts are nothing new in the criminal law; as Coomber (2003) points out, it is obviously easier for the law to define illegal conduct than it is for the law to start defining complex terms such as 'racism' or 'hate'. To this end, the term 'hate crime', like the term 'racism', encompasses a much used but little understood concept, or set of concepts.

Looking beyond Europe, hate crime legislation is most comprehensively endorsed in the United States; and it is this North American approach, or model, that is being promoted at some levels in the EU – notably through the OSCE's Decision on Tolerance and Non-Discrimination (No. 4/03), which was adopted by the foreign ministers of the 55 OSCE participating states (that includes the EU25) as a result of a meeting in 2003 in Maastricht. The OSCE's ODIHR office has itself developed a working definition of hate crime which reads:

> A hate crime can be defined as: (a) any criminal offence, including offences against persons or property, where the victim, premises, or target of the offence are selected because of their real or perceived connection, attachment, affiliation, support or membership of a group as defined in Part B; (b) A group may be based upon a characteristic common to its members, such as real or perceived race, national or ethnic origin, language, colour, religion, sex, age, mental or physical disability, sexual orientation or other similar factor. (OSCE/ODIHR 2005: 12)

Using this working definition and a North American-led group of police officers and academics, ODIHR initiated a pilot 'Law Enforcement Officer Programme on Combating Hate Crime' in Hungary and Spain (ODIHR 2005).

Whether a hate crime approach to combating racist and religiously motivated crime will be adopted in more EU member states has yet to be established. However, promotion of a hate crime model needs to be critically addressed at the European level before it can be offered as a 'solution' for an effective response to racist violence and crime.

Critiquing hate crime

Besides the lack of a clear definition of 'hate' in existing hate crime legislation, a first critique that can be levelled at hate crime legislation is its emphasis on offender motivation – which is, typically, a difficult area to prove in a court of law, and is also questionable with respect to its focus on an offender's thought processes. The critique here is, why should thought be punished in addition to the actions of an offender, and how can the hate motivation of an offender – minus evidence of language, graffiti and witnesses – be determined? Also, the deterrent effect of hate crime legislation, as opposed to its symbolic impact, is questioned by some commentators (Jacobs and Potter 1998; Iganski 1999).

At present, a number of European countries have legislation that recognises racist discrimination and intolerance as factors that can provide for enhanced sentencing in particular offences, but does not look specifically at the perpetrator's hate motivation. Given what is known about the nature of racist offending it is apparent that a great deal of racist crime is not committed by people who are members of extreme right-wing groups with some political or group ideology promoting hate; for example, the EUMC's report on racist violence in EU member states (2005) indicates that in Sweden, for the period 1997–2002, police figures show that only 15 per cent of xenophobic crime and 20 per cent of anti-Semitic crime is perpetrated by extremist 'White Power' groups. Nor can it be readily said that those belonging to these groups are in fact themselves motivated by hate (Ray *et al.* 2003; Virtanen 2002). Of more concern is the fact that a large part of 'petty' racist crime – such as graffiti and name-calling – is committed by young people and children (Webster 1997). Therefore, the usefulness of adopting hate crime legislation that might encompass these types of offender, but not necessarily these types of offence, is questionable for the impact that the 'hate' offender label can have on young people.

Another criticism is that by encompassing a wide range of victim groups within hate crime legislation, the emphasis on the plight of specific groups – such as racial and ethnic minorities – is undermined as all groups become potential victims of hate crime. As an (unintentional) result of having wide-ranging hate crime legislation, the impact of the hate label is in danger of being diluted as the law applies equally to a broad swathe of victim groups. Yet the counter argument to this is why should only one or two groups be singled out as the potential victims of hate crime legislation and others not. Again, the historical legacy of discrimination in individual countries reflects why the victimisation of certain groups has been prioritised in their legislation – black and minority ethnic people in England and Wales, and Jewish people in Germany. Still, even the most wide-ranging hate crime legislation may leave out certain groups, which, again, can be misinterpreted to mean that some people are more important than others as victims of crime.

At its heart, hate crime legislation purports to send out a clear message from the state and society that hate-motivated crimes are unacceptable – not only for the impact they have on the individual victim but for the impact they have on his/her 'community'. But which victim community or communities benefit from hate crime laws is, according to some commentators (Jacobs and Potter 1998; MacNamara 2003), dependent on the strength of the group or groups lobbying on their behalf. According to MacNamara (2003: 527), who levels a strong critique against New York's Hate Crimes Act 2000, an advocacy group can call public and political attention to its cause by overstating the incidence of a particular problem. MacNamara goes on to ask, 'How prevalent are hate crimes?' by looking at available police statistics as evidence of the extent of the problem, and in so doing overstates the idea that official criminal justice statistics are a reliable indicator of the extent of hate crime – if this were the case many European countries would be able to state, on the basis of their limited or non-existent data on racist crime, that there is no problem in their country.

As a counterpoint to MacNamara's limited interpretation of official criminal justice statistics, Hall (2005) critically explores the process of police data collection on hate crime in his comparative overview of policing responses to hate crime in London and New York City – two cities of similar size with similarly diverse minority populations. His research shows that the counting of hate crimes is manifestly different between the two cities: in 2001, for example, 20,628 'hate crimes' were recorded in London and only 484 for New York City. Much of this difference is explicable in relation to the very generous victim-centred definition of a racist incident that the police currently employ in England and Wales, when compared with the more stringent police-centred procedures for identification of a hate crime adopted by the Hate Crimes Task Force in New York. What lies also at the heart of these very different figures for hate crimes and racist incidents, when comparing the cities of New York and London, is the extent to which the justice system in each city has adopted a victim-centred approach to recording crime.

A 'victim-centred model': the UK approach

Rather than focus on offender motivation and/or police-determined interpretations of a reported incident, the working definition of a racist incident in England and Wales focuses on whether the victim or any other person considers a particular incident to be 'racist'. From here it is the duty of the police to record publicly reported racist incidents, after which the Crown Prosecution Service takes over and applies stringent evidential rules to determine whether particular crimes can be considered to be racially or religiously aggravated.

In 2005, following on from the adoption of a generous victim-centred definition of a racist incident in England and Wales, the Association of Chief Police Officers (ACPO) adopted a definition of a hate incident as: 'Any incident, which may or may not constitute a criminal offence, which is perceived by the victim or any other person, as being motivated by prejudice or hate'.[23] This was accompanied by a definition of a hate crime which reads: 'Any hate incident, which constitutes a criminal offence, perceived by the victim or any other person, as being motivated by prejudice or hate.' This replaced ACPO's earlier (2000) definition of a hate crime, which was: 'a crime where the perpetrator's prejudice against any identifiable group of people is a factor in determining who is victimised'.[24] Herein, the 2005 ACPO definitions of a hate incident and a hate crime have developed – like the definition of a racist incident – to place the victim's perception of the incident centre-stage, but with the addition that the victim should perceive the incident as motivated by prejudice or hate. Notably, as Hall comments (2005: 11), the ACPO definitions provide for the policing of hate crime as it impacts on any identifiable group, and therefore extend well beyond what the criminal law currently recognises as specific offences against particular groups in society; for example, the Criminal Justice Act 2003 allows for homophobia and disability 'hate' to be taken into account as aggravating factors in sentencing, but does not make crimes against these groups specific offences. In this regard, the ACPO definitions do not reflect either current legislation or actual policing practices in England and Wales, which are framed around policing racially and religiously aggravated incidents.

Currently, the application of this victim-centred definition of a racist incident means in practice, for England and Wales, that a lot of racist incidents are being recorded when compared with other countries which remain with a police-centred definition (EUMC 2005). The result is that the criminal justice system in England and Wales, and particularly in the capital, has to process a significant number of recorded incidents to determine whether they are crimes. The focus of public and political attention, in the aftermath of the Lawrence Inquiry, means that police action (or inaction) in this area is under intense scrutiny in England and Wales when compared with other European countries. Yet, as Hall (2005) argues in his comparison of policing resources in London and New York, the system in England and Wales is currently overloaded by reported incidents that do not warrant investigation as racially and religiously aggravated offences. As a result, serious cases are in danger of being lost under the weight of reported incidents, as the police simply do not have the resources to manage their workload. Herein, if other hate incidents – identified in the first place by the victim – were to be given equal priority alongside what the police already have to consider under the existing model that is used for the policing of racist incidents, then the policing of hate crime could simply not function without the injection of new resources.

Any consideration of adopting a hate crime response to racist and religiously aggravated crime, in England and Wales and other European countries, should centrally examine the limitations and possibilities of a country's existing mechanisms for responding to crime committed against certain groups in society, and should look at the lessons learned from those countries that have moved towards a hate crime model. Undoubtedly, legislative recognition of hate crime sends out a strong political message that certain crimes are being taken very seriously by the State. Yet without good data collection, which is able to inform us about the actual extent and nature of these types of crime – and primarily whether they are motivated by 'hate' – it is difficult to establish where the offence category of a 'hate crime' is most needed and where it would be most effective.

The current way in which racist incidents are identified and recorded in England and Wales would not be sustainable if transferred to a more comprehensive hate crime model that remains with a victim-centred approach. Herein, perhaps the role of the police in identifying which incidents should be recorded as hate incidents needs to be looked at again with a view to making sure that the 'hate' label is attributed to the most serious incidents as they impact on victims. The approach to identification of and data collection on racist, xenophobic and anti-Semitic crime in other European member states, such as Germany and Sweden, should be considered by those seeking to critique the UK approach for what they offer in terms of workable models for recording serious hate offences. Having said this, it would be a very brave politician in England and Wales who suggests that the reforms for recording racist incidents that were established as a result of the Lawrence Inquiry should, in any form, be reconsidered along the lines of the earlier role played by the police as 'gatekeepers' in determining what crimes were registered as racist.

Concluding comments

In presenting a critical overview of existing legislation, policy and criminal justice data collection mechanisms for racist and religiously motivated crime, this chapter has set out to highlight the current disparity that exists in most EU member states between the law in the books and the law in action. The absence of comprehensive data on 'racist' crime in most EU member states indicates clearly that the law is not being applied in practice, and that governments are often failing to prioritise criminal justice responses to these serious crimes. As a result, the needs of victims of racist crime are not being recognised or addressed across much of Europe.

Yet the hate crime model, which is being promoted in some quarters in Europe, does not offer a panacea solution to the low status that is afforded to racist crime in many member states. Reflecting on the particular histories that have shaped recognition and prioritisation of particular hate crimes in different European countries – be this anti-Semitism or general racist crime – the chapter has sought to show that a 'one model fits all' approach cannot work in a diverse Europe. Instead, and given that legislation *does* exist in EU member states to combat racist crime, the practical application of existing legislation needs to be a new focus, or a renewed focus, of the police and governments in EU member states.

Given the general low status of criminal justice data collection on racist crime in many parts of Europe, there is an obvious need for 'joined-up justice' in Europe that is able to promote the application of the law in practice, and to see it reflected in criminal justice data collection on racist crimes. The barriers to data collection on ethnic monitoring offered in many member states should be addressed with reference to examples in other countries that do collect criminal justice data on ethnicity and use it to reveal experiences of victimisation by ethnicity. However, this kind of data collection requires a level of trust in state institutions that is absent in some EU member states. Herein, the history of twentieth-century Europe cannot be forgotten.

In comparison with many other European countries, the US and the UK have more in common with respect to the emphasis they place on the 'counting' of racist and hate crimes. According to Jacobs and Potter (1998), the US's Hate Crime Statistics Act 1990 was promoted in the hope that better data collection would enhance criminal justice responses to the problem of hate crime. The need for accurate crime counting was also fundamentally wedded in the UK and the US to the 'new managerialist' call for economic, efficient and effective justice. Yet what the two systems end up counting is very different, and is primarily a reflection of the victim-centred approach to the first stage of crime counting that currently exists in England and Wales. To this end, any promotion of better data collection on racist crime in Europe should not only refer to enhancement of police intelligence in this area, but should also critically address the role that victims do and do not play in the identification and reporting of crime under different systems. Recognising that the police and courts are reliant on the public's willingness to report crime and to co-operate with the authorities, the victim should not be overlooked in this process.

Jenness and Grattet (2005) specifically look at the policing of hate crimes in the US from the standpoint of the 'law-in-between' – by which they mean the organisational policies and structures that provide intermediary linkages between legislation (the law in the books) and officer discretion (the law in practice). To this end they focus on the role of environment, community demands, operational capacity, and the degree to which an organisation is aligned with a new proposal, to see how an organisation can adapt to innovative ideas and implement policy. In other words, how organisations (in this case the police) make innovation (in this case hate crime legislation) operational (in this case implemented in practice – which should be reflected in data collection). Like Jacobs and Potter (1998), Jenness and Grattet (also writing about the US) recognise the importance of community demands on whether hate crime legislation is transferred into hate crime policies. In this regard, the role of certain victim lobby groups – both historically and contemporarily – is important when looking at what legislation is in place and how it is implemented at the level of the police organisation and the police officer on the street.

In the context of Europe, aside arguably from the UK, Jenness and Grattet's observations are, as yet, some way off. Although important minority and racism-focused NGOs do exist in many member states, their political impact is limited. Also, the development of victim-centred justice, let alone minority-centred justice, is underdeveloped in many parts of Europe in comparison with the UK and the US. However, as Europe's immigrant communities increase, and as the children of these immigrants settle and come (it can be expected) to demand certain rights – provided they are awarded citizenship – then we might begin to see more calls for effective justice responses to these communities as victims, and as victims of racist crime.

This brief overview of different legislative, policy and data collection practices has illustrated the extent to which racist crime is and is not responded to as a serious social ill in Europe. The results have shown that there is still much room for improvement in this area in many EU member states, and that victims of racist crime will have to wait some time before their victimisation receives due recognition and an adequate response. To some extent England and Wales offers a 'good practice' example for other member states, but one that is difficult to replicate in diverse criminal justice jurisdictions. At the same time it is apparent when comparing data collection mechanisms in England and Wales with those in other countries that the UK system is at full capacity and, perhaps, is not serving the interests of those for which it was intended. To this end, England and Wales can also learn from other countries that have more focused data collection practices. However, this should only be done without losing sight of the important victim-centred approach to combating racist crime that England and Wales has been at the forefront of promoting in Europe.

Further reading

For an overview of what is known about the nature and extent of racist violence and crime in the European Union's 25 member states, readers are recommended to look at the FRA's online InfoBase (http://fra.europa.eu) and the following EUMC reports, all of which are available online: *Racist Violence in 15 EU member states* (2005); *Policing Racist Crime and Violence* by Oakley (2005); EUMC Annual Report 2006, Part II, chapter on Racist Violence and Crime. The OSCE/ODIHR online report *Combating Hate Crimes in the OSCE Region* (2005) also provides a good insight into the problems of data collection in this area in a wider geo-political context (http://www.osce.org). For the UK, readers should look at the section on victims in the UK Home Office's annual online report *Statistics on Race and the Criminal Justice System*, and the 2006 online Home Office report by Jansson, *Black and Minority Ethnic groups' experiences and perceptions of crime, racially motivated crime and the police: findings from the 2004–05 British Crime Survey* (www.homeoffice.gov.uk/rds).

Notes

1 EUMC (2005) Racist Violence in 15 EU member states, Chapter 2, 'Legal Approaches to Racist Violence', pp. 42–3 (print version) (http://fra.europa.eu) (report written by chapter's author).
2 (http://www.coe.int/T/e/human_rights/ecri/1-ECRI/)
3 United Nations Universal Declaration of Human Rights, Article 2 (http://www.un.org/Overview/rights.html).
4 United Nations International Convention on the Elimination of all Forms of Racial Discrimination (http://www.ohchr.org/english/law/cerd.htm). Although ICERD does not refer in its text to religious discrimination, the UN Committee on the Elimination of Racial Discrimination (CERD), which is the body responsible for the implementation of ICERD, has addressed religious aspects of discrimination as they concern particular ethnic groups.
5 (http://www.coe.int/T/E/Com/About_Coe/Human_rights.asp).
6 (http://www.coe.int/T/e/human_rights/ecri/1-ECRI/).
7 (http://www.coe.int/T/e/human_rights/Minorities/2._FRAMEWORK_CONVENTION_%28MONITORING%29/1._Texts/H%281995%29010%20E%20FCN M%20and%20Explanatory%20Report.asp#TopOfPage).
8 In December 2003, the decision was made at EU level to extend the mandate of the EUMC by transforming it into the EU's Fundamental Rights Agency.

9 The Racial Equality Directive focuses on the prohibition of racial and ethnic discrimination in the fields of employment, education, social security, health care and access to goods and services (http://ec.europa.eu/comm/employment_social/fundamental_rights/pdf/legisln/2000_43_en.pdf).

10 The Employment Equality Directive focuses on the principle of equal treatment in employment and training irrespective of religion or belief, disability, age or sexual orientation (http://ec.europa.eu/comm/employment_social/fundamental_rights/pdf/legisln/2000_78_en.pdf).

11 Council Decision of 27/11/00 (2000/750/EC).

12 COM (2001) 664 final.

13 In June 2006 – under the Austrian Presidency of the EU, and with the co-organisation of the EUMC and the European Commission – a high level seminar was held, in Vienna, to resurrect discussions concerning the Framework Decision on Combating Racism and Xenophobia.

14 ACPD *Good Practice Guide for Police Responses to Racial Incidents*, cited in MPS (Metropolitan Police Service) submission to Part I of the Stephen Lawrence Inquiry (Macpherson 1999: 205).

15 Based on officially recorded criminal justice statistics for the EU25, as reported by the EUMC (see online EUMC InfoBase (http://fra.europa.eu).

16 Source: EUMC (2006) Annual Report, chapter on racist violence and crime; note – the EUMC's online InfoBase contains some revised information on racist violence and crime, which the EUMC received after the Annual Report went to press (see http://fra.europa.eu). For a fuller account of data collection in the area of racist violence and crime in the 'old' EU 15 member states, see the EUMC's report on 'Racist Violence in 15 EU member states' (April 2005).

17 (http://fra.europa.eu). At the time of writing (May 2007) the FRA now collects data and information related to six core areas: legislation, employment, education, housing, racist violence and crime and health.

18 (http://eumc.europa.cu/eumc/index.php?fuseaction=content.dsp_cat_content&catid=3fb38ad3e22bb&contentid=4582d9f4345ad).

19 See: (http://www.thecst.org.uk/).

20 EU Directive on Data Protection – 95/46/EC, paragraph 26 (http://europa.eu.int/comm/internal_market/provacy/law_en.htm).

21 Council Directive 2000/43/EC.

22 (http://www.homeoffice.gov.uk/rds/pdfs06/rdsolr2506.pdf) *'Black and Minority Ethnic Groups' Experiences and Perceptions of Crime, Racially Motivated Crime and the Police: Findings from the 2004-05 British Crime Survey'*, Home Office online report 25/06.

23 ACPO (2005) *Hate Crime: Delivering a Quality Service – Good Practice and Tactical Guidance* (http://www.ac.po.police.uk/asp/policies/Data/Hate%20Crime.pdf).

24 ACPO (2000) *Guide to Identifying and Combating Hate Crime* (http://www.asylumsupport.info/publications/acpo/hatecrime.pdf

References

Bleich, E. (2003) *Race Politics in Britain and France: Ideas and Policymaking since the 1960s*. Cambridge: Cambridge University Press.

Bowling, B. (1998) *Violent Racism*. Oxford: Clarendon Press.

Bowling, B. and Phillips, C. (2002) *Racism, Crime and Justice*. London: Longman.

Brienen, M.E.I. and Hoegen, E. (2000) *Victims of Crime in 22 European Criminal Justice Systems*. Nijmegen: Wolf Legal Productions.

Coomber, A. (2003) 'The Council of Europe: Combating Racism and Xenophobia', in *European Strategies to Combat Racism and Xenophobia as a Crime*, European Network Against Racism (ENAR), pp. 17–26.

Crawford, A. and Goodey, J. (2000) *Integrating a Victim Perspective within Criminal Justice: International Debates*. Dartmouth: Ashgate.

Croall, H. and Wall, D. (2002) (eds) 'Hate crimes', *Criminal Justice Matters*, 48.

Dummett, A. (1997) *Racially Motivated Crime: Responses in Three European Cities*. London: CRE.

EUMC (2005) *Racist Violence in 15 EU member states: A comparative Overview of Findings from the RAXEN National Focal Points Report 2001–2004*. Vienna: EUMC.

Fyfe, N.R. (2001) *Protecting Intimidated Witnesses*. Aldershot: Ashgate.

Goldston, J. (2001) 'Race and Ethnic Data: A Missing Resource in the Fight against Discrimination', in A. Krizsán (ed.) *Ethnic Monitoring and Data Protection: The European Context*. Budapest: Central European University, pp. 19–41.

Goodey, J. (2005) *Victims and Victimology: Research, Policy and Practice*. London: Longman.

Hall, N. (2005) *Hate Crime*. Cullompton: Willan Publishing.

Holdaway, S. (1999) *Police, Race Relations*, position paper for the Commission on the Future of Multi-Ethnic Britain. London: Runnymede Trust.

Home Office (2004) *Strength in Diversity: Towards a Community Cohesion and Race Equality Strategy*. London: Home Office.

Home Office (2006) *Statistics on Race and the Criminal Justice System*. London: Home Office.

Iganski, P. (1995) 'Why make hate a crime?', *Critical Social Policy*, 19(3): 386–95.

Jacobs, J.B. and Potter, K. (1998) *Hate Crimes: Criminal Law and Identity Politics*. New York: Oxford University Press.

Jenness, V. and Grattet, R. (2005) 'The law-in-between: The effects of organizational perviousness on the policing of hate crime', *Social Problems*, 52(3): 337–59.

Krizsán, A. (2001) (ed.) *Ethnic Monitoring and Data Protection: The European Context*. Budapest: Central European University.

Lees, S. (1997) *Ruling Passions: Sexual Violence, Reputation and Law*. Buckingham: Open University Press.

Lentin, A. (2004) *Racism and Anti-Racism in Europe*. London: Pluto Press.

MacNamara, B.S. (2003) 'New York's Hate Crimes Act of 2000: Problematic and redundant legislation aimed at subjective motivation', *Albany Law Review*, 66: 519–45.

Macpherson, W. (1999) *The Stephen Lawrence Inquiry: Report of an Inquiry by Sir William Macpherson of Cluny*, Cm 4262. London: The Stationery Office.

Nickel, R. (2003) 'The current standards of protection through criminal legislation in the EU member states: A general overview', in *European Strategies to Combat Racism and Xenophobia as a Crime*. European Network Against Racism (ENAR): 5–16.

Oakley, R. (2005) *Policing Racist Crime and Violence*. Vienna: EUMC.

ODIHR (2005) *Report on the Implementation of the Pilot Programme in the Republic of Hungary and Kingdom of Spain*. Warsaw: Law Enforcement Officer Programme on Combating Hate Crime.

OSCE/ODIHR (2005) *Combating Hate Crimes in the OSCE Region*. Warsaw: OSCE.

Ray, L., Smith, D. and Wastell, L. (2003) 'Understanding Racist Violence', in E.A. Stanko (ed.) *The Meanings of Violence*. London: Routledge, pp. 112–29.

Rowe, M. (2004) *Policing, Race and Racism*. Cullompton: Willan Publishing.

Simon, P. (2005) 'Measurement of Racial Discrimination: The Policy Use of Statistics', in *Data to Promote Equality*. Ministry of Labour: Finland, pp. 77–100.

Virtanen, T. (2002) 'Cycles of Racist and Xenophobic Violence among the Youths in Finland', in T. Virtanen (ed.) *Youth and Racist Violence in the Nordic Countries* (www. abo.fi/~tivirtanen/) (accessed 14 October 2004).

Webster, C. (1997) *Local Heroes: Racial Violence Among Asian and White Young People.* Leicester: Leicester University.

Wergens, A. (1999) *Crime Victims in the European Union.* Umeå: The Crime Victim Compensation and Support Authority.

Witte, R. (1996) *Racist Violence and the State.* London: Longman.

Wrench, J. (2005) 'The Measurement of Discrimination: Problems of Comparability and the Role of Research', in *Data to Promote Equality.* Ministry of Labour: Finland, pp. 56–76.

Chapter 17

Victims of corporate crime

Dave Whyte

Introduction

Whether in the form of being exposed to illegal pollution, being ripped off by goods that have been sold at illegally inflated prices, being made ill by sub-standard or out-of-date food, or having our pensions stolen, the illegal-activity of private corporations[1] has a major impact upon our lives. It is no longer controversial in criminology to assert that the social and economic costs of corporate crime tend to exceed the corresponding costs of other forms of crime. Corporate crime injures and kills many times more people than interpersonal violence (Box 1983; Slapper and Tombs 1999; Whyte 2004). Researchers in the US have estimated that the total economic cost of corporate crime is perhaps as much as 20 times the cost of 'mainstream' crime (Albanese 1995; Friedrichs 1996). Although we are very often unaware of being victimised, the sheer magnitude and encroachment of offending by business into our everyday lives means that everyone reading this chapter is likely to have been victimised many times over by corporate crime.

Despite some recognition by victimologists that abuses of power by states and corporations cannot legitimately be ignored by research into victims (Walklate 1989; Elias 1994: 24–6) analyses of the crimes of the powerful remain pretty much absent from victimology, with a few notable exceptions (for example Lynch and Stretesky 2001; Slapper and Tombs 1999: 96–101; Croall 1995, 2007a, 2007b). While some victims groups – most notably Victim Support – have become mainstreamed in the criminal justice system, the victims of corporate crime remain largely untouched by victim–centred reforms and remain outside the remit of specialist victim agencies (Mawby and Walklate 1994; see also Croall 2007a).

Benjamin Mendelsohn, one of the founding fathers of victimology, who in the late 1930s/early 1940s coined the terms 'victimology' and 'victimity', would most probably not have approved of this state of affairs. Mendelsohn (1947) was concerned with establishing an analytical approach to the types of victimisation that are produced by political decisions, by the use of technology, and by 'accidents' as well as by 'crime'. The millions of victims created by the Second World War and the Nazi Holocaust provided some impetus to the project of victimology in the early years of its infancy in the 1940s. It is arguable, then, that the founders of victimology envisaged that the victims of crimes of the powerful would fall squarely within the analytical focus of victimology. [2]

The ideal victim

Despite the early overtures to a broad definition of crime 'victims', the victims of corporate crime remain largely absent from the project of victimology. Victims of corporate crime, in other words, have never been granted 'ideal victim' status; they cannot be described as 'a person or category of individuals who – when hit by crime – *most readily* are given the complete and legitimate status of being a victim' (Christie 1986: 18, emphasis added). The concept of the ideal victim identifies key features of the 'ideal' victimising event, features that normally must be present in order to guarantee public sympathy for the victim: the victim is weak; the victim is carrying out a respectable project; the victim is in a place where she could not possibly be blamed for being; the offender is physically dominant and 'bad'; the offender is unknown to the victim; and finally, the victim needs to be unopposed by counter-powers strong enough to silence the victim. Those who meet those criteria are typically the 'victims' that attract public and media attention and sympathy.

To Christie's typology we can add another dimension: the ideal victim is generally the victim of interpersonal crime. In other words, typically a victim of crime committed by individuals against other individuals. Offenders in corporate crimes rarely fit the profile of 'ideal' offenders, most commonly constructed as 'a dangerous man coming from far away' (1986: 26).

Christie's observations raise key questions for victimology:

- who is granted victim status and why?
- who has the power to define victims as deserving of public sympathy and state support?
- how is the definition and construction of the ideal victim challenged and refined?

Richard Quinney (1972/1994) famously attempted to address those questions in an earlier article, 'Who is the Victim?'. In this analysis, dominant conceptions of the victim are limited to a narrow range of crimes – primarily murder, aggravated assault, forcible rape and robbery. In other words, this conception actively excludes types of crime associated with powerful offenders such as consumer frauds or war crimes. Victim status, therefore, cannot be taken for granted; our conceptions of the victim and of victimisation are optional, discretionary and not innately given. Some of the general observations in Quinney's early work actually presaged, very accurately, the development of contemporary victim discourses. We can see this most clearly in his insights into how victims are systematically used to legitimise or vindicate criminal responses by criminal justice agencies and by government. More than 30 years on, Garland (2001: 143) noted:

> [I]f victims were once the forgotten, hidden casualities of criminal behaviour, they have now returned with a vengeance, brought back into full public view by politicians and media executives who routinely exploit the victim's experience for their own purposes. The sanctified person of the suffering victim has become a valued commodity in the circuits of political and media exchange.

The symbolic victim, or the 'ideal' victim, then, is of value to those involved in the construction of a generally accepted or consensus view of how the criminal justice system should respond to crime (see also Miers 2000). In this sense, the use of particular images and discourses around victimhood has provided states and state institutions with an alibi for the development and expansion of criminal justice systems. It is an alibi that has enabled the state to play a greater role in ordering social relationships by 'governing' through crime (Crawford 1997; Coleman 2004) ostensibly on behalf of the victim. Quinney's assertion that '[t]he victim, a concrete one, apart from the state itself, is held up as a defence of the social order' (1972/1994: 316) thus retains a powerful resonance.

Neo-liberalism, social ordering and the victim

The assault of the 'new right' or 'neo-liberal' governments of the early 1980s upon an overbearing 'nanny' state combined powerfully with an authoritarian populist crusade against some forms of criminality to place the victim at the centre of political discourse (Elias 1993). This ideological elevation of the victim was, in turn, connected to a neo-liberal shift in the relationship between the citizen and the state (Walklate 2003: 120–4; see also Walklate 2006), whereby responsibility for absorbing the costs of welfare was resocialised and transferred back to individuals. The privatisation of public amenities and state industries in the 1980s, in particular the privatisation and contracting out of local authority services, re-enforced this process of individualising welfare or *responsibilisation* as it has become known in neo-Foucauldian criminology (O'Malley 1992; Garland 2000). The victims that were located at the heart of the criminal justice system during this period were not *all* victims, but those that cohered well with the intensification of a 'war on crime' (or more accurately, a war on *some* crimes, since white collar and corporate crime have never been the focus of generalised wars on crime and have by and large been absent in new penology agendas; Braithwaite 2003).

Emile Durkheim taught us that crime helps produce and reproduce a particular moral order. One way of understanding why some victims and not others have been placed at the heart of the criminal justice system is to explore their relationship to the prevailing social and moral climate. This adds another dimension to our understanding of the 'ideal victim'. So, for example, youth crime epidemics are commonly connected to a lack of parental discipline on one hand and a lack of respect for authority on the other. Similarly, the origin of political violence in the UK has been connected to a breakdown in respect for British traditional values among particular sections of the population (Burnett 2006). Arguably, an explicit attempt to connect the origins of crime – and their victims – to a crumbling moral order is present in all wars on crime of the past quarter century.

The victims of high-volume property crimes, burglary, robbery and other thefts, are easier to conceptualise as ideal victims when compared to victims of corporate crime precisely because in liberal democracies, the right to own and enjoy property is inscribed into all aspects of social life, not least the institutions of law.[3] As long as liberal democracies are structured around a system of private property relations, this means that violations of property rights must remain socially unacceptable in those societies. In other words, property offences violate the social and moral order – as well as the legal order – of liberal democracies. This feature of liberal democracies also ensures that corporations, because of the central role they play in upholding and facilitating the system of private property ownership, hold a position that is relatively privileged in the moral order (Glasbeek 2002).

The practical problem that confronts us in 'seeing' corporate crime, then, is a problem of social and moral ordering. As the discussion in this chapter has already noted, it is a problem that is deeply embedded in the way that knowledge about corporate victimisation is accumulated and represented. The next section of this chapter illustrates this process of knowledge construction by exploring in more detail how some of the most devastating forms of corporate crime remain invisible.

Victims of corporate killing

There are at least three types of corporate activity that cause death on a scale that exceeds the 800–900 people murdered in incidents of interpersonal violence every year in the UK. First, the number of people killed as a result of injuries and illnesses caused by work is huge, yet only very sketchily subject to quantitative assessment. One group of researchers based at the University of Stirling estimates that at least 24,000 people die every year from occupational cancers alone (*Hazards*, No. 92, November 2005). This figure rises dramatically when we add other major causes of occupational death such as deaths that result from sudden injury (1200–1500 each year in the UK; Tombs 1999), deaths that result from exposure to other toxins (such as mercury or lead) and deaths that result from long-term musculoskeletal strains.

Second, according to Department of Health estimates, the deaths of at least 24,000 people every year in the UK can be attributed to poisoning by various forms of environmental air pollution. Because of the lack of reliable data, this is certainly an underestimate. It does not, for example, include deaths related to carbon monoxide, ozone, NO2, 1,3-Butadiene, or lead pollution (Department of Health 1998).

Third, corporations can be held responsible for large numbers of food-related illnesses and deaths. The full scale of food poisoning related deaths remains unknown and official data are yet less complete than the two categories already examined. Food poisoning-related deaths are relatively invisible, partly because we do not have the data available to document anything like the full range of food-related deaths. And this is a task that requires some commitment, not least because of the complex way that food infection affects human health. While between 100 and 200 people in the UK die directly as a result of Salmonella and Campylobacter every year, this does not quite capture the full scale of food poisoning related deaths. This scale is more accurately represented by considering that if an individual is infected by food bacteria such as Salmonella or Campylobacter, then that person is three times as likely to die of any other condition or disease within a year of the food infection (Helms *et al.* 2003).

We therefore know that tens of thousands of people are killed by working, by breathing and by eating, although the data are nowhere near complete enough to be able to estimate this death toll with any accuracy. The dearth of data creates another problem for us: given that the substantive issue we are concerned with is corporate crime. Can we assume that these deaths result from *corporate* activity? Well, we can say with some degree of certainty that a large majority of deaths in the first category are caused by employers, and most of those will be profit-making business organisations of some hue (Tombs and Whyte 2007). The absence of accurate data in the second category makes it more difficult to estimate the level of deaths caused by *corporate* pollution. It is not so easy to separate the institutional from the individual sources of environmental pollution (the key example of the latter being personal vehicle use). However, since the data available to us suggest that the bulk of emissions of the largest known killers such as nitrogen oxide, fine particles emissions and sulphur dioxides can be identified as having commercial sources (Coleman *et al.* 2005) we can assume that most environmental pollution is caused directly by corporations as opposed to private individuals. Food poisoning-related deaths, as noted above, are notoriously difficult to quantify, since neither the cause nor the source of infection can always be determined. According to government estimates, however, around half of all food poisoning cases can be attributed to food consumed outside the home (UK Parliament 2003). Although it is possible to argue that the majority of those cases are caused by food sold by outlets that are owned or franchised by large corporations, there is no data that allow us to quantify those cases precisely.

In sum, then, although we can safely assume that the majority of people killed in the categories of death noted above were killed directly as a result of corporate activity, the best we can say is that those deaths can be counted in their tens of thousands. In other words, although we know that corporate killing is a very significant social problem, the first difficulty that confronts us is that the available data do not allow us to know precisely what the scale of the problem is.

Corporate victimisation in crime statistics

The second difficulty we have in recognising corporate crimes as 'crimes' is that they are rarely processed and recorded as crimes. When they are treated as crime, they are more likely to be subject to alternative administrative procedures or informal warnings (Slapper and Tombs 1999; Tombs and Whyte 2007).

In the case of environmental pollution-related deaths it is highly unlikely that *any* result in prosecution. This is partly because cases of deaths brought forward by pollution are not generally subjected to any process of investigation and partly because of the complexities of investigating and prosecuting such a case. Unless the victim lives or works close to a major source of pollution, it may be difficult to identify a link between the source of the pollution and the victim. However, even in cases where identifying a source may be possible, prosecution for causing a death is likely to be difficult to pursue unless there has been a breach of regulations. One issue that takes us out of the scope of criminal process is that much of the air and water pollution that has a deadly effect is often legalised – it is permitted by government licence.

It is lack of investigation, rather than lack of prosecution that renders most deaths caused by work invisible. The first filter in this process is the fact that only a small minority of deaths are reported to the Health and Safety Executive (HSE) or other regulatory authorities. A very low percentage of all deaths caused by sudden injury – the most visible category of deaths at work – are dealt with by the regulatory authority. In 2002/03, 68 deaths were prosecuted by HSE. If we use Tombs' estimates cited above, this may be as little as a twentieth of all deaths caused by sudden injury. If we include the deaths resulting from long-term illness and disease caused by work, this figure represents a tiny fraction of all deaths. The second filter in the process is that not all of the small proportion of deaths that *are* investigated will be deemed prosecutable by investigators. Despite the likelihood that between two-thirds and three-quarters of all deaths caused by working result from criminal breaches of safety law, only around a quarter reach the courts (Tombs and Whyte 2007).

Prosecutions of food-related deaths by regulators are similarly rare. Many if not most food poisoning cases are likely to be a direct result of *criminal* breaches of food hygiene and food safety legislation. A Food Standards Agency (2001) report found that 45 per cent of all inspections of premises used for food preparation and sale uncover breaches of food safety law that lead to formal enforcement action. Very few of those, however, are ever prosecuted. The same report noted that around half of all local authorities failed to lay one single prosecution for breaches of food law in 2000/01.

In the majority of cases, we therefore have little idea about whether the deaths caused by corporate activity might have involved criminal breaches of the law, because they are rarely investigated as such. Even when they are investigated, regulatory agencies tend to prosecute only as a last resort (Hawkins 2002), not least because the dominant regulatory approach is to seek compliance rather than strict enforcement of the criminal law (Pearce and Tombs 1990; Davis 2004).

Even in cases where corporate crimes are investigated and processed as crimes, they are not systematically recorded in government crime statistics (see Tombs 1999). This is partly because in the UK Home Office recorded crime figures are derived from the returns made by police forces. No returns are requested from the various national regulatory agencies (in the cases noted above, the HSE, the Food Standards Agency and the Environment Agency/Scottish Environmental Protection Agency) or from local authority regulators. Corporate crime data sources therefore remain as fragmented as the complex multitude of agencies that separately collate and publish their data. However, questions on corporate crime have never been included in official victim surveys such as the British and Scottish Crime Surveys.

As other contributions to this volume note, victim surveys emerged in the early 1970s as a method of uncovering the 'dark figure' of crime. The US National Crime Survey was established in 1972 and the British Crime Survey (BCS) in 1982. From its beginnings, the BCS faced a challenge from critical criminologists for the narrow definition of crime that it adopted, particularly in relation to the exclusion of sexual violence, domestic violence and white-collar crime.

The victimised corporation

The lack of data that are available to allow us to know anything much about the victims of corporate crime contrasts starkly with the burgeoning data and academic research on business as a victim (as opposed to perpetrator) of crime. Despite claims about the under-representation of crimes against business in the literature (Burrows 1997) and in crime statistics (Taylor 2003), reviews of the literature indicate a major surge in the research since the mid 1990s (Hopkins 2002), including the emergence of international surveys of crime against business (Frate 2004). The Home Office now organises a regular Commercial Victimisation Survey to complement the British Crime Survey (Shury 2002) and research reports on various aspects of business victimisation are now commissioned regularly (for example Levi et al. 2005; Taylor 2004).

The literature generally paints a picture of the toll of business victimisation as more ubiquitous and economically damaging than offences committed against individuals (for example, Hill 2004). It is an assertion that has gained some currency in criminology over the past decade. Thus, for example, Shapland notes that '[t]he prevalence of crime in the retail sector is higher than for residents' (Shapland 1995: 263; see also Felson and Clarke 1997).

Businesses, by positioning themselves as victims of crime, similarly contribute to a more generalised, hegemonic, reconstruction of the notion of victimhood. Discourses around business crime are characterised by a sentiment that implores us to think of business as part of a broader 'community of victims'. Thus, as David Frost, the Director General of the British Chambers of Commerce notes: 'Business is at the heart of any vibrant community and therefore crime against business is an attack upon the fabric of the whole community' (Frost 2004). The reconstruction of victimhood thus allows business to assert that a crime against business is a crime against all of us. We all suffer price rises as a result of shoplifting, breaking and entering businesses, the general hiking up of insurance premiums, and so on.

The movement against 'business crime' can be conceptualised as part of a process of responsibilisation. This conceptualisation is empirically supported by the proliferation of government–business partnerships set up to deal with crimes against business, indicated by the 195 local business crime partnerships in the UK listed on the Action Against Business Crime website (http://www.brc.org.uk/aabc/index.htm). The current effort to reduce business crime is being organised on a scale that is certainly unprecedented. And its primary purpose is of course to reduce crimes against business. But this is by no means the only social effect of this proliferation.

The way that crime control efforts are directed have wider impacts upon the way that crime is constructed as a social problem. Sim (2004), commenting on the enduring discourse of the 'victimised state', has argued that the redefinition of the state, or particular branches of the state, as 'victim' plays a 'central and complex ideological role ... in constructing and positioning state servants as always the victims and never the victimisers'. The key effect of victimised state discourses is that they allow the state to remobilise effort around the repair of a moral order, invariably in need of a 'further injection of law and order' (2004: 126), to distract attention from the institutionalised nature of violent state practices and to allow the state to virtually monopolise the debate about violence and danger (2004: 127). Similarly, a victimised business discourse places corporations at the heart of debates about victimisation. As the clamour for more public–private sector resources to be diverted towards crime control grows, corporations are progressively empowered to dominate the law and order debate (Coleman 2004).

To achieve victim status, businesses must assert a 'personality' beyond their juridical status as a legal person. This is unlikely to be fully achieved since corporate victims 'lack human vulnerability, having no bloodied faces to display, no feelings to be injured, no fears to be allayed, no lifestyles to be undermined' (Young 2002: 134). First, it is not the business itself that suffers the consequences of violence against its employees but more often than not the most vulnerable front-line workers within the organisation that suffer violence. Second, businesses are much better able to absorb the costs of crime precisely because they are corporations and not individuals. Businesses can offset the costs of thefts or shoplifting by redistributing costs across the business, they are better placed to insure themselves against major thefts, and the rules of incorporation generally give the owners of private companies legal protections which indemnify them against losses. Yet, through their emergent role in crime reduction partnerships, corporations come to debates on crime from an increasingly powerful position that has served to heighten our awareness of various forms of business victimisation, and begins to concretise the hitherto abstract concept of 'crimes against business'.

This is significant when we return to a discussion of crime committed *by* business, since, despite a growing public awareness of the devastating social impact of corporate offending (Tombs and Whyte 2003a) many forms of corporate victimisation appear to us in a relatively abstract form. This remains the case because of the difficulties associated with identifying corporate offenders outlined already in this chapter. We are discouraged from thinking about major harms – such as illness caused by work, pollution or food poisoning – as having been produced by corporate activity. Rather, they are typically constructed as 'accidents' rather than harms that are preventable and avoidable. The way that the *law* constructs those harms further discourages us from considering them as 'crimes' when compared, for example, to interpersonal crimes (Tombs 2007). Thus, we do not think about our employer or our local supermarket as a habitual criminal, despite the fact that they routinely break the law in ways that are harmful to us (Slapper and Tombs 1999; Box 1983). In short, at the same time as the bid for corporate victimhood gathers momentum, there remain key ideological barriers in place that prevent corporate criminals being regarded as 'usual suspects'.

Criminology's traditional concern with the 'victimising event' acts as a mechanism that is highly effective in obscuring corporate offending even if it is not immediately obvious to us. It was the search for a set of empirical indicators of 'victim precipitation' (how the victim contributes to the offence by provoking the offender or creating the necessary conditions for the offence to occur) that was the dominant mode of empirical research in victimology until the 1970s. This mode of research emphasised the closely observed interaction between 'criminal' and 'victim' around a small set of very specific 'crime events'.

As Walklate notes, conventional criminology generally views crime as a series of atomised occurrences that exist in isolation from the ongoing, ever-present power relationship between the victim and the offender (2003: 127–9). A point made consistently by feminist criminologists is that an analysis of male violence is incomplete if only conceptualised in the former sense. Male violence can only be understood as part of an ongoing state of unequal *gendered* power relations (2003: 127–9). In corporate crimes, a concept of a 'victimising event' is also of limited value precisely because the relationship between the victim and the offender is also based upon an ongoing relationship of unequal power.

The relationship between workers and their employer in the workplace is unequal precisely because the employee is in a subordinate position to the employer and at the same time relies upon regular employment for her or his livelihood. Safety conditions in the workplace might be negotiated between both sides, or may not be, depending upon the strength of collective organisation in the workplace. Vulnerability to be disciplined or ultimately sacked can discourage workers from taking steps to actively resist unsafe working regimes (Woolfson *et al.* 1996). Similarly, the commercial relationship between buyer and seller in the market place is not an equal one. In most contemporary markets an increasing number of sellers enjoy a privileged market position because of trends towards *monopolisation* (the domination of the market by a small number of businesses or group of jointly-owned businesses) and *cartelisation* (the illegal agreement between different businesses to apply a uniform price or surcharge to a particular good or service). The existence of monopolies and cartels limits the real choice of the buyer to find a safe or reasonably priced product elsewhere. Recent high-profile examples of price fixing in the UK have involved criminal conspiracies by household names, including well-known toy manufactures and distributers, airlines and high street sellers and manufacturers of electrical goods. The six largest milk companies in Scotland are, at the time of writing this chapter, under investigation for an overpricing scam which, it is alleged, involved the sale of milk to schools at illegally inflated prices (*The Scotsman*, 7 September 2006).

In such cases, often it is the offender that has a monopoly on information about the costs of production. Precisely the same point can be made about the safety of a product. Consider the example of contaminated food. If a consumer reads a newspaper report about a supermarket being prosecuted for selling contaminated chicken, that person can of course go to another supermarket. But often such cases go unreported and even when they are reported, they are newspaper stories and may therefore be limited in the detail (never mind the accuracy) that they carry about the case. Assuming that the knowledge is accurate and it does reach the consumer, a subsequent issue is that the consumer has limited ability to establish whether their chosen supermarket imposes higher standards of meat preparation than the criminal supermarket reported in the newspaper. How would the consumer know?

The chances of the consumer buying uncontaminated chicken may be increased if it is bought from a butcher who gets it from a known reputable source, rather than from an anonymous supplier who deals in mass-produced meat. The problem is that the former tend to be much more expensive, and it may take resources that the average person does not have readily available to find out where their food comes from or assess its safety (see also Croall 2007b).

The fact that consumers may have to pay a higher price for safer, better-quality goods, or may have to use resources that are beyond the means of the majority of people, alerts us to a relationship between 'ability to pay' – or relative economic power – and the likelihood of being exposed to corporate crime. In the workplace, a parallel observation can be made. It is the most casualised workers who are the least likely to be insured against injury or to have access to compensation schemes. At the same time, casualised, unskilled workers tend to be exposed to high risks at work because their relatively subordinate economic position can affect their ability to resist those risks. When a worker has less relative economic power, she has less opportunity to oppose dangerous work regimes by organising resistance with other workers. In lower-wage economies, or in labour markets when employment terms are shorter, workers will be in a weak position to seek safer work elsewhere. On the other hand, where workers are in a relatively more powerful position, they are better positioned to resist dangers in the workplace. This point is supported by a body of evidence that demonstrates a positive relationship between a strong trade union presence in the workplace and a reduced chance of being injured or killed by working (Tombs and Whyte 2007). Similarly, there is a close relationship between structural inequalities and the likelihood of our exposure to pollution. Friends of the Earth's (1999) study *Pollution Injustice* concluded that the poorest families are on average twice as likely to have a polluting factory in their neighbourhood. The study showed that exposure to pollution is intensified at the bottom of the social hierarchy. A total of 662 of the UK's largest factories were located in areas where the average household income was less than £15,000, yet there were only five located in areas where the average income was £30,000 or over.

Each of those examples point to the centrality of social class as a determining structure in shaping the chances of victimisation. However, this is not to imply that conflicts around corporate crime are not mediated by other social cleavages of inequality. Womens' structured vulnerability as consumers and as workers is central to understanding the unequal distribution of corporate crime victimisation along lines of class *and* gender (Croall 1995; Haantz 2000; Szockyj and Fox 1996; Wonders and Danner 2002). This work has documented how cosmetic and health products that are particularly targeted at women are often relatively untested and unregulated. Key examples here are those products that intervene in womens' bodies and mental health. Products that have caused harm to women on a devastating scale include those associated with pregnancy (e.g. Thalidomide), menstruation (tampons with associated risks of TSS), physical appearance (silicon breast implants, diet products) and psychological health (tranquillisers) (Szockyj and Fox 1996).

Occupational segregation and differentiation in working conditions leaves women more vulnerable to offences committed by their employer than men (Croall 1995). More than half of all employed women in Britain work in three broad categories of industry: the distributive trades (shops, mail order, warehouses); miscellaneous services (laundries, catering, dry cleaning, etc.); and professional and scientific (typists, secretaries, teachers and nurses). The first two sectors are notoriously casualised and most jobs in those sectors are part-time (Hakim 1993). Because women tend to be employed in more casualised, part-time work in comparison to men they are less likely to have the protection of a trade union to bargain and represent them on safety matters – or on other aspects of the law: unfair dismissal/sex discrimination and so on. Relative lack of representation also means that we are less likely to know about some of the hazards associated with women's work: for example, the new evidence of industrial injuries associated with RSI and relatively unknown hazards associated with the combined effect of chemicals in cleaning. Research by NGO, the Women's Environmental Network has demonstrated how women in the beauty and hairdressing industries are routinely exposed to cocktails of cosmetic chemicals whose combined effects are largely unresearched (see http://www.wen.org). In global terms, women's work is increasingly concentrated in dangerous industries, not least garment manufacture and some forms of highly hazardous agricultural industries (see http://www.women-ww.org/index.html).

The chances of being poisoned or injured by working may increase or decrease depending upon the way that production is organised and controlled by regulatory standards in a particular country. As regimes of consumption and production have grown in concert with the expansion of global markets, the ability of corporations to locate abroad as producers, sellers, investors and so on has been enhanced. The expression of global markets creates opportunities for producing products in, and exporting products to, other countries. It is the way that those markets are structured that both creates inequalities and intensifies vulnerabilities to corporate activity. As some forms of hazardous production are moved abroad to less developed economies, this intensifies the pressure on workers in developed countries to compete. One way of competing is to drop standards in working conditions and in the production process. Cheaper production very often means less stringent safety or environmental standards. This is a social process that is known popularly as the 'race to the bottom'.

Similarly, the trading relationship between countries is always shaped by the degree of inequality between their economies. The phrase 'product dumping' is used to describe how sub-standard or cheaper goods are placed in foreign markets to gain a market advantage, to drive prices of competitors, and perhaps even simply to offload goods that do not meet regulatory standards in stronger economies. The cost of the 'race to the bottom' precipitated by product dumping in less-regulated economies is often paid for by consumers and the public in the form of exposure to untested goods or exposure to goods that are sub-standard or too harmful to be sold in developed economies. This is precisely what happened in the case of the Dalkon Shield, a contraceptive IUD device produced by the pharmaceutical company A.H. Robbins in the 1970s and 1980s. The company marketed and advertised using falsified claims about its safety, despite senior management being made aware that the device carried serious health risks. In the US alone, it is reported that the Dalkon Shield injured 235,000 women, killed 33 and caused 200 cases of spontaneous septic abortion. Soon after it began to discover problems in the US, A.H. Robbins began an aggressive export policy to 'dump' the devices on third world economies. Subsidised by the government agency USAID, as part of its policy of promoting birth control in the poor south, the company sold millions of unsterilised Dalkon Shields in the third world, eventually distributing a total of 4.5 million in 80 countries. They did so in the knowledge that less-developed countries would have even lower standards of regulation, and even less access to product information than the US (Mintz 1985).

The market processes that create and reinforce vulnerability are evident not only in developing countries by also *within* populations in the most advanced economies. This is evidenced by the creation of unequal exposure to vulnerability between different groups in the developed world. A social division that Bullard (1994) calls 'environmental apartheid', for example, structures the vulnerability of black people in the US to toxic poisons in their neighbourhood. He notes that in eight southern states, three-quarters of hazardous waste landfill sites are located in predominately African American communities. Around 60 per cent of African-Americans across the US live in neighbourhoods with abandoned toxic waste sites.

We therefore need to think in terms of how gender and race interact with social class to expose particular groups to highly differentiated levels of vulnerability to corporate crime. Vulnerability to corporate crime is initially determined by – and then reinforced by – the relative location of victims in asymmetrical relations of production, distribution and consumption.

Conclusion

In his ground-breaking text Silently Silenced (2004), Thomas Mathiesen sets out a framework for understanding how mechanisms of silencing resistance to power in advanced capitalism act in ways that are not immediately obvious to us. It is a framework that is useful for structuring our understanding of how corporate crime victimisation remains absent from mainstream corporate crime agendas. Silencing can be found in the various techniques that act to 'pulverse' the 'totality' of and the 'context' for social relationships. Pulverisation occurs when the context for an event is isolated from the event itself. There are echoes here of Fromm's (2003: 216–217) remarks on how 'facts', when they are isolated from a structuralised whole, paralyse our ability to think critically. The example Mathiesen uses is the death of oil workers in the North Sea. When those deaths occur, he argues, fundamental questions tend to arise which establish a relationship between the profit motive and the lack of safety on oil platforms. Those links are pulverised precisely because 'when *many* people perceive such a totality or context, the activity itself begins to be threatened' (ibid.: 37; emphasis in the original). Thus, Mathiesen argues that the process of silencing can take place without mobilising any particular apparatus.

In the case of the victims of corporate crime, as we have seen, the silence of criminologists and victimologists is not a function of an obvious apparatus, but stems on one hand from a systematic exclusion from crime agendas of data and knowledge about corporate offending. On the other hand, it stems from a related failure to understand and define this form of victimisation as a crime amidst the cacophony of noise that surrounds other selected groups of crime victims. At the same time the discourse of the victimised corporation allows business organisations to pulverise the totality of the relationship between business activity and crime. It is pulverising effect that can be measured by the fact that we now have several regular national business victim surveys (organised by business associations and by the Home Office as part of the BCS) and we are yet to have one single comprehensive victim survey of corporate crime in this country commissioned by the Home Office or any other organisation (Tombs and Whyte 2003b). This, we might say, is silencing by creating noise. Under such conditions, it is less likely that we will be in a position to challenge the ubiquity of corporate offending noted throughout this chapter. Who, for example, has ever objected to National Semi Conductor's involvement in the Scottish Business Crime Centre (http://www.sbcc.org.uk/public/Memberships/tlsg,jsp) on the basis of evidence that the company knowingly exposed workers to carcinogenic chemicals at its plant in Greenock (see for example McCourt 2006).

Crucial to understanding how this process of silencing currently operates is an appreciation of the moral and political elevation of a so-called free-enterprise society and the process of business reification. The 'bonfire of controls' that stripped away many of the protections afforded to workers and consumers (Tombs 1996) during this period included: the attacks upon workers trade union rights and consequent erosion of national bargaining privatisation; financial deregulation; tightened controls on public spending and so on, have at the same time combined to produce conditions that allow some forms of corporate crime to flourish. The pensions and endowments mortgage thefts of the late 80s and early 90s that created victims of corporate crime by the million were directly produced by financial deregulation policies (Fooks 2003a and 2003b). 'Corporate manslaughter' in the UK became a major issue of public concern following a series of disasters that included Kings Cross, Piper Alpha, the Marchioness, and the Clapham and Purley train crashes. Each of those 'disasters' made clear the fatal contradictions between safety and profits and became symbolic of the state of the economy after almost a decade of Thatcherism (Tombs and Whyte 2003a; Tombs 1995: 348–351).

Crucially, it was the noise made by the organisations that represent the victims of those crimes that was the key factor in forcing the issue of corporate killing onto the political agenda. Although the UK's new Corporate Manslaughter and Corporate Homicide Bill has been weakened by years of corporate lobbying, it is hardly likely that there would have been such a bill in the first place had there been no campaign by the trade unions and by organisations such as Disaster Action (http://www.disasteraction.org.uk/) the Simon Jones Memorial Campaign (http://www.simonjones.org.uk), the Hazards Campaign (http://www.hazsardscampaign.org.uk) and the Centre for Corporate Accountability (http://www.corporateaccountability.org/), all of whom crucially brought into public view the privileged treatment of corporate killers within the criminal justice system. Perhaps they do not appear on *Crimewatch UK* or feature very often in dramatisations of crime in episodes of *Taggart*, *Regus* or *The Bill*, but the fact the victims of corporate crime continue to organise opposition tells us that they are unlikely to remain silenced, or their campaign for justice pulverised.

Researchers who recognise that the prevailing wind in criminology is pulverising our ability to understand the problem of crime might take inspiration from the second Islington Crime survey. This was one victim survey that *did* ask respondents about their exposure to corporate crimes. In this study 19 per cent of respondents reported having been deliberately overcharged for goods or services they had purchased over a 12 month period, and 5 per cent reported being victim of a dangerous incident at work (30 times the rate normally reflected in official statistics; Pearce 1990). This is precisely the type of activity criminologists need to engage in if we are to resist our 'silent silencing'.

Acknowledgement

This chapter owes an incalculable debt to the insights I have gained from working with Steve Tombs. Many of the insights here are his; any mistakes are mine alone.

Further reading

Croall, H. (2001) *Understanding White Collar Crime*. Buckingham: Open University Press.
Slapper, G. and Tombs, S. (1999) *Corporate Crime*. Harlow: Longman.
Szockyj, E. and Fox, J. (1996) *The Corporate Victimisation of Women*. Boston, MA: Northeastern University Press.
Tombs, S. and Whyte, D. (2007) *Safety Crimes*. Cullompton: Willan Publishing.

Notes

1 In this chapter, the term 'corporation' is used throughout. The term is used to mean private sector, for-profit business organisations. For a definition of corporate crime, see Tombs and Whyte 2006.

2 In this respect, it is also worth noting that most criminologists who were contemporaries of Mendelsohn would have been aware of the publication of Edwin Sutherland's influential text *White Collar Crime* in 1949.

3 The famous cliché that 'property is nine tenths of the law' is reflected in the fact that 95 per cent of crimes recorded by the police are property related (Lacey and Wells 1998, cited in Norrie 2001).

4 See http://www.disasteraction.org.uk/

5 See http://www.simonjones.org.uk

6 See http://www.hazardscampaign.org.uk

7 See http://www.corporateaccountability.org/

References

Albanese, J. (1995) *White Collar Crime in America*. Englewood Cliffs, NJ: Prentice Hall.

Allen, J., Forrest, S., Levi, M., Roy, H. and Sutton, M. (ed. D. Wilson) (2005) *Fraud and Technology Crimes: Findings from the 2002/03 British Crime Survey and 2003 Offending, Crime and Justice Survey*, Home Office Online Report 34/05. London: Home Office.

Box, S. (1983) *Power, Crime and Mystification*. London: Routledge.

Braithwaite, J. (2003) 'What's wrong with the sociology of punishment', *Theoretical Criminology*, 7(1): 5–28.

Bullard, R. (1994) *Dumping in Dixie: Race, Class, and Environmental Quality*. Boulder, CO: Westview Press.

Burnett, J. (2006) 'From Community Cohesion to Community Coercion', paper presented to Social Impacts of the War on Terrorism seminar, Melbourne Trades Hall 13–14 July.

Burrows, J. (1997) 'Criminology and Business Crime: Building the Bridge', in M. Felson and R. Clarke (eds) *Business and Crime Prevention*. Monsey, NY: Criminal Justice Press.

Christie, N. (1986) 'The Ideal Victim', in E. Fattah (ed.) *From Crime Policy to Victim Policy: Reorienting the Justice System*. London: Macmillan.

Coleman, R. (2004) *Reclaiming the Streets: Surveillance, Social Control and the City*. Cullompton: Willan Publishing.

Coleman, R., Tombs, S. and Whyte, D. (2005) 'Capital, crime control and statecraft in the entrepreneurial city', *Urban Studies*, 42(13).

Crawford, A. (1997) *The Local Governance of Crime: Appeals to Community and Partnerships*. Oxford: Clarendon.

Croall, H. (1995) 'Target Women: Womens' Victimisation from White Collar Crime', in R. Dobash and L. Noakes (eds) *Gender and Crime*. Cardiff: Cardiff University Press.

Croall, H. (2007a) 'White Collar and Corporate Victimisation', in P. Francis, P. Davies and C. Greer (eds) *Victims and Society*. London: Sage.

Croall, H. (2007b) 'White Collar and Corporate Victimisation', in H. Pontell (ed.) *Contemporary Issues in White Collar Crime*. Dordrecht: Springer.

Davis, C. (2004) *Making Companies Safe: What Works?* London: Centre for Corporate Accountability.

Department of Health (1998) *Quantification of the Effects of Air Pollution on Health in the United Kingdom*, Committee on the Medical Effects of Air Pollutants. London: The Stationary Office.

Elias, R. (1993) *Victims Still: The Political Manipulation of Crime Victims*. London: Sage.

Elias, R. (1994) 'Paradigms and Paradoxes of Victimology', in C. Sumner, M. Israel, M. O'Connell and R. Sarre (eds) *International Victimology: Selected Papers from the 8th International Symposium*. Canberra: Australian Institute of Criminology.

Felson, M. and Clarke, R. (1997) *Business and Crime Prevention*. Monsey, NY: Criminal Justice Press.

Food Standards Agency (2001) *Draft Report on Local Authority Food Enforcement in the UK*. London: FSA.

Fooks, G. (2003a) 'In the Valley of the Blind the One-eyed Man is King: Corporate Crime and the Myopia of Financial Regulation', in S. Tombs and D. Whyte (eds) *Unmasking the Crimes of the Powerful: Scrutinising States and Corporations*. New York: Peter Lang.

Fooks, G. (2003b) 'Contrasts in tolerance: The peculiar case of financial regulation', *Contemporary Politics*, 9(2): 127–42.

Frate, A. (2004) 'The International Crime Business Survey: Findings from nine Central-Eastern European cities, *European Journal on Criminal Policy and Research*, 10(2–3): 137–61.

Friends of the Earth (1999) *Pollution Hits the Poor Hardest*, press release, 26 April.

Friedrichs, D. (1996) *Trusted Criminals: White Collar Crime in Contemporary Society*. Belmont, CA: Wadsworth.

Fromm, E. (2001) *Fear of Freedom*. London: Routledge.

Frost, D. (2004) 'Foreword' *Setting Business Free from Crime: A Crime Against Business Survey*. London: British Chambers of Commerce.

Garland, D. (2000) 'The culture of high crime societies: Some preconditions of recent law and order policies', *British Journal of Criminology*, 40: 347–75.

Garland, D. (2001) *The Culture of Control: Crime and Social Order in Contemporary Society*. Chicago: University of Chicago Press.

Glasbeek, H. (2002) *Wealth by Stealth: Corporate Crime, Corporate Law and the Perversion of Democracy*. Toronto: Between the Lines.

Haantz, S. (2000) *Women and White Collar Crime*. National White Collar Crime Centre (available on request from webteam@nw3c.org).

Hakim, C. (1993) 'The myth of rising female employment', *Work Employment and Society*, 7(1).

Hawkins, K. (2002) *Law as Last Resort: Prosecution Decision Making in a Regulatory Agency*. Oxford: Oxford University Press.

Helms, M., Vastrup, P., Gerner-Smidt, P. and Molbak, K. (2003) 'Short and long term mortality associated with foodborne bacterial gastrointestinal infections: Registry based study', *British Medical Journal*, 15 February, no. 326: 357–60.

Hill, S. (2004) *Setting Business Free from Crime: A Crime Against Business Survey*. London: British Chambers of Commerce.

Hopkins, M. (2002) 'Crimes against businesses: The way forward for future research', *British Journal of Criminology*, 42(4).

Lacey, N. and Wells, C. (1998) *Reconstructing Criminal Law*, 2nd edn. London: Butterworth.

Lynch, M. and Stretesky, P. (2001) 'Toxic crimes: Examining corporate victimization of the general public employing medical and epidemiological evidence', *Critical Criminology*, 10: 153–72.

Mathiesen, T. (2004) *Silently Silenced: Essays on the Creation of Acquiescence in Modern Society*. Winchester: Waterside Press.

Mawby, R. and Walklate, S. (1994) *Critical Victimology*. London: Sage.

McCourt, J. (2006) 'Worker Health at National Semiconductor, Greenock (Scotland): Freedom to Kill?', in T. Smith, D. Somerfeld and D. Pellow (eds) *Challenging the Chip: Labour Rights and Environmental Justice in the Global Electronics Industry*. Philadelphia: Temple University Press.

Mendelsohn, B. (1947) 'New bio–psychosocial horizons: Victimology', *American Law Review*, 13.

Miers, D. (2000) 'Taking the Law into their own Hands: Victims as Offenders', in A. Crawford and J. Goodey (eds) *Integrating a Victim Perspective within Criminal Justice: International Debates*. Aldershot: Ashgate.

Mintz, M. (1985) *At Any Cost: Corporate Greed, Women and the Dalkon Shield*. New York: Pantheon.

Norrie, A. (2001) *Crime, Reason and History: A Critical Introduction to Criminal Law*, 2nd edn. London: Butterworth.

O'Malley, P. (1992) 'Risk, power and crime prevention', *Economy and Society*, 21: 252–275.

Pearce, F. (1990) 'Commercial and Conventional Crime in Islington', in A. Crawford, T. Jones, T. Woodhouse and J. Young (1990) *The Second Islington Crime Survey*. London: Middlesex Polytechnic Centre for Crimnology.

Pearce, F. and Tombs, S. (1990) 'Ideology, hegemony and empiricism', *British Journal of Criminology*, 30(4).

Quinney, R. (1972/1994) 'Who is the Crime Victim?', in P. Rock (ed.) *Victimology*. Aldershot: Dartmouth.

Shapland, J. (1995) 'Preventing Retail–Sector Crimes', in M. Tonry and D. Farrington (eds) *Building a Safer Society: Strategic Approaches to Crime Prevention–Crime and Justice: A Review of Research*. Chicago: University of Chicago Press.

Shury, J., Speed, M., Vivian, D. and Kuechel, A. (2002) *Crime Against Retail and Manufacturing Premises: Findings from the 2002 Commercial Victimisation Survey*, Home Office Online Report 37/05. London: Home Office.

Sim, J. (2004) 'The Victimised State and the Mystification of Social Harm', in P. Hillyard, C. Pantazis, S. Tombs and D. Gordon (eds) *Beyond Criminology: Taking Harm Seriously*. London: Pluto.

Slapper, G. and Tombs, S. (1999) *Corporate Crime*. Harlow: Longman.

Szockyj, E. and Fox, J. (1996) *The Corporate Victimisation of Women*. Boston, MA: Northeastern University Press.

Taylor, J. (2004) *Crime Against Retail and Manufacturing Premises: Findings from the 2002 Commercial Victimisation Survey*, Home Office Research Findings 259. London: Home Office Research, Development and Statistics Directorate.

Taylor, N. (2003) 'Under reporting of crime against small businesses: Attitudes towards police and reporting practices', *Policing and Society*, 13(1).

Tombs, S. (1995) 'Law, resistance and reform: "Regulating" safety crimes in the UK', *Social and Legal Studies*, 4(3).

Tombs, S. (1996) 'Injury, death and the deregulation fetish: the politics of occupational safety regulation in UK manufacturing industries', *International Journal of Health Services*, 26(2): 309–26.

Tombs, S. (1999) 'Death and work in Britain', *Sociological Review*, 47(2): 345–67.

Tombs, S. (2007 forthcoming) '"Violence", safety crimes and criminology', *British Journal of Criminology*.

Tombs, S. and Whyte, D. (2003a) 'Two steps forward, one step back: Towards accountability for workplace deaths?', *Policy and Practice in Health and Safety*, 1(1).

Tombs, S. and Whyte, D. (2003b) 'Scrutinising the Powerful? Crime, Contemporary Political Economy and Critical Social Research', in S. Tombs and D. Whyte (eds)

Unmasking the Crimes of the Powerful: Scrutinising States and Corporations. New York: Peter Lang.

Tombs, S. and Whyte, D. (2006) 'Corporate Crime', in E. McLaughlin and J. Muncie, (eds) *The Sage Dictionary of Criminology*, 2nd edn. London: Sage.

Tombs, S. and Whyte, D. (2007) *Safety Crimes*. Cullompton: Willan Publishing.

UK Parliament (2003) *Postnote: Food Poisoning*. London: Parliamentary Office of Science and Technology.

Walklate, S. (1989) *Victimology: The Victim and the Criminal Justice Process*. London: Routledge.

Walklate, S. (2003) *Understanding Criminology: Current Theoretical Debates*, 2nd ed. Buckingham: Open University Press.

Walklate, S. (2006) 'Community Safety and Victims: Who is the Victim of Community Safety?', in P. Squires (ed.) *Community Safety: Critical Perspectives on Policy and Practice*. Bristol: Policy Press.

Whyte, D. (2004) 'Corporate Crime and Regulation', in D. Wilson and J. Muncie (eds) *Student Handbook of Criminal Justice*. London: Cavendish.

Wonders, N. and Danner, M. (2002) 'Globalisation, State-Corporate Crime and Women: The Strategic Role of Women's NGOs in the new World Order', in G. Potter (ed.) *Controversies in White Collar Crime*. Cincinnati, OH: Anderson.

Woolfson, C., Foster, J. and Beck, M. (1996) *Paying for the Piper: Capital and Labour in Britain's Offshore Oil Industry*, London: Mansell.

Young, R. (2002) 'Testing the Limits of Restorative Justice: The Case of Corporate Victims', in C. Hoyle and R. Young (eds.) *New Visions of Crime Victims*. Oxford: Hart.

Chapter 18

Cultural victimology: are we all victims now?

Gabe Mythen

Introduction

In recent years both the idea of the victim, and the material structures through which victimisation is defined, have increasingly been shaped and influenced by cultural forces. To grasp both the processes through which meanings are attributed to victims and the institutional networks that emerge in response to victimhood, due consideration needs to be given to the cultural framework within which notions of criminality and victimisation are located. In this contribution dominant understandings of criminal victimisation are situated in the contemporary context and analysed in relation to broader macro-social shifts. Drawing primarily on examples from the UK, the changing place of the victim in society is considered through an evaluation of prevalent political discourses, media representations and established modes of crime control. The chapter is underpinned by the belief that victimology requires a robust theoretical framework to broach current problems and issues surrounding the place and role of the victim in the criminal justice process. In order to advance research in the area of cultural victimology, it begins by addressing the relationship between given understandings of the victim and the operation of cultural processes. Having highlighted the gravitation towards culture within criminology, it goes on to explore the ways in which the media represents and influences the range – and, moreover, the narrowness – of meanings commonly attributed to victims. From here, the cultural construction of the terrorist threat in the UK is utilised as a way of tapping into the institutional tendency to use the figurehead of the victim as a way of organising and regulating social activity. Centring on the shaping of 'new terrorism', the chapter elucidates how cultural institutions play a major role in defining crime risks and circulating dominant ideas about victimisation. The example of 'new terrorism' is used to bring into view current debates about the 'risk society' and the generation of a 'culture of fear'. By unpicking the work of Beck and Furedi, I suggest ways in which the cultural can be more firmly factored into victimology. Having scrutinised both the utility and the limitations of these macro theories, I move on to discuss how the cultural issues that remain might meaningfully be addressed in the future. In the final section some speculative comments are made on the ways in which the hegemonic discourse of 'new terrorism' feeds contemporary imaginings of the universal victim and reveals the explicitly political uses to which the crime victim is being put. However, before looking at these possibilities, it is first necessary to consider the evolving meaning of the victim and to highlight the conceptual movement toward culture within criminology.

From cultural criminology to cultural victimology?

Up until the late twentieth century, expenditure on crime control in most western nations had been skewed towards preventing crime, rather than resourcing the needs of victims. This unevenness was reflected in mainstream criminology which has been offender rather than victim focused. Although criminological interest in victims is far from novel, it is fair to say that the victim has been sidelined in administrative criminology in favour of a focus on criminals, sentencing and preventative legislation. It is only relatively recently that victims of crime have been taken seriously as subjects of study within criminology (Williams 2005: 493). In the 1970s and 1980s, reported crime rates rose in the UK and one of the products of this was a rise in public and institutional concern about victims of crime. In the last two decades, the victim has moved from the margins to the centre of debates about crime and violence, with interest in victimisation in the academe rising alongside the growth in political initiatives oriented towards the victim and the expansion of victim support networks (Zedner 2002: 420).

Of course, the turn towards the victim is also the result of a deeper and wider set of macro transitions (see O'Malley 2006; Walklate 2007). One of the outcomes of these transitions has been an attempt to reduce crime rates by raising awareness about crime and informing the public about strategies of victim avoidance. An unfortunate consequence of such consciousness-raising initiatives has been a net rise in public fears about crime and mounting numbers of people classifying themselves as victims of crime. In 1979–80 the total number of claims to the UK Criminal Injuries Compensation Authority (CICA) stood at around 22,000. In 2003–04, over 70,000 applications were received and more than £2 million paid out to victims of violent crime.[1] In the 1980s and 1990s government, state agencies and policy researchers became progressively interested in victims, both as identifiable individual parties and collective marginalised groups. Accordingly, the plight of the 'victim' has ascended the political ladder, so much so that the category of victim acts as a key instrument of penal repression and policy formation around law and order (see Garland 2001; Rock 2002). Not only has the victim become more visible in political debates about crime, victims' rights have assumed a pivotal role in public policy-making. As we shall see, a sharper focus on the victim has knock-on effects for the treatment of offenders who are increasingly situated by and through their relationship with the victim (see Hudson 2003: 87; Williams 2004: 89).

As O'Malley (2006: 52) observes, the current political accent on the victim is bound up with a concatenation of social transformations, including the extension of risk as a technology for organising human behaviour: 'the victim ... became a new subject of risk, to be worked with and upon in order to correct ignorance, vulnerability and misunderstanding'. The ways in which individuals and agencies respond to the problem of crime is not restricted to the issue of how to deal with offenders. Instead, the criminal justice system now considers the ways in which society responds to victims of crime as an integral part of constructing and delivering 'justice'. Bearing this point out, in recent years the suffering of victims has been used to provide leverage for new legislation, such as Megan's Law in the United States and the UK 2005 Prevention of Terrorism Act.

Having commented briefly on the ascendance of the victim, let us now turn to culture. Culture is one of the most untidy and contested concepts in the social sciences, being open to multifarious definitions (Barker 2000: 35). It is hardly surprising then that there has been an element of confusion in the criminological canon over what is meant by culture and how it might be marshalled to enhance the victimological agenda. Naturally, we cannot hope – nor did we ought – to impose a single definitive meaning on culture. Following Raymond Williams (1981), here we conceive of culture as way(s) of life that involve institutions and modes of cultural production, including the organisation of signs and symbols through which sense-making takes place. In this context, culture can be viewed as the collective symbolic environment in which individuals and social groups interact and generate meaning (see Ferrell 2005: 140). It needs to be recognised that within the broad church that is culture, different methodological approaches can be taken, according to one's research questions and theoretical trajectory (O'Brien 2005: 606). Putting aside these methodologies and trajectories, it is incontrovertible that culture has become an increasingly popular unit of analysis within the social sciences (McRobbie 2005). The 'cultural turn' that emerged in the 1980s highlights both the academic trend toward using culture as an explanatory concept and its broader centrality within society (du Gay *et al.* 2002).

But what utility and resonances does culture have for criminology in general and victimology specifically? If we travel with Williams' earlier definition of culture – as both a way of life and a site of meaning-making through symbolic practices – it follows that culture is at the heart of the process of victimisation, from the habitual activities of offenders to institutional modes of caring for those who suffer crime. Being or becoming a victim is not a neat or absolute journey. Acquiring the status of victim involves being party to a range of interactions and processes, including identification, labelling and recognition. As Tulloch (2006) implies, victims of crime can find themselves passed through various victimological phases in the media, from heroic survivor to political agitant. As such, the contemporary politics of crime victimisation cannot be *other* than a cultural issue and one which provokes considerable moral conflicts at an individual and a societal level (Ferrell 2005: 153).

Given all of this, it is not difficult to state the case for a working up of the cultural within criminology, particularly in the area of victimology. Indeed, running parallel with advances in related social science disciplines, culture has already impacted on criminology. Thinkers such as Jeff Ferrell (1999, 2005), Mike Presdee (2000) and Keith Hayward (2004) have been at the forefront of a shift towards the cultural. We can agree with Hayward and Young (2004: 259) that the rise of cultural criminology points to an increasing emphasis on 'crime and its control in the context of culture; that is, viewing both crime and the agencies of control as cultural products – as creative constructs'. Cultural criminology is vitally concerned with the construction of criminality, the different ways in which human beings create meaning through law-breaking activity and the symbolic aspects of transgression and regulation. Thus, cultural criminology has been alert to the power of the media in contemporary culture and the salience of symbolic images in shaping dominant understandings of criminalisation, crime control and victimisation (see Greer 2005: 174).

Despite having its finger on the social pulse, it is fair to say that cultural criminology remains a scattered field of loosely connected approaches, ranging from studies of urban culture to the association between risk-taking and criminality (Ferrell 1999; Lyng 2004). Yet one can see how the core set of concerns developed within cultural criminology can be appropriated and utilised in the study of victims: for instance, to inspect the way in which victims are geographically and experientially located, institutionally labelled and represented in the media. Looking at things the other way around, cultural criminology is equally well equipped to consider the ways in which victims come to recognise themselves *as victims* through engagement with cultural products and practices. Thus, it is possible to argue that cultural criminology might profitably open out from an emphasis on the meaning of crime for subcultural actors, to scrutinise how the victim is culturally constructed and socially remade. In order to pursue this objective, the modes through which the victim is politically assembled and symbolically deployed, can be examined. This venture in no way amounts to a dismissal of the victim, either in ideological or material terms. To be clear from the outset, the violence suffered by victims of crime should not be belittled. Nor should it be assumed that political opinion leaders are hell-bent on a programme of mass indoctrination that renders an acquiescent public fearful. Clearly, the experience and the politics of victimisation are far more complex than this.

The universal victim: making up 'new terrorism'?

The mass media has historically been identified as an important source of information about crime and a vehicle through which victimisation is rendered visible. Given the current presence of media technologies, it is likely that the media play an increasingly central role in informing and cultivating people's everyday perceptions of crime, disorder and victimisation (see Banks 2005; Mythen and Walklate 2006a). It has commonly been argued that – far from reflecting objective crime realities that exist 'out there' – the political economy in which the media operate, the professional interests of journalists and the technical needs of the production process mean that news-making is an inherently selective and partial activity. In practice, this means that 'certain values, interests and beliefs are promoted, while others are downplayed, or even actively suppressed' (Greer 2005: 158). This matters greatly in a context in which the media are driven by financial imperatives such as market share, advertising revenue and profit margins (Mythen 2004). Given such an economic compulsion, the need to produce marmalade-dropping headlines is omnipresent, leading to emotive sensational coverage of crime issues designed to captivate and titillate audiences. The production of crime news impacts not only upon people's knowledge of crime but also on their attitudes towards victims and offenders. The classic research of Cohen (1972) and Hall *et al.* (1978) articulates the cycle through which repeated portrayals of law-breaking subcultures can stimulate moral panics about deviant groups. Despite the diversity and multiplicity of media forms in contemporary society, the sources that people use most frequently for information about crime and violence – such as national broadcast news and daily newspapers – can serve to promote anxieties and uncertainties about crime. Through representations of crime victimisation, the media creates symbolic identities for sufferers of crime (see Ferrell 2005: 149). Within this *mise en scène*, the needs and interests of victims can be re-presented – and, on occasion, *mis*represented – to satisfy the preferences of multimedia conglomerations and/or the objectives of self-seeking politicians (see Mawby and Walklate 1994). This point is sublimely illustrated by the media theorist John Tulloch (2006) who found himself party to all manner of media demands as a consequence of surviving the 7/7 bombings in London. Tulloch's story forces us to think long and hard about how victims are ascribed roles and what the ramifications of victim identities are for understanding the nature and causes of crimes such as terrorism. Unpacking the contemporary problem of 'new terrorism' enables us to glimpse the ways in which both criminality and victimisation are culturally constructed. In order to illumine some of these processes, let us turn to the role of politicians and the media in the symbolic construction – or 'making up' – of new terrorism.

So, what is meant by 'new terrorism'? How does 'new' terrorism differ from 'old' terrorism? At the turn of the millennium a cluster of security experts and academics were busy tracking the formation of 'new' or 'postmodern' forms of terrorism (see Lacquer 2000; Lesser *et al.* 1999). Outside of the field of security studies, their discussions went relatively unnoticed in the social sciences. Predictably enough, post September 11 the spotlight fell on academics and intelligence experts who had been studying the changing nature of terrorist groups. Following this lead, the expression 'new terrorism' began to be used by journalists, policy-makers and politicians keen to distinguish between the activities of new radical Islamic groups and older European organisations such as ETA, the IRA and the UVF. A number of factors are said to separate out new terrorist groups such as Al Qaeda and Jemaah Islamiyah from their European predecessors. It is claimed that new terrorist groups operate using a cellular system, attempt to stage high lethality attacks across the globe and have access to an extensive array of dangerous weapons. Further, such groups are defined by their amorphous aims, disparate organisational structure and diverse financing (Morgan 2004; Lesser *et al.* 1999). The attacks launched by new terrorist groups indiscriminately target the general public to cause maximum impact and intensify fearfulness. Insofar as it is questionable whether a meaningful divide between 'new' and 'old' terrorism is defensible, the idea of new terrorism has proved attractive to politicians seeking to explain a step change in armed conflicts and civil unrest (see Mythen 2007). A sequence of incidents on European soil, including bomb attacks in the UK, Turkey and Spain have propelled terrorism forward as an imperative issue, with the problem of new terrorism steepling up the political agenda in many western nations (Furedi 2005; Welch 2006).

In the UK it is evident that a deal of governmental work has been done to keep security high on the media agenda and to make the public more aware of the terrorist threat. During his tenure, Jack Straw made reference to 'an ever changing, ever present danger', while his successor David Blunkett claimed, 'Al Qaeda is on our doorstep and threatening our lives'.[2] More recently, both the current Home Secretary and the Prime Minister have compared the threat of new terrorism to that of Nazism in the mid-twentieth century (Blair cited in Waugh 2004: 5; Reid 2006). Such pronouncements are designed to universalise the threat: anyone and everyone is endangered. While raising public awareness about the terrorist threat may be considered a sensible precautionary measure, the terrorist risk should be properly contextualised. As Ripley (2006: 5) notes, 'last year car crashes claimed the lives of an estimated 40,000 people in America. Terrorists? Zero.' While the risks are not strictly comparable, such bald statistics do reveal quite a bit about what counts as dangerous in political terms. Looking at the amplification of risks such as terrorism it becomes clear that high-ranking politicians have sought to gain consent for criminal justice policies by utilising and manipulating the symbol of the victim (see Mythen and Walklate 2006a). Indeed, at times it seems that degrees of exposure to crime and differential victimisation have become so obscured in political debates in the UK that 'the public' and 'the victim' have become almost interchangeable. The universalisation of the terrorist threat extends way beyond national boundaries. As the outgoing Secretary-General of the UN, Kofi Annan (2001) observed some time ago, 'new threats make no distinction between races, nations or religions. A new insecurity has entered every mind, regardless of wealth or status'. This appeal to the commonality of risk is significant, as the summons to take up the role of victim encourages us *all* to reflect on our lived experience in a way that invites anxiety.

The political construction of crime risks – and the associated making up of the victim – does not happen in isolation and is itself cultivated and vectored by other institutions such as the mass media. Although the range of technologies and forms dictates that media outlets cannot convey uniform security messages, there is a detectable moral dimension embedded within dominant (re)presentations of the terrorist risk. The narrative framing of the terrorist risk has acted as a conduit for establishing what Peelo and Soothill (2000: 136) have termed the 'mass endorsement of morality'. The military reprisal – namely the 'war against terrorism' – is ideologically stitched together by a range of symbolic signifiers, conjuring up emotive images of a battle between good and evil waged against 'terror networks' and 'rogue states' (Lilleker 2006: 108; Mythen 2005). Although the media's moral endorsement of common- sense political assumptions is principally governed by economic imperatives rather than hegemonic desire, the danger is that the representation of the terrorist threat veers out of kilter with the probability of harm. To this end, problems of exaggeration and misrepresentation loom large. New terrorist groups such as Al Qaeda are cast as a bloodthirsty enemy bent on maximal destruction and perpetually seeking victims. At the same time, long-standing ethnic conflicts in the Middle East become cackhandedly subsumed into debates about how western nation states can best expunge 'new terrorism'.

It is evident that terrorist attacks attain meaning through cultural norms and practices. Geographically proximate events – such as 9/11 and 7/7 – become touchstones for discussions about national and individual security, while others such as the Beslan seige in Northern Ossetia drift out of the media lens. It is estimated that during the present conflict in Iraq, an attack by insurgent forces takes place every 15 minutes with the total number of Iraqi civilians killed in the conflict currently standing at 48,343 (Goldenberg 2006: 18).[3] This means that the total death toll of civilians killed in the 2005 London bombings is being surpassed each and every day in Iraq. Despite this, the constant media prompts to 'think security' relate to a threat to the British nation. The terrorist victim we are invited to imagine is an affluent white urban Christian Anglo-Saxon, not an impoverished Baghdadi Muslim. Not only do such cues articulate a deficient notion of the victim, they also perpetuate the notion of a non-white 'terroristic other'.

Understanding the universal victim: theoretical perspectives

Having considered both the contemporary place of the victim in society and some of the ways in which the terrorist threat is being politically universalised, it is now necessary to ask whether theoretical approaches can help us understand changes in political attitudes towards victimisation and transformations in social policy. To this end, I point up two perspectives that may help us establish a firmer grip on the cultural dynamics underpinning the construction of the universal victim, namely the risk society thesis associated with Ulrich Beck (1992, 1999) and the culture of fear approach delineated by Frank Furedi (2002, 2005). Both Beck's and Furedi's work seeks to reveal the cultural impacts of macro-social changes on contemporary lived experience. However, as we shall see, the two authors have very different ideas about who might be a victim, under what circumstances and why. Prior to dealing with the victimological issues, it is first necessary to provide capsule accounts of each thinker's argument.

In perhaps the most well-known contribution to risk theory, Beck (1992) graphically recounts the destructive impacts of risk on everyday life. Ironically – given current usage within criminology – Beck has little explicit to say about either crime or victimisation. Although Beck's thesis is firmly rooted in the tradition of Germanic sociology, various components have been extracted to explore issues of penal control, policing and social justice (see Feeley and Simon 1995; Ericson and Haggerty 1997; Hudson 2003). Following this tradition, I wish to show here how the risk society thesis can enable us to envisage the darkening silhouette of the universal victim and the ways in which the cultural politics of victimisation is being unfurled. Beck's summary of the changing nature of social threats – and its associated social consequences – is supported by the 'three pillars of risk' (Mythen 2004: 17). First, Beck contends that contemporary threats have greater temporal and spatial mobility than the natural hazards that blighted traditional cultures. The de-territorialised dangers of the risk society – environmental pollution, AIDS, and new terrorism – effectively smash the boundaries of time and space. As far as criminal justice is concerned, the globalisation of crime means that 'national security is, in the borderless age of risks, no longer national security' (Beck 2002: 14). Second, the risks delineated above are potentially catastrophic. Not only do such threats span the globe, they also generate irremediable effects that victimise people far and wide. Third, the sheer force of 'worst imaginable accidents' undermines existing modes of institutional regulation. As the risks get bigger and more explosive, our capacity to manage them diminishes. As a corollary, extant mechanisms of insurance, welfare provision and criminal legislation effectively short-circuit.

For Beck, the fluctuating nature of social hazards disrupts established patterns of social distribution and transforms the content of politics. Growing awareness of the harm caused by manufactured risks promotes a shift in political focus within capitalist societies away from the positive problems of acquiring 'goods' – such as income, health care and education – towards avoiding 'bads'. This ground shift is suggestive of a wider point about social distribution. While the logic of the traditional class society is sectoral – some win and some lose – the logic of the risk society is universal: ultimately everyone loses (see Mythen 2005). As Beck (1996: 32) puts it, 'there are no bystanders anymore'. The foremost dangers of the world risk society – ecological collapse, nuclear warfare and global terror networks – render us all potential victims, regardless of place, race, gender or class. The spread of risk – both as material harm and cultural ideology – has facilitated both a distributional and an ideational transition from the positive acquisition of social goods to the negative avoidance of social bads. This ideational shift is reinforced by the media's capacity to 'socially explode' risks that would otherwise be secreted from the public. Thus, in a perverse way, the universality of threats serves to democratise the distribution of risk. On a perceptual plain, this is indicative of a movement away from differential class-consciousness towards a universal risk-consciousness. Beck reasons that the pervasiveness of risk has a dual cognitive effect. At one level, people become more reflexive about their social practices and learn to self-manage the trials and tribulations of everyday life. At another, heightened awareness of risk serves to foment anxieties about threats that are out of the sphere of individual control.

The risk society thesis has obvious connotations for victimology, drawing out a number of prescient trends which shape dominant notions of the victim and influence attitudes towards the regulation and management of crime. On balance, Beck (1992) has been vindicated in predicting a shift in orientation away from goods towards a preoccupation with bads. Rather than trying to tap into collective desires for the good, the language of politics increasingly delves into individualised insecurities and fears (see Lilleker 2006: 108; Rigakos and Hadden 2001: 63). Further, the mega-hazards depicted in the risk society thesis have unquestionably served as wider moral points of reference, both within and outside of academia. Discussions about the side-effects generated by capitalist modernisation and technological development are essentially bound up with establishing acceptable levels of risk and mitigating exposure to harm. The media has played a key role in raising public awareness about a range of risks and providing advice about how to guard against dangers. Yet the more we become sensitised to risk, the more threats we perceive and the more vulnerable we feel. While feelings of vulnerability may have positive political effects – say, in relation to modifying individual practices that produce environmental harm – they can also spark unnecessary fears and foster suspicion. As Beck is aware, ontologically speaking, the rise in risk-consciousness is something of a double-edged sword.

An emphasis on the deleterious aspects of risk is also central to Furedi's work on the culture of fear. Furedi's (2002) approach demonstrates that the tendency to view social experience through the prism of risk can discourage social participation and cultivate a victim-oriented compensation culture. Furedi believes that a preoccupation with victimisation is symptomatic of a wider tendency to focus on the damaging features of the modern age. For him a culture of fear is operating in western nations, encouraged by state institutions and promoted by those working within the media and security industries. This culture of fear is characterised by rising fears about crime and sporadic moral panics about extreme but rare acts of violence and/or sexual perversion (Furedi 2002: 23). Furedi posits that the current cultural preoccupation with risk is deeply troubling. First, so far as scientific, technological and social developments are concerned, the balance between positive advances and negative consequences becomes distorted. Second, media emphasis on high-impact but low-probability risks encourages individuals to become more inward-looking. Furedi (2002: 5) claims that these processes constitute one aspect of a wider set of cultural changes that encourage victimhood in all of us: 'being at risk has become a permanent condition that exists separately from any particular problem ... by turning risk into an autonomous, omnipresent force in this way, we transform every human experience into a safety situation'. According to Furedi, the establishment of a culture of fear signals a ground-shift away from adventurous risk-taking towards a pessimistic morality of low expectation. In such a climate, social institutions become hooked on the negative effects of risks that are unlikely to materialise. At the same time, the institutional fixation with risk situates citizens as active risk managers and views human interactions as little more than a series of potentially dangerous situations. Thus, people become schooled in undertaking personal risk assessments weighing up the 'what if?' questions. Such 'what if?' questions lead us to hypothetically imagine ourselves as victims and reflect on various means of victim avoidance. For Furedi, a society obsessed with risk endlessly produces *faux* victims. It also elides that contemporary western cultures are comparatively secure and safe environments. Like Beck, Furedi's attempt at theory-building leads him to produce a caricatured version of events. Nevertheless, despite its blemishes, Furedi's thesis allows us to identify the growing formation of a victim culture and also to locate this within a broader social and historical framework. Although overstated, the culture of fear pins down the movement towards a more anxious, compensation-oriented culture.

Furedi's work locks on to institutional attempts to share the burden of responsibility for crime risks with the general public through various awareness campaigns and partnerships. Further, he is more attuned than Beck to the ways in which media news values assist the articulation of dominant ideologies. What is accentuated in Furedi's analysis – but downplayed in the risk society theory – is the way in which moral panics about crime are used to piggy-back political interests and to pave the way for new legislation. For Beck, the social explosion of hazards in the media is a positive phenomenon, which heightens risk awareness and leads to public calls for preventative action. Yet Beck's 'social explosiveness' is decoded by Furedi as media sensationalism about outlying risks that are unlikely to eventuate. Furedi is also wise to the cultural production of the universal victim, but in a different way from Beck. While the universal arc of Beck's thesis leads him to argue that the notion of the bystander has disappeared, Furedi justly warns that different people have different degrees of risk-proneness. A daily commuter living in central London and working in the City is more likely to be a victim of terrorism than a home-based market gardener in Stroud. Insofar as Beck's thesis depicts a global society vulnerable to novel and catastrophic risks, his habit of universalising threat obscures the differentiated material distribution of risks and ignores the strong link between forms of cultural stratification and patterns of victimisation. The 'global' spread of terrorism is strikingly uneven, with terrorist attacks being concentrated in certain areas. Even within recognised danger zones risks are not democratically dispersed. We only need take a cursory glance at the disparity in casualties between western military personnel and Iraqi civilians to remind ourselves of the unevenness of risk. What is more, the way in which similarly harmful events receive uneven attention indicates that who counts as a victim is an issue that is up for grabs. Comparing responses to a terrorist related aeroplane crash in Niger with one that took place in Scotland around the same time, Soyinka (2004: 2) observes that 'even in death, where all victims are surely considered equal, some continue to die more equally that others. Dying over Scotland, no matter what your pedigree, enhances your value over dying over African soil.'

Contra the Beckian idea that risk acts as a mechanism for human emancipation, it might be argued that acceptance of living in a 'risk society' has been expedient for neo-liberal politicians and served to bolster social control. Institutional technologies can ostensibly reduce risk, yet they can also extend the tentacles of governance. In some senses then, Beck's theory – and its appeal to the universal victim – sits inadvertently, but comfortably, with the regulatory aspirations of government, law enforcers and legislators. A social environment in which a greater number of people feel themselves to be victims is also problematic in other ways. The mushrooming culture of victimhood potentially inhibits our capacity to differentiate between victims and muddies political priorities (see Cole 2007). If everyone is a victim of crime then nobody is. Degrees of victimhood can thus be flattened out and concreted over, ignoring the undulations of class, ethnicity, age, gender and location. People have different levels of vulnerability and different degrees of exposure to different types of crime. In this sense, the idea of the universal victim is something of a *canard*, particularly given that in many instances primary victimisation serves as a predictor of future victimisation (Shaw and Pease 2000). Since its inception in 1982, the British Crime Survey has persistently indicated that some cultural groups are more at risk than others. In short, the risk of victimisation will vary according to community, lifestyle and cultural grouping. To cite one example, the survey has successively reported that both Asians and Afro-Caribbeans are more likely to be victims of violent crime than white people: 'the general risks of victimization disguise the greater real risks for some groups. Individuals within certain groups may fall victim to many offences in a year whereas others in different subgroups may never, or only very rarely, experience a crime' (Williams 2004: 92).

Given their totalising pitch, both Beck's and Furedi's theoretical contributions lack subtlety and tend to imagine an undifferentiated public. In both narratives the subject is an increasingly anxious, security-conscious and risk-aware citizen, albeit one that is politically catalysed in Beck's version and paralysed in Furedi's. Applied in the criminological context, the cultural factors that define perceptions of crime risks such as age, gender, ethnicity and class are obscured. The resilience of such factors in shaping understandings of risk means that victims of the same crime may react and respond to their victimisation in markedly different ways (Zedner 2002: 429). Going down a level further, those suffering multiple victimisation might experience their victimisation in various shades of activity, passivity and/or indifference. While Furedi's 'culture of fear' chimes with a society at once fixated and appalled by various violent threats – such as terrorism, paedophilia and nuclear warfare – the idea of an all-embracing 'culture of fear' is theoretically simplistic and empirically wanting. This said, Furedi's work has been ably refined by criminologists interested in the fear of crime. For instance, Murray Lee (2001) shows us that fear of crime is influenced by social structures and crucially directed by lived experience and habitus. To understand fears about crime and the individual process of 'victim positioning' we need to address the cultural articulations through which fears about crime and violence are propagated. Further, as Tudor (2003: 249) reasons, we would do well to recognise the role of institutions in reinforcing notions of safety and harm:

> If our cultures repeatedly warn us that this kind of activity is dangerous … then this provides the soil in which fearfulness may grow. Indeed, the very constitution of the ways in which we experience and articulate fear is significantly dependent upon the channels of expression made available to us by our cultures. That is particularly apparent where 'new' fears emerge and become widespread in relatively short periods of time.

Clearly, the range, mix and depth of cultural processes at play will vary between different forms of criminal activity, different contexts and different places. It needs also to be remembered that empirical studies indicate that the media is far from a one-way instrument of communication about crime (see

Chadee and Ditton 2005; Ditton *et al.* 2004). The media may set the agenda on certain political issues and reinforce existing cultural values, but it does not determine people's perceptions of crime. Media moguls are not able to tell people what to think, but they can tell them what to think *about*. Given divergent public opinion around the risk of crime victimisation in general and terrorism specifically, it is perhaps more sensible to speak of different *cultures* of fear. We need to be cognisant that 'the public' is constituted by risk-averse individuals *and* various cultures of pragmatism and resistance in which the anxieties projected by dominant groups are refuted and opposed.

Governance, control and the cultural politics of the victim

Having considered the potentialities and pitfalls of macro theories in understanding the changing context in which notions of victimisation are set, it is now necessary to consider the contemporary cultural politics of the victim. Drawing on UK examples, let us inspect the articulation between foreign and domestic policies on terrorism and the broader cultural meaning of victimisation.

As part of its obligation to provide safety and security for citizens the state has a keen interest in the management of crime and the well-being of victims. The judicial system seeks justice for victims through the punishment of offenders and government agencies are responsible for overseeing compensation schemes for victims and supplying funding to various victims groups. There are, of course, many social pluses that have emerged out of a more victim-centred focus within politics, policing and criminology. In the UK, increased awareness of the plight of victims has led to the establishment of action groups, informed more progressive ways of punishing offenders and directed attention towards the policing of areas where victims are concentrated. However, there are also drawbacks to political ventures that place the victim at the heart of crime prevention and civil regulation. In order to reflect on some of these drawbacks, we now consider the interplay between a victim-centric political culture, media discourses of risk and authoritarian modes of social control.

As discussed earlier, the current emphasis on the victim in matters of criminal justice has not developed in a vacuum and can be explained in relation to a host of social factors. The work of Furedi and Beck is instructive in pinpointing some of these factors, including the diffusion of individualisation and responsibilisation, the prevalence of risk discourses and ever-deepening institutional incursions into the private sphere. As we have seen, the media is a critical vehicle through which victimisation is flagged and assumptions about offenders reinforced. This is not to suggest that politicians and/or the media have the capacity to determine people's thoughts – less still their actions – in any uniform manner. Clearly, reflexive individuals think and (inter)act in ways that ensure that prescribed social roles are not passively taken up. Putting some big hermeneutic questions to one side, it is evident that politicians have traded on risk in order to raise awareness about global threats, be they around crime, terrorism, AIDS or the energy crisis. As far as victimology is concerned, what this does is to reframe understandings of victimisation and raise the bar of entry under which people feel victimised. Risk prevention campaigns may raise awareness of risk but they can also exacerbate feelings of insecurity. As Burkitt (2005) argues, it is likely that the continual reinforcement of the terrorist threat by the British government has heightened rather than attenuated people's anxieties. People's perceptions of the terrorist threat are shaped not only by the level of risk but also extant assumptions, underlying values and political world-views. History suggests that politicians and public officials are not beyond manipulating the media agenda in pursuit of their own ideological or professional ambitions (Ferrell 2005: 140; Hall *et al.* 1978). This means that what is defined as criminal and who is cast as a victim are subject to cultural and political shaping: 'suspect people do not have (actually) to commit crimes to be identified as criminal, nor do respectable people have to experience crime to identify themselves as (potential) victims' (Hudson 2003: 65). Through their day-to-day working practices, various institutional actors working within the media, politics, the police and the criminal justice system build different categories of victim: blameless victims, feckless victims, deserving victims. So too are classes of offender defined and criminal groups labelled. Over the course of time, both government and the media have pilloried particular 'folk devils', homing in on symbolic displays to reinforce deviance attachments (Ferrell 2005: 152).

Such processes of inclusion and exclusion are not limited to the realms of politics and crime control. As Young (1999, 2003) reasons, there has been a distinct motion from an inclusive society to a more exclusive culture, characterised by side-taking and vindictiveness. To shine a light on who is 'in' and who is 'out', we might reflect on the exhaustive media coverage of Muslim 'problems' since 7/7, ranging from religious extremism and alienated youth to violent families and the infamous veil dispute. Rendering young British Asians as 'other', sections of the media have clumsily cast Muslims as a problem group to be feared and ostracised, reinforcing stereotypes and cementing imagined divides (Mythen and Walklate 2006b). These ethnic divides are not simply ideological but have a material reality, manifested in domestic crime control policies. Mediated security cues give out clear indicators of which groups are victims and which aggressors. This takes us a step further in our understanding of the universal victim, suggesting that both 'us' and 'all' can paradoxically carry exclusionary meanings (Walklate 2007: 21). To cite one example, just concerns have been voiced by civil rights groups about the uneven implementation of the stop and search law in the UK. The number of Asian and black males stopped and searched in London under section 44 of the Terrorism Act 2000 rose more than twelve-fold after the 7 July bombings (Dodd 2005). Such examples of racial profiling are now being ingrained in policy and imperil the rights and liberties of ethnic minority groups. As Hudson (2006) warns, the perils of 'white man's justice' loom large. On a global canvas, the ideology of exclusion is written out via the war on/against terror(ism). The either/orism of Anglo-American foreign policy stands as a case in point: you are either with us, or against us. Through such power plays, deeply defined lines are drawn between a righteous 'us' and an undeserving and criminal 'them' (Hudson 2003; Mythen and Walklate 2006a).

The narrative of the war against terrorism decrees that terrorist activities take no account of national boundaries and have no militaristic imperative. 'They' are the aggressors and 'we' the victims. Where previously an emphasis was placed on correcting the lax behaviour of victim-prone individuals, against the steel glint of new terrorism society *en masse* is vulnerable. It follows then that all must be vigilant, all alert. Casting back to Furedi's aperture on the incitement to self-manage risk, the current political cues are akin to a call to arms to a victimised – nay, terrorised – society. As the Home Secretary John Reid (2006) put it: 'the struggle has to be at every level, in every way and by every single person in this country'. Such attempts to mobilise an illusory society of victims slot easily into the framework of Furedi's culture of fear, but are also resonant of Garland's (2001) 'culture of control'. Garland draws parallels between the United States and the United Kingdom in terms of the way in which the victim is employed as a potent symbol in the management of crime. In becoming responsibilised around crime, people are asked to monitor and evaluate their own risks in order to avoid becoming a victim. Logically, it is in the citizens' best interest to form partnerships with crime control agencies to improve the prospects of security. Yet despite evidence of responsibilisation, perhaps the differential notion of the victim is gradually being replaced by the idea of the universal victim. At the very least, seemingly conflicting tales of universalisation and individualisation are simultaneously being told, most notably around the terrorist threat. The 'war against terrorism' suggests that *society* is threatened by the terrorist other, while simultaneously demanding that the *individual* acts as a day-to-day foot soldier of security management.

Against the argument marshalled here, it could be argued that terrorism is an extreme and atypical criminal act. As such, it may be unwise to hang too many conclusions about the current state of the victim on a solitary example. Yet the making up of the universal victim glimpsed through the prism of the terrorist risk is symptomatic of a much wider and deeper process of victim creation. The process of identifying oneself as a victim is enabled at a structural level through a burgeoning number of bodies and agencies. In 2007 the UK government will establish a Commission for Equality and Human Rights (CEHR) that will formally protect six groups: women, ethnic groups and disabled people, plus those defined by sexual orientation, age, and religion. While such moves are doubtless progressive in their endeavour to defend marginalised groups, they also fuel a victim-slanted culture. As Green (2006: 6) warns, we are in danger of creating a nation of victims, with officially protected groups covering 73 per cent of the population. When victim groups encompass such a large swathe of the population, we can almost dispense with the term 'public' and replace it with 'victim'. Green (2006: 29) believes that an identifiable 'victimocracy' is being constructed, in which similar crimes are attributed different status according to their cultural valency. Crimes that transgress the boundaries of cultural acceptability – such as the atrocities of 7/7 – are treated differently from distant crimes with equally dreadful consequences. Those left suffering with the mental and physical scars of 7/7 are somehow more visible, more accepted and designated higher status as victims than the thousands of nameless and faceless Iraqis who have perished since Allied forces set about the quest to 'liberate' their country. It is precisely because the survivors of 7/7 were party to an attack that deeply offended the moral sensibilities of 'ordinary people' that the UK government decided to increase the compensation paid out to victims. What is at stake here is essentially a moral judgement about degrees of suffering, gauged in terms of cultural proximity and perceived psychological impact rather than physiological disability. Such common-sense logic assumes that victims of terrorism are more important and deserving of sympathy than victims of other violent crimes – and definitely more than, say, victims of corporate homicide. Some victims are indeed more equal than others.

Returning to Garland (1996), it is clear that an assemblage of practices and policies are involved in the formation of a 'crime complex', in and through which the proclivities of dominant political, military, economic and cultural interests meet. What is pertinent to the present debate is the relationship between the discourse of new terrorism and the configuration of domestic crime policies. In the UK, dominant discourses of (in)security have been used to justify a number of political decisions that have generated material effects. At an economic level, the British government has drastically increased the amount spent on national security, beefing up security measures, passing through anti-terrorist legislation and orchestrating a campaign to inform the public about emergency situations (Kearon *et al.* 2007).[4] If citizens accept the provocation to see themselves and the nation at threat, objections to legislative changes can be devalued and deflected. It would appear that protection of the (imagined) victim is being utilised as an integral part of the broader armoury of the 'crime problem', designed to enhance social control and to bring citizens to order. We are lamentably heading towards a situation in which not spying on strangers, not being unsuspicious of neighbours and failing to monitor the behaviour of ethnic minority groups is seen as tantamount to victim precipitation. At present, the symbolic creation and ideological invention of the universal victim are serving to cloud the real issues that actual victims of crime face and detracting from the core responsibilities of the state such as providing practical help, material resources and emotional support for those affected by crime. Revising Simon's (1997) idiom, there is more than a suggestion that neo-liberal states such as the US and the UK are seeking to 'govern through terrorism'.

Conclusion

It would seem fitting to draw matters to a close by considering the implications of our discussion for the study of victims and the development of an agenda for cultural victimology. As far as the study of victims is concerned, it is clear that there is work to be done if we are to properly appreciate how people live with (the threat of) victimisation. Homing in on the representational and ideational dimensions, this chapter has advocated the selective use of theoretical perspectives to pin down the cultural trends that influence the ways in which people situate themselves as victims of crime. In this regard, aspects of both Beck's and Furedi's contributions are revealing in painting the larger picture on which crime, victimisation and regulation feature. Yet simply ascribing to one or the other perspective in an attempt to grasp the forces that affect the experience of victimisation is short-sighted. While macro theories are important tools in the development of victimology, their generality affords them only partial utility across different contexts and situations. Theoretical perspectives can help us travel partway in understanding both the mediation of the crime threat and the universalisation of victimhood, but it is critical that the lopsided impacts of crime across populations do not become veiled. Thus, we need to take on board some of the general contextual elements of these theories and put them to work to extend criminological knowledge. Contra the political pull of the universal victim, the expansion of victimology can foster greater appreciation of the ways in which people *experience* victimisation. Without doubt, the 'place sensitive', subjective aspects of what it *feels* like to be a victim deserve a continuing place in criminology (see Banks 2005; O'Malley 2006: 51; Walklate 2007). We cannot assume either that we *are* all victims, or that victims of similar crimes attribute the same *meanings* to their victimisation. The risks and fears associated with being or feeling like a victim are not simply a result of being located at the sharp end of criminality. While the experiential aspects of victimisation can be addressed by ramping up micro-level empirical forays, it is important that victimologists are alert to the macro structural effects of victim-centric forms of regulation and punishment. The ongoing politicisation of victims, the tendency for media organisations to pay lip-service to the universal victim and the hasty implementation of anti-terrorist legislation all indicate that a critical and inquisitive criminological imagination is required to interrupt the drive to manufacture consent. At present, there is a very real possibility that ubiquitous historical happenings – such as terrorism and victimisation – are being categorised as atypical and manipulated for political ends.

In relation to the bulking up of cultural victimology, it would be misguided to see culture as a magic explanatory bullet through which the experiences of all victims can be deciphered. The cultural lens does have its uses, but simply tossing blanket academic categories over diverse patterns of everyday life can muffle people's understandings of their own lived experience. As O'Brien (2005: 607) counsels: 'it is too easy to forget that terms like "culture" are part of the way that social scientists describe the world, rather than what the world actually comprises'. There is no need to deify the cultural within criminology or to exaggerate its possibilities for victimology. Rather, the cultural needs to be one facet of a holistic victimology that also takes account of social, economic, political, geographical and technological factors. Quite reasonably, debates will continue about the extent to which such factors can be disentangled. As we have seen, when we get down to the fine grain of separating the cultural wheat from the political chaff, the analytical units begin to shade into one another. This said, it is important that victimology takes culture seriously enough to grapple with the connections between perceptions of crime, media representations and the political economy of risk. There is no solitary cultural fix that can be added to reinvigorate extant understandings of the victim. Due to its inherent diversity, culture can be operationalised in various ways and employed at many different levels. To give examples, a cultural inflection within victimology might encourage research into representations of crime victims in popular culture, forms of cultural resistance to victim categorisation, the discursive deconstruction of the language of victimisation and the symbolic production of the victim. This list is far from exhaustive, but it does indicate areas of cultural analysis that might be built up to get a rounder picture of the fears and feelings that cluster around victimisation. Given the complexities involved in defining and analysing the explicitly cultural aspects of victimology, it would not do to end with too tidy an argument. Nevertheless, it does seem that advancing a more holistic approach to victimology and developing cultural victimology ride in tandem.

In conclusion, as the example of 'new terrorism' shows, it is not beyond politicians to noisily invite us to position ourselves as hypothetical victims, while the real sufferers are silently crushed elsewhere. In such a climate, the advancement of a victimological agenda that asks searching and oppositional questions is essential if criminology is to retain credibility and edge. It may not be too far-fetched to suggest that the road we are presently travelling down will lead us into a cul-de-sac in which over-surveyed citizens are indelicately classified as either offenders or victims. Such a dystopic view is disquieting and requires that those within the criminological tradition probe and interrogate the motives and policies of powerful institutions. Understanding the cultural construction of the victim and its relationship with regimes of social control is but one avenue to pursue. Are we all victims now? No. But they're working on it.

Further reading

Bourke, J. (2005) *Fear: A Cultural History*. London: Virago.
Cole, A. (2007) *The Cult of True Victimhood: From the War on Welfare to the War on Terror*. Stanford, CA: Stanford University Press.
Furedi, F. (2005) *Politics of Fear: Beyond Left and Right*. London: Continuum.
Lee, M. (2001) 'The genesis of fear of crime', *Theoretical Criminology*, 5(4): 467–85.
Mythen, G. and Walklate, S. (2006) 'Communicating the terrorist risk: Harnessing a culture of fear?', *Crime, Media, Culture: An International Journal*, 2(2): 123–42.
Walklate, S. (2007) *Imagining the Victim of Crime*. Maidenhead: Open University Press.

Notes

1 See www.cica.gov.uk.
2 See, respectively, Whittikar, D. (2001) *The Terrorism Reader* (London: Routledge) and Morris, N. (2004) 'The politics of fear', *Independent*, 23 November.
3 See www.iraqbodycount.net for an estimate of the current number of casualties.
4 In the UK, government expenditure on national security will rise from £1 billion to £2.1 between 2004 and 2008.

References

Annan, K. (2001) Nobel Lecture, Oslo, 10 December.

Banks, M.O. (2005) 'Spaces of (in)security: Media and fear of crime in local context', *Crime, Media, Culture: An International Journal*, 1(1): 169–87.

Barker, C. (2000) *Cultural Studies: Theory and Practice*. London: Sage.

Beck, U. (1992) *Risk Society: Towards a New Modernity*. London: Sage.

Beck, U. (1996) 'Risk Society and the Provident State', in B. Szerszinski, S. Lash and B. Wynne (eds) *Risk, Environment and Modernity: Towards a New Ecology*. London: Sage, pp. 27–43.

Beck, U. (1999) *World Risk Society*. London: Sage.

Beck, U. (2002) 'The silence of words and the political dynamics in the world', *Logos*, 1(4): 1–18.

Burkitt, I. (2005) 'Powerful emotions: Power, government and opposition in the "War on Terror"', *Sociology*, 39(4): 679–95.

Chadee, D. and Ditton, J. (2005) 'Fear of crime and the media: Assessing the lack of relationship', *Crime, Media, Culture: An International Journal*, 1(3): 322–32.

Cohen, S. (1972) *Folk Devils and Moral Panics: The Creation of Mods and Rockers*. London: MacGibbon and Gee.

Cole, A. (2007) *The Cult of True Victimhood: From the War on Welfare to the War on Terror*. Stanford, CA: Stanford University Press.

Ditton, J., Chadee, D., Farrall, S., Gilchrist, E. and Bannister, J. (2004) 'From imitation to intimidation: A note on the curious and changing relationship between the media, crime and fear of crime', *British Journal of Criminology*, 44: 595–610.

Dodd, V. (2005) 'Asian men targeted in stop and search', *Guardian*, 17 August.

Ericson, R. and Haggerty, K. (1997) *Policing the Risk Society*. Toronto: University of Toronto Press.

Feeley, M. and Simon, J. (1995) 'True Crime: The New Penology and Public Discourse on Crime', in T. Blomberg and S. Cohen (eds) *Punishment and Social Control: Essays in Honour of Sheldon L. Mesenger*. New York: Aldine De Gruyter.

Ferrell, J. (1999) 'Cultural criminology', *Annual Review of Sociology*, 25: 395–418.

Ferrell, J. (2005) 'Crime and Culture', in S. Hale, K. Hayward, A. Wahidin and E. Wincup (eds) *Criminology*. Oxford: Oxford University Press, pp. 139–56.

Furedi, F. (2002) *Culture of Fear: Risk Taking and the Morality of Law Expectation*. London: Continuum.

Furedi, F. (2005) 'Terrorism and the Politics of Fear', in S. Hale, K. Hayward, A. Wahidin and E. Wincup (eds) *Criminology*. Oxford: Oxford University Press, pp. 307–22.

Garland, D. (1996) 'Governmentality and the problem of crime', *Theoretical Criminology*, 1(2): 173–214.

Garland, D. (2001) *The Culture of Control: Crime and Social Order in Contemporary Society*. Oxford: Oxford University Press.

du Gay, P., Hall, S., Janes, L., Mackay, H. and Negus, K. (eds) (2002) *Doing Cultural Studies*. London: Sage.

Goldenberg, S. (2006) 'Every 15 minutes an attack in Iraq', *Guardian* 30 September.

Green, D. (2006) *We're (Nearly) All Victims Now! How Political Correctness is Undermining Our Liberal Culture*. London: Civitas.

Greer, C. (2005) 'Crime and Media', in S. Hale, K. Hayward, A. Wahidin and E. Wincup (eds) *Criminology*. Oxford: Oxford University Press, pp. 157–82.

Hall, S., Critcher, C., Jefferson, T., Clarke, J. and Roberts, B. (1978) *Policing the Crisis: Mugging, the State and Law and Order*. London: Macmillan.

Hayward, K.J. (2004) *City Limits: Crime, Consumer Culture and the Urban Experience*. London: Glasshouse Press.

Hayward, K. and Young, J. (2004) 'Cultural Criminology: Some Notes on the Script', *Theoretical Criminology*, 8(3): 259–73.

Hudson, B. (2003) *Justice in the Risk Society*. London: Sage.

Hudson, B. (2006) 'Beyond white man's justice: Race, gender and justice in late modernity', *Theoretical Criminology*, 10(1): 362–86.

Kearon, T., Mythen, G. and Walklate, S. (2007 forthcoming) 'Making sense of the terrorist risk: Public perceptions of emergency advice', forthcoming in *Security Journal*.

Lacquer, W. (2000) *The New Terrorism: Fanaticism and the Arms of Mass Destruction*. London: Oxford University Press.

Lee, M. (2001) 'The genesis of fear of crime', *Theoretical Criminology*, 5(4): 467–85.

Lesser, I., Hoffman, B., Arquilla, J., Ronfeldt, D., Zanini, M. and Jenkins, B.M. (1999) *Countering the New Terrorism*. California: RAND.

Lilleker, D. (2006) *Key Concepts in Political Communication*. London: Sage.

Lyng, S. (2004) 'Crime, edgework and corporeal transaction', *Theoretical Criminology*, 8(3): 359–75.

Mawby, R. and Walklate, S. (1994) *Critical Victimology*. London: Sage.

McRobbie, A. (2005) *The Uses of Cultural Studies*. London: Sage.

Morgan, M. (2004) 'The origins of new terrorism', *Parameters*, Spring edition: 29–43.

Mythen, G. (2004) *Ulrich Beck: A Critical Introduction to the Risk Society*. London: Pluto Press.

Mythen, G. (2005) 'From goods to bads? Revisiting the political economy of risk', *Sociological Research Online*, 10(2): http://www.socresonline.org.uk/10/3/mythen. html.

Mythen, G. (2007) 'The Postmodern Terrorist Risk: Plus Ça Change, Plus C'est la Même Chose?', in T. Owen and J. Powell (eds) *Reconstructing Postmodernism: Critical Debates*. Nova Science Publications: New York.

Mythen, G. and Walklate, S. (2006a) 'Communicating the terrorist risk: Harnessing a culture of fear?', *Crime, Media, Culture: An International Journal*, 2(2): 123–42.

Mythen, G. and Walklate, S. (2006b) 'Towards a Holistic Approach to Risk and Security', in G. Mythen and S. Walklate (eds) *Beyond the Risk Society*. Berkshire: Open University Press/McGraw-Hill.

O'Brien, M. (2005) 'What is cultural about cultural criminology?', *British Journal of Criminology*, 55: 599–612

O'Malley, P. (2006) 'Criminology and Risk', in G. Mythen and S. Walklate (eds) *Beyond the Risk Society: Critical Reflections on Risk and Human Security*. Berkshire: Open University Press, pp. 43–60.

Peelo, M. and Soothill, K. (2000) 'The place of public narratives in reproducing social order', *Theoretical Criminology*, 4(2): 131–48.

Presdee, M. (2000) *Cultural Criminology and the Carnival of Crime*. London: Routledge.

Rigakos, G. and Hadden, R. (2001) 'Crime, capitalism and the "risk society": Towards the same olde modernity?', *Theoretical Criminology*, 5(1): 61–84.

Ripley, A. (2006) 'Risk: How much are we willing to take?', *Time*, 13 August.

Reid, J. (2006) 'Reid makes Nazi terror comparison', *Guardian*, 31 October.

Rock, P. (2002) 'On Becoming a Victim', in C. Hoyle and R. Young (eds) *New Visions of Crime and Victims*. Oxford: Hart Publishing.

Shaw, M. and Pease, K. (2000) *Preventing Repeat Victimization in Scotland: Some Examples of Good Practice*. Edinburgh: SECR.

Simon, J. (1997) 'Governing Through Crime', in L. Friedman and G. Fisher (eds) *The Crime Conundrum: Issues in Criminal Justice*. Boulder, CO: Westview Press.

Soyinka, W. (2004) *Reith Lecture 1*. London: BBC News.

Tudor, A. (2003) 'A (Macro) Sociology of Fear?', *Sociological Review*, 51(2): 238–56.

Tulloch, J. (2006) *One Day in July: Experiencing 7/7*. London: Little Brown.

Walklate, S. (2007) *Imagining the Victim of Crime*. Maidenhead: Open University Press.

Waugh, P. (2004) 'Blair: Britain must never be afraid to fight terrorists', *Independent*, 13 March.

Welch, M. (2006) 'Seeking a safer society: America's anxiety in the war on terror', *Security Journal*, 19: 93–109.

Williams, B. (2005) 'Victims', in S. Hale, K. Hayward, A. Wahidin and E. Wincup (eds) *Criminology*. Oxford: Oxford University Press, pp. 494–507.

Williams, K. (2004) *Textbook on Criminology*. Oxford: Oxford University Press.

Williams, R. (1981) *Culture*. London: Fontana.

Young, J. (1999) *The Exclusive Society*. London: Sage.

Young, J. (2003) 'Merton with energy, Katz with structure: the sociology of vindictiveness and the criminology of transgression', *Theoretical Criminology*, 7(3): 389–414.

Zedner, L. (2002) 'Victims', in M. Maguire, R. Morgan, and R. Reiner (eds) *The Oxford Handbook of Criminology*. Oxford: Oxford University Press, pp. 419–56.

Conclusion

Sandra Walklate

In the aftermath of 7 July 2005 the Home Office presented its consultation document *Rebuilding Lives* to Parliament. In that document (also referred to in the Introduction and Overview) a number of claims are made concerning the delivery of services to victims of crime and a number of promises made about the future of that service delivery. For example, the Ministerial Foreword states:

> The good news is that the number of people who are victims of crime has fallen by 40% compared to ten years ago. And if people are the victims of crime, their experience of the criminal justice system is vastly improved. For example, the Code of Practice for Victims of Crime means that victims will be regularly updated about the progress of their case. When victims, or witnesses, have to go to court, they are helped throughout the process by Witness Care Units, the Witness Service, and new measures in court which make giving evidence less traumatic. Victims now have the opportunity to make a personal statement of how the crime has had an impact on them, and there has been a radical reform of sentencing. Many more victims are now receiving support from Victim Support and other organisations than in the past.

It is important to state, as does Miers in Chapter 13, that much of the impetus for this document was a result of a politically embarrassing awareness of the deficiencies in the operation of the Criminal Injuries Compensation Authority in the aftermath of 7 July both in terms of what it could consider as compensatable injuries and in relation to how much compensation might be considered appropriate. However, it is also important to note that this document forms part of a continuing commitment, under New Labour, to rebalance the criminal justice system, with that rebalancing meaning looking for ways in which to lend greater weight to the role of the victim in the criminal justice process. As the chapters in this handbook have documented, this rebalancing takes a number of different shapes and forms, from the reorientation of the work of criminal justice professionals, to the voice given to the victim (witness) in court, to the dispositions available from the court, to the role of the various voluntary organisations who have embraced working with victims of crime. Moreover, it is a process that has some international dimensions. However within this rebalancing exercise it is possible to observe a number of other processes in play.

First, again as contributors to this volume have illustrated, it is possible to observe the impact of globalisation. This is evident in a number of ways. The economic conditions of the early 1980s marked the beginning of what Feeley and Simon (1994) were to call 'actuarial justice'. In the UK these economic conditions dictated that the agencies of the criminal justice system were to be subjected to, for the first time, the demands of efficiency, effectiveness and value for money. As a result not only was the world of business and its associated management practices introduced to the criminal justice system (hence actuarial justice), agencies were encouraged to look to the management practices of other criminal justice systems in other countries to improve local practices. As Garland (2001) has documented, much of that looking elsewhere has involved, for England and Wales, especially looking west across the Atlantic rather than looking east to Europe. This westward-looking barometer has taken its toll on the criminal justice system as a whole in the UK particularly from the early 1990s, as all political parties embraced penal populism as a way of securing election to government. The continued rise in the prison population, the use of electronic tagging, zero tolerance policing, private prisons, are a few examples of this westward-looking agenda. This agenda is particularly evidenced in the UK in relation to the victim of crime by the embrace, in principle, of the victim impact statement, popular in the United States and elsewhere, that is discussed in the chapters by Sanders and Jones, and Booth and Carrington. However, policies with a global reach have also emanated from Australia and New Zealand in the form of restorative justice, discussed by Dignan.

The influence of the restorative justice agenda, in particular, is remarkable, so much so that researchers have commented that despite the fact that no one seems to have a clear idea of what counts as restorative justice (see, for example, Miers 2004), these are policy initiatives that have a good deal of 'swagger' (McEvoy et al. 2002). How and why that has happened need not concern us here (but see Walklate 2005) but what is evident is that the processes of governance articulated by Rhodes (1997), despite the more detailed analysis offered by Jones and Newburn (2007) addressing how well policies travel, now have global dimensions. In addition it is also important to note that over this same period of time the nature and range of victim-oriented research has also grown apace. Crucial to this has been the ever more refined use and development of the criminal victimisation survey methodology, not only epitomised by its contemporary use to measure the nature and extent of violence against women in both national (see Walby and Myhill 2001; Piipsa 2003) and international settings (see International Violence Against Women Survey, HEUNI), but also exemplified by the work of the International Criminal Victimisation Survey discussed by Van Dijk and Groenhuijsen in Chapter 14. As mentioned in the Introduction to Part Four, these global developments and interlinkages are not without their problems, not least of which is understanding how and under what circumstances policies travel in this way and what socio-economic and cultural condition might permit or inhibit their ability to deliver on the political claims that are made for them (see also Jones and Newburn 2007).

The second process it is possible to observe in this rebalancing agenda is the return to gothic horror commented on by Valier (2004) and alluded to by Godfrey and Kearon in Chapter 1. The symbolic use of the crime victim for political and policy purposes has served to capture and capitalise on the emotional. This symbolism has, however, real consequences in both contemporary policy initiatives as well as in mediated portrayals of (criminal) victimisation. Karstedt (2002: 302) notes:

> Judges in the United States were the first to remake the courts and the criminal justice system as a public space of emotions. Offenders were ordered by courts to wear T-shirts in public that identified them as thieves. Young offenders had to apologise on their knees to their victims with members of the community present. Sexual offenders had to erect signs on their front lawn warning the public about the inhabitant; another court order sent the victims of a burglary to the house of the offender to take from it what they liked.

In the UK we have seen the emergence of 'named and shamed' offenders whose pictures appear on leaflets distributed to households in their neighbourhood alongside the interesting observation that while crime rates appear to have gone down the fear of crime remains relatively high, leading Cavender (2004: 346) to suggest that the media's role, and the narrative that has been sustained in the media about crime, has been central to this. In the re-emergence of the gothic horror approach to crime, there has been a slippage from a concern with the moral culpability or otherwise of the offence to a concern with the moral culpability or otherwise of the offender. This process is commensurate with the 'culture of control' commented on by Garland (2001). Moreover, in the aftermath of the terrorist attacks of 9/11, 3/11 and 7/7, and the emergence of what Valier (2004) calls 'teletechnologies', the media have played their part in this gothic horror that excavates our fears.

Cavender (2004: 346) argues that in the UK and US over the last 25 years:

> The public had genuine concerns that reflected a changing social reality. But, the media reinforced and reproduced the public's attitudes. The media provided the organising frame, the narrative structure, the story line, and they kept it up for 25 years. Perhaps this is why the public's fear of crime has declined so little despite a decline in the crime rate. Crime has become an ever-present part of our symbolic reality.

This 'ever-present part' is very visual and this visual culture plays upon people's feelings. For example, it is now commonplace for the chief investigating officer at the conclusion of a trial in particularly gruesome or problematic cases to speak to awaiting reporters about the evil of the offenders and the road to recovery for the victim and/or victim's family, quite often drawing on a wide-ranging emotional repertoire. Moreover, as Valier (2004) points out, visual culture travels rapidly and can be viewed in locations and circumstances a long way from their point of production. For example, the events that followed the publication of contentious cartoons of the prophet Mohammed in Denmark in early 2006 that resulted in widespread demonstrations across the Muslim world and elsewhere illustrates the power of such visual technology. Media images of hostages, videotapes of beheadings, at-the-scene broadcasts of terrorist acts (*qua* 11 September 2001) are all intended to move us, to encourage us to place ourselves next to the victim.

The excavation of such feelings from newspaper headlines, television programmes, internet websites and so on arguably has been a crucial component of the rise of penal populism. Anger, guilt, shame, fear, and as Young (2003) would say, vindictiveness, are some of the key feelings that have been given expression in recent years, much of which has had a wider impact in its televised reporting than perhaps was once the case. This observation is not intended to imply that criminal events do not take their toll on people's emotions. From post-traumatic stress syndrome to anger in the aftermath of criminal victimisation (especially for men, see Ditton *et al.* 1999) and a whole range of emotional bus stops in between, crime can and does harm people. What is important about appreciating the anger, guilt, shame and vindictiveness referred to here, and other feelings that have been tapped in this process (Hodgson 2005), is the way that they are being harnessed both politically and in the criminal justice system as justification for victim-oriented policies.

This excavation of feelings has ensured a high public profile on sentiments about crime, especially those sentiments expressed by the victim. As McMillan (2004: 383) states in the aftermath of September 11, 'Suddenly, the national identity of each American was reappraised as inherently dangerous, an invitation for victimisation', with those same representations being used to endorse an imagery of the national hurt, of harm done, to the American body (see also Cole 2007). Such appeals and representations not only potentially misrepresent the chances of victimisation but also simultaneously maximise the harm done. In the UK this is increasingly expressing itself as a strategy of responsibilisation as part of the process of harnessing a culture of fear (Mythen and Walklate 2006). As they argue, it is evidently the case that the 'war on terrorism', as it has been framed by the media and politicians, has become the means whereby the state has sought to extend its powers over us all (what Innes 2002 has called 'control creep'; see also Head 2004 on Australia). This has resulted not only in the increased targeting of young Asian males as those to be feared by the media and in criminal justice practice but has also impacted on us all in creating the potential of a unitary victimhood (see Mythen in this volume).

Of course, this discussion is not intended to imply that the impact of crime does not elicit an emotional response in the individuals affected by it. It does (see *inter alia* Maguire and Bennett 1982; Ditton *et al.* 1999; Kearon and Leach 2000; Spalek 2006: chapter 5; Tulloch 2006). However, the harnessing of emotion in the interests of politics and policy on the one hand and the expressive role given to emotion by some of the recent policy interventions within the criminal justice system as a part of the contemporary rebalancing agenda on the other, are issues worthy of further reflection. Karstedt (2002: 304) observes:

> In Britain public demands for representation of the emotions of victims in the criminal justice system have been widely supported. Their sorrow, rage, and anger, feelings of vengeance need to be voiced, and 'healed' by the sanction imposed on the offender. This imbalance in the collective emotional mood thus easily intrudes into the criminal justice system, where decisions disadvantage actual offenders.

It is a moot point whether or not giving expression to the emotions of victims in the criminal justice system has wide support. Such support may vary considerably with respect to what kind of crime and under what kind of circumstances (the emotional response witnessed during the trial for those convicted of the murder of James Bulger in 1993 being a case in point). However, what is less equivocal is what this re-emergence of the emotional implies for questions of justice.

In an earlier piece on the emotionality of law Laster and O'Malley (1996) suggest that these processes hark back to pre-modern times when the victim (complainant) had space to give vent to their feelings as part and parcel of their responsibilities in relation to the process of prosecution, as Godfrey and Kearon commented in Chapter 1. In their view, the Enlightenment put emotionality in opposition to rationality, and while during the late twentieth century there has been an increasing preoccupation with actuarial justice (Feeley and Simon 1994), at the same time the patterns of consumption that have put the needs of the individual to the fore, as a moral good in and of themselves, have been accompanied by an increasing political sensitivity to (public) sensibilities. Laster and O'Malley (1996) go on to document how the law in Australia, especially around rape and domestic violence, reflect a concern with these sensibilities. In these laws, they argue, this is articulated by the desire contained within them to assert the central importance of human dignity. In this way, they suggest, it is possible to trace the beginnings of a transformation of the legal subject, so long having been the 'rational man' (see also Naffine 1990), into a legal subject that might be differently informed.

This analysis raises some interesting questions: one, of whether or not the law can act as a vehicle for social change or is merely reflective of it, is an issue to which we shall return below. This question notwithstanding, Laster and O'Malley's (1996) analysis is suggestive of a 'double movement' (Polanyi 2001) in which, as McMylor (2006) argues, the big threat to us all is capitalism and the processes associated with it. In relation to the discussion here, it reminds us to situate this return to the emotional in the criminal justice system within the wider capitalist global process that appears to be producing the effect (among the Anglo-speaking axis at least) that there is no other way of seeing and responding to the impact of the global expansion except in terms of the economic (see also Green in this volume). Of course, as McMylor (2006) is at pains to point out, the concept of the 'double movement' serves precisely to encourage us to think about other options. Moreover, within the processes of actuarial justice this re-emergence of the emotional has consequences both in the routine, mundane, everyday work of the criminal justice system (as, for example, in what a police officer is expected to do when dealing with a person who has been a victim of a burglary), and in relation to the bigger questions of terrorism, *qua* the discussion above. However, another question might be: what are the implications for justice of this recourse to the emotional?

Justice as a concept can be differently defined, as it can be differently practised. As Cook (2006: 1) observes, 'Justice is a concept that many of us take for granted: its meaning and existence are assumed to be the foundation of the "British way of life" and integral to the society in which we live.' So while much criminological and legal research, along with people's experience of the criminal justice system, clearly indicates that not all people are equal before the law, one of the principles of justice in the liberal democratic tradition is that the law should apply equally to everyone. And it is this principle that the recourse to the emotional challenges. At the root of this challenge is the question it raises about the status of the criminal justice system as a public good.

A public good is a good, like education or health that we all have a vested interest in. For example, Waldron (1993: 358) suggests that a public good is 'something which is said to be valuable for human society without its value being adequately characterisable in terms of its worth to any or all of the members of the society considered one by one'. The value of public goods, then, is not reducible to their aggregate value for each member of society but what they are worth to everyone together. In other words, they are irreducibly *social*. Public goods represent something more than their economic worth. Their value lies in what we all take from their meaning to us in the way in which Cook (2006), quoted earlier, implies. In other words, it is in all our interests, as victims, witnesses, or as offenders, that the criminal justice system operates with those collective interests in mind. Indeed, as Karstedt (2002) intimates, in this recourse to the emotional the space for such collective claims has changed shape and it is within this changing shape that the criminal justice system is being increasingly compromised. There are, however, other tensions here. The contemporary social condition is not only a global one, it is a highly diverse one, as populations and goods move and are moved around the world in the interests of capital. So the question is raised how, within that kind of socio-economic and cultural climate, can such difference and diversity be accommodated? How can an interest in the commonalities between people (Bauman 2000) be sustained? How, if at all, can the criminal justice system accommodate difference? This returns us to the question of the role of the law and the criminal justice system as a vehicle for change, mentioned above.

The recourse to the law as a vehicle for change is not impossible but is fraught with difficulties. The difficulties that can result in this recourse to law range from the unintended consequences of how the law is used (*qua* Smart 1989), to the problems in facing 'white man's law' (Hudson 2006) in the face of difference, to the potential of the co-option of laws in the interests of the state (Chesney-Lind 2006) to the interests of the victim potentially overriding those of the offender (Williams 2005). Such difficulties, and the practice issues that may ensue from changing the law, have not prevented continued energy and emphasis being placed on the symbolic power of the legal. This is illustrated by the focus of the feminist campaigns discussed in Chapters 5 and 6 and the work directed towards religiously motivated and hate crime discussed in Chapter 16 intimates. Yet as the discussion on hate crime in the chapter by Goodey illustrates, and the current reactions to the attrition in rape cases suggests (see Cook and Jones in this volume and HMIC/CPSI 2007), much of the change that might make a difference to these respective victim voices lies in facilitating social and cultural change, not just legal change. However, it is not just campaigning and/or pressure groups that persist in this legal reference point. The government itself uses the same reference point, as McRobbie (2006: 82) points out. Moreover, in the context of criminal victimisation and some of the policies discussed in this volume, this recourse to the law has resulted in pitting the victim against the offender. O'Malley (2004: 325) expresses some of the concerns associated with this dualism in this way:

> Certain persons are defined primarily in terms of their purely negative and dangerous status as threats to others (victims) and accordingly are incapacitated. Therapeutics are abandoned or become subordinate to a regimen of risk reduction. Risk avoidance negativity has been taken as the hallmark of risk in criminal justice, just as it has in critical and liberal analysis of government more generally.

And, in the context of the criminological (and here read also victimological) response to this, he says that 'They assume that risk can only be imagined and operationalised as a zero-sum: a game between potential victims and potential offenders, in which the risks to one party are created by the other'. O'Malley argues, for example, that while instituting devices such as Megan's Law may say much about our sense of morality, there is little evidence that these kinds of strategies reduce the risk of sexual victimisation. He further observes that:

> If the risk is defined as a social problem in terms of society that is culturally and socially saturated with sexual violence, then neither the victim–offender binary nor the exclusionary response appear adequate or even productive. (O'Malley 2004: 325)

This is a view that shares some similarity with the harm done/social justice approach of Hillyard *et al.* (2005) and returns us to the question of what we understand by justice, or as the government White Paper (2002) might say, *Justice for All*. Consequently we can see that there are tensions between accommodating difference, whether that be the difference experienced by an individual victim in relation to the impact that a crime has had on them and the emotions generated, or difference in terms of reconstituting the legal subject as being someone other than the rational man of law. If justice and the criminal justice system, are a public good, then it is the public nature of this good that needs to be debated, not the law *per se*.

Nevertheless, some might argue that, in the aftermath of terrorist activities that take no account of national boundaries and have no militaristic imperative, such a debate is highly unlikely since indeed we are all victims now (see also Green, Chapter 4). This universal victim (Mythen, Chapter 18) is reflected in the either/or-ism of international politics: you are either with us, or against us. (The 'us' in this case, of course, being the United States.) An either/orism, that as Mythen and Walklate (2006: 129) argue:

> relates to a potentially disparate collection of ideas, about – amongst other things – foreign policy, national security, warfare, and electronic systems of monitoring and crime prevention. Thus, in the UK the 'war against terrorism' metaphor is not simply extending into national policies about immigration, detention, identity cards, policing and surveillance, it actually appears to be driving them.

Thus rendering problematic not only individuals but nation states, countries and creeds. And, of course, in these processes victims are created, by both the action and the inaction of the state in the interests of security. While this is a view open to dispute it is equally the case that the events of the last five years raise all kinds of questions for criminology, and victimology, in relation to who is the criminal and who is the victim. But, the question remains, how do we manage difference? In the context of global terrorism difference appears to have been managed by the creation of a third category, the 'unlawful combatant' (Freedland 2006). Within this middle way option (in Beck's terminology), or what has come to be called the Third Way in the UK, it is possible to observe the rise and rise of cosmopolitanism.

Beck (2006) argues that cosmopolitanisation is multidimensional and demands multiple loyalties. He goes on to state that cosmopolitanism 'basically means the recognition of difference, both internally and externally' (2006: 57). It is a view of the contemporary social world that regards the either/or-ism of sameness/difference debates as constituting false alternatives preferring to deal with 'the both/and principle' (2006: 57). So, for example, 'cosmopolitan realism rests on a twofold negation: it negates both the universalism of and the essentialist insistence on ethnic difference' (2006: 61). Beck's audience for his interpretation of cosmopolitanism is clearly political and European. Somewhat in contrast, Benhabib's (2002) work on cosmopolitanism focuses on the 'we' question: who are 'we' and how do 'we' exist in a reflective relationship with 'the other'? In other words, how do we learn from each other through deliberative and democratic processes, and through that learning accommodate difference? In some respects these are exactly the tensions that we have observed in efforts to respond to the victim of crime at the level of policy rather than practice. These policies operate not on the both/and principle but still with the either/or principle. You are either victim or an offender (*qua* Miers on criminal injuries compensation, for example). Though as Williams and Goodman, and Dunn in this volume articulate, at the level of practice things can look somewhat different. In all of this there potentially is another victim here. That victim is justice: for both the victim and the offender.

The discussion above clearly intimates that some of the struggles and tensions that exist in endeavouring to respond to the victim of crime are located in wider social processes. In this Conclusion I have unashamedly engaged in 'opportunistic theorising', to quote Rock from Chapter 2. I have situated victimology and victimological concerns squarely within the sociological domain and its contemporary preoccupation with cosmopolitanism, in the interests of pursuing a critical stance towards victimology and its concerns. The increasing tendency to take account of difference, whatever form that difference takes, while arguably possible in the local domain of the wide range of support work that exists to help people in difficult circumstances, when writ large hits the brick wall of a criminal justice system rooted in the modernist principles of 'white man's justice' (Hudson 2006). Those modernist principles reflect principles of justice that assume a majoritarian world-view. In other words: justice is in all our interests and we can all agree on what that might look like. It taps part of what Bauman (2000) refers to when he talks about the commonalities of the human condition. Interestingly, this kind of majoritarian view is also to be found in the work of Beck. It also taps into the work of Harre (1979), who argued that one of the basic drivers of the human condition was the search for respect, to be treated with dignity. As I have argued elsewhere (Walklate 2004), this is also what the crime victim looks for. In the face of co-option, silence and silencing (Mathiesen 2004) and the complex management of sovereignty in the interests of the hegemonic capitalist state (Walklate 2007), it is a moot point whether or not such a search for respect is possible within the current cosmopolitan turn. There are those who would argue that the celebration and claims of difference have driven diversity policies and practices and have contributed to the compensation culture of fear (Furedi 2002; Green 2006) have gone too far in making victims of us all, reflecting an interesting twist on the notion of universal victimhood. Such claims notwithstanding, it might help if victimology took a little more note of the problems and possibilities that the debates on cosmopolitanism raise. This handbook may be one step in this direction.

References

Bauman, Z. (2000) *Liquid Modernity*. Oxford: Polity.

Beck, U. (2006) *Cosmopolitan Vision*. Cambridge: Polity.

Benhabib, S. (2002) *The Claims of Culture*. Princeton, NJ: Princeton University Press.

Cavender, G. (2004) 'Media and crime policy: A reconsideration of David Garland's Culture of Control', *Punishment and Society*, 6(3): 335–48.

Cole, A. (2007) *The Cult of True Victimhood: The War on Welfare to the War on Terror*. Stanford, CA: Stanford University Press.

Chesney-Lind, M. (2006) 'Patriarchy, crime and justice: Feminist criminology in an era of backlash', *Feminist Criminology*, 1(1): 6–26.

Cook, D. (2006) *Criminal Justice and Social Justice*. London: Sage.

Ditton, J., Farrall, S., Gilchrist, E. and Pease, K. (1999) 'Reactions to victimisation: Why has anger been ignored?', *Crime Prevention and Community Safety: An International Journal*, 1(3): 37–54.

Feeley, M. and Simon, J. (1994) 'Actuarial Justice: The Emerging New Criminal Law', in D. Nelken (ed.) *The Futures of Criminology*. London: Sage.

Furedi, F. (2002) *Culture of Fear*. London: Continuum.

Freedland, J. (2006) 'No, international law doesn't have to be dumped because of Al Qaeda', *Guardian*, 5 April.

Garland, D. (2001) *The Culture of Control*. Oxford: Polity.

Green, D. (2006) *We're (Nearly) all Victims Now*. London: Civitas.

Harre, R. (1979) *Social Being*. London: Blackwell.

Head, M. (2004) *Australian government uses Madrid bombings to justify further police-state powers* (www.wsws.org).

Hillyard, P., Pantazis, C., Tombs, S., Gordon, D. and Dorling, D. (2005) *Criminal Obsessions: Why Harm Matters more than Crime*, Monograph 1. London: Crime and Society Foundation.

HMIC/CPSI (2007) *Without Consent*. London: HMIC.

Hodgson, C. (2005) 'Angry or what? Experiences of being a victim of crime', *British Journal of Community Justice*, 3(3): 50–6.

Hudson, B. (2006) 'Beyond white man's justice: Race, gender and justice in late modernity', *Theoretical Criminology*, 10(1): 29–47.

Innes, M. (2002) 'Control creep', *Sociological Research Online*, 6(3) (www.socresonline. org.uk/6/3/innes.html).

Jones, T. and Newburn, T. (2007) *Policy Transfer and Criminal Justice*. Maidenhead: Open University Press.

Karstedt, S. (2002) 'Emotions and criminal justice', *Theoretical Criminology*, 6(3): 299–318.

Kearon, T. and Leach, R. (2000) 'Invasion of the body snatchers: burglary reconsidered', *Theoretical Criminology*, 4(4): 451–73.

Laster, J. and O'Malley, P. (1996) 'Sensitive New Age laws: The reassertion of emotionality in law', *International Journal of the Sociology of Law*, 24: 21–40.

Maguire, M. with Bennett, T. (1982) *Burglary in a Dwelling*. London: Heinemann.

Mathiesen, T. (2004) *Silently Silenced*. Winchester: Waterside Press.

McEvoy, K., Mika, H. and Hudson, B. (2002) 'Introduction: Practice, performance and prospects for restorative justice', *British Journal of Criminology*, 42(3): 449–75.

McMillan, N. (2004) 'Beyond representation: Cultural understandings of the September 11 attacks', *Australian and New Zealand Journal of Criminology*, 37(3): 380–400.

McMylor, P. (2006) 'Economics and Risk', in G. Mythen and S. Walklate (eds) *Beyond the Risk Society*. Maidenhead: Open University Press.

McRobbie, A. (2006) 'Vulnerability, violence and (cosmopolitan) ethics: Butler's "Precarious Life"', *British Journal of Sociology*, 37(1): 69–86.

Miers, D. (2004) 'Situating and researching restorative justice in Great Britain', *Punishment and Society*, 6(1): 219–30.

Mythen, G. and Walklate, S. (2006) 'Communicating the terrorist threat: harnessing a culture of fear?', *Crime, Media, Culture: An International Journal*, 2(2): 123–42.

Naffine, N. (1990) *Law and the Sexes*. London: Allen and Unwin.

O'Malley, P. (2004) 'The uncertain promise of risk', *The Australian and New Zealand Journal of Criminology*, 37(3): 323–43.

Piipsa, M. (2003) 'Violence against women as conveyed by surveys: The Finnish case', *Journal of Scandinavian Studies in Criminology and Crime Prevention*, 3: 173–93.

Polanyi, M. (2001) *The Great Transformation: The Political and Economic Origins of our Time*. Boston: Beacon Press.

Rhodes, R.W. (1997) *Understanding Governance*. Buckingham: Open University Press.

Smart, C. (1989) *Feminism and the Power of Law*. London: Routledge.

Spalek, B. (2006) *Crime Victims: Theory, Policy and Practice*. London: Palgrave.

Tulloch, J. (2006) *One Day in July: Experiencing 7/7*. London: Little, Brown.

Valier, C. (2004) *Crime and Punishment in Contemporary Culture*. London: Routledge.

Walby, S. and Myhill, A. (2001) 'New methodologies in researching violence against women', *British Journal of Criminology*, 41(3): 502–22.

Waldron, J. (1993) *Liberal Rights: Collected Papers 1981–91*. Cambridge: Cambridge University Press.

Walklate, S. (2004) 'Justice for All in the 21st Century: The Political Context of the Policy Focus on Victims', in E. Cape (ed.) *Reconcilable Rights? Analysing the Tensions between Victims and Offenders*. London: Legal Action Group.

Walklate, S. (2005) 'Researching restorative justice: Politics, policy and process', *Critical Criminology*, 13: 165–79.

Walklate, S. (2007) *Imagining the Victim of Crime*. Maidenhead: Open University Press.

Williams, B. (2005) *Victims of Crime and Community Justice*. London: Jessica Kingsley.

Young, J. (2003) 'Merton with energy, Katz with structure: The sociology of vindictiveness and the criminology of transgression', *Theoretical Criminology*, 7(3): 389–414.

Glossary

ACPO Association of Chief Police Officers. An umbrella organisation that comprises the membership of all chief police officers of the rank of Assistant Chief Constable, Deputy Chief Constable, and Chief Constable of police forces throughout England and Wales.

Acturial justice A way of thinking and managing the criminal justice system that relies upon a calculative approach to risk and a risk assessment approach to offenders.

Adversarialism This refers to the conduct of the criminal trial in which the defence and the prosecution face each other as two individuals in opposition and the function of the court is to be convinced of the strength or otherwise of the arguments, beyond reasonable doubt, presented to it by these two individuals. It implies the right to confront the accused with the evidence against them as well as the right to cross-examine the accused and any witnesses.

BCS British Crime Survey. First conducted in 1982, now conducted annually and an integral part of measuring and understanding the nature, extent and impact of crime based on response from a sample of the general population.

CICA Criminal Injuries Compensation Authority. The body whose responsibility it is in England and Wales to handle claims made to it as a result of criminal victimisation.

Civic trust The belief that people have that the criminal justice system, or indeed any arm of the state, is there to protect them.

Conferencing Often considered to be one facet of restorative justice, conferencing focuses on bringing all parties to an offence together so that they can voice their opinions and experiences of it and look to some agreed solution with the intended outcome of reintegrating the victim and the offender into the wider community.

Continuum of violence Associated with the work of Kelly (1988) this concept was devised to capture a sense of women's experiences and understandings of sexual violence that can range from the everyday experience of sexual harassment, stalking, sexual verbal abuse to more 'serious' but routine 'domestic violence' that can result in murder.

Culture of control A concept devised by Garland (2001) to capture the contemporary emphasis within UK and US criminal justice policy with a punitive response to offending behaviour and the wider processes that have been put in place to ensure that the responsibility for responding to and managing offending behaviour is widely dispersed between different organisations and wider society.

Cultural criminology A marriage of cultural studies and criminology, cultural criminology focuses on the way in which cultural representations of crime interplay with, and become a source of information about, people's experience of crime and the criminal justice system.

Culture of fear Associated with the work of Furedi (1997, 2002) in the UK and Glassner (1999) in the US, this concept refers to the ways in which the contemporary preoccupation with safety in both societies has taken its toll on cultural processes, and resulted in an increased individual fearfulness of people, places and activities.

Cosmopolitanism This concept has philosophical origins but in contemporary social and political commentary is taken to raise the question of how it is possible not only to take account of difference but also to learn, reflectively, from the appreciation of difference.

Critical victimology Differently interpreted by different writers within the field of victimology. Some use the label to highlight the interactive nature of criminal victimisation, while others use it as a vehicle to separate the academic victimologist from the campaigning voice. More recently it has largely been associated with the work of Mawby and Walklate (1994) and Walklate (2007) who have used this term to draw attention to the importance of understanding the underlying social mechanisms and processes that result in the patterning of the criminal victimisation that we see as well as that which we do not see.

Deserving victim This reflects the idea that some people are victims through no fault of their own, while others are not – they have in some way contributed to what has happened to them and therefore 'deserve' the outcome. It is an idea that has its roots in the historical distinction between the 'deserving' and the 'undeserving' poor that informs much of the welfare system response in England and Wales. It was built upon in the 1960s in the formation of the (then) Criminal Injuries Compensation Board in the forms of deserving and undeserving victims. The idea of the undeserving victim can be perpetuated in a range of criminal justice practices, from the response of police officers to incidents of domestic violence to the allocation of awards by the Criminal Injuries Compensation Authority.

Family impact statement A statement taken from family members in the aftermath of a crime of murder or manslaughter and designed to document the impact that the loss of the person concerned has had on the family, with the intention of such documentary evidence being read out in court.

Gender The social expectations of masculinity and femininity that are associated (though not exclusively) with being male or female.

Governance A concept developed in the work of Rhodes (1997) that highlights the changing nature and processes associated with the work of governments. It particularly focuses on the way in which decisions contemporarily are influenced by pressure groups, individuals and other vested interests who are not elected but nevertheless wield significant power.

Hate crime A term used to describe crimes that can be attributed to the feelings of the offender towards particular victim characteristics. Hate crimes can be racist, sexist, homophobic or religiously motivated.

Hegemonic masculinity Ideological and practical processes that endorse men as being the dominant sex in gender relations.

Hypermasculinity Exaggerated forms and expressions of masculinity.

ICVS International Criminal Victimisation Survey. First conducted in 1988, there have been several sweeps of this survey including an increasing number of countries. Usually conducted as a telephone sample survey of the general population in each country it is used to compare and contrast levels of criminal victimisation and levels of satisfaction with the services offered to them by victims of crime. The most recent of these surveys was conducted in 2004 and at the time of writing has yet to report from all the participating countries.

Ideal victim A concept constructed by Christie (1986) designed to capture the stereotypical characteristics of being a victim that would guarantee a sympathetic response from not only the criminal justice system but also the wider community. Put rather simply it taps into the fairy-tale image of Little Red Riding Hood, that is someone young, innocent, out doing good deeds, being violated by the archetypal stranger.

Indigenous justice Used to refer to those kinds of community-based response to offending behaviour that predate criminal justice system interventions. Introduced as a result of colonisation, it has nevertheless been sustained by those communities who comprise people whose heritage belongs to the country concerned. A way of engaging in the possibilities of restorative justice noted in Canada, Australia and New Zealand.

Innocent victim Connected with the concepts of 'ideal victim' and 'deserving victim', this is particularly pertinent to understanding the practices of the Criminal Injuries Compensation Authority, which demand the victim be innocent of involvement in the incident for which they are making a claim. Any evidence that the victim may have been partly responsible for what happened to them can be used to either reduce the claim being made or invalidate it.

Inquisitorialism A legal system designed to determine the likelihood of an event having occurred rather than seeking to prove beyond reasonable doubt what might have occurred. This system implies a different relationship between the victim(s) and the offender(s) from that found in an adversarial system of justice.

Liberal feminism Concerned with questions of equality between men and women and how best to achieve equality. It is a view of male/female relationships that presumes everyone should have an equal chance to achieve their potential and is concerned to eliminate discriminatory practices that may stand in the way of this.

Lifestyle A concept derived from the work of Hindelang, Gottfredson and Garofalo (1978) that has informed much criminal victimisation survey work. It focuses on how people spend their time, doing what, as indicators of lifestyle that can be measured and related to the risk of criminal victimisation. It is a way of thinking about lifestyle that is incident-focused rather than process-focused.

New terrorism This term has emerged since 9/11 to distinguish the contemporary threat of terrorist activities from earlier forms of terrorism. The contemporary preoccupation with terrorism is considered 'new' because of the advent of the phenomenon of the 'suicide bomber'.

NOVA National Organisation of Victim Assistance, the US umbrella organisation that co-ordinates services and acts as a pressure group for victims of crime.

Mediation Considered to be one facet of restorative justice, mediation brings the victim and offender together with a mediator to facilitate processes of apology or making amends. Mediation tends to be informal and can occur either before, during or after the more formal criminal justice response.

Orality The verbal tradition of the adversarial criminal justice process that requires that all participants in a criminal trial make their contribution verbally.

Patriarchy A concept employed by radical feminism to delineate the structure of male power over women.

Positivist victimology A term first coined by Miers (1989) to describe the way in which much conventional victimological work took as its main focus of concern the non-random patterning of criminal victimisation and reflected a preoccupation with interpersonal crimes of violence and those incidents which the victim might have contributed to.

Postmodern feminism For this version of feminism, women's 'otherness', difference, and diversity, are aspects of their lives to be celebrated and not marginalised. As such it promotes a critical stance to the procedures, practices and language that result in the marginalisation of women.

Radical feminism A strand of feminist thought that focuses on the ways in which women are dominated and controlled by men especially by, or through the threat of, sexual violence.

Radical victimology A strand of victimological thought that takes as part of its central problematic the role of the state and state actors in producing victims and reflects a preoccupation with all kinds of victimisation, not just that defined by the law. It is a version of victimology that aligns itself with questions of human rights.

Rape crisis The feminist-inspired voluntary organisation that supports women who have been subjected to sexual assault and/or rape.

Repeat victimisation The recognition of the phenomenon of repeat victimisation grew in popularity in the mid-1990s. It is concerned with the ways in which the pattern of victimisation is not random but is predictable; the most certain indicator of being a likely victim of crime is having been a victim of crime before. It has resulted in an enormous amount of energy being devoted to how best identify those most likely to be the victim of further victimisation and how best to respond in the light of this information.

Responsibilisation Associated with the work of Garland (2001), this term refers to the ways in which responsibility for the control of crime has been dispersed among a wide range of bodies and authorities, including individual members of society and state authorities, to work in partnership to tackle the problems of crime and social order.

Restorative justice A catch-all term that encompasses a range of different interventions, all concerned to ensure the more active involvement and participation of the victim in dealings with the offender. One underlying principle of restorative justice is to reintegrate both the victim and the offender into the community with a focus on ways of making amends for what has happened.

Risk society Used by Beck (1992), among other social theorists, to delineate the preoccupation of contemporary western societies with precaution and safety.

Routine activity theory This views crime as the outcome of three factors: a motivated offender, a suitable victim and the absence of capable guardians. It is largely associated with the work of Felson (1998).

SAMM Support After Murder and Manslaughter. A voluntary organisation that operates under the wing of Victim Support, its distinct area of concern and support being those families whose lives have been affected as a result of victimisation consequent to the crimes of murder or manslaughter.

Second-wave feminism A phrase usually used to refer to the 'revitalisation' experienced by the feminist movement in the 1960s.

Sentencing circles Rather like conferencing features in programmes concerned with the implementation of Indigenous justice, sentencing circles give voice to all the parties on whom a particular crime has had an impact though they have a stronger community input on the outcome for the victim and the offender.

Sex A biologically based categorisation usually assigned to people at birth based on observable sexual characteristics.

Socialist feminism This version of feminism is concerned to understand how women are both oppressed by capitalism and dominated by men simultaneously.

Survivor The term favoured by the feminist movement to capture the ways in which women routinely and actively resist the oppression they experience on a day-to-day basis. Historically put in opposition to the concept of victim, though contemporarily there is greater awareness that the process of moving from being a victim to a survivor can be quite complex on an individual level, and is not necessarily achieved by everyone. However this is still an important term for political purposes.

Universal victim A notion of the victim derived from risk society theory, which presumes that we are all equally exposed to the bad consequences of contemporary society.

Victimisation Understanding the processes associated with the impact of crime.

Victimocracy A term coined by Green (2006) to describe the current voice and power given to the victims' movement.

Victims' Advocate An individual who presents the family impact statement in cases of murder and manslaughter in England and Wales to the court.

Victims' Code of Practice A statement of good practice that came into operation in April 2006 subsequent to the Domestic Violence, Crime and Victims Act 2004. It outlines practices that all agencies within the criminal justice process who come into contact with victims of crime need to put in place in order to ameliorate the secondary victimisation experienced at the hand of the criminal justice system itself.

Victim impact statement A statement taken from the victim of crime documenting the harm done to them by their experience. These statements are used at different points in the criminal justice system depending upon the jurisdiction in which they are being used, sometimes to inform sentencing decisions, though not always.

Victim Personal Statement Scheme (Victim statement of opinion) This scheme has operated in England and Wales since 2001. It requires that the police take a statement from the victims about the harm done by a crime at the point at which the crime occurred; then at a later date, should the case be taken to court, to consider any longer-term impact. The statements form part of the case file that is taken to court and may be referred to by the judge or the magistrate along with other aspects of the file.

Victim precipitation An early victimological concept that takes into account the nature of the victims' behaviour as a contributory factor in what happened to them.

Victim Support A UK based organisation that seeks to offer victims of crime assistance in the aftermath of an event.

Vulnerability This concept is used to highlight the way in which crime can have a differential impact on different categories of people.

Witness Care Unit Usually situated within the Crown Court and staffed by the police and the Crown Prosecution Service, these units operate in England and Wales to facilitate the management of witnesses for the criminal justice system and to ensure that people are able to give their evidence to the best of their ability.

Women's Refuge A feminist-inspired movement that offers places of safety to women and children escaping from domestic violence.

References

Beck, U. (1992) *The Risk Society*. London: Sage.

Christie, N. (1986) 'The Ideal Victim', in E.A. Fattah (ed.) *From Crime Policy to Victim Policy*. London: Macmillan.

Felson, M. (1998) *Crime and Everyday Life*, 2nd edn. Thousand Oaks, CA: Pine Forge Press.

Furedi, F. (1997, 2002) *The Culture of Fear*. London: Continuum.

Garland, D. (2001) *The Culture of Control*. Oxford: Polity.

Glassner, B. (1999) *Culture of Fear*. New York: Perseus Books.

Green, D. (2006) *We're (Nearly) All Victims Now!* London: Civitas.

Hindelang, M.J., Gottfredson, M.R. and Garofalo, J. (1978) *Victims of Personal Crime*. Cambridge, MA: Ballinger.

Kelly, L. (1988) *Surviving Sexual Violence*. Oxford: Polity.

Mawby, R. and Walklate, S. (1994) *Critical Victimology*. London: Sage.

Miers, D. (1989) 'Positivist victimology: A critique, part 1', *International Review of Victimology*, 1(1): 1–29.

Rhodes, R.W. (1997) *Understanding Governance*. Buckingham: Open University Press.

Walklate, S. (2007) *Imagining the Victim of Crime*. Maidenhead: Open University Press.

Index

Added to a page number 'f' denotes a figure,'t' denotes a table and 'n' denotes notes.

Witness Assistance Service (NSW), 393
Witness Care Units, 219, 222, 223, 233,
    285, 287–8, 291, 385, 501
witness satisfaction surveys, 288
Witness Service, 222, 244, 265, 289
Witness Support, 222
Witness and Victim Experience (WAVE)
    survey, 211
witnesses
    adversarial systems, 284, 406
    behaviour and performance of, 290
    impact of attending court, 267
    inquisitorial systems, 299, 300
    support services, 221
    see also vulnerable and intimidated
        witnesses
Wolfgang, Marvin, 44, 45
'woman question', 180, 190, 196
woman-to-man violence, 185
woman-to-woman violence, 185
women
    abuse of black, 156
    abuse of elderly, 154
    characterised as victim-prone, 178
    corporate crime, 456–7
    definition of rape, 128, 129
    experience of criminal justice process,
        203
    fear of victimisation, 182
    focus on violence against, 119
    harm through victimisation, 98–9
    likelihood of victimisation, 98
    predictions of domestic violence, 159
    rational response to victimisation,
        182–3
    supporting rape victims, 133–4
    surviving victimisation, 187
    see also female criminality; female
        offenders; female violence;
        indigenous women

Women, Crime and Criminology, 44
'women who kill', 186
Women's Aid, 47, 177, 272–3
Women's Aid refuges, 186, 247
Women's Environmental Network, 457
Women's Liberationsts, media dismissal
    of, 130
Women's Refuge, 502
women's rights, fight for, 131
working conditions, corporate crime, 457
World Society of Victimology, 3, 41–2, 54
written evidence, inquisitorial systems,
    284, 299

young men
    likelihood of victimisation, 95
    low income and offending, 102
    risk-harm axis, vulnerability, 93
young offenders, probation services, 225
young people
    assessment of competence, 271
    stereotyping, 97
    Victim Support consultation with,
        274–5
    victimisation, 95, 96, 263
Young People's support pack, 270–1
young witnesses, intimidation of, 267
youth conferencing, 406
youth crime, 449
Youth Justice and Criminal Evidence Act
    (1999), 126, 135, 139, 223, 225, 246,
    287, 292
Youth Justice and Criminal Evidence Bill
    (1998), 135
youth offender panels (YOPs), 325
youth offending teams (YOTs), 225, 326
youth victimology, 96

Zero Tolerance, 137–8, 139
Zito Trust, 187, 245